Blue Book of
Guitar Amplifiers™
1st Edition

Text by Zachary R. Fjestad
Edited by S.P. Fjestad

$24.95
Publisher's Softcover
Suggested List Price

Publisher's Limited
Edition Hardcover
Suggested List Price - $44.95

D0807860

136 52342

1st Edition Blue Book of Guitar Amplifiers™

Publisher's Note: This book is the result of nonstop and continual guitar amplifier research obtained by attending guitar shows, communicating with dealers and collectors throughout the country each year, following the marketplace through want ads and web sites, and staying on top of trends as they occur. This book represents an analysis of prices for which both recently manufactured and collectible amplifiers have actually been selling for during that period at an average retail level.

Although every reasonable effort has been made to compile an accurate and reliable guide, guitar amplifier prices may vary significantly depending on such factors as the locality of the sale, the number of sales we were able to consider, famous musician endorsement of certain makes/models, regional economic conditions, and other critical factors.

Accordingly, no representation can be made that the guitar amplifiers listed may be bought or sold at prices indicated, nor shall the editor or publisher be responsible for any error made in compiling and recording such prices.

Blue Book Publications, Inc.
8009 34th Avenue South, Suite 175
Minneapolis, MN 55425 U.S.A.

Orders only: 800-877-4867 (U.S.A. and Canada only)
Phone: 952-854-5229
Fax: 952-853-1486
Email: guitars@bluebookinc.com
Web site: http://www.bluebookinc.com

ISBN No. 1-886768-35-8
Library of Congress ISSN Number - pending as this edition went to press
Published and printed in the United States of America

Distributed in part by Music Sales Corporation and Omnibus Press
257 Park Avenue South, New York, NY 10010 USA
Phone: 212.254.2100 Fax: 212.254.2013 Email: 71360.3514@compuserve.com

Cover Design & Layout - Thomas D. Heller & Clint Schmidt
Fender Custom Shop amp on front & back covers courtesy of Willie's American Guitars
Fender Stratocaster on rear cover courtesy of George McGuire
Production Manager & Cover Photography - Clint Schmidt
Manuscript Production - Zachary Fjestad
Executive Assistant Editor - Cassandra Faulkner
Proofing - Heather Mohr, Cassandra Faulkner, Zachary Fjestad, & S.P. Fjestad
Printer - Phoenix Color, Hagerstown, MD

Front & Back Cover Explanation: You may be asking yourself why is that amp on the front cover. To make a short story long, this is our third attempt at creating a cover for this book. With rejections from two other ideas, due to high ranking officials, this is what we came up with. It's not vintage, but you have to admit, it's pretty cool.

This is a Fender amp that looks vintage, but in fact is brand new! That's right, this is a Two-Tone model (No. 082-2000-000) straight out of Fender's custom shop. It features many different styles that Fender has used over the years including a top-mounted chrome control panel from the tweed era, the black and blonde Tolex, and a Fender logo that was used for a short time in the early 1960's. Then on the inside, a new design for a chassis is used. This is a Blues Junior chassis with 3 X 12AX7 preamp tubes and 2 X EL84 power tubes that produces 15W of power. It also has two Eminence speakers, one a 12 inch and one a 10 inch. The cabinet is the selling point for this product. The amp is covered in two different colored tweeds and the grille cloth is shaped like a trapezoid. It makes you wonder if the Master Builder slipped and sawed the board at a 45 degree angle. Whatever they did, it works. Not only do you get a tube amp, there are several features from different eras on the exterior. Courtesy Willie's American Guitars.

What is better than playing through a Fender amp? Playing a Fender guitar through a Fender amp. The Fender Stratocaster wasn't Leo's first design, but to date, is by far his most popular. With Fender testing their guitars and their amps interchangeably, it's only natural to have these two pieces tweaked to sound the best when played through each other. This particular model is a 1974 Fender Stratocaster, serial number 552445, finished in Lake Placid Blue. Note the large Fender logo on the headstock. Courtesy George McGuire.

CONTENTS

GENERAL INFORMATION

As this edition goes to press, the following titles/products are currently available, unless otherwise specified:

Online subscriptions and individual downloading services for the *Blue Book of Gun Values*, *Blue Book of Modern Black Powder Values*, *Blue Book of Airguns*, *Blue Book of Electric Guitars* and *Blue Book of Acoustic Guitars*.

Blue Book of Gun Values, 23rd Edition by S.P. Fjestad (ISBN No. 1-886768-31-5 1,680 pages)

Colt Black Powder Reproductions & Replicas by Dennis Adler (ISBN: 1-886768-11-0)

2nd Ed. *Blue Book of Modern Black Powder Values* by Dennis Adler (ISBN: 1-886768-32-3)

2nd Ed. *Blue Book of Airguns* by Dr. Robert Beeman & John Allen (ISBN 1-886768-30-7)

Blue Book of Electric Guitars, 7th Edition, edited by S.P. Fjestad (ISBN 1-886768-26-9)

Blue Book of Acoustic Guitars, 7th Edition, edited by S.P. Fjestad (ISBN 1-886768-25-0)

Blue Book of Guitars **CD-ROM** (ISBN: 1-886768-27-7)

Blue Book of Pool Cues, 2nd Edition, by Brad Simpson, edited by Victor Stein and Paul Rubino (ISBN: 1-886768-12-9)

If you would like to get more information about any of the above publications/products, including the *Blue Book of Electric Guitars* and the *Blue Book of Acoustic Guitars*, simply check our web site.

We would like to thank all of you for your business in the past – you are the reason(s) we are successful. Our goal remains the same – to give you the best products, the most accurate and up-to-date information for the money, and the highest level of customer service available in today's marketplace. If something's right, tell the world over time. If something's wrong, please tell us immediately – we'll make it right.

FACES BEHIND THE PHONE

Many of you may want to know what the person on the other end of the telephone/fax/email looks like, so here are the faces that go with the voices.

S.P. Fjestad – Editor & Publisher

Zach Fjestad – Author & Guitar Researcher

Cassandra Faulkner – Executive Assistant Editor

Tom Stock - CFO

Clint Schmidt – Art Director

John Andraschko – Technology Director

John Allen – Associate Editor & Firearms Researcher

Beth Marthaler – Operations Manager

Katie Sandin - Operations

Heather Mohr - Operations

GENERAL INFORMATION

While many of you have probably dealt with our company for awhile, it may be helpful for you to know a little bit more about our operation and what we are currently publishing. We are also the leaders in online informational services on collectibles. As this edition goes to press, the following titles/products/services are currently available.

Online Guitar, Amp, and Gun Services: www.bluebookinc.com

1st Edition *Blue Book of Guitar Amplifiers*, by Zachary R. Fjestad, edited by S.P. Fjestad
7th Edition *Blue Book of Electric Guitars*, edited by S.P. Fjestad, text by Gurney Brown
7th Edition *Blue Book of Acoustic Guitars*, edited by S.P. Fjestad, text by Gurney Brown
7th Editions *Blue Book of Guitars*, CD-ROM includes information from both guitar books, - and sophisticated inventory program for fretted instruments, amplifiers, pedals/effects, etc.

2nd Edition *Blue Book of Pool Cues*, by Brad Simpson, edited by Victor Stein and Paul Rubino

23rd Edition *Blue Book of Gun Values* by S.P. Fjestad
GunTracker 2.3, CD-ROM firearms inventory software program
Colt Black Powder Reproductions & Replicas by Dennis Adler
2nd Edition *Blue Book of Airguns* by Dr. Robert Beeman & John Allen, edited by S.P. Fjestad
2nd Edition *Blue Book of Modern Black Powder Values* by Dennis Adler

---

If you would like to order or get more information about any of the above publications/products, please check our web site or contact us at:

Blue Book Publications, Inc.
8009 34th Avenue South, Suite 175
Minneapolis, MN 55425 U.S.A.
www.bluebookinc.com
bluebook@bluebookinc.com
800-877-4867 (toll free domestic)
952-854-5229 (non-domestic) • Fax: 952-853-1486

Since our phone system is equipped with voicemail, you may also wish to know extension numbers which have been provided below:

Ext. No.: 11 - Tom Stock	Ext. No.: 18 - Katie Sandin
Ext. No.: 12 - John Andraschko	Ext. No.: 19 - Cassandra Faulkner
Ext. No.: 13 - S.P. Fjestad	Ext. No.: 20 - Art Department
Ext. No.: 14 - Honored Guest	Ext. No.: 22 - Heather Mohr
Ext. No.: 15 - Clint Schmidt	Ext. No.: 24 - Break Room
Ext. No.: 16 - John Allen	Ext. No.: 25 - Beth Marthaler
Ext. No.: 17 - Zach Fjestad	Ext. No.: 27 - Shipping

Office hours are: 8:30 a.m. - 5:00 p.m. CST, Monday - Friday.
Orders Only: 800-877-4867 Phone No.: 952-854-5229
Additionally, an after hours answering service is available for ordering.
Fax No.: 952-853-1486 (available 24 hours a day)
Email: guitars@bluebookinc.com (checked several times daily)
Web site: http://www.bluebookinc.com

We would like to thank all of you for your business in the past - you are the reason(s) we are successful. Our goal remains the same, to give you the best products, the most accurate and up-to-date information for the money, and the highest level of customer service available in today's marketplace. If something's right, tell the world over time. If something's wrong, please tell us immediately.

ACKNOWLEDGEMENTS

After you've had a good chance to go through this book, many of you are going to want to know how did we come up with the information and values for this book? A simple question, and a difficult answer. For currently manufactured guitar amplifiers, we gather as much factory information as possible on model specifications and current MSRs. This also includes any options that may be available, in addition to trying to provide you with a short company history and other useful information. Please refer to the Trademark Index for a complete listing of companies/trademarks with contact information.

On recently discontinued and vintage guitar amplifiers, this research process becomes more complex. The people/companies listed below are very knowledgeable within their specific area(s), and have helped us tremendously with both specific information and up-to-date pricing. Rick Wilkiewicz is our vintage pricing editor, and he has spent many long hours gathering both information and current pricing on most major trademark vintage amplifiers.

The people below have generously given us their time to help us with this project, and are truly experts within the guitar amplifier industry. Both the Author & Publisher of this new 1st Edition *Blue Book of Guitar Amplifiers* would like to thank these people/companies listed below, since without them, this book would be a lot thinner! If you think you might have something significant to contribute to this project, please submit your information directly to us (see page 5 for contact info).

Pricing Editor, Rick Wilkiewicz, at recent Dallas Guitar Show.

Vintage Pricing Editor - Rick Wilkiewicz
Head Photographer - Clint Schmidt
Nate Westgor & Crew from Willie's American Guitars
Mark Sampson
Larry Meiners - Flying Vintage
Paul Jernigan & Rich Siegle of Fender USA
Kenny Rardin & Bruce Barnes - solidbodyguitars.com, Inc.
Jeff Krumm & crew - Savage Audio
Mark Dupree
Tim Fletcher & Steve Russell
David Eden from Eden Electronics
Dave Boze
George McGuire
Gurney Brown
Michael Soldano

Paul Reed Smith
John Beeson
David Wilson from *ToneQuest*
Laura Rausch - PRS Guitars
Dave Rogers & Eddy Thurston - Dave's Guitar Shop, LaCrosse, WI
Morphine Mark & crew - Dallas Guitar Show
Don & Jeff Lace - Lace Guitars/Rat Fink Amplifiers
Keith Smart - Zemaitis Guitar Owners Club
Jason Scheuner - Ultrasound Amps
Trent Salter - *Musician's Hotline*
Rick Kessel - *MMR Magazine*

The following books have been a tremendous help that I find myself going back for reference, almost daily.

Thanks again for those who have already done a book on amplifiers. We know it's a tough job coming up with this material, and your books are always appreciated.

The Fender Amp Book by John Morrish
Fender Amps - The First Fifty Years by John Teagle & John Sprung
Ampeg - The Story Behind the Sound by Gregg Hopkins & Bill Moore
The History of Marshall by Michael Doyle
The Tube Amp Book 4.1 Edition by Aspen Pittman
Amps! - The Other Half of Rock 'n' Roll by Ritchie Flieger

FOREWORDS

Finally! All I can say is finally. For everyone who's been waiting for the *Blue Book of Guitar Amplifiers*, it is finally here. It's been an ongoing process for almost a year now, but the idea for the project has been around for a long time. In fact, I think I was still waiting for my driver's license when the idea was being considered seriously. Indeed, the need for a book like this is evident, due to people inquiring at every show. Now it's finally here, and has many new features that Blue Book Publications has never used before.

A first for Blue Book, is individual model pictures on many amps. This way, identifying your model is easier with a picture below the description. We also have price ranges. In the past, all prices were one set value. With this industry being a lot broader, we felt that putting these amps into a range would perform more accurately.

This book is also available in several formats. It can be purchased as a paperback for the traditionalists, as a CD-ROM, and as an online subscription. An online subscription allows, this information to be downloaded from the Internet by using your email address and password. After all, good information never sleeps!

My first amplifier was a small Harmony that I borrowed from my uncle Steve. After learning how to play, I upgraded to a Fender Princeton Chorus, which is my amp to this day. I really thought I had something, but now I realize there are so many choices with amplifiers, it's almost endless.

This project has truly been a rewarding and informal experience (I had to buy new fitted hats, my brain was getting so big!), but of course I couldn't have done it without the help and support of many people. Rick Wilkiewicz and Gurney Brown have helped out with the text immensely.

The author (L), a rocket scientist, and the publisher, at the recent summer NAMM show. Only one has figured out $E=MC^2$! Photo courtesy Rick Kessel, *MMR Magazine*

Jeff and the superb crew at Savage Audio have been a huge help in getting pictures in this book. The great staff at Blue Book has helped throughout the project.

I wouldn't be writing any of this if it wasn't for an uncle who offered me this opportunity at this age. Thanks S.P., it beats bagging groceries! I have to thank my parents for putting up with the constant noise coming from my guitar amp in the basement. (Some people think I'm all right!) I can't forget the one person who gave me the final push when I decided to start this project. Katie, who always supported my crazy idea and still never laughs at my jokes, thanks kiddo. There are several other people who have had faith in me, but there simply isn't enough room to list everyone, so Thanks!

Enjoy reading the new *Blue Book of Guitar Amplifiers* (finally), that is the most up-do-date book of it's kind on that market. It's all you players out there that make this project possible. Maybe now that this is over, I can finally plug my guitar back in (I think the strings are rusted solid!), then again the second edition is right around the corner...

Sincerely,

Zachary R. Fjestad
Author
Blue Book of Guitar Amplifiers

While the *Blue Book of Guitars* took 4 years to get from an idea to a printed product (1994), this 1st Edition *Blue Book of Guitar Amplifiers* has taken only 9 months from start to finish! This is what can happen when one person can exclusively focus on a large project, and all of today's high-tech publishing horsepower can work its magic on premise.

Originally, the *Blue Book of Guitars* got started because a friend of mine died, and his widow wanted me to pay her a fair price for his guitars. After visiting several shops locally, while everybody knew exactly what they'd pay me for them, nobody exactly volunteered what they were actually worth. Seven editions and 80,000 books later, both the *Blue Book of Acoustic Guitars* and the *Blue Book of Electric Guitars* have established themselves as the industry leaders for comprehensive guitar information and up-to-date pricing.

About a year ago, a friend visited the office, and commented on how many guitar books were in our library - approx. 8 linear feet, and most of these titles were not in print even 10 years ago. When he asked me how many amp books were on the shelf, my comment surprised him - "Maybe 10-12, 4-5 that we really use." After checking Amazon.com for guitar amplifier books, only 9 titles came up, and 3 of those are out of print! Hmmm, maybe a *Blue Book of Guitar Amplifiers* is needed.

Even though my first concert was the Beatles in Minneapolis in August 1966, and I'll never forget what their 4-5 Voxs did through a primitive (by today's standards) PA system, seeing Eric Clapton with Cream a few years later at a smaller venue plugged into his 3 screaming, bite your balls loud Marshall double stacks proved to me that a guitar amp is at least, or more important, than the guitar when amplified.

In closing, I would like to thank my very talented nephew, Zachary, for taking a corporate idea and turning it into this important 1st Edition. Before joining our staff, many people warned me, "Don't hire a relative or a friend - you'll live to regret it, especially a kid his age." After doing all the typing and most of the research himself on this project nonstop during the past year, I can't tell you how proud I am of this accomplishment. Zach has attended many industry trade and guitar shows with me during the past 8 years, and now, he is also the author of both guitar books. Maybe someday, he can even teach me how to play guitar!

This publication, like any other from Blue Book Publications, Inc., is a work in progress, and future editions will have more information and up-to-date pricing on guitar amplifiers. Thank you for supporting this 1st Edition, and above all else, stay plugged in, and let the good tone roll!

Sincerely,

S.P. Fjestad
Editor & Publisher
Blue Book of Guitar Amplifiers

HOW TO USE THIS BOOK

This new 1st Edition *Blue Book of Guitar Amplifiers*™ can provide you with both comprehensive information and up-to-date pricing for guitar amplifiers. Much of the information in this book is simply not available anywhere else, and this section explains how to use this book.

The prices listed in the 1st Edition *Blue Book of Guitar Amplifiers*™ are based on average national retail prices for both currently manufactured and vintage guitar amplifiers. This is NOT a wholesale pricing guide - prices reflect what you typically see on an amp's price tag.   More importantly, do not expect to walk into a music store or pawn shop, and think that the proprietor should pay you the retail price listed in this text. Dealer offers on most models could be 20%-50% less than the values listed, depending upon desirability, locality, and profitability.

Currently manufactured guitar amplifiers are typically listed with the manufacturer's suggested retail (MSR), a 100% price (may reflect market place discounting), and in most cases, includes prices for both Excellent and Average condition factors. Please consult the digital color **Photo Grading System**™ (pages 33-48) to learn more about the condition of your guitar amplifier.

For your convenience, an explanation of amplifier condition factors, how to convert them, and descriptions of individual condition factors appear on pages 31-32 to assist you in learning more about amplifier grading, and individual condition factors. Please read these pages carefully, as the values in this publication are based on the grading/condition factors listed. **Remember, the price is wrong if the condition factor isn't right.**

All values within this text assume original condition. From the vintage marketplace or (especially) a collector's point of view, any repairs, alterations, modifications, "enhancements," "improvements," "professionally modified to a more desirable configuration," or any other non-factory changes usually detract from an amplifier's value. Please refer to page 31 regarding an explanation on alterations/modifications, repairs, and other possible problems which have to be factored in before determining the correct condition. Depending on the seriousness of the modification/alterations, you may have to go down a condition factor or two when re-computing price for these alterations. Determining values for damaged and/or previously repaired amplifiers will usually depend on the parts and labor costs necessary to return them to playable and/or original specifications. Once again, the grading lines within the 1st Edition reflect the Excellent and Average condition factors only.

We have designed an easy-to-use (and consistent) text format throughout this publication to assist you in finding specific information within the shortest amount of time, and there is a lot of information! Here's how it works:

To find a particular guitar amplifier in this book, first identify the name of the manufacturer, trademark, importer, or brand name. Refer to this listing within the correct alphabetical section. Next, locate the correct category name, then look at the individual model and submodel listings, typically listed in chronological and alphabetical sequence. Once you find the correct model or sub-model under its respective heading or subheading, determine the amplifier's original condition factor (see the Photo Grading System™ on pages 33-48). For the correct value, simply look under the corresponding condition column. Special/limited editions usually appear last under a manufacturer's heading. In order to save time when looking up a particular model, you may want to look first at the Index on pages 300-303. Also, a thorough Trademark Index is located on pages 290-295 – it is the only up-to-date and comprehensive listing of current guitar amplifier manufacturers in print – use both of them, they can be very helpful!

A grading line will appear at the top of each page where applicable. This grading line is once again standard for the

GRADING	100%	EXCELLENT	AVERAGE

Blue Book of Guitar Amplifiers™, and reflects the 100% value (this price could represent any industry discounting). Next to 100%, left to right, are the standard Excellent and Average condition factors. These two condition factors will hopefully eliminate some of the "grading graffiti" on these types of amplifiers, where other condition descriptions might be confusing or misleading.

HOW TO USE THIS BOOK

A pricing line will typically be located directly underneath the model or submodel description. You will notice in the 1st Edition *Blue Book of Guitar Amplifiers* features a similar price line format throughout. Typically, it includes the Mfg.'s Sug. Retail (MSR) on currently manufactured amplifiers, a 100% price (this may reflect industry discounting, if any) and, if applicable, a range price for both Excellent and Average condition factors. When the following price line is encountered:

GRADING		100%	EXCELLENT	AVERAGE
MSR	$995	$700	$475 - 550	$350 - 400

it automatically indicates the amplifier is currently manufactured and the manufacturer's suggested retail price (MSR) is shown left of the 100% column. **The 100% price on a new amplifier is what a consumer can typically expect to pay for that amplifier, and may reflect a discount off the manufacturer's suggested retail price (MSR). The values for the remaining Excellent and Average condition factors represent actual selling prices for used instruments in these two conditions.**

An "N/A" instead of a price means that a firm market price is either **Not Available** for that particular amplifier and/or condition factor.

A price line with 2 price ranges listed (as the example below demonstrates) indicates a discontinued, out of production model with ranges shown for Excellent and Average condition factors only. 100% prices have intentionally not been listed, since the longer an amplifier has been discontinued, the less likely you will find it in 100% condition. On popular, non-custom, factory discontinued models within the past several years, 100% values (new condition) will typically be no higher than 70% of the last MSR. 100% pricing on desirable, low production discontinued models from well-known makers and/or small companies will normally be priced closer to the last Manufacturer's Suggested Retail Price (MSR) for that model.

GRADING	100%	EXCELLENT	AVERAGE
	N/A	$2,150 - 2,400	$1,550 - 1,800

Obviously, "MSR" will not appear in the left margin, but a model note may appear below the price line indicating the last manufacturer's suggested retail price.

While the current Manufacturer's Suggested Retail price is included on current models whenever possible, the last suggested retail price for discontinued models may appear in smaller typeface to the right, directly underneath the price line:

Last MSR was $795.

There are a few things to remember when looking at models listed in this book:

All wattages are listed as RMS (Root Mean Square) unless otherwise specified. Companies almost always use this when they produce an amp. We find that the RMS rating is listed on almost every amp. Peak power is important, but many manufactures don't even list it. If it is an important fact in the model, we will do everything to include it.

Speakers are all in inches, such as 12" or 15". Since 99.9% of speakers are circle in shape, all speakers with the number listing are assumed circles. If they are oval, such as the Ampeg Echo unit, or something else (The Fender Bantam Bass, Trapezoidal), they will be listed accordingly. When there are more than one speaker they will be listed like this: 2 X 12" indicates two 12" speakers.

Most of the time tube configurations are split up into pre amp/power/rectifier. These are then split into how many tubes are in each section. Some amps are listed as "all-tube chassis," which means that the amp section is all power. This does not involve the rectifier all of the time. When referring to an all-tube chassis it is usually the preamp and power section of the amp. Rectifier is usually listed as what it is, tube or solid-state.

When speakers are not listed, it can be assumed that the amp is a head unit only. Most of the time, we list whether it is a head-unit or a combo.

ANATOMY OF A GUITAR AMPLIFIER

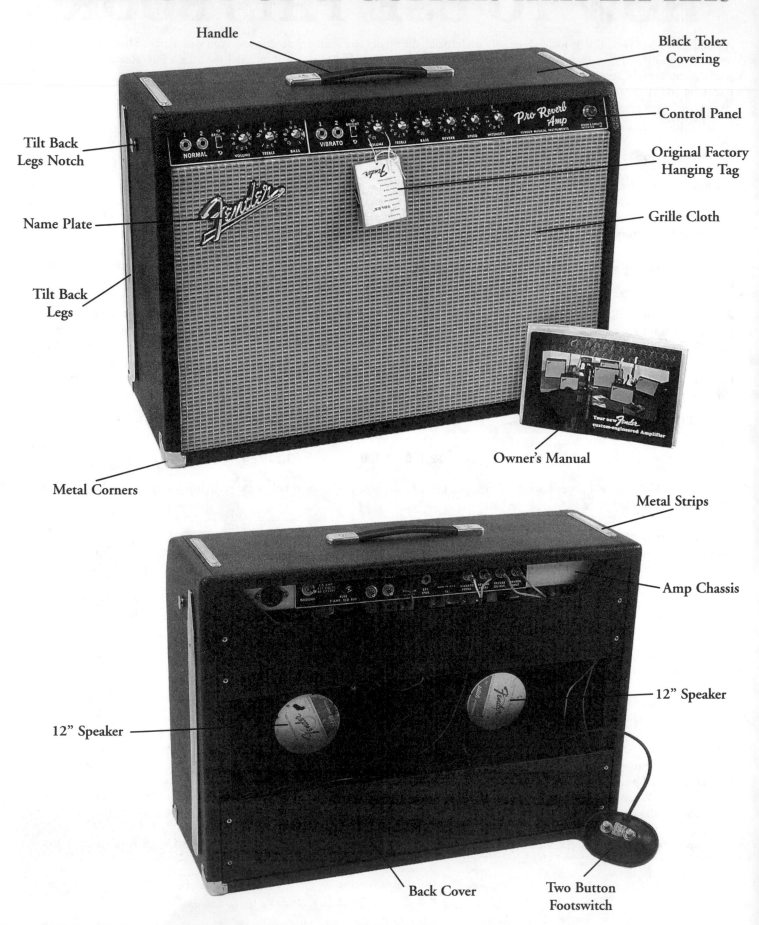

Handle

Black Tolex Covering

Control Panel

Tilt Back Legs Notch

Original Factory Hanging Tag

Name Plate

Grille Cloth

Tilt Back Legs

Owner's Manual

Metal Corners

Metal Strips

Amp Chassis

12" Speaker

12" Speaker

Back Cover

Two Button Footswitch

ANATOMY OF A GUITAR AMPLIFIER

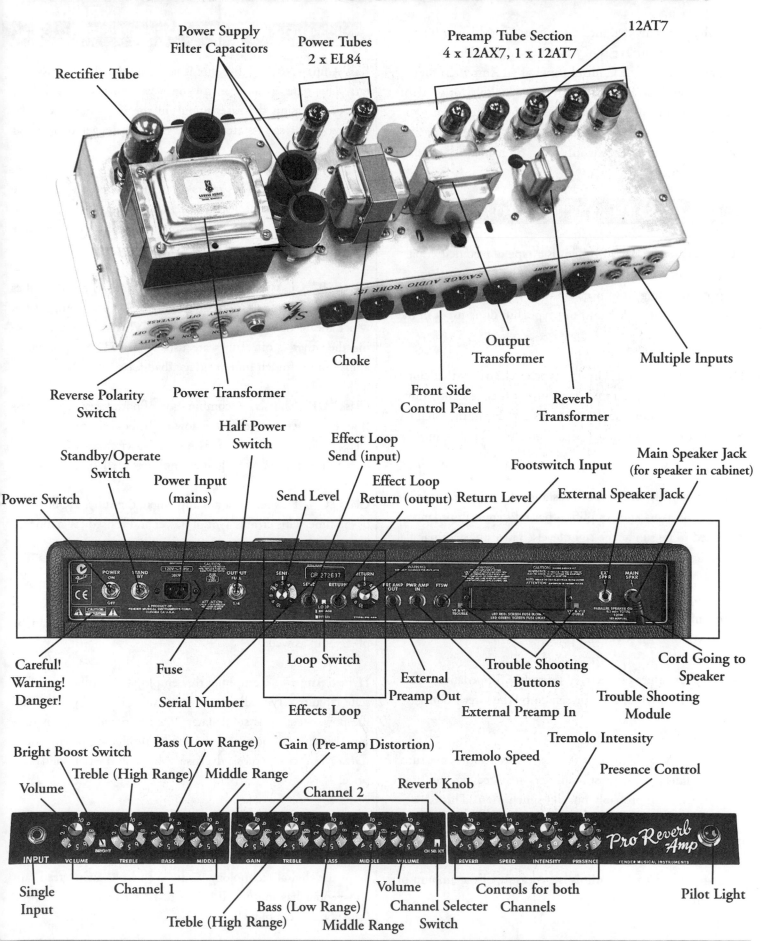

Power Supply Filter Capacitors

Rectifier Tube

Power Tubes 2 x EL84

Preamp Tube Section 4 x 12AX7, 1 x 12AT7

12AT7

Choke

Output Transformer

Multiple Inputs

Reverse Polarity Switch

Power Transformer

Front Side Control Panel

Reverb Transformer

Standby/Operate Switch

Half Power Switch

Effect Loop Send (input)

Footswitch Input

Main Speaker Jack (for speaker in cabinet)

Power Switch

Power Input (mains)

Send Level

Effect Loop Return (output)

Return Level

External Speaker Jack

Careful! Warning! Danger!

Fuse

Loop Switch

External Preamp Out

Trouble Shooting Buttons

Cord Going to Speaker

Serial Number

Effects Loop

External Preamp In

Trouble Shooting Module

Bright Boost Switch

Bass (Low Range)

Gain (Pre-amp Distortion)

Tremolo Intensity

Treble (High Range)

Middle Range

Tremolo Speed

Presence Control

Volume

Channel 2

Reverb Knob

INPUT

Channel 1

Single Input

Bass (Low Range)

Treble (High Range)

Middle Range

Volume

Channel Selecter Switch

Controls for both Channels

Pilot Light

Blue Book of Guitar Amplifiers™ - First Edition   11

GLOSSARY

This glossary is divided into 5 sections: General Amplifier Glossary, Different Types of Amplifiers, Amplifier Components, On the Control Panel of an Amplifier, and Coverings and Grille Cloths. If you are looking for something and can't find it in one section, please check the others. You may also want to refer to Anatomy of A Guitar Amplifier (pages 10-11) for visual identification on many of the terms listed below.

GENERAL AMPLIFIER GLOSSARY

AC (Alternating Current) - This is a type of electricity that comes out of a wall outlet. It flows in a back and forth motion, switching from negative to positive several times in a second. Amplifiers plug into this type, but don't use it in the circuitry.

DC (Direct Current) - This is a type of electricity that comes from a battery, for example. The current is consistently flowing in one direction. Most amplifiers use this in the circuitry. A rectifier is the component that converts AC power into DC power.

Impedance - The amount of resistance that a component is rated at. Speakers and Amplifiers have different impedances and need to be run at the right levels. This runs with parallel and series connections as well.

Peak Power - This is the most wattage an amp can put out. Companies typically don't list this one for specs. They will list only RMS or both RMS and peak.

Ohms - A measure of electrical resistance. Impedance is listed in Ohms. This symbol is represented by the Greek Omega sign.

RMS (Root Mean Square) - This is a power rating measured in watts. This is what most amplifiers are rated at, even thought they can probably put out much more. This is an average rating and is probably the best way to get an accurate measurement out of an amp.

Wattage - In an amplifier, this is a measure of the amount of power an amp puts out.

DIFFERENT TYPES OF AMPLIFIERS

Bass Amps - An amplifier that is made specifically for bass guitars. There are certain controls on a bass amp such as limiter and compression that are unique to the instrument. Can be either tube or solid-state and are generally bigger than guitar amps.

Class "A" Chassis - This refers to an amp where the tubes are always on. This is the least efficient way of producing sound, but sounds the best. These amps typically produce low wattages.

Class "B" Chassis - This refers to an amp where the tubes switch on and off. This chassis usually uses a push/pull design, which means the tubes turn on and off. When one tube is working the other is off. Tubes are usually placed in pairs. These amps put out much more wattage than Class A.

Class "A/B" Chassis - A combination of both Class A and Class B amps. When the volume is low the tubes will remain on in Class A. When the volume is higher it switches to Class B to create more power. Most guitar amplifiers are like this today.

Class "C" - This refers to an amp where the tubes are off most of the time. This creates a lot of power and is used for radio and other amplification where the sound isn't as important.

Guitar Amps - Amplifiers that are voiced to sound best by a guitar. Most amplifiers produced on the market today are usually aimed for guitars. Different instruments usually can be plugged in as well.

Hybrid Amps - An amplifier that employs both tube and solid-state circuitry. Typically the preamp stage is run by tubes and the power section is solid-state. The advantage of this is tube sound is created, but money saved by producing it with solid-state. Most companies advertise tube sound at a solid-state price.

Modeling Amps - A recent design where several different amp sounds are programmed into one amplifier to make literally hundreds of sounds available at your fingertips. Most of these amps use digital technology. Some even have digital read-outs and Fender has motorized knobs to be set to a desired sound (talk about technology!).

GLOSSARY

P.A. (Public Address) **Amp** - An amp that is voiced for taking all kinds of instruments be amplified into one box. Typically they'll have several inputs and have several outputs for many speakers.

Solid-State (Also known as transistor) - An amplifier that uses diodes and semiconductors instead of vacuum tubes. These amps feature several more components than a tube amp. Traditionally solid-state amps are the budget models that don't sound as good, or have the response of a tube.

Vacuum Tube (Also known as a Valve in England) - A glass "tube" that is sealed containing electrodes and cathodes (among other components) that generates sound by passing electrons back and forth. Tubes were used in all amps until solid-state came around in the 60's. Now tubes are used in the higher priced amps that produce a warmer sound.

AMPLIFIER COMPONENTS

Cabinet - A box (or other enclosure) that houses the amplifier, speakers, or both. This is usually constructed out of wood (most of the time, not mahogany or rosewood) and enclosed in a covering. Unlike guitars, most amps aren't made out of high-quality wood (who sees it anyway?).

Channel - A circuit in an amplifier that is in someway separate from one set of controls to another. Sometimes this is done by different inputs, different knobs, or a physical switch to change between different sets of controls. A channel is used for creating different sounds from one amp without having to change the settings on the dials.

Chassis - The brains of the amplifier. This is where all the electronic components, tubes, and controls for the amp is housed. This is usually a narrow metal box that typically takes up less than 20% of the entire cabinet.

Combo - An amplifier that houses both the chassis and the speaker in one enclosure.

Covering - The material that wraps the cabinet on an amplifier.

Grille - The covering on the front of the amp. This is usually a cloth material or a metal. This covers the speaker from damage and dust.

Head-Unit - An amplifier where the chassis is housed in it's own enclosure. There are no speakers within the cabinet. Useful to keep the heat of tubes away from a speaker, and for the ability to use different speaker cabinets.

Power-Amp Tube - A vacuum tube that turns the audio wave into physical sound, "makes the power." This is where the sound is generated into larger watts.
Examples: 6L6, EL34, KT88, 6550, EL84, 6V6.

Pre amp Tube - A vacuum tube that is in the pre amp stage of an amp. The sound is shaped and toned by these tubes. Examples: 12AX7, 12AT7, ECC81, 7025, 12AY7.

Rectifier - A solid-state or tube unit that converts AC power into DC power, which an amplifier can use. On old and small-wattage amps it is usually a tube. On newer designs and high-watt amps it is a solid-state design. The rectifier has no direct contact with the sound, therefore a reliable solid-state rectifier can be used and no sound difference is noticed. Examples (tubes): 5AR4, GZ34, 5U4.

Speaker - The component that the sound is projected from. Most of the time it is a round unit with 8,10,12 or 15 inch speaker (excluding the Fender Bantam Bass and Ampeg Echo unit).

Speaker Enclosure - A cabinet that is strictly speakers. Marshall made this famous with the 4-12" cabinet. There is usually one input to bring the sound from a head unit or combo. This is useful to keep the weight of an amp down, and stacking 10 combo units would just look stupid.

Tilt-Back Design - This is an amp that has a cabinet that is built to sit at an angle. This way the sound can be projected upward instead of straight out.

ON THE CONTROL PANEL OF AN AMPLIFIER

Bass - The low end sound typically found in the equalization section on an amplifier. Also a Bass is a guitar that produces

GLOSSARY

notes an octave lower than a regular guitar. A bass amplifier can be for either a bass guitar, or in older models to get a lower sound.

Bright Switch - A switch that boosts the high-end of the tonal range on an amp. Early models sometimes had a push-pull feature on the volume or treble knob. There are also Deep and Boost switches for bass and middle, respectively.

Chorus - An effect that is similar to vibrato combined with reverb. When in effect it sounds like a watery effect. Controls are typically depth and rate.

Compression - An control, typically associated with bass amps. It compresses the range of sound to make the loud and soft sounds not so far apart.

Control Knobs - These are knobs, typically on the control panel, that control the level of different effects and volumes on the amp. The most frequent type is a round knob that is numbered 1-10.

Control Panel - The panel where the inputs, control knobs, switches and other buttons are located. On most amps there is a front and back control panel. The back control panel is for less used equipment such as the effects loop, footswitch jack and fuses. The front control panel usually has volume and tone knobs along with input jacks. Some control panels are on top of the amp as well.

Distortion - An effect that happens when a tube starts to clip. This sound is sort of dirty and heavy. Associated with rock and heavy metal, typically.

Effects Loop - A circuit that features an in and out jack for external effects to be plugged in. This is usually on the back of an amp, and sometimes links in with the pre amp, instead of before the amp.

Footswitch - A remote box connected by a cord that has buttons to turn certain effects on or change channels on the amp. Now they have digital footswitches where all of the amps digital effects can be accessed by your foot.

Gain - Sometimes a control on a distortion or overdrive circuit.

This controls the amount of distortion that goes into the preamp.

Half Power Switch - A switch that can take the power of an amplifier and reduce it in half and sometimes to ¼ power. If you have a 100W amp you could switch it down to 50W or less when you need the sound, but no so much power.

Input - The place where the instrument or other object is plugged in to the amplifier. Usually a ¼" jack for most guitar and bass guitars. For mics and other higher audio, a multi-prong XLR jack may be used. Sometimes there are multiple inputs on an amp.

Limiter - A control that limits the sound of an amp (usually bass amps) from going to high. It saves the amplifier as well as your ear.

Mains - The place on the amp where the AC power comes in. Older amps usually have the cord permanently attached to the amp, where amps today feature a male end on the amp itself.

Master Volume - A control that can control the overall volume of the amplifier. This works to be able to turn down the distortion without losing any. The MV control can also govern the volume over more that one channel.

Middle - A control that usually cuts or boosts the mid-range of the equalization. This is a more recent control on amps (intoduced in the late 1950's).

Overdrive - Usually a second channel on an amp that provides gain and distortion. This could also be available in an effect pedal.

Pilot Light - Indicates that the amplifier is on in either the operate or stand-by mode. Typically found on the front control panel.

Power Switch - Turns the power on to the amp.

Presence - A control that typically boosts the upper frequencies on an amp equalization circuit.

Reverb - An echo effect that is typically run by springs. This is usually run by a dwell control.

GLOSSARY

Standby Switch - A switch that enables the amp to be shut off from sound but the tubes are still on. A tube takes a long time to heat up and this switch allows the amp to be shut off from operation but is still running (like a car in neutral). This only works with a tube amplifier since there is nothing to warm up in a solid-state amp.

Tone - The different pitch of a sound that an amplifier produces.

Treble - The high end sound that is usually in the equalization section. Produces a high, almost tinny sound when turned up high.

Tremolo - A pulsating effect that changes the volume (loud/soft). If it were graphed out as a wave it would look like a sine wave. This is usually controlled by a speed and intensity factor.

Vibrato - A pulsating effect that changes the pitch (tone). Don't get this confused with Tremolo and vice-versa. This is usually controlled by a speed and intensity factor.

Volume - The loudness of the sound of an amplifier. Some amps have Master Volumes, which is the overall volume on the whole amp. Pre amp volume is the volume level when the tone goes into the equalization and such.

Blue Check - A covering used by Ampeg during the 1960's. This is a blue covering that has a checkboard type pattern. These amps look really sharp when they are in good shape.

Levant - A covering that was used by Marshall. This is reminiscent of Tolex, but it had its own texture to it. It was also available in colors such as red, orange, and purple. This covering was switched to Elephant in the mid 1970's.

Textured Covering - A covering that has a rough feel to it. When you look at it some parts are actually slightly higher than others. This gives a covering that appears very random. Most coverings are done like this.

Tolex - A covering developed by Fender. This is a covering that looked like leather. It is a fairly smooth surface but has design on it. Tolex been produced in many different colors including white, cream, brown, and black. This is still in use by Fender today.

Tweed - A famous covering (not sure if it's been patented) on amps made in the 1950's and 60's. It is a brown and yellow design that is usually diagonal. The feature that makes it original is that it is a cloth design. When it rips, it will come apart like a sweater.

ABBREVIATIONS

b	Bass	i	Intensity (tremolo or vibrato)	PPGS	Photo Percentage Grading System
bs	Bright Switch	inst.	instrument	r	Reverb
c	Contour	kits	Kick in the shorts	s	Speed (tremolo or vibrato)
Ch.	Channel	l	Low	ss	Solid-state
d	Depth (tremolo or vibrato)	m	Middle	Ser. No.	Serial number
ds	Deep Switch	mic	Microphone	t	Treble
e	Edge	mfg	Manufactured	trem	Tremolo
EQ	Equalizer	MSR	Manufacturer's Suggested Retail	v	Volume
f or freq.	Frequency	MV	Master volume	vib	vibrato
FS	Footswitch	N/A	Not Applicable	w/	with
g	Gain	OD	Overdrive	w/o	without
h	High	p	Presence	w/in	within

An Introduction to Guitar Amplifiers by David Wilson from *ToneQuest*

David Wilson is the publisher of *The ToneQuest Report* - an inspirational monthly resource for guitarists, and *The Players Guide to Ultimate Tone*. He was given his first guitar (an Epiphone acoustic) at the age of 11, and soon graduated to a 1964 National Westwood electric, and his first of many amps - a Fender Deluxe Reverb. The ensuing molecular restructuring of young David's essence remains in full force today, prompted by the genius of a man who couldn't play a lick on the guitar, but he sure could build an amplifier.

To quote Todd Sharp, one of the most talented guitarists and amp techs I know, "Amplifiers are liberators and enablers that are absolutely necessary to transmit that deep, up-from-the-bottom stuff communing between you and your guitar." In skilled hands, amplifiers are indeed instruments that create a magical and utterly inspiring dynamic interplay with the guitar and the guitarist. This mysterious melding of electrons, wood, flesh, and soul continues to be explored today with more passion and creativity than in any period during the relatively short history of the guitar amplifier.

If you truly love guitar amps, this is your time, for we have been blessed with an abundance of riches that grows larger and more diverse with every passing day. We are living in the golden era of guitar amplification - right here, right now - and a comprehensive guide to guitar amplifiers new and old has never been needed more. Thanks to the creativity of so many talented players, technicians, and designers who share our passion for the guitar amplifier, this guide is destined to remain an enduring work in progress, for at this very moment, someone is dreaming up another new amp!

But where did it all begin? Who built the first guitar amp? What was it, exactly, and how did the first guitar amplifier sound? We'll never truly know the answer to any of these questions, but I think we may safely assume that the first guitar amplifier was created with an old radio set. It would have been a fairly easy task to connect an electric guitar to a radio amplifier and speaker, and many amp builders first turned to an old family radio in their youthful quest to discover just how an amplifier worked (and their discoveries were often shocking).

With this in mind, perhaps a nod should be given to the fathers of radio, including (but not limited to) Guglielmo Marconi, Max Braun, and General Electric engineers Chester Rice and Edward Kellog, who developed the design for an AC powered radio that became the 1926 RCA Radiola. Bell Labs was also instrumental in the development of moving coil speakers, and James B. Lansing and his brother survived the Great Depression making speaker cones and winding voice coils at home for their 6 inch and 8 inch speakers destined for home radio sets. In truth, the guitar amplifier has many fathers and it continues to evolve today, but its heritage began with the tube amplifiers developed for radio.

While we can't be certain of the identity of that first adventurous solder

David Wilson, Editor & Publisher of *ToneQuest*, shown with one of his favorite amps, a Fender Black Face Pro Reverb.

jockey who plugged a guitar into an amplifier, we do know that Gibson was one of the first companies to produce small guitar amplifiers such as the 1936 EH150 1x12 'suitcase' amp. The amplifiers of the day were typically small and moderately powered, using field coil speakers and metal vacuum tubes common in radio circuits of the time, and these early amps were often used by lapsteel players. In addition to Gibson, Magnatone and National amps were popular early amps. Leo Fender first began building guitar amplifiers during WWII, and the Fender Dual Professional was the first production amplifier built with two speakers. In the 1950's, guitar amplifier manufacturing in America expanded dramatically. Why? Back to the radio again! America was awash in music ranging from hillbilly bluegrass records to Texas swing, blues, country, jazz, and rock & roll.

> "We are living in the Golden Era of guitar amplification, right here, right now."

The radio not only made music accessible - it stimulated America's appetite for live music, which supported local and regional bands that could deliver the hits on Saturday night at the local dance hall. Fender and Gibson initially led the charge, but the Valco Company of Chicago also produced thousands of inexpensive (and increasingly treasured) amplifiers under the Alamo, Airline, Silvertone, Supro, Ohau, National, Guild, and Gretsch nameplates. Soon, more companies joined in with names like Ampeg, Standel, Rickenbacker, Flot-o-Tone, Danelectro, Premier, and DeArmond, among others. By the late '50s the electric guitar was king bee, and guitar amplifiers were indeed the great enablers of electric guitar tone.

Thanks to bands like Hank Marvin and The Shadows, the popularity of the electric guitar also skyrocketed in England and Europe. Prior to 1960, British musicians were unable to buy American amps or guitars due to an embargo on imports, and a new industry was created to serve the European market. The early British and German amplifiers used very simple, single-ended Class A designs, and they were often housed in cabinets that are beautifully crafted works of art. In fact, many of them resemble radios... Principal British makers included Selmer, Elpico, Vox, Watkins, WEM, Fenton-Weil, and later, Marshall. The German Klemt and Dynacord amps are also significant; they are well built, very unique, and still overlooked and undervalued in today's vintage market.

All of the British and German amps used tubes (valves, as they say in England), that were different from those typically chosen by American manufacturers - usually EL84's and EL34's, followed by KT66's and KT88's in some of the larger Marshall amps. Compared to American amplifiers, the early European amps have a more compressed, harmonically rich tone, and they saturate very quickly - a nice touch if you enjoy mondo overdrive, but don't look for much clean headroom.

In 1963, the Beatles changed everything. The great 'guitar explosion' of the '60s was ignited by the chimey jangle of John and George's guitars played through Dick Denny's 'candy panel' Vox AC30 amplifiers. While teenaged girls were swooning over the Fab Four singing "I Want to Hold Your Hand," their boyfriends were thinking, "I wanna play the guitar," and play they did. The British Invasion ultimately spawned competition among amp manufacturers on both sides of the Atlantic, and this was a wonderful thing for guitarists. Strange new amplifiers arrived on America's shores with names like Marshall, Vox, Hiwatt, Orange, Laney, and Matamp (although not always in large numbers).

In 1964, Fender introduced reverb throughout their entire 'blackface' line, and amplifiers were generally becoming bigger, louder, and more refined. In reality, however, most of us young garage band wannabes were playing "House of the Rising Sun" through Fender Deluxe Reverbs, Ampeg Reverb-o-Rockets, or the odd Gibson Lancer. Our heroes may have played classic Marshall Super Leads or Twin Reverbs, but these amps were too big for the station wagon, and much too stout for Dad's wallet.

A few years later, the Stones put Ampeg SVT and V4 stacks on the map, Eric Clapton adopted MusicMan amps, and most of us were playing bigger Fender or Marshall amps. Then along came a race car mechanic and complete tonefreak named Randall Smith, father of the Mesa Boogie Mark I. This 'little' behemoth made a huge impact with its high gain, overdriven tone in a compact and portable 1x12 cabinet, and the Boogie Mark I launched a wave of imitators as companies rushed to hop on the Boogie bandwagon.

Thanks in large part to Randall Smith, all of the major manufacturers began to build amplifiers with channel switching, boost circuits, and more power. This trend continued into the '80s, and new features and designs continue to be introduced in amplifiers today. Modeling amps have arrived, offering the promise of a variety of selectable vintage tones through the wonders of digital technology, and for many companies, their focus will remain on creating increasingly versatile, modern amplifiers at a price point that is accessible to novice and pro alike.

The 1990's can also be considered the decade of the boutique amp

builder, especially where point-to-point, hand-built, all-tube amps are concerned. After nearly 50 years, one might sensibly ask what could possibly be left to explore in analog amplifier design? What drives the demand for boutique amps that cost thousands of dollars, when you can still buy a perfectly respectable Fender for a few hundred? The answer lies in the supply and demand dynamic driving the vintage amplifier market. When classic vintage amplifiers like the 1959 Fender Bassman, the Marshall JTM45 Plexi, and the Vox AC30 were cheap and demand was low, there were no boutique builders. We didn't need them, and in fact, we didn't want any of those stinkin' old road dog amps.

The same thing can be said of old Stratocasters, Teles, and Les Paul guitars that cost thousands today. Once upon a time, new was cool, and old was just old. But things changed. We grew older. The old classics began to be recognized for what they were - classics, built in limited quantities, and when they were gone, they were gone (and a lot of them were leaving the U.S. for collectors in Japan). We also discovered just how magical many of the old amps sounded. Enter the boutique builder. With prices for clean, unmodified vintage amplifiers steadily rising, a new market was created for amplifiers that were, tonally speaking, "as good as vintage." Lately, we've even christened a few current production boutique amplifiers as being "better than vintage," (with credit to Sheryl Crow guitarist Peter Stroud for having coined the term). With so many visionaries now recreating the classics or improving on classic designs, it would seem as if we guitarists are sittin' in high cotton.

> "Although we may never know who created the first guitar amplifier, we can safely assume that it was probably created from an old radio set."

But how can you make the right choice when there are clearly more new models of amplifiers being built today than one person could possibly audition? Is there a 'best' among so many worthy contenders? Well, yes... there is a 'best' for you, and it is simply whatever sounds right to you. If you have acquired this guide with the intention of researching amplifiers that you intend to own and play, I urge you to play as many amps as you can. Keep an open mind, and try to learn something from every experience, whether you like a particular amp or not.

As an artist, it pays to expand your depth of vision. Blindly following someone's latest idea of 'the best' is a losing game that will only distract you from the real reason you first picked up a guitar, which was to make sounds, and eventually, music. It's a lifelong journey. I've played hundreds of amps new and old, and while many of them have absolutely captivated me, I am under no illusion that any of them may be 'better' than my 1968 Pro Reverb. What others may think of my amp is not important. The speakers and faceplate have been changed, it's been tweaked by Mr. Sharp, and as such, it is of no value to fastidious collectors, but it's the right amp for me, and I am always inspired by it.

There are more great amplifiers new and old for you to explore than ever before, and the odds of capturing inspiring guitar tone through an amplifier are definitely in your favor. This guide has been created to help you do just that. Quest forth...

David Wilson is the publisher of *The ToneQuest Report* - an inspirational monthly resource for guitarists, and The Players Guide to Ultimate Tone. *The ToneQuest Report* is available by subscription only. For more information, visit www.tonequest.com, or call 1-877-MAX-TONE toll-free in the USA. ∎

An Interview with Michael Soldano

Michael Soldano was making his own design of boutique amps way before boutique amps became fashionable, or became a sizable cottage industry. Originally influenced by soaking up all the information he could from discarded tube amp books from the Seattle Public Library, he went on to repair, modify, and finally, build what he thought would be the perfect guitar amplifier, with an amazing overdrive sound.

His first amp to bear the Soldano brand name appeared on his first Super Lead Overdrive (SLO), which was built for a friend of his in 1986. It was an immediate success, and set a new industry standard for high gain guitar amps during the late 80's. From the very beginning, Soldano amps were known for their killer high gain tone. Soldano's unrelenting pursuit of both quality (he uses only the finest components) and reliability have become legendary, and as he says, "I build stuff that won't break" - no small statement considering what guitar players can/will do to abuse an amplifier. For more information on Soldano Custom Amplification's current model lineup and answers for frequently asked guitar amp questions, please visit www.soldano.com.

Q/A Article:

Q: How did you originally get started in the amp business and explain how this initial hobby has evolved into a career, now culminating with Soldano Custom Amplification?

A: Initially, like a lot of people in this business, I was just a guitar player looking for a better sound. Actually, I started building guitars before amps. As a result of that, customers were asking me if I could repair their amps. I had a very, very basic knowledge of electronics, but nothing to write home about. Mostly, I just looked for the broken part to replace. I started doing repairs and, of course I got curious, wondering what would happen if I modified different things. Then I started doing little mods, and actually got really interested in it, so I taught myself electronics out of books. I went to the Seattle Public Library and checked out all the books they had on the subject. Luckily, I got a lot of discards from the library when they decided that technology was obsolete, because my mom worked for the library system.

Q: I read about that story a little bit. Didn't you literally pick up some amp books out of a basket that was going to recycling or something?

Michael Soldano from Soldano Custom Amplification working his booth at a recent Anaheim NAMM show.

A: Exactly! To me, that's an outrage, because technology is never obsolete. Even if we don't use it anymore it should be kept on record. The library was just chucking these books on vacuum tube stuff. Fortunately, my mom worked for the library system at the time, so whenever some book like that went by on its way to the dumpster; she'd grab it for me.

I learned most everything I know about vacuum tube technology from reading books for theory and experimenting on amps for the practical aspect. As things evolved, I started playing more and I started realizing how bad my sound was, and how I knew it could be better. I started modifying an old Silver Face Fender 50 watt Bassman, which is a good test mule. I did some mods on that. Then, I modified some of my friends' Marshalls.

> "There seemed to be a shortage of good amp people, so I started Soldano Custom Amplification."

After that, I decided to build an amp from scratch. Several experiments in that direction yielded various results and finally, I landed on what eventually became the 100 watt Super Lead Overdrive. I built one for myself, and it was fabulous - I loved it. Friends of mine heard it and said it was an incredible amp, and could I build them one? I said "Sure, why not? I'll order the parts to do it." So I built three of these amps and nobody could come up with the money, except one guy, a friend of mine, Tommy Martin.

At this point in my life, I already had been working in an autobody shop on and off ever since high school, and was getting tired of banging fenders out on cars as a day job. "I need to do something different." I thought, so I went to L.A. and started a guitar business. I packed everything up in my van, moved to L.A., and opened a little shop on Melrose. When I got there, I realized that everybody and their brother was doing guitar work, so I decided the guitar thing was not the place to be. There was just so much competition, people were working for peanuts. Yet, there seemed to be a shortage of good amp people, so I started Soldano Custom Amplification, which was mostly doing Marshall mods, and I was hoping to maybe manufacture the SLO 100. After attempting to get my amps into various shops, finally, a friend of mine, Tony Antidormi showed one to Steve Lukather. Steve tried it out, loved it, and bought it on the spot. Then the word spread that there was this great new amp in town, and overnight Soldano Custom Amplification became a major player in the world of high gain guitar amplification. It's really quite amazing. I never planned on it being that way.

Q: How effective are today's modeling amps at replicating the vintage sounds of older Fenders, Marshalls, Vox, etc.?

A: You'll be surprised to hear that I think they've done a fairly decent job, but I'm going to qualify that. I think the only guys that have nailed the modeling thing is Line 6. But, here's where I'll qualify it. It's better than I thought it could ever be, but that doesn't mean it's great. In other words, I never thought it could even be close to any good, just because of the whole concept of digital modeling. I just thought, "no way." But that said, if you're some kid sitting in your bedroom recording directly onto a four track without a studio, and you don't even have the luxury of micing speakers, because the noise will piss off the neighbors or whatever, I find the modeling amps are fairly decent tool, because they have the voicing of the speaker, amp, and everything built into it to make this pseudo believable amp sound. For doing little demo tapes in your bedroom, it really doesn't sound bad, because it mimics the overall essence of the amp by virtue of taking snapshots of sound and letting you cut and paste them note by note onto your tape.

Modeling amps don't work when you're trying to play them live, because they are nothing but a cardboard cutout of the amp they're supposed to represent. They don't react with you as a guitar player in any way that the original amp did. It's more noticeable on the high gain models than on the vintage models. The vintage models are fairly clean and linear. You would not expect to have much interaction between your guitar and the amp. You crank up a clean sound on a Vox AC-30 and unless it's really loud, you're not going to get any feedback out of the guitar. It's just going to be this clean, jangly, bright pop sound. In this case, a modeling amp isn't going to do too bad of a job, because it's not asked to do anything more than simulate these classic sounds.

A high gain amp will feed back readily, because it has so much gain. It can take the weakest signal in the world and amplify it a million times. That's where you get your sustain and your notes that will hang on forever, because the amp is so sensitive that any sound of influence in the guitar's pickup will cause it to feedback. Well, in a modeling amp there

is no gain. It's simulating a highly saturated guitar sound, and all you're getting is what an amp sounds like when it's really saturated, without actually creating oodles of gain. It's drawing a picture of what oodles of gain looks like. When you stand in front of one of those modeling amps, you'll be disappointed when trying to make it react to what your fingers are doing on the fretboard. On a real high gain amp, you have this extreme interaction that's happening between you, the guitar, and the amp. It's not going to happen in this cutout, because it's only a mirage of the real thing. It's like a hologram or something. It's not going to respond like a real high gain amp will because it has no gain - it's like a synthesizer. The guitar in this situation isn't anything more than a trigger. The signal comes from the guitar. The processor and the modeling amp sense that it's an A#, and then it picks through its little library of simulations for what a Soldano playing an A# sounds like, and spits that out that snapshot of tone into the speaker. So, that's where the problem lies with modeling amps. They don't play like a real amp. They sound kind of close from a two dimensional place, but they aren't it.

Q: Do you consider speakers to be 50% of an amp's tone? Also, what do you look for when selecting speakers for Soldano Amps?

A: I don't know if I'd say 50%, but yes, I'd say speakers play a huge role in the way an amp sounds. You could have a really great sounding amp and plug it into some bad speakers and that amp is going to sound bad. You can take a normal sounding amp and improve it somewhat by playing it through better speakers, if it happens to be equipped with bad ones. Speakers are very important. There are all different types of speakers, and speakers are very subjective, because everybody has a different idea of what they want to hear.

When I'm selecting speakers for my amps, I look for something that's reliable and can handle the power, because nothing's worse than having blown speakers. And with today's technology, there's no excuse for a blown speaker, because we have much better material for the voice coils, and better manufacturing methods. The first thing I look for in a speaker is one with a suitable power rating, and then I look for voicing. For guitars, I like speakers that are going to have a good low-end response and that actually will roll off the top-end. All speakers will roll off top-end anyway - it's just a part of the equation, but some are better at reproducing top-end (like P.A. speakers) than others.

A guitar amp, even a tube guitar amp is capable of producing some upper-end harmonics that can somewhat be painful or tiring to the ear. So, I look for a speaker that will help roll off some of that top-end a little bit, that will help shape the sound and give it a little violin-y tone, but not to the point where it sounds muffled, of course. You want clarity. I've been using speakers that have been based on old British designs,

> "The word spread that there was this great new amp in town, and overnight Soldano Custom Amplification became a major player in the world of high gain guitar amplification."

Celestion being the most noted. I'm not a big fan of the modern Vintage 30's, because they have this hard, upper midrange thing that I find annoying. The old "greenback" has a really nice roundness to it, where they actually had this kind of "thunk" on the low-end that was cool and yet had a defined, not shrill, top-end.

Eminence Corporation is manufacturing all of the speakers that we currently use now. It's a company that will work with me. I might say that one speaker has too much high-end and they retool it to make something different. So, I just look for something that has a nice musical tone, not necessarily something that's efficient. I don't care about efficiency in a speaker, because I have amps that put out over 100 watts. I have amps that put out 50 watts, as well, and they can get plenty loud that way, so I'm not looking for high sound pressure levels, which you would be looking for in a P.A. speaker where you're trying to get the most efficiency out of your available amplifiers. With guitars, it's almost better to have less efficiency, because you can crank the amp harder without the sound pressure getting so high that it's tearing your head off. For the vintage amplifiers, I love the new reissue Jensens. I think they did a brilliant job - they sound exactly like the originals, some of which I've been fortunate enough to own. They're beautiful speakers, but they're very bright on the top-end, but it's a very musical top-end. In other words, it's not shrill and unlistenable, but it's limited to a certain kind of sound. I wouldn't use it for heavy metal, for example, but if you're looking for a more vintage vibe, the new Jensens nail it perfectly.

Q: Explain how electronics can age to produce the vintage tone many amp manufacturers are trying to duplicate today.

A: Electronics do age, but it's more the designs of the older amps that make them sound the way they do than the components aging. Resistors and capacitors will drift in value a little bit.

Q: That's what I was wondering. Things go in and out of tolerance a little bit. Does that happen more over time, or is that something that happens right away? I was thinking that the tolerances, as they drift out of specs, could produce some of this vintage tone, but that's really the question that I had.

A: And it's a valid question, and it's a hard one to answer. Pots can get scratchy and dirty, but that's not going to change the sound, except when you're turning the knobs, and you hear the scratchiness. Resistors are also known to change value, but not a lot. For example, I've taken apart some of the really old amps where the resistors are still exactly what they're supposed to be for specs. Nothing's changed at all. Capacitors do tend to change over time, especially those older ones where the dielectric breaks down, like in power filters, and have less capacitance than they originally had. I have been told that transformers can absorb moisture in the paper that separates the windings,

changing the tone. It's really hard to say. You'll see on the Internet information about transformers "wearing out." That's a bunch of crap, since there's nothing in a transformer to wear out. It's just a bunch of copper wire wrapped around an iron bobbin. There are no moving parts. There's no actual wearing there. Either the thing's working or it's shorted out and dead. In the whole aging process, the tubes wearing are probably more noticeable than anything.

Q: I know you're going to like this next question. Where do you draw the line on a vintage amp's originality? Do you feel replacing such components as filter capacitors, vacuum tubes, etc. hurt the value from a collector's standpoint, or does actually add value from a player's standpoint?

A: Yes and yes. I'm totally about people being able to play their amps, though I feel it's true that you're going to change its originality if you replace some original parts to keep it working well. On the other hand, hard core collectors are going to thumb their nose and say that you ruined it by replacing anything. I equate it the same as a vintage guitar. Say you have an old Stratocaster where the frets are so worn down that they're right into the wood of the fingerboard and you can't play the instrument anymore. How valuable is that guitar if you can't play it? Yank the damn frets out, and refret it so you can play it. I feel the same way about guitar amps. If you can't use the amp anymore, it's pointless to own it, unless you just like to have a room or museum full of nice virginal originals, which I can relate to as well.

> "My biggest concern with a new design is reliability. I build stuff that won't break. I'm all about quality and reliability."

I know that sometimes it's fun to collect things, because it is an original and it is pristine and beautiful. You might be perfectly okay with having something you can never put electricity into (that might fry, because it has shorted filters), but you just want it, because it's so perfect and original. I respect people who are into that, but as a player, I want to be able to play the stuff. I feel that it should not hurt the amp's value to change parts to keep it playable, but it does make it less original, so I can see this from a hard core collector's point of view. It's less original, therefore it's less valuable, but I would put the value on whether it's playable, and if it's still playable, it should be worth more. But that gets into a whole argument on where the value is. I feel an amp should be playable - the collectors think it should be pristine and perfect.

Q: Do you play much? If so, outside of Soldano, what are your favorite amps to plug into?

A: I do play. I don't play as much as I'd like to, but I do play in a friend's band right now. It's a lot of fun playing out, and we have a good time. Outside of my own amps, I have a collection of other brands of amps I've collected over the years that I'm rather fond of. I like Hiwatts, and have a 200 watter. A friend of mine has a beautiful mid-70's 100 watter that's absolutely amazing. I have a really nice, late 50's Fender Vibrosonic that I use for surf tone. It has a big 15-inch JBL D130 in it, it's all original, and it's the ultimate surf amp. It's got that sound. I've got an old brown face Fender Reverb that I plug into it that's got Dick Dale written all over it. One amp that's also tough to beat, but you do have to use some kind of an overdrive pedal (I use my all tube Supercharger pedal), is the mid-70's JMP master volume Marshalls, not the Plexis, but the ones that had master volumes. Those things, for a good old rock and roll work horse amp, are pretty tough to beat. They're a little bright and a little shrill in their stock form, but if you put any kind of gain pedal in front of them, they're a pretty good rock amp. They're a little chunky, and have that classic British sound.

Q: What's the strangest tone you've ever listened to out of an original amp?

A: My 120 watt Sound City. This model has all active, all tube tone controls. You can get some of the most hideous sounds out of that amp that you've ever heard - it's unbelievable. Each tone control is like a volume knob for that frequency. It also has a lot of gain in each frequency, so if you crank up the bass and the top end, it sounds like some horrible distortion box, but in a cool 60's psychedelic kind of way. I think that's the oddest sounding amp I've ever messed with. The Oranges are interesting in that they have this filter in them called the FAC control that's basically a stepped high-pass filter, and you can get some weird voicing when combining this with its bass and treble controls. It has a rather unique EQ in it also.

Q: What's your favorite output tube configuration?

A: I'm a really fan of the 6L6/5881. That's what I use with everything I build practically. I think that the 6L6 was one of the most musical audio tubes ever designed and built. It combines many things of all tubes in a nice balance, whereas the EL 34's have a really round and warm, fuzzy thing going. It's almost too warm and fuzzy, and the bottom end is kind of weak. The 6550, on the other hand, has a bottom end like a sledgehammer, but it's way too cold and sterile sounding. The 6L6 is both. It has a warm, musicalness to it, and yet it has a clear and solid bottom, which I find hard to get with EL 34's. When you get into the bigger power stuff, like hi-fi amps, KT88's are wonderful, but strictly for hi-fi. I don't know I'd be all that thrilled about a KT88 equipped guitar amp, because I think it would be too hard.

Q: When you're designing a new amp, what are your primary considerations, (without getting too technical) and do you have a price point from the start?

A: My biggest concern with a new design is always tone, of course. But since that's a given, the next consideration is reliability. I build stuff that won't break. I'm all about quality and reliability. That's my number one thing. Lately, price point has become an issue, only because I've seen the market more driven by pricing. When I designed the 100-watt Super Lead Overdrive, which is our flagship amp, the Ferrari of the Soldano line, price was no object. This is a no compromise amp - I simply set out to build the world's best guitar amplifier, in my mind, anyway. I didn't compromise on anything. It's a very pricey amp, and these days it lists for over $3,599. That's because the parts are extremely expensive and it's a bit labor intensive to build, but that's what makes it a great amp. On my newer designs, I do think about price, because regardless of what anybody says, people have a threshold on what they can afford. Today's amp marketplace is somewhat driven by pricing, because there is so much competition out there. In that respect, I still use the best parts I can get for a given price range, and I won't allow my quality to drop below a certain level, which means my prices will never drop below a certain level also.

Q: That brings us to the next question. What do you consider to be the minimum tolerances of such amp components as resistors, capacitors, output transformers, etc. in order for an amplifier's tone to sound consistent in a production line environment?

A: The 100-watt Superlead Overdrive is all mil-spec. Because of the fact that they are readily available and they don't cost any more than anything else, I think resistors should all be either one or two percent tolerance (that's what Soldano uses), because now we have the technology to make resistors like that all day. Capacitors, again, because there is not point in ignoring technology, five to ten percent tolerance is as bad as you should let it get. It doesn't have to be any better than five percent, but it should not be any less than ten percent on capacitor values.

> "Forget point-to-point wiring. It's only labor intensive. A well designed circuit board will make a more superior product than any point-to-point amp could ever be."

That's why, when you plug in any of the amps that I make, they all sound identical. In other words, you could have an SLO that you bought fifteen years ago and if it gets stolen and I build you a new one, it's going to sound exactly like your fifteen year old one, because there is no variance in the component tolerances. If you go in a store and there are three of my amps, all three are going to sound the same with the only variation being the tubes, but the Russian tubes we are using nowadays are very consistent. So, we're finding we have very good consistency that way.

Q: I know that you are a no-compromise guy and weren't satisfied with some of your amp designs that were produced by Yamaha in the 1980's, because of modifications to reduce cost. What are some of the most common things mass production amp manufacturers do to cut corners?

A: Well, the worse thing they do is scrimp on transformer size and on power supply filter capacity. Transformers are expensive, because they sell them by the pound (i.e., how much copper or iron is in them). A lot of the companies are making their transformers smaller, trying to reduce costs. As a result, they're not getting the good bass response they should get from the output transformer, and the power transformers are running hotter, because they're pulling the same amount of power through thinner wires and a smaller core and relying on today's higher temperature insulating materials. While this is perfectly acceptable engineering, in a guitar amp where you're trying to build something that can work in any kind of adverse condition, I feel you shouldn't cut it that close to the line.

Many companies also cut costs on filter capacitors. A perfect example of this is the 100-watt Marshalls. In the mid-70's, they had more than ample filter capability, because they had a whole bank of filter caps. As the years went by and they were trying to cut costs, they just kept removing capacitors. The theory being, if an old Fender works fine on 25 microfarads, we can do it, too. You can think of capacitors in the power supply as the storage battery. They're what provide a power reserve for when you hit those passages where you're really attacking the amp, especially in the low frequency stuff, or when you're doing a lot of percussive runs on the low strings. If you don't have a lot of filter capacity, the voltage will drop as you hit those lower frequency notes. When that happens, the amp looses power and falls on its face, creating a spongy sound, and it loses its tightness. Now, if that's a desired design feature, then go ahead and run with it. A lot of companies are just doing that. Another thing, and this is what pisses me off about the Yamaha thing, is that companies are taking out the filter chokes from the power supply. This is okay on smaller amps, because the slight voltage drop you have across the resistor that replaces the choke is negligible. But in a high powered amp, replacing the choke with a large power resistor is also going to aggravate that problem of the voltage drop when the amp needs the power the most.

The other thing some companies do to cut costs of course, is just plain crappy construction. Instead of using screws to hold the circuit boards in place, they use snap-in plastic standoffs. Instead of having soldered connections, they're using slip-on spade terminals - just so they can have monkeys assembling these things. These cost savings and short cuts will eventually come back to bite them in the ass, because it's going to reduce their reliability and durability. Additionally, instead of using plywood cabinets, they're using particle board.

Q: How about speakers, Michael, are they just quoting speakers by spec and the cheapest price gets them in the cabinet, or how do you feel about that?

A: On the really cheap amps that's probably the case. They'll buy inexpensive speakers made overseas that are adequate for transistor radios. It's surprising how inexpensive good speakers really are. You can buy a very high quality speaker from Eminence for not very much money. Because of the perceived value of speakers, I think amp makers will spend more money on speakers, just so they can say, "Hey, we're using Celestions." They're paying the price when they're buying Celestions, because people buying an amp will spend a few extra dollars if it has Celestions in it. So, that's one area where I notice they don't chince so much. It seems like most companies are using good quality speakers.

Q: Do you feel some of today's new crop of advanced ax-grinders is actually looking for tone that's completely new and unique as opposed to getting the same old vintage sounds?

A: I definitely think so. I don't listen much to a lot of the new bands, because I just don't dig the style that much. But bands, like Korn and Limp Biscuit and such, are doing a whole new kind of guitar sound. They're using drop tunings and doing these bass-y kinds of things. I've even noticed in some of the magazine articles that these guys are running fifteen-inch speakers in sub-bass cabinets, with massive amounts of power. These new guitarists are really trying to do something different.

> "Modeling amps don't work when you're trying to play them live, because they are nothing but a cardboard cutout of the amp they're supposed to represent, and they don't play and react like a real amp."

There are a lot of guys still trying to sound like 1950's Mississippi bluesmen, but there's also this whole flock of new players that are really trying to chisel out their own defined sound. It may not necessarily appeal to my taste, but I'm happy to see that they're not just copying everything that's been done a million times before them.

So, yes, I think there is a new breed of guitar player out there. Seven string guitars are in vogue now - for a while it was seven strings with an extra high string, but now it's seven strings with an extra low string.

I think there's a conscious effort for the new generation to find their own sound. I don't think there's anything that's been done that's quite as revolutionary as when Jimi Hendrix plugged a Strat into a Marshall and cranked it wide open with an Octavia pedal. But, I think these guys are trying to create their own nitch and separate themselves from what's preceded them.

Q: What do you consider to be the top five vintage amps of all time?

A: Definitely at the top of the list would be the "410 Tweed" Fender Bassman, because that's the one that started it all for everybody. Everything that's ever been made is based on that. That's where Marshalls came from, that's even where Soldanos came from.

Q: So, that's your "holy grail" of amplifiers?

A: Well, I don't know that it's the "holy grail" in that it sounds amazing or anything, but it's the foundation that everything else sprang from. After that, on a time line, you'd get into the Plexi-Marshalls, which were just an English-made Fender Bassman. They didn't change the circuit at all. If you compare the schematics, a 50-watt JTM45 is just a Fender Bassman.

Q: I didn't know that.

A: Yeah, it is. It's exactly… In fact, that's all a JTM45 is - a Ken Bran, Jim Marshall built Fender Bassman. The reason is that Fenders were very expensive in England. Jim Marshall had a music store and noticed that all the players wanted in the early 60's were Fender amps, but they couldn't afford them. So he just said, "Well, hell, let's built clones of Fenders here in England, so we can sell them at an affordable price." So, that's what a JTM45 is - a Fender Bassman. I'd say the Plexi-Marshalls, not because they're unique In design or anything, but because they started that whole head/cabinet separation, the "look of rock," so to speak, the stack of cabinets. That was all part of the Marshall deal, with Pete Townshend leading the charge.

Moving beyond that, I'm a huge Hiwatt fan, just because of the absolute beauty of construction of those Hiwatts. As far as setting a benchmark for craftsmanship, the early Hiwatts were some of the most beautiful amps, internally, you ever set your eyes on. They were constructed like works of art. They're incredible, and have been the inspiration for the things I've done.

From there, I'd probably have to fast forward a ways to the 70's and I'd have to say the flagship amp would be the Boogie Mark I, because Randall Smith, who I have to credit as being the first one to purposely go after designing a high gain design to sustain and distort specifically, redefined the whole sound of what guitar amps could do.

The next flag after that would be in fifteen years, when I designed the 100 watt Super Lead Overdrive, which I think was the next step beyond what Randy already started with the Boogie.

Q: Really, that was the original high wattage, high gain amplifier, right?

A: Yeah, he was really the first to do that. Marshall had high power amps, but they didn't necessarily distort. They only reason they distorted was because guys were turning them wide open and all the distortion was happening in the power tubes. Randall Smith was the first guy to say, "Hey, let's overdrive the pre amp and let the pre amp make the sound distortion, so we can turn the volume down with a master, but still get that sound." So, he set the pace for everything that followed since. A couple of other notables along the way, just because of uniqueness in design, would be the Orange, because they had a very cool, physical look to them, but they were just another loud, clean

amp, just like everything that was being made then. The Fender Twin will also always remain in the annals of amp history, because it's so versatile. It had two twelve inch speakers. It had reverb. It had vibrato. It did it all, except distort, but it was an amp that was made for so many years that many players cut their teeth on it. It'll always be one of histories great marks in the amp world.

Q: Do you have any closing remarks, Michael?

A: I could go on for days! Amps are a very subjective thing. Every amp has its own voice, whether it be an old vintage little 20 watt lap steel amp from the 30s, or a high gain Soldano for that matter, or a Bogner, or a VHT. The most important thing is that people buy amps that work for them and for what they want to do. In other words, get an amp that fits what you're doing stylistically, playing-wise. Just because you're in a rockabilly band, don't feel you have to buy an old vintage Fender, just because that's what rockabilly guys do. Play what works for you!

If you're playing an older amp and it isn't working for you or it's not reliable enough, buy a modern amp that does do what you want it to do and don't be afraid to create your own style. I think a lot of people buy vintage amps because they think that's what they have to do to be cool. "I play the blues; therefore, I must play an old Fender." There are a lot of other amps out there that can do what a Fender does and do it better, plus you can still buy inexpensive replacement parts. They're more reliable and more versatile and won't conk out on you in the middle of a gig. I feel that people should open their minds a little more when they're amp shopping. The other thing is, and this is important: don't believe everything you read on the Internet, because the Internet is a vast quagmire of misinformation regarding amps. There are a lot of people on the Internet that, due to anonymity, have become self-proclaimed experts and they really don't know what the hell they're talking about. It's one of those things where a little knowledge is more dangerous than none at all. And the whole voodoo thing about point-to-point wiring versus circuit boards? Forget point-to-point wiring. It's only labor intensive. A well designed circuit board will make a more superior product than any point-to-point amp could ever be. If you want to know more about that and other things, check out the tech articles on our web site, www.soldano.com. ∎

> "The worse thing many companies do when trying to cut costs is to scrimp on transformer size and on filter capacitor capacity."

Paul Reed Smith Interview:
A Guitar Maker's Perspective

Paul Reed Smith's ears are probably worth an easy $2 million. When you hook them up to his musically powered brain, you can double that. And when you factor in his guitar playing skills, what he knows and has sacrificed for his most sacred word - TONE, he should probably be a monetary level demanded by many of today's top professional athletes.

While he can be very easy going, whimsical, and downright comical at times (his clinics bring this out), when the word tone comes up, you better be deadly serious, and you better know what you're talking about. Paul is very fussy about everything between his guitar strings and speaker cone, and his amplifier knowledge is very extensive. Nothing gets taken for granted. We feel fortunate to be able to feature Paul Reed Smith in this 1st Edition *Blue Book of Guitar Amplifiers*. If you would like to obtain more information about his guitars, please refer to the current edition of the *Blue Book of Electric Guitars*.

Q/A Article:

Q: Given your success and intolerance for bad tone and knowing that you're pretty much a one guitar guy, do you have a favorite amp? If so, what is it and do you have it in your basement?

A: When I play rhythm guitar, I plug into an old Silver Face Super Reverb. There are several amps that I use on the road. I like playing through Mesa Boogie Triple Rectifiers. I like playing through Soldano SLO 100's. I like playing through Marshall 2000's. I have played through some great amplifiers on the road that have sounded just fine, but generally, Marshalls and Boogies and some other stuff are what get used on the road. The amps I use at home, the amps I use in my band, and the amps I use to record with solo tone wise are Koch amps. I don't like them - I love them.

I have gotten similar beautiful tones out of the other amps I've mentioned, however. For some reason, for rhythm guitar I like Super Reverbs. I like them through 212 cabinets. I like them through the 410's that the old ones came with, and for some reason I like the Silver Face ones better than I like the Black Face ones. Everybody says, "Black Face this," and "Black Face that." I don't know what it is, but I've never heard a Silver Face Super that was original that I didn't like. This guy, Steve from MN, gave me a non-master volume Silver Face that had one of the speakers replaced and it still sounds good. I plug that amp into 212 cabinets. For a rhythm guitar, it breaks up nicely. It's a good amp. It records extremely well. The Koch amps sound really

Paul Reed Smith and his newest sensation - the Singlecut Dragon IV.

good through PA systems, they sound really good without PA systems, and they sound really good recorded. Some people find them a little too compressed. I find people compress it anyway when they record it, so I don't need to use a compressor. Carlos Santana has some Dumble Overdrive Specials that I like; there's one in particular that I really like. I'm picky about Overdrive Specials, but that's a whole other land. There are also some amps that are out now, specialty amps, that sound really good. There are some boutique makers that are making really good sounding amps. So, without listing all the boutique guys, they are worth checking out, also.

> "If you want your amp to sound better, become a better guitar player!"

Q: Because PRS guitars have never been more popular, do you have any general words of wisdom for your customers in terms of purchasing the right amp for their new PRS guitar?

A: It depends so much on the player. They need to listen to the amp they are interested in before they buy. Fender makes a reissue Super Reverb I like. It's a nice sounding amplifier.

Q: The people at Tonequest also really like the sound of this new reissue Super Reverb.

A: It's a good amp, but I still like my old Silver Face better. I thought that Richie Fliegler and the whole Fender crew did a good job on the reissue of the Super. There's a Fender that I played through at their booth the other day. I thought it sounded absolutely beautiful; I don't remember the model name. I guess my point is it's important to plug into it. Marshall makes a good clean channel in the Marshall 2000, which is a really good amp overall. The clean channel in a Triple Rectifier sounds beautiful also. There are a lot of really good amps out there, and my recommendation is play through them before you buy one." A music store is a carpeted environment. A stage is a hard floor environment. I recommend that you try to put an amp in a room that's fairly hard floored and turn it up a little bit, because amps sound very different in a carpeted room than they do sitting on a hard floor. Everybody usually gets very surprised when they play a gig on a hard floor and the amps sounds so bright they ask what happened. Well guess what? It's up eight or nine dB on the high end because of the room. I would be careful about that kind of thing.

Q: If a person has $3,000 to spend on a guitar and amp, do you think they should spend approximately ½ on the guitar and ½ on the amp?

A: I'd rather not go down that road. Some guys have a magic amp and they're looking for a magic guitar. Some guys have a magic guitar and they're look for an amp. Some guys need both. I'm picky about what I like. A good amp sounds good with the knobs in any position. Bad amps, typically, have to have the knobs in one position and you still can barely tolerate it. It's true for guitars, too. More important than any amount of money you spend on getting the right guitar/amp combination, is that if you really want to get a better sound and tone, the first place to start is by learning how to play better through more practice and a good teacher.

Q: That's an interesting point.

A: That should be the first point. Learn how to play better. If the Beatles had to use the Super Reverbs or the Vox AC30, would the tune sound the same? Yes. If "Good Day Sunshine" was recorded with different amps, would it have still sounded great? Yeah.

Q: You've been in the amp business before with your HG-70 head and HG-212 combo, both of which used solid state electronics. Any plans to get back into the amp business, this time with a tube design? It seems like a logical move, given the popularity of your instruments.

A: Maybe. We have a very large inventory of new, old stock tubes that I bought up a while back.

A: Stockpiling tubes, are you?

A: I did, even though we got to the party really late.

A: We inventoried a very large amount of tubes, and I was very careful about which ones I bought and which ones I didn't. I'm happy with the ones I bought. I don't know. I'm going to take my time if we decide to make an amp again.

Q: Do you have a favorite output tube configuration, or don't you think it makes that much difference overall?

A: Of course it makes a difference. The 6L6 and the EL34's usually sound different. I find much more of a variance between the manufacturers of tubes and how you bias them. In my amp, I'm using old Siemans EL34's and I'm really careful about how I bias them. They are supposed to be biased between twenty-five and thirty-five; I bias them between thirty-three and thirty-four. There's a real difference in how they're biased. Groove Tubes just sent me some of the new 6L6's they're making, but I haven't heard them yet. I need to try them. My friend, Ralph, really prefers 6L6's over EL34's. I don't know why I prefer EL34's over 6L6's, except that I've probably been playing Marshalls and EL34 amps all my life. It gets simple. How does the amp sound? Does it sound good, or does it sound bad? Do you like the way the amp sounds? Is it more musical than it used to be with the other amp, or is it less musical? My friend, Mike Ault just bought an amp with 6L6's in it. It sounds beautiful. Remember, the tube's just one piece of an amp. How's it biased? What's the configuration? What kind of output transformers? What kind of speaker cabinet? Who knows how many effects boxes are in front of it? It just goes on and on. It's a whole chain. When talking about output tubes, we are looking at one small piece of a long chain, so it's hard for me to say that everything with a 6L6 sounds good and everything with an EL34 sounds bad. It just doesn't work that way.

> "A good amp sounds good with the knobs in any position. A bad amp can barely be tolerated if the knobs are in its best position."

Q: Do you feel that an amp's speakers are at least as important as the electronics, and do you feel have a favorite make/model of speaker?

A: I like Celestion Vintage 30's. I like them for rhythm guitar. I like them for solo guitar. They can be a little too bright. I found a way to darken them up when you buy them, which I'm experimenting with. It kind of works, but in general, Vintage 30's sound good to me. I've used the 75-watt Celestian speakers and they've always sounded pretty good to me too. I've messed around a lot with these new Jensons. I haven't had much luck with them, but a lot of other people have. I really like the 10's that came in Silver Face Supers, but they're a vintage speaker for rhythm guitar. If I were to pick, I would put two Vintage 30's in an open back cabinet.

Q: What do you think of today's high tech modeling amplifiers? Do they do a good job on amplifying older Marshalls, Fenders, Voxs and other vintage makes/models?

A: Yes and no. Do they sound as good as the other things? Yes and no. The Line 6 has a different character than the Johnson, which has a different character than the old Korg A2 or the new Vox. I don't have experience with the Cybertwin and many other modeling amplifiers, so I can't tell you about that, but they all have a different thing about them. We used a Pod in our booth and David Grissom was playing through it. We had to do a couple of things to make it sound like a recorded amplifier, but we were able to get a pretty good sound out of it, after messing with it for a while. The Johnson has a different tone. If I had to pick out of all of them, Korg used to make something called an A2 with a Nashville card. It sounded absolutely beautiful.

Q: It must make you pretty happy that so many of today's killer guitar players now prefer PRS instruments. Have you noticed that any of them have a common amplifier of choice, or are they all over the board in what they want for an amp?

A: No. Musicians are as much all over the board for amps as they are for guitars. There are an awful lot of bands not playing PRS's. If you were to ask the industry, as a whole, what's the choice of these bands? They'd probably say a PRS through a Triple Rec, but there are millions of guys that don't play PRS's and don't play Triple Recs. Thank God we live in America. Thank God we have a choice. Steve Morris played through a metal knob V4 in the Dixie Dregs in the early days. It sounded good. Eric Clapton played into a straight 100-watt Marshall. It sounded good. I've heard Warren Haynes through a SLO 100. It sounded good. I've heard David Gilmore, from Pink Floyd, play through a Fender top. It sounded good. You've heard the Koch amp I used during my clinic at Dave's Guitar Shop (LaCrosse, WI) last year. It doesn't even sound like a guitar anymore - the tone is more like a violin. It sounds good. Ralph plays on Boogies. Bogner makes a really nice amp called a Shiva. This is a really nice amp. To answer your question, I'm picky, but there are a lot of things you could use as a musician. Let's go back one step. It's an AMPLIFIER. It's amplifying your guitar, so you can hear it.

Q: Point well taken. I saw Carlos Santana recently in Saint Paul - what's he currently using?

A: He's playing through Dumble Overdrive Specials and Boogies. He's using Mark 1's and Dumbles at the same time. What a sound!

Q: Obviously, if anyone has a trademark sound these days, it's Carlos Santana, but the way the stage was set up, all the amps were in the back, so we couldn't see what he was using for an amplifier.

A: The cabinets were underneath the drum riser and the amps were behind that in racks. There were about ten amps behind there. He has a row of cabinets that were as long as the stage, but you can't see them because of the cloth hanging in front of the drum riser.

Q: Are they all mic'ed then? What's the mix on all this when they get them set up? There's probably some serious snake oil treatment going on, isn't there?

A: He's got a lot going on. He's got that Boogie mic'ed up, which you can see. It's the only cabinet you can see. Then he has a whole bunch of other stuff running, too, but he's using Boogies and Dumbles.

Q: Who are your favorite guitar players today? Do you see and fads or trends right now in amplifiers?

A: Jeff Beck, Jeff Beck, and did I mention Jeff Beck? I'll tell you why. He's playing so well right now. I like Eric Johnson, I like Carlos Santana, and I like Eric Clapton. I really like Tommy Emmanual, Robben Ford, and David Grissom as well. David's a very good guitar player, frighteningly good; he's one of the best guitar players I've ever seen in my life. Mark Tremonti I like a lot. He's a really good guitar player. I also have some guitar players I play with regularly that I like.

Q: Any of these guys you mentioned are all over the board in amplifiers, right?

A: I could tell you what all those guys use.

Q: What did Jeff Beck use for an amp?

A: He uses a Marshall 2000. He bought it at Guitar Center.

Q: What's Eric Johnson using right now?

A: He's mostly using Marshalls and Fenders.

A: The last time I saw Robben Ford, I know he was using a Dumble.

Q: How about David Grissom, is he still using a Marshall?

A: David's playing through Marshalls and there's another amp he really likes. He plays through a Matchless sometimes.

Q: Are you big on Monster cable and other fat wire alternatives, or do you think that for the average guitar player a $9 twelve-foot cord would be just fine?

A: I like the Whirlwind leader 18-footer. But if I were to pick a cable, I'd pick a Whirlwind leader 25-foot cable, and then I'd check it one direction and check the other direction and use it the way it sounds the best. They sound different one direction than the other. It is not bullshit. I have a guess as to the physics of why, but I'll keep it to myself.

> "There are a lot of really good amps out there, and my recommendation is play through them before you buy one."

That's my choice from guitar to pedal or guitar to amp, not for pedal to amp.

Q: What's your choice for pedal to amp?

A: I don't know. I don't have a good choice.

Q: That brings up another point. A lot of your endorsers, are they very sensitive about their cables, too, or do they just take whatever the roadie gives them to plug into?

A: I find very few people talking to me at length about cables. I'm very sensitive about what cables I use.

Q: What's your favorite group of all time and why?

A: It's the Beatles! How could it possibly be any other band? Do you want to know why I think that? Because their writing was so gifted. They were grounded, beautiful, had teamwork, knew what they were doing, honed their craft, it just goes on and on and on. No band ever grew more in their history. The Beatles grew with every record. Could you imagine? They were writing tunes in the cab on the way to the studio that we'll remember for the rest of our lives. It was just one of those combinations of people and intelligence and skill level. It was awesome. They were awesome.

Q: What are your top five most desirable amplifiers from a tone standpoint, either new or vintage? I think I know what some of the answers are, but I'm going to let you fill in the blanks.

A: A Fender Silver Face Super Reverb, an early Dumble Overdrive Special (make sure you find a good one by playing it first before you buy), a Koch Multi-Tone 100 (with the right tubes), and a late Marshall Plexi or early metal face 50 (again, be fussy and look a long time for a good one). An early Ampeg SVT bass amp would have to be my last choice, because, in term of bass amps, it's just a good amp. There are also some Boogie amps I like, but you're limiting me to five amps - that's not very fair. One of the reasons I don't like your question about five amps, is that there are very few of them I would use, because I like the new amps with the high gain.

Q: Like you mentioned, you might have to listen to more than a few early Marshalls or Dumbles to really get a good one. With today's boutique manufacturers, they're more consistent, aren't they?

A: They are way more consistent in tone and they sound pretty good all the time. A friend of mine just bought a boutique amp. It sounds beautiful. I'd say these custom builders are bringing the art back.

Q: What else are you up to right now?

A: I'm very involved in building a studio. I've been getting into microphones and computer based recording. I didn't spend all this time with all this amp stuff recently so I couldn't record. We have all the songs ready. I'm ready to go. It's a very interesting time for me.

Q: What is your most recent accomplishment or what are you working on right now, pretty seriously?

A: I'm working on improving the sound of the guitars. I've come up with some ideas for how to control a guitar. I'm concerned about making sure that the people that have ordered our guitars get a very good one. We're always working on quality. That's important to me. I've been working on redefining the way I play also. Again, if you want to get good sound and improve your tone, you must learn how to play better.

Q: Do you think amps twenty-five years from now will be confined to emulating the tones of the 20th century, or do you think there's going to be some breakthrough sounds that nobody has ever heard of before that sound cool? I know that's a theoretical question, but do you think guitar amps are really ready to change? Do you think the industry is ready to change?

> **"Most new boutique amps are way more consistent in tone than older vintage amplifiers, and they sound pretty good all the time."**

A: It's changing right now. For awhile, modeling amps were real hot, and now people are going back to regular amps. Modeling amps are going to be around forever, they're not going away. Getting good tubes is really difficult, so manufacturers are fighting tube problems all the time. The tubes can be microphonic, they can sound bad and sometimes they're brittle. I think the industry will always shift. You'll have digital effects in your amp; you'll have effect loops, etc. I like the new gain thing, but will it evolve over time? Yes. Are musicians going back to plain old good tones? Yes. There's also this triple rectifier thing that's good. I think that will morph over time, just like rap has now morphed into people singing. Will amps be emulated successfully over a long period of time? I don't know. Toasters are the same as they were twenty years ago, because the design works. They look a little more modern, but they're still a toaster. If you're trying to brown a little bit of bread or amplify a guitar, will it change that much? Yes, some. Who knows what genius is going to show up? I'm open to change. Did we all predict this thing that happened with ADAT and digital recording? This industry will always evolve, but where its going exactly in the future is anybody's guess.

Q: Thanks again Paul, for taking the time to do this interview, and hope to see you and Sam again sometime soon. ∎

An Amp Dealer's Perspective with John Beeson

John Beeson has been dealing in guitars and amplifiers since the mid 1960's, while he was still in high school and college. Being from the Midwest, his take on the marketplace for guitar amplifiers is tempered with decades of experience acquired in a retail environment. His store, The Music Shoppe, was established almost 30 years ago, and he has been attending NAMM (National Association of Musical Merchandisers) shows since the early 70's.

John is an easy going guy with a very good working knowledge on what to look for when buying, selling, or trading new and vintage amplifiers. It was his suggestion to put in color images regarding the various conditions of both guitar amplifier covering material and face fabrics. He has also provided us with many important tips on how non-originality on vintage amps can affect the desirability and price.

He's always a pleasure to talk to at the various guitar shows, where he also has a lot of experience based on years of exhibiting. More importantly, he has seen a lot of major amp trends come and go, and is well suited to inform us on the current state of the guitar amplifier industry.

John Beeson from The Music Shoppe in Terre Haute, IN, flanked by the other part of the guitar amplifier equation - guitars!

Q/A Article

Q: John, your store, The Music Shoppe, was established during the early 70's in Terre Haute, IN, and even before that, you were buying and selling both guitars and amplifiers. Also, you've been attending NAMM (National Association of Musical Merchandisers) shows for over 30 years, and have a real feel for the industry. Please explain to us a little bit about the evolution of amplifiers and what's been popular from the early 60's to present day.

A: The Music Shoppe was established in 1973. I started dealing with guitars and amps in the late 60's while still in high school and during college. I started attending NAMM shows in 1971 when they were located in Chicago each summer.

During this time, many of the amp companies were moving toward solid state technology. Marshall and Fender, two of the major manufacturers, were still very strong in the tube market, but they were even working on solid state designs at the time. I feel companies were moving in this direction, because of the cost factor. Solid state was cheaper to produce and helped create the huge success of the Vox and Kustom amps of the 1960's. Quality control, at that time, was very poor compared to today's standards. Large numbers of amps would come into a dealer and be defective. Today, the manufacturer works harder on the design and quality of their products. Most large manufacturers today offer a wider selection of amps than in the early 70's. Small practice amps up to full stacks, or solid state to full tube class "A" amps are now available. Also, many companies are successfully recreating retro tube amps that sound very good.

Q: It seems that many serious amp hounds today are really focused on originality and condition. Given the fact that many tube amps have had their filter capacitors and other electronic components replaced to keep

> "Amp quality control in the 1960's was very poor compared to today's standards. Large numbers of amps would come into a dealer and be defective."

them working, how do you feel this affects their values?

A: Many tube amps built in the 50's, 60's, and 70's wear out and fail from use over time. (i.e.: Capacitors dry up.) Therefore, these components must be replaced. Finding original parts can become difficult at times, so non-original components must be used. When an amp has any changes, this can affect its value. Most buyers of vintage amps will not take an amp completely apart. They will check cosmetics such as original grille cloth, tolex, speakers, and most importantly, the tone of the amp. Most will ask if any internal changes have been made, but seldom does the seller know if or how many have been made.

Q: It seems the top of the vintage amp marketplace today in terms of price are those original "cream puff, trailer queens" that are never used or even plugged in because the owners are scared of damaging something. Do you think these amps deserve a huge premium over those that are still in excellent condition, but may have some non-original components/items?

A: It is wonderful to find a totally original vintage amp in pristine condition, but many of these amps do not sound as good as the ones with many bruises and years of great music played through them. An amp that just sits or is stored away for years can have more problems than the one that is played daily. Capacitors can dry up, speakers can dry rot, and pots will fill with dust. I feel a mint old amp should be played and enjoyed, just be more careful when transporting, so the outside will remain mint. An amp in total mint condition will bring a higher price than one that is beat up.

Q: Some people are now restoring vintage amps, including replacing the grille cloth, speakers (if necessary), and perhaps even upgrading some electronic components. Again, how do you think this affects their value, from both a player and collector standpoint?

A: Replacing electronic components and speakers will possibly upgrade the sound of many vintage amps, but this will take value away. Replacing grille cloth, tolex, and speakers can destroy half, if not more, of the value of any vintage amp. The collector who wants a vintage amp wants the piece to be in original condition, no matter how beat up it looks. The player wants the amp to sound original. That is why he will buy a certain model. Modifications will take away much of the value!

Q: What seems to be the trend today regarding new amps, and what's your average price point?

A: The trend with young guitar players is to get as much distortion as they can get in an amp. In my store, that is one of the first things they ask for. The second is power. The seasoned guitar players want tube amps and are looking for tone. We carry amps ranging from beginner student models starting at $79 up to class "A" tube amps for $3000.

Q: When someone brings in an older, major trademark vintage amp, what do you look for before deciding its value? Also, which older makes/models do you seem to see come through the shop on a regular basis?

A: When determining a value on a vintage amp, one must look at how desirable it is and what the market is presently bringing on the certain piece. This will always give a good idea on the value of the amp.

Today, as with most stores that deal with vintage amps, you don't see any one model walk in on a regular basis. We still see many Fender, Gibson, and Marshall amps, but not as many as we saw in the 70's and 80's.

Q: Would you rather have 10 guitars and 2 amps or 5 guitars and 5 amps?

A: I would always rather have many different types of guitars and a couple of quality tube amps. There are many styles of good guitars and with a good amp, these guitars will come alive.

Q: Being in the business for as long as you have, what amp(s) would you recommend for the average beginning player looking for his/her first amp? Currently, how many amp lines do you carry in stock?

A: For a beginner, I would recommend a small, inexpensive amp. This way, if he or she does not stick with the guitar, they can recover the expense easier. As the young guitarist progresses, they will find on their own what features they want. Most will learn from friends and reading guitar publications and catalogs. Many will buy an amp to emulate the sound of their favorite guitar player.

As far as amps we carry, our main new amps are Crate and Ampeg, but we sell more used and vintage amps than anything.

Q: Do you think today's high tech modeling amps do a good job of replicating the tone of older Marshalls, Fenders, Voxs, and other vintage makes/models?

A: The new modeling amps are okay. You cannot reproduce the exact sound of an old amp, you can only come close. For example, if you took Vox AC 30's, there would be different on each characteristics. Amp tones will change due to aging components and speaker fatigue. A tube amp's

tone will vary after the tubes and speaker is heated up. Modeling amps offer a very wide range of guitar amp sounds in one package.

Q: What do think overall of the inexpensive, solid-state amplifiers coming in from Asia today?

A: The small solid-state amps coming in from Asia sound very good for what they are. They are aimed at beginner and intermediate players or players who want a small practice amp. Price also plays a desirable factor with these amps.

Q: What are your most popular amp makes/models today, and how much of a difference does a large advertising/marketing campaign make in what your customers think/want? Will good hype overcome bad tone?

A: Popularity varies, so I can only speak on our market. Peavey is still strong, but not as it was ten years ago. Crate, for us, is very good, Fender and Marshall are also very strong.

Large advertising by any manufacturer is always great. People will buy a lot just from a picture. The catalogs have proven this.

Good hype will overcome bad tone, but only once. Many companies have come and gone, due to major hype and a poor product.

Q: On amp repairs, how do you fix the older 70's and 80's solid state-amps?

A: The store has a good repair department for guitars and amps, and we can handle most problems. Some problems we find are 80's MOSFET amps and finding old Ampeg transformers.

Q: How have such major chains as the Guitar Center, Mars Music, and catalog houses such as Musician's Friend affected your amp business over the last decade?

A: The large box stores and catalogs have not affected our business much. Customers will always buy where they feel most comfortable. They will always look at price, service, dealer knowledge of the product, and availability.

Q: What do you consider to be the 5 most desirable vintage amplifiers today?

A: My favorite vintage amps are:
- 1964 Fender Super Reverb
- 1965 Fender Twin Reverb
- 1964 Fender Deluxe Reverb
- Any Marshall 50 watt plexi with Marshall 4x12 cab with 25 watt green back speakers
- Mid 60's Vox AC 30's with top boost ■

> "While wonderful to find a totally original vintage amp in pristine condition, many of these amps do not sound as good as ones with wear and tear and years of use."

INTERESTED IN CONTRIBUTING?

The good thing about publishing a book on an annual basis is that you generally find out what you don't know. Each new edition will be an improvement on the last. Even though you can't do it all in one, 10, or even 20 editions, accumulating the new information is an ongoing process, with the results being published in each new edition.

The *Blue Book of Guitar Amplifiers* has been the result of non-stop and continual guitar amplifier research, obtained by getting the information needed from manufacturers, amp dealers and collectors, trade magazines, and off the Internet (must be documented however). Also, of major importance is speaking directly with acknowledged experts (both published and unpublished), attending guitar/amp shows, reading books, catalogs, and company promo materials, gathering critical and up-to-date manufacturer information at the NAMM Shows and directly from the manufactuters, observing and analyzing market trends by following major vintage dealer, and collector pricing sheets.

If you feel that you can contribute in any way to the material published herein, you are encouraged to submit hard copy regarding your potential additions; revisions, corrections, or any other pertinent information that you feel would be beneficial if published. Unfortunately, we are unable to take your information over the phone (this protects both of us). Earn your way into the ranks of the truly twisted, and join the motley crew of contributing editors - your information could make a difference! We thank you in advance for taking the time to make this a better publication.

All materials sent in for possible inclusion into upcoming editions of the *Blue Book of Guitar Amplifiers*™ should be either mailed, faxed, or emailed to us at the address listed below:

Blue Book Publications, Inc.
Attn: Guitar Contributions
8009 34th Avenue South, Ste. 175
Minneapolis, MN 55425 USA
Fax: 952-853-1486
Email: guitars@bluebookinc.com
Web: http://www.bluebookinc.com
If you're emailing us an image, please make sure it is in TIF or JPEG format. Poor quality images cannot be used for publication.

QUESTIONS, CORRESPONDENCE AND APPRAISALS

Do you have a question about a guitar amplifier? Can't find your make/model listed in the book on our web site? The color/feature is not listed? What it worth? These are the most common questions we get when conducting research. There also may be guitar amplifiers that won't be listed within th publication because of space considerations. Because expanded research uncovers model variations and new companies, there will always be some gr area within the text. Not believing in ivory towers and one-way traffic, this publisher offers a mechanism for the consumer to get further informatic about models not listed in the text. No book can ever be totally complete in a collectible field as broad as this. For that reason, we offer this correspondence service along with an appraisal service.

The Correspondence/Appraisal information service is as follows:

If you don't own the current *Blue Book of Guitar Amplifiers*, there is a $10 charge for information given over the phone or through email. If you own the current Blue Book, there is no charge for a model that is not listed or for other information. There is a $20 charge for a written appraisal on guitar or amplifier (regardless if you own a current Blue Book).

For the appraisal service, we need to see good quality color images (preferably by email) and a complete description of the guitar amplifier(s). Th includes the manufacturer, model, markings, serial number, color, and any other considerations that may be helpful when determining more inform tion on the amp in question. The specifications for emailed images are 72 pixel/inch, JPEG, RGB, Quality: 5-Medium, Baseline Optimized. Phot should include an overall shot of each side, serial number, chassis, tubes, speakers (on amps), pickups, inside the soundhole, headstock (on guitars), e Poor quality images cannot be properly used for determining value. If you can't see it, neither can we!

Payment can be made by a credit card or through the mail by a check or money order. In addition to payment, be sure to include your address ar phone number, giving us an option of how/when to contact you for best service. To keep up with this constant onslaught of correspondence, we have large network of dealers and collectors who can assist us. Payment must accompany your correspondence and will be answered in a FIFO (first in fir out) system. Typical turnaround time on this service is 10-14 business days. Thank you for your patience; it's a big job. All correspondence regardir information and appraisals should be directed to:

Blue Book Publications, Inc.
Attn: Guitar/Amp Correspondence
8009 34th Ave. S. Ste #175
Minneapolis, MN 55425, U.S.A.
Phone: 952.854.5229
Fax 952-853-1486
guitars@bluebookinc.com
www.bluebookinc.com

Vintage Guitar Amplifiers - What to Look For by Dave Boze

Originally published in *The ToneQuest Report* and edited for this publication.

An increasing number of amplifiers are being purchased today over the Internet without the new owners seeing or hearing them. Most of these transactions involve older amps (Fenders, Ampegs, Marshalls, Voxs, etc.) and aside from the varying descriptions offered by the sellers, who really knows what may be going on inside these purported cream puffs? What potential surprises should a prospective buyer look for? What are the questions you need to ask before you buy?

As many of the most desirable vintage guitars have become increasingly rare and expensive, it was inevitable that amplifiers would attract the attention of collectors. However, during the last 4 years, the collecting frenzy has truly caught up with vintage guitar amps. People are finally starting to realize that in many cases, these older amplifiers are much rarer than the vintage guitars that they're spending $2,000 - $150,000 for!

Now that the word is out, the potential for some unpleasant problems exists. You'll notice that most vintage instrument dealers won't sell an amp with a warranty, for example. Why? Well, aside from the fact that amplifiers can be unexpectedly temperamental even after having been serviced, shipping can wreak havoc on an amp, even in the absence of any visible signs of damage. And unfortunately, a lot of people don't pack amplifiers properly. So the mint, just serviced, killer amp that you bought on Ebay could arrive looking mint and sounding like a cat on fire!

LOOKING UNDER THE HOOD

If you want to a buy one of the more valuable and collectible models, it is crucial to know what you're getting "under the hood." For example, Blackface control panels can be bought today for around $100, along with some new grille cloth and poof- someone's Silverface amp worth $750 is now cosmetically transformed to a Blackface model worth $1,500. Does this go on? It must. Transformers can be changed (and they often are) speakers reconed, cabinets recovered and even new cabinets aged and recovered to look 30 years old. Would someone really do that? Think of the money involved when you're dealing with a $3,500 Vibroverb or a $6,000 '59 Bassman. Now, I'm not crying wolf and telling you that everyone who has an amp for sale is out to screw you, but sometimes I wonder if many of the sellers of all of these suddenly hot amps know if the amp they are selling is "original."

The point is, I'd want to know before I spent $1,000 or more on an amplifier, or anything else. So know what you're buying, or pass!

When it comes to evaluating an amp before you buy, there are several critical things you want to verify to the best of your ability. Amps are different from guitars in that changed parts in guitars will usually reduce the selling price, but changed, missing, or altered parts in amps can be hard to detect and they can dramatically alter the tone of the amp (as well as the selling price, if you know.) Somethings are more important than others and in some cases an altered amp may even be more desirable than an original! More on that in a moment...

THE CABINET

Does it have the original covering? Is the tolex or tweed in good condition? Tweed is tough to recondition, but black tolex can usually be brought back to life with a little know-how. Even if the covering is shot and unsalvageable, you may wish to consider buying the amp at a bargain price and having it professionally restored. I run across a lot of amps with missing back panels. Not to worry, you can get some made if needed, and they will look perfect.

TRANSFORMERS

One of the key components in the classic sound of old tube amps is the way that the original transformers were made. Most were manufactured using paper bobbins and the coils were carefully interleaved together to allow the maximum transfer of sound. You'll find that in almost all new boutique amps, transformer construction is quite similar to those found in vintage amplifiers of yesteryear.

To me, original transformers have been a very important consideration, especially in 1950's amps, since exact repro copies were more difficult to find. Having said that, a much better selection of new reproduction transformers is now available and they are very close to OEM transformers. In regard to power transformers, it is critical that the voltages match the specs of the original, and in output transformers, you certainly want to have the correct impedance to match your speakers and similar construction to the original to produce authentic vintage sound. Virtually all transformers are dated, so you can verify their originality.

SPEAKERS

Original speakers can be a significant benefit to tone, or not, and almost always a determining factor in price. Most people who really know amps will tell you that the sound of an original Celestion in a Marshall, a Bulldog in a Vox, or a Jensen in a Fender is the sound that defines those amps.

Reconed speakers are highly variable. Be cautious in this area, because I have heard some reconed speakers that sound fantastic, and others that sound horrible, depending on the type of voice coil and paper that were used. There are also instances when original speakers may not be desirable. A new speaker can dramatically enhance the sound of many amps, sometimes even those with their original speakers.

INTERNAL CIRCUITRY

This is an area rife with controversy, but here's my 2 cents worth:

Electronic parts wear out, primarily as a result of age, use, and heat. Also remember that in the 1950's, electronic parts were not manufactured to nearly the same tolerances that they are today; plus or minus 20% was the norm for some parts. Electrolytic capacitors definitely have a shelf life, and when they leak, they can wreak havoc in an amp in terms of tone and noise, and they can even cause transformers to fail. With time, coupling caps can leak DC into tone circuits - not good. Power resistors can drift, especially those that are near a heat source, and when they do, they can disrupt voltages throughout the amp, negatively affecting tone. Some manufacturers used cheap parts to cut costs (the brown chocolate drop coupling and tone capacitors are an example). So, if some parts are changed, that can be a good thing.

TUBES

Original tubes are in almost all cases absolutely worthless unless the amp was hardly ever played. Occasionally, I'll see lots of life left in original tubes, but for the most part, an amp that has been played will need new tubes. Tubes are mechanical components that wear out.

GRILLE CLOTH

The new repro cloth is very good and you can even acquire aged cloth now. Contrary to what anybody tells you, Fender never used black grille cloth on any Tweed, Brown, White, or Black tolex amp (from the 1950's through 1970's).

Don't get too hung up on "changed" amps that you intend to play - especially if you have access to a good amp tech. Just be aware that originality should normally affect the final purchase price. Most players have Silverface Fender amps converted to Blackface circuits because many people believe that doing so tremendously improves the tone. So here's a case where an altered amp may have more value than an amp in original condition.

Above all, keep in mind that amps are for TONE! I've heard many absolute beaters produce the most fabulous tone that you could imagine. As a player rather than a collector, I get much less hung up on cosmetic condition and internal changes as long as the amp is running great and produces killer tone.

But it is important to know what you're buying, particularly when you're dealing with an amp you haven't seen or heard, and won't, until it's yours.

EXPLANATION AND CONVERTING GUITAR AMPLIFIER GRADING SYSTEMS

Rating the condition factors of guitar amplifiers can be very subjective if done properly while using the grading perimeters listed in this section. When grading vintage amplifiers, many things must be taken into consideration to get the correct grade, and the following descriptions will help you out when sorting through these grading criteria. Remember, the price will be wrong if the grade isn't right!

This 1st Edition *Blue Book of Guitar Amplifiers* lists 100%, Excellent, and Average condition factors, followed by the equivalent numerical grades/percentages, and ending with the corresponding page number(s) where that grade can be seen. While not listed in this text, Mint, Below Average, and Poor condition are also defined below.

Included in this section are examples of things that can affect the pricing and desirability of vintage guitar amplifiers, but it's almost impossible to accurately ascertain the correct condition factor (especially true on older models) without knowing what to look for – that means having the amplifier available for a physical inspection. Even then, three experienced amp dealers/collectors may come up with slightly different grades, not to mention different values, based on different reasons. Described below are the major condition factors to consider when accurately grading an amplifier. Also, please study the Photo Grading System digital color photos carefully on pages 38-48 to learn more about the factors described below.

GUITAR AMPLIFIER CONDITION FACTORS WITH EXPLANATIONS

100% condition (new, 10, page 38) - in this publication, 100% refers only to factory new condition. This includes all factory materials, including warranty card, owner's manual, and other items that were originally included by the manufacturer. On currently manufactured amps, the 100% price refers to an amplifier not previously sold at retail. Even though a new amplifier may have only been played through twice, it no longer qualifies as 100%. On out-of-production amplifiers, the longer an amp has been discontinued, the less likely you are to find one in 100% condition. Most amps that are several years old can no longer be considered 100%, and Mint condition would be a better way of describing these "near new" amplifiers. Remember, there are no excuses for 100% condition - period.

Mint Condition (not listed, 9.8, 98% or greater, page 39) - even though this condition factor is not listed in this book, it is important to consider. Mint condition is typically used when describing either a currently manufactured amp that's in like-new condition, but has been previously sold at retail, or a vintage amplifier that for whatever reason(s), has been used very little and was extremely well cared for. In vintage circles, Mint condition is sometimes referred to as a "cream puff," "cherry," or simply "WOW! Where did you find this?" Mint prices on recently manufactured amps are typically about halfway between the Excellent and 100% prices. On vintage amps, a pristine, original, mint amplifier may be worth several times more than a similar model in Excellent condition. However, since this condition factor is only infrequently encountered with vintage amps, and can be interpolated easily with recently manufactured amps, this condition factor is intentionally not included in this book for these reasons.

Excellent Condition (9.0 to 9.5, 90% - 95%, page 40) - very light observable wear, normal scratching and light dings on cabinet, corners may have slight wear, and grille cloth might show a little deterioration. This condition factor assumes the amp is 100% original - any tubes and other components that have been replaced, non-factory alterations, and potential modifications should be listed within the description, everything must work OK, and on a recently manufactured amp, everything should look close to new. On a vintage amp, more scratching, corner wear, grille fabric deterioration, and some non-original components (tubes mostly) typically enter into evaluation of this condition factor.

Average Condition (6 to 8.5, 60% - 85%, pages 41-42) - more serious exterior wear, including noticeable nicks, scratches and gouges, dirty/slightly worn grille cloth, light fading or tarnishing of exposed face plate metal (if any), a few normal components (tubes, resistors, filter capacitors, not potentiometers, speakers, power transformers, etc.) may have also been replaced/repaired, but no non-factory alterations or modifications. Visibly, an Average condition amplifier will noticeably have some mileage on it, but still must be in perfect working order. Anything that needs to be done to the amp in order for it to be in correct working condition must be subtracted from the Average condition price.

Below Average Condition (not listed, 3.5 - 5.0, 35% - 50%, page 43) - cabinet typically in very worn condition, with much damage occurring to the outside while being used frequently as a road warrior. Normally, this condition factor is encountered on a vintage amplifier only, as the only way this condition might describe a recently manufactured amp is if it had been both used and abused on a regular basis since it was new. Below Average Condition guitar amplifiers should still work, even though many internal components may have been replaced and/or repaired. Except for early, desirable models of Fender. Marshall, Vox, Ampeg, etc., there isn't much collectibility in this condition factor. The playability remaining in an amp in Below Average Condition will typically dictate the price tag. Typically, subtract 20% - 30% from the Average price to figure out a Below Average Condition price.

Poor Condition (not listed, 0 - 3, 0% - 30%, page 44) - basically, this means beat up or extremely hard usage, and the amp may or may not work. If not in working condition, the price should reflect what the parts are worth now. In other words, an amp in Poor Condition usually means that its gigging days are close to over, and family members should be notified, since an electronic retirement home or recycling center is probably the next and last stop. Never pay a premium for this condition, unless major trademark desirability and rarity factors are such that few specimens ever come up for sale annually.

An array of American Classics! Fender was certainly not the first amp company out there, but hands down revolutionized the amp industry. This collage displays amps from the 1940's until the mid 1960's. Leo's first amps, the K&F model is listed as the earliest. Woodie's, TV-front, wide-panel tweed, narrow panel tweed, brownface, and blackface are all included. Starting at the bottom and going clockwise we have a late 1940's Princeton "Woodie" amp, a wide-panel tweed Princeton from about 1953, an early 1960's Brownface Princeton, the famed Blackface Super Reverb from the mid 1960's, a late 40's Champion 800 sitting on the Super Reverb, an early 60's Brownface Vibroverb (half-hidden), an early 60's Showman amp with cabinet, a late 40's Princeton "Woodie" with blue grille cloth, a TV-front Princeton or Deluxe from the early 1950's, a Princeton Reverb Blackface circa 1965, a wide-panel Deluxe from circa 1953, an early 60's Concert brownface, a K&F amp (technically non-Fender) from circa 1946, that is sitting on a late 50's Bassman narrow-panel tweed, and a Dual Professional from the late 40's or early 50's. Image courtesy John Peden.

Marshall JTM45's from the 1960's. For you Marshall hard cores that only like the early stuff, keep your pants on. These are the Marshall JTM 45 amps from the mid 1960's. The amp on top of the pile is a highly collectible 1962 JTM 45 off-set chassis. Only three of these are known to exist (and Jim Marshall has one of them). The two amps below that are from circa 1963 with all white control panels. The next two down are MK II's from 1964/65. The white one on the left is one of six that was made for Brian Poole and the Tremolos. The bottom two amps are also MK II's and are from 1965. These have the gold block logo and the new script logo that is still used today. On all these amps, the condition is surprisingly good. When you have amps this collectible, condition gets less important (this isn't for all cases though.) For many collectors and players alike, these are the best Marshall amps ever produced. That is what makes them so valuable on today's market. Courtesy solidbodyguitar.com Inc.

Close-up the 1965 Marshall JTM45 Plexi with script logo. This is one of the favorite amps of many musicians and collectors alike. Plexi means that the control panel is made out of gold plexi-glass. These "Plexi" amps can be thought of the desirability of Blackface Fenders compared to other Fenders. They have that sound that so many musicians love. The Plexi front only lasted a few years until it was changed to an aluminum front in the early 70's. Courtesy solidbodyguitar.com Inc.

Marshall, Park, and CMI Color Amplifiers. Marshall was one of the first companies to use colored Levant covering on their amps. We have four amps from Marshall in red, white, and blue, and orange. The Red Marshall is a 1967/68 100W Super Lead (Model 1959) in excellent condition. The White Marshall is a 100W Lead produced later than the Red Super Lead. Marshall also produced their amps under other names during the 60's and 70's. Two of these are Park and CMI. The Park is a 1965 45W top-mount amp that is covered in Orange Levant, which is simply is a JTM 45 chassis with a Park nameplate on the front. CMI was a project in the late 1970's for Marshall, that also featured different name plates attached to the amp. This is a dark blue CMI combo with 2-12" speakers. Not many of these CMI amps show up anywhere. Colored Marshall Amps are more collectible to those who get a bang out of the odd-ball stuff. Courtesy solidbodyguitar.com Inc.

Early 1960's Vox AC30 with Vox AC2. Vox has produced one of the most highly sought after amp models with its AC-30. We have early (circa 1960) Vox amps covered in the desirable fawn-colored covering. The AC-30 has 2-12" speakers and is still produced to this day. The AC-2 is an amp that not many people know about. This is obviously much smaller than the AC-30, but is still a good little amp. Circa 1963, Vox started covering their amps in a black material. These are also collectible amps, but the fawn models tend to be the more desirable color. Courtesy solidbodyguitar.com Inc.

Ampeg mid 1960's B-15N Portaflex. Ampeg has one of the most innovative designs with the Portaflex. These amps were both piggy-back and combo units. For transportation, the head comes off the top of the cabinet, is turned over, and is stored safely inside the cabinet. For playing, the head is simply flipped over and sits on top of the cabinet completely separate from the speaker. Not only do these amps sound great, they have a lighted "Ampeg" plate that sticks up on the chassis. For a while in the 60's, Ampeg offered a personalized name plate that could be attached when ordering a new amp. I have yet to find a "Zach" lighted plate, but I'll keep looking. These amps were covered in the famed "Blue Check" covering, which was used from circa 1962-67. Keep in mind that Everett Hull disliked Rock and Roll, and no Ampeg amp was ever designed for hard rock guitar that was becoming popular in the 60's. Most RMS wattages are rated low, and what these amps can put out is usually much higher. Courtesy Savage Audio.

New Savage Blitz 50. 100% condition. The Savage Blitz 50 is a new amp from a boutique amplifier company. Note that this amp is perfect from the factory (since we took the picture there). There are no marks, scuffs, tears, or other blemishes. Also note later in the PPGS the Savage Chassis in 100% condition.   Courtesy Savage Audio.

New Ultrasound AG50DS2. 100% condition. This new Ultrasound is a digital acoustic amp covered in brown. There are no marks at all on this amp. Typically 100% amps are less than five years old, or brand new. Unless the amp has not been played after a period of five years or more, wear starts to show and it moves to the excellent category. Courtesy S.P. Fjestad.

1967 Fender Pro Reverb. Mint condition. For all those who love the Fender Blackface (and who doesn't?), here is a collector's ultimate find. This Pro Reverb was actually found in a church, and we don't mean in the closet collecting dust. This was used in the Gospel band, probably at volume 2 for most of its life. Church bands typically don't gig outside very often, so transportation of equipment was rare if ever. Transportation produces the most wear on an amp, because typically most people don't have a cover for it. Every guitar usually has a case. There are no marks to really speak of in this amp. If it were only a couple of years old it would be a 100% amp. Since it is over 35 years old, natural aging puts it in the mint category. Notice the hanging tags and owner's manual still with the amp as well as the footswitch. This isn't your every day find. There are tons of Pro Reverbs out there, but to find one in this condition is extremely rare. An amp in mint condition like this will have a major premium over the excellent condition. Courtesy solidbodyguitar.com Inc.

1960's Gibson GA-79. Excellent condition. As far as amplifiers go, the GA-79 was Gibson's finest work. It really sounds great as an amp and has the speakers angled to give 180 degrees of sound. It is also a stereo amp. These have become increasingly collectible as of late. This one has only minor blemishes here and there. Art director Clint Schmidt commented that it looks like an end table at his grandma's. I had to agree with him. Courtesy solidbodyguitar.com

1970's Mesa Boogie MK IIB. Excellent condition. The Mesa Boogie is housed in a wood cabinet. There is no chance to recover this amp unless you are real handy with the sander, which means you are probably getting the original thing. The Boogie amps were built like a tank and weigh about as much. For being a 12 inch combo, this little devil is deceiving. The wicker grille is pretty cool; it reminds me of an old lamp shade. Courtesy Savage Audio.

Orange OR-120 head and 4-12" speaker cabinet. Average condition. Orange debuted in England during the late 1960's. The owner had come across a bunch of orange Levant covering for cheap and purchased it to start making amps. Not being able to come up with a name for the company, they decided to name it after the color of the amps. They were all in Orange Levant from then on (and still are today). This amp shows average wear that an amp this big would have. There are nicks and tears all over the head and cabinet, however the cabinet shows more wear than the head. The head unit has the mains (voltage) selector. This is a plug that you pull out to select what voltage is being used. Courtesy Willie's American Guitars.

Hiwatt Lead 30. Average condition. Hiwatt amps were another great sounding product that came out of England. They are reminiscent of Marshall, but had their own tone. This is a combo with 1-12 inch speaker. The covering of this amp is in pretty average shape with a couple of big tears. It still plays though, which is more important anyway. Courtesy Willie's American Guitars.

Mid 1970's Fender Super Reverb. Average condition. A Fender Silverface amp can be purchased for much less money than the more desirable Blackface. Blackface and silverface amps are very similar in chassis and often it's tough to tell the difference. Hard-cores always beg to differ that Blackface is much better when in reality the chassis' were sometimes identical. In some cases the price tag is twice as much on a blackface compared to a silverface. Of course CBS mangement had nothing to do with this… Courtesy of S.P. Fjestad

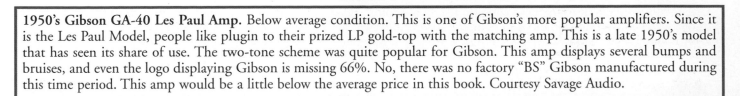

1950's Gibson GA-40 Les Paul Amp. Below average condition. This is one of Gibson's more popular amplifiers. Since it is the Les Paul Model, people like plugin to their prized LP gold-top with the matching amp. This is a late 1950's model that has seen its share of use. The two-tone scheme was quite popular for Gibson. This amp displays several bumps and bruises, and even the logo displaying Gibson is missing 66%. No, there was no factory "BS" Gibson manufactured during this time period. This amp would be a little below the average price in this book. Courtesy Savage Audio.

1958 Fender Bassman 5F6-A. Poor condition. This amp has seen better days. The Fender Bassman Narrow Panel Tweed is a highly desirable amp. This particular model looks like it was burned alive and lived to tell about it. The tweed is very discolored, ripped, and the grille is very dirty. The one thing this amp has going for it is that it works. The condition of the amp heavily alters the price and puts it in the poor condition category. There is proof to this being a legendary amp, as Fender has produced a reissue in the custom shop of the 1959 Bassman for several years now. Courtesy solidbodyguitar.com Inc.

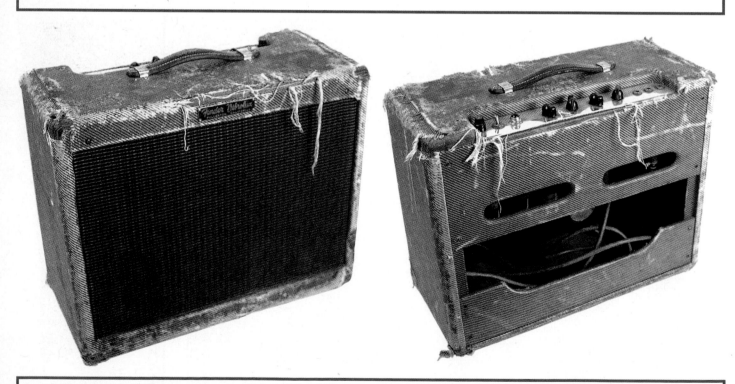

Late 1950's Fender Vibrolux. Poor condition. This Vibrolux is also a narrow panel tweed. Even though this amp has more of the original color in it, it still is in poor condition. In fact, it has probably has been lightened some. The tweed is physically coming apart on the amp, sort of like a sweater unraveling. The corners of the amps are down to the cabinet, and even that is worn. This is an indication of heavy use (and abuse) over the years. This amp is also in poor condition. Note that if these amps didn't work at all, the condition would be around 0. In both cases here it's a good thing these amps can't handle guns. Courtesy Willie's American Guitars.

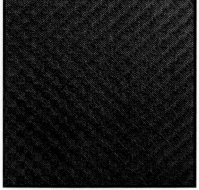

Ampeg Blue Check covering
(Excellent condition)

Fender Black Tolex
(Excellent condition)

Fender Black Tolex
(Average condition)

Fender Tweed
(Excellent condition)

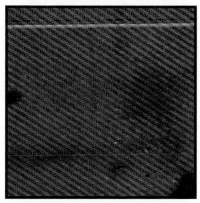

Fender Tweed
(Average condition)

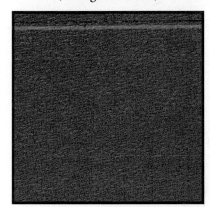

Fender Brown Tolex
(Excellent condition)

Marshall Black Levant
(Excellent condition)

Marshall Black Levant
(Average condition)

Orange covering
(Average condition)

Mesa Boogie Wood
(Average condition)

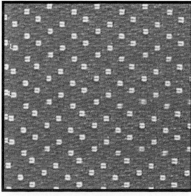

Gretsch Electromatic (late 1950's)
(Average condition)

Kustom Tuck and Roll
(Average condition)

Ampeg grille 70's era
(Excellent condition)

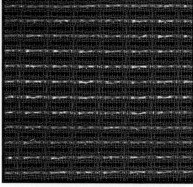

Fender Blackface grille
(Excellent condition)

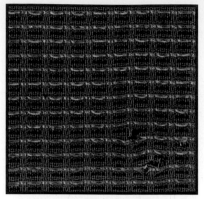

Fender Blackface grille
(Average condition)

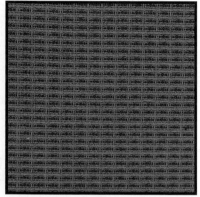

Fender Wheat grille
(brownface)(Average condition)

Fender Tweed grille
(Excellent condition)

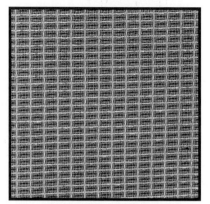

Fender Silverface grille
(Average condition)

Marshall Basketweave grille
(Excellent condition)

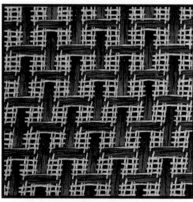

Marshall Chequerborad grille
(Excellent condition)

Marshall grille cloth
Half the grille has been replaced.

Marshall Black grille
(Excellent condition)

Vox grille
(Excellent condition)

Gibson grille
(Average condition)

Photo Grading System™

Mid 1960's Chassis from a Fender Twin Reverb. This is the chassis from the very popular Twin Reverb, Blackface series. Everything in this chassis is original (except tubes). Note how the wiring looks old and all the resistors have almost a yellowing to them. Note the tubes and power transformer in the top photo. The power tubes on this amp are 4 X 5881 Sovtek's. If you look closely you can see that only 2 of the 6 preamp tubes are installed. If you plugged this amp in right now, it wouldn't work.

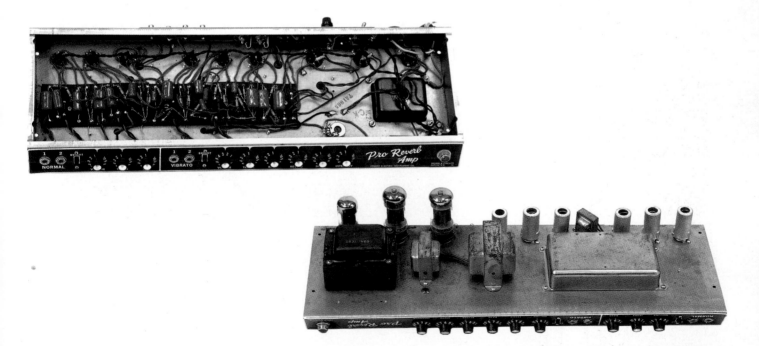

Mid 1960's Chassis from a Fender Pro Reverb. This amp has been completely gone through. This is like overhauling an engine. With an engine you put new rings, gaskets, and sometimes bore the cylinders. On an amp, wiring, resistors, filter capacitors, and other components can go bad or simply wear out. This is what going through an amp, consists of. When an amp starts to go bad, there are a lot of electric signal paths that can leak and voltage starts to get off. Then it's time to do an overhaul. The replacement of tubes can be thought of as changing oil on a car. Tubes are meant to be replaced when the amp starts to sound muddy and such. On the inside of this amp, notice the orange components compared to the original Twin Reverbs. There were absolutely no modifications done to this amp, but it'll probably sound better than when it came from the factory.

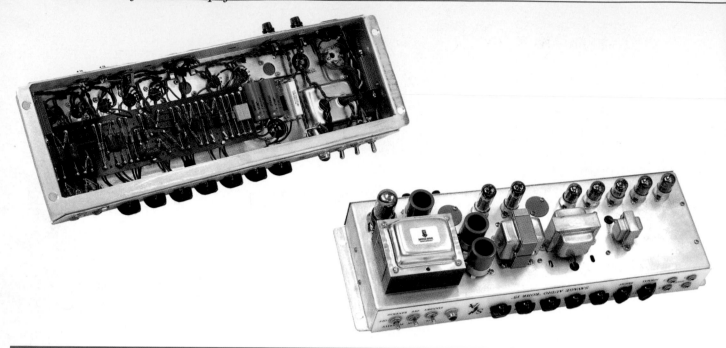

Savage Rohr 15 Chassis. This amp freatures point-to-point connections, and is completely hand-wired. It takes an enormous amount of time to build one of these. As opposed to the tube Fender amps listed on the previous page, this one looks more orderly and clean in the layout and construction. The tube set-up consists of (left to right), the rectifier, power tubes: 2 X EL34, preamp tubes 4 X 12AX7 and 1 X 12AT7. The other pieces of equipment are left to right, the power transformer (the big one), the choke, the output transformer, and the small one is the reverb transformer. To describe everything on the inside that makes an amp work is a completely different book. This amp is ready to go and is waiting for a cabinet to be installed in.

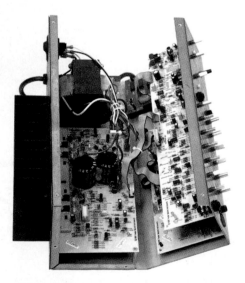
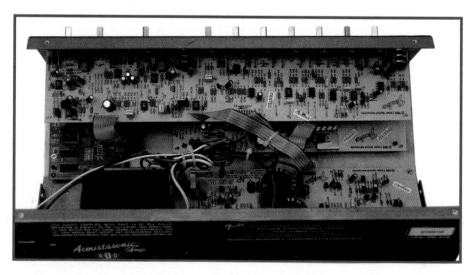

Fender Acoustasonic Chassis. Solid-state is a whole different animal. No tubes means that all the sound and power has to come from transistors and solid-state parts. As you can see, the inside contruction is modular like a computer, and many repair people hate to work on them. This particular model has the SFX effects, which are digital. What this means is that the effects are processed with ones and zeros. Sometimes the fix-it shop for an older solid-state amps is the dumpster. There is so much room for error and so many places to find it that sometimes it's just not worth it. This amp currently is producing no sound at the speakers. It could be something as simple as a resistor or it could be stuck somewhere in the middle of the circuit board jungle. Taking a look at this picture and going further to the schematics is a campaign to why tube amps are that much better. I guess the tone has something to do with it as well.

Section A

A.R.T. (APPLIED RESEARCH AND TECHNOLOGY)

Amplifiers and professional audio signal processing equipment currently produced in Rochester, New York. The A.R.T. trademark was established in 1984.

A.R.T. produces a full line of audio equipment including rack-mounted equalizers, reverb units, tube processors, microphone preamps, and other audio products. Artists such as Robben Ford and Eric Johnson have used these effects and processors over the years. There are several tube preamp and processor products that they have to offer and they run between a variety of prices. For more information, refer to their web site (see trademark index).

ACOUSTIC

Amplifiers currently distributed by the Samick Music Corporation in the City of Industry, California. Amplifiers previously produced by the Acoustic Control Company in the late 1960's through the early 1980's. The Acoustic trademark was reborn in 2001 by Samick.

Acoustic tube and solid-state amplifiers were intoduced in the late 1960's. Their claim to fame was the 360 bass amp, which could efficiently relocate a small house, if needed. The 360 could power up to four speaker cabinets (the 360 is strictly a pre-amp, and each speaker cabinet had a 200W power amp), thus producing up to 800W of bass, very impressive.

Acoustic, at its time, was a very futuristic amplifier company. They found themselves in the middle of the transistor versus tube war that was going on in the 1970's. Essentially, they were the only company that had solid-state products that could compete with the big dawgs (Marshall, Fender, Sunn) of the day. Acoustic established themselves as a bass amp company (even though they made several guitar amps). The bass amps were extremely clean sounding and Acoustic had several innovations including the "Variamp" control and the "Electronic Tuning Fork."There were distortion effects, which were supposed to be fuzz sounds, but became more annoying than anything.The company folded in the mid 1980's as not many guitar players were drawn in by their products and other companies such as SWR and Hartke were coming around. Acoustic was more "old school" and offered the deep bass sound when bass players were starting to look for the more mid-range sound. With the movie *Josie and the Pussycats,* the Acoustic trademark was revived in 2001 with the re-introduction of the 360.

(The Author would like to thank Mark Dupree for his contributions to this section.)

GRADING	100%	EXCELLENT	AVERAGE

ELECTRIC TUBE AMPLIFIERS

160 Wattage unknown, tubes chassis preamp: 3 X 7025, 12AT7, power: 4 X 6L6, mfg. 1970's.

	N/A	$225 - 275	$175 - 200

For a while the tubes were 2 X 7025 and 2 X 12AT7.

164/165 - 100W (switchable to 60W), 1-12" combo, all tube chassis, preamp: 12AX7's, power: 6L6's, dual channels, reverb, front control panel, various contols and switches, wood cabinet, mfg. 1970's.

	N/A	$250 - 300	$175 - 200

The 164 and 165 both appear to be the same amp with minor differances.

G-60T - 60W, 1-12" speaker, all-tube chassis, preamp: 1 X 12AT7, 2 X 12AX7, power: 2 X 6L6, two switchable channels, reverb, front brown control panel, two inputs (low and high), seven brown knobs (v1, v2, t, m, b, r, MV), effects loop, footswitch, external speaker jacks, brown tolex covering, brown grille, mfg. late 1970's.

	N/A	$160 - 210	$120 - 140

G-100T - 100W (switchable to 50W), head-unit only, tubes chassis, preamp: 3 X 7025, 12AT7, power: 4 X 6L6, dual channels, reverb, copper control panel, two inputs (high and low), eight black and silver knobs (v1, v2, t, m, b, presence, reverb, master), 5-band equalizer, parallel effects loop, black covering, brown grille, mfg. late 1970's.

	N/A	$175 - 225	$125 - 150

ELECTRIC SOLID-STATE AMPLIFIERS

The Solid-State Acoustic models are divided up into the different model numbers.

Models 100 - 149

114 - 50W, 2-10" speakers, solid-state combo, reverb, bright, master volume, black tolex covering, black grille, mfg. late 1970's.

	N/A	$225 - 275	$175 - 200

***115** - Similar to the 114 except has 1-12" speaker, mfg. late 1970's.

	N/A	$225 - 275	$175 - 200

116 - 75W, 1-15" speaker, solid-state combo, bright, boost, black tolex covering, black grille, mfg. late 1970's.

	N/A	$250 - 300	$175 - 225

120 - 125W, head-unit only, solid-state, black control panel with blue stripe, 5-band equalizer, mfg. late 1970's - early 1980's.

	N/A	$175 - 225	$125 - 150

124 - 100W, 4-10" speaker, solid-state combo, reverb, master volume, 5-band equalizer, bright switch, black tolex covering, black grille, mfg. 1970's.

	N/A	$300 - 350	$225 - 275

***125** - Similar to the 124 except 2-12" speakers, mfg. 1970's.

	N/A	$300 - 350	$225 - 275

GRADING	100%	EXCELLENT	AVERAGE

* 126 - Similar to the 124 except is a bass amp with 1-15" speaker, mfg. 1970's.

	N/A	$275 - 325	$200 - 250

134 - 100W, 4-10" speakers, solid-state combo, dual channels, reverb, vibrato, front black control panel with blue stripe, four inputs (two per channel), nine black knobs (Ch. 1: v, b, t, Ch. 2: v, b, t, r, s, i), bright switches, black covering, mfg. 1970's.

	N/A	$225 - 275	$150 - 195

136 - 110W, 1-15" Eminence speaker with folded horn-cabinet, solid-state combo, dual channels, front black control panel with blue stripe, four inputs (two per channel), six black knobs (v, b, t, for each channel), black covering, mfg. 1970's.

	N/A	$275 - 325	$200 - 250

Models 150 - 350

150 - 110W, head-unit only, solid-state chassis, dual channels, vibrato, reverb, front black control panel with blue stripe, two inputs, silver various knobs (v, b, t), black covering, mfg. mid 1970's.

	N/A	$275 - 350	$175 - 225

Later models had black knobs and these models had 125W output.

220 BASS - 160W, head-unit only, solid-state, high and low gain, bright, boost, 5-band equalizer, black control panel, black covering, black grille, mfg. mid 1970's.

	N/A	$200 - 250	$150 - 175

* 230 - Similar to the 220 Bass except is a guitar amp without boost or high/low inputs, but has reverb and master volume, mfg. mid 1970's.

	N/A	$200 - 250	$150 - 175

260 - Wattage unknown, head-unit only, solid-state chassis, two channels, tremolo, front black and blue control panel, four inputs, seventeen silver knobs, various buttons and switches, black covering, mfg. mid 1970's.

	N/A	$175 - 250	$125 - 150

320 BASS - 300W, head-unit only, solid-state, 5-band equalizer, preamp in/out, dual channels, black covering, mfg. 1970's.

	N/A	$275 - 325	$200 - 250

* 330 - Similar to the 320 Bass except is a guitar amp with reverb, mfg. 1970's.

	N/A	$275 - 325	$200 - 250

360 Bass

This is by far the flagship model for Acoustic. This amp is notorius for pumping out large amounts of bass that could be heard clearly at great distances. This amplifier (and cabinet) used the folded-horn cabinet design and the power-amp was in the bottom of the cabinet with the speakers. This meant that the preamp was a separate unit that acted as the head. By having the speaker mounted backwards in a chamber and blowing sound into a giant bin, made lots of bass in not-so-much space. This amp was so loud that there was a warning label on the back that stated "prolonged use could lead to hearing loss." These amps are also very, very heavy; don't move them unless you have to. For the actual speaker cabinet description, refer to the speaker cabinet section.

360 Preamp head-unit only (power amp is in the speaker cabinet), solid-state chassis, single channel, fuzz, front black control panel with blue stripe, two inputs (high and low), nine knobs (v, t, b, variamp balance, effect, fuzz attack, fuzz gain, electronic tuning fork course, and fine), bright/normal switch, switch for tuning fork and ground rocker, black covering, mfg. 1970's.

Acoustic Model 360
courtesy Savage Audio

Acoustic Model 360
courtesy Savage Audio

	N/A	$575 - 750	$425 - 525

* 370 - Similar to the 360 except has 375W output, dual channels, and a five band equalizer,

	N/A	$575 - 750	$450 - 550

360 BASS AMPLIFIER (CURRENT PRODUCTION) - 950W (2 475W power amps), head-unit only, dual channels, black and blue control panel, high and low inputs, 16 silver knobs (Ch A: level, low, mid, contour, high, fuzz level and attack, tuning fork level and pitch, Ch B: level, low, mid, high, direct out level, low and high crossover's), harmonically time aligned, convection cooled, effects loop, foot pedal, mfg. 2001-current.

$849	$475 - 600	$375 - 450

GRADING	100%	EXCELLENT	AVERAGE

*** FH-118, VL-810T, VL-215, FL-410T** - Speaker cabinets used to match up with the series 360 bass head. The numbers correspond to the number and how big the speakers are in the cabinet. The FH-118 is recommended to match up with the VL-810T and the VL-215 with the FL-410T.

400 Series

400 - 375W, stereo power amp only, solid-state, dual power supplies, high speed fan cooling, rack mount, black control panel, mfg. 1970's.

	N/A	$250 - 300	$175 - 225

450 LEAD/BASS - 300W, head-unit only, solid-state chassis, dual channels, front black control panel, two inputs, six black knobs (v, t, m, b, distortion control, aux. v), lead/bass switch, normal/bright switch, five-band equalizer, black covering, mfg. late 1970's.

	N/A	$250 - 300	$200 - 230

470 BASS - 300W, head-unit only, solid-state, dual channels, reverb, tremolo, built in distortion, black control panel, 12 black or white knobs including bass, treble, and mid controls, 5-band equalizer, line in & out, black covering, no grille, mfg. late 1970's.

	N/A	$300 - 350	$250 - 275

833 - 200W, power amp only, solid-state, rack mount, mfg. late 1970's.

	N/A	$125 - 150	$75 - 100

Speaker and P.A. Cabinets

The 800 series are all PA cabinets with these following models and corresponding speakers: The 804 has 2-12" and 3-8" speakers with 2 piezo horns and a sealed column. The 806 has 1-15", a midrange horn, a piezo horn, and a front loaded tuned reflex. The 807 has 2-12", a midrange horn, 2 piezo horns, and a front loaded tuned reflex cabinet. The 808 has 2-15" speakers with 3 midrange horns, 2 piezo horns, and a front loaded tuned reflex. The 811 has 1 sectional horn with 6 piezo horns. The 812 has 4-15" speakers and front loaded tuned reflex. The 813 has 2-15" speakers with 1 midrange horn and 2 piezo horns. All of the models are PA cabinets and have black tolex covering and a black grille.

301 POWERED CAB - 200W powered cab, speaker cabinet that matches the 360 head-unit, 1-18" speaker in a baffle unit, large blue panel front, black covering, mfg. 1968-1972.

	N/A	$450 - 550	$300 - 400

301 SPEAKER CAB - 300W, passive cab speaker cabinet that matches the 370 head-unit, 1-18" speaker in a baffle unit, small blue panel front, black covering, mfg. 1970's.

	N/A	$250 - 300	$150 - 180

401 - 2-12" speaker cabinet, front loaded sealed horn, black tolex covering, black grille, mfg. 1970's.

	N/A	$175 - 200	$125 - 150

402 - 2-15" speaker cabinet, front loaded vented baffle, tuned reflex, black tolex covering, black grille, mfg. 1970's.

	N/A	$175 - 200	$125 - 150

403 - 4-12" speaker cabinet, sealed system, black tolex covering, black grille, mfg. 1970's.

	N/A	$200 - 225	$150 - 175

407 - 2-15" speaker cabinet with midrange horns, front loaded sealed horn, black tolex covering, black grille, mfg. 1970's.

	N/A	$200 - 225	$150 - 175

408 - 4-15" speaker cabinet, tuned combination reflex, black tolex covering, black grille, mfg. 1970's.

	N/A	$200 - 250	$150 - 175

ACOUSTIC IMAGE

Amplifiers currently produced in Raleigh, North Carolina.

Acoustic Image is a company that hasn't been on the market for long, but have already produced some quality guitar and bass amplifiers. Dr. Rick Jones is the founder and president of the company. He felt that the products out for acoustic instruments weren't good enough and that the demand was great enough to develop a product that was of the finest quality. Acoustic Image uses this philosophy: "Acoustic Image products are designed and built to meet the specific needs of professionals for natural, powerful and practical sound reinforcement." For a full description of their products, what makes their products different, retailers, and specs visit the Acoustic Image web site (see Trademark Index).

ACOUSTIC SOLID-STATE AMPLIFIERS

Currently Acoustic Image has four series of amplifiers in production and are set to release the Acoustic Image Series II shortly. These amps are very small and lightweight. The Acoustic Image line starts with the **Clarus 1** and **1R**. These are 300W amplifier heads and are only six pounds in weight! The R indicates reverb in a model. The **Clarus 2** and **2R** is slightly bigger in wattage. The **Contra** and **Contra R** are bass units with the speaker combined for a weight of only 25 lbs! The **Coda** and **Coda R** are for electric and acoustic instruments but have the speaker for a combo unit of 25 lbs also. Look for more information on upcoming editions of the Blue Book of Guitar Amplifiers.

AGUILAR

Amplifiers currently produced in New York City, New York.

Aguilar makes a wide variety of bass power amps, preamps, and speaker cabinets. They also have some effects such as the Direct Box. The head amplifiers are tube along with one hybrid. These are high quality amplifiers but they also cost a premium. All of the amps are rack mount, but can be used otherwise such as with the Aguilar cabinets.

ELECTRIC TUBE AMPLIFIERS

Aguilar features three different amp heads. There are two all-tube models the **DB359** and **DB728.** The DB359 is a bass, rack mountable amp that uses the same preamp tube section of the famous DB680. It features 200W output, a tube array of: 2 X 12AX7 & 12AU7 for preamp and 4 X 6550C for power. The

DB359 is a 2-space rack mount and retails for $2,095. The DB728 has 400W output with the same preamp tubes as the DB359 but has 8 X 6550C power tubes. This is a 4-space rack mount and retails for $2,750. There is a hybrid model **DB750** amp that has 3 X 12AX7 and a 12AU7 tubes in the preamp with a solid-state power section. This amp has a variety of controls, takes up 2 spaces for a rack mount, and retails for $2,295.

PRE-AMPLIFIERS

There are four preamps currently offered by Aguilar. The **DB680** is a tube preamp, rack-mounted unit. It features 2 X 12AX7/7025 and 3 X 12AU7 for tubes. This is a 2-space rack mount that retails for $1,995. The **DB659** is another tube preamp that has less features than it's bigger brother the DB680. The tube section consists of 2 X 12AX7 and only takes up one space in a rack. The retail on this is $975. There is also an outboard preamp, the **DB924**, and an onboard, the **OBP1**. The DB924 has a volume, treble, and bass controls and retails for $229. The OBP1 mounts right onto a bass guitar and has two bands of boost for the guitar. The retail on this is $139.

BASS SPEAKER CABINETS

There are five different speaker cabinet models offered by Aguilar. All are constructed with strong cabinets and high-quality speakers. The **GS-112** has a 1-12" speaker, 300W handeling, and retails for $529. The **GS-212** has 2-12" speakers, can handle 600W, and retails for $899. The **GS-115** has 1-15" speaker, is rated at 400W, and the price tag is $749. The **GS-210** has 2-10" speakers, accepts up to 350W, and retails for $799. The grandaddy of them all is the **GS-410**, which has 4-10" speakers handeling up to 700W of thunder, and retails for a meager $1,149.

AIRLINE
Amplifiers previously produced by Valco in Chicago, Illinois.

Airline was the name that Valco amplifiers were produced under in the 1950's and 60's. These amps were fairly inexpensive when they were produced and still carry that today, however they are becoming slightly more collectible. For more information refer to the Silvertone, Supro, or National as these were also names that Valco used.

ALAMO
Amplifiers previously produced in San Antonio, Texas. The Alamo trademark was established circa 1947 and lasted to around 1982.

Alamo was founded around 1947 by Charles Eilenberg. He started the company Southern Music in San Antonio, Texas and began making guitars and amplifiers. By 1950, the company was producing instrument cases, tube amplifiers, and lap steel guitars. Alamo continued to produce tube amplifiers throughout the fifties and sixties. In 1970, they stopped producing tube amps and jumped on the solid-state bandwagon. The company produced amps and guitars through the 1970's when the company folded in 1982. There are numerous guitar amplifier models under the Alamo name. Look for more information on Alamo amplifiers in upcoming editions of the Blue Book of Guitar Amplifiers.

(Source: Michael Wright, Vintage Guitar Magazine & Guitar Stories Volume Two)

Alamo Electra Model 25-70
courtesy Savage Audio

Alamo Electra Model 25-70
courtesy Savage Audio

ALEMBIC
Amplifiers currently produced in Santa Rosa, California. The Alembic trademark was established in 1969 and they produce Guitars, Basses, Pre-Amps, and a variety of other products.

The Alembic company is known for making top-end pre-amps along with other guitars and such. All of the components are high quality and the sound is of an unbelievable tone. The first F-2B preamp unit shipped out of the factory in 1969.

PRE-AMPLIFIERS

There are three different pre-amps offered by Alembic currently. The **F-1X** is a tube driven pre-amp with a 12AX7 tube. It features bright and boost switches along with tone controls and gain effect. The F-1X along with all of the Alembic amps are rack-mount units and take up one space. The **F-2B** is Alembic's claim to fame as far as the amp industry. This was the amp introduced in the late 1960's. This amp is generally used as a stereo amp and has a complete tube preamp section. Originally this amp was inspired by the Fender Dual Showman. The F-2B has some more controls and features than its younger brother the F-1X. There are two channels to get the stereo effect. The other Alembic preamp currently being produced is the **SF-2** which stands for the Superfilter. There are two tunable active filters in the amp which gives a large range. There are a possible three channels, and the stereo mode can mix two of them together. It is a switchable mono/stereo amplifier that can also be used as a stand-alone unit.

ALESSANDRO

Amplifiers currently produced in Huntington Vally, Pennsylvania.

George Alessandro has taken high-end technology and applied it to guitar amplifiers. Alessandro is mainly a high-end amplifier company that produces some fine amplifiers. They produce all-tube amps with circuits developed by George, himself. Alessandro offers amp heads and speaker cabinets along with a variety of other products. All of their amps have a base price, but can be custom fit to a customer's needs. See their web site for all of the options and specifications (see trademark index). All of the cabinets for the amps and speakers are made of high-grade woods that can be upgraded and changed on request. Needless to say, these amps are only for the serious amp enthusiast, and an amp head/speaker cabinet can easily run $5,000, if not more.

ELECTRIC TUBE AMPLIFIERS

The **Redbone** and **Bloodhound** series were the first introduced by Alessandro. The Redbone has a 55W output and retails for $2,600. This model is also available as the Redbone Special, which gives it more options in the pre-amp for more range between clean and distortion. The Bloodhound model has 55W output, 12AX7 preamp tubes, and retails for $2,200. There are four newer models with a wider range of playability. The **Beagle** is a 10W amp with 2 classic EL84 output tubes, and retails for $2,400. The **Basset Hound** is a bass amp with 60W output coming from 2 X 6550 power tubes. This model helps electric basses sound more like an upright and it retails for $2,600. The **English Coonhound** is a Class-A amp with 20W output coming from 4 X EL84 output tubes. This amp is an English sounding amp and retails for $2,800. The **Plott Hound** is one of the most advanced amplifiers in the Alessandro range with a cross between English and American sounds. It has 10W output coming from 2 X 6V6 tubes and retails for $2,400.

The upgrade options are something to take note of Alessandro amplifiers. If you're looking for an amp made out of fine woods the options here are endless. For about $500 (less on other types of wood), custom woods can be used to create an amp and speaker cabinet. Curly Maple, Flame Maple, Quilted Maple, Mahogany, Quilted Mahogany, Walnut, Cherry, and Rosewood are all options. There are also other options that can be applied to the chassis of the amp. A pre-amp and power amp upgrade is possible for around $1,000. Silver wire, a gold-plated chassis, a solid pure silver chassis and a solid-gold chassis is available at the price of $50,000! (How much is gold per ounce?!)

SPEAKER CABINETS

Like the amp heads, Alessandro produces matching speaker cabinets of the same caliber wood. There are four models available including configurations of 1 X 12, 2 X 12, 4 X 10, and 4 X 12. All of these cabinets come unloaded without any speakers at a base price of $800. The speakers used in the cabinets are either Celestion G12H or Celestion "Bulldog" Alnico speakers. All speakers and wood options are a cost upgrade and these can all be viewed on the Alessandro web site.

ALLEN

Amplifiers currently produced in Walton, Kentucky.

The Allen Amplification company makes tube amplifiers similar to the blackface Fender amps of the mid 1960's. They are known for making quality amplifiers with the vintage edge to them. Allen amplifiers are available to buy completely assembled or as a kit where the customer can assemble them at a discounted price. This is because all Allen amps assembled at the factory are wired point-to-point by hand and is quite time consuming. If the customer provides his/her own tubes, speakers, etc. there is also a discount in price.

ELECTRIC TUBE AMPLIFIERS

Allen offers four different models of amplifiers that can be bought fully assembled or as a kit. The **Accomplice** is a 20 amp combo available with one 12" or two 10" speakers.This amp has a striking resemblence to a Blues Jr. and the chassis will fit the cabinet of the Jr. The Accomplice is available with a number of options and retails for $1,299. The **Old Flame** is a 40W amp combo that comes with either 2-10" or 4-10" speakers. It is also available as a head-unit only. There are a list of options for this model and it starts at $1,249. The **Tone Savor** is an 80W amp that is similar to the mid 1960's blackface Fender models. This model is the most powerful offered by Allen and has a number of options. It is available as a head or a combo with 2-12" speakers. The retail is $1,349 for the head and $1,649 for the combo. The **Class Act** is the smallest amp that is also available as a head or a combo. The Class Act has 10W ouptut max, a bottom mounted chassis, and in combo version comes with 1-12" speaker. This amp retails for $899 for the head and $999 for the combo. For all prices and other options check the web site for Allen Amplification (see trademark index). Allen also offers a complete line of U.S. made replacement transformers for vintage Fender amps, the Allen C1045 10" guitar speaker and quality repairs of vintage Fenders.

AMPEG

Amplifiers currently produced in St. Louis, Missouri. Distributed by St. Louis Music of St. Louis, MO. The Ampeg trademark was established circa 1945 in Chicago, Illinois.

Charles Everett Hull was born on January 17, 1904 in Wisconsin. A constructive and energetic young man, Everett developed an interest in playing bass guitar when he could find no one else to do the job in his band. He had played around in the 20's and 30's with numerous bands and his own orchestra. After playing an upright bass for some time, he noticed that during bass solos the sound was remarkably quiet. He knew that a microphone would work on the outside of the instrument, but would pick up unwanted sounds such as hitting it with his bow. A light went on in Hull's head and one late night he took out the peg that holds up the bass guitar on the bottom, fixed up a microphone inside of the bass with coat hangers, ran it through a radio, and the Amplifier-Peg was born. Everett's wife, Gertrude, named the new invention "Ampeg," which was short for Amplifier Peg. Popularity picked up on the invention and in 1946 Everett applied for a patent, which was granted a year and a half later.

In 1946, Everett moved to Newark, New Jeresy to pursue his amplifier invention. Everett had been selling a Dynaco hi-fi amp, but wanted to design his own amp specifically for bass instruments. Everett met Stanley Michael in New York and the two of them opened The Michael-Hull Electronics Labs in 1946. Here they offered the "Ampeg" for the bass and the Michael-Hull Bassamp. This partnership that seemed to be a good matchup dissolved in 1948 as they were both unhappy. Everett ended up with the company and moved it to New York where the company was renamed The Ampeg Bassamp Co. After a few years of rough times and small business, the Ampeg company started to expand and grow. This involved a move to a new factory in New York in 1954, and another move in 1957. In 1956 The name was shortened to simply the Ampeg Company. This year Everett's right hand mand started to work for Ampeg. Jess Oliver came into Ampeg when they were still at the cramped little shop to buy an Ampeg. Everett offered him a job, and he accepted in 1956, as they became friends. With Oliver, Ampeg amps began to sell regularly and business appeared to be booming. Money had always been a problem at Ampeg and continued up into the 60's. Ampeg had grown so much that they had to move to Linden, New Jersey. Models were rolling off of the shelf at this point, and in the early 60's Ampeg released their first guitar, a stand-up bass.

Times began to get rough as Oliver's and Hull's partnership went sour over a compensation deal. Oliver then was fired or quit and still we don't really know what happened. Avnet was in the process of buying but they pulled out in fall of 1966. The company ,Unimusic, then bought out more than 50 percent of Ampeg's stock in the fall of 1967. The company was under new ownership, but Everett was still president. As many top-officials left Ampeg,

Hull began to get upset with the way things were going and still didn't like Rock & Roll music. He ended up resigning in the fall of 1968. This was the start of the downward spiral for Unimusic. Things going askew, Unimusic sold to Magnavox in 1971 as part of the Selmer division.

In the '70's, Ampeg was still of good quality, but they didn't keep up with the times. Their tube amps were hardly updated over the time when Magnavox was in charge. A few solid-state amps were introduced, but not enough. The Linden factory was closed in 1974 and moved the manufacturing to Jefferson City, Tennessee. Magnavox just wasn't a good "marriage" with Ampeg and they never made any money on them. Lots of things changed at this point. Ampeg did have a lot of endorsers including The Rolling Stones and Fleetwood Mac, but without new product, Ampeg made no large impact in the 1970's. The only breakthrough Ampeg had in this decade was what Dan Armstrong created.

Ernie Breifel started Music Technology Inc. (MTI) in 1977 as a wholesaler that imported instruments. MTI was looking to expand the corporation and in 1980 Ernie and MTI bought Ampeg from Selmer-Magnavox. This finished a deal that Ernie had tried to do back in the late 50's, but he didn't like how Hull worked and refused to deal with Ampeg. At this point the Japanese market was in high swing for instrument makers. Ampeg followed suit and started to make amps overseas. These new amps that they were making just didn't have the same sound that the old Ampeg amps had, and they weren't well received by the public. The old term "Three Strikes and you're out" happened in 1985. MTI ended up filing for bankruptcy and the name was up for sale again. Gene Kornblum of St. Louis Music (SLM) was there to purchase the company in the bankruptcy court. When SLM went to move all of the stock out of Long Island, all Ampeg had was two truckloads of odds and ends, very little inventory. In short, SLM had very little to go on. SLM had started to distribute Crate amps in the 70's and Ampeg was brought in for the higher end of amplifiers. It only took one model, the SVT-100 made of old MTI heads, but it brought Ampeg back into the market. In 1987, Ampeg introduced 14 new bass and guitar amps at the NAMM show. The sign that Ampeg was back into the majors was their new "Monster" bass amp. This amp stood nine feet tall, weighed in at 718lbs, and had 600W running into 32 10" speakers! It is now a world record.

As the 1990's rolled around SLM, and Ampeg were both going strong with new products and endorsers joining consistently. Ampeg was keeping up with technology and what other companies were doing. That is something that they really failed to do in the70's and early 80's. Now Ampeg amps are distributed throughout 40 countries, they have made reissue amps from the glory days and continue to take the Ampeg pride into the new century.

Source for Ampeg History: Ampeg The Story Behind the Sound by Gregg Hopkins & Bill Moore.

DATING AMPEG AMPLIFIERS

In dating Ampeg Amplifiers, there are several different schemes to be used. The good thing about Ampeg is that when they changed their models, they all changed at the same time. This means that it is fairly easy to determine the range of year by just looking at the outside of the amp. Like all U.S.A. made amps, the speakers, transformers, and potentiometers have date codes on them. This along with the serial number on the amp can help narrow down the year of manufacture.

There are six distinctive periods in the Ampeg line. Each period has a different way of identifying the year made. Note that each different period is approximately during each different ownership. The chart here should be of some help.

Individual Amp Identification (Dates)

Pre 1953 - These amps can only be dated by the EIA (Electronics Industries Association) codes on the speakers and other parts. No serial numbers were used during this time. Michael-Hull amplifiers were made between 1946-48. When Hull started on his own, the name was switched to Ampeg and were mostly wood amps with Ampeg written across the grille.

1953-Mid 1965 - In 1953, the first Serialization system was introduced. This was a six digit number like this YMMNNN which was the last digit of the year, month, and number of production. Since there is a possibility of overlap here, cosmetics are a huge factor in determining the year. The year 1953 could be 1963 since only the last digit was used. Ampeg changed their cosmetics several times in the late 50's and by determining whether the amp is black, blue, gray or tan will identify the year.

1965-1969 - In early 1965 a new serialization system went into effect. The old one lasted on certain models for about six months. This system was also six digits. This system here was strictly numerical and started at 000001. It ran for about five years and ended with 092000. This chart is fairly accurate:

Serial Number	Year	Serial Number	Year	Serial Number	Year
000001-020000	1965	049000-075000	1967	080000-090000	1969
020000-049000	1966	075000-080000	1968		

1970-1979 - By 1970, Ampeg was in turmoil and in the process of selling to Magnavox. It was only fitting to introduce a third serialization system. At this point in time there isn't enough information about the serial numbers to accurately date with them. The best way to do that is by the cosmetics and when they were used over the decade. There is a small list of what Selmer and Ampeg changed during this time. The first feature is the control panel. From 1968-1972, a blue control panel was used. In 1972 until 1975, the control panel was changed to black with square corners. In 1976, the panel was horizontally split with rounded corners (This was started in 1973 on solid-state models). The second feature is the addition of a distortion knob which occured in 1976. The third are the "white rocker switches", which replaced the "black rocker switches." These were changed on solid-state amps in 1973 and on tube amps in 1976. The final feature was the "a" logo. It was metal from 1968-1972, and plastic from 1973 on.

1981-1985 - This is the MTI period of production. These are probably the hardest to date by year. This is because of overseas production with no EIA numbers and the fact that fourth serialization system is not reliable. There is not enough information to determine the specific year. The approximation between 1981-1985 can be assumed since all of these were made then and it was a short enough period where a few years doesn't concern the value much.

Post 1985 - These are the amps during the St. Louis Music period, which is still in production today. Here the fifth serialization system and code that's in practice today was introduced. This is the best way to identify the date of manufacture. A 10 digit number is used as a serial number, which contains lots of information. The number is set up like this LLLCYMNNNN. LLL stands for the model, C stands for the country. U is U.K., Y is Europe, W is Worldwide, and D stands for domestic (U.S.). The Y is a year code that is a letter. A is 1988, B is 1989, C is 1990, and so on. What happened before 1987 for the year is unclear (as very few amps were made because of bankruptcy for MTI). The M is a number code for January-October. Jan is 1, Feb is 2, Oct is 10, fill in the blanks. For November and December the letters A and B were used respectively. The last 4 numbers (N) are the actual serial number for the instrument. Example? Certainly. Serial number on a B-15R is AJYDB60626. This is a U.S. amp made in June of 1989 and its serial number 626. It's a piece of cake when you learn how to do it.

Date Codes on Potentiometers

On every American made potentiometer (pots), there is a date and manufacture code. This code consists of six or seven digits. The first three indicate the manufacture and the last three or four indicate the date it was made. If there are six digits, the fourth digit indicates the last number of the year, and the fifth and sixth digit indicate the week of that year. If there are seven digits, the fourth and fifth indicate the last two digits of the year it was made, and the sixth and seventh indicate the week of that year. Usually the numbers were separated by a hyphen after the third digit.

The most common pots manufactures and their numbers are as following: CTS (137), Stackpole (304), Clarostat (140), Cetralab (134), Bourns (381), and Allen Bradley (106). Examples of how this system works are: pot# 140-6421= a Calrostat pot made int the 21st week of 1964, 137-711= a CTS pot made in the 11th week of 1947 or 1957. When there are possibilities of two different years, refer to the amplifier and see what years it was manufactured.

GRADING	100%	EXCELLENT	AVERAGE

There are several instances to make sure that this system is accurate. The pots must be original. If they have been replaced, they are not going to be an accurate way to determine the date of the amplifier. The pots show that the amp was not made before the date on the pot, but could be made much later than that date.

ELECTRIC TUBE AMPS

Our greatest attempt has been made to try to break up the Tube amps into sensible categories. Ampeg really didn't have model series until the early sixties when the Universal series was released. We have broken up the early models into time periods, as are miscallaneous amps in the sixties and amps throughtout the seventies and eighties. There are series of amplifiers that begin to show up in the 1960's, and most of these are pretty self-explanatory. If a certain amp isn't listed under a series, check the misc. models for that time period. Every attempt has been made to include every Ampeg amp in an easy format.

Michael-Hull Series

This was the series that Stanley Michael and Everett Hull started when they opened their shop. These were bass amps made to be used with the "Ampeg" inside of a stand up bass. There were two models, the Michael-Hull Bassamp and the Model 770 Bassamp. There are only two known survivors of the Michael-Hull era. The early model Bassman had a plywood cabinet with mahogany veneer, which was very classy. The chassis was on one side of the cabinet. The controls were on a slanted control panel on the back of the amp. The speaker is covered by a bass clef sign. This amp had two channels, 18W output, tubes consisting of 2 X 6SC7 preamps, 2 X 6L6 outputs, and a 5U4 rectifier. There was 1-12" GE Alinco V speaker. The control panel had a number of knobs.

The Model 770 Bassman was very similar to the first run, except for the fact that it was covered with what they call "mother-of-toilet-seat," which was much shinier than mahogany. The tubes were also changed from 6SC7 preamps to 3 X 6SN7's. This version had an even more elaborate control panel and a new vent to let heat escape out the back.

It is very hard to put a price on these, since only a few were made. The best price is how bad someone really wants one!

Early Amps 1949-1955

Since the early amps weren't released with any direction towards a series, the best way to do it is by the year they came out. There were only a few released during these years so they're easy to identify.

SUPER 800 BASSAMP - 18W, 1-12" GE Alnico V speaker, tubes: 2 X 6BG6 power tubes, 2 X 6SN7 preamp, 5U4 rectifier, top control panel, three "chicken head" knobs (v, b, t), all controls on the panel, a sensitivity control, brown cocoa vinyl covering, brown grille with Ampeg logo silk-screened onto it, mfg. 1949-1951.

	N/A	$400 - 500	$275 - 350

This model had a bottom mounted chassis, and speedometer cables that ran to the chassis from the control panel to run the poteniometers. It was a very good amp for its time.

* **Model 815 Bassamp** - Similar to the Super 800 Bassman except has 1-15" Alnico V Jensen speaker, new engraved polished aluminum control panel, mfg. 1951-55.

	N/A	$400 - 475	$275 - 350

There are three different versions of this amp. The second one, which was introduced in 1952 and ran until 1954. It featured a change in tubes to 4 X 6V6 power tubes and 3 X 6SJ7 preamps, and the vinyl covering was changed to a dot tweed. The third version ran from 1954-55, which went back to the 6BG6 tubes, and a voltage regulator was added. The speedometer cables were finally discontinued and replaced with wires (talk about technology!).

MODEL 500 & 700 GUITAR AMPS - These amps were introduced in 1950 as the first guitar amps for Ampeg. These amps are very similar to the Super 800 Bassman and Model 815 Bassman. There is only one known survivor of these models, therefore it's hard to come up with information or a value on it.

TONY MOTTOLA "DANGER" GUITARAMP - 20W, 1-12" Jensen Concert Speaker, different from the Super 800 and Model 500 Guitaramps as it was shallower and the speaker sat higher, each amp was made differently, used by the jazz guitarist of the time, mfg. 1953-55.

	N/A	$475 - 600	$325 - 425

600 GUITARAMP - 10W, 1-12" Jensen Concert Alnico V speaker, virtually unknown in today's market, went along with the Tony Mottola and Johnny Smith models, no examples are known to exist today, mfg. 1955-57.

Mid Fifties Amps (1955-1960)

As 1955 came around, Ampeg started to make some innovative and important changes. There are a few things to remember during this period up until about 1960. Ampeg now had the new Baxandall tone circuit. This made two separate chassis inside the amp, but it reduced production costs. This was big for Ampeg as they had a chance to expand choices and use the modular design. The problem with the amps around this time is that by using the same chassis for many different amps, it was difficult to decipher model numbers, as they weren't often listed on the amp. Model numbers were listed by the type of amp. If it was a Bassamp, the series were numbered 800 (8000 has also been discovered). Accordiamps were 7000 and 400 numbers, and Guitaramps were 6000. In 1958, the model numbers were all 3 digits the 6000 went to 600 and the 7000 went to 700. A couple of other notes to help: Tremolo was only available in the guitar and accordion amps and Bassamps had deeper cabinet with the slanted control panel. In 1956, the logo changed and the p in Ampeg now went through the line underneath the logo.

JS-35 FOUNTAIN OF SOUND - 20W or 30W, 15" JBL speaker, tubes: 3 X 6SJ7 preamps, 2 X 6L6/5881 ouputs, silver control panel, five black knobs, three inputs, navy blue covering, gray grille, sat on four legs, speaker pointed upward, mfg. 1955-1960.

	N/A	$650 - 850	$400 - 600

The JS-35 stood for Johnny Smith as this amp replaced the old one in his name. This amp looks like a pool table.

* **JS-20 Fountain of Sound** - Similar to the JS-35, except the pre-amp section was changed to 6SJ7 tubes, the OC3 voltage regulator was added, mfg. 1957-58.

	N/A	$600 - 800	$400 - 550

* **JS-30 Fountain of Sound** - Similar to the JS-20 Fountain of Sound, except has 30W output, mfg. 1957-58.

	N/A	$650 - 850	$400 - 600

DOLPHIN - 15W, 1-12 Jensen Alnico speaker, 2 X 6SN7 pre-amps, 2 X 6V6 outputs, 1 X 5Y3 rectifier, top control panel, one channel, tremolo, chrome control panel, six control knobs (pickup matching, tremolo intensity, tremolo speed, v, t, b,) footswitch jack, black vinyl covering, square plastic grille cloth with a horizontal bar in the middle, mfg. 1956-1960.

	N/A	$300 - 400	$225 - 300

In 1957, the covering changed to gray bookbinding-type and a dark gray swirl grille. In 1958 the covering was changed to the Navy Random Flair. This amp along with the Zephyr and the Continental were all in a "series" together.

* ***Dophin II (6015)*** - Similar to the Dolphin except has two channels, mfg. 1956-1960.

	N/A	$325 - 450	$250 - 315

ZEPHYR I (6020) - 20W, 1-15" Jensen speaker, tubes: 3 X 6SN7 pre-amps, power: 2 X 6L6 or 5881, 5U4 rectifier, OC3 voltage regulator, one channel, top chrome control panel, controls for one channel, black vinyl covering, square plastic grille cloth with horizontal bar in the middle, mfg. 1956-59.

	N/A	$350 - 425	$250 - 325

In 1957, the ouptut was raised to 25W, the covering changed to gray bookbinding-type, and a dark gray swirl grille. In 1958 the covering was changed to the Navy Random Flair. This amp along with the Continenetal and the Dolphin were all in a "series" together.

* ***Zephyr Duette (6020)*** - Similar to the Zephyr I except has two channels, mfg. 1956-58.

	N/A	$350 - 450	$250 - 325

CONTINENTAL I - 30W, 1-15" Jensen coaxial speaker, 3 X 6SN7 pre amps, 2 X 6L6 or 5881 outputs, 5U4 rectifier, OC3 voltage regulator, one channel, top chrome control panel, controls for one channel, black vinyl covering, square plastic grille cloth with horizontal bar in the middle, mfg. 1956-59.

	N/A	$350 - 450	$275 - 325

In 1957, the output was raised to 35W, the covering changed to gray bookbinding-type, and a dark gray swirl grille. In 1958, the covering was changed to the Navy Random Flair. This amp along with the Zephyr and the Dolphin were all in a "series" together.

* ***Continental Duette (6030)*** - Similar to the Continental I except has two channels, mfg. 1956-58.

	N/A	$350 - 450	$275 - 335

JUPITER (720), RHAPSODY (435-S), & NEW YORKER (440-S) - 15W, 20W, & 30W respectively, these amps are identical to the Dophin, Zephyr, and Continental except that they are voiced for accordians, refer to the amps listed above for specs, mfg. 1956-1961.

MODEL 820 BASSAMP - 20W, 1-15" speaker, tubes: 3 X 6SN7 pre-amps, 2 X 6L6 or 5881 outputs, Stancor transformers, top control panel with knobs for one channel, sensitivity control, black vinyl covering, square plastic grille with horizontal bar, mfg. 1956-58.

	N/A	$350 - 425	$275 - 325

* ***Model 830 Bassamp*** - Similar to the Model 820 Bassamp except has 30W output, mfg. 1956-58.

	N/A	$375 - 450	$275 - 350

* ***Super Comboamp (833)*** - Similar to the Model 830 Bassamp except has 40W output, 2-15" Jensen Alnico speakers, three channels, 4 X 6L6GC pre-amp tubes, mfg. 1956-1961.

	N/A	$700 - 900	$500 - 650

This amp changed its model name to the 833 Comboamp in 1958 and to the 950-C Supercombo amp in 1959. There are only about six of these made ever. This amp looks to be two model 835 amps welded together.

* ***Model 822 Bassamp*** - Similar to the Model 820 Bassamp except has two channels, mfg. 1957-58.

	N/A	$375 - 450	$275 - 350

* ***Model 835 Bassamp*** - Similar to the Super Comboamp except it is only about half of that since the Super Comboamp appears to be two Model 835 amps welded together, mfg. 1959-1961.

	N/A	$350 - 435	$250 - 325

There are other models of Bassamps such as the Model 824, 825 and 825D that have been discovered, but they were never in an Ampeg catalog. Keep in mind this may happen to other models as well.

Universal Series

This is one of the first official series released by Ampeg. They called them Universal because they could be used for both accordion and guitar. The first two amps released in the series in 1957 were the Rocket and Mercury. In 1958, the Jet model was added and stayed in the Ampeg line until 1970. The series stayed the same until 1959 when the Mercury was replaced by the Big M. Other amps were changed in other lines for Ampeg as well. The Universal series remained unchanged throughout 1960.

R-12 ROCKET - 12W, 1-12" speaker, tubes: 3 or 4 X 6SN7 pre-amps, 2 X 6V6GT outputs, 5Y3 rectifier, one channel, tremolo, top black control panel, four black knobs (v, tone, s, i) four inputs, cream or yellow bookbinding covering, red or watermelon colored grilles, mfg. 1957-1965.

	N/A	$325 - 375	$225 - 275

In mid 1958, the covering was changed to the Navy Random Flair and the grille was changed to a gray with a white swirl.

* ***R-12A Rocket*** - Similar to the M-12 Mercury except produced as an updated version of the R-12 Rocket.

	N/A	$325 - 375	$225 - 275

* ***Reverberocket R-12R*** - Similar to the R-12 Rocket except has 15W output, tubes consisting of: 2 X 6SL7 & 2 X 6SN7 octal pre-amps, 2 X 6V6GT outputs, spring reverb, mfg. 1961-1963.

	N/A	$450 - 550	$350 - 425

* ***R-12R-B*** - Similar to the Reverberocket R-12R except has 7591A power tubes, mfg. 1964-65.

	N/A	$425 - 525	$325 - 400

GRADING	100%	EXCELLENT	AVERAGE

M-12 MERCURY - 15W, 1-12" speaker, tubes: 3 or 4 X 6SN7 pre-amps, 2 X 6V6GT outputs, 5Y3 rectifier, two channels, tremolo, top black control panel, six black knobs (Ch. 1: v, t, Ch. 2: v, t, Both: s, i), four inputs, cream or yellow bookbinding covering, red or watermelon colored grilles, mfg. 1957-1963.

| | N/A | $325 - 400 | $250 - 300 |

M-12A Mercury - Similar to the M-12 Mercury except produced as an updated version of the M-12.

| | N/A | $325 - 400 | $250 - 300 |

J-12 JET - 12W, 1-12" speaker, 3 or 4 X 6SN7 pre-amps, 2 X 6V6GT outputs, 5Y3 rectifier, one channel, top black control panel, two black knobs (v, tone) two inputs, cream or yellow bookbinding covering, red or watermelon colored grilles, mfg. 1958-1963.

Ampeg Jet J-12
courtesy Savage Audio

Ampeg Jet J-12
courtesy Savage Audio

| | N/A | $300 - 350 | $225 - 275 |

In 1958, the Jet's covering changed to the Navy Random Flair like all Ampeg amps at that time. In 1962, the Covering changed to Blue Check. There were a few models made in 1959 and 1960 with the Tin logos.

J-12A Jet - Similar to the J-12 Jet, except has 7591A power tubes, mfg. 1964 only.

Ampeg J-12A
courtesy Willie's American Guitars

| | N/A | $275 - 350 | $200 - 250 |

J-12T Jet - Similar to the J-12A, except has 2 X 6BK11 pre-amp tubes, mfg. 1965 only.

| | N/A | $275 - 325 | $200 - 250 |

J-12D Jet - Similar to the J-12T, Jet except has a solid-state rectifier instead of a 5Y3GT, mfg. 1965-66.

| | N/A | $250 - 300 | $175 - 225 |

This model was changed back to the J-12 Jet in 1966 until it was discontinued in 1967. Some J-12D's had 7868 pre-amp tubes. For the J-12R Reverbojet see the Golden Glo series in the Ampeg tube section along with the Jet II.

M-15 BIG M - 20W, 1-15" Jensen speaker, tubes: 3 X 6SN7 pre-amps, 2 X 6L6 outputs, 5Y3 rectifier, two channels, top control channel, six black knobs, Navy Random Flair covering, gray grille cloth, mfg. 1959-1965.

| | N/A | $325 - 400 | $250 - 300 |

GRADING	100%	EXCELLENT	AVERAGE

Misc. Amps Late 50's through Early 60's

The amps listed in this section are the amps that weren't released in a common series. Ampeg then became a more organized company and began to release amps in a series more during the 1960's. There are other models where there isn't any information on including the **518 Dolphin Special**, the **Model 435 SN**, the **Model 635-S Zephyr**, the **Model 720-SN Jupiter II**, and the **625-SN Constellation**. Most of these amps are submodels of more popular models and often have minor differences or were made at a different time period. Look for more information on these models on upcoming editions of the Blue Book of Guitar Amplifiers.

625-D MANHATTEN - 25W, 2-12" Jensen speakers, tubes: pre-amp: 2 X 6CG7, 12AU7, & 6SL7, output: EL37, 5U4 rectifier, OC3 voltage regulator, dual channels, top chrome control panel, 6 black knobs (v, b, t, for each channel), Navy Random Flair covering, gray grille, mfg. 1959-1961.

N/A	$475 - 600	$375 - 450

SUPEREVERB MODEL R-15R - 15W, 1-15" Jensen C15N speaker, tubes: pre-amp 7025, power: 2 X 7591A, similar to the Reverberocket, mfg. 1963-64.

N/A	$475 - 625	$350 - 450

Portaflex Series

The Portaflex or "flip top" series debuted in 1960. This was a new innovation, which gave new life to Ampeg in the 1960's. This new series offered, a closed back, tuned-port cabinet, the head actually flipped out of the cabinet and rested on top of it, a reflex baffle to dampen the speaker, the amp head was separate for better cooling and it could be stored in the cabinet for easy transport, and kept important components away from heat of the tubes. The first amps in this series were the A-15 and the B-15. These were exactly the same amps, the A-15 was for accordions and the B-15 for guitars. At the end of 1960, the B-15 was changed to the B-15N. The Portaflex series was very successful and lasted into the 1970's. Some of these models offer a lighted Lucite nameplate.

A-15 & B-15 PORTAFLEX - 25W, 1-15" speaker, tubes: 2 X 6SL7 pre-amps (one for each channel), 6SL7 phase inverter, 2 X 6L6GC outputs, 5U4G rectifier, dual channels, piggyback unit, chrome control panel, three input jacks (one for stereo), four black knobs (v1,v2, t, b), navy random flair covering, gray grille, mfg. 1960-61.

N/A	$525 - 650	$400 - 475

The A-15 was designed for accordions even though it was the same amplifier. The B-15 was redesigned and renamed the B-15N in 1961.

* **B-15N Portaflex** - Similar to the B-15 Portaflex except with a redesigned circuit, which included tone controls for each channel, a pre-amp tube for each channel, and the stereo jack removed for a bright and normal jack on channel one, gray covering early then blue check, gray grilles, mfg. 1961, reintroduced in 1968 until 1980.

Ampeg B-15
courtesy Savage Audio

Ampeg B-15
courtesy Savage Audio

Ampeg B-15
courtesy Savage Audio

N/A	$600 - 750	$450 - 525

Check later in the Portaflex section for later model B-15N.

* **B-15NB Portaflex** - Similar to the B-15N except a few resistors and capacitors were changed, the rectifier was changed to a solid-state diode, blue check covering, gray grille cloth, mfg. 1962-63.

N/A	$550 - 650	$425 - 500

* **B-15NC Portaflex (1964)** - Similar to the B-15NC Portaflex except the rectifier was changed back to a tube, mfg. 1964 only.

N/A	$575 - 675	$450 - 525

* **B-15NF Portaflex** - Similar to the B-15NC Portaflex except output raised to 30W, output tubes changed to 2 X 6L6GC, new printed circuit board, inside was changed to a single baffle, mfg. 1965-67

N/A	$500 - 600	$375- 450

B-15ND PORTAFLEX - 50W, 1-15" CTS speaker, matching 1-15" extension cabinet, tubes: pre-amp: 2 X 6SL7, power: 2 X 7027A, 7199 phase inverter, solid-state rectifier, two channels, front chrome control panel, six black knobs (v, b, t, for each channel), black vinyl covering, blue and silver grille, light-up Lucite logo, mfg. 1967 only.

N/A	$600 - 750	$450 - 550

* **B-15NC Portaflex (1967-68)** - Similar to the B-15ND Portaflex except is all in one vertical cabinet (2-15" speakers),mfg. 1967-68.

N/A	$500 - 600	$375 - 450

GRADING	100%	EXCELLENT	AVERAGE

B-15N PORTAFLEX (1968-1980) - 50W, 1-15" speaker, tubes: pre-amp: 2 X 6SL7, power: 2 X 7027A, s.s. rectifier, front control panel, two input jacks, black vinyl, blue/silver grille, no chrome grille strips, no light-up logo, new "a" logo, mfg. 1968-1980.

| | N/A | $450 - 525 | $350 - 400 |

This amp is a revamped model of the B-15NF. New circuit board design.

* B-15S Portaflex - Similar to the new B-15 Portaflex except is slightly larger, 60W output, tubes: pre-amp: 2 X 12AX7, 12DW7, 12AU7 phase inverter, power: 2 X 7027A, solid-state rectifier, response switch, mfg. 1971-77.

| | N/A | $450 - 525 | $350 - 400 |

* B-15T Portaflex - See Solid-State section in Ampeg.

B-15X PORTAFLEX - 50W, 1-15" speaker, all tube chassis, pre-amp: 7199, 6D10, power: 7027A's, dual channels, reverb, vibrato, portaflex design, front chrome control panel, four inputs, nine black knobs (Ch. 1: v, b, t, r, s, i, Ch. 2: v, b, t), blue check covering, gray grille, mfg. 1964-65.

| | N/A | $450 - 550 | $375 - 425 |

B-12N PORTAFLEX - 25W, 1-12", tubes: 2 X 6SL7 pre-amps (one for each channel), 6SL7 phase inverter, 2 X 6L6GC outputs, 5U4G rectifier, dual channels, piggyback unit, silver control panel, three input jacks (one for stereo), four black knobs (a volume for each channel, t, b), navy random flair covering, gray grille, mfg. 1960-61.

| | N/A | $425 - 500 | $325 - 400 |

In 1962, the Blue Check covering was introduced. The circuit is identical to that of the B-15N (1961) except with a smaller cabinet.

B-12X PORTAFLEX - 25W, 1-12" speaker, tubes: preamp: 2 X 6SL7, power: 2 X 6L6GC, dual channels, reverb, vibrato, both only on one channel, Navy Random Flair covering, gray grille, mfg. 1961-64.

| | N/A | $450 - 525 | $350 - 425 |

In 1962, Blue Check covering was introduced. This was the first Portaflex amplifier specifically designed for guitars. This amp had a separate reverb cabinet that had an oval speaker (early) and 2-4" speakers (later), tubes: 6SL7 preamp, 6V6GT power.

* B-12XY Portaflex - Similar to the B-12X except tubes were changed to 6D10 preamps & 7591A powers for the reverb unit, 7027A power tubes for the main unit, output raised to 50W, mfg. 1965-68.

| | N/A | $450 - 525 | $350 - 400 |

In 1965 the cabinet was changed to 2-12" speakers and the tubes were changed to preamp: 4 X 12AX7, 7199 phase inverter, power: 2 X 7027A, 5AR4 rectifier.

SB-12 PORTAFLEX - 22W, 1-12" Jensen C12N speaker, tubes: pre-amp: 2 X 12AX7, power: 2 X 7868, single channel, blue check covering, gray grille, mfg. 1965-1971.

| | N/A | $425 - 500 | $325 - 400 |

This was a close but not an exact replacement for the B-12N. This amp was specifically designed for the Ampeg Baby Bass.

B-18N PORTAFLEX - 50W, 1-18" speaker, tubes: preamp: 2 X 6SL7, 7199 phase inverter, power: 2 X 7027A, 5AR4 rectifier, dual channels, front chrome flip-up control panel, six black knobs, Blue Check covering, gray grille, mfg. 1963-67.

| | N/A | $525 - 650 | $425 - 500 |

* B-18X Portaflex - Similar to the B-12XY except has an 18" speaker, with a midrange horn, reverb, vibrato, mfg. 1966-67.

| | N/A | $500 - 600 | $400 - 475 |

* BT-18L Portaflex - See Solid-State series in Ampeg.

Echo Series

In 1961, Ampeg figured that folks who owned an amp that didn't have reverb should be offered this option without having to buy a new amplifier. The Echo Satellite ES-1 was the solution. This was a separate cabinet that hooked up directly to the speaker from another amp without reverb. The reverb unit would then sit separately and create reverb. Eventually combo Echo models derived from this unit.

ES-1 ECHO SATELITE - 6W, 1-8" oval speaker early, 2-4" speakers later, tubes: pre-amp: 6SL7, power: 6V6GT, top control panel, one knob for reverb, Navy Random Flair covering, gray grille, mfg. 1961-63.

| Oval Speakers | N/A | $275 - 325 | $200 - 225 |
| 2-4" Speakers | N/A | $200 - 250 | $150 - 180 |

In 1962, Blue Check covering introduced.

ET-1 ECHO TWIN - 30W (2 x 15W) stereo amplifier, 2 seperate power amps, tubes: 2 X 6V6GT output, tremolo reverb, front chrome control panel, controls for each, Navy Random Flair covering, gray grille cloth, mfg. 1961-63.

| | N/A | $475 - 575 | $400 - 450 |

In 1962 Blue Check covering introduced.

* ET-1-B Echo Twin - Similar to the ET-1 Echo Twin except has 7591A output tubes and a 5Y3GT rectifier, mfg. 1963-64.

| | N/A | $475 - 550 | $400 - 450 |

This model replaced the original ET-1 Echo Twin.

ET-2 SUPER ECHO TWIN - 30W (2 X 15) Stereo amplifier, 2-12" Jensen C12Q speakers, tubes: pre-amp: 4 X 6SL7, power: 2 X 2 X 6V6GT (two seperate power amps) 2 X 5Y3 rectifiers, two channels, vibrato, reverb, top control panel, seven knobs (v, & tone for each channel, s, i, reverb depth), channel selector switch, footswitch, blue check covering, gray grille, mfg. 1962-63.

| | N/A | $750 - 875 | $600 - 675 |

* ET-2-B Super Echo Twin - Similar to the ET-2 except the power tubes are 2 X 7591A, mfg. 1964 only.

| | N/A | $725 - 850 | $575 - 650 |

EJ-12 ECHO JET - 12W, 1-12" CTS Alnico speaker, tubes: pre-amp: 6D10, power: 2 X 7591, 5Y3GT rectifier, top control panel, tone control, blue check covering, gray grille, mfg. 1963-64.

| | N/A | $425 - 500 | $350 - 400 |

This was a reverb unit but it could be used as an amplifier as well. It is similar to the Ampeg Jet.

GRADING	100%	EXCELLENT	AVERAGE

* EJ-12A & EJ-12D - Similar to the EJ-12 Echo Jet EJ-12 except features a different pre-amp section, mfg. 1964 only.

	N/A	$425 - 500	$350 - 400

Gemini Series

This was a new line introduced from Ampeg in 1964. It was the first series of amps to have front-facing controls and a horizontally mounted chassis. These were combo amps that used the back panels to alter the sound and tone by removing parts of it, or the whole panel. The amps were generally covered with the blue check covering, had a black and tan with silver grille cloth (all blended together it looks gray), and a chrome control panel.

G-12 GEMINI I - 22W, 1-12" speaker, tubes: pre-amp: 12AX7 & GCG7, power: 2 X 7591A, solid-state rectifier, 7199 phase inverter, dual channels, chrome front control panel, four inputs, two for accordion, two for guitar, nine black knobs (v, t, b for each channel, reverb intensity, tremolo s & i), blue check covering, gray grille, mfg. 1964-68.

	N/A	$350 - 400	$275 - 325

A bright switch was on the treble control that was a push/pull switch, reverb was only available on the first channel, but there have been models made between 1966-67 with another reverb pot.

* GS-15 Gemini II - Similar to the G-12 Gemini I except has a 15" speaker, a fixed-bias power section, increased output to 30W, mfg. 1965-68.

	N/A	$350 - 400	$275 - 325

* GS-15R Gemini VI - Similar to the GS-15 Gemini VI except is a single channel version and designed for accordions, mfg. 1966-67.

	N/A	$325 - 375	$250 - 300

* GV-15 Gemini V - Similar to the GS-15 Gemini II except has vibrato, front control panel, black covering, blue/silver grille, mfg. 1968-1971.

	N/A	$300 - 350	$225 - 275

Later in 1968 the Gemini V added a printed circuit board, ultra high and lo controls, output raised to 35W, and an Altec 418B speaker available as an option.

GS-12 ROCKET 2 - 12W, 1-12" speaker, tubes: preamp: 12AX7, 7199 phase inverter, power: 2 X 6V6GT, one channel, tremolo, reverb, front control panel, two inputs, five black knobs (v, tone, reverb, s, i), blue check covering, gray grille, mfg. 1965-67.

Ampeg Rocket 2 G2-12
courtesy Willie's American Guitars

	N/A	$325 - 400	$250 - 300

This amp replaced the R-12 Rocket from the Universal series. This amp featured the new Repeat Percussion effect. Ampeg also offered a model identical to this one with 4 inputs instead of 2 called the Gemini IV.

REVERBEROCKET GS-12R 2 - 18W, 1-12" speaker, tubes: preamp: 12AX7, 7199 phase inverter, 6U10 reverb tube, power: 2 X 6V6GT, one channel, front chrome control panel, two inputs, six black knobs (v, t, b, reverb intesity, tremolo s & i), blue check covering, gray grille, mfg. 1965-1970.

	N/A	$325 - 400	$250 - 300

Golden-Glo Series

The Golden-Glo series was introduced in 1967. This completely new series was more new in the cosmetics than anything else. These amps were covered in black and had a brown grille. The three models offered in this odd color were the Reverberocket III, Jet II, and Reverbojet. All of these models derived from older, popular ones with the cosmetic changes. It's hard to describe this amp without seeing it, since Ampeg had never had anything look like this before. It has a black covering with the brown straw-like grille. The grille sticks out about three inches from the rest of the amp and on top of this protusion sits the control panel which is a top-mount. The amp rises another six inches from that, and is finished in wood-grain. The control panel is gold which must be where the name comes from. These amps would probably look good next to an old cabin or a Woody station wagon. In this case a picture is the best way to describe the amp.

JET II - 12W, 1-12" speaker, 12AX7 pre-amps, 2 X 6V6GT outputs, solid-state rectifier, one channel, top gold control panel, three black knobs (v, tone, tremolo) two inputs, black covering, brown straw grille, mfg. 1967-1968.

	N/A	$250 - 300	$175 - 225

J-12R REVERBOJET - 15W, 1-12" speaker, tubes: pre-amp: 2 X 12AX7, 6U10 reverb, power: 2 X 7591A, solid-state rectifier, top gold control panel, two inputs, four black knobs (v, t, b, reverb), VU meter on control panel, black covering, brown straw grille, mfg. 1967-68.

	N/A	$300 - 375	$225 - 275

GRADING	100%	EXCELLENT	AVERAGE

GSC-12R REVERBEROCKET III - 18W, 1-12" speaker, tubes: pre-amp: 2 X 6SL7 & 2 X 6SN7, power: 2 X 6V6GT, spring reverb, top gold control panel, two inputs, eight black knobs, black covering, brown straw grille, light-up lucite logo (red) mfg. 1967-1968.

	N/A	$300 - 400	$225 - 285

This was the only model to have the light-up logo like that of the Portaflex's. This amp was derived from the Reverberocket GS-12R. There have been models found when the model was spelled Reverborocket.

New Tube Amps Intoduced in 1969

1969 was the beginning of turmoil around Ampeg as Unimusic was having trouble and would have to sell again in 1971. The corporates at Unimusic decided that they should intoduced some new product to get things rolling again. In 1969 seven new models were introduced, and lik the old days, they were released all as single amps, not in a series. The models that came out were the B-25, B-25B, B-22X Jupiter-22, B-42X Jupiter 42, GV-22 Gemini 22, G-20 Gemini 20, and the infamous SVT. Since there is no series we just grouped them during the time that they were released.

B-25 - 55W, 2-15" speaker cabinets with a head-unit, guitar amp, tubes: pre-amp: 2 X 12AX7, 1 X 7199 phase inverter, power: 2 X 7027A, 5AR4 rectifier, two channels, front control panel, 8 black knobs (Ch 1: v, b, t, Ch 2: v, b, t, ultra high, ultra lo), black covering, blue/gray grille, mfg. 1969 only.

	N/A	$325 - 375	$250 - 300

* B-25B- Similar to the B-25 except designed for bass guitars, mfg. 1969-1980.

	N/A	$325 - 375	$250 - 300

B-22X JUPITER 22 - 55W, 2-12" combo, tubes: pre-amp: 4 X 12AX7, 1 X 6CG7, 1 X 7199 phase inveter, power: 2 X 7027A, 5AR4 rectifier, front control panel, two bright and normal inputs for each channel (4 total), 9 knobs (v, t, b, Ultra high, Ultra Lo, tremolo, vibrato, reverb, afterbeat) black covering, blue/gray grille, mfg. 1969-1971.

	N/A	$325 - 375	$250 - 300

Altec 417B speakers were an option.

* B-42X Jupiter 42 - Similar to the B-22X except in a head/cabinet version with 4-12" speakers, mfg. 1969-1970.

	N/A	$375 - 425	$275 - 325

Altec 417B speakers were an option.

GV-22 GEMINI 22 - 35W, 2-12" speakers, combo amp tubes: preamp: 12AX7 & GCG7, power: 2 X 7591A, solid-state rectifier, 7199 phase inverter, dual channels, four inputs, silver front control panel, nine black knobs (v, t, b for each channel, r, tremolo s & i), black covering, blue/gray grille, mfg. 1969-1972.

	N/A	$300 - 350	$225 - 275

Altec speakers were an option.

* G-20 Gemini 20 - Similar to the G-20 Gemini 20 except in a 2-10" speaker combo, no vibrato, mfg. 1969-1972.

	N/A	$275 - 325	$200 - 250

Altec speakers were an option.

Super Vacuum Tube (SVT) Model

This massive amplifier made its debut in 1969 along with six other models, but this one lasted much longer than all the rest. There is a good reason for this as it was possibly the best bass amplifier Ampeg designed. It started out in 1969 as just an amp, not a guitar or bass amp, and by 1974 it was listed in Ampeg catalogs as a bass amp. This was truely a monster with 300 Watts of power, 14 tubes driving it and 16 speakers to disperse the noise. There have been many changes and refinements to this hog, but the spirit still remains after over 30 years of the SVT.

For the models SVT-400T, SVT-200T, SVT-140TC, and the SVT-70T see the solid-state section of Ampeg.

SUPER VACUUM TUBE (SVT) - 300W head unit, 16-10" speakers (8-10" speakers in a cabinet, 2 cabinets, there were four seperate compartments for each pair of speakers), tubes: pre-amp: 4 X 12DW7, 12AX7, 6C4, power: 6 X 6550, 12DW7 phase inverter, 2 X 12BH7 followers, solid-state rectifier, two channels, four inputs, seven knobs (Ch.1: v, t, m, b, Ch. 2: v, t, b), black covering, blue/gray grille, mfg. 1969-current.

Ampeg SVT
courtesy Savage Audio

Ampeg SVT
courtesy Savage Audio

1969-1974	N/A	$2,000 - 2,300	$1,500 - 1,800
1975-1980	N/A	$1,700 - 2,000	$1,400 - 1,600
1981-1990	N/A	$1,600 - 1,900	$1,300 - 1,500
1991-2001	$1,950	$1,575 - 1,850	$1,250 - 1,450
MSR $2,199	$1,350	$1,000 - $1,200	$775 - 925

Early models were equipped with 6 X 6146 power tubes, but were discontinued shortly after the SVT was introduced, because they ran too hot. There was a recall issued in 1972 to update all of the amps with the 6146 tubes and other modifications. When MTI took over in the early 1980's they had the SVT's made in Japan with Japanese parts. The amp was changed from 12DW7 preamps to 12AX7's. When SLM took over in 1986 the production of the SVT moved back to the U.S. The preamp tubes were changed back to the 12DW7's and there were only 500 made over a five year period in the "Skunkworks" department. In 1986, the name was changed to SVT-HD for head unit. In the late 1990's, the model was changed to the SVT-AV (Anniversary) to match the model of the 1970's.

SVT-100 - 100W, head unit with an 8-10", 4-10", 1-15 & 1-10", and a 1-18" cabinet, tubes: preamp: 3 X 12AX7, power: 4 X 6550, single channel, front black control panel, two inputs, six black knobs (v, MV, b, m, t, p), bs, gain switch, black covering, black grille, mfg. 1986-1992.

	N/A	$400 - 500	$275 - 350

This amp was a butchered V5 amp from the MTI days and made into a bass amp. When SLM bought Ampeg they received a slug of V5 heads. They made a small component change in the preamp and had a new bass amp. None of these amps were built from scratch.

SVT-II - 300W, rack mount, similar to the SVT original model in circuitry, includes a footswitchable 6-band equalizer, mfg. 1989-1994.

	N/A	$750 - 900	$575 - 650

SVT-III - See Electric Hybrid Listing at the end of the Ampeg section.

SVT 4 - 1600W, mono, tube preamp, little information known.

	N/A	$800 - 950	$675 - 750

SVT-300 - 300W, power amp only, similar to the SVT original with 6 X 6550 output tubes, mfg. 1991-95.

	N/A	$750 - 900	$600 - 675

This amp was meant to be mated with the SVT-IIP preamp to make a complete rack system.

SVT CLASSIC - 300W, head-unit only, tubes: preamp: 4 X 12DW7, 12AX7, 6C4, power: 6 X 6550, 12DW7 phase inverter, 2 X 12BH7 followers, solid-state rectifier, two channels, two inputs, six black knobs (g, b, m, freq, t, limiter), black covering, black grille, mfg. 1994-current.

MSR	$2,149	$1,200	$1,000 - 1,150	$750 - 925

V-4B - 100W, head-unit only, 4 X 6L6GC output tubes, single channel, two inputs, six black knobs (gain, b, m, freq., t, master), black tolex covering, black grille, mfg. 1995-2000.

MSR	$1,199	$725	$525 - 675	$450 - 500

Pro Series

These are the current Ampeg head-only units that are for rack units. These are derived from the SVT of many years ago but have a lot of updated material that sets it separate from the older amps. There are four speaker cabinets that are currently being offered by Ampeg. These are all meant to be teamed up with the Pro series head-units. The **PR-810H** has 8-10" speakers, handles 2400W and retails for $2,499. The **PR-410HLF** has 4-10" speakers, can take 1200W of power, and retails for $1,399. The **PR-410H** is the same as the HLF except is in 8 Ohms resistance and retails for $1,299. The **PR-15H** has a 15" speaker, 800W, and retails for $1,149. All the enclosures have at least one horn in them.

There are also rack spaces available for head units. The **PR-RC4** is a four space and retails for $299. The **PR-RC3** is a three space, which retails for $249.

SVT-2PRO - 300W, four-space rack mount, all tube chassis, 6 X 6550 output, single channel, black front control panel, single input, seven black knobs (g, drive, b, m, freq, t, MV), nine-band equalizer, tuner out, mute switch, effects loop, various switches, black covering, mfg. 1999-current.

MSR	$2,399	$1,499	$1,125 - 1,400	$975 - 1,075

SVT-3PRO - 450W, two-space rackmount head, tube preamp, tube driven MOSFET power-amp, single channel, seven black knobs (g, b, m, freq, t, MV, tube gain), nine-band equalizer, mute switch, tuner out, line out, effects loop, black covering, mfg. 1999-current.

MSR	$1,329	$785	$525 - 700	$385 - 450

SVT-4PRO - 1600W, three-space rackmount head, tube preamp, tube driven MOSFET power-amp, single channel, front black control panel, ten black knobs (g, compression, b, m, freq., t, line out level, master, freq., balance), ultra high and low boosts, nine band equalizer, various switches, mute switch, tuner out, black covering, mfg. 1999-current.

MSR	$1,799	$999	$700 - 875	$550 - 650

SVT-5PRO - 1350W, 3-space rackmount head, tube preamp, MOSFET power amp, single channel, front black control panel, one input, 15 black knobs, various buttons, black covering, new 2002.

MSR	$1,799	$950	$700 - 850	$550 - 650

SVT-PRO - Preamp only, single-space rackmount, tube chassis, front black control panel, six black control knobs (g, drive, b, m, freq, t), nine-band equalizer, bright switch, various switches and jacks, mfg. 1999-current.

MSR	$699	$350	$250 - 325	$200 - 235

SVT-BSP - Preamp only, single-space rackmount, tube chassis, dual channels, front black control panel, one input, 12 black control knobs (Clean: g, b, m, t, v, OD: gain, b, m, freq., t, v, MV), channel switching and combining, black covering, mfg. 1999-current.

MSR	$699	$350	$275 - 335	$200 - 250

Tube Amps in the 70's

AC-12 - 20W, 1-12" speaker, accordion amp, tubes: preamp: 12AX7, 6U10, 12DW7, power: 2 X 7591, one channel, reverb, tremolo, silver front control panel, two inputs, six black knobs (v, b, t, reverb, s, i), black covering, blue/gray grille, mfg. 1970 only.

	N/A	$175 - 200	$125 - 150

* **GU-12** - Similar to the AC-12, except it didn't have a negative-feedback loop, mfg. 1971-73.

	N/A	$175 - 200	$125 - 150

The AC-12 was a new amp designed for Accoridans that flopped. Ampeg took the circuit from this and made it into a new guitar amplifier that replaced the Rocket II. This was the last amp that Ampeg made especially for accordians (and probably for the better).

GRADING	100%	EXCELLENT	AVERAGE

VT-22 - 100W, 2-12" CTS or Eminence speakers, combo, tubes: preamp: 2 X 12AX7, 6K11, 12DW7, reverb: 6CG7, 12AX7, power: 4 X 7027A, 12AU7 phase inveter, solid-state rectifier, two channels, front silver control panel, two inputs, six silver knobs (v for each channel, t, m, b, r), Ultra Hi and Lo switches, black covering, blue/gray grille, mfg. 1970-1980.

	N/A	$400 - 450	$300 - 350

Altec 417-8C speakers were an option.

* V-4 - Similar to the VT-22 except was the head unit with a 4-12" cabinet (or two to make a stack), the cabinet is totally sealed, 4-12" CTS or Eminece ceramic magnet speakers, mfg. 1970-1980.

	N/A	$525 -600	$400 - 475

Altec 417-8C speakers were an option.

* V-4B - Similar to the V-4 (mostly circuitary) but labeled a bass amp, had a 2-15" cabinet, mfg. 1971-1980.

	N/A	$500 -575	$375 - 450

This model had Altec 421A speakers at first and they were switched over to Electo-Voice 200W speakers.

V-3 - 55W, head unit with a 4-12" speaker cabinet, guitar amp, tubes: preamp: 2 X 12AX7, 7199 phase inverter, power: 2 X 7027A, 5AR4 rectifier, two channels, front control panel, six silver knobs (Ch 1: v, b, t, Ch 2: v, b, t), ultra high and lo switches, black covering, blue/gray grille, mfg. 1970-71

	N/A	$375 - 425	$300 - 350

This amp was derived from the circuit of the B-25 made a year earlier. The only two changes were the cabinet was changed to 4-12" and the negative feedback loop was removed.

V-2 - 60W, head unit with a 4-12" ported cabinet, Eminence or CTS speakers, tubes: preamp: 3 X 12AX7, 6K11, 12DW7, 6CG7, power: 2 X 7027A, 12AU7 phase inverter, two channels, reverb, front silver control panel, two inputs, seven silver knobs (v for each channel, t, m, b, r), black covering, blue/gray grille, mfg. 1971-1980.

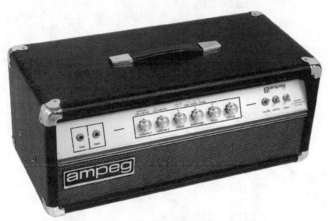

Ampeg V-2
courtesy Savage Audio

Ampeg V-2
courtesy Savage Audio

	N/A	$375 - 425	$300 - 350

* VT-40 - Similar to the V-2 except is a comb unit with 4-10" CTS speakers, mfg. 1971-1980.

	N/A	$375 - 425	$300 - 350

These models were derived from the VT-22 and V-4 to put out smaller wattages but to have a stack. V-2 had Altec 417-8C speakers as an option, and the VT-40 had Altec 425-8A as an option. The early VT-40 had a top mounted control panel and a vertical chassis.

V-9 - 300W head unit with a 9-10" speaker cabinet, tubes: preamp: 2 X 12BH7, 4 X 12DW7, 12AX7, 6CG7, power: 6 X 6550, reverb, distortion, dual channels, front control panel, black covering, blue/gray grille, mfg. 1975-1980.

	N/A	$800 - 1,000	$600 - 750

This amp was generally an SVT designed for guitars and keyboards. The speaker cabinet was divided up into three parts and each one was sealed from the others.

MTI Tube Amps 1980's

When MTI bought Magnavox in 1980, they completely overhauled their line. They introduced new lines and all the amps had a cosmetic makeover to black covering with a black grille. The only surviving model of the Magnavox days was the SVT. All amps were made overseas in Japan as well. MTI released six new tube amps at this time the V3SC, V3HD, V5SC, V5HD, V7SC, and the V7HD. The model description here stood for what each one had in terms of speakers. the SC's were combo's and the HD's were head units. The combos had 1-12" speaker for the VS3C and 2-12" for the other two.

V3SC - 50W, 1-12" combo unit, tubes: preamp: 4 X 12AX7, 12AT7, power: 2 X 6550, two channels, reverb, front black control panel, two inputs, nine black and silver knobs (Ch. 1: pre and post volume, Ch.2: v, Both: b, m, t, presence, reverb, MV), Mid-shift switch, E.Q. Shift switch, black covering, black grille, mfg. 1981-85.

	N/A	$225 - 275	$150 - 200

* V3HD - Similar to the V3SC except is the head-unit version, could be used with one or two 4-12" V-series speaker cabinets, mfg. 1981-85.

	N/A	$175 - 225	$125 - 150

V5SC - 100W, 2-12" speakers, tubes: preamp: 3 X 12AX7, power: 4 X 6550, single channel, front black control panel, two inputs, six black and silver knobs (Pre v, MV, b, m, t, presence), bright switch, gain switch, black covering, black grille, mfg. 1981-85.

	N/A	$300 - 350	$225 - 275

GRADING	100%	EXCELLENT	AVERAGE

* V5HD - Similar to the V5SC except is the head unit version, used with V-series 4-12" cabinets, mfg. 1981-85.

| | N/A | $200 - 250 | $150 - 180 |

V7SC - 100W, 2-12" speakers, tubes: preamp: 4 X 12AX7, 12AT7, power: 4 X 6550, dual channels, reverb, front black control panel, two inputs, nine black and silver knobs (Ch. 1: pre and post volume, Ch.2: v, Both: b, m, t, presence, reverb, MV), Mid-shift switch, E.Q. Shift switch, black covering, black grille, mfg. 1981-85.

| | N/A | $325 - 375 | $250 - 300 |

* V7HD - Similar to the V7SC except is the head unit version, used with V series 4-12" cabinets, mfg. 1981-85.

| | N/A | $225 - 275 | $150 - 200 |

VT Series Tube Amplifiers

St. Louis Music started to make tube amps for Ampeg again with the release of the VT series in 1989. The feature on these amplifiers was a "Multi-stage Musical Instrument Amplifier Having Distortion Modes" which meant, after a long breath, that you could change between distortion and normal modes while having the gain stage working in both modes. This design actually received a patent.

VT-60 - 60W, 1-12" combo, 6L6GC power tubes, mfg. 1989-1991.

| | N/A | $325 - 375 | $250 - 285 |

* VT-60H - Similar to the VT-60 except in a head-unit only version, mfg. 1989-1992.

| | N/A | $250 - 300 | $175 - 225 |

VT-120 - 120W, 1-12" combo, 6L6GC power tubes, mfg. 1989-1992.

| | N/A | $375 - 425 | $275 - 320 |

* VT-120H - Similar to the VT-120 except in a head-unit only version, mfg. 1989-1992.

| | $N/A | $225 - 275 | $200 - 250 |

VL Series Tube Amplifiers

The VL series amplifiers were supposed to be the finest amps offered by Ampeg at the time in 1991. They were even so good that they came with a key to stop unauthorized use. An important feature of these amps were the fact that either 6550 or EL34 tubes could be used to change sound with a flick of a switch. All of these VL models were head units only and were meant to be paired with four different speaker cabinets; the V412TV with Celestion Vintage 30's, V412TC with Celestion G12T-75, the SS412A with Ampeg Custom, and the SS212 with Celestion G12K-85 speakers. The SS212 had only 2-12" speakers while all of the rest had 4-12" speakers.

VL501 - 50W, head-unit only, tubes, single channel, black covering, black grille, mfg. 1991-92.

| | N/A | $225 - 275 | $150 - 200 |

* VL1001 - Similar to the VL501 except has 100W output, mfg. 1991-93.

| | N/A | $250 - 300 | $200 - 230 |

VL502 - 50W, head-unit only, two channels, reverb, black covering, black grille, mfg. 1991-95.

| | N/A | $250 - 300 | $200 - 225 |

* VL1002 - Similar to the VL502 except has 100W output, mfg. 1991-95.

| | N/A | $275 - 325 | $225 - 250 |

VL503 - 75W, 1-12" combo, tubes, three channels, reverb, black covering, black grille, mfg. 1993-95.

| | N/A | $425 - 475 | $300 - 350 |

This amp could use both kinds of tubes but when EL34 tubes were used the output dropped to 50W

Diamond Blue Series

In 1995 Ampeg did an overhaul to their line. A lot of the old models were discontinued and the new ones introduced this year were covered in blue check covering as they were in the 1960's. They also released some reissue models. These were more like amps that looked old but had modern day circuits.

J-12T REISSUE - 15W, 1-12" Ampeg vintage speaker, all-tube Class A chassis, preamp: 2 X 12AX7, power: 2 X EL84, single channel, tremolo, reverb, top silver control panel, two inputs (guitar and accordian), five black knobs (v, tone, s, i, r), vintage diamond blue vinyl covering, sparkle-weave grille cloth, 30 lbs., mfg. 1995-current.

| MSR | $599 | $425 | $300 - 350 | $225 - 260 |

On the control panel it says "Jet II," which the amp is also known as.

SJ-12R SUPER JET - 50W, 1-12" combo, all tube Class AB chassis, preamp: 2 X 12AX7, power:2 X 6L6 Groove Tubes, single channel, reverb, tremolo in the SJ-12T, top chrome control panel, two inputs, five black knobs (v, t, m, b, r), footswitch included, vintage diamond blue vinyl covering, sparkle-weave grille cloth, 40 lbs., mfg. 1996-current.

| MSR | $829 | $600 | $425 - 500 | $325 - 375 |

* SJ-12T - Similar to the SJ-12R except has tremolo circuit, with s and i controls, mfg. 1996-current.

| MSR | $829 | $600 | $450 - 500 | $350 - 400 |

R-12R REVERBEROCKET - 50W, 1-12" combo, all tube chassis, preamp: 3 X 12AX7, power: 2 X 6L6 Groove Tubes, dual channels, reverb, top chrome control panel, two inputs (guitar & accordion), seven black knobs (g, v, t, m, b, MV, r), effects loop, gain control, vintage diamond blue vinyl covering, sparkle-weave grille cloth, 45 lbs., mfg. 1996-current.

| MSR | $979 | $699 | $500 - 600 | $400 - 450 |

* R-212R Reverberocket - Similar to the R-12R except has 2-12" speakers, 55 lbs., mfg. 1996-current.

| MSR | $1,099 | $775 | $600 - 700 | $500 - 550 |

GRADING	100%	EXCELLENT	AVERAGE

* *R-50H Reverberocket* - Similar to the R-12R Reverberocket except in head-unit only version, front mounted control panel, 34 lbs., mfg. 1997-current.

	MSR	$949	$675	$525 - 575	$400 - 450

* *R-412TA/BA* - Speaker cabinet to match the R-50H Reverberocket with 4-12" Ampeg Vintage Speakers, 84 lbs., mfg. 1997-current.

	MSR	$749	$525	$375 - 450	$285 - 325

SR-212RT SUPEROCKET - 100W, 2-12" Celestion Vintage 30 speakers, all tube Class AB combo, preamp: 3 X 12AX7, power: 4 X 6L6 Groove Tubes, dual channels, reverb, tremolo, top chrome control panel, two inputs, nine black knobs (g, v, t, m, b, master, r, s, i), line out/in, vintage diamond blue vinyl covering, sparkle-weave grille cloth, new 2002.

	MSR	$1,499	$1,075	$800 - 900	$650 - 725

B-15R - 100W, 1-15" driver & horn, all-tube chassis combo, Portaflex design, single channel, front chrome control panel, two inputs, ultra hi and lo switches, six black knobs (g, b, m, freq, t, MV), various switches, vintage diamond blue vinyl covering, sparkle-weave grille cloth, mfg. 1999-current.

	MSR	$2,549	$1,850	$1,350 - 1,600	$1,025 - 1,175

For B-100R and B-50R models see solid-state section.

ELECTRIC SOLID STATE AMPS

Ampeg introduced its solid-state line of amplifiers at the 1966 NAMM show. This was right around the time that Fender and other companies were jumping on the bandwagon and turning some of their popular models into solid-state ones. The first models came from the B-15 and B-18 and were turned into BT-15 and BT-18 respectively. The first solid-state amps were not very durable and often failed quickly. After some more work and design, this line started to turn around by the early 70's. During the 1970's, Ampeg relied heavily on the development of solid-state amps as they only released one new tube amp after 1971. Since solid-state amps were cheaper to make, Ampeg liked to make them. Out of all of the companies that made solid-state, Ampeg was one of the most successful.

First Series Solid-State

There were seven amps released initially. These were all Portaflex's, had two channels, a volume, bass, and treble control for each channel. These amps had a new "electrominescent" control panel which made the panel light up with a blue glow. This was caused by high voltage running into a plastic plate, which made the control panel dangerous. These amps had blue covering, a silver grille, and a silver control panel that lit up blue. On all of the amps in this series the cosmetics were changed in mid 1967. The solid-state models were changed to a black pebbled textured vinyl covering, the blue and gray grillecloth, and a stamped steel chassis. The electroluminescent display was still used.

BT-15 - 50W, 1-15" Portaflex, solid-state chassis, multi-purpose amp, basic controls, mfg. 1966-1970.

	N/A	$200 - 225	$150 - 175

* *BT-15D* - Similar to the BT-15 solid-state chassis Portaflex except has a matching extension cabinet with another 15" speaker, mfg. 1966-68.

	N/A	$250 - 275	$175- 200

* *BT-15C* - Similar to the BT-15D except has 2-15" speakers column style, mfg. 1967-68,

	N/A	$250 - 275	$175 - 225

* *BT-18* - Similar to the BT-15 except has an 18" speaker, mfg. 1966-68.

	N/A	$225 - 250	$175 - 200

T-15 - 50W, 1-15" Portaflex, solid-state, reverb, tremolo, knobs for those, mfg. 1966-67.

	N/A	$200 - 250	$140 - 175

Another variant of the BT-15.

* *T-15D* - Similar to the T-15 except has 85W, and came with an extension 15" cabinet, mfg. 1966-68.

	N/A	$225 - 275	$165 - 200

* *T-12T* - Similar to the T-15 except has 2-12" speakers, mfg. 1967-68.

	N/A	$225 - 250	$175 - 200

* *T-12D* - Similar to the T-12T except has an extension cabinet with 2-12" speakers, output increased to 85W, mfg. 1967-68.

	N/A	$250 - 300	$200 - 225

Solid-State Portaflex Amplifiers

In 1967 Ampeg gave the solid-state innovation another run with the ever-so-popular Portaflex amps in transistor form. There were six new solid-state models released for the 1967 catalog. This included the GT-15C, BT-140, the ST series and a PA amp. The ST series consisted of three of the same amps with different speaker configurations. The PA amp was extremely unpopular and was discontinued early after its introduction. In 1969, Ampeg discontinued the Portaflex design in favor of the piggyback design.

GT-15C - 100W, Portaflex with 2-15" Altec speakers, solid-state guitar amp, two channels, ultra hi and lo switches, silver control panel, four inputs, black covering, blue/gray grille, mfg. 1967-68.

	N/A	$250 - 300	$200 - 225

This model has column style speakers.

BT-140 - 100W, Portaflex with 2-15" JBL D140F speakers, solid-state bass amp, two channels, hi and lo switches, silver control panel, black covering, blue/gray grille, mfg. 1968-1971.

	N/A	$300 - 350	$250 - 275

The BT-140 was essentially a GT-15C but made for bassists. This model has column style speakers.

ST-22L GLADIATOR - 120W, Portaflex with 2-12" Altec 417A speakers, two channels, tremolo, vibrato, reverb, silver panelescent control panel, four inputs (two per channel), nine black and silver knobs (Ch. 1: v, t, b, s, i, r, Ch. 2: v, t, b,) black covering, blue/gray grille, mfg. 1967-69.

	N/A	$300 - 350	$250 - 275

GRADING	100%	EXCELLENT	AVERAGE

* **ST-25L Olympian** - Similar to the ST-22L Gladiator except has a cabinet with 2-15" Altec 418A speakers, mfg. 1967-1970.

	N/A	$300 - 350	$250 - 275

* **ST-42L Colossus** - Similar to the ST-22L Gladiator except has a cabinet with 4-12" Altec 417A speakers, mfg. 1967-1970.

	N/A	$350 - 400	$275 - 325

This was Ampeg's second effort at a half-stack amp but also failed like the B-12XTC.

Solid-State Piggyback Amplfiers

In 1969 Ampeg changed from their popular Portaflex design to the traditional Piggyback design. At the same time they were working on getting new models out, they still continued some of the better-sellers from previous years. The BT-25 and BT-25L were the first two new amps of 1969 in this series.

BT-25 - 120W, Piggyback with 2-15" CTS speakers, solid-state guitar amp, two channels, silver control panel, four inputs, black covering, blue/gray grille cloth, mfg. 1969-1971.

	N/A	$225 - 275	$190 - 215

* **BT-25L** - Similar to the BT-25 except has Altec Lansing speakers, mfg. 1969-1970.

	N/A	$250 - 300	$200 - 225

SST - 120W, Piggyback with 2 speaker cabinets, each one with 4-12" 417B Altec speakers, solid-state amp with 42 transistors and 10 diodes, two channels, reverb, vibrato, tremolo, silver front control panel, four inputs (two for each channel), 11 black and silver knobs (Ch 1: v, t, b, vibrato s, i, tremolo s, i, reverb intensity, Ch. 2: v, t, b), reverb on/off controls, Ultra hi and lo controls, midrange frequency select, black covering, blue/gray grille, mfg. 1969-1970.

	N/A	$450 - 500	$350 - 400

This amp had the power amp built into the speaker cabinets making the head light and the cabinets heavy. There were input jacks, level control and an on/off switch on the cabinet.

* **SBT** - Similar to the SST except a bass amp with 2-15" Altec 421A speakers in two cabinets, mfg. 1969-1971.

	N/A	$400 - 450	$300 - 350

V-6B - 240W, Piggyback with 2-15" cabinet, solid-state bass amp, single channel, front control panel, two inputs, four knobs (v, b, m, t), Ultra hi switch, modular components, black covering, blue/gray grille, mfg. 1974-1980.

	N/A	$400 - 450	$300 - 350

G-60 - 120W, Piggyback with a 6-10" ported speaker cabinet, solid-state chassis, two channels, reverb, tremolo, front control panel, four inputs, (two per channel), 11 knobs (Ch.1: v, b, m, t, Ch 2: v, b, m, t, reverb, s, i), black covering, black grille, mfg. 1975-1980.

	N/A	$375 - 425	$275 - 325

B-40 - 120W, Piggyback with a sealed 4-10" speaker cabinet, solid-state bass amp, two channels, front silver control panel, four inputs, two per channel, eight black and silver knobs (Ch. 1: v, b, m, t, Ch 2: v, b, m, t), selective midrange switch, ultra-hi switch, tuned reflex speaker design, black covering, black grille, mfg. 1973-1980.

	N/A	$350 - 400	$250 - 300

Solid-State Combo Amplifiers

Ampeg finally released combo amps in solid state form in 1971. The first was the small GT-10. Then in 1973, five new amps with the similar chassis were released. The series were cleverly named so the amp could be identified by just looking at the model number. There were two bass amps labled by the "B" and three guitar amps labeled "G." The numbers indicated the speaker configuration. The first number was how many speakers there were and the last number indicated what size speakers they were in inches. The G-30, G-50, B-30, B-50, and B-80N were all part of MTI's ownership.

GT-10 - 15W, 1-10" combo, solid-state, one channel, reverb, silver top control panel, two inputs, four black knobs (v, t, b, r), black covering, blue/gray grille, mfg. 1971-1980.

	N/A	$95 - 120	$60 - 85

B-115 - 120W, 1-15" combo, solid-state bass amp, two channels, front silver control panel, four inputs(two per channel), eight black and silver knobs (Ch. 1: v, b, m, t, Ch 2: v, b, m, t), selective midrange switch, ultra-hi switch, tuned reflex speaker design, black covering, black grille, mfg. 1973-1980.

	N/A	$160 - 185	$120 - 140

* **B-410** - Similar to the B-115 except has a completely sealed 4-10" combo, mfg. 1973-1980.

	N/A	$180 - 210	$130 - 160

G-212 - 120W, 2-12" combo, solid-state guitar amp, two channels, reverb, tremolo, front silver control panel, four inputs, two per channel, eleven black and silver knobs (Ch 1: v, t, m, b, Ch 2: v, t, m, b, Both: r, s, i), open back, ultra hi and midrange switch for each channel, black covering, black grille, mfg. 1973-1980.

	N/A	$175 - 215	$125 - 150

Altec speakers were available as an option.

* **G-412** - Similar to the G-212 except has 4-12" speakers in a sealed cabinet, mfg. 1973-1980.

	N/A	$200 - 250	$160 - 185

Altec speakers were available as an option. Casters were standard.

* **G-410** - Similar to the G-212 except has 4-10" speakers, mfg. 1973-1980.

	N/A	$195 - 235	$160 - 180

Altec speakers were available as an option. Casters were standard.

SOUNDCUBE (MODEL 8850) & BUSTER (MODEL 8851) - These are two amps that were listed as mini amps. Each of these amps operated on AC or DC power. The soundcube was in the shape of a cube with the "a" logo on the side and the Buster is taller and looks a lot like a Pignose. Each amp has one knob and one input. Both of these amps were introduced in 1975. The Buster was discontinued by the end of the year, while the Soundcube lasted until 1977.

GRADING	100%	EXCELLENT	AVERAGE

G-100 - 20W, 1-10" combo, solid-state guitar amp, one channel, front silver control panel, two input jacks, three black and silver knobs (v, b, t), black covering, blue/gray grille, mfg. 1976-1980.

	N/A	$80 - 95	$60 - 75

* B-100 - Similar to the G-100 except a bass amp with a heavier magnet in the speaker, mfg. 1976-1980.

	N/A	$85 - 100	$65 - 80

* G-110 - Similar to the G-100 with the addition of reverb and tremolo 3 knobs added (reverb, s, i), mfg. 1978-1980.

	N/A	$100 - 120	$75 - 90

G-18 - 10W, 1-8" combo, solid-state guitar amp, one channel, front control panel, two input jacks, three black and silver knobs (v, b, t), black covering, blue/gray grille, mfg. 1977-1980.

	N/A	$75 - 90	$55 - 70

G-115 - 175W, 1-15" JBL speaker, solid-state guitar amp, one channel, front control panel, two input jacks, ten black and silver knobs (v, t, m, b, mid-frequency, presence, sensitivity, r, s, i), black covering, blue/gray grille, mfg. 1979-1980.

	N/A	$165 - 190	$130 - 150

G-30 - 30W, 1-12" combo, solid-state guitar amp, two channels, distortion, reverb, front black control panel, two inputs, six black knobs (v, b, m, t, MV, reverb), distortion switch, black covering, black grille, mfg. 1981-1985.

	N/A	$130 - 150	$110 - 125

* G-50 - Similar to the G-30 except has 50W output, mfg. 1981-85.

	N/A	$140 - 165	$115 - 130

* B-30 - 30W Similar to the G-30 except a bass amp with 1-15" speaker, mfg. 1981-85.

	N/A	$125 - 150	$110 - 125

* B-50 - Similar to the G-30 except a bass amp with 50W output, mfg. 1981-85.

	N/A	$140 - 160	$110 - 130

* B-80N - Similar to the G-30 except a bass amp with a 12" or 15" speaker, 80W output, mfg. 1981-85.

	N/A	$160 - 185	$120 - 140

Solid-State SVT Amplifiers (SLM)

In 1987 Ampeg was now being run in full swing by St. Louis Music. They then introduced a slug of new amps and four of these were new solid-state SVT's. More were to be produced in the following years.

SVT-70T - 70W, 1-15" combo, solid-state guitar amp, mfg. 1987-89.

	N/A	$180 - 200	$140 - 160

* B-15T - Similar to the SVT-70T except it has 100W output and 15" Ampeg or Electrovoice speaker, mfg. 1988-1992.

	N/A	$190 - 215	$150 - 175

This model was to reintroduce the B-15 Portaflex. It had the same circuit as the SVT-70T, but wasn't successful at all.

* SVT-15T - Similar to the B-15T except has a 1-15" tuned-port cabinet, combo, mfg. 1989-1992.

	N/A	$195 - 215	$150 - 170

SVT-140TC - 140W (2 X 70) 4-10" sealed speaker cabinet, stereo solid-state bass amp, mfg. 1987 only.

	N/A	$210 - 250	$175 - 200

This model was also available as a head-unit only.

SVT-100T - 100W, 2-8" combo, solid-state bass amp, mfg. 1990-92.

	N/A	$175 - 200	$140 - 165

SVT-200T - 200W, 4-10" sealed speaker cabinet, solid-state chassis, mfg. 1987 only.

	N/A	$260 - 295	$210 - 235

SVT-350T - 350W, 2-10" combo, ported cabinet with horn, solid-state bass amp, mfg. 1989-1991.

	N/A	$265 - 300	$220 - 250

SVT-350H - 350W, head-unit only, solid-state chassis, single channel, front black control panel, single input, five black knobs (g, b, m, t, MV), nine-band equalizer, effects loop, black tolex covering, black grille, mfg. 1995-current.

MSR	$899	$640	$475 - 550	$350 - 400

SS Solid-State Amplifiers (SLM)

St. Louis Music released five new amplifiers in 1987 denoted the SS series. These were all guitar amps with varying wattages according to the model number. The models consisted of the SS-70, SS-150, SS-35, SS-140C and the SS-70C. All of these amps had two channels, reverb and a couple were available as heads or combos (SS-70, SS-150, and SS-140C). The SS-70 and the SS-150 were both 1-12" combos, the SS-70C had 2-10" speakers, and the SS-140C has 2-12" speakers. These amps lasted sporadically until 1992, with some models lasting longer than others. Prices for these amps are around $100-$300, depending on condition and how demanding the certain model is.

VH Series Solid-State

Another new patent that Ampeg received was for their new Varying Harmonics circuitry. This was a circuit in solid-state amps that could sound like tube distortion by using multiple harmonic textures. There were three different models in this series the VH-150, VH-70, and the VH-140C.

VH-140C - 140W (2 X 70), 2-12" Celestion speakers, solid-state combo, black covering, black grille, mfg. 1992 only.

	N/A	$280 - 325	$225 - 260

GRADING	100%	EXCELLENT	AVERAGE

* VH-140CH - Similar to the VH-140C except is in head-unit version, mfg. 1992-95.

	N/A	$190 - 225	$150 - 175

VH-70 - 70W, 1-12" combo, solid-state chassis, black covering, black grille, mfg. 1992 only.

	N/A	$210 - 240	$170 - 195

VH-150 - 150W, head-unit only, solid-state chassis, two channels, reverb, black covering, black grille, mfg. 1991-92.

	N/A	$210 - 250	$175 - 200

"B" Series Bass Heads

All of these models are rackmount, solid-state head units for bass guitars. It should be noted that early models have a different style control panel that is black with white racing stripes and blue lettering. In 2000, the front was changed to a solid black and gray control panel. There are also three different speaker cabinets currently being offered by Ampeg to match up with these bass heads. If you notice, the model name describes what the enclosure has. BSE stands for B Series Enclosure, the number indicates how many speakers and what size are included, the following letter indicates if it has a tweeter, horn, or the extend low end. The **BSE-115T** has 1-15" speaker, a tweeter, can handle 400W of power and retails for $549. The **BSE-410H** has 4-10" speakers, a horn, can take 400W of power, has a three position horn switch, and retails for $679. **BSE-410HLF** is like the BSE-410H except has an extended low end design and retails for $849. There are also two BXT Bass Speaker Enclosures, which are on the higher end. The **BXT-115HL4** has 1-15" Phantom "A" speaker, a horn can handle 400W and retails for $899. The **BXT-410HL4** has 4-10" speakers plus a horn and handles 1200W. This model retails for $1,149.

B-2R - 350W, head-unit only, solid-state rackmount, single channel, gray control panel, single input, five black knobs (g, b, ultra mid, t, MV), nine-band equalizer, XLR balanced line out, effects loop, preamp out/power amp in, black metal covering, mfg. 1998-current.

MSR	$769	$550	$400 - 450	$325 - 350

B-4R - 1000W, head-unit only, solid-state rackmount, single channel, gray control panel, two inputs, nine black knobs (g, style, b, ultra mid, t, effects mix, master, freq. balance), nine band equalizer, XLR balanced line out, effects loop, preamp out/power amp in, black metal covering, mfg. 1998-current.

MSR	$1,399	$999	$725 - 825	$600 - 650

B-5R - 500W, head-unit only, solid-state rackmount, dual channels, gray control panel, two inputs, eleven black knobs (Clean: v, style, b, ultra mid, t, Overdrive: gain, style, v, Both: v, FX blend, MV), XLR balanced line out, effects loop, preamp out/power amp in, black metal covering, footswitch, mfg. 1998-current.

MSR	$1,199	$850	$625 - 675	$500 - 550

"B" Series Bass Combos

These models are like that of the B series rackmount heads, except these are in combo form. Early models have a black front with white racing stripes and blue lettering.

B-2 - 200W, 1-15", solid-state combo, single channel, gray control panel, five black knobs (g, b, ultra mid, t, MV), three black buttons, nine-band equalizer, XLR balanced line out, effects loop, preamp out/power amp in, optocoupler limiter, external speaker jack, black Tolex covering, black metal grille, 87 lbs., mfg. 1998-2000.

	$775	$550 - 625	$450 - 500

This model was also offered as the B-248 which had 4-8" speakers with a tweeter.

Last MSR was $1,099.

B-3 - 150W, 1-15", solid-state combo, single channel, gray control panel, single input, six black knobs (g, drive, b, ultra-mid, t, MV), nine-band equalizer, XLR balanced line out, effects loop, preamp out/power amp in, optocoupler limiter, black Tolex covering, black metal grille, 68 lbs., mfg. 1998-2001.

	$625	$450 - 500	$350 - 375

Last MSR was $879.

* B-328 - Similar to the B-3 except has 2-8" speakers with a tweeter, 57 lbs., mfg. 1998-2001.

	$625	$450 - 500	$350 - 375

Last MSR was $879.

B-3158 - 150W, 1-15" & 1-8" with a biampable feature (100W drive the 15" and 50W are sent to the 8"), single channel, gray control panel, single input, seven black knobs (g, b, ultra-mid, t, v, bi-amp, MV), nine-band equalizer, XLR balanced line out, effects loop, preamp out/power amp in, optocoupler limiter, black Tolex covering, black metal grille, 84 lbs., mfg. 1998-2001.

	$800	$575 - 650	$450 - 500

Last MSR was $1,099.

Bassamp Series

These amplifiers were introduced in the late 90's with the BA-112 and the BA-115. The names of these amps come from the classic B series amps of the 1950's and 1960's. In 2001, new models were introduced along with two amps with digital signal processing.

BA-110 - 30W, 1-10" speaker, solid-state combo, tilt back cabinet design, single channel, black control panel, two inputs, four black knobs (v, l, m, h), cd input, line out, headphone jack, contour button, black tolex covering, black cloth grille with white trim, 32 lbs., mfg. 2001-current.

MSR	$379	$265	$195 - 225	$150 - 175

BA-112 - 50W, 1-12" speaker, solid-state combo, tilt back cabinet design, single channel, black control panel, two inputs, five black knobs (v, s, t, m, b), cd input, line out, headphone jack, black tolex covering, black cloth grille with white trim, 39 lbs., mfg. 1997-current.

MSR	$499	$350	$250 - 300	$175 - 200

Add $20 for the Anniversary Model Limited Edition (offered in 2001 only).

GRADING	100%	EXCELLENT	AVERAGE

BA-115 - 100W, 1-15" speaker, solid-state combo, tilt back cabinet design, single channel, black control panel, two inputs, six black knobs (g, MV, t, ultra mid, b), cd input, XLR line out, headphone jack, black tolex covering, black cloth grille with white trim, 62 lbs., mfg. 1997-current.

	MSR $599	$425	$325 - 375	$250 - 300

BA-115SP - 105W, 1-15" speaker with Piezo tweeter, solid-state combo, 16 digital effects, tilt back cabinet design, single channel, black control panel, two inputs, nine black knobs (v, style, l, m, h, level, Effects: select, adjust, level), cd input, XLR line out, headphone jack, foot-switch, black tolex covering, black cloth grille with white trim, 62 lbs., mfg. 2001-current.

	MSR $749	$525	$400 - 450	$325 - 375

* **BA-210SP** - Similar to the BA-115SP except has 200W output and 2-12" speakers, 76 lbs., mfg. 2001-current.

	MSR $969	$690	$550 - 625	$450 - 500

Misc Solid-State Amplifiers

Ampeg has released a lot of models and when St. Louis Music took over even more models were available. If you haven't found a small model that wasn't very popular, chances are it may be in here.

AP3550 - 350W, power amp only, mfg. 1992-93.

	N/A	$240 - 280	$185 - 220

AP6500 - 1300W (2 X 650), stereo power amp, mfg. 1992-95.

	N/A	$425 - 475	$325 - 375

Diamond Blue Series (Solid-State)

B-100R ROCKET BASS - 100W, 1-15" speaker, solid-state combo bass amp, single channel, top chrome control panel, two inputs, six black knobs (g, b, low mid, high mid, t, MV), line in and out, headphone jack, vintage diamond blue vinyl, sparkle-weave grille cloth, mfg. 1996-current.

	MSR $699	$499	$350 - 425	$275 - 325

B-50R ROCKET BASS - 50W, 1-12" speaker, solid-state combo bass amp, single channel, top chrome control panel, two inputs, five black knobs (v, b, low mid, high mid, t), line in and out, headphone jack, vintage diamond blue vinyl, sparkle-weave grille cloth, mfg. 1997-current.

	MSR $549	$399	$250 - 300	$200 - 235

Portabass Series

This is a new series unveiled in 2002. These new amplifier heads feature MDT, which is Micro Dynamic Technology. Ampeg is advertising these new amplifiers as "Less is More." There is less weight, less size and out of this they created more power and more tone. The first amplifier in this series is the PB-250 which is a 250W solid-state head and weighs only a mere 14 lbs! At this point, this is the only head unit with a price tag on it and it retails for $899. The PB-800 and PB-8000R rackmount units are on their way as well. There are three different speaker cabinets built specifically for the Portabasses. There are gig bag cases available for these head-units. More information is on the way about the PB-800 and PB-8000R in upcoming editions of the *Blue Book of Guitar Amplifiers*.

PB-250 - 250W @ 4 Ohms (150W @ 8 Ohms), head-unit only, solid-state MDT power amp, single channel, front gray control panel, two inputs (normal and padded), seven black knobs (gain, l, l/m, h/m, h, effects blend, MV), four black buttons, line out level control, silver covering, 14 lbs., new 2002.

	MSR $899	$650	$475 - 550	$375 - 425

ELECTRIC HYBRID AMPS

In the early 1990's, like most amplifier companies, Ampeg jumped on the bandwagon and released some amps that had a cross of tubes and solid-state components to produce sound. This happened in 1990 with the AX models. These amps didn't last very long in the line, but Ampeg experimented and also released the B-1, B-2 and B-3 Bass series of amps with this kind of circuit.

AX-44C - 44W (2 X 22), 2-8" speakers, hybrid combo, preamp tubes: 12AX7's, solid-state power section, two channels, reverb, mfg. 1990 only.

	N/A	$220 - 250	$175 - 200

AX-70 - 70W, 1-12" combo, hybrid, preamp tubes: 12AX7's, solid-state power section, two channels, mfg. 1990 only.

	N/A	$195 - 225	$150 - 180

ASHDOWN ENGINEERING

Amplifiers currently produced in Essex, England. Ashdown amplifiers are distributed in North and South America by HHB Communications in Los Angeles, California and Toronto, Ontario Canada.

Ashdown Engineering is a relatively young company with an array of models ranging from acoustic amps to bass amps. Mark Gooday was the managing director of Trace Elliot back in the mid 1980's. After Trace Elliot was sold to Kaman Music in 1992, he worked for Kaman for the next five years on a contract. After his tenure at Kaman and Trace Elliot, Mark left the company in 1997. He took the skills and knowledge he had and decided to develop a bass amp that brought back real tone and style. Mark worked with old friends and started up his new company which he called Ashdown after his wife's family name. The first amps made were named as Klystron Bass Maginfier from a movie. The Klystron name had to be dropped as another company of years ago had used it. Only 200 units were shipped with the Klystron name. After this, the Acoustic Radiator amps made their debut. Now Ashdown Engineering is a world-known amplifier maker and their company grows daily. Ashdown Amplifiers have a VU meter on almost every one of their models, which is almost unique to the company.

ACOUSTIC AMPLIFIERS

The two different series of Acoustic Amps are the radiator series. They are all listed under the Acoustic Radiator Series, with the only differance being the Reso series has a metal casing.

Acoustic Radiator Series

ACOUSTIC RADIATOR 1 (AAR-1V-R) - 60W, 1-8" driver speaker with dual tweeter array, solid-state combo, single channel, vertical control panel on right side of amp, one input, six cream knobs (output, reverb, notch frequency, t, b, input level), numerous buttons for acoustic effects, wood cabinet, basket weave grille, 13 lbs., mfg. 1999-current.

Ashdown Acoustic Radiator
courtesy Ashdown

Ashdown Acoustic Reso 1
courtesy Ashdown

MSR	$899	$650	$475 - 525	$375 - 425

Add $200 for cherry and walnut wood covering.

Add $100 for burgandy bookbound covering.

This model is available in walnut, cherry, and burgandy bookbound wood coverings. A black vinyl and polished "Bakelite" finish is also available. The burgandy bookbound covering has a hinged mesh grille. Walnut and burgandy bookbound covering were both discontinued in 2002. Cherry Model is known as the AAR-1C-R.

Reso 1 (AAR-1RESO) - Similar to the Acoustic Radiator 1 except is finished in a classic, polished metal "Resonator" style cabinet, 14 lbs., mfg. 1999-current.

MSR	$1,399	$999	$725 - 825	$600 - 650

ACOUSTIC RADIATOR 2 (AAR-2V) - 120W, 1-8" driver speaker with dual tweeter array and 1-8" bass radiator, solid-state combo, dual channels, reverb, top cream control panel, four inputs (Ch.1: active, piezo, Ch. 2: Low 1/4", XLR), 17 cream knobs (Ch. 1: input level, b, m, t, Ch. 2: input level, tube selector, b, m, t, Both: Mid Feedback Notch (F & Q), Low Feedback Notch (F & Q), reverb level for each channel, reverb type, output level), equlizer, VU meter, phase shifter, various other buttons, wood cabinet finish, basket weave grille, 34 lbs., mfg. 1999-current.

Ashdown Acoustic Radiator 2
courtesy Ashdown

Ashdown Acoustic Reso 2
courtesy Ashdown

MSR	$1,499	$1,075	$750 - 850	$550 - 625

Add $225 for cherry and walnut wood covering.

Add $100 for burgandy bookbound covering.

This model is available in walnut, cherry, burgandy bookbound, carbon fibre, polished "bakelite", and black vinyl. Walnut and burgandy bookbound covering were both discontinued in 2002. The Cherry Model is known as the AAR-2C.

GRADING	100%	EXCELLENT	AVERAGE

* Acoustic Radiator 2-12H - Similar to the Acoustic Radiator 2 except has 1-12" speaker with a high-frequency horn, mfg. 1999-2001.

| | $1,050 | $750 - 850 | $550 - 650 |

* Reso 2 (AAR-2RESO) - Similar to the Acoustic Radiator 2 except is finished in a classic, polished metal "Resonator" style cabinet, 35 lbs., mfg. 1999-current.

| MSR | $1,999 | $1,399 | $950 - 1,150 | $750 - 850 |

BASS AMPLIFIERS

Currently there are two flavors in the Ashdown Bass series. The ABM Series (Ashdown Bass Magnification) are the higher end amps. The MAG series are more affordable, without all the features of the ABM's.

ABM (Ashdown Bass Magnification)

Originally, these models all had pale blue control panels along with black speakers. In 2002 the speakers were changed to the Ashdown Blueline speakers that appear blue through the grille. Add $90 for the grille cloth option on all of the following models. In 2002, the whole series was designated with an EVO behind the model number (i.e. ABM-C110-300 EVO)

ABM-C110-300 (EVO) - 300W, 1-10", solid-state combo, one channel, blue control panel, two inputs (high and low), seven black knobs (input, input mix, b, m, t, sub-harmonic level, output level), 4-band equalizer, various push buttons, two outputs, black vinyl covering, black grille, 55 lbs., mfg. 2000-current.

Ashdown ABM-C110-300 EV0
courtesy Ashdown

| MSR | $1,449 | $1,025 | $750 - 875 | $650 - 700 |

In 2002, the output was raised to 320W.

ABM-C115-300 (EVO) - 300W, 1-15", solid-state combo, one channel, blue control panel, two inputs (high and low), seven black knobs (input, input mix, b, m, t, sub-harmonic level, output level), 4-band equalizer, various push buttons, two outputs, black vinyl covering, black grille, 57.2 lbs., mfg. 2000-current.

| MSR | $1,579 | $1,125 | $800 - 950 | $675 - 750 |

In 2002, the output was raised to 320W.

* ABM-C115-500 (EVO) - Similar to the ABM-C115-300 except has 500W output, 61.6 lbs., mfg. 1999-current.

| MSR | $1,799 | $1,275 | $900 - 1,050 | $700 - 800 |

In 2002, the output was raised to 575W.

ABM-C210-300 (EVO) - 300W, 2-10" speakers, solid-state combo, one channel, blue control panel, two inputs (high and low), seven black knobs (input, input mix, b, m, t, sub-harmonic level, output level), 4-band equalizer, various push buttons, two outputs, black vinyl covering, black grille, 77 lbs., mfg. 2000-current.

| MSR | $1,599 | $1,125 | $825 - 950 | $650 - 775 |

In 2002, the output was raised to 320W.

* AMB-C210H-500 (EVO) - Similar to the ABM-C210-500 except has 500W output and a horn along with the speaker, 83.6 lbs., mfg. 2000-current.

| MSR | $1,999 | $1,425 | $1,025 - 1,200 | $850 - 950 |

In 2002, the output was raised to 575W.

ABM-C410H-500 (EVO) - 500W, 4-10" speakers & high-fidelity horn, solid-state combo, one channel, blue control panel, two inputs (high and low), seven black knobs (input, input mix, b, m, t, sub-harmonic level, output level), 4-band equalizer, various push buttons, two outputs, black vinyl covering, black grille, mfg. 2000-current.

| MSR | $1,999 | $1,399 | $1,025 - 1,200 | $850 - 950 |

In 2002, the output was raised to 575W.

GRADING	100%	EXCELLENT	AVERAGE

ABM-300 (EVO) - 300W, head-unit only, solid-state combo, one channel, blue control panel, two inputs (high and low), seven black knobs (input, input mix, b, m, t, sub-harmonic level, output level), 4-band equalizer, various push buttons, two outputs, black vinyl covering, black grille, mfg. 2000-current.

Ashdown ABM-300 EV0
courtesy Ashdown

	MSR	$1,199	$850	$625 - 700	$550 - 600

Output was increased to 320W in 2002.

* ABM-500 (EVO) - Similar to the ABM-300 except has 500W output, mfg. 2000-current.

	MSR	$1,599	$1,125	$800 - 950	$675 - 725

Output was increased to 575W in 2002.

* ABM-900 (EVO) - Similar to the ABM-300 except has 900W output and cooling slits on the front control panel, mfg. 2000-current.

	MSR	$2,299	$1,625	$1,200 - 1,400	$1,000 - 1,100

Output was increased to 575W + 575W in 2002.

ABM SPEAKER CABINETS - There are several speaker cabinets to match up with the ABM heads. Each model corresponds to the number and size of the speaker, along with the second set of numbers indicating how much power it can handle. There is the **ABM-115-300** which is a 300W cabinet with 1-15" speaker, which retails for $699, the **ABM-210H** which handles 300W into 2-10" speakers and retails for $779, the **ABM-410H** which is rated at 650W into 4-10" speakers and a horn costs $999, the **ABM-115-500** is the same as the ABM-115-300 except has 500W and goes for $649, the **ABM-1510HX** which has 1-10", 1-15", and a horn that deals with 450W. The **ABM-BP1510** which has1-15", 2-10", and a horn, can handle 600W, which goes for $1,199. The **ABM-810** has 8-10" speakers and can handle 1200W, which sells for $1,999. This is also known as the backbreaker or walletbreaker, take your pick. The ABM-SUB was also available between 2000-01 but prices aren't established.

MAG Bass Series

This series is designed for the player who doesn't need all the bells and whistles of the ABM series. For a reasonable price, bass players get a classic sound. Like the ABM series, there is a wide variety of combos, heads, and speaker cabinets. All combo models have black metal grilles. The older models only had 200W output and in 2002 they switched them over to 265W.

MAG-200 - 200W, head-unit only, solid-state combo, one channel, black control panel, two inputs (high and low), eight black knobs (input, b, 220Hz, m, 1.6KHz, t, Sub-harmonics level, output), effects loop, deep, bright, and EQ switches, output D.I post EQ XLR input, gray carpet covering, mfg. 2000-01.

N/A	$550	$495

* MAG-250 - Similar to the Mag-200 except has 265W output, white control panel, 18.7 lbs., new 2002.

Ashdown MAG-250
courtesy Ashdown

	MSR	$699	$499	$350 - 400	$250 - 285

* MAG-C115-250 - Similar to the MAG-200 head unit except is in combo form with 1-15" speaker, mfg. 2000-01.

	MSR	$999	$699	$500 - 600	$400 - 450

* MAG-C210T-250 - Similar to the MAG-200 head unit except is in combo form with 2-10" speakers and a tweeter, mfg. 2000-01.

	MSR	$1,099	$775	$575 - 675	$475 - 525

GRADING	100%	EXCELLENT	AVERAGE

* MAG-C410T-250 - Similar to the MAG-200 head unit except is in combo form with 4-10" speakers and a tweeter, mfg. 2000-01.

Ashdown MAG-C410T-250
courtesy Ashdown

MSR	$1,299	$925	$700 - 800	$575 - 625

All of the above models in combo form are available as just the speaker cabinets. That is, the MAG-C115-200 is available as the MAG-115-200. Prices are according.

MAG-400 - 500W, head-unit only, solid-state combo, one channel, black control panel, two inputs (high and low), eight black knobs (input, b, 220Hz, m, 1.6KHz, t, Sub-harmonics level, output), effects loop, deep, bright, and EQ switches, output D.I post EQ XLR input, gray carpet covering, mfg. 2000-current.

MSR	$899	$635	$475 - 550	$375 - 425

MAG-MON-10-200 - 200W, 1-10" speaker, wedge monitor combo, solid-state combo, one channel, black control panel, two inputs (high and low), eight black knobs (input, b, 220Hz, m, 1.6KHz, t, Sub-harmonics level, output), effects loop, deep, bright, and EQ switches, output D.I post EQ XLR input, gray carpet covering, black metal grille, mfg. 2000-01.

		$800	$600 - 675	$475 - 525

* MAG-MON-15-200 - Similar to the MAG-MON-10-200 except has 1-15" speaker, mfg. 2000-01.

		$850	$625 - 700	$525 - 560

* MAG-MON-12-200 - Similar to the MAG-MON-10-200 except has 1-12" speaker, mfg. 2000-01

MSR	$1,169	$825	$600 - 700	$500 - 550

Electric Blue Series

These amplifiers are what you could call the entry level for Ashdown. These are basic combo amplifiers that are solid-state and have the basic features. There is rumor that these amplifiers exist in 130W form but aren't found in the catalogs.

EB12-150 - 150W, 1-12" speaker, solid-state combo, single channel, front blue control panel, two inputs, eight black knobs (input, b, m, t, two other equalizers, output, level), various buttons and switches, black carpet covering, black metal grille, 36.3 lbs., mfg. 2001-current.

MSR	$699	$499	$375 - 425	$300 - 335

* EB-15-150 - Similar to the EB12-150 except has a 15" speaker, 41.8 lbs., mfg. 2001-current.

MSR	$749	$525	$400 - 450	$325 - 375

* EB-210T-150 - Similar to the EB12-150 except has 2-10" speakers + tweeter, 58.3 lbs., mfg. 2001-current.

MSR	$899	$640	$475 - 525	$375 - 425

ELECTRIC GUITAR AMPLIFIERS

Just recently, Ashdown released some quality tube amplifiers known as the Peacemaker series.

GRADING	100%	EXCELLENT	AVERAGE

Peacemaker Series

PEACEMAKER 100 - 130W, head-unit only, all-tube chassis, hand-wired, preamp: 5 X 12AX7, power: 4 X EL34, front silver control panel, two inputs, seven silver knobs (g1, g2, b, m, t, p, MV), standby and mains switches, black tolex covering, 70.4 lbs., mfg. 2001-current.

Ashdown Peacemaker 100 Head
courtesy Ashdown

MSR	$2,999	$2,250	$1,800 - 2,000	$1,450 - 1,600

* Peacemaker 50 - Similar to the Peacemaker 100 except has 70W and 6550 power tubes, 68.2 lbs., mfg. 2001-current.

		$1,999	$1,500 - 1,700	$1,200 - 1,350

PEACEMAKER 60 - 60W, 2-12" Celestion Vintage 30 speakers, all tube Class A chassis, three channels (gain boost on channel 2), front silver control panel, single input, 13 silver knobs (Ch.1: gain, t, m, b, v, Ch. 2: gain, t, m, b, v, Master: r, v1, v2), black tolex covering, silver grille, 46.2., mfg. 2001-current.

Ashdown Peacemaker 60 Combo
courtesy Ashdown

MSR	$1,399	$999	$700 - 800	$600 - 650

* Peacemaker 60R - Similar to the Peacemaker 60 except in head-unit only version, 30.8 lbs., mfg. 2001-current.

MSR	$999	$699	$500 - 600	$400 - 450

* Peacemaker 40 - Similar to the Peacemaker 60 except has 40W output and 1-12" Celestion speaker, 37.4 lbs., mfg. 2001-current.

MSR	$999	$725	$525 - 600	$425 - 475

* Peacemaker 20 - Similar to the Peacemaker 60 execpt has 20W output, 1-10" Celestion V10 speaker, and one less volume knob, 28.6 lbs., mfg. 2001-current.

MSR	$899	$650	$475 - 550	$400 - 425

Section B

BGW

Amplifiers and other audio equipment currently produced in Hawthorne, California. The BGW trademark was established in 1971.

BGW makes a full line of rack-mount amplifiers along with other audio equipment including computers, subwoofers, and other rack-mount accessories. There are several different model lines including the Professional series, the Grand Touring series, the Performance series, the BGW Millennium series, the C series, the GT series, VX series, and the X series. Each series of models have their own features and wide price range. For the full product line, options, and prices take a look at the BGW web site (see trademark index).

BADCAT

Amplifiers currently produced in Corona, California.

Badcat amplifiers were founded in 2001 by James Heidrich and his wife Debbie. Mark Sampson, who was associated with Matchless amps, is the designer of these Badcat amps. They offer top-of-the-line amplifiers for a premium price. Badcat is known for having some of the finest Class A amplifiers on the market. They are all-tube, hand built, and hand wired to ensure perfection. All amps are offered with a variety of colors including black, burgundy, white, gray, and slate green. For a listing of all options and specifications visit the Badcat web site (see Trademark Index).

ELECTRIC TUBE AMPLIFIERS

Bad Cat currently offers two series of tube amplifiers, the Cub Series and the Cat Series. The Cub series are the smaller amps and the Cat series are the more elite amps.

GRADING	100%	EXCELLENT	AVERAGE

Cub Series

Originally the Cub series was introduced, but later the series was updated to the Cub II series.

CUB (II) - 15W, 2-10" or 1-12" combo, tubes: preamp: 3 X 12AX7, power: 2 X EL84, 5AR4 rectifier, single channel, front control panel, two inputs, six chicken head knobs (v, b, t, reverb, cut, master), choice of color covering, corresponding grille, current mfg.

	MSR	$2,019	$1,475	$1,050 - $1,200	$850 - 925

In 2002, the original Cub model was modified with more controls and effects and renamed the Cub II.

* Cub (II) Reverb - Similar to the Cub model except has reverb, 2 more 12AX7 tubes, and controls for the reverb, current mfg.

	MSR	$2,479	$1,750	$1,225 - 1,425	$975 - 1,125

HOT CAT - 30W, 1-12", 2-10", and 2-12" combo's and a head unit available, Class A power, tubes: preamp: 4 X 12AX7, power: 2 X EL34, 5AR4 rectifier, dual channels, front control panel, two inputs, 8 chicken head knobs (v, g, e, level, b, t, brilliance, MV), choice of color covering, corresponding grille, current mfg.

	MSR	$2,599	$1,850	$1,400 - 1,600	$1,100 - 1,250

Add $360 for the 1-12" or the 2-10" combo units.

Add $500 for the 2-12" combo unit.

Cat Series

BLACK CAT - 30W, head-unit or 2-12" combo, all tube chassis, preamp: 3 X 12AX7, EF86, power: 4 X EL84, 5AR4 rectifier, dual channels, front control panel, four inputs (two per channel), seven chicken knobs (Ch 1: v, b, t, Ch. 2: v, 5-position tone, cut, master volume), choice of color covering, corresponding grille, current mfg.

	MSR	$2,699	$1,900	$1,500 - 1,700	$1,100 - 1,250

Add $500 for the 2-12" combo version.

* Black Cat Reverb - Similar to the Black Cat except has reverb, 2 more 12AX7 tubes, and control for reverb.

	MSR	$2,999	$2,100	$1,700 - 1,900	$1,300 - 1,500

Add $500 for the 2-12" combo version.

* Wild Cat - Similar to the Black Cat Reverb except has 40W output and 2 X EL34 tubes instead of EL84, current mfg.

	MSR	$2,999	$2,150	$1,750 - 1,950	$1,325 - 1,525

Add $500 for the 2-12" combo version.

BALDWIN
See BURNS

BELTONE

Amplifiers previously produced in Canada or Japan.

Beltone amplifiers were produced during the 1960's or 1970's. They were either produced in Japan, Canada, or a combination of the two. Very little is known about these amplifiers or the company. Any information can be submitted directly to the publisher for upcoming editions of the *Blue Book of Guitar Amplifiers*.

BIG M
Amplifiers previously produced in England by Marshall.

Big M is one of five other tangents Marshall had (CMI, Park, Kitchen Marshall, and Narb). The story behind Big M is a result of the name Marshall already being used in Germany. When Marshall started to get big, products were being built for other countries, including Germany. The Germans had the name Marshall on a line of trumpets, and Jim wasn't able to use the name. In 1966, he started building amps for Germany under the name "Big M." These are Marshall amplifiers with a different name on the cover. By 1968, Jim had bought the rights to Marshall in Germany and stopped producing the Big M products.

Big M reappeared in 1975, in the American market. The marketing execs. decided that building amps in America would bring prices down, and thus boost sales. The second run of Big M amplifiers were manufactured in Long Island, New York. They made solid-state and tube heads, for lead and bass applications. They also made some speaker cabinets with some new features, such as the extended frequency enclosure. These units were cheaper and maybe partly because they had Eminence speakers, instead of Celestions. The second run of Big M lasted less than a year and they were discontinued. Big M never made a third comeback.

(Courtesy of Michael Doyle, The History of Marshall)

BLOCKHEAD
Amplifiers currently produced in New York.

Blockhead is a boutique amplifier company that produces Marshall recreation amps. The JTM-45 Marshall amps of the early 1960's are some of the most sought after amps and have awesome sounds. Blockhead has taken those designs and recreated them to exact replicas. Even real tone hard cores would have a tough time telling a JTM-45 apart from a Blockhead amp. Even the cabinets look like Marshall. Instead of spending oodles of time and money looking for an early JTM-45 just for the tone, Blockhead provides an alternative that is much cheaper. For more information and pricing please refer to the Blockhead web site (see trademark index).

BLUES PEARL
Amplifiers currently produced in Soddy Daisy, Tennessee.

Blues Pearl makes quality tube amplifiers. R. Hudson has been in the electronics industry for many years now and started his own company making amplifiers. This was started when customers would come in and want their amplifier modified to a new tone. With great tone and a competitive price, Blues Pearl has been able to turn back to high-quality tube amplifiers.

ELECTRIC TUBE AMPLIFIERS

Currrently there are five amplifiers in production. The **Texas Tornado** is a 20W model with either 2-10" or 1-12" speakers and retails for $1,295. The **Verbrasonic** has 40W and is a bigger brother to the Texas Tornado. This amp offers 2-10" Jensen speakers, 6L6 power tubes, and lists for $1,395. The **Blues Master** is a dual channel amp that is driven by 6L6GC power tubes to deliver 40W of power. This amp has 3-10" Jensen speakers and goes for $1,495. The **Diablo**, which appears to be like the Blues Master has 40W of power but 4-10" Jensen speakers and costs $1,595. The Hombre is an amp that will "Take you to Texarkana" according to the Bluespearl web site (which was not up at time of publication). The amp consists of 1-15" speaker, dual channels, 40W from 6L6GC tubes, and goes for $1,495. All amplifiers are available with custom options (such as coverings). Check the web site for further details (see Trademark index).

BLUE TONE
Amplifiers currently produced in the United Kingdom.

Blue Tone are producing amplifiers with tube technology to get vintage tube sound. They focus on making their amps as "old school" so players can adjust the sound by a volume and tone knob, rather than digital technologies and such. They aim to make their amplifiers like vintage models of the 1960's and use a circuit called Virtual Valve Technology. For more information refer to the website (see Trademark Index).

BOGNER
Amplifiers currently produced in North Hollywood, California.

Reinhold Bogner is the man behind Bogner amps. He moved from Germany to Los Angeles in 1989. He had been building amplifiers overseas for some time before he came to the U.S.A. After earning the trust of many famed musicians, including Eddie Van Halen, he started Bogner amplification. He now builds a complete series of tube amplifiers that are of high quality. They also have speaker cabinets and accessories to match up with their amps. For more information, please refer to the Bogner web site (see Trademark Index).

BRUCE BENNETT MUSIC LABS
Custom Amplifiers currently produced in Rossville, Georgia.

From the mind that made Warrior guitars comes a line of amplifiers called Bennett. These are amplifiers and cabinets that can be made to specifications. The 410 Bass Cabinet for example is a 1200W model with 4 Eminence speakers and a tweeter. The price on this runs for $859. Most of these amps are made custom for the customer. For further information, contact their web site (see Trademark Index).

BRUNETTI
Amplifiers currently produced in Modena, Italy. These amplifiers are distributed by Salwender International of Orange, California in the U.S.

Brunetti Amplifiers are hand-made in Italy by Marco Brunetti. Each amplifier is hand crafted from start to finish and tested at the factory. Marco has designed each model according to the market needs and the best design out there. Brunetti makes a full variety of tube amplifiers, rack-mount amplifiers, rack-mounted effects, preamps, and speaker cabinets. Brunetti amplifiers are distributed in many countries in Europe as well as the U.S.

ELECTRIC TUBE AMPLIFIERS

Currently Brunetti offers two combo amplifiers the **Maranello** and the **MC2** (squared). The Maranello is the smaller model with 25W output, 1-12" Jensen speaker, and a tube array of 3 X 12AX7 preamps and 2 X EL84 power. The Maranello has two channels which offer an array of features and effects. The MC2 has 60W output, 1-12" Celestion speaker, tubes that consist of 4 X 12AX7 for the preamp section, and 2 X EL34 for the power. This amp has three channels with two having distortion. This amp also features reverb for all channels, a Harmonic Shape Mirror, and a foot pedal microprocessor.

There are two tube amp heads being offered as well by Brunetti. The **059** is a 120W amp that has 6 X 12AX7A tubes for preamp and 4 X EL34 for output. The 059 offers three channels (clean, crunch, and solo) and a number of features and effects on its red control panel (18 black knobs in all!). The other tube head amp is the **XL R-evo**, which is an improved version of the XL amp (now discontinued). The XL R-evo has 120W output (switchable to 60W) driven by 5 X 12AX7A and 2 X EL34 for output. This amp has three switchable channels (clean, boost, X-lead) and a number of effects and features.

Currently there are two power amplifiers in production by Brunettii. The **Silver Bullet** is a 60W, two channel amp, that has 2 X 12AX7 & 5814A tube for preamps, and 4 X EL34 tubes for output. Total ouput is 120W (60 for each channel). The only controls are volume and presence. The **Rockit** is a 120W output total amp (switchable to 60W and 40W). The tubes are 2 X 5814A's and this has power level and spectral response controls. Both of these amps are rack units with the Rockit being 1 space.

Brunetti MC²
courtesy Brunetti

Brunetti 059
courtesy Brunetti

Brunetti Silver Bullet
courtesy Brunetti

SPEAKER CABINETS AND PREAMPS

Brunetti offers three different speaker cabinets that can be matched up with any one of their heads. The **XL-Cab** is a 4-12" speaker cabinet that can handle 400W and has 12" Jensen Custom speakers. The XL-Cab can be run at 400W in mono or 200W in stereo. The **Dual-Cab** has 2-12" Jensen Custom speakers and can handle 200W in mono and 100W in stereo. The **XL-Mini Cab** has 1-12" Jensen Custom speaker and can handle 100W. All cabinets are designed with a "Half Back Open" system and are constructed of hard-plywood that is hand assembled. They are all covered with black tolex covering and have black grilles with the Brunetti Logo in white letters on the middle.

There are a wide variety of premaps that are in current production and that have been discontinued. The **Mille**, which is currently in production, is a three channel preamp. It has three channels (clean, crunch, and lead shine) with a fourth branching out (lead fat). The tubes for this are 6 X 12AX7's. The control panel is blue with several silver knobs and the unit takes up two rack spaces. The **Centouno** is a three channel preamp driven by 3 X 12AX7 and 1 X PCF82 tubes. The control panel on this is silver with blue knobs and it takes up one rack space. Other units include the **Matrix**, the **RPS 300**, the **Mister B**, and the **Van der Graal**. All of these models are currently not in production. For further information refer to the Brunetti web site (see Trademark Index).

BUDDA

Amplifiers currently produced in San Rafael, California.

Budda are handcrafted amplifiers that are often built to order. They make tube amps, speaker cabinets, effects, and will soon offer accessories. The amps are wired by hand point-to-point and offer superb sound from the tubes that power it. These amps all sell at a premium, but are very high quality built. Typically the wait time on a Budda amp is between six to eight weeks. For a full model line and information visit the Budda web site see (Trademark Index).

ELECTRIC TUBE AMPLIFIERS

Budda makes both combo and head-only amplifiers. All Budda tube amplifiers have a class AB power section. The **Verbmaster** series has six different models in the line. The Verbmaster 18 comes in a head unit only, 1-12" or a 2-12" combo. The Verbmaster 18 sports 18W of power, has a tube section of: 3 X 12AX7 & 1 X 12AU7 for the preamp, 2 X EL84 power tubes, and a 5U4 rectifier tube. Features include dual reverb settings, normal and high gain inputs, treble, bass, and volume controls and an effects loop with Slave out. The Verbmaster 18 head unit costs $1,450, the 1-12" retails for $1,650, while the 2-12" goes for $1,800. The Verbmaster 30 has some more horsepower than the 18. This model also comes in a head-unit only, 1-12" or 2-12" combo. The Verbmaster has 30W output coming from 4 X 6L6 high grade tubes. The preamps are the same as the Verbmaster 18 as are the controls. The head-unit lists at $1,700, the 1-12" version has a $1,900 price tag, and the 2-12" model goes for $2,050.

The **Twinmaster** is the smaller brother to the Verbmaster. This model is 18W and comes in three versions: a head-unit, 1-12" combo, and a 2-12" combo. The tube section in this series consists of: 2 X 12AX7 preamps, 2 X EL84 power tubes, and a 5U4 rectifier. The features on these amps include: normal & high inputs, treble, bass, volume controls, and effects loop with slave out, and a custom purple anodized chassis. The price on the Twinmaster head starts at $1,200 and the two combo units both retail for $1,400.

The **Superdrive** series is a higher grade of amplifiers that offers two channels, one that offers killer distortion. In this series there are nine possible combinations. There are three different wattages including 18, 30, and the massive 80. All three come in head-units, 1-12" and 2-12" combos. The controls are the same on all of the models in the Superdrive series and they include: treble, mid, bass, rhythm volume and master volume. All models are dual channels (rhythm & hi-gain), have a drive control and effects loop. The preamp tubes on all models are 12AX7 high grades. The power tubes for the Superdrive 18 are 2 X EL84 with a 5U4 rectifier. The 30 has 4 X EL84 and the rectifier. The 80 has 4 X 6L6GC power tubes to get the 80W of power, and a solid-state rectifier. The prices run

GRADING	100%	EXCELLENT	AVERAGE

as follows: The Superdrive 18 head retails for $1,400, the 1-12" combo for $1,600, and the 2-12" for $1,750. The 30W model head prices at $1,700, the 1-12" combo for $1,900, and the 2-12" combo for $2,050. The 80W bigdawg goes at $2,200 for the head unit, $2,300 for the 1-12" and $2,450 for the 2-12" combo.

Budda Superdrive Combo
courtesy Budda

Budda Verbmaster Combo
courtesy Budda

SPEAKER CABINETS

Budda makes their own speaker cabinets to match the amplifier heads. All the cabinets are made of pine with great durability. Currently Budda offers six different options, but they also will build a canbinet to a customer's specs as well. Three of the cabinets offer 12" speakers with the conifgurations of 1, 2, or 4 speakers. Two of the cabinets have either 2 or 4 10" speakers and the **1210** model has 2-10" and 2-12". Prices start at $360 and run up to $975.

BURNS

Amplifiers previously produced in Britain in the 1960's. Baldwin-built Burns were produced from 1965-1972 in Booneville, Arkansas.

James O. Burns has produced many guitars and amplifiers in Britain from the 1940's-1980's. More known for his guitars, Burns has many original ideas such as the 24-fret fingerboard and other features on the guitar.

After making guitars for many years, Burns released his first line of amplifiers in 1961. The idea for an amplifier came from the first Hawaiian guitar that Burns made. An amplifier would be needed to amplify the sound of the guitar. In the 1950's, Burns made a number of one-time amplifiers, but nothing that went into production as a model line. In the early 1960's, Burns had become a very big name in guitars in Britain so they tried their luck with a line of guitar amplifiers. Jim Burns bought a slug of empty TV cabinets to encase his new amplifiers. Burns made both tube and solid-state amplifiers.

(Courtesy: Paul Day, The Burns Book)

ELECTRIC SOLID-STATE AMPLIFIERS

Information on a lot of these models are scarce. The *Blue Book of Guitar Amplifiers* strongly suggests getting a second opinion when buying or selling any Burns amplifiers as the market pricing on these amps aren't widely spread.

Early Models

Along with the models listed here there have been some models that only a few were made and they never went into production. The "Bassmaster" Bass amp was a piggyback amp that was designed by Gordon Chandler. Because of a lot of problems in the prototype stage, the amp never went into production.

TELE-AMP - 15W, 1-12" speaker with a treble and mid-range units, dual channels, tremolo, top control panel, four inputs (two per channel), five controls (v1, v2, tone, tremolo depth, tremolo speed), cabinet that was designed for televisions, grille that resembles the front of a T.V., mfg. 1961-63.

	N/A	$300 - 400	$225 - 275

This was the first production model Burns. The name comes partly from the fact that the housing for the amplifier was an empty television cabinet. There were some modifications done to the amp as production went on, including the addition of the treble and mid-range speaker units (early models didn't have them).

BISON - 24W, 1-15" Jensen speaker, solid-state, dual channels, top control panel, four inputs (two per channel), six controls (Ch. 1: v, tone, tremolo depth, tremolo speed, Ch. 2: v, tone), tone switches, grayish covering, light cloth grille, mfg. 1962-63.

	N/A	$250 - 325	$200 - 225

BISON BASS COMBO - 35W, 2-12" Jensen Bass speakers, solid-state, tremolo, dual channels, top control panel, four inputs (two per channel), six controls (Ch. 1: v, tone, tremolo depth, tremolo speed, Ch. 2: volume, tone), grayish covering, light grille cloth, mfg. 1962-63.

	N/A	$450 - 600	$325 - 400

The Bison and Bison Bass models were both manufactured by the Supro company in U.S.A. and imported by the Barnes & Mullins company. The only thing separating the Supro from the Burns models was the name of "Burns Bison" on the amp.

Orbit & Double 12 Series

Even though these two series have separate names, they share many of the same features. Their cabinets are very similar, they both have the leather handles, and the Orbital and Super Orbital speakers were made by the Fane company. Essentially these amps are all in the same series with the differences mainly com-

GRADING	100%	EXCELLENT	AVERAGE

ing from wattages, and speaker configurations. When the Orbit 75 was released by Baldwin-Burns in 1966, the amp was available with 10 different cabinet color options. A new Automatic Power Control was featured.

ORBIT 2 COMBO - 40W, 1-12" "Orbital" speaker, solid-state, dual channels, vibrato, rear-top control panel, four inputs (two per channel), seven silver knobs (Ch 1: v, b, t, s, i, Ch 2: v, t), black covering, aluminum metal grille, mfg. 1963-65.

| | N/A | $500 - 650 | $350 - 450 |

ORBIT 3 COMBO - 60W, 3-10" speakers, solid-state, dual channels, vibrato, rear-top silver control panel, four inputs (two per channel), seven silver knobs (Ch. 1: v, 6-way tone select, t, s, i, Ch. 2: v, t), black covering, aluminum metal grille, mfg. 1963-65.

| | N/A | $550 - 700 | $400 - 475 |

* Orbit 3 Reverb Combo - Similar to the Orbit 3 Combo except has reverb and reverb dimension control on channel 1, mfg. 1963-65.

| | N/A | $550 - 700 | $400 - 475 |

DOUBLE 12 COMBO - 60W, 2-12" speakers, solid-state, dual channels, vibrato, rear-top silver control panel, four inputs (two per channel), eight silver knobs (Ch.1: v, 6-way tone select, t, s, i, Ch. 2: v, b, t), black covering, aluminum metal grille, mfg. 1963-65.

| | N/A | $500 - 700 | $350 - 450 |

* Double 12 Reverb Combo - Similar to the Double 12 Combo except has reverb with a reverb dimension control, mfg. 1963-65.

| | N/A | $550 - 750 | $400 - 500 |

ORBIT 75 COMBO - 75W, 2-12" heavy-duty speakers, solid-state, dual channels, top front control panel, four inputs (two per channel), nine black and silver knobs (Ch. 1: v, b, t, i, s, reverb dimension, Ch. 2: t, b, v), light covering, black cloth grille, mfg. 1966-late 1960's.

| | N/A | $500 - 600 | $350 - 425 |

The Orbit 75 was the first model released under the Baldwin-Burns name after the buyout in 1965. The Orbit series and the Double 12 series were condensed to become the Orbit 75. This new model was quite different then the earlier Burns models including the changes of: a front control panel, back-mounted speakers, and a new cloth grille. The cost of this model in 1966 was 156 pounds (in England).

Sonic Series

The Sonic series was a line of amplifiers that were marketed as more of a budget model. These models were targeted to be used with the budget guitars of the same caliber. Most of these amps have only a few controls and features.

SONIC 20 COMBO - 20W, 2-10" Orbital speakers, solid-state, dual channels, top black control panel, two inputs (one per channel), six silver knobs (Ch. 1: v, t, i, s, Ch. 2: t, v), dark covering, light cloth grille, mfg. 1964-65.

| | N/A | $200 - 250 | $135 - 165 |

SONIC 25 COMBO - 25W, 2-10" speakers, solid-state, dual channels, front black control panel, two inputs (one per channel), six black and silver knobs (Ch. 1: v, t, i, s, Ch. 2: v, t), dark covering, black cloth grille, mfg. 1966.

| | N/A | $225 - 275 | $150 - 200 |

SONIC 30 COMBO - 30W, 1-12" Orbital speaker, solid-state, top black control panel, two inputs (one per channel), six silver knobs (Ch. 1: v, t, i, s, Ch. 2: t, v), dark or light covering, light cloth grille, mfg. 1963-65.

| | N/A | $250 - 300 | $150 - 200 |

SONIC 35 COMBO - 35W, 1-12" heavy-duty speaker, solid-state, dual channels, vibrato, front control panel, three inputs (two for channel one, one for channel two), eight black and silver knobs (Ch. 1: v, b, m, t, i, s, Ch. 2: v, t), dark covering, dark grille cloth, mfg. 1966.

| | N/A | $250 - 300 | $160 - 200 |

SONIC 50 COMBO - 50W, 2-12" Orbital speakers, solid-state, dual channels, vibrato, top black control panel, four inputs (two per channel), eight black and silver knobs (Ch. 1: v, b, t, i, s, Ch. 2: v, b, t), dark covering, light grille cloth, mfg. 1963-65.

| | N/A | $275 - 350 | $200 - 240 |

SONIC 55 COMBO - 55W, 2-12" heavy-duty speakers, solid-state, dual channels, vibrato, top front control panel, four inputs (two per channel), nine black and silver knobs (Ch. 1: v, b, t, i, s, 3-way tone select, Ch. 2: v, b, t), various coverings with various cloth grilles, mfg. 1966.

| | N/A | $275 - 350 | $200 - 250 |

Misc Amplifiers

Burns has also made several P.A. amplifiers and speaker cabinets to go along with their amplifier line. There is also a wide assortment of vibrato units, cases, strings, machine heads, and pickups that they made.

DOUBLE B BASS AMPLIFIER - 75W, piggyback and cabinet with 2-18" speakers, solid-state, single channel, front black and silver control panel, two inputs, three black and silver knobs (v, b, t), black covering, dark grille cloth for cabinet, mfg. 1965-66.

| | N/A | $500 - 700 | $300 - 375 |

INTERNATIONAL COMBO - 80W, 3-12" speakers, solid-state, dual channels, vibrato, front control panel, four inputs (two per channel), various knobs, mfg. 1965-66.

| | N/A | $525 - 700 | $325 - 400 |

* International Reverb Combo - Similar to the International except has reverb and a reverb dimension control, mfg. 1965-66.

| | N/A | $550 - 750 | $400 - 475 |

NOTES

Section C

CMI (CLEARTONE MUSICAL INSTRUMENTS LTD.)

Amplifiers previously made in Birmingham, England. The CMI label was a part of Marshall. Production of these amplifiers occurred mainly between 1976-1977.

The Cleartone Musical Instrument Ltd. Company (CMI) was a distribution company established in 1965. Jim Marshall bought into the company in 1967 and took over the company in 1969 when it was finacially indebted to him. Later in the 1970's, Marshall decided to introduce a new line of amps to run alongside its other brother Park. Park amplifiers had been made for Johnny Jones since 1965, but were essentially Marshall amps with a different name on them. CMI amplifiers were introduced around 1976 and followed Marshall design very closely. To this day there is speculation why they would introduce a new line of amplifiers that were almost identical to Park. Most of CMI amplifiers were in the PA industry, but they did make some guitar amps. These amps are just another production name by Marshall, but house another good design. CMI proved to be unsuccessful as a cheaper amp and was discontinued around 1977.

(Source for CMI history: Michael Doyle, The History of Marshall: The Illustrated Story of "The Sound of Rock"

ELECTRIC TUBE AMPLIFIERS

The CMI line didn't last very long and only a few models were made. These models are rare, and are somewhat collectable. There are other PA amps and miscallaneous amplifiers made but very little information is known about them. A lot of amp barely made it past the prototype stage. Since these amps show up rarely (I've seen one), pricing is highly unstable. We suggest getting a couple opinions, if you do find one.

MODEL 1037 - 50W, head-unit only, lead & bass application, tubes: preamp: 3 X ECC83, power: 2 X EL34, dual channels, two inputs per channel for a total of four, silver control panel, six black and silver knobs (presence, b, m, t, v1, v2), black covering, mfg. 1976-77.
   Some of these models were available with 12AX7 preamp tubes. Blue vinyl covering was also available.

MODEL 1038 - 100W, head-unit only, lead & bass application, tubes: preamp: 3 X ECC83, power: 4 X EL34, dual channels, two inputs per channel for a total of four, silver control panel, six black and silver knobs (presence, b, m, t, v1, v2), black covering, mfg. 1976-77.
   Some of these models were available with 12AX7 preamp tubes. Blue vinyl covering was also available.

MODEL 1070 - 50W, combo, tubes: 3 X ECC83, power: 2 X EL34, tremolo, dual channels, two inputs per channel, black covering, mfg. 1976-77.

CMI Combo
courtesy solidbodyguitar.com, Inc.

CMI Combo
courtesy solidbodyguitar.com, Inc.

CALLAHAM VINTAGE AMPLIFIERS

Amplifiers currently produced in Winchester, Virginia.

Callaham Vintage Guitars creates vintage reproduction amplifiers and solid body electric guitars. Callaham feels that these amplifiers aren't copies, but are some of the best sounding amplifiers that are on the market. These amps feature hand, point-to-point wiring, all-tube chassis', wooden cabinets, and components that are of the finest quality. Rather than pay extreme prices on the vintage market, Callaham figures to offer reproduction amplifiers that people want at a more reasonable price. Currently they offer three amplifiers named after their power tubes. Their retail prices range from $1,335 - 1,460. Visit the web site for more information on how to order an amplifier (see trademark index).

CARR AMPLIFIERS

Amplifiers currently produced in Pittsboro, North Carolina.

Carr Amplifiers began when Steve Carr started producing amps out of his repair shop in 1998. Steve Carr is a guitarist and engineer. He reparied amps in Chapel Hill before producing his own. Carr Amplifiers is now located in a converted 50's chicken hatchery located 15 miles south of Chapel Hill. The company employs four craftsmen builders. Carr's philosophy is to combine the best vintage sound with the modern technology and products. They spend hours selecting components and testing amplifiers to get the best sound possible out of an amplifier.

ELECTRIC TUBE AMPLIFIERS

Carr has custom colors that they offer. Their standard colors are black or cream tolex.

   Add $200 for Custom Colors, which include Wine, Cowboy, Green, Purple, Red, CoCoa, and Orange.

GRADING	100%	EXCELLENT	AVERAGE

HAMMERHEAD 1-12 COMBO - 25W, 1-12" speaker combo, all-tube chassis, preamp: 2 X 12AX7EH, power: 2 X EL-34, single channel, top control panel, single input, four black knobs (v, MV, impact, grip), various color covering, diamond shaped grille cloth, mfg. 2000-current.

	MSR	$1,395	$999	$750 - 850	$650 - 700

* *Hammerhead 2-12 Combo* - Similar to the Hamerhead 1-12" Combo except has 2-12" speakers, mfg. 2000-current.

	MSR	$1,595	$1,125	$850 - 1,000	$675 - 750

* *Hammerhead 2-10 Combo* - Similar to the Hamerhead 1-12" Combo except has 2-10" speakers, mfg. 2000-current.

	MSR	$1,595	$1,125	$850 - 1,000	$675 - 750

RAMBLER 1-12 COMBO - 28W, 1-12" speaker combo, all-tube chassis, preamp: 3 X 12AX7, 1 X 12AT7, power: 2 X 6L6GC, single channel, reverb, top control panel, single input, seven black knobs (v, b, t, m, r, depth, s), pentode/triode switch, footswitch, various color covering, parallelogram shaped grille cloth, mfg. 1999-current.

	MSR	$1,995	$1,450	$1,100 - 1,300	$900 - 1,000

* *Rambler 2-12, 2-10", & 1-15" Combo* - Similar to the Rambler 1-12" Combo except have 2-12", 2-10", or 1-15"speakers respectively, mfg. 1999-current.

	MSR	$2,195	$1,575	$1,200 - 1,400	$975 - 1,050

SLANT 6V HEAD - 40W, head-unit only, all-tube chassis, preamp: 4 X 12AX7, 2 X 12AT7, power: 4 X 6V6, dual channels, reverb, front control panel, single input, ten black knobs (Ch.1: v, t, m, b, r, Ch. 2: v, MV, t, m, b), pentode/triode switch, gain-mode switch, footswitch, various color covering, brown grille cloth, mfg. 1998-current.

	MSR	$2,295	$1,650	$1,200 - 1,400	$1,000 - 1,100

Add $200 for FX loop on all Slant 6V models.

* *Slant 1-12 Combo* - Similar to the Slant 6V head except in combo form with 2-12" speakers, mfg. 1998-current.

	MSR	$2,395	$1,699	$1,250 - 1,450	$1,025 - 1,125

* *Slant 6V 2-12, 2-10", & 1-15" Combo* - Similar to the Slant 6V 1-12" Combo except have 2-12", 2-10", or 1-15"speakers respectively, mfg. 1998-current.

	MSR	$2,595	$1,850	$1,400 - 1,600	$1,150 - 1,250

DOUBLE POWER 6V HEAD - 80W, head-unit only, all-tube chassis, preamp: 4 X 12AX7, 2 X 12AT7, power: 4 X 6L6, dual channels, reverb, front control panel, single input, ten black knobs (Ch.1: v, t, m, b, r, Ch. 2: v, MV, t, m, b), pentode/triode switch, gain-mode switch, footswitch, various color covering, brown grille cloth, mfg. 1998-current.

	MSR	$2,595	$1,850	$1,400 - 1,600	$1,150 - 1,250

* *Double Power 6V 2-12 Combo* - Similar to the Double Power 6V head except in combo form with 2-12" speakers, mfg. 1998-current.

	MSR	$2,895	$2,100	$1,600 - 1,850	$1,300 - 1,450

IMPERIAL HEAD - 60W, head-unit only, all-tube chassis, preamp: 3 X 12AX7, 1 X 12AT7, power: 4 X 6L6GC, single channel, reverb, tremolo, top control panel, single input, seven black knobs (v, b, t, m, r, depth, s), pentode/triode switch, footswitch, various color covering, pointed shaped grille cloth, mfg. 2000-current.

	MSR	$2,395	$1,699	$1,250 - 1,450	$1,025 - 1,125

* *Imperial 2-12 & 1-15" Combo* - Similar to the Imperial head except in combo form with 2-12" or 1-15"speakers respectively, mfg. 2000-current.

	MSR	$2,595	$1,850	$1,400 - 1,600	$1,150 - 1,250

* *Imperial 4-10" Combo* - Similar to the Imperial head except in combo form with 4-10"speakers respectively, mfg. 2000-current.

	MSR	$2,795	$1,999	$1,500 - 1,750	$1,200 - 1,350

EL MOTO - 88W, head-unit only, all-tube chassis, preamp: 4 X 12AX7, power: 4 X EL34, two channels, front black control panel, single input, nine black knobs (Ch. 1: v, MV, t, m, b, Ch. 2: v, t, b, overall MV), reverse trapezoid head shape, various color covering, brown grille, mfg. 2000-current.

	MSR	$2,295	$1,650	$1,225 - 1,425	$1,000 - 1,100

Add $200 for FX loop.

SPEAKER CABINETS

Carr offers speaker cabinets that can be matched up to their heads. There are mainly 2-12" and 4-10" cabs. These cabinets are also available in all the custom colors. For more information on speaker cabinets, refer to the Carr web site (see trademark index).

CARVIN

Amplifiers currently produced in San Diego, California.

Carvin is known for making quality guitars, amplifiers, and other accessories from a mail-order catalog. Carvin advertises that they are the number one factory direct music store. Carvin offers a variety of products to amplify guitars and basses. They make combo amplifiers, head-only amplifiers, rack-mounted units, and speaker cabinets. For a complete list of everything Carvin has to offer, visit their web site and request a catalog (see trademark index).

ELECTRIC TUBE AMPLIFIERS

Carvin has three series of tube amplifiers including the Vintage, Stevie Vai (Vai Legacy), and Master Tube Series.

GRADING	100%	EXCELLENT	AVERAGE

C

Vintage "All Tube" Series

The 212 Bel Air and the 112 Nomad both have extension cabinets available with the same speaker configurations as the corresponding amplifiers.

212 BEL AIR - 50W, 2-12" GT12 speakers, tubes: 5 X 12AX7 preamps, 4 X EL84 outputs, dual channels, reverb, top brown control panel, one input, 10 chicken head knobs (Ch. 1: v1, b, m, t, Ch. 2: soak, v2, b, m, t, mv), selector switch for channels, acoustic presence knob on back panel, effects loop, footswitch, vintage tweed diagonal covering, brown cloth grille, mfg. current mfg.

MSR	$1,095	$600	$425 - 500	$325 - 400

Add $20 for cover.

* 112 Nomad - Similar to the 212 Bel Air except has 1-12" speaker, current mfg.

MSR	$895	$525	$375 - 450	$275 - 325

Add $20 for cover.

VINTAGE 16/5 TRIODE - 16W (switchable to 5W in triode operation), 1-12" GT12 speaker, tubes: 3 X 12AX7 preamp, 2 X EL84 output, single channel, reverb, top brown control panel, one input, six chicken head knobs (soak, v, b, m, t, reverb), footswitch, vintage tweed diagonal covering, brown cloth grille, new 2002.

MSR	$679	$375	$275 - 325	$200 - 250

Add $20 for cover.

VL (Vai Legacy) Series

The VL series is a signature series after legendary guitarist Steve Vai. These amps are built by Carvin along with Steve's specifications and ideas. The amps are switchable from 100W down to 50W and besides the stock EL84 tubes, there is a switch to change to either 5881 or 6L6GC tubes.

VL100 VAI LEGACY - 100W, head-unit only, tubes: 5 X 12AX7A preamps, 4 X EL84 output, dual channels (clean & overdrive), bottom black control panel, one input, 11 chicken head knobs (r, Clean: t, m, b, v2, OD: p, t, m, b, drive1, v1), 50W/100W switch, footswitch, black lavant covering, black metal grille, current mfg.

MSR	$1,595	$850	$650 - 750	$525 - 600

Add $20 for cover.

Carvin offers VL speaker cabinets to match up with the VL head. The C412T and C412B are 4-12" Celestion G12 Vintage 30 speakers in a matching cabinet to the VL100 head. Putting two cabinets and a head creates a true Marshall-like stack. The speaker cabinet alone retails for $995 (100% $499). Carvin also offers a special price for a half stack at $2,495 retail (100% $1,200) and a full stack for $3,495 retail (100% $1,700). All speaker cabinets have see through black metal grilles.

* VL212 Vai Legacy - Similar to the VL100 Head-unit except in combo form with 2-12" Celestion G12 Vintage 30 speakers, current mfg.

MSR	$1,895	$999	$725 - 850	$600 - 700

Add $20 for cover.

The control panel is the same as the VL100 Head-unit except it is exactly reversed. An extension cabinet is available for the VL212. The C212E cabinet has 2-12" Celestion G12 Vintage 30 speakers and is valued at $325 in 100% condition.

MTS (Master Tube Series)

MTS3200 - 100W (switchable to 50W), head-unit only, tubes: 5 X 12AX7A preamp, 4 X 5881 output, dual channels (clean & crunch), silver control panel, one input, eleven silver knobs (r, p, Ch. 2: t, m, b, v, Ch. 1: t, m, b, drive, v), effects loop, footswitch, black vinyl covering, black metal grille, current mfg.

MSR	$1,195	$625	$450 - 550	$350 - 425

The MTS3200 Head has two cabinets to match up to it. The 412T (slanted) and the 412B (straight) both have 4-12" GT12 speakers in a matching black vinyl covered and metal black grille cabinet. The speaker enclosures list for $695.

* MTS3212 - Similar to the MTS 3200, except is in combo form with 2-12" speakers, current mfg.

MSR	$1,295	$725	$525 - 650	$400 - 475

The MTS 3212 has an extension cabinet (model VE212) to match. It has 2-12" GT12 speakers and is in a matching cabinet. The value of this in 100% condition is $219. The controls are reversed on the MTS combo version from the head unit.

ELECTRIC SOLID-STATE AMPLIFIERS

In the Carvin Solid-State series there are the following model series: the SX series, the Pro Bass series, Red Eye Series, and Red Line series. The last three of those series are all bass amplifiers.

SX Series

SX50 - 50W, 1-12" combo, solid-state, digital effects, dual channels, front black and silver control panel, one input, 12 black knobs (Ch. A: v, drive, b, m, t, Ch. B: v, b, m, t, Effects: level, adjust, select), 256 24-bit digital effects, footswitch, black vinyl covering, black metal grille, current mfg.

MSR	$495	$325	$225 - 275	$150 - 185

Add $20 for cover.

* SX100 - Similar to the SX50 except has 100W output, current mfg.

MSR	$595	$375	$275 - 325	$200 - 250

Add $20 for cover.

C

GRADING	100%	EXCELLENT	AVERAGE

SX200 - 100W, 2-12" GT12 speakers, solid-state, digital effects, dual channels, front black and silver control panel, two inputs, 15 black knobs (Ch. A: v, drive, b, m, t, p, Ch. B: v, b, m, t, p, Effects: input, output, adjust, reverb select), 256 24-bit digital effects, footswitch, effects loop, black vinyl covering, black metal grille, current mfg.

MSR	$795	$475	$375 - 425	$300 - 330

Add $20 for cover.

* SX200H - Similar to the SX200 except is the head-unit only, current mfg.

MSR	$599	$350	$250 - 300	$195 - 225

Add $20 for cover.

Pro Bass Series

PRO BASS 100 - 100W, 1-10" or 1-15" speaker, solid-state bass combo, black control panel, one input, seven black and red knobs (v, b, g, freq, t, comp, gate), three white push buttons, black Dura Tuff II covering, black metal grille, current mfg.

MSR	$395	$280	$200 - 250	$150 - 175

Add $50 for the 15" speaker option.

PRO BASS 200 - 160W, 1-15", solid-state bass combo, black control panel, one input, seven black and red knobs (v, b, g, freq, t, comp, gate) 5-band equalizer, three white push buttons, tweeter pad control on back, black Dura Tuff II covering, black metal grille, current mfg.

MSR	$695	$425	$325 - 375	$250 - 275

Red Eye Series

RC210 RED EYE COMBO - 600W, 2-10" heavy-duty drivers plus red eye horn, solid-state bass combo, tilt-back cabinet, black front control panel, two inputs, 13 red knobs, 9-band equalizer, various white buttons, black Dura Tuff II covering, black metal grille, current mfg.

MSR	$1,395	$850	$625 - 750	$500 - 575

* RC210-18 - Similar to the RC210 except has an 18" extension cabinet, current mfg.

MSR	$2,090	$1,200	$800 - 950	$650 - 725

Add $20 for cover.

The RC210 features the series III R600 bass amp head.

* RL6815 Cyclops - Similar to the RC210 Red Eye except has different speaker configuration of 1-15" woofer, 2-8" mid-range drivers, and the red-eye horn driver, current mfg.

MSR	$1,495	$950	$700 - 800	$475 - 550

Add $25 for cover.

Red Line Series

Along with the two head units in the Red Line Bass series, there are a few speaker cabinets to go along with it. There are a number of configurations and options in this series. The **RL410T** "Redeye" is a cabinet with 4-10" and a horn driver, which retails for $695. The **RL118** cabinet has 1-18" woofer and retails for $695 as well. The **RL210T** cabinet has 2-10" and a horn driver, which retails for $495. The **RL115** sports 1-15" woofer and goes for $595. The "big daddy," the RL810, has 8-10" drivers along with a horn driver and sells retail for a measly $1,295. For full special combos (cabinets with heads) visit the Carvin web site.

R600 - 600W bridged, head-unit only, solid-state bass amp, black front control panel, two inputs, 13 red knobs, 9-band equalizer, various white buttons, black Dura Tuff II covering, current mfg.

MSR	$1,195	$650	$450 - 525	$350 - 425

* R1000 - Similar to the R600 except has 1000W output bridged, current mfg.

MSR	$1,395	$750	$550 - 650	$425 - 475

ACOUSTIC SOLID-STATE AMPLIFIERS

AG100D - 100W, 1-12" AG12 200W driver with a horn tweeter, solid-state combo, three channels, black front control panel, three inputs (one per channel), several gray knobs, five-band equalizer, various effects, 256 digital effects, hunter green vinyl covering, black metal grill, current mfg.

MSR	$895	$499	$350 - 400	$275 - 320

CORNELL
Amplifiers currently produced in Essex, United Kingdom.

Cornell amplifiers are located in Europe, and they produce quality guitar amplifiers. They have a series of production amplifiers out, but they do take a peek into the custom amp industry. These are generally all-tube amplifiers with various controls and effects. For more information on Cornell amplifiers please refer to the web site (see trademark index).

CORNFORD AMPLIFICATION
Amplifiers currently produced in Kent, England.

Cornford amplifiers just recently appeared in the U.S. after being in England for a while. Cornford produces tube amplifier head and combo units. They also make a series of speaker cabinets. A lot of design and testing goes into Cornford amps to make them the best possible. For more information on Cornford amps please refer to the web site as (see trademark index).

GRADING	100%	EXCELLENT	AVERAGE

CRATE

Amplifiers currently produced overseas. Crate Amplifiers are distributed by St. Louis Music in St. Louis, Missouri. The Crate Trademark was established in 1979.

Crate has produced many amplifiers since 1979. The Crate trademark started out in the early 1980's when the entire guitar industry was at a time of rebuilding. By 1989, Crate had received its first award, and they haven't looked back since. Out of the last seven years, Crate has received the American Amplifier Line Award five times. With many amplifer models and low prices, Crate is able to keep bringing new products to the market rapidly. Most of Crate's amps are small solid-state models, but recently they have expanded to other tangents in the amplifier business. The Blue Voodoo series are tube amps that are reminiscent of Marshall stacks. Crate has also recently developed a digital modeling amp.

ELECTRIC TUBE AMPLIFIERS

Crate has three series of tube amplifiers, the Vintage Club, the Blue Voodoo, which includes the Sammy Hagar model, and the V series.

Vintage Club Series

This series of amps was introduced in 1994. These are combo amps that are all Class A or Class AB chassis and come in up to 50W output. Some of these amplifier models were available in blonde covering instead of black and had a brown grille.

VC508 - 5W, 1-8" Celestion speaker, all tube Class A chassis, preamp: 12AX7, power: EL84, single channel, top silver control panel, one input, three silver knobs (g, tone, v), line out, painted black cabinet, black metal grille, 18 lbs., mfg. 1994-current.

MSR	$279.99	$195	$150 - 180	$115 - 135

VC3112B - 30W, 1-12" Crate Vintage speaker, all tube Class A chassis, preamp: 4 X 12AX7, power: 4 X EL84, dual selectable channels, dual reverb, top silver control panel, one input, 10 silver knobs (Ch. A: v, t, b, Ch. B: g, t, m, b, level, rA, rB), effects loop, footswitch, black tolex covering, black cloth grille, 48 lbs., mfg. 1994-2001.

	$575	$400 - 475	$300 - 350

Last MSR was $799.99.

VC5212B - 50W, 2-12" Crate Vintage speakers, all tube Class AB chassis, preamp: 4 X 12AX7, power: 4 X EL84, dual selectable channels, dual reverb, top silver control panel, one input, 10 silver knobs (Ch. A: v, t, b, Ch. B: g, t, m, b, level, rA, rB), effects loop, footswitch, black tolex covering, black cloth grille, 63 lbs., mfg. 1994-2001.

	$650	$475 - 550	$375 - 425

Last MSR was $899.99.

* VC50 - Similar to the VC5212B, except is in head-unit only, mfg. 1994-99.

	$450	$300 - 350	$240 - 275

VC6112 - 60W, 1-12" Crate Vintage Speaker, all tube chassis, preamp: 5 X 12AX7, power: 2 X EL34, dual selectable channels, dual reverb, silver front control panel, two inputs, 14 silver knobs (g, b, m, t, MV, r, p all for each channel), mid, bass, and boost switches, parallel effects loop, footswitch, black Tolex covering, black grille, mfg. 1994-2000.

	$650	$475 - 550	$400 - 450

* VC6212 - Similar to the VC6112 except has 2-12" speakers, mfg. 1994-2000.

	$675	$495 - 575	$375 - 425

Blue Voodoo Series

BV120H/HB/HR - 120W, Full-size head unit only, all tube chassis, preamp: 4 X 12AX7, power: 4 X 6L6, dual selectable channels, dual reverb, black front control panel, one input, 12 black and silver knobs (Ch. 1: v, h, m, l, Ch. 2: g, h, m, l, v, Both: r1, r2, p), effects loop, line out, footswitch, available in blue covering with gold cosmetics (H), black covering with silver cosmetics (HB), "Red Rocker" covering with silver cosmetics, 52 lbs., mfg. 1996-current.

MSR	$1,099.99	$775	$550 - 650	$450 - 500

Add $75 for the Sammy Hagar "Red Rocker" covering.

The Red Rocker head unit retails for $1,199 and was introduced circa 2000.

BV412 SERIES SPEAKER CABINETS - There are currently eight different speaker cabinets offered to match up with the BV120 head unit. The difference between these are the covering colors and speakers. The retail starts at $699.99 for 120W units and $949.99 for 280W units (stereo). Add another $50 for Celestion Vintage 30 speakers. These cabinets are available in the red, blue, or black coverings.

V Series

Essentially, the V series replaced the discontinued Vintage Club amps. These new amps have the DSP digital modeling effects along with new cosmetics that look pretty sharp. All of these amps have tube circuits that are equipped with Groove Tubes. A cover is available for each model and you can add 10% to the price if the cover is included and is in excellent shape. For a complete listing of the DSP effects visit Crate's web site.

V1512 - 15W, 1-12" V-series speaker, all tube Class A chassis, preamp: 3 X 12AX7A, power: 2 X EL84, single channel, reverb, top black control panel, single input, six silver knobs (g, t, m, b, level, r), black covering, black grille, "15" logo on front, 38 lbs., new 2002.

MSR	$599.99	$425	$275 - 325	$215 - 240

VFX5112 - 50W, 1-12" V-Series speaker, all tube Class AB chassis, preamp: 4 X 12AX7A, power: 2 X EL34, dual channels, DSP effects, top black control panel, single input, 12 silver knobs (Ch A: v, t, m, b, Ch. B: g, t, m, b, level, Master: DSP mode, DSP level, p), 16 digital effects, footswitch, line in/out, 16 or 8 Ohm, extension speaker jack, black covering, black grille "50" logo on front, 48 lbs., new 2002.

MSR	$999.99	$699	$500 - 600	$400 - 450

* VFX5212 - Similar to the VFX5112 except has 2-12" speakers, 58 lbs., new 2002.

MSR	$1,099.99	$750	$525 - 625	$425 - 475

GRADING	100%	EXCELLENT	AVERAGE

ELECTRIC SOLID-STATE AMPLIFIERS

Crate have made many solid-state amps since they introduced the first wooden "Crate" model in the late 1970's. We have listed some of the early models, the DX digital series, the GX series, the GFX series, and the Taxi & Limo series. Please view the subcategories for these following models.

Early Models

Crate has produced many amplifiers since the late 1970's. It is impossible to list every one that has been made. There will be as many amps as we can list in this edition, but check further editions for more model listings and information.

Generally Crate amps were named after the way the physical cabinet looked; like a wooden crate. Many early models are like this. It appears that the first Crate amps were designated with the intials "B" for bass amps, "CR" for guitar models, and "G" for later guitar models. For other models that aren't listed, prices can be generally between the $75 and $200 range.

This Crate G-600 head-unit can usually be bought for $100 in mint shape.

Crate G-600 (Head Unit)
courtesy Dave's Guitar Shop

CR-1 - Wattage unknown, 1-12" speaker, solid-state combo, single channel, front green control panel, two inputs, four black knobs (g, b, t, MV), line out, natural wood cabinet, black metal grille, mfg. late 1970's-early 1980's.

	N/A	$150 - 200	$100 - 125

   * CR-1R - Similar to the CR-1 except has reverb circuit with reverb controls, mfg. late 1970's-early 1980's.

	N/A	$150 - 180	$100 - 125

CR-110 - Wattage unknown, 1-10" speaker, solid-state combo, dual channels (normal and overdrive), black and white front control panel, two inputs (high and low), six black and silver knobs (OD: level, g, Clean: level, b, m, t), footswitch, black covering, black grille with wood bar, mfg. early 1980's.

	N/A	$100 - 135	$75 - 90

   * CR-112 - Similar to the CR-110 except has 1-12" speaker and reverb, circuit with control, mfg. early 1980's.

	N/A	$125 - 150	$85 - 105

DX Digital Series

The DX series was introduced in 1999 and won the Amplifier of the year In 2000. These amps have on board digital modeling technology that provides 16 different amp voices and 16 effects (for a complete listing visit the Crate we bsite). You can then program 10 channels with these different effects. Crate also sells the DXJFC footpedal for $149.99 (retail) to control the channels. The DXFC MIDI Footpedal can store up to 128 channels and retails for $279.99.

DXB112 - 30W, 1-12" Crate Guitar Driver speaker, solid-state combo, 10 user-programmable channels, 16 digital effects, 16 amp voices, top brushed copper control panel, single input, ten black knobs (MV, Amp voice selection, g, b, m, t, channel level, effects selection, effect adjust, r), footswitch, MIDI in, external speaker, headphone jack, CD input, black covering, black with copper grille, mfg. 2001-current.

MSR	$549.99	$399	$275 - 325	$200 - 225

DXJ112 - 60W, 1-12" Crate Vintage Driver speaker, solid-state combo, 10 user-programmable channels, 16 digital effects, 16 amp voices, front brushed copper control panel, single input, eleven black knobs (MV, Amp voice selection, g, b, m, t, channel level, effects selection, effect adjust, r level, r depth), footswitch, MIDI in/out, stereo line in, line out, stereo headphone jack, black covering, black with copper grille, mfg. 1999-current.

MSR	$699.99	$500	$350 - 425	$275 - 325

   * DX212 - Similar to the DXJ112 except has 100W output and 2-12" speakers, mfg. 2000-current.

MSR	$899.99	$650	$475 - 550	$375 - 425

GX Series (Heads & Combos)

This series of amps have been very popular for Crate as far as solid-state goes. Along with the combos there are a couple of head-units that they make. There are also speaker cabinets to match up with these. There are two full size cabs the **GX412S** and the **GX412R**, which each include 4-12" Crate speakers and weigh 74 lbs. These each retail for $659.99. There are two compact sized cabs (to match the compact 1200H head) which are the **GX412XS** and the **GX 412XR**, which have 4-12" speakers, and weigh 54 lbs. These retail for $469.99. The only difference between the two in each set is one is slanted (S) and the other is straight (R). Note that this series has changed cosmetically from year to year but the electronics are generally the same.

GX15 - 12+W, 1-8" Crate speaker, solid-state combo, dual selectable channels, front black control panel, six gray knobs (OD: g, level, Clean: level, l, m, h), headphone jack, ext. speaker jack, black covering, black grille, 15 lbs., mfg. 1990's - current.

MSR	$109.99	$75	$35 - 45	$20 - 30

GRADING	100%	EXCELLENT	AVERAGE

* GX15R - Similar to the GX15 except has reverb effect and control for reverb, 16 lbs., mfg. 1990's - current.

MSR	$149.99	$100	$55 - 70	$40 - 50

GX20M - 20W, 1-10" Crate speaker, solid-state combo, dual selectable channels, reverb, mono chorus, front black control panel, seven gray knobs (OD: g, level, Clean: level, l, m, h, r), headphone jack, ext. speaker jack, black covering, 21 lbs., black grille,

MSR	$249.99	$175	$115 - 135	$90 - 100

* GX20C - Similar to the GX20M except has 2-6" speakers for stereo chorus, mfg. late 1980's-early 1990's.

	N/A	$100 - 125	$70 - 85

GX30M - 30W, 1-12" Crate speaker, solid-state combo, dual selectable channels, reverb, mono chorus, front gray control panel, single input, ten gray knobs (OD: g, shape, level, Clean: level, l, m. h, Both: r, d, rate), footswitch, headphone jack, external speaker jack, black covering, black grille, 24 lbs., mfg. 1990's-current.

MSR	$299.99	$210	$135 - 155	$110 - 120

GX65 - 65W, 1-12" Crate speaker, solid-state combo, three selectable channels, reverb, front gray control panel, single input, eleven gray knobs (OD: g1, g2, shape, l, h, level, Clean: level, l, m, h, level), footswitch, headphone jack, external speaker jack, black covering, black grille, 34 lbs., mfg. 1990's-current.

MSR	$399.99	$275	$160 - 195	$130 - 150

* GX212 - Similar to the GX65 except has 120W output and 2-12" Crate speakers, 50 lbs., mfg. 1990's-current.

MSR	$499.99	$350	$225 - 275	$180 - 210

GX900H - 90W, head-unit only, solid-state, three selectable channels, reverb, front black control panel, single input, 12 black and silver knobs (rA, rB, Ch B: level, h, m, l, Ch A: l, h, m, l, g2, g1), effects loop, footswitch, bright switch, black covering, black grille, 33 lbs., mfg. 1990's-current.

MSR	$589.99	$400	$250 - 325	$200 - 225

* GX2200H - Similar to the 900H except has 220W output, 41 lbs., mfg. 1990's-current.

MSR	$659.99	$450	$275 - 325	$230 - 255

GX1200H - 120W, compact head-unit, solid-state, three selectable channels, reverb, front black control panel, single input, eleven gray knobs (OD: g, shape, l, h, level, Clean: level, l, m, h, r1, r2), effects loop, footswitch, black covering, black grille, 25 lbs., mfg. 1990's-current.

MSR	$459.99	$300	$215 - 245	$180 - 200

GFX Series (Heads & Combos)

This series of amps include the "Flexwave Evolution 5" preamp in each model. New for 2002, the upper three models now have a built in chromatic tuner and the model names have a T at the end of them now. The 2200HT head unit can be matched up with heads from the GX series (see GX series).

GFX15 - 12+W, 1-8" Crate speaker, solid-state combo, two selectable channels, DSP, front black control panel, single input, seven gray knobs (OD: g, level, Clean: level, l, m, h, DSP mode), headphone jack, external speaker jack, black covering, gray grille, 15 lbs., mfg. 1990's-current.

MSR	$199.99	$135	$90 - 105	$75 - 85

GFX20 - 20W, 1-10" Crate speaker, solid-state combo, two selectable channels, DSP, front black control panel, single input, seven gray knobs (OD: g, level, Clean: level, l, m, h, DSP mode), headphone jack, external speaker jack, black covering, gray grille, 21 lbs., mfg. 1990's-current.

MSR	$329.99	$215	$150 - 170	$125 - 140

GFX30- 30W, 1-12" Crate speaker, solid-state combo, two selectable channels, DSP, front black control panel, single input, seven gray knobs, two blue knobs, (OD: g, shape, level, Clean: level, l, m, h, DSP mode, level), headphone jack, external speaker jack, footswitch, black covering, gray grille, 24 lbs., mfg. 1990's-current.

MSR	$379.99	$250	$165 - 190	$140 - 155

GFX50TT (TWO TONE) - 50W, 1-12" Crate speaker, solid-state combo, independent two player operation (two channels), DSP, front black control panel, two inputs, 15 gray knobs, 2 blue knobs (Ch. A & Ch. B each have v, g, t, m, b, level, effects, DSP mode, DSP level, CD input level), headphone jacks, black covering, gray grille, 34 lbs., mfg. 1997-current.

MSR	$529.99	$350	$230 - 275	$195 - 220

I know what you're thinking, and it's also a favorite of mine including the two player operation.

GFX65T - 65W, 1-12" Crate Custom speaker, solid-state combo, three selectable channels, DSP, front black control panel, single input, 10 gray knobs, 2 blue knobs (OD: g1, g2, shape, l, h, level, Clean: level, l, m, h, DSP: level, mode), 16 digital effects, footswitch, external speaker jack, chromatic tuner, black covering, gray grille, 44 lbs., mfg. 1997-current.

MSR	$539.99	$360	$250 - 280	$200 - 225

This model used be strictly the GFX65 without the Chromatic tuner. The GFX65T was introduced in 2002.

GFX120T - 120W, 1-12" Crate Custom speaker, solid-state combo, three selectable channels, DSP, front black control panel, single input, 10 gray knobs, 2 blue knobs (OD: g1, g2, shape, l, h, level, Clean: level, l, m, h, DSP: level, mode), 16 digital effects, footswitch, external speaker jack, chromatic tuner, black covering, gray grille, 34 lbs., mfg. 1997-current.

MSR	$579.99	$400	$250 - 280	$210 - 235

* GFX212T - Similar to the GFX120T except has 2-12" speakers, 50 lbs., mfg. 1997-current.

MSR	$659.99	$450	$275 - 325	$225 - 255

Both of these models had the chromatic tuner introduced in 2002. Before that they didn't have the "T" in the model.

GRADING	100%	EXCELLENT	AVERAGE

GFX2200HT - 220W, solid-state full size head, three switchable channels, DSP, front black control panel, single input, 13 black and silver knobs (Ch A: g1, g2, l, m, h, level, Ch. B: l, m, h, level, DSP: mode, level A, level B), footswitch, bright switch, chromatic tuner, black covering, black grille, 41 lbs., mfg. 1997-current.

	MSR	$779.99	$525	$325 - 375	$250 - 300

Taxi & Limo Series (Battery Powered)

The Taxi & Limo amps are battery operated for use on the go. The first amps were introduced in 1998 and more have been added along the way. These amps have a 120V AC Wall Charger and some have a 12V DC car charger. The TX50DBE even has Crate's DSP effect.

TX15 - 15W, 1-8" Crate woofer with Crate piezo tweeter, solid-state combo, angled cabinet (3 positions), dual channels, top black control panel, two inputs (one per channel, one normal, one 1/4"-XLR combo), six black and yellow knobs (v1, v2, l, l/m, h/m, h), CD input, headphone jack, 120V Wall charger/adapter, black covering, black steel grille, 20 lbs., new 2002.

	MSR	$199.99	$135	$80 - 100	$60 - 75

TX30BE/TX30E - 30W, 1-8" Crate woofer with Crate piezo tweeter, solid-state combo, angled cabinet (3 positions), dual channels, top black control panel, two inputs, seven black and yellow knobs (Ch 1: level, tone, Ch 2: g, l, m, h, level), insert/effects loop, headphone jack, black or yellow covering, black steel grille, 17 lbs., mfg. 1998-current.

	MSR	$329.99	$225	$145 - 170	$110 - 125

TX50DBE - 50W, 1-10" Crate woofer with Crate piezo tweeter, solid-state combo, angled cabinet (3 positions), three channels (two instrument, one mic), top silver control panel, three inputs (one XLR, two normal), ten gray and three blue knobs (Ch 1: g, level, shape, Ch 2: l, m, h, level, Mic: level, l, m, h, three blue DSP knobs), insert/effects loop, headphone jack, footswitch, CD inputs, black covering, black steel grille, 17 lbs., mfg. 1998-current.

	MSR	$529.99	$375	$275 - 325	$200 - 235

* **TXB50E** - Similar to the TX50DBE except, is specified for bass instruments, has no piezo tweeters, smaller control panel, 22 lbs., new 2002.

	MSR	$529.99	$375	$250 - 300	$175 - 210

BX, BXF, & KX Bass and Keyboard Amps

There are a number of amplifiers in these lines and there isn't simply enough room at this point to publish them all. For a complete listing of models contact the Crate web site (see trademark index). There will be more in depth information in upcoming editions of the *Blue Book of Guitar Amplifiers*.

ACOUSTIC SOLID-STATE AMPLIFIERS

Currently, Crate has one line of Acoustic amps, simply named the Acoustic Series. Please refer the Acoustic Series subcategory for model listing.

Acoustic Series

The Acoustic Series have a lot of the features that the electric counterparts have; including the DSP effect. The models that don't have DSP have a darker covering. All the models from the CA60 up have the ability to have an instrument as well as a microphone to be in use at the same time.

CA30 - 30W, 1-8" High Fidelity speaker with a Crate special design tweeter, solid-state slanted front combo, dual channels, spring reverb, brown control panel, two inputs, seven black knobs (g1, g2, l, m, c, h, r), line out, effects loop, mahogany tolex covering, brown grille, 28 lbs., mfg. 1995-current.

	MSR	$359.99	$250	$150 - 200	$100 - 125

* **CA30D** - Similar to the CA30 except has the DSP digital effect (more knobs), spruce tolex covering, mfg. 1997-current.

	MSR	$399.99	$275	$175 - 225	$115 - 140

CA60 - 60W, 2-6.5" Crate High Fidelity speakers, Crate tweeter, solid-state slanted front combo, dual channels, stereo chorus, reverb, feedback elimination circuit, front brown control panel, three inputs, 15 brown knobs (Inst: g, l, m, h, f, cut, rev/eff send, d, rate, Vocal: g, l, h, rev/eff send, Master: rev return, level), line out, footswitch, mahogany tolex, brown grille, 38 lbs., mfg. 1995-current.

	MSR	$649.99	$450	$250 - 300	$200 - 225

* **CA60D** - Similar to the CA60 except has the DSP digital effect (more knobs), spruce tolex covering, mfg. 1997-current.

	MSR	$729.99	$500	$300 - 350	$250 - 280

CA112D - 125W, 1-12" Dual Voice Coil sub with tweeter, solid-state tilt back cabinet combo, three channels, feedback elimination circuit, stereo chorus, DSP effects, front brown control panel, four inputs, 18 brown knobs (Inst: g, l, m, c, h, f, cut, rev/eff send, Mic: g, rev/eff send, Aux: g, rev/eff send, Chorus: d, rate, Effects mode, rev/ret, eff/ret, level out) 5-band equalizer, effects loop, line out with knobs, footswitch, spruce tolex covering, brown grille, 42 lbs., mfg. 1997-current.

	MSR	$969.99	$675	$400 - 475	$325 - 375

* **CA125D** - Similar to the CA112D except has 2-8" high-fi speakers with tweeters, mfg. 1997-current.

	MSR	$969.99	$675	$425 - 475	$325 - 380

Section D

DANELECTRO

Amplifiers previously produced in Red Bank, New Jersey from 1953-58 and in Neptune, New Jersey from 1958-1969. The company was folded in 1969 until 1998 when it was revived as the Danelectro Corporation of Laguna Hills, California. Danelectro amplifiers are currently produced in Asia and distributed by the Danelectro Corporation.

The Danelectro company was started by Nathan I. Daniels in 1948. Danelectro only produced amplifiers for the first five years that the company was in business. The first guitar was released in 1953. In the first five years or so, Danelectro released around a dozen amplifiers. Danelectro kept producing new models here and there until the demise of the company in 1969. Most amps are small wattage tube amplfiers but were at an affordable price. In 1998, when Danelectro was revived, they started producing amplifiers again that are currently in production.

(Source for Danelectro history: Paul Bechtoldt and Doug Tulloch, Guitars From Neptune; and Mark Wollerman, Wollerman Guitars.)"

GRADING	100%	EXCELLENT	AVERAGE

ELECTRIC TUBE AMPLIFIERS

Danelectro tube amps are split up into the different time periods that they were in production.

Early Models

MAESTRO (SUPER VIBRAVOX) - 20W, 1-12" speaker, seven tube chassis, dual channels, top mounted control panel, three inputs, brown simulated leather covering, light brown four-leaf clover grill design, leather handle, Danelectro emblem on bottom of amp, mfg. 1948-1958.

	N/A	$325 - 450	$250 - 300

In 1952, the Maestro output was increased to 25W. In 1956, a model number (#78) was assigned to the amp.

SPECIAL (VIBRAVOX) - 15W, 1-12" Alnico V speaker, six tube chassis, 3 X 6SJ7, 2 X 6V6GT, 6X5GT single channel, top mounted control panel, three inputs, four knobs (v, tone, s, vibrato strength), brown simulated leather covering, four-leaf clover design light brown speaker grille, mfg. 1948-1958.

	N/A	$350 - 450	$225 - 275

ENVOY - 10W, 1-12" speaker, six tube chassis, AC/DC power supply, top control panel, three inputs, two knobs (v, tone), brown simulated leather covering, light brown four-leaf clover grille cloth design, mfg. 1948-1952.

	N/A	$300 - 400	$200 - 250

LEADER - 10W, 1-12" Alnico V speaker, five tube chassis, single channel, top control panel, three inputs, two knobs (v, tone), brown simulated leather covering, light brown four-leaf clover grille cloth design, mfg. 1948-1958

	N/A	$300 - 400	$200 - 250

In 1956, a model number (#48) was assigned to the amp.

TWIN TWELVE (SUPER VIBRAVOX) - 30W, 2-12" heavy-duty speakers, eight tube chassis, dual channels, vibrato, top control panel, three inputs, various control knobs (v, vibrato controls, etc.), brown simulated leather covering, dual light brown four-leaf clover grille cloth designs, mfg. 1949-1969.

	N/A	$450 - 550	$300 - 350

In 1952, output was increased to 50W.

SUPER CONSOLE - 50W, 3-12 auditorium type loudspeakers, dual channels, rear control panel, six inputs (three per channel), six knobs (v, b, t for each channel), brown simulated leather covering, diagonal woven light brown grille, four leaf clover speaker opening, mfg. 1951-55.

	N/A	$500 - 750	$350 - 450

The Super Console had three removable speaker cabinets that could be placed as extension cabinets. This is truly a unique design as the amp was supplied with 100 feet of cable to move the speakers or keep them in the cabinet.

CHALLENGER - 30W, 1-15" Alnico speaker, seven tube chassis, dual channels, eight control knobs, light brown simulated leather covering, dark grille cloth, mfg. 1950's.

	N/A	$400 - 500	$300 - 350

COMMANDO - 30W, 8-8" speakers, nine tube chassis, dual channels, control panel on inside of amp, six total inputs (three per channel), six knobs (v, b, t for each channel), electronic vibrato with two controls, dual cabinets that swing apart, brown simulated leather covering, brown cloth grille, mfg. 1956-1960.

	N/A	$500 - 700	$375 - 450

In later 1956, the covering was changed to gray, but there are a few white ones out there as well.
This model had a massive number of speakers at eight. To get this all into a combo amp, they placed two cabinets (each cabinet with four speakers enclosed), that were placed back to back. In another words, it was a double faced amp with sound projecting from the front and the back. The amp would separate in the middle for access to the controls and the guts of the amp.

THE MASTER-SLAVE SYSTEM - 30W, 1-15" Alnico V speaker, 7 tubes (4 preamp, 3 power), dual channels, vibrato, six total inputs (three per channel), eight knobs (two vibrato controls, v, t, b for each channel), light covering, dark grille, mfg. 1956-late 50's.

MASTER	N/A	$400 - 550	$275 - 350
SLAVE	N/A	$200 - 300	$100 - 150

This model was a cousin of the stack system. The Master amp came with the amp and a speaker. The Master could be used by itself for a total output of 30W. A slave, as the name states, operates from the Master. The master had a power amp in it and hooks up to the master amp as an extension cabinet except the power was then increased to another 30W. More and more slave cabinets could be added for an unlimited number of watts or cabinets. Not exactly a Marshall stack, but it was a start.

GRADING	100%	EXCELLENT	AVERAGE

Models Introduced in 1962

All models were changed at this point in time to reflect, the familiar Danelectro look. The upper line models, such as the Twin's, the Centurion, and the Explorer all had a piggyback design that was all in a combo package. This was done by completely separating the tube chassis on the top from the speaker cabinet on the bottom. This way the entire chassis was shielded from any foreign hum or noise.

TWIN TWELVE (MODEL 300) - 30W, 2-12" speakers, eight tube chassis combo, dual channels, vibrato, reverb, top control panel, nine black knobs, black covering, light diagonal grille cloth, mfg. 1962-64.

N/A	$300 - 400	$225 - 275

In 1964, output was raised to 40W.

TWIN FIFTEEN (MODEL 217) - 60W, 2-15" speakers, nine tube chassis combo, 5 preamp tubes, 4 X 6L6 output tubes, dual channels, vibrato, top control panel, various control knobs, black covering, light diagonal grille cloth, mfg. 1962-64.

N/A	$350 - 450	$250 - 300

CENTURION (MODEL 275) - 15W, 1-12" speaker, seven tube chassis combo, dual channels, vibrato, reverb, top control panel, four inputs (two per channel), eight black knobs (v, b, t for each channel, vibrato, reverb), black covering, light diagonal grille cloth, mfg. 1962-64.

Danelectro Centurion (Model 275)
courtesy Willie's American Guitars

Danelectro Centurion (Model 275)
courtesy Willie's American Guitars

N/A	$275 - 350	$175 - 225

EXPLORER (MODEL 291) - 30W, 1-15" speaker, seven tube chassis combo, dual channels, vibrato, top control channel, four inputs (two per channel), eight black knobs (v, b, t for each channel, vibrato controls), black covering, light diagonal grille cloth, mfg. 1962-64.

N/A	$300 - 375	$200 - 250

VISCOUNT (MODEL 143) - 12W, 1-12" speaker, six tube chassis combo, single channel, vibrato, back mounted control panel, three input jacks, various control knobs, white covering, dark grille cloth, mfg. 1962-64.

Danelectro Viscount (Model 143)
courtesy Harry Browning

Danelectro Viscount (Model 143)
courtesy Harry Browning

N/A	$200 - 250	$150 - 175

CORPORAL (MODEL 132) - 10W, 2-8" speakers, four tube chassis combo, single channel, back control panel, three inputs, two knobs (v, and tone), white covering, dark grille cloth, mfg. 1962-64.

N/A	$175 - 235	$125 - 145

CADET (MODEL 123) - 5W, 1-6" speaker, three tube chassis combo, single channel, rear control panel, two inputs, two knobs (v, and tone), white covering, dark grille cloth, mfg. 1962-69.

N/A	$150 - 200	$100 - 125

GRADING	100%	EXCELLENT	AVERAGE

D

New "D" Models Introduced in 1965

In 1965, Danelectro introduced a whole new line of amplifiers. All old amplifiers were discontinued except for the small Cadet model. These new models had new true Piggyback designs with an amp head sitting on top of the speaker cabinet. This differs from the earlier "piggyback" design as there are two separate cabinets instead of a separation in one cabinet.

DS-100 - 100W, 6-10" Jensen speakers, piggyback design, tubes, dual channels, reverb, vibrato, top silver control panel, four inputs (two per channel), nine knobs (Ch. 1: v, b, t, Ch. 2: v, b, t, r, vibrato speed, vibrato strength), black covering, brown cloth grille, mfg. 1965-69.

| N/A | $350 - 425 | $250 - 300 |

DS-50 - 50W, 3-10" Jensen speakers, piggyback design, tubes, dual channels, reverb, vibrato, top silver control panel, four inputs (two per channel), nine knobs (Ch. 1: v, b, t, Ch. 2: v, b, t, r, vibrato speed, vibrato strength), black covering, brown cloth grille, mfg. 1965-69.

| N/A | $300 - 375 | $225 - 275 |

DM-25 - 25W, 1-12" Jensen speaker, piggyback design, tubes: 6X4, 3 X 12AX7, 2 X 7189, 6FQ7 or 6C67, dual channels, reverb, vibrato, top silver control panel, four inputs (two per channel), nine knobs (Ch. 1: v, b, t, Ch. 2: v, b, t, r, vibrato speed, vibrato strenth), two button footswitch, black covering, brown cloth grille, mfg. 1965-69.

Danelectro DM25
courtesy Harry Browning

Danelectro DM25
courtesy Harry Browning

| N/A | $275 - 350 | $175 - 225 |

DM-10 - 10W, 1-8" Jensen speaker, tube combo, single channel, vibrato, top silver control panel, two inputs, four knobs (v, tone, vibrato speed, vibrato strength), black covering, brown cloth grille, mfg. 1965-69.

| N/A | $150 - 200 | $100 - 125 |

ELECTRIC SOLID-STATE AMPLIFIERS

Danelectro put out only one model (that we know about) that was solid-state in the 60's. They did come roaring back in the 90's with their new transistor models. (See corresponding sections below.)

Vintage Solid-State Models

DTR-40 - 40W, 2-10" speakers, solid-state combo, dual channels, vibrato, top silver control panel, four inputs (two per channel), eight knobs (Ch. 1: v, b, t, Ch. 2: v, b, t, vibrato speed, vibrato strength), black covering, brown grille, mfg. 1965-69.

| N/A | $250 - 400 | $150 - 200 |

Current Solid-State Models

The new Danelectro company has released some new budget-line guitar amplifiers. There is the unbelievably cheap **Honeytone** amplifier which sells for $39. The **Dirty Thirty, Nifty Fifty, and Nifty Seventy** are all small wattage amps for cheap prices. With prices starting at $79 going up to $149 you can get an amp for relatively cheap. All of these models have a variety of controls, features, and color options. Danelectro has recently offered the new **Amp in a Bag**. This is a guitar gig-bag that comes with an amp inside of it. Remember you get what you pay for. For a complete listing visit the Danelectro website.

DEAN MARKLEY

Amplifiers currently produced in San Diego, California.

Dean Markley currently produces smaller solid-state amplifiers, along with their wide variety of other products in the music industry. Dean has been in the business with strings and amps for over 25 years now. Typically these are basic solid-state amps with basic controls at an affordable price. Most of these amps aren't collectible, but very useful as an amplifier. Dean Markley Amplifiers usually show up in the $100-200 range. Look for more information in upcoming editions of the *Blue Book of Guitar Amplifiers*.

Dean Markley K-20
courtesy Kaler Hendricks

Dean Markley K-20
courtesy Kaler Hendricks

DEMETER

Amplifiers currently produced in Van Nuys, California.

The roots of Demeter date back to 1980 when John Demeter, Rob Robinetter, and Phil Van Allen designed their first FET direct box. They started the company Innovative Audio and continued to make different audio products and in 1990 the company was renamed Demeter Amplification. More guitar related amplifiers started to surface in the early 1990's. Now in the 21st century, Demeter has a full range of products which include guitar combo amps, power amps, preamps, and other audio effects.

ELECTRIC TUBE AMPLIFIERS

The TGA-3 is essentially the amplifier that Demeter lists as their claim to fame. This amp was introduced around 1985 and included such features as three channels and a stereo effects loop. This amp lasted into the 1990's. There aren't enough of these amplifiers to determine a price yet.

Currently Demeter offers the TGA-2 series amplifiers, which in a sense are of the TGA-3 descent. These amps are available in six different combinations including the choice between 50 and 100 Watt power outage and as a head unit, or a 1 or 2-12" combo. The model number indicates what configuration the amplifier is. The first three numbers and first number are TGA-2 for the model line. This is followed by a dash then a T or C which indicates head or a combo unit respectively. The next two or three numbers are how much power they put out (50 or 100) and the final indication is the speaker configuration (obviously there will be no numbers for the head-units). Retail prices for these amps are as follows: **TGA2-T50** - $1,799, the **TGA2-T100** - $1,999, the **TGA2-C50-112** $1,999, the **TGA2-C50-212** - unknown, the **TGA2-100-112** - $2,299, the **TGA2-100-212** - $2,499. All of these amplifiers include the same controls and offer Eminence speakers, where applicable. There are also speaker extension cabinets available for these amps made by Demeter.

For a full line of all that Demeter visit Demeter's web site (see Trademark Index). Look for more information in upcoming editions of the *Blue Book of Guitar Amplifiers*.

DIAZ

Amplifiers currently produced in California, U.S.A.

Diaz amplifiers are hand made units that were previously made by Cesar Diaz. Cesar was a native of Puerto Rico who has been involved in the music business since he was six years old. He came over to the United States with Johnny Nash in 1969. In the U.S., he became one of the best "amp doctors" for many musicians including Stevie Ray Vaughan, Eric Clapton, and Keith Richards. He was also the amp technician for Bob Dylan (guitarist G.E. Smith, who was Diaz's long time friend), and later the guitar player in Dylan's band. Cesar left Dylan in 1993 to concentrate on making Diaz amps. There are several stars who own Diaz amps including Billy Gibbons, Jimmy Vivino, and R.E.M., Collective Soul, and Joan Osborne have used the Diaz tremolo device the Tremodillo. Cesar Diaz passed away on April 26, 2002.

ELECTRIC TUBE AMPLIFIERS

Diaz made a number of different tube amplifiers that sold at a premium. The Vibramaster, which is a tremolo and reverb unit, started the pricing at $1,500. This doesn't even have an internal power amplifier! The P-XX is a 20W amp that can serve as a practice amp as well as a performer (at $2,500 it had better). The CD-30 is an amp that has 35W of output and sold for $3,500. Then the next price point for Diaz was $4,500 for the Classic Twin, a 100W performer. The top of the line amp was the CD-100 at a mere $5,000. Most of Diaz's amplifiers were available as combos or head-units and extension speaker cabinets were also available. For a full lineup of Diaz check out the Cesar Diaz website. Keep in mind that Cesar passed away in 2002 and it is uncertain what will happen to these amplifiers and the company.

DIEZEL

Amplifiers currently produced in Munich, Germany. Diezel Amplifiers are distributed by Salwender in Orange, California.

Peter Diezel and Peter Stapfer came up with the Diezel head unit over five years ago and speaker cabinets to go with them. These amplifiers are pricy, but Salwender, who distributes them, can't keep them in stock. Diezel amps are all tube amps with four separate pre-amps within the unit. For someone who likes a lot of options in an amplifier a Diezel definitely has that. Such bands as Guns n' Roses, Tool, Fuel, and others use Diezel amps. Check the Salwender web site for a full catalog and history of the company (see trademark index).

GRADING	100%	EXCELLENT	AVERAGE

ELECTRIC TUBE AMPLIFIERS

Currently there are two amplifier head-units available from Diezel. The **VH4** is a mono amplifier with 90 or 160W output. There are four channels with bass, mid, treble, and volume in each. The Chassis consists of an all-tube circuit, and in the 4-tube power section, there are several different tubes that can be used including, EL34's, 6L6's, and 5881's among others. This unit retails for $4,250. The **VH4S** is the same in set-up as the VH4 except in a stereo version. This amp puts out 45W per side and a total comination of 80W. This unit retails for $4,600. There are also four different speaker cabinets offered by Diezel, which include 2 4X12 cabinets, and 2 2X12 cabinets.

DINOSAUR

Amplifiers and other products currently produced in China. Dinosaur products are distributed by Eleca International Inc. in Walnut, California.

Dinosaur amplifiers are made overseas in China and sold throughout the United States. Dinosaur makes tube and solid-state amplifiers at a competitive price. They also offer guitars, pedals, effects, and a number of accessories. For a complete catalog and description of products visit the distributors web site (see trademark index).

ELECTRIC TUBE AMPLIFIERS

There are two different tube amplifiers offered by Dinosaur. The **DG-30VR** is a 30W amp with an 8" speaker and a tube chassis that consists of 1 X 12AX7 & 1 X 6F2 for preamp and 2 X 6V6GT for power. There is a simple three band equalizer. The **DG-60VR** is a 60W unit with a 10" speaker, and a tube chassis of: 3 X 12AX7 preamp, 2 X 6L6GC power. This amp has more features such as gain, reverb, and presence added to the three band EQ. These amps are covered in an attractive wood covering, with a gold control panel, and a black grille.

ELECTRIC SOLID-STATE AMPLIFIERS

Dinosaur has several models in the solid-state genre. The **DG-Series** are guitar amps that come in all varieties of sizes and wattages. Like most solid-state lines, these amps start at 10W as a "plain jane" and climb all the way up to 200W with all the bells and whistles. The **DB-Series** are bass amps that like the DG-Series have many models from low wattage up to high. There are also Stereo Chorus Amps, Guitar Effect Amps, and Lead Amplifiers. Dinosaur has a complete catalog with their products, or visit their web site for more information.

DR. Z

Amplifiers currently produced in Maple Heights, Ohio.

Dr. Z amplifiers are handmade units that are of high quality. Every amplifier is wired point-to-point and are made with the finest materials out there. Dr. Z offers a lot of options as far as guitar amplfiers goes. There are some combos, some head amps, and speaker cabinets. There are quite a few possibilities when it comes to matching up heads and speaker cabinets. All of the models are available in black, red, or blonde cabinets. Check the Dr. Z web site for a complete listing of what they have to offer (see trademark index).

ELECTRIC TUBE AMPLIFIERS

There are quite a few different models in the Dr. Z amplifier line. These are split up into the following series **Carmen Ghia, KT-45, MAZ series, Z-28 series, Prescription Series, Misc Amps, and speaker cabinets**. Starting December 1, 2001, all amplifiers and cabinets were available with black, red, or blonde covering. Dr. Z. amps typically sell quite close to the actual retail price.

Carmen Ghia Series

CARMEN GHIA HEAD - 18W, head-unit only, all-tube chassis, preamp: 5751, 12AX7, power: 2 X EL84, 5Y3 rectifier, single channel, front black control panel, single input, two white chicken head knobs (v, tone), choice of color covering, gray grille, current mfg.

MSR	$799	$650	$500 - 575	$400 - 450

* Carmen Ghia Combo - Similar to the Carmen Ghia head-unit except in combo form with 2-10" speakers, mfg. 2001-current.

MSR	$1,099	$899	$650 - 775	$500 - 575

KT-45 Series

KT-45 - 45W, head-unit only, all-tube chassis and solid state rectifier, preamp: EF86, 12AX7, power: 2 X EL34, single channel, front black control panel, single input, three white knobs (v, b, t), choice of color covering, gray grille, current mfg.

MSR	$1,399	$1,250	$850 - 1,025	$650 - 750

MAZ Series

MAZ-18 JUNIOR - 18W, head-unit only, all tube chassis, preamp: 4 X 12AX7, 1 X 12AT7, power: 2 X EL84, GZ34 rectifier, single channel, reverb, front black control panel, single input, seven black knobs (v, t, m, b, cut, MV, r), choice of color covering, current mfg.

MSR	$1,299	$1,125	$800 - 950	$575 - 700

* MAZ-18 Junior 1-12 - Similar to the head-unit except in combo form with 1-12" speaker, current mfg.

MSR	$1,549	$1,450	$1,000 - 1,200	$800 - 900

* MAZ-18 Junior 2-10 - Similar to the head-unit except in combo form with 2-10" speakers, current mfg.

MSR	$1,549	$1,450	$1,000 - 1,200	$800 - 900

MAZ-38 SENIOR - 38W, head-unit only, all tube chassis, preamp: 4 X 12AX7, 1 X 12AT7, power: 4 X EL84, GZ34 rectifier, single channel, reverb, front black control panel, single input, seven black knobs (v, t, m, b, MV, cut, r), choice of color covering, gray grille, current mfg.

MSR	$1,499	$1,200	$900 - 1,050	$750 - 825

GRADING	100%	EXCELLENT	AVERAGE

* MAZ-38 Senior 1-12 (Studio Deluxe) - Similar to the MAZ-38 head-unit except in combo form with 1-12" speaker, current mfg.

| MSR | $1,649 | $1,399 | $950 - 1,150 | $750 - 850 |

* MAZ-38 Senior 2-12 (Invasion) - Similar to the MAZ-38 head-unit except in combo form with 2-12" speakers, current mfg.

| MSR | $1,849 | $1,550 | $1,100 - 1,300 | $825 - 950 |

* MAZ-38 Senior 2-10- Similar to the MAZ-38 head-unit except in combo form with 2-10" speakers, mfg. 2001-current.

| MSR | $1,649 | $1,399 | $950 - 1,150 | $750 - 850 |

Z-28 Series & Misc Amplifiers

Z-28 HEAD - 22W, head-unit only, all tube chassis, preamp: 1 X EF86, 1 X 12AX7, power: 2 X 6V6, tube rectifier, single channel, front black control panel, one input, three knobs (v, b, t), choice of color covering, mfg. 2000-current.

| MSR | $1,149 | $950 | $700 - 825 | $550 - 625 |

* Z-28 Combo - Similar to the Z-28 head-unit except in combo form with 4-10" speakers, mfg. 2000-current.

| MSR | $1,549 | $1,200 | $850 - 950 | $675 - 750 |

MAZERATI HEAD - 30W, head-unit only, all tube chassis, preamp: 1 X 5751, 1 X 12AX7, power: 4 X EL84, 5Y3 rectifier, single channel, front black control panel, single input, two knobs (v, tone), choice of color covering, current mfg.

| MSR | $1,099 | $850 | $600 - 700 | $475 - 550 |

PRESCRIPTION HEAD - 45W, head-unit only, all tube chassis, preamp: 3 X 12AX7, power: 4 X EL84, GZ34 rectifier, dual channels, front black control panel, four black knobs (v, t, m, b), 3-way bright switch, expand switch, footswitch boost, choice of color covering, gray grille, current mfg.

| MSR | $1,399 | $1,200 | $900 - 1,050 | $700 - 800 |

* Prescription Combo - Similar to the Prescription head except in combo form with 2-12" speakers, current mfg.

| MSR | $1,799 | $1,525 | $1,100 - 1,300 | $850 - 950 |

There is also a 1-12" combo advertised but no pricing on it.

ROUTE 66 - 32W, head-unit only, all tube chassis, preamp: 1 X EF86, 1 X 12AX7, power: 2 X KT66, GZ34 rectifier, single channel, front black control panel, single input, three black knobs (v, t, b), choice of color covering, gray grille, current mfg.

| MSR | $1,399 | $1,250 | $925 - 1,050 | $750 - 850 |

SRZ-65 HEAD - This amp was just released. Look for more information in upcoming editions of the *Blue Book of Guitar Amplifiers*.

Dr. Z Speaker Cabinets

Currently, Dr. Z has three different speaker cabinets in production. The 1-12" cabinet is available as an open or closed back and retails for $449. The 2-12" cabinet is named "Z-Best." This cabinet is Thiele Ported and retails for $749. The third cabinet option currently, is a 4-10" enclosure that retails for $649.

DUMBLE
Amplifiers currently produced in California.

Howard Dumble began producing amplifiers circa 1963. He has built only approximately 200 amps in 40 years, and they are extremely collectible. Some people consider this amp to be one of the most desirable amp that there is. The model to take note of is the Overdrive Special Amp. Collectors and players feel it is one of the best amps out there. Prices for these amps on today's market are over $12,000, and that might be low. Dumble amps have been purchased in the last few years from anywhere between $10,000-15,000. We suggest getting second and third opinions if you stumble upon a dumble (no pun intended).

Section E

EBS

Amplifiers currently produced in Solna, Sweden. EBS amplifiers are distributed by Brooklyn Gear in Brooklyn, New York. The EBS trademark was established in 1988.

The EBS company makes amplifiers and equipment for bass guitars. The company started in 1988 in Sweden, and the staff consists mostly of bass players. This way they are able to work with the product and perfect the sound. EBS makes combo amplifiers, head units, speaker cabinets, pedal effects, and preamps. Visit the EBS web site for a complete line-up and list of options (see trademark index).

ELECTRIC BASS AMPLIFIERS & SPEAKER CABINETS

EBS currently offers rack-mount preamps and heads, combos, and speaker cabinets. "Fafner the Dragon" is a tube loaded amp head. This model is named the **TD600** and has a continuous output of 500W (600W at a 2 Ohm load). The **EBS-1** series are preamps for rack units. The EBS combo units are split into two series, the "**Drone**" and the "**Gorm.**" The Drone series are 150W amplifiers with either a 12" or 15" speaker, and a variety of controls. The Gorm amps have a bit more power (350W to be exact) and have a bit more options. The Gorm's are available in three different configurations, with 1-15" speaker, 2-10" speakers, or 4-10" speakers. There are eight different speaker cabinets in production currently. They start out with a cabinet of 1-15" and go along the line with 2-10", 4-10" and at the "super size" an 8-10" or 4-12" giant cabinet are available. For complete specifications and other information refer to the EBS web site.

EMC

Amplifiers previously produced in the 1970's-1980's.

Not much information is known about this company and what they produced. Any information about this company can be submitted directly to the publisher.

GRADING	100%	EXCELLENT	AVERAGE

B-150 - Wattage unknown, 1-15" speaker, solid-state chassis, dual channels, four inputs (two per channel), six black and silver knobs (v, b, t, for each channel), black covering, blue/gray grille cloth, mfg. 1970's.

EMC B-150
courtesy S. P. Fjestad

	N/A	$100 - 150	$50 - 75

EDEN, DAVID

Amplifiers currently produced in Montrose, Minnesota. David Eden amplifiers are distributed by Eden Electronics. The David Eden Trademark was established in 1976.

David Eden Amplifiers are bass amplifiers that are built with high quality specifications. The amplifiers are known as the World Traveler series and can be used as a rack-mount unit or not. There are David series speaker cabinets and a CXC solo series. All models are hand built in the upper midwest of the United States. For a full line and information on the company visit the Eden Electronics web site (see trademark index).

ELECTRIC BASS AMPLIFIERS

TIME TRAVELER - 330W, head-unit only, solid-state chassis, single channel, front gold control panel, two inputs, two blue knobs, two gray knobs, three red knobs, various buttons, various outputs, headphone jack, black casing, 15 lbs., new 2002.

MSR	$970	$699	$500 - 575	$400 - 450

WT-400 TRAVELER PLUS - 400W, head-unit only, solid-state chassis, single channel, compressor, front gold control panel, single input, two blue knobs, one gray knob, eight red knobs, headphone jack, black casing, 13 lbs., current mfg.

MSR	$1,230	$899	$700 - 800	$550 - 625

WT-500 HIGHWAYMAN - 500W (2 X 250W), head-unit only, solid-state chassis, single channel, compressor, front gold control panel, single input, two blue knobs, two gray knobs, eight red knobs, various buttons, headphone jack, various outputs, effects loop, black casing, 20 lbs., current mfg.

MSR	$1,440	$1,050	$800 - 900	$650 - 750

GRADING	100%	EXCELLENT	AVERAGE

WT-600 ROADRUNNER - 600W (2 X 300W), head-unit only, solid-state chassis, single channel, crossover, compressor, front gold control panel, single input, two blue knobs, two gray knobs, nine red knobs, various buttons, headphone jack, various outputs, effects loop, black casing, 22 lbs., current mfg.

MSR	$1,748	$1,250	$950 - 1,100	$775 - 875

WT-800 WORLD TOUR - 800W (2 X 400W), head-unit only, solid-state chassis, single channel, crossover, compressor, front gold control panel, single input, two blue knobs, two gray knobs, nine red knobs, various buttons, headphone jack, various outputs, effects loop, black casing, 26 lbs., current mfg.

MSR	$1,976	$1,425	$1,100 - 1,300	$900 - 1,000

WT-1000 BASS POWER AMP - 1000W (2 X 450W), head-unit only, solid-state chassis, single channel, front gold control panel, single input, two blue knobs, two red knobs, various buttons, various outputs, black casing, 26 lbs., current mfg.

MSR	$1,190	$850	$700 - 775	$600 - 650

WP-100 NAVIGATOR - preamp only, head-unit, solid-state chassis, single channel, compression, front gold control panel, two blue knobs, eight gray knobs, eight red knobs, various buttons, headphone jack, various outputs, effects loop, black casing, 12 lbs., current mfg.

MSR	$1,010	$725	$550 - 650	$450 - 500

VT-300A ALL TUBE BASS AMP - 300W, head-unit only, all tube chassis, 4 X EL34 or 4 X 6550 power tubes, single channel, front gold control panel, two inputs, two blue knobs, six red knobs, black casing, 40 lbs., current mfg.

MSR	$2,498	$1,799	$1,300 - 1,500	$1,050 - 1,150

SPEAKER CABINETS

Eden is probably equally as famous for their speaker cabinets in comparison to the amplifiers. On their current pricelist there is over a dozen of models. These come in several different configurations and sizes. For more information on the speaker cabinets and the pricing, please refer to the Eden Electronics web site. More information is to come about Eden speaker cabinets.

EDWARD AMPLIFICATION

Amplifiers currently produced Stoney Creek Ontario, Canada.

Edward Amplifiers are small tube amplifiers that are of high quality and many options. The Edward Amplification company describes their product as "products for those who want low power amplification for harmonically rich distortion created by driving the output tubes to the edge." Edward amplifiers are all available with a variety of color and grille options along with electronic options. The cabinets, in a sense, resemble early tweed amplifiers. For a complete list of pricing for amps and options visit the Edward Amplification web site (see trademark index).

ELECTRIC AMPLIFIERS & SPEAKER CABINETS

Edward Amplification has two amplifiers in production, one a combo and the other a head unit. The **ED** guitar amp is a 14W, single channel amp with a single Celestion 25W Greenback speaker. The controls on this amp are relatively basic with volume, bass, treble, reverb, and tremolo. There is a low and high gain stage to get that distortion factor. Among other features are line in and out, external speaker jacks, footswitch with assignable options, and a wide array of colors for the covering. The **HED** model is the other amplifier in the Edward lIne. This is the same as the ED except in a head-unit only. The amplifier cabinets are reminsic of a Fender Narrow Panel Tweed. The options is where Edward Amplification stands alone. When ordering an amplifier there are five different options. First a choice between two or three spring reverb is offered at no cost. Second option is the speaker choice, starting with the basic Celestion Greenback up to a Celestion Blue (five different speakers in all). The third option is the handle and grille color. The fourth option is the cabinet color (eight to choose from). The last option gives the owner the choice of what switches the footswitch will control on the amp. There are 12 different combinations that control the gain, boost, reverb, and tremolo. Those crazy Canucks!

The retail on the HED is $1,399 and $1,499 on the ED. The Shoulder, a separate 1-12" speaker cabinet retails for $599. Prices vary for all of the options so check the web site for those. There are also hard and soft covers available for Edward amps.

EGNATER

Amplifiers currently produced in Pontiac, Michigan.

Egnater Amplifiers have been around since 1980. They are responsible for custom amplifier combos and heads, and most recently the M4 Pre-Amp that has changeable modules.

ELECTRIC AMPLIFIERS

Egnator has a tube amplifier with moduling effects in a head or combo version. Both of these models have the same specifications, which include: 50W output, two channels (including modeling effects), a power tube section that is switchable (EL34, 6L6, 5881, KT66, 6550, and KT88), and effects loops. Reverb is optional and a footswitch is included. The combo unit is available with a 1-12" or 2-12" speakers. Pricing is as follows: 50W Head unit is $2,000, for the 1-12" combo it's $2,300, and the 2-12" combo is $2,500.

The M4 PRE-AMP follows the technology that has taken amplifier companies into the 21st Century. This certain model is different than most modeling amps that are out there because you can actually plug in four different module units. This system works as a rack-mount deal and the four module units can be taken out by two simple screws and changed with another for a different sound. This system starts out for $2,000. For a full list of options and sounds you can get out of the unit refer to the website (see trademark index).

There are also two speaker cabinets available in the forms of a 2-12" cabinet or a 4-12" cab. Options include: closed or open back (closed standard) and a choice of Jensen or Celestion speakers. The 2-12" retails for $750, and the 4-12" goes for $1,100.

ELECTRO-HARMONIX

Amplifiers and other products currently produced in New York City, New York. The Electro-Hamonix trademark was established in 1968 and revived in the 1990's.

GRADING	100%	EXCELLENT	AVERAGE

The Electro-Harmonix company was founded by Mike Matthews in 1968. The company went under in 1985 and was revived by the same man in the early 1990's. Electro-Harmonix currently only has one amplifier and one speaker cabinet, but they are more known for their accessories. These include tubes, speakers, cables, and other pedal effects. For a complete listing of their accessories, visit their web site (see trademark index).

ELECTRIC SOLID-STATE AMPLIFIERS

There is little known about early Electro-Harmonix amplifiers. One such model is the Mike Matthews Dirt Road Special. This is a simple solid-state amp with tremolo and gain. This amp is also named after the founder of the company.

MIKE MATTHEWS DIRT ROAD SPECIAL - 25W, 1-12" Celestion speaker, solid-state chassis, phase shifter, single channel, top black control panel, single input, four black knobs, black covering, black grille, mfg. mid 1970's.

Electro-Harmonix
(Mike Matthews Dirt Road Special)
courtesy S. P. Fjestad

Electro-Harmonix
(Mike Matthews Dirt Road Special)
courtesy S. P. Fjestad

Electro-Harmonix
(Mike Matthews Dirt Road Special)
courtesy S. P. Fjestad

N/A	$300 - 375	$225 - 275

The one amplifier that is currently offered at Electro-Harmonix is the **Freedom** Amplifier. This is an 8" speaker combo that is battery operated and can be recharged. The controls on the amp are volume, tone, and bite to get a lot of sound out of a little amp. The amplifier also features a preamp output and comes in a hand crafted pine cabinet with a brown grille. The current Freedom amp is based off of the original Freedom amp back in the 1970's that was one of the first guitar amplifiers to be battery-operated.

Electro-Harmonix also offers a speaker cabinet with 4-10" speakers. This enclosure features a hand-crafted pine box, four Electro-Harmonix 10CS speakers and a removable brown grille.

ELK

Amplifiers previously produced in Japan during the 1960's.

Elk amplifiers were made during the 1960's overseas in Japan. Not much is known about this company and models aren't very common. There are five models that we know of. They are the Custom Series, which included the Custom Amp 30, the Custom 150-L, and the Custom 150-S. The Viking series consists of the Viking-100 and the Viking-50. Features and specifications are unknown about these amplifiers, but they had similarities to Fender amplifiers of the same era.

(Source: Rittor Books, 60's Bizarre Guitars)

EMERY SOUND

Amplifiers currently produced in California.

Emery Sound Amplifiers are hand built by Curt Emery in California. All amplifiers are available at the best price, sold direct from Emery, the company itself. Emery amps are all tube amps that are sold as just the chassis, and they sell the speaker cabinet for the amp seperately. There is also a combo amplifier available. For ordering and product information visit the Emery Sound web site (see Trademark Index).

ELECTRIC TUBE AMPLIFIERS

There are two different amplifiers available from Emery Sound. Emery makes low wattage amps that require smaller tubes. This means by using a 6G6 power tube wide open, the output is about 2W. The **Microbaby** is the smallest wattage amp I can remember seeing with 2W of power (and a half power switch!). The features are 6G6 tubes but can be switched with 6K6 or 6V6 tubes. The chassis on these amps are completely exposed. There are only two knobs (v, tone), and the normal jacks for a head-unit. The Microbaby retails for $1,099. The **Superbaby** and the **Spotlight** are the same amp in electronics, the only differance being the Spotlight has a speaker. These are 8W amps with a variety of tube options. In fact, Emery offers a **Mad Scientist** kit that includes 10 different tubes (a possibility of 36 combinations) and a mohagany rack to experiment with different sounds. The Superbaby and Spotlight both have two controls (v, tone) and basic head-unit jacks. The Superbaby retails for $1,099. The Spotlight has 1-8" speaker and retails for $1,799. A speaker cabinet for the head-units are available as a 1-10" for $570.

All of the models listed are available to be purchased factory direct, where the prices are cheaper. For all these prices and more options and details, refer to the Emery Sound web site (see Trademark Index).

ENGL

Amplifiers currently produced in Germany. Engl Amplifiers are distributed in the United States by JI Concept. The Engl company was established circa 1984.

Edmund Engl to this day still believes in building the most innovative, cutting edge amplifiers. Engl debuted their first amplifier The Straight at the Frankfurt Music Fair in 1984. Engl has been producing fine tube amplification for two decades now, and have added to their arsenal immensely. Engl now has a line of amplifiers, cabinets, and accessories. For all the options and models, visit the Engl web site (see Tademark Index).

ELECTRIC TUBE AMPLIFIERS

Engl doesn't even bother with solid-state, so tube is all they have. The original Engl amp is the **Straight 50**. This amp is what started it all for Engl back in the 80's, but they don't produce it any longer. Look for more information in upcoming edtions of the *Blue Book of Guitar Amplifer*.

Savage Series, Fireball, & Ritchie Blackmore Model

SAVAGE SPECIAL EDITION (E 660) - 100W, head-unit only, all-tube chassis, preamp: 5 X ECC83, power: 4 X 6L6GC, 1 X ECC83, four channels, six basic sounds, reverb, gain, front control panel, single input, 22 black and gray knobs, MV, line out, several jacks, black tolex covering, current mfg.

MSR	$2,899	$2,350	$1,800 - 2,050	$1,400 - 1,550

SAVAGE 120 (E 610) - 120W, head-unit only, all-tube chassis, preamp: 5 X ECC83, power: 2 X 6550, 1 X ECC83, four channels, six basic sounds, 19 black and gray knobs, various switches and jacks, line out, black tolex covering, current mfg.

MSR	$2,449	$1,950	$1,500 - 1,700	$1,200 - 1,350

RITCHIE BLACKMORE SIGNATURE 100 (E 635) - 100W, head-unit only, all tube chassis, preamp: 3 X ECC83, power: 4 X 5881, 1 X ECC83, four channels, front silver control panel, single input, nine black chicken head knobs (clean, lead, b, m, t, p, MV, Master A Lo Gain, Master B Hi Gain, various switches, line out, various jacks, black covering, current mfg.

MSR	$1,599	$1,150	$900 - 1,000	$775 - 850

FIREBALL (E650) - 60W, head-unit only, all tube chassis, preamp: 3 X ECC83 power: 2 X 6L6GC, two channels, front silver control panel, single input, seven black chicken head knobs (g, b, m, t, p, MVA, MVB), various switches, FX loop, line out etc., black covering, current mfg.

MSR	$1,299	$950	$750 - 850	$600 - 700

Classic Series

There are two Classic amps, one is a head and one is a combo. There are also speaker cabinets that are designed for the Classic Head. The 2-10" cabinet has Celestion Vintage 10 speakers and retails for $599. The 4-10" cabinet has Jensen Alnico speakers and retails for $799.

CLASSIC SERIES HEAD (E 355C) - 50W, head-unit only, all tube chassis, preamp: 3 X ECC83, power: 2 X 5881, two channels, reverb, front black control panel, single input, nine cream chicken head knobs (lo gain 1, hi gain 2, b, m, t, r1, r2, MV1, MV2), bright and depth switch, lo/hi switch, line out, FX loop, various jacks, cream covering, brown grille, current mfg.

MSR	$1,399	$1,000	$800 - 875	$650 - 700

* Classic Series Combo (E 350C) - Similar to the Classic Series Head except has 1-12" speaker in combo form, current mfg.

MSR	$1,599	$1,125	$900 - 1,000	$750 - 825

Sovereign, Screamer, & Thunder Series

SOVEREIGN 100 VINTAGE (E 360) - 100W, 1-12" speaker combo, all tube chassis, preamp: 5 X ECC83, power: 4 X 5881, four channels, reverb, MV, front silver control panel, single input, 18 black and silver knobs, FX loop various output jacks, black covering, metal grille, current mfg.

MSR	$1,999	$1,500	$1,100 - 1,300	$850 - 1,000

SCREAMER 50 HEAD (E 335) - 50W, head-unit only, all tube chassis, preamp: 4 X ECC83, power: 2 X 5881, four channels, reverb, MV, front silver control panel, single input, nine black knobs (clean, lead, b, m, t, p, r, MV1, MV2), various jacks and switches, black covering, metal grille, current mfg.

MSR	$1,199	$925	$725 - 800	$625 - 675

* Screamer 50 Combo (E 330) - Similar to the Screamer 50 Head unit except in combo form with 1-12" V80 speaker, current mfg.

MSR	$1,299	$975	$750 - 850	$600 - 775

THUNDER 50 COMBO (E 320) - 50W, 1-12" Celestion V80 speaker combo, all tube chassis, preamp: 4 X ECC83, power: 2 X 5881, three channels, reverb, MV, front silver control panel, single input, seven black knobs (Clean, b, m, t, r, v, MV), various output jacks, black covering, metal grille, current mfg.

MSR	$1,099	$850	$600 - 700	$475 - 550

* Thunder 50 Head (E 325) - Similar to the Thunder 50 Combo except in head-unit only form, current mfg.

MSR	$899	$675	$525 - 600	$425 - 475

Rack-Mount Units

Engl has a couple rack mount units. Two of them are pre-amps. The first one is the **Midi Tube Preamp 580**, which can almost fuse atoms. This unit can be remotely controlled by a computer, and up to 256 presets can be stored. Officially a modeling amp, this amp can almost do it all. It does have a 4 X ECC83 preamp circuit, and a variety of controls. This isn't for the novice as the retail on this machine is $3,049 (I hope they have an exchange policy if you don't like it!). There is a more simple **4-channel preamp** that retails for $699. It has 2 X ECC83 for tubes and lots of controls for a wide array of playing possibilities.

There are two power amps in the rack line. The **840/50** is a 2 X 50W stereo amp with 1 X ECC83 preamp tube and 2 X 5881 for power on each side. This amp retails for $1,299. The **930/60** is a 2 X 60W stereo amp with a few more options than its younger brother. Instead of 5881 power tubes it has 6L6GC. This particular model goes for $1,699.

SPEAKER CABINETS AND ACCESSORIES

Engl also offers speaker cabinets to match up to the head-units. For the Classic Series speaker cabinets please refer to the Classic Section under Electric Tube Amplifiers. Full size cabinets are available in 4-12" units only, but with 4 different options. For a retail price of $799 you can get the **E 412 SG**, which has V60 Celestion speakers in a straight cabinet, or the **E 412 SS**, which is a slanted cab. The higher end cabinets are the Pro-series which feature Vintage 30 Celestion speakers. For $1,149 the **E 412 VG** is straight where the **E 412 VS** is slanted. There are also compact cabinets where a 1-12" or 2-12" combination is available. The **E 212 S** is a slanted cabinet with V60 Celestion's and retails for $699. The **E 112 S** is also slanted but only has 1 V60 and goes for $449. The **E 212 V** has Vintage 30 speakers and is straight. Price is $749 on that. The **E 112 V** only has one speaker. Note that the Vintage 30 speakers only come in straight cabs and the V60 speakers are in slanted styles.

For all the accesories that are available for Engl products visit their website (see Trademark Index).

ENHANCER

Amplifiers currently produced in Waxahachie, Texas.

Enhancer is possibly the only trademark in the book where there amplifier doesn't run on electricity. In a way the Enhancer amplifies an amplifier, hence their name. The Enhancer is a hollow box where an amplifier sits. The amp is angled upward, and the sound resonates inside the box. The sound is then projected out of the opening in the front right underneath the amplifier. This increases sound greatly without even touching the volume knob on the amp itself. Currently Enhancer makes their amps in different sizes to fit some of the more popular amps such as a Fender Super Reverb.

Enhancer Model E-LG
courtesy S. P. Fjestad

Enhancer Model E-LG
w/Fender Super Reverb
courtesy S. P. Fjestad

EPIPHONE

Amplifiers currently produced in Asia since 1983. Epiphone is a division of Gibson Musical Instruments in Nashville, Tennessee. The Epiphone trademark was established in 1930 and was purchased in 1958 by Gibson. Production of Epiphone instruments lasted in the U.S. until 1969 where it moved to Japan in 1983.

The Epiphone company was founded in the late 1920's as the The Epiphone Banjo Co. Anastasios Stathopoulo, his wife Marianthe, and son Epaminondas (Epi) were the three that started making instruments when they moved to the U.S. from Greece in 1903. Their first products were banjos, ukeleles and other instruments of the like. In 1931, the Masterbuilt series of guitars released and this was the first line of guitars for Epiphone. When the first band of electric guitars came out in the mid 1930's, there was a need to amplify the sound. In 1941, the first line of Epiphone amplifiers made their debut. These first three models were the Dreadnaught, Zephyr, and Century.

Shortly after the release of the amplifiers, Epi Strathopoulo, the founder of Epiphone, died of Leukemia in 1943. In a sense this was the beginning of the end for Epiphone. Orthie Stathopoulo took over as president, but couldn't get things going as well again. Frixo Stathopoulo, his brother, and Ortho were in constant friction and it took its toll on the company. In 1951, there was a labor strike at the plant that stopped production for several months. After this Ortho part of his share and the production moved to Philadelphia. The 1950's were especially rough for Epiphone. Frixo died leaving the rest of the company already in turmoil to Orphie. New guitar manufactures and the lack of Epiphone to keep up with that led Orphie going to Ted McCarty, Gibson's president, to talk about selling the company. Gibson and Epiphone signed a deal and Gibson got a lot more than what they bargained for! Instead of going to New York and Philadelphia to get just the bass violin production, the trucks returned with the bass violin material, and all the jigs and what not for making guitars and some works in progress. For less than the cost of a mid-sized car today, Gibson bought its rival for $20,000. This would turn out to be the most profitable assest of Gibson.

During the 1950's throughout the sale and turmoil of Epiphone, no new amplifiers were introduced. As the Epiphone manufacturing plant was moved to Kalamazoo amplifier production became a factor again. More models were released in the 1960's until production was moved to Japan in 1970. Amplifier production would be halted until the late 1990's when models were introduced as budget amplifiers.

ELECTRIC TUBE AMPLIFIERS

Electar Models

Epiphone jumped into the electric guitar market under the Electar name in 1935. Shortly thereafter, Electar amplifiers emerged for Epiphone. Nat Daniels was responsible for making the first Epiphones. These first Electar models were made by Daniels and by a suitcase company. The suitcase company supplied the cabinets and Daniels made the chassis to go inside of them.

GRADING	100%	EXCELLENT	AVERAGE

ELECTAR MODEL - Unspecified wattage, 1-8" speaker, tube chassis, single channel, rear control panel, three inputs (two for instruments, one for microphone), on/off switch, later models have volume and tone controls, black leatherette covering, black grile, mfg. 1936-37.

	N/A	$275 - 325	$200 - 240

This model was available as an AC model or as an AC/DC power supply. The front and rear panels were detachable.

ELECTAR MODEL C - Unspecified wattage, 1-10" speaker, tube chassis, single channel, rear control panel, on/off switch, volume control, grey linen covering, airplane cloth grille, "E" logo on the grille, mfg. 1936-39.

	N/A	$300 - 350	$225 - 275

This model was available as an AC/DC power input. In 1937, a tone control was added and an AC only model was made available.

ELECTAR MODEL M - 15W (AC), 10W (AC/DC), 1-12" speaker, tube chassis, rear control panel, two input jacks, on/off switch, grey linen airplane cloth, brown grille with metal "E" logo, mfg. 1936-39.

	N/A	$325 - 375	$250 - 285

In 1937, the output of the DC version was raised to 15W and a special AC/DC model was available, which had a high fidelity speaker and an additional filter. In 1938, a volume control was added.

ELECTAR SUPER AC/DC - 30W (AC/DC power), 1-12" speaker, tube chassis, rear control panel, three inputs (two for instruments, one for microphone), on/off switch, tone control, black Keratol covering, brown speaker covering with metal E logo, mfg. 1936-39.

	N/A	$350 - 425	$250 - 300

In 1937, an AC only model was available. In 1938, a volume control was added.

Coronet, Century, Zephyr, & Dreadnaught Models

CORONET - Unspecified wattage, unspecified speaker, unspecified tubes, single channel, two input jacks, on/off switch, volume control, gray linen covering, "E" logo on the grille, mfg. 1939-1949.

	N/A	$300 - 375	$225 - 275

In 1941, the cabinet was changed to a wood with walnut finish. We promise that this amp was "specified."

CENTURY - Unspecified wattage (until 1949), 1-12" speaker, tube chassis, single channel, three inputs, on/off switch, volume control, wood maple covering with "E" logo on grille, mfg. 1939-1957.

1939-1948	N/A	$300 - 350	$240 - 275
1949-1954	N/A	$325 - 375	$250 - 300
1955-1957	N/A	$350 - 400	$275 - 310

In 1949, wattage was found at 14W, vibrato was added to some models, covering was changed to a tweed plastic fabric with the "E" logo, tone control was added, cabinet size was increased, and it was only available as an AC model. In 1954, vertical slots were added to the grille. In 1955, output was increased to 15W, a channel was added, another input jack was added (two per channel), covering was changed to a yellow plastic linen, and a footswitch for the vibrato was available.

ZEPHYR - Unspecified wattage (until 1949), 1-12" speaker, AC/DC power, tube chassis, single channel, on/off switch, three input jacks, volume and tone controls, wood cabinet, "E" logo on grille, mfg. 1939-1957.

1939-1949	N/A	$350 - 400	$250 - 300
1950-1954	N/A	$350 - 425	$275 - 325
1955-1957	N/A	$325 - 400	$250 - 300

In 1949, wattage set at 20W, vibrato available as an option with controls for speed and intensity, and the AC/DC option was discontinued. In 1950, vibrato was standard, and wood cabinet was made of walnut veneer. In 1954, a footswitch for vibrato was an option. In 1955, output was increased to 30W, the speaker was upped to 1-15", a second channel was added with another input jack, volume and tone controls for each channel, and covering was changed to a yellow plastic linen with a brown grille.

DREADNAUGHT (ZEPHYR DREADNAUGHT) - Unspecified wattage (until 1949), 1-12" speaker, tube chassis, single channel, three input jacks (two for instrument, one for microphone), on/off switch, volume and tone controls, wood cabinet, "E" logo on grille, mfg. 1939-1957.

	N/A	$300 - 400	$225 - 275

When the Dreadnaught was released in 1939, it was a Zephyr that had more power. In 1949, it became its own name, the Dreadnaught, vibrato was an option, AC/DC was discontinued, covering was changed to a walnut veneer and output was stated to be 30W. In 1950, Vibrato was standard. In 1954, the speaker was upgraded to 1-15", the covering was changed to a tweed plastic linen, and a footswitch was available. In 1955, output was increased to 50W, the speaker configuration was change to 2-12", and the covering was changed to a yellow plastic linen.

KENT - 6.5W, 1-10" speaker, tubes, single channel, two input jacks, on/off switch, volume control, tweed plastic covering, "E" logo on the grille, mfg. 1949-1950.

	N/A	$275 - 350	$200 - 250

New Epiphone Amps Introduced in 1961 Under Gibson

After Epiphone was bought by Gibson in 1957/1958 the entire line went under renovation. The old amps were all discontinued and a new line was introduced in 1961. Some of these models carried the old names, and some new ones were introduced. It should be noted that the new Epiphone amplifiers were the same in circuitary as their Gibson counterparts.

When the new Epiphone amplifiers were introduced in 1961, almost all of them had corresponding Gibson cousins. There is little information on Epiphone amplifiers since no one really cared after Gibson bought them out and made them the cheaper line. There are models that correspond with each other, but the numbers rarely match up. It would make sense but I suppose Gibson figured this would be a bang-up idea in marketing, since people wouldn't be able to catch on to the identical models in two different lines. More information and research is underway for future editions.

As far as pricing, it is similar to Gibson, but lower proportionally. Gibson and Epiphone Amps of the 1960's can be compared to Gibson and Epiphone today.

EUPHONIC AUDIO

Amplifiers currently produced in New Jersey. The Euphonic Audio trademark was established in 1995.

Euphonic Audio began designing musical equipment in 1995. Larry Ullman and John Dong are at the helm of this company, and they believe to get the best possible sound out of their products, they're going to need feedback from players. Real life situations are what make these products unique. Euphonic offers a slug of speaker cabinets, power amps, pre amps, combos, and the Rumble Seat was introduced in 1999. The latest design by Euphonic Audio is the CXL-110. For a full listing of what Euphonic Audio has to offer, refer to the Euphonic Audio web site (see Trademark Index).

EVANS CUSTOM AMPLIFIERS

Amplifiers currently produced in Burlington, North Carolina.

The Evans Custom Amplifier company was established in 1962 and are still producing quality amplifiers to this day. Many musicians play their products (see thier pricelist for a complete listing of over 90 artists). Evans makes three different types of amplifiers, for archtops, jazz, and steel. They also have a full line of speaker cabinets. For a complete listing of what Evans has to offer, or to request some information refer to the web site (see Trademark Index).

E

NOTES

Section F

FENDER

Amplifiers currently produced in Corona, California (U.S.), Mexico, Japan, Tianjin (China), and Korea. Distributed by the Fender Musical Instruments Corporation of Scottsdale, Arizona. The Fender trademark established circa 1946 in Fullerton, California.

Clarence Leonidas Fender was born in 1909, and raised in Fullerton, California. As a teenager he developed an interest in electronics, and soon was building and repairing radios for fellow classmates. After high school, Leo Fender held a bookkeeping position while he still did radio repair at home. After holding a series of jobs, Fender opened up a full scale radio repair shop in 1939. In addition to service work, the Fender Radio Service store soon became a general electronics retail outlet. However, the forerunner to the Fender Electric Instruments company was a smaller two-man operation that was originally started as the K & F company in 1945. Leo Fender began building small amplifiers and electric lap steels with his partner, Clayton Orr Doc Kaufman. Leo and Doc produced their first amplifier and steel guitar in 1945. Kauffman left K&F in early 1946 and Leo Fender took over. Leo then formed the Fender Electric Instrument company in 1946, located on South Pomona Avenue in Fullerton, California. By 1947, Fender produced the model 26 and shortly thereafter came the Super. In 1948, the new Fender amps looked to improve cabinet construction. The Champion student amplifier was introduced at this time. Increased demand meant it was time to expand to a new warehouse.

Soon Fender's inventive genius began designing new models through the early 1950's and early 1960's. The Fender Bassman Amp was unveiled in 1951. This paved way to a new, formidable line of amplifiers. In 1952, the Twin Amplifier was introduced. This amplifier consisted of two 12" speakers and became the top model of the line. With the success of this line, Fender was forced to move again in 1953. The Tweed amplifiers became very popular in the 50's. In 1955, Fender developed an amp using the new effect of tremolo. They named the amp the Tremolux. Fender often would release a new guitar with a new amplifier. In 1958, the Jazzmaster was released as was the Vibrasonic amp. This amp was a completely new design. It had a front facing control panel, and its covering was made by the General Tire & Rubber Company. This allowed for these amps to take a lot of abuse and not a lot of wear. The Reverb Unit, Twin Reverb, and the Showman debuted in the early 60's.

By 1964, Fender's line of products included electric guitars, basses, steel guitars, effects units, acoustic guitars, electric pianos, and a variety of accessories. Leo's faltering health was a factor in putting the company up for sale, and first offered it to Don Randall (the head of Fender Sales) for a million and a half dollars. Randall opened negotiations with the Baldwin Piano & Organ company, but when those negotiations fell through, offered it to the conglomerate CBS (who was looking to diversify the company holdings). Fender (FEIC) was purchased by CBS in December of 1964 for thirteen million dollars. Leo Fender was kept on as a special consultant for five years, and then left when then contract was up in 1970. Due to a ten year no compete clause, the next Leo Fender designed guitars did not show up in the music industry until 1976 (Music Man).

While Fender was just another division of CBS, a number of key figures left the company. Forrest White, the production manager, left in 1967 after a dispute in producing solid state amplifiers. Don Randall left in 1969, disenchanted with corporate life. George Fullerton, one of the people involved with the Stratocaster design, left in 1970. Obviously, the quality in Fender products did not drop the day Leo Fender sold the company. Dale Hyatt, another veteran of the early Fender days, figured that the quality on the products stayed relatively stable until around 1968 (Hyatt left in 1972). But a number of cost-cutting strategies, and attempts to produce more products had a deteriorating effect. This reputation leads right to the classic phrase heard at vintage guitar shows, "Is the amp pre-CBS?"

In the early 1980s, the Fender guitar empire began to crumble. Many cost-cutting factors and management problems forced CBS to try various last ditch efforts to salvage the instrument line. In March of 1982, Fender (with CBS' blessing) negotiated with Kanda Shokai and Yamano Music to establish Fender Japan. After discussions with Tokai (who built a great Fender Strat replica, among other nice guitars), Kawai, and others, Fender finally chose Fuji Gen Gakki (based in Matsumoto, about 130 miles northwest of Tokyo). In 1983, the Squier series was built in Japan, earmarked for European distribution. The Squier trademark came from a string-making company in Michigan (V.C. Squier) that CBS had acquired in 1965.

In 1984 ,CBS decided to sell Fender. Offers came in from IMC (Hondo, Charvel/Jackson) and the Kaman Music Corporation (Ovation). Finally, CBS sold Fender to an investment group led by William Schultz in March for twelve and a half million dollars. This investment group formally became the Fender Musical Instruments Corporation (FMIC). As the sale did not include production facilities, USA guitar production ceased for most of 1985. It has been estimated that 80% of the guitars sold between late 1984 and mid 1986 were made in Japan. Soon after, a new factory was built in Corona, California, and USA production was restored in 1986 and continues to this day.

In 1990, the Fender (FMIC) company built an assembly facility in Mexico to offset rising costs of oriental production due to the weakening of the American dollar in the international market. Fender also experimented with production based in India from 1989 to 1990. The Fender (FMIC) company currently manufactures instruments in China, Japan, Korea, Mexico, and the U.S.

As reported in the March 1998 edition of MMR, Fender CEO Schultz sent out a letter to Fender dealers (dated January 9, 1998) which discussed the company establishing a "limited number" of Fender mail-order catalog dealers. Fender has announced specific guidelines as to what is allowed in mail-order catalog sales. Most importantly, Fender "announced a minimum advertised price (MAP) policy applicable to mail-order catalogs only," stated Schultz, "The MAP for mail-order catalogs is set at a maximum 30 percent off the Fender suggested retail price, and will be enforced unilaterally by Fender". What this does to the Fender retail price overall is basically lower the bar - but the impact on regular guitar stores has not been fully realized. While it's one thing to buy because of a discounted price through a catalog, it's a different situation to walk into a dealer's shop and be able to "test drive" a guitar before it is purchased. Retail music stores have to be aware that there is now an outside source (not under their control) that dictates minimum sales prices - the national catalogs. Of course, retail shops still control the maximum sale price applied to an instrument. Readers familiar to the *Blue Book of Amplifiers* will note both the Manufacturer's suggested retail price and the appropriate discounted price (100% listing) under currently produced models.

In 1999, Fender changed a significant number of Model Numbers (SKU's). An attempt has been made to update as many of these as possible, but you may encounter a few that have not been changed. We will continue to monitor these changes and stay up-to-date.

In August of 2002, Fender expanded its power once again by buying the Gretsch company. This buy-out goes into effect January 1, 2003. Now Fender has Guild, Benedetto, DeArmond, Squier, Sunn and the newly acquired Gretsch.

(Source for earlier Fender history: Richard R. Smith, Fender: The Sound Heard 'Round the World)

DATING FENDER AMPLIFIERS

When trying to determine the date of an amplifiers production, it is useful to know a few things about feature changes that have occurred over the years. The following information may help you to determine the approximate date of manufacture of a Fender amplifier by visual observation, without having to handle (or disassemble) the instrument for serial number verification. Check a number of these procedures together to try to get the right year. Sometimes parts weren't used for a time and the amps are actually newer than the dates on certain procedures may indicate.

1946-1948: Solid-wood, uncovered cabinets.

1946-1953: TV-front model which looked like that of a loudspeaker.

1953-1958: Tweed amplifier with the controls on top.

1958-current: The Normal combo shape that was introduced in the 1960's and is used to this day.

In 1957, Fender introduced the use of treble, bass, middle, and presence controls.

Around 1960, Tolex amps were introduced on some models and by 1964 no Tolex models were being produced.

Around 1963, Blackface was introduced on most models, which has a black control panel, black tolex covering, and a silver grille.

Around 1968, Silverface was introduced on most models, which featured silver control panels, black tolex covering, and a silver with blue sparkle grille.

1981: Blackface was introduced for a brief period again, and by 1982, a whole new line of amplifiers was introduced.

Date Codes on Speakers

Date codes were stamped on almost all speakers in early Fender amplifiers. The date stamped on the speaker was a clue to when the amp was manufactured. Fender used mostly Jensen speakers in their amps until the early 60's. At this time when production increased greatly, other speakers had to be used. They started to use Oxford and JBL speakers along with Jensen's. Most of Fender's speakers were made by Jensen, Oxford, or JBL, until the CBS takeover in 1965.

The number stamped on the speaker is a code for the company who made the speaker and the date of manufacture. Jensen used the number 220 and Oxford used the number 465. These were the first three numbers in the date code. The second set of numbers, usually followed by a hypen, indicated the date the speaker was manufactured. The fourth digit in the code stands for the year, while the fifth and sixth digit stand for the week in the year it was made.

Examples of this: 465-831 is an Oxford speaker made in the 31st week of 1958. 220-424 is a Jensen speaker that was made in the 24th week of 1954 (or 1964). There are instances like this when the number could overlap and stand for two different decades. The best way to tell which one is real is by the common knowledge of the amp. If it's a Deluxe Reverb Balckface, we know it was only made between 1963 and 1968. Another way is to look at the label on the speaker. The old Jensen label was changed in the late 1950's. It takes experience and a knowledge of the product to be able to get the hang of it.

On Blackface Fender amps with gold label Jensen speakers, they should say Fender on the speaker. If the Jensen label doesn't have Fender on it, it is likely that the speaker has been replaced.

Here are some examples of Blackface era speakers. The gold ones with Fender on the back appear to be authentic. The other gold label Jensen's are suspicious of being not original. The number on the speaker is the date code.

Date Codes on Tube Charts

On Fender Amplifiers made after 1953, there is a date code stamped onto their tube charts. These charts are found on the inside cabinet of combo models, and on the amp head of piggy-back models. This date code is rubber stamped in ink, and consists of two, small letters. The first letter stands for the year, and the second letter indicates the month of manufacture. The procedure can be found by this chart:

A	1951	JANUARY
B	1952	FEBURARY
C	1953	MARCH
D	1954	APRIL
E	1955	MAY
F	1956	JUNE
G	1957	JULY
H	1958	AUGUST
I	1959	SEPTEMBER
J	1960	OCTOBER
K	1961	NOVEMBER
L	1962	DECEMBER
M	1963	
N	1964	
O	1965	
P	1966	
Q	1967	

This code starts on January 1951, even though it was not introduced until 1953.

GRADING	100%	EXCELLENT	AVERAGE

Here are some examples of what Fender tube charts look like. The Super Reverb has a date code of QH, which means it was produced August of 1967. The other two tube charts are from later models (Silverface's). After Silverface amps were introduced, they stopped putting production codes on them.

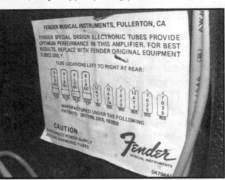

Date Codes on Potentiometers

On every American made potentiometer (pots), there is a date and manufacture code. This code consists of six or seven digits. The first three indicate the manufacture and the last three or four indicate the date it was made. If there are six digits the fourth digit indicates the last number of the year, and the fifth and sixth digit indicate the week of that year. If there are seven digits, the fourth and fifth indicate the last two digits of the year it was made, and the sixth and seventh indicate the week of that year. Usually the numbers were separated by a hyphen after the third digit.

The most common pots manufactures and their numbers are as following: CTS (137), Stackpole (304), Clarostat (140), Cetralab (134), Bourns (381), and Allen Bradley (106). Examples of how this system works are: pot# 140-6421= a Calrostat pot made in the 21st week of 1964, 137-711= a CTS pot made in the 11th week of 1947 or 1957. When there are possibilities of two different years, refer to the amplifier and see what years it was manufactured.

There are several instances to make sure that this system is accurate. The pots must be original; if they have been replaced, they are not going to be an accurate way to determine the date of the amplifier. The pots show that the amp was not made before the date on the pot, but could be made much later than that date.

ELECTRIC TUBE AMPS

Fender amplifiers are what started Leo's business. The first amplifier was a simple tube amp with a small speaker. To this date, there are literally hundreds of different amplifiers, including many tube amps. Throughout the years there have been many variations in the different series of Fender amps. Most amp gurus know what a Blackface is from a Silverface and so on. For eveyone else, here's a brief overview. The first Fender amps (excluding oddballs) were the wood cabinets, dubbed "woodies," which had a metal bar over the grille. Later on in the late 1940's and early 1950's, the covering was changed to a vinyl and the look of the amps were known as TV front, since they looked like a TV set of that era. Around 1952-3 Tweed amplifiers were introduced, first as wide panels. This meant the top and bottom panels on the amplifiers were wider (than a narrow model in the late 1950's). The late 50's had the look of the narrow panel. Wide panel and narrow panel can be compared and a difference noticed. Tolex is a covering that was introduced around 1959 on some amps and by 1961 was standard on almost all Fenders. A tolex amp featured some of the most extreme changes that Fender has ever done. Amps were now in a tolex covering, had a front mounted control panel, and looked completely different than any Fender amp before. Brownface was the first tolex amp. This meant that the control panel (face) was a brown in color and the actual covering was either a white, cream, or brown. 1964 brought the most popular amps for Fender, the Blackface look. The control panel was then black with black tolex covering, and a silver grille. These were only made for about five years and are the most desirable among collectors. In or around 1968 Silverface was phased in (right after CBS took over, what a coincidence), and this lasted up until 1980. Features on these models had a silver control panel on black tolex and a silver/blue grille. These amps were practically the same as Blackface in schematics, but not nearly as desireable to collectors (In fact we had a tough time finding someone with a Silverface collection!). During the limbo years of the 80's, Blackface was introduced again to try to revive Fender, but to little or no avail. After many other experiments, the 90's brought Blackface in with vigor. Now all Fender amplifiers are Blackface once again. Even you know what a Silverface is from a Blackface now!

American Tube Series

HOT ROD AMPLIFIERS - These are amplifiers that were previously covered in tweed, but in 2000 were switched to Black Toles covering. There are three models in the series and they include the Hot Rod DeVille 410, Hot Rod DeVille 212, and the Hot Rod Deluxe. These amps feature three selectable channels, normal, drive and more drive. Tubes include: 2 X 6L6 Groove Tube output tubes, 3 X AX7 preamp tubes. They all have a top silver control panel, two inputs, bright switch, eignt black pointing knobs (v, drive, t, b, m, master, reverb, p), preamp out and power amp in, power and standby switches, two button footswitch, narrow panel vintage cabinet, black tolex covering, silver grille, mfg. 2000-current.

* ***Hot Rod DeVille 410 (No. 021-3201-000)*** - 60W into 4 or 8 Ohms, 4-10" Eminence speakers.

MSR	$1,099.99	$750	$450 - 550	$375 - 425

* ***Hot Rod DeVille 212 (No. 021-3200-000)*** - 60W into 2 or 4 Ohms, 2-12" Eminence speakers.

MSR	$1049.99	$700	$425 - 525	$350 - 400

* ***Hot Rod Deluxe (No. 021-3202-000)*** - 40W, 1-12" Eminence speaker.

MSR	$799.99	$550	$375 - 425	$300 - 350

BLUES JUNIOR (No. 021-3205-000) - 15W, 1-12" Eminence speaker, tubes: 2 X EL-84 Groove Tube output tubes, 3 X AX7 preamp tubes, reverb, top silver control panel, one input, FAT switch, six black pointer knobs (r, MV, m, b, t, v,), one button footswitch, narrow panel vintage cabinet, black tolex covering, silver grille, mfg. 2000-current.

MSR	$550	$349	$275 - 325	$225 - 250

Add $19 for cover.

GRADING	100%	EXCELLENT	AVERAGE

PRO JUNIOR (No. 021-3203-000) - 15W, 1-10" Eminence speaker, tubes: 2 X 12AX7, 2 X EL84 Groove Tube output tubes, single channel, top chrome control panel, one input, two pointer knobs (volume, tone), narrow panel vintage cabinet, black textured vinyl with silver grille cloth, mfg. 1994-current.

MSR	$420	$299	$200 - 250	$165 - 195

Add $19 for cover.

Sometime in the late nineties, the preamp tubes were changed to 3 X 12AX7.

Bandmaster Series

BANDMASTER (TV Front) - 15W, 1-15" Jensen, tubes: 2 X 6SJ7,6SN7 or 6SL7, 2 X 6L6, top control panel, two pointer knobs (v, & tone), early tweed covering, cloth grille, mft. 1952 only.

N/A	$2,500 - 3,000	$2,000 - 2,400

It would be almost identical to the Bassman of the same time.

This model is extremely rare, and there are doubts that it actually exists.

BANDMASTER (Wide Panel) - 15W, 1-15" Jensen's, tubes: 2 X 6SJ7, 6SN7, or 6SL7, 2 X 6L6, top control panel, two pointer knobs, (v, & tone), diagonal tweed covering, cloth grille, mfg 1952-54.

N/A	$2,900 - 3,500	$2,400 - 2,800

BANDMASTER (Narrow Panel) - 15W, 3-10" Jensen's, tubes 12AY7, 12AX7, 2 X 6L6G, 5U4G rectifier, top control panel, five pointer knobs, (Mic, v, Inst, v, t, b, p), diagonal tweed covering, brown tweed-era grille, mfg. 1954-1960.

Fender Bandmaster (Narrow Panel)
courtesy Dave Rogers

Fender Bandmaster (Narrow Panel)
courtesy Dave Rogers

N/A	$3,500 - 4,500	$2,500 - 3,200

BANDMASTER (Tolex) - 30W, 3-10" Jensen's, vibrato, tubes: 5 X 7025, 2 X 6L6GC, silicon rectifier, brownface control panel, nine brown knobs (Norm, b, t, v, Vibr. b, t, v, s, i, Both, p), brown tolex covering, brown tweed-era grille, mfg. 1960-61.

N/A	$3,200 - 4,000	$2,500 - 3,000

The 1960 version has controls in reverse order. This model has virtually the identical chassis to the Concert, Pro, and Vibrasonic.

BANDMASTER (Piggy-back) - 40W, 1-12" speaker, vibrato, tubes: 4 X 7025, 2 X 12AX7, 2 X 5881, silicon rectifiers, brownface control panel, nine brown knobs, (Norm, v, b, t, Vibrato, v, b, t, s, i, Both p), cream tolex covering, maroon grille, mfg. 1961-67.

Fender Bandmaster (Piggy-back)
courtesy Dave's Guitar Shop

Fender Bandmaster (Piggy-back)
courtesy Dave's Guitar Shop

1961-64 BROWN	N/A	$1,200 - 1,500	$900 - 1,100
1965-67 BLACK	N/A	$700 - 900	$525 - 650

In late 1962, the 2 X 12" cabinet was introduced. In 1965, blackface was introduced with black tolex covering, a silver grille, and a black control panel.

GRADING	100%	EXCELLENT	AVERAGE

BANDMASTER (Silverface) - 40W, 2-12" speakers, vibrato, tubes: 2 X 7025, 12AX7, 12AT7, 2 X 6l6GC, silicon rectifiers, Silverface control panel, eight silver top knobs, (Norm, v, b, t, Vibrato, v, b, t, s, i), black tolex covering, silver grille, mfg. 1968-1974.

Fender Bandmaster
courtesy Savage Audio

Fender Bandmaster
courtesy Savage Audio

N/A	$500 - 650	$400 - 475

Output was increased to 45W in 1970. The picture doesn't include the speaker cabinet.

* Bandmaster Reverb - Similar to Silverface Bandmaster, except, 45W, tubes: 3 X 7025, 2 X 12AT7, 12AX7, 2 X 6L6GC, rectifier 5U4GB, and nine silver knobs (added a bs), mfg. 1970-1981.

Fender Bandmaster Reverb
courtesy George McGuire

Fender Bandmaster Reverb
courtesy George McGuire

N/A	$550 - 700	$425 - 525

In 1976, underlining in name plate is removed, and a master volume switch with distortion switch is added. Speakers are mounted diagonally as well. In 1981, output is raised to 70W.

Bassman Series

BASSMAN (T.V. Front) - 26 watts, 1-15" Jensen, tubes: 2 X 6SJ7, 6SL7, 2 X 6L6, top control panel, two pointer knobs (v, & tone), closed back with circle ports, chassis is on the bottom of the cabinet, early tweed covering, cloth grill. Mfg. 1951-52.

N/A	$2,500 - 3,000	$1,900 - 2,400

* Bassman (Wide panel) - Similar to the Bassman TV front except has a wide panel cabinet with diagonal tweed covering, mfg. 1952-54.

N/A	$2,500 - 3,200	$2,000 - 2,400

In 1956, mid-range, four jacks, and two volumes were added. Power tubes changed to 2 X 5881 and the rectifier changed to GZ34.

BASSMAN (Narrow panel) - 50W, 4-10" Jensen P-10R's, tubes: 12AY7, 2 X 12AX7, 2 X 6L6G, 2 X 5U4G, top control panel, four pointer knobs (v, b, t, p), diagonal tweed covering, brown tweed-era grille, mfg. 1954-1961.

Fender Bassman SF6-A
courtesy solidbodyguitar.com, Inc.

Fender Bassman SF6-A
courtesy solidbodyguitar.com, Inc.

N/A	$3,200 - 4,200	$2,500 - 3,000

A mint Bassman amp (this means perfect) can bring as much as $6,000. This is one of the most desirable amps that Fender has ever produced, which is why there is a reissue model.

GRADING	100%	EXCELLENT	AVERAGE

BASSMAN (Piggyback) - 50W, 1-12" Jensen, tubes: 4 X 7025, 2 X 5881, GZ34 rectifier, two channels, brownface control panel, seven brown knobs (Ch. 1: v, t, b; Ch 2: v, t, b, Both: p), cream tolex covering, maroon grille, mfg. 1961-64.

	N/A	$1,250 - 1,600	$975 - 1,200

In 1962, the 2 X 12" cabinet is introduced. Tubes in later models may be different. They may inlcude 3 X 7025, 12AT7, and 2 X 6L6GC. Silicon rectifiers were also used. In 1964, the presence switch is removed and a bright switch is added.

BASSMAN (Blackface) - 50W, 2-12" Jensen's, tremelo, tubes: 3 X 7025, 12AT7, 6L6GC, GZ34 rectifier, two channels, blackface control panel, dual inputs, six silver knobs (Ch. 1: v, t, b; Ch. 2: v, t, b), black tolex covering, silver grille, mfg. 1964-68.

Fender Bassman (Blackface)
courtesy Dave Rogers

	N/A	$700 - 900	$525 - 650

* Bassman (Silverface) - Similar to the Blackface Bassman, except has silverface control panel, mfg. 1968-1979.

	N/A	$500 - 650	$400 - 475

In 1970, the 2 X 15" was introduced. The Silverface was renamed the Bassman 50 in 1972.

SUPER BASSMAN (SUPER BASSMAN II) - 100W, 2-15" speakers, tubes: 2 X 7025, 12AT7, 4 X 6LGC, silicon rectifiers, two channels, bass and normal, silverface control panel, four inputs (two bass and two normal), seven silver-top knobs (Bass: v, t, b, Norm: v, t, m, b) deep and bright switches for both channels, black tolex covering, silver grille, mfg. 1969-1971.

	N/A	$550 - 675	$450 - 525

Add $250-350 for the Super Bassman's second cabinet.

The Super Bassman I came with one cabinet, the Super Bassman II came with two cabinets. This was the first big bass amp, and was later renamed the Bassman 100.

BASSMAN 10 - 50W, 4-10" Jensen's, tubes: 2 X 7025, 12AT7, 2 X 6L6GC, silicon rectifiers, two channels, silver control panel, four inputs, eight silver-top numbered knobs (Ch. 1: v, t, b; Ch. 2: v, t, b, b, both m),bs, ds, black tolex covering, silver grille, mfg. 1972-1982

	N/A	$375 - 450	$325 - 365

In 1981, the blackface control panel became standard, and the output was increased to 70W.

BASSMAN 20 - 20W, 1-15" Jensen, tubes: 2 X 7025, 2 X 6V6GTA, blackface control panel, single input, one channel, four silver-top numbered knobs (v, t, b, m), black tolex covering, silver grille, mfg. 1982-1983.

	N/A	$275 - 325	$210 - 250

BASSMAN 50 - 50W, 2-15" speakers, tubes: 2 X 7025, 12AT7, 2 X 6L6GC, silicon rectifier, silverface control panel, six silver-top numbered knobs (Bass, v, t, b, Norm, v, t, b), bs, ds, black tolex covering, silver grille, mfg. 1972-76.

Fender Bassman 50
courtesy Savage Audio

Fender Bassman 50
courtesy Savage Audio

	N/A	$400 - 475	$325 - 375

Master volume was introduced in 1974 and included a Master Volume control.

GRADING	100%	EXCELLENT	AVERAGE

BASSMAN 70 - 70W, 4-10" speakers in a cabinet, tubes: 3 X 7025, 12AT7, 2 X 6L6GC, two channels, silicon rectifier, silverface control panel, seven silver-top numbered knobs (Bass: v, t, b, Norm: v, t, b MV), bs, ds, black tolex covering, silver grille, mfg. 1977-79.

	N/A	$425 - 500	$350 - 400

BASSMAN 100 - 100W, 4-12" speakers in a cabinet, tubes: 2 X 7025, 12AT7, 2 X 6L6, silverface control panel, eight silver-top numbered knobs (Bass: v, t, b, Norm: v, t, b, m, MV), black tolex covering, silver grille, mfg. 1972-79.

	N/A	$450 - 525	$375 - 425

BASSMAN 135 - 135W, 4-10" speakers in a cabinet, tubes: 2 X 7025, 12AT7, 4 X 6L6, silverface control panel, nine silver-top numbered knobs (Bass: v, t, m, b, Norm: v, b, m, MV), bs, black tolex covering, silver grille, mfg. 1979-1983.

	N/A	$425 - 500	$350 - 400

BASSMAN 300 (No. 021-3302-010) - 300W, head-unit only, all tube chassis, preamp: 12AX7's, power: 6 X 6550, dual channels, compression, front black control panel, single input, eleven black knobs, 10-band graphic equalizer, black covering, black metal grille, new 2002.

MSR	$1,699	$1,200	$900 - 1,050	$700 - 800

Blues Series

BLUES DEVILLE - 60w, 4-10" speakers, tubes: 3 X 12AX7, 2 X 6L6, top control panel, seven pointer knobs (v1, v2, b, m, t, p, r), diagonal tweed covering, brown tweed-era grille, mfg. 1993-late 1990's.

Fender Blues Deville
courtesy George Maquire

	N/A	$450 - 550	$375 - 425

In 1994, the 2-12" cabinet was introduced.

* **Blues Deluxe** - Similar to Blues Deville, except has 40W output, and one 12" speaker, mfg. 1993-late 1990's.

	N/A	$325 - 375	$250 - 300

Bronco Series

BRONCO - 5W, 1-8" speaker, tubes: 2 X 12AX7A, 6V6GTA, vibrato, silverface control panel, two inputs, five pointer knobs (v, b, t, s, i), black tolex covering, silver grille, mfg. 1968-1974.

	N/A	$225 - 275	$175 - 210

Last MSR was $94.50

Output was raised to 6W in 1972.

The Bronco matches the schematics and manuals of the Vibro-Champ. These are basically the same amplifiers with a different name on them. The Bronco has red lettering while the Vibro-Champ has blue lettering.

* **Bronco (Solid State)** - Refer to the Solid-State listing in the Fender section.

Champ Series

CHAMPION 800 (TV Front) - 4W, 1-8" Jensen, tubes: 6SJ7 preamp, 6V6 power, 5Y3 rectifier, gray-green Hammerloid finish with white marking, two inputs one volume pointer knob, gray-green linen, gray grille, mfg. 1948-1949.

	N/A	$500 - 600	$425 - 475

This is the rare version that came before the Champion 600. It is estimated that only 100 of these amps were made.

GRADING	100%	EXCELLENT	AVERAGE

CHAMPION 600 (TV Front) - Similar to Champion 800, except has 1-6" Jensen, has two-tone brown and white textured vinyl covering, and a brown clothe grille, mfg. 1949-1953.

Fender Champion 600 (TV Front)
courtesy Dave Rogers

Fender Champion 600 (TV Front)
courtesy Dave Rogers

N/A	$500 - 700	$400 - 450

This model was also known as the Student or the Student 600.

CHAMP (STUDENT, Wide Panel) - Similar to Champion 600, except has diagonal tweed covering, and a brown clothe grille, mfg. 1953-54.

Fender Champ (Student) (Wide Panel)
courtesy Dave Rogers

Fender Champ (Student) (Wide Panel)
courtesy Dave Rogers

N/A	$500 - 650	$400 - 450

This model was called the student in the catalog, and was renamed due to other claimants to that name. Earlier versions of this model had the "600" logo on the control plate, later ones had "Champ Amp" on the plate.

CHAMP (Narrow Panel) - 4W, 1-6" Jensen, tubes, tubes: 12AX7, 6V6GT, 5Y3GT, top control panel, two inputs, one volume pointer knob, tweed covering, brown tweed-era grille, mfg. 1954-1964.

1955 Fender Champ (Narrow Panel)
courtesy Dave Rogers

1955 Fender Champ (Narrow Panel)
courtesy Dave Rogers

1964 Fender Champ (Narrow Panel)
courtesy Dave Rogers

N/A	$700 - 800	$450 - 525

Some later models came with black tolex covering, and a silver sparkle grille (early 1960's). A choke was added to the high-voltage filter section and the use of negative feedback was used,

GRADING	100%	EXCELLENT	AVERAGE

CHAMP (Tolex) - 4W, 1-8" speaker, tubes: 12AX7, 6V6GT, 5YTGT, blackface control panel, two input jacks, three silver-top knobs (v, t, b), black tolex covering, silver grille, mfg. 1964-1979.

Fender Champ (Tolex) courtesy Savage Audio	Fender Champ courtesy solidbodyguitar.com, Inc.	Fender Champ courtesy solidbodyguitar.com, Inc.

1964-67	N/A	**$300 - 400**	**$200 - 250**
1968-1979	N/A	**$180 - 225**	**$130 - 160**

Output increased to 5W in 1965, Silverface introduced in 1968, Output increased to 6W in 1972.

VIBRO CHAMP- 4W, 1-8" speaker, tubes: 2 X 12AX7, 6V6GT, 5Y3GT, vibrato, blackface/silverface control panel, two input jacks, five silver-top knobs (v, t, b, s, i), black tolex covering, silver grille, mfg. 1964-1982.

Fender Vibro Champ courtesy solidbodyguitar.com, Inc.	Fender Vibro Champ courtesy solidbodyguitar.com, Inc.

1964-67	N/A	**$350 - 500**	**$250 - 300**
1968-1979	N/A	**$240 - 275**	**$195 - 225**

Output increased to 5W in 1965, Silverface introduced in 1969, Output increased to 6W in 1972.

CHAMP II- 18W, 1-10" speaker, tubes: 2 X 7025, 2 X 6V6GTA, silicon rectifiers, bs, new blackface control panel, four silver-top knobs (v, t, b, mv), black tolex covering, silver grille, mfg. 1982-85.

N/A	**$250 - 275**	**$195 - 230**

This model was a cheaper version of the Super Champ and featured completely new circuitary.

GRADING	100%	EXCELLENT	AVERAGE

CHAMP 12 -12W, 1-12" Eminence, tubes: 2 X 12AX6, 6L6, blackface control panel, two inputs, tape inputs, line output, headphone jack, six red knobs (t, b, v, overdrive gain, v, r), black tolex covering, black grille, mfg. 1986-1992.

Fender Champ 12
courtesy Savage Audio

Fender Champ 12
courtesy Savage Audio

| N/A | $250 - 300 | $200 - 235 |

This model came with five custom coverings, including red, white, gray, and snakeskin besides the standard black.

SUPER CHAMP - 18W, 1-10" speaker, tubes: 2 X 7025, 2 X 6V6GTA, silicon rectifiers, reverb, hot rod lead channel, new blackface control panel, one input jack, six silver-top knobs (v, t, b, r, lead level, MV), black tolex covering, silver grille, mfg. 1982-85.

| N/A | $450 - 600 | $375 - 425 |

This amp uses reverb and switching lead sound using the reverb drive as an extra pre-amp.

*** Super Champ Deluxe** - Similar to the Super Champ except, has an Electro-voice speaker, solid oak cabinet, brown cloth grille, brown knobs, brown control panel, padded cover included, mfg. 1982-85.

| N/A | $800 - 1,000 | $400 - 550 |

CHAMP 25 S/E & CHAMP 25 - SEE HYBRID AMP SECTION.

Concert Series

CONCERT - 40W, 4-10" Jensen's, tubes: 5 X 7025, 2 X 6L6GC, vibrato, brownface control panel, four inputs, two normal, two vibrato, nine brown knobs (norm, v, t, b, vibrato, v, t, b, s, i, both p), brown tolex covering, light brown grille, mfg. 1959-1963.

Fender Concert (Brownface)
courtesy Dave Rogers

Fender Concert (Brownface)
courtesy Dave Rogers

| N/A | $1,200 - 1,500 | $900 - 1,100 |

The earliest Concerts had a center volume control, which was a transition period. In 1961, the light brown grille was changed to maroon, which was then changed to a richer shade of brown. In 1962, one 7025 tube is replaced with two 12AX7's, and the 6L6GC tube is replaced by a 5881, the grille changed to a wheat-colored cloth.

GRADING	100%	EXCELLENT	AVERAGE

* Concert (Blackface) - Similar to the Concert except the tremolo circuit is changed to 12AX7, 7025, 12AT7, 2 X 6L6GC, the presence control is taken off and replaced with a bright switch and the control panel changed to blackface with black and silver knobs, black tolex covering and a silver grille, mfg. 1963-65.

Fender Concert (Blackface)
courtesy Dave Rogers

Fender Concert (Blackface)
courtesy Dave Rogers

	N/A	$800 - 950	$600 - 750

CONCERT II (112) - 60W, 1-12" speaker, tubes: 5 X 7025, 2 X 12AT7, 2 X 6L6GC, two channels, new blackface control panel, two inputs, eleven silver-top knobs (Ch.1, v, t, m, b, Ch.2, v, gain, master, t, m, b, r, p), channel switching, effects loop, black tolex covering, silver grille, mfg. 1982-85.

	N/A	$350 - 425	$275 - 325

This model was available as a combo or with a separate head.

* Concert II (210) - Similar to the Concert II 112, except has 2-10" speakers.

	N/A	$375 - 450	$300 - 350

* Concert II (410) - Similar to Concert II 112, except has 4-10" speakers.

	N/A	$400 - 475	$325 - 375

CONCERT (POST CBS) - 60W, 1-12" speaker, tubes: 2 X 12AT7, 4 X 12AX7, 2 X 6L6, two-selectable channels, new blackface control panel, two inputs, 12 silver-top knobs (Ch.1, v, t, m, b, Ch.2, gain 1, gain 2, v, t, b, m, Both, mix, r), effects loop, line out jack, foot switch, black tolex covering, silver grille, mfg. 1993-mid 1990's.

	N/A	$375 - 425	$325 - 360

This model was derived from the Super 60 in the late eighties.

Deluxe Series

DELUXE (MODEL 26) - 10W, 1-10" Jensen, tubes: 6SC7, 6N7, 2 X 6F6, 5Y3, top black control panel with white lettering, three pointer knobs (instrument volume, mic. volume, and tone), polished wood cabinet, colored felt with vertical chrome strips, mfg. 1946-48.

Fender Model 26 Deluxe
courtesy solidbodyguitar.com, Inc.

Fender Model 26 Deluxe
courtesy solidbodyguitar.com, Inc.

	N/A	$900 - 1,200	$700 - 850

Also known as the "woodie." Some of these models had two strips instead of the more common three on the front. This model was sometimes called the Model 26. This name appears on the control panel of the Deluxe and Professional amps.

GRADING	100%	EXCELLENT	AVERAGE

DELUXE (TV FRONT) - 10W, 1-12" Jensen, tubes: 6SC7/6N7, 2 X 6V6, 5Y3, top control panel, three pointer knobs (instrument volumen, mic. volume, and tone), early tweed covering, dark brown cloth grille, mfg. 1948-1953.

Fender Deluxe (TV Front)
courtesy Dave Rogers

Fender Deluxe (TV Front)
courtesy Dave Rogers

| N/A | $1,150 - 1,500 | $950 - 1,100 |

Some of these models have a deep back panel. In 1949, the vertical tweed and dark brown grille was replaced with diagonal tweed and brown linen cloth.

DELUXE (WIDE FRONT) - 10W, 1-12" Jensen, tubes: 2 X 6SC7, 2 X 6V6, 5Y3, top control panel, a separate on/off switch, extra speaker jack, negative feedback loop, three pointer knobs (instrument volume, mic. volume, and tone), diagonal tweed covering, dark brown grille cloth, mfg. 1953-55.

Fender Deluxe (Wide Panel)
courtesy Dave Rogers

Fender Deluxe (Wide Panel)
courtesy Dave Rogers

| N/A | $1,200 - 1,600 | $975 - 1,150 |

Model numbers 5B3 and 5C3 are virtually identical. In 1954 some of the 5D3 models use minature 12AX7 and 12AY7 preamp tubes, and the negative feedback loop was removed. This was the end of metal tubes that were replaced by glass tubes.

DELUXE (NARROW PANEL) - 15W, 1-12" Jensen, tubes: 12AX7, 12AY7, 2 X 6V6, 5Y3, top control panel, four inputs, three pointer knobs (instrument volume, mic. volume, tone), ground switch, diagonal tweed covering, brown tweed-era grille, mfg. 1955-1960.

Fender Deluxe (Narrow Panel)
courtesy Dave Rogers

Fender Deluxe (Narrow Panel)
courtesy Dave Rogers

| N/A | $1,800 - 2,400 | $1,000 - 1,500 |

When the model was changed to 5F3 from 5E3 the half of the 12AX7 tube was being used, leaving the other half as another preamp stage. This means the other half could be used to create higher gain. It is known for Deluxe models to distort at low volumes.

GRADING	100%	EXCELLENT	AVERAGE

DELUXE (BROWNFACE)- 15W, 1-12" Jensen, tubes: 7025, 2 X 12AX7, 2 X 6V6, GZ34, front brown control panel, four inputs (two normal, two bright), six brown knobs (Norm: v, t, Bright: v, t, both, s, i), external speaker jack, brown tolex covering, light brown grille, mfg. 1961-63.

Fender Deluxe (Brownface)
courtesy Dave Rogers

Fender Deluxe (Brownface)
courtesy Dave Rogers

| N/A | $850 - 1,025 | $675 - 750 |

Tremolo operates on both channels.

DELUXE (BLACKFACE) - 20W, 1-12" Jensen, tubes: 2 X 7025, 12AX7, 12AY7, 2 X 6V6, GZ34, , front, blackface control panel, four inputs, two normal, two vibrato, eight silver-top knobs (norm, v, b, t, vibrato, v, b, t, s, i), black tolex covering, silver grilee, mfg. 1963-66.

Fender Deluxe
courtesy Savage Audio

Fender Deluxe
courtesy Savage Audio

| N/A | $600 - 800 | $500 - 575 |

Models AA763 and AB763 are almost identical. In 1966, some amps get the underlined Fender nameplates on the grilles. Tremolo operates on bright channel only.

DELUXE REVERB - 20W, 1-12" speaker, tubes: 3 X 7025, 2 X 12AT7, 12AX7, 2 X 6V6, GZ34, tremelo on only one channel, front blackface control panel, four inputs, (two normal, two vibrato), nine silver-top knobs (norm, v, b, t, vibrato, v, b, t, r, s, i), black tolex covering, silver grille, mfg. 1963-68.

Fender Deluxe Reverb (Blackface)
courtesy Dave Rogers

Fender Deluxe Reverb (Blackface)
courtesy Dave Rogers

| N/A | $1,350 - 1,650 | $950 - 1,250 |

This amp was introduced at the same time as the regular Deluxe but lasted longer. In 1966, the Fender nameplate was put on the front.

GRADING	100%	EXCELLENT	AVERAGE

Deluxe Reverb Silverface - Similar to the blackface version of the Deluxe Reverb, except the GZ34 rectifier was removed, has a sliverfaee control panel, and a 1200 pF capacitor is on the grids of each of the power tubes, which cures instability that was on earlier models, mfg. 1968-1979.

Fender Deluxe Reverb (Silverface)
courtesy George Maquire

Fender Deluxe Reverb (Silverface)
courtesy George Maquire

N/A	$800 - 1,000	$600 - 750

DELUXE REVERB II - 20W, 1-12" speaker, tubes: 5 X 7025, 12AT7, 2 X 6V6GTA, tremolo, distortion and channel switching, front blackface control panel, two inputs, 11 silver-top control knobs (Ch.1, v, t, b, Ch.2, v, g, MV, t, m, b, r, p), preamp output and power amp input jacks, hum balance control, black tolex covering, silver grille, mfg. 1982-85.

N/A	$425 - 475	$350 - 400

Harvard Series

HARVARD - 10W, 1-10" speaker, tubes: 6AT6, 12AX7, 2 X 6V6, 5Y3 rectifier, top numbered control panel, two pointer knobs (v, t), three inputs, diagonal tweed covering, brown tweed-era grille, mfg. 1955-61.

Fender Harvard (Narrow Panel)
courtesy Dave Rogers

Fender Harvard (Narrow Panel)
courtesy Dave Rogers

Fender Harvard (Narrow Panel)
courtesy Dave Rogers

N/A	$775 - 925	$650 - 750

The Harvard is shown in some catalogs with 8" speakers, and some with 10" speakers, and both were used at different times during the production of the amp. The Harvard was discontinued in 1961 when the Princeton and the Champ were too close in price to justify another amp in between.

Princeton Series

PRINCETON (MODEL 26) - 4.5W, 1-8" Jensen or Utah, tubes: 6SL7, 6V6, 5Y3, no control panel, only two jacks in the back, no on/off switch, polished wood cabinet, colored cloth grille with vertical chrome strips, mfg. 1946-48.

N/A	$850 - 975	$700 - 825

This model never had the name "Princeton" on the amp, this model was named this because it is very close to the Princeton amps to follow. The chassis was quite similar to that of the earlier K&F model.

PRINCETON (TV FRONT) - 4.5W, 1-8" Jensen, tubes: 6SL7, 6V6, 5Y3, top control panel, two input jacks, two pointer knobs (volume and tone, an on and off switch was part of the tone control), fuse holder, new jeweled control pilot light, early tweed covering, brown cloth grille, mfg. 1948-1952.

N/A	$700 - 850	$600 - 675

This model's circuitary is virtually identical to that of the Model 26 Princeton.

GRADING	100%	EXCELLENT	AVERAGE

PRINCETON (WIDE PANEL) - 4.5W, 1-8" Jensen, tubes: 6SL7, 6V6, 5Y3, top control panel, two input jacks, two pointer knobs (volume and tone), diagonal tweed covering, brown cloth grille, mfg. 1952-54.

Fender Princeton (Wide Panel)
courtesy Dave Rogers

Fender Princeton (Wide Panel)
courtesy Dave Rogers

N/A	$700 - 850	$600 - 675

This model also had the same circuitry of earlier Princetons with the exception of the preamp tubes becoming 6SC7 in 1953 and 12AX7 in 1954. It is known that 200 Princetons were taken apart and used for the first Mesa Boogie amps.

* Princeton (Narrow Panel) - Smiliar to the Princeton Wide Panel except the front of the amp had narrow tops and bottoms, and has brown tweed-era grille, mfg. 1954-1961.

Fender Princeton
courtesy solidbodyguitar.com, Inc.

Fender Princeton
courtesy solidbodyguitar.com, Inc.

N/A	$700 - 850	$600 - 675

This model's cabinet was enlarged in 1956, which was also used for the Harvard. The Champ then used the old Princeton box.

PRINCETON (BROWNFACE/BLACKFACE) - 12W, 1-10" Jensen, tubes: 7025, 12AX7, 2 X 6V6, 5Y3, tremolo, front brownface control panel, two input jacks, four brown knobs (v, t, s, i), ground switch on back, completely new design from earlier Princeton, brown tolex covering, light brown grille, mfg. 1961-69.

Fender Princeton (Brownface)
courtesy Dave Rogers

Fender Princeton (Blackface)
courtesy Dave Rogers

1966 Fender Princeton (Blackface)
courtesy Dave Rogers

	100%	EXCELLENT	AVERAGE
BROWNFACE	N/A	$625 - 800	$525 - 600
BLACKFACE	N/A	$450 - 700	$350 - 425

GRADING	100%	EXCELLENT	AVERAGE

In 1963, the covering was changed to Black Tolex, silver grille, blackface control panel with white or black knobs. In 1964, separate bass and treble controls were introduced. Around 1966, the Fender nameplate was put on the grille.

* *Princeton (Silverface)* - Similar to the blackface Princeton except has a silverface control panel, five silver-top knobs (bass and treble were now seperate knobs), everything else identical to the blackface Princeton which didn't change for the 15 years of its life, mfg. 1969-1979.

	N/A	$300 - 375	$225 - 275

PRINCETON REVERB - 12W, 1-10" speaker, tubes: 7025, 2 X 12AX7, 12AT7, 2 X 6V6, 5U4, tremolo, blackface control panel, two inputs, six silver-top knobs (v, t, b, r, s, i), black tolex covering, silver grille, mfg. 1964-1981.

Fender Princeton Reverb (Blackface)
courtesy Dave Rogers

Fender Princeton Reverb (Blackface)
courtesy Dave Rogers

1964-67	N/A	$750 - 1,000	$600 - 725
1967-73	N/A	$600 - 700	$475 - 550
1974-81	N/A	$475 - 550	$400 - 450

In 1966 the Fender underlined nameplate is added on the grille, In 1968, the control panel was changed to silver, blue cloth, and aluminum trim was added. A three position ground switch was added in 1970. The underline on the namplate was dropped in the mid-seventies. A boost-pull knob pot was added shortly around 1978, in 1980, blackface with silver grille again, became an option.

Pro Series

PROFESSIONAL (MODEL 26) - 15W, 1-15" Jensen, tubes: 6SC7/6N7, 2 X 6L6, 5Y3 power tubes, back control panel, three inputs, one mic, two instruments, three pointer knobs (mic v, inst v, tone), polished wood cabinet, red, blue or gold grilles, with vertical chrome strips, mft. 1946-47.

	N/A	$1,000 - 1,400	$750 - 950

This model was also known as the Model 26 which was the same as the Princeton and Deluxe. Some of these models use a field-coil speaker, which has no permanent magnet.

PRO AMP (TV FRONT) - 15W, 1-15" Jensen, tubes: 3 X 6SC7, 2 X 6L6G, 5U4G, top black control panel, four inputs, two instrument, two mic, three pointer knobs (mic v, inst v, tone), early tweed covering, brown cloth grille, formerly known as the Professional, mfg. 1948-1952.

	N/A	$1,200 - 1,500	$950 - 1,100

In 1950, the removoable back paneling, which was originally a solid rectangle, had two holes cut in it, to let heat escape from the tubes.

PRO AMP (WIDE PANEL) - 15W, 1-15" Jensen, tubes: 12AY7, 12AX7, 2 X 6L6G, 5U5G, top control panel, four inputs, two instruments, two mic, three pointer knobs (mic v, inst v, tone), spare speaker jack in back, standby switch, diagonal tweed covering, brown cloth grille, mfg. 1952-1954.

	N/A	$1,300 - 1,600	$1,000 - 1,200

GRADING	100%	EXCELLENT	AVERAGE

PRO AMP (NARROW PANEL) - 26W, 1-15" Jensen, tubes: 2 X 12AY7, 12AX7, 2 X 6L6, 5U5G, top control panel, four inputs, two instrument, two mic, three pointer knobs (mic v, inst v, tone), ground switch added to panel, negative feedback removed, diagonal tweed covering, brown tweed-era grille, mfg. 1954-1960.

Fender Pro Amp
courtesy Savage Audio

Fender Pro Amp
courtesy Savage Audio

N/A	$1,300 - 1,650	$1,000 - 1,250

The circuitry in this model was still linked with earlier models. In 1956, bass, treble, and presence controls were added. In 1957, a new nameplate was introduced.

PRO AMP (BROWNFACE) - 25W, 1-15" Jensen, tubes: 5 X 7025, 2 X 6L6GC, tremolo, brownface control panel, four inputs, two normal and two vibrato, nine brown knobs (Norm, v, t, b, s, i, Vibrato, v, t, b, Both, p), brown tolex covering, light brown grille, mfg. 1960-63.

Fender Pro Amp (Brownface)
courtesy Dave Rogers

Fender Pro Amp (Brownface)
courtesy Dave Rogers

N/A	$950 - 1,300	$750 - 875

In late 1960, the tubes were changed and included 4 X 7025, 2 X 12AX7, 2 X 5881. This amp is almost identical to the Vibrasonic, except for the speaker and that was about $200 cheaper than theVibrasonic.

PRO AMP (BLACKFACE) - 25W, 1-15" speaker, tubes 2 X 7025, 12AX7, 12AT7, 6L6GC, 5U4GB, tremolo, front black control panel, four inputs, two normal, two vibrato, bright switches, eight silver-top knobs (Norm, bs, v, t, b, Vibrato: bs, v, t, b, s, i), AC outlet on back panel, black tolex covering, silver grille, mfg. 1963-65.

Fender Pro Amp
courtesy Savage Audio

Fender Pro Amp
courtesy Savage Audio

N/A	$725 - 850	$575 - 700

This model faded out after the Pro Reverb amp was introduced. The Pro-Amp was on the cover of any Fender owner's manual for amps.

GRADING	100%	EXCELLENT	AVERAGE

PRO REVERB (BLACKFACE) - 40W, 2-12" speakers, tubes: 3 X 7025, 12AX7, 2 X 12AT7, 2 X 6L6GC, GZ34, tremolo, reverb, black control panel, four inputs, two normal, two vibrato, nine silver-top knobs (Norm: bs, v, t, b, Vibrato: bs, v, t, b, r, s, i), tilt back legs, black tolex covering, silver grille, mfg. 1965-67.

Fender Pro Reverb
courtesy solidbodyguitar.com, Inc.

Fender Pro Reverb
courtesy solidbodyguitar.com, Inc.

	N/A	$1,250 - 1,500	$950 - 1,100

* Pro Reverb Silverface - Similar to Pro Reverb blackface except 5U4GB tube changed to GZ34, sliverface plate with blue lettering, and a blue cloth grille, mfg. 1967-1981.

1967-69	N/A	$900 - 1,100	$750 - 850
1970-73	N/A	$725 - 850	$600 - 675
1974-1981	N/A	$600 - 700	$495 - 575

In 1972, the output is increased to 45W by using a different rectifier, and increased voltage in the output stage. In 1976, a master volume knob is added and a pull distortion switch. In 1981, the Pro Reverb went back to the blackface. At this time the output was raised to 70W, the tubes were changed to 4 X 7025, 2 X 12AT7, 2 X 6L6, had twelve black knobs with a middle added to each channel.

PRO REVERB (NEW VINTAGE SERIES) - See Pro-Tube listing in the Fender section.

Pro-Tube Series (New Vintage)

PROSONIC (No. 021-1007-000) - 60W, 2-10" Celestian speakers, all-tube circuitry, three-way rectifier switch, dual selectable channels (normal and drive), all-tube reverb, blackface control panel, two inputs, channel switch, eight black knobs (v, gain 1, gain 2, t, b, m, master, r), effects loop, two button footswitch, black tolex covering, silver grille, mfg. 1996-2001.

	$799	$575 - 675	$495 - 550

Last MSR was $1,599.99.

* Prosonic Head (No. 021-2007-000) - Similar to Pronsonic except head unit only. mfg. 1996-2001.

	$650	$450 - 525	$375 - 425

Last MSR was $1299.99.

The Prosonic/Tone-Master Enclosure was meant to be used with this. Refer to the Custom Shop section for the Tone-Master enclosure.

PRO REVERB (No. 021-5500-000) - 50W (switchable to 12), 1 - 12" Jensen C12N speaker, 2 X 6L6 Groove Tube ouput tubes, 7 X 12AX7 preamp tubes, 12AT7 tube, tremolo, reverb, front black control panel, one input, 13 silver-top knobs (Ch.1, v, t, m, b, Ch.2, gain, t, b, m, v, Both: r, s, i, p), switchable channels, external speaker jack, effects, loop preamp jacks, tilt-back legs, black tolex covering, silver grille, cover included, new 2002.

Fender Pro-Reverb (Pro-Tube Series)
courtesy Fender

Fender Pro-Reverb (Pro-Tube Series)
courtesy Fender

Fender Pro-Reverb (Pro-Tube Series)
courtesy Fender

MSR	$1,500	$1,025	$750 - 850	$625 - 700

GRADING	100%	EXCELLENT	AVERAGE

CONCERT REVERB - 50W (switchable to 12W), 4-10" Special design Fender Eminence speakers, tubes: 12AT7, 7 X 12AX7 preamps, 2 X 6L6 groove tube outputs, tube tremolo, dual selectable channels (normal and drive), blackface control panel, 13 silver-top knobs, (v, t, m, b, etc.), foot switchable FX loop with send and return level controls, four-button footswitch, external speaker jack, tilt-back legs, cover included mfg. 2002-current.

Fender Concert Reverb (Pro-Tube Series)
courtesy Fender

Fender Concert Reverb (Pro-Tube Series)
courtesy Fender

MSR	$1,800	$1,250	$800 - 925	$675 - 750

TWIN AMP (No. 021-5700-000) - 100/25W, 2-12" Eminence speakers, tubes: 4 X 6L6 Groove tube output tubes, 7 X 12AX7 preamp tubes, 12AT7, two channels with overdrive reverb, tremolo, effects loop, blackface control panel, two input jacks, 14 silver-top knobs (Ch.1:v, gain, t, b, m, v, Ch.2: gain, t, b, m, v, Both: mix, r, p), the volume knobs had a push/pull switch for channel switching, four buton footswitch, black tolex covering, silver grille, mfg. 1995-current.

Fender Twin Amp (Pro-Tube Series)
courtesy Fender

Fender Twin Amp (Pro-Tube Series)
courtesy Fender

MSR	$1,700	$1,199	$625 - 750	$525 - 600

In 2002, two input jacks were changed to one input jack.

CUSTOM VIBROLUX REVERB - 40W, 2-10" Jensen P-10R speakers, tubes: 2 X 6L6 Groove Tube output tubes, 5 X 12AX7 preamp tubes, 12AT7 tube, two independent channels (normal and bright), reverb, vibrato, nine cream knobs (Norm: v, t, b, Bright: v, t, b, r, Both: s, i), cream tolex covering, wheat grille, tilt-back legs, two-button footswitch, mfg. 1995-current.

MSR	$1,420	$775	$575 - 650	$500 - 550

In the late 90's, blackface was introduced with a black control panel, silver grille, and black tolex covering.

GRADING	100%	EXCELLENT	AVERAGE

Showman Series

SHOWMAN (Piggy-back) - 85W, 1-12" or 1-15" JBL, tubes: 4 X 7025, 2 X 12AX7, 4 X 5881, tremolo, brownface control panel, four inputs, two normal, two vibrato, nine white or brown knobs (Norm: v, t, b, Vibrato: v, t, b, s, i, Both: p), elaborate porting system, tilt-back legs, cream tolex covering, maroon grille, mfg. 1961-1969.

Fender Showman (Piggy-back)
courtesy Dave Rogers

Fender Showman (Piggy-back)
courtesy Dave Rogers

Fender Dual Showman (Piggy-back)
courtesy Dave Rogers

Brownface (1961-63)	N/A	$1,200 - 1,600	$975 - 1,150
Blackface (1964-67)	N/A	$850 - 1,000	$695 - 800
Silverface (1967-69)	N/A	$650 - 750	$550 - 600

This model was available with a 12" or 15" speaker. Some early models have a 6 X 7025 and 4 X 6L6GC tube configuration. In 1962, the grille is changed to a wheat color. In 1964 blackface is introduced with black control panel, black tolex covering, and silver grille. The bright switch replaces a presence control, tube configuration is changed to 2 X 7025, 12AT7, 12AX7, and 4 X 6L6GC. In 1969, Silverface is introduced with silver control panel, blue cloth grille, and aluminum trim. The Showman is virtually the Twin amplifer in Piggy back version.

* Dual Showman - Similar to the Showman except has 2-15" JBL speakers, and a change in the transistors and resistors in the output transfomer.

Brownface (1961-63)	N/A	$1,250 - 1,600	$975 - 1,150
Blackface (1964-67)	N/A	$850 - 1,000	$695 - 800
Silverface (1967-69)	N/A	$650 - 750	$550 - 600

* Super Showman, Showman 112, 212, 115, and 210 - See the Solid State listing in the Fender section.

DUAL SHOWMAN REVERB (PIGGY-BACK) - 100W, 2-15"JBL speakers, tubes: 3 X 7025, 2 X 12AT7, 12AX7, 4 X 6L6GC, two channels, reverb, vibrato, silverface control panel, four inputs, two normal and two vibrato, 11 silver-top knobs (Norm: bs, v, b, m, t, Vibrato: bs, v, b, m, t, s, i, r), bright switches on each channel, remote footswithces for vibrato and reverb, black tolex covering, silver grille, mfg. 1969-1979.

N/A	$650 - 750	$575 - 625

This model was also sold as the Dual Showman Reverb Bass. In 1972 master volume was added. In 1976 a distortion switch was added. This amp is virtually the Twin in piggy-back form.

DUAL SHOWMAN (POST CBS VERSION) - 100W, 4 X 12" speakers, tubes: 4 X 12AX7, 1 X 12AT7, 4 X 6L6GC, channel switching, effects loop, high gain preamp, three-position damping control, black control panel, four inputs, ten red knobs (Ch.1:v, t, m, b, Ch. 2: gain, t, m, b, p, v), black tolex covering, black grille, mfg. 1987-1994.

N/A	$500 - 575	$425 - 475

In 1990, the Dual Showman was changed to the Dual Showman SR, which had reverb. In 1992, a 25 watt switch and parallel channel mode was installed. This made it possible for all the controls to be working at once.

GRADING	100%	EXCELLENT	AVERAGE

Super Series

DUAL PROFESSIONAL (SUPER) - 16W, 2-10" Jensen's, tubes: 3 X 6SJ7, 2 X 6L6, 5U4, top numbered control panel, four inputs, two instruments, one mic, one lo-gain, three pointer knobs (mic v, inst v, tone), fuse holder, and red pilot light, V-front cabinet, early tweed covering, dark brown grille with vertical chrome strip in middle, mfg. 1946-1952.

Fender Super Amp
courtesy solidbodyguitar.com, Inc.

Fender Super Amp
courtesy solidbodyguitar.com, Inc.

| 1946-49 | N/A | $1,300 - 1,600 | $900 - 1,175 |
| 1950-52 | N/A | $2,000 - 2,500 | $1,600 - 1,875 |

This amp was renamed the Super in 1947. The 3 X 6SJ7's are changed to 3 X 6SC7's. The tubes are converted over to 12AX7 and 12AY7 as soon as these are available. A TV front Super was never made. In 1952, the V front is taken away, There are some Super amplifiers of this time with 6V6 tubes.

SUPER (WIDE PANEL) - 20W, 2-10" Jensen's, tubes: 2 X 12AY7, 12AX7, 2 X 6L6G, 5U4G, top numbered control panel, four inputs, three pointer knobs (mic v, inst v, tone), diagonal tweed covering, brown tweed-era grille, mfg. 1952-54.

| | N/A | $2,000 - 2,500 | $1,500 - 1,900 |

SUPER (NARROW PANEL) - 20W, 2-10" Jensen's, tubes: 2 X 12AY7, 12AX7, 2 X 6L6G, 5U4G, top numbered control panel, four input jacks, four pointer knobs (Mic v, inst v, t, b), ground switch, diagonal tweed covering, brown tweed-era grille, mfg. 1954-1960.

Fender Super Amp (Narrow Panel)
courtesy Dave Rogers

Fender Super Amp (Narrow Panel)
courtesy Dave Rogers

| | N/A | $2,500 - 3,500 | $1,500 - 2,000 |

Some of these models have 6V6 tubes. In 1955, the nameplate changes to script type. In 1956, the namplate is changed to Super Amp script. In 1958, a presence control is added.

GRADING	100%	EXCELLENT	AVERAGE

SUPER (BROWNFACE) - 30W, 2-10" Jensen's, tubes: 5 X 7025, 2 X 6L6GC, 5U4G, tremolo, brownface control panel, four inputs, two normal, two vibrato, nine brown knobs (Norm: v, b, t, Vibrato: v, b, t, s, i, Both: p), brown tolex covering, brown grille, mfg. 1960-64.

Fender Super Amp (Brownface)
courtesy Dave Rogers

Fender Super Amp (Brownface)
courtesy Dave Rogers

	N/A	$1,250 - 1,600	$950 - 1,200

From 1962, some amps were made with 5881 output tubes and could produce 45W output. The Super amp was replaced by the Super Reverb.

SUPER REVERB - 40W, 4-10" speakers, tubes: 3 X 7025, 12AX7, 2 X 12AT7, 2 X 6L6GC, tremolo, reverb, blackface control panel, four inputs, two normal, two vibrato, bright switch, 11 silver-top knobs (Norm: bs, v, t, m, b, Vibrato: v, t, m, r, s, i), black tolex covering, silver grille, mfg. 1964-1982.

Fender Super Reverb (Blackface)
courtesy Dave Rogers

Fender Super Reverb (Blackface)
courtesy Dave Rogers

Fender Super Reverb (Silverface)
courtesy S. P. Fjestad

1964-1967	N/A	$1,600 - 2,200	$1,025 - 1,250
1968-1972	N/A	$875 - 1,100	$700 - 825
1973-1981	N/A	$700 - 850	$525 - 650

In 1968, Silverface was introduced with a silver control panel, blue cloth, and aluminum trim. In 1970, the output was raised to 45W. In 1976, a master volume knob and distortion switch was added. In 1981, the output was raised to 70W and the silverface went back to the blackface, with a black control panel, and silver grille.

* Super Six Reverb - See the Twin Series listing in the Fender section.

SUPER 60 - 60W, 1-12" Eminence, tubes: 2 X 12AX7, 12AT7, 2 X 6L6, black control panel, two input jacks, eight red knobs (Ch. A: v, t, m, b, Ch. B: v, gain, Both: p, r), black tolex covering, black grille, mfg. 1988-1990.

Combo	N/A	$250 - 300	$210 - 240
Head	N/A	$200 - 230	$170 - 190

The red knobs on this amp were replaced by black ones shortly after the amp was introduced. This unit was available as a head-unit only or as a combo.

* Super 112 - Similar to the Super 60, except has overdrive channel, and a notch filter, Celestian speakers an option, mfg. 1990-93.

	N/A	$250 - 300	$210 - 235

* Super 210 - Similar to Super 210, except has 2-10" speakers, mfg. 1990-93.

	N/A	$275 - 325	$225 - 255

SUPER AMP (PRO-TUBE SERIES) - 60W, 4-10" with AlNiCo magnets, tubes: 4 X 12AX7, 2 X 12AT7, 2 X 6L6, new blackface control panel, two input jacks, 12 silver-top knobs (Ch.1: v, t, b, m, Ch.2: gain 1, gain 2, t, b, m, v, Both: Mix, r), black tolex covering, silver grille, mfg. 1992-late 1990's.

	N/A	$475 - 525	$400 - 450.

GRADING	100%	EXCELLENT	AVERAGE

Tremolux Series

TREMOLUX (NARROW PANEL) - 15W, 1-12" Jensen speaker, tubes: 12AY7, 2 X 12AX7, 2 X 6V6, 5U4 rectifier, electric tremolo, top numbered control panel, four input jacks, five pointer knobs (Mic v, Inst v, tone, speed, depth), tremolo foot control switch, diagonal tweed covering, brown tweed-era grille, mfg. 1955-1960.

Fender Tremolux
courtesy solidbodyguitar.com, Inc.

Fender Tremolux
courtesy solidbodyguitar.com, Inc.

Fender Tremolux
courtesy solidbodyguitar.com, Inc.

N/A	$1,400 - 1,800	$950 - 1,100

In the later models, they may have different phase inverter and tremolo circuits. The nameplate changed in 1957. This was the first Fender amp with an electric tremolo unit.

TREMOLUX (PIGGY-BACK) - 30W, 1-10" speaker, tubes: 2 X 7025, 2 X 12AX7, 2 X 6L6GC, GZ34 rectifier, tremolo, front brown-face control panel, four input jacks, two bright, two normal, tremolo worked on both channels, eight cream knobs (Bright: v, t, b, Norm: v, t, b, Both: s, i), cream tolex covering, maroon grille, mfg. 1961-66.

Fender Tremolux (Piggy-back)
courtesy Dave Rogers

Fender Tremolux (Piggy-back)
courtesy Dave Rogers

Fender Tremolux (Piggy-back)
courtesy Dave Rogers

1961-63	N/A	$1,100 - 1,275	$825 - 975
1964-67	N/A	$775 - 875	$650 - 725

In 1962, the 1-10" speaker was changed to 2-10". In 1963, the maroon grille was changed to a wheat grille and later that year the handle was changed to black. In 1964, Blackface was introduced with a black control panel, black tolex covering, and a silver grille. A bright switch was added and the preamp tubes changed to a 12AX7 and a 12AT7. This amp used the same chassis as the Bandmaster, Concert, Pro, and Vibrolux of the same era.

Twin Series

TWIN (WIDE PANEL) - 15W, 2-12" Jensen Concert Series speakers, tubes: 2 X 6SC7, 6J5 for tone controls, 6SC7 driver, 2 X 6L6 output, top numbered control panel, four input jacks, four pointer knobs(Mic v, Inst v, b, t), diagonal tweed covering, brown cloth grille, mfg. 1952-54.

N/A	$3,200 - 3,800	$2,600 - 3,100

This was the first wide panel amp for Fender and the first to offer dual tone controls.

GRADING	100%	EXCELLENT	AVERAGE

TWIN (NARROW PANEL) - 50W, 2-12" Jensen speakers, tubes: 3 X 12AY7, 12AX7, 2 6L6, 2 X 5Y3GY rectifer, top numbered control panel, four input jacks, five pointer knobs (Mic v, Inst v, b, t, p), diagonal tweed covering, brown tweed-era grille, mfg. 1954-1960.

Fender Twin (Narrow Panel)
courtesy Dave Rogers

Fender Twin (Narrow Panel)
courtesy Dave Rogers

N/A	$3,500 - 4,200	$2,800 - 3,200

In 1955, the rectifers were changed to 2 X 5U4G and later on to a GZ34. In 1956, a mid-range control is added along with bright and normal inputs. In 1958, the pre-amp and driver tubes were changed to a 12AY7 and 2 X 12AX7, and the output tubes are changed to 4 X 5881. This is model 5F8-A, and power output was reported at 85W. The control panel now had six knobs. A few of the very late (1960) models were covered in brown tolex with the top control panel. Some collectors say early Twin's had 2-10" speakers.

If you can find one of these in mint condition (good luck) they can go over $6,000.

TWIN (BROWNFACE) - 90W, 2-12" Jensen's, tubes: 4 X 7025, 2 X 12AX7, 4 X 6L6GC, solid state rectifier, tremolo, front brownface control panel, four input jacks, two normal, two vibrato, nine cream knobs (Norm: v, t, b, Vibrato: v, t, b, s, i, Both: p), cream tolex covering, maroon or wheat colored grille, mfg. 1960-63.

Fender Twin Amp (Brownface)
courtesy Willie's American Guitars

Fender Twin Amp (Brownface)
courtesy Willie's American Guitars

N/A	$3,100 - 3,750	$2,700 - 3,000

Model number 6G8A changed the tube schematics to 6 X 7025 and 4 X 6L6. There are many different variants of this model over its 11 year existence. There are a few amps made with brown tolex covering and a smaller box. The Twin was phased out when the Twin Reverb was introduced.

GRADING	100%	EXCELLENT	AVERAGE

TWIN REVERB - 85W, 2-12" Jensen's, tubes: 3 X 7025, 2 X 12AT7, 12AX7, 4 X 6L6GC, bright, reverb, vibrato, front blackface control panel, four input jacks, two normal, vibrato, bright and middle switches, 11 silver-top knobs (Norm: v, t, m, b, Vibrato: bs, v, t, m, b, r, s, i), black tolex covering, silver grille, mfg. 1963-1982.

Fender Twin Reverb (Blackface)
courtesy Dave Rogers

Fender Twin Reverb (Blackface)
courtesy Dave Rogers

Fender Twin Reverb (Silverface)
courtesy S. P. Fjestad

1963-67	N/A	$1,500 - 2,000	$950 - 1,250
1968-70	N/A	$850 - 1,100	$675 - 800
1971-82	N/A	$650 - 750	$525 - 600

In 1968, the Silverface is introduced with silver control panel, blue cloth grille, and aluminum trim. The Silverface is the same as the Blackface in the schematics. In 1973 the output is raised to 100W and a master volume control is added. In 1976 a push/pull distortion switch was added to the master volume control and JBL speakers becsme an option. In 1981, Blackface was reintroduced as it was in the mid-sixties, and the ouptut was raised to 135W. The tube schematics were changed to 4 X 7025, 2 X 12AX7, and 4 X 6L6GC.

* Super Six Reverb - Similar to Twin Reverb except has 6-10" speakers, has 100W output since it was introduced in 1972, removable casters on the side, uses a series-parallel connection, master volume, mfg. 1972-79.

	N/A	$525 - 625	$425 - 485

* Quad Reverb - Similar to Twin Reverb except has 4-12" speakers, master volume, mfg. 1972-79.

	N/A	$500 - 600	$400 - 450

SUPER TWIN - 180W, 2-12" speakers, tubes: 2 X 7025, 12AT7, 12AU7A, 12AX7A, 6 X 6L6, front black control panel, two inputs, elaborate equilization system, new active electronics, 12 silver-top knobs, (v, t, m, b, p, distortion, output level, and five-way equilization), black tolex covering, black grille with white trim, mfg. 1975-76.

	N/A	$400 - 450	$325 - 375

* Super Twin Reverb - Similar to Super Twin except has reverb unit, tube schematics were changed to: one 7025 was replaced with two sections of a 6C10 triple triode, the reverb driver was a 6CX8 pentode, mfg. 1977-1980

	N/A	$425 - 475	$350 - 400

This model replaced the Super Twin in 1977.

TWIN REVERB II - 105W, 2-12" speakers, tubes: 4 X 7025, 2 X 12AT7, 2 X 6L6GC, three-stage distortion, channel switching, rear mounted effects loop, new blackface control panel, two inputs, 12 silver-top knobs (Ch.1: v, t, m, b, Ch.2: v, gain, master, t, m, b, r, p), black tolex covering, silver grille, mfg. 1982-86.

	N/A	$550 - 650	$450 - 525

Note-production of this amp stopped in 1985 at the end of CBS ownership, but were still sold though 1986. This amp was also available in a head/cabinet version.

THE TWIN (POST-CBS) - 100W, 2-12" Eminence speakers, tubes: 2 X 12AT7, 5 X 12AX7, 4 X 6L6, two channels with overdrive, low power switch, reverb, black control panel, four input jacks, two for each channel, eleven red knobs (Ch.1: v, t, m, b, Ch.2: gain, t, m, b, p, v, r), most knobs had pull switches, effects loop, foot switch, black tolex covering, black grille, mfg. 1987-1994.

	N/A	$475 - 550	$395 - 450

This model was available in white, grey, red, or snakeskin on a special order. In 1992, the black grille was replaced with a silver grille, and the red knobs were replaced with black ones.

GRADING	100%	EXCELLENT	AVERAGE

Vibrasonic Series

VIBRASONIC (BROWNFACE) - 25W, 1-15" JBL speaker, tubes: 5 X 7025, 2 X 6L6GC, tremolo, two channels, brownface control panel, four inputs, two normal, two vibrato, nine brown knobs (Norm: b, t, b, Vibrato: b, t, v, s, i, Both: p), brown tolex covering, brown tweed-era grille, mfg. 1959-1963.

Fender Vibrasonic (Brownface)
courtesy Dave Rogers

Fender Vibrasonic (Brownface)
courtesy Dave Rogers

N/A	**$1,100 - 1,400**	**$875 - 1,025**

This amp had a reversed control layout at first but went back to the original design shortly thereafter. In 1961, the grille turned to maroon, and in 1962, it turned to wheat. Later models used 2 X 12AX7 tubes in the tremolo circuit rather then the 7025 and 5881 tubes. This amp was a very close relative to the Pro amp with vibrato and a 15" JBL speaker.

VIBROSONIC (SILVERFACE) - 100W, 1-15" speaker, tubes: 3 X 7025, 2 X 12AT7, 12AX7, 4 X 6L6GC, reverb, vibrato, silverface control panel, four inputs, two normal, two vibrato, bright switches, 12 silver-top knobs (Norm: v, t, m, b, Vibrato: v, t, m ,b, r, s, i, Both: master volume), black tolex covering, silver grille, mfg. 1972-1981.

N/A	**$550 - 650**	**$450 - 525**

No that's not an error in spelling, it is the Vibrosonic. This amp was released nine years after the original Vibrasonic was released, but it is more simliar to the twin, quad, and super-six reverb amps. It doesn't have a lot to do with the original Vibrasonic. In 1974, a less expensive JBL D-130F was offered for a speaker. In 1976, a distortion switch was added to the master volume knob. In 1979, the JBL speaker was replaced with a 15" Electro-voice.

Vibrolux Series

VIBROLUX (NARROW PANEL) - 10W, 1-10" Jensen, tubes: 2 X 12AX7, 2 X 6V6, 5Y3 rectifier, tremolo, top black control panel, three inputs, four pointer knobs (v, tone, s, depth), diagonal tweed covering, brown tweed-era grille, mfg. 1954-1961.

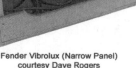

Fender Vibrolux (Narrow Panel)
courtesy Dave Rogers

Fender Vibrolux (Narrow Panel)
courtesy Dave Rogers

Fender Vibrolux (Narrow Panel)
courtesy Willie's American Guitars

N/A	**$1,200 - 1,500**	**$800 - 1,000**

GRADING	100%	EXCELLENT	AVERAGE

VIBROLUX (BROWNFACE/BLACKFACE)

VIBROLUX (BROWNFACE/BLACKFACE) - 30W, 1-12" Jensen's, tubes: 2 X 7025, 2 X 12AX7, 2 X 6L6GC, two channels, vibrato, front blackface control panel, four inputs, two normal, two bright, eight brown knobs (Norm: v, t, b, Vibrato: v, b, t, Both: s, i), tremolo works on both channels, brown tolex covering, light brown grille, mfg. 1961-64.

Fender Vibrolux (Brownface)
courtesy Dave Rogers

Fender Vibrolux (Brownface)
courtesy Dave Rogers

Fender Vibrolux (Blackface)
courtesy Dave Rogers

1961-63	N/A	$1,000 - 1,250	$825 - 975
1964	N/A	$1,200 - 1,500	$900 - 1,075

In 1964, the Blackface was introduced with a black control panel, black tolex covering, and a silver grille. The speed and intensity controls are changed to work on only the vibrato channel, both channels get a bright switch, and the 12AX7 is replaced with a 12AT7. In 1966, the nameplate changes. The Vibrolux and the Tremolux are virually identical.

VIBROLUX REVERB

VIBROLUX REVERB - 35W, 2-10" Jensen's, tubes:3 X 7025, 2 X 12AT7, 12AX7, 2 X 6L6GC, two channels, vibrato, reverb, blackface control panel, four inputs, two normal, two vibrato, bright switches, nine silver-top knobs (Norm: v, t, b, Vibrato: v, t, b, r, s, i), black tolex covering, silver grille, mfg. 1964-1982.

Fender Vibrolux Reverb
courtesy Savage Audio

Fender Vibrolux Reverb
courtesy Savage Audio

1963-67	N/A	$1,500 - 2,000	$950 - 1,200
1968-1973	N/A	$900 - 1,200	$725 - 850
1974-1981	N/A	$650 - 850	$550 - 625

In 1965, Silverface was introduced with a silver control panel, blue cloth grille, and aluminum trim. In 1970, output was increased to 40W.

GRADING	100%	EXCELLENT	AVERAGE

Vibroverb Series

VIBROVERB (BROWNFACE) - 35W, 2-10" Oxford speakers, tubes: 4 X 7025, 2 X 12AX7, 2 X 6L6GC, GZ34 rectifier, reverb, vibrato, brownface control panel, four input jacks, two normal, two bright, nine brown knobs (Norm: v, t, b, Bright: v, t, b, r, Both: s, i), tilt-back legs, brown tolex covering, light brown grille, mfg. 1963 only.

Fender Vibroverb (Brownface)
courtesy Dave Rogers

Fender Vibroverb (Brownface)
courtesy Dave Rogers

N/A	$3,000 - 3,800	$2,500 - 2,900

VIBROVERB (BLACKFACE) - 40W, 1-15" speaker, tubes: 3 X 7025, 12AX7, 2 X 12AT7, 2 X 6L6GC, GZ34 rectifier, two channels (normal and vibrato), four input jacks, two for each channel, blackface control panel, bright switches, nine silver-top knobs (Norm: v, t, b, Vibrato: v, t, b, r, s, i), black tolex covering, silver grille, mfg. 1963-64.

Fender Vibroverb (Blackface)
courtesy Dave Rogers

Fender Vibroverb (Blackface)
courtesy Dave Rogers

N/A	$2,500 - 3,500	$1,500 - 2,000

This version of the Vibroverb was completely different from the first version with different circuitary in the phase inverter and tremolo. Fender stopped making this amp in fall of 1964, however models were still sold through early 1965. This model was replaced by the Vibrolux Reverb.

Vintage Reissue Series

'65 SUPER REVERB (No. 021-7600-000) - 40W, 4-10" Jensen P-10R Alnico speakers, tubes: 2 X 6L6 Groove Tube output tubes, 5AR4 rectifier tube, 4 X 12AX7 preamp tubes, 2 X 12AT7 tubes, dual channels, vibrato, reverb, black control panel, four inputs, two normal, two vibrato, 10 silver-top knobs (Norm: v, t, b, Vibrato: v, t, m, b, r, s, i), two-button footswitch (reverb and vibrato), tilt back legs, black textured vinyl, silver grille, mfg. 2001-current.

MSR	$1,700	$1,150	$725 - 825	$625 - 700

In 2002 the output was increased to 45W.

'65 TWIN REVERB REISSUE (No. 021-7300-000) - 85W, 2-12" Jensen speakers, tubes: 4 X 12AX7, 2 X 12AT7, 4 X 6L6GC, reverb, vibrato, blackface control panel, four inputs, two normal, two vibrato, bright switches, 11 silver-top knobs (Norm: v, t, m, b, Vibrato: v, t, m, b, r, s, i), two button footswitch for reverb and vibrato, tilt-back legs, black tolex covering, silver grille, mfg. 1991-current.

MSR	$1,500	$999	$650 - 725	$550 - 625

'59 BASSMAN REISSUE (No. 021-7100-000) - 45W, 4-10" 8Ohm Jensen P10R speakers, tubes: 2 X 6L6 Groove Tube output tubes, 2 AX7 preamp tubes, plug in 8 pin tube rectifier, dual channels (normal and bright), top chrome control panel with numbers to 12, 4 inputs, two per channel, five pointer knobs (Norm v, Bright, v, t, m, b), diagonal tweed covering, Oxblood grille cloth, mfg. 1990-current.

MSR	$1,420	$925	$600 - 725	$500 - 575

GRADING	100%	EXCELLENT	AVERAGE

VIBROVERB '63 REISSUE (No. 021-7200-000) - 40W, 2-10" speakers, tubes: 4 X 12AX7, 2 X 12AT7, 2 X 6L6GC, solid-state rectifier, vibrato, reverb, two channels (normal and bright), brownface control panel, four input jacks, two for each channel, nine brown knobs (Norm: v, t, b, Bright: v, t, b, r, Both: s, i), brown tolex covering, light brown grille, mfg. 1990-95

	$725	$550 - 625	$475 - 525

Last MSR was $1,079.99.

'65 DELUXE REVERB VINTAGE REISSUE - 22W, 1-12" speaker, tubes: 3 X 12AX7, 2 X 12AT7, 2 X 6V6, 5AR4, tremolo, front blackface control panel, four inputs, two normal, two vibrato, nine silver-top knobs (Norm, v, b, t, Vibrato, v, b, t, r, s, i), black tolex covering, silver grille, mfg. 1993-current.

Fender Deluxe Reverb Reissue (Blackface)
courtesy George Maquire

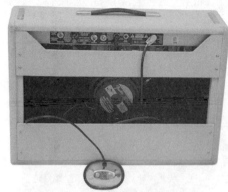

Fender Deluxe Reverb Reissue (Blackface)
courtesy George Maquire

MSR	$1,140	$750	$525 - 575	$450 - 500

This amp is a reissue of the pre-CBS Deluxe Reverb released in vintage series.

Misc. Tube Amps

K&F - 3W, 1-8" or 1-10" speaker, tubes: 6N7, 6V6, 5Y3, no controls, gray crackle paint, corse mesh or cloth, mfg. 1945-46.

	N/A	$475 - 525	$400 - 450

This amp was the first produced by Leo Fender. The K&F was meant for steel type guitars. It sometimes would have one volume knob. This model was found with two different sized speakers. This is an extremely rare amplifier.

WHITE - 3W, 1-8" speaker, tubes: 12AX7, 6V6, 5Y3 rectifier, top numbered control panel, two pointer knobs (volume, tone), grey fabric covering, blue-black grille, mfg. 1955 only.

	N/A	$475 - 525	$400 - 450

This was an amp produced by Leo Fender, but didn't bear the Fender name. The White was a student amp that came with a matching steel guitar, and was a tribute to Forest White.

30, 75, & 140 - These short lived amps, were Fender's first real try into channel switching, modern sound, and distortion. These models featured different speaker configurations, tubes: 3 X 7025, 2 X 12AT7, 2 X 6L6GC, silicon rectifiers, hi/lo power switch, two channels (rhythm, and lead), dual pedal switch, reverb, bright switches, eight silver top knobs (clean: v, t, m, b, with pull-knob boosts, lead drive, r, lead level, master volume), two input jacks, blackface control panel, black tolex covering, black grille, mfg. 1980-82.

* 30 - 30W, 2-10" or 1-12" speakers (The 2-10" was $20 more), nine silver-top knobs (Norm: v, t, b, Reverb, gain, t, m, b, r, v), mfg. 1980-81.

	N/A	$350 - 400	$275 - 325

Last MSR was $675.

* 75 - 75W, 1-12" speaker Fender special design or E-V speaker standard in combo, or your choice of various performance matched Fender speaker cabinets, available in piggyback or combo, switchable power from 75W to 15W.

Combo	N/A	$400 - 450	$325 - 375
Piggy Back	N/A	$425 - 475	$350 - 400
Head Only	N/A	$210 - 250	$170 - 195

Last MSR was $1,245.

Add $40 for 4-10" cabinets instead of 12".

* 140 - 135W, head only, came with a 4-12" cabinet enclosure, control panel consisted of eight silver top knobs (v, t, m, t, r, 5 band equalizer, lead drive, lead level, master volume), had 4 X 7025 instead of 3, and 4 X 6L6GC instead of 2, mfg. 1980 only.

Piggy Back	N/A	$475 - 550	$395 - 450
Head Only	N/A	$275 - 300	$215 - 250

This amp was spendy and was replaced shortly after it was introduced by the 300 PS. There is little information about this amp.

300PS - 300W, amp sold with a 4-12" cabinet, tubes: 2 X 7025, 12AT7, 6V6, 4 X 6550, black control panel, two input jacks, twelve silver-top numbered knobs (v, t, m, b, p, 5-way equalizer, distortion, output), black tolex covering, black foam grille, mfg. 1975-79.

	N/A	$525 - 600	$425 - 495

This amp was also available as the 300PS Bass with a larger cabinet. This amp was offered through the release of the B-300, which is a solid state amp.

GRADING	100%	EXCELLENT	AVERAGE

400 PS BASS - 435W, 18" horn cabinet, tubes: 6 X 7025, 12AT7, 6 X 6550, separate head and cabinet, black control panel, four input jacks, two bass, two normal, bass and bright switches, 11 numbered knobs (Bass, ds, v, t, b, Norm: bs, v, t, m, b, s, i, master volume), three power output jacks, black tolex covering, black foam grille, mfg. 1970-75.

| | N/A | $500 - 600 | $400 - 475 |

The three output jacks boasted to have three 145W output, when you could get all the power out of one. There were three amplifers within the model and they all came together to drive the massive cabinet. This was Fender's response to the power race in bass amplifiers in the 1970's.

BANTAM BASS - 50W, Yamaha plastic cone speaker non-circular, tubes: 2 X 7025, 12AT7, 2 X 6L6, 5U4 rectifier, two channels (bass and normal), silverface control panel, four input jacks, two per channel, seven silver-top knobs (Norm: v, b, t, Vibrato: v, b, t, s, i, r), bright switches, black tolex covering, silver grille, mfg. 1969-1971.

Fender Bantam Bass
courtesy Greg Wells

Fender Bantam Bass
courtesy Greg Wells

| | N/A | $425 - 500 | $350 - 400 |

The Bantam was replaced by the Bassman ten in 1972. This amp featured a very odd speaker made by Yamaha. This speaker was very rare to get a replacement, if it was ever blown, and working Bantam amps with original speakers are very rare in today's market.

Add $100 for original Yamaha speaker.

MUSICMASTER BASS - 12W, 1-12", tubes: 12AX7, 2 X 6V6GTA, silverface control panel, two black plastic knobs with silver skirts, volume and tone control only, black tolex covering, silver grille, mfg. 1970-1982.

Fender Musicmaster (Silverface)
courtesy Savage Audio

Fender Musicmaster (Silverface)
courtesy Savage Audio

| | N/A | $140 - 165 | $110 - 125 |

The Musicmaster is one of the earliest versions using a phase inverter. Around 1976, the nameplate lost the tail. In 1982, blackface was reintroduced for its final year of existance. This model was replaced by the Bassman 20.

STUDIO BASS - 200W, 1-15" Electrovoice, tubes: 2 X 7025, 12AT7, 12AU7A, 12AX7A, 6 X 6L6, new blackface control panel, two inputs, 12 silver-top knobs (v, t, m, b, p, distortion, output level, five-way equalization), black tolex covering, black grille, mfg. 1977-1980.

| | N/A | $450 - 500 | $350 - 425 |

This amp combined the equalization system of the 300 PS with the Super Twin to create a bass amp with these features.

GRADING	100%	EXCELLENT	AVERAGE

Custom Shop Models

The Fender Custom shop was introduced in 1993, and was created to bring back vintage models and put some modifications to them. It was also partly created to design the odd-ball models that custom-shops are known for doing. The first amps are styled like the early 60's brownface amps with cream tolex covering. Later on, Fender started to produce other amps like old vintage such as the woodies, and a narrow panel tweed. Some new ideas have been introduced as well.

VIBRO-KING (No. 081-1000-000) - 60W into 2 Ohms, 3-10" Celestian speakers, tubes: 5 X 12AX7 preamps, 6V6 Groove Tube driver tube, reverb, vibrato, brownface control panel, two inputs, nine cream knobs (dwell, mix, tone, v, t, b, m, s, i), FAT switch, footswitch, cream tolex covering, brown grille, mfg. 1993-current.

	MSR	$2,850	$1,425	$975 - 1,200	$800 - 950

Add $21 for cover.

* Vibro King 212 Enclosure (No. 081-3004-000) - Speaker enclosure for the Vibro-King amp, handles 140W, 2-12" Celestian speakers, same covering as Vibro-King.

	MSR	$610	$399	$275 - 300	$225 - 250

Add $21 for cover.

TONE-MASTER (No. 081-2000-000) - 100W into 4, 8, or 16 Ohms, head-unit only, 3 X 12AX7 preamp tubes, dual channels, brownface control panel, one input, nine cream knobs (Ch. 1 v, t, b, m, Ch. 2 gain, t, b, m, v), FAT switches, effects loops, footswitch, cream tolex covering, brown grille, mfg. 1993-current.

Fender Tonemaster
courtesy solidbodyguitar.com, Inc.

Fender Tonemaster
courtesy solidbodyguitar.com, Inc.

	MSR	$2,300	$1,150	$800 - 900	$700 - 775

* Tone Master 212 Enclosure (No. 081-3000-000) - 2-12" Celestian G2180 speakers designed for the tone master head, matches the tone master style (designed as piggy-back).

	MSR	$700	$450	$325 - 375	$250 - 300

Also available as the Tone Master 212 V30 (No. 081-3003-000) enclosure which is the same as the regualar enclosure except has 2-12" Celestian Vintage 30 speakers, and is the same retail price.

* Tone Master 412 Enclosure (No. 081-3001-000) - 4-12" Celestian Vintage 30 speakers in a cabinet designed for the Tone-Master, and matches the tone master style (designed as piggy-back).

	MSR	$700	$525	$425 - 475	$350 - 400

DUAL PROFESSIONAL (No. 081-1005-000) - 100W, into 4 or 2 Ohms, 2-12" Celestian speakers, tubes: 4 X 12AX7 preamps, 6V6 Groove Tube reverb driver tube, dual channels, reverb, vibrato, brownface control panel, two inputs, ten cream knobs (dwell, mix, tone, volume A, volume B, t, m, b, s, i) three switches for FAT and channel switching, two button footswitch, effects loop, cream tolex covering, brown grille, mfg. 1995-current.

	MSR	$3,000	$1,599	$1,075 - 1,300	$875 - 1,025

On all Custom Shop Amps add $21 for cover, $26 for Tone-Master 412 enclosure, or $19 for Tone-Master head unit

RUMBLE BASS (No. 081-2100-000) - 300W at 2 or 4 Ohms, head unit only, tubes, dual channels, brownface control panel, nine cream knobs, three inputs, lots of power, cream tolex covering, brown grille, mfg. 1994-98.

	N/A		$800 - 950	$650 - 750

Last MSR was $2,399.99.

Designed to run with a Rumble-Bass 410 Full-Range Speaker Enclosure (No. 081-3100-000), which has 4-10" special design cast-frame speakers, and can handle 600W. It was also designed for the Rumble-Bass 410 SUB Speaker enclosure (No. 081-3101-000) which has 4-10" special Fender design steel frame speakers, and can also handle 600W. They both last retailed for $799.99. With the head, speaker, and sub cabinets you're looking at a $4,000 bill.

GRADING	100%	EXCELLENT	AVERAGE

CUSTOM SHOP MASTER BUILT GUITAR AMPLIFIERS - These are amplifiers from the custom shop that are built in limited quantities. These are all tube amps, hand crafted, and are a true custom shop creation. Introduced in 2000, these models include vintage woody amps, a narrow panel tweed, and a brand new concoction called the two tone. All of these amps are built for outstanding quality with that vintage look. There is the Woody Junior Exotic and Woody Pro Exotic which are wood cabinets with the metal strips on the panel. The Woody Junior Ash and Woody Pro Ash are 50's models with narrow panel front, covered in ash and white gloss paint, with a brown grille. The Bass Breaker is similar to the mid 50's Bassman, with narrow panel tweed, but through brand new Celestian speakers. The Two Tone is a completely different amp than what Fender has ever had before. It has top control panel, but the controls are in the front, the grille is slanted at the top and the covering is black on the sides, and white on the top and bottom. Truly a unique style with quality circuitry. For prices and model numbers check the Fender web site.

Fender Two-Tone Custom Shop Amp
courtesy Dave's Guitar Shop

Fender Two-Tone Custom Shop Amp
courtesy Dave's Guitar Shop

ACOUSTIC AMPLIFIERS

Fender has only made solid-state amplifiers for acoustics up to this point. There aren't any tube amps strictly for acoustic guitars. The Acoustasonic series was introduced in 1998 for acoustic guitars and a possible microphone.

Acoustasonic Series

ACOUSTASONIC SFX (No. 022-1301-000) - 2 X 80W into 8 ohms, 1-8" 8 ohm Fender Special Design Foster Culver speaker, 1-10" Fender Special Design speaker, solid state combo, two independent channels (instrument and microphone), XLR input for mic, onbard digital signal processor with 32 stereo digital presets, insert patch points for external signal processors, one input for instrument channel, two for mic, seventeen black-top knobs (Instrument: gain, t, m, b, string dynamics, feedback notch, DSP send, SFX, DSP return, MV, Mic: gain, t, m, b, feedback notch, DSP send, DSP effects), bypass switches, brown textured vinyl, wheat grille cloth, mfg. 1998-current.

MSR	$930	$650	$475 - 525	$400 - 450

    Add $21 for cover (No. 005-0246-000).

ACOUSTASONIC PRO - 160W (2 X 80), 2-8" special design & high frequency horn, dual notch filters, 1 special piezo horn, solid-state combo, dual processing, 99 digital multi-effect presets two independent channels (instrument and microphone), XLR input for mic, 18 black-top knobs (Inst: gain, t, m, b, channel send, return, attack, string dynamics, feedback notch 1 & 2, Mic: gain, t, m, b, channel send, return, both: Master and auxillary level), auxillary inputs, presets, four button footswitch, brown tolex covering, wheat grille Mfg. 1998-2000.

	$875	$675 - 750	$575 - 650

Last MSR was $1,249.

ACOUSTASONIC JR. (No. 022-1302-000) - 2 X 40W, 2-8" Fender special design Foster Culver speakers, 1 piezo horn, solid state combo, two independent channels (Inst. and Mic/Inst), reverb, stereo chorus, stereo FX loop, brownface control panel, three inputs, one 1/4" for each channel and a XRL on the mic, 13 black knobs (Inst: v, t, m, b, feedback notch, string dynamics, Mic: v, t, b, reverb send, both: r, depth, master volume) three switches, brown tolex covering, wheat grille, Mfg 1998-Current.

MSR	$620	$400	$275 - 325	$240 - 265

    Add $21 for cover (No. 005-0249-000).

ACOUSTASONIC 30 (No. 022-1303-000) - 30W, 1-8" Fender special design Foster Culver speaker & 1 piezo horn, solid state combo, two independent channels (Inst. and Mic), chorus, reverb, two inputs, XRL for mic, brownface control panel, ten black knobs (v, t, m, b, string dynamics, chorus, Mic: v, t, b, Both: reverb) optional footswitch, line out, portable floor wedge design (sits at an angle), brown tolex covering, wheat grille Mfg 2000-current.

MSR	$450	$275	$220 - 245	$190 - 205

ELECTRIC SOLID-STATE AMPLIFIERS

Fender has produced thousands of solid-state amplifiers over the years. These aren't necesarily more desireable or collectible, but the later models all offer great features and sounds. Since they have tried solid-state a few times, we divided them up into their respective series. The first series were the amps that were based off of popular tube models that crashed and burned shortly after their introduction. The second and third series followed later on, with the third series finally taking off. If you notice there are no pictures in this section, it is because nobody has any solid-state amps! If you have a collection of early Fender solid-state models please contact the publisher directly.

First Series Solid-State

Fender released its first solid-state series under CBS management in the summer of 1966. This series of amplifers featured some of Fender's most popular tube amps and transformed them into transistors versions. The first three models were the Dual Showman, Twin Reverb, and the Bassman. A solid-state reverb unit and PA system were also introduced in this series. These amps were completely different than anything Fender had tried before and sported a silver control panel at a 45 degree angle, cylindrical flat-topped knobs, and aluminum trim around the speaker cabinets that would become standard for all Fender amps later on. These models had "Fender" spelled in black letters along the top of the grille and the words SOLID STATE printed in bold red letters. In 1967, Fender announced four new solid-state combos. These amps didn't last long and the whole project was called off in 1971.

DUAL SHOWMAN (SOLID-STATE) - 100W, 2-15" JBL speakers, solid-state, piggy-back style, two channels, normal and vibrato, silverface control panel, two inputs for each channel, bright switches, 11 silver-top knobs (Norm: style, v, t, b, Vibrato: style, v, t, b, s, i, reverb), the style control gives tone settings of pop/normal/CW-RR, black tolex covering, silver grille with aluminum trim, mfg. 1966-68.

N/A	$375 - 450	$300 - 350

* Twin Reverb (Solid-State) - Similar to the Dual Showman except has 2-12" speakers mounted on top of each other, solid-state combo, mfg. 1966-69

N/A	$375 - 450	$300 - 350

BASSMAN (SOLID-STATE) - 100W, 3-12" JBL speakers, piggy-back style, silver control panel, two inputs, four silver-top knobs (style, v, t, b), the style controlled the tone for four positions: Bass Boost 1, Bass Boost 2, Guitar Normal, and Guitar Bright, black tolex covering, silver grille with aluminum trim, mfg. 1966-1971.

N/A	$350 - 415	$275 - 325

SUPER REVERB (SOLID-STATE) - 50W, 4-10" speakers, solid-state, dual channels, vibrato and normal, four inputs, two per channel, ten silver-top control knobs (Norm: v, t, b, Vibrato: style, v, t, b, reverb, s, i), the style control switches to three tone settings: pop, normal, CW/RR, bright switches, black tolex covering, silver grille, aluminum trim, mfg. 1967-69.

N/A	$375 - 425	$300 - 350

* Pro Reverb (Solid-State) - Similar to the solid-state Super Reverb except has 2-12" speakers, mfg. 1967-69.

N/A	$350 - 400	$275 - 325

VIBROLUX REVERB (SOLID-STATE) - 35W, 2-10" speakers, solid-state, reverb, vibrato, silver control panel, dual channels, four inputs, two per channel, bright switches, nine silver-top knobs (Norm: v, t, b, Vibrato: v, t, b, s, i, reverb), black tolex covering, silver grille with aluminum trim, mfg. 1967-69.

N/A	$325 - 375	$250 - 300

DELUXE REVERB (SOLID-STATE) - 25W, 1-12" speaker, solid-state, vibrato, reverb, dual channels, silver control panel, four inputs, two per channel, bright switches, nine silver-top knobs (Norm: v, t, b, Vibrato: v, t, b, s, i, reverb), black tolex covering, silver grille with aluminum trim, mfg. 1967-69.

N/A	$275 - 325	$210 - 250

Super Showman

Fender then started to experiment with other solid-state ideas. The Super Showman replaced the Dual Showman in 1969. This amp had many features including new technology with powered speakers. This was an amp that was designed for everyone in the band to use that same amp. The head had a built in E tuner, and a master volume the could control the combine the output of the three individual preamps. Fender used the idea of channel patching as well with the Super Showman. If only one person was using the amp, they could patch the channels together with short cords and use all the effects at athe same time. Each speaker cabinet had a volume control on it. This amp had a lot of power, however it was very spendy and very large. It only lasted for two years.

SUPER SHOWMAN - 140W, 4-12"or 8-10" speakers, solid state (49 transistors and 19 diodes), reverb, vibrato, new dimension IV effect, black/aluminum control panel, three channels, six inputs, two per channel, 18 silver numbered knobs (Ch 1.: v, b, m, t, fuzz, Ch. 2.: v, b, m, t, dimension IV, Ch. 3: s, i, r, t, m, b, v, MV), black tolex covering, silver grille, mfg. 1969-1971.

* Super Showman XFL-1000 - This model had the 4-12" speaker cabinet with head.

N/A	$425 - 475	$325 - 400

* Super Showman XFL-2000 - This model had the 8-10" speaker cabinet with head.

N/A	$425 - 475	$325 - 400

Zodiac Series

The Zodiac series was designed after the first series of solid-state amps and supposedly improved. There were four models in the series all named after Zodiac signs including: Libra, Capricorn, Scorpio, and the Taurus. These amps featured JBL speakers, alligator skin covering, and a new control panel. Other than that there were few changes beside cosmetics from the old amps. These amps were offered just under two years and very few of them were actually manufactured. They are actually very rare today, but hardly collectible. Maybe if they made an amp for my sign, Cancer, I might pick it up as a souvernere. Besides that these amps don't hold much value as collectibility. All models came with a remote footswitch for vibrato and reverb.

LIBRA - 105W, 4-12" JBL speakers, solid-state (28 transistors, 13 diodes), dual channels, reverb, vibrato, black/aluminum control panel, four inputs, two for each channel, bright switches, ten numbered black knobs with silver skirts (Norm: v, t, b, Vibrato: v, t, m, b, reverb, s, i), ground and power switch on front, optional casters, black alligator covering, silver grille, mfg. 1969-1971.

N/A	$325 - 375	$275 - 300

F

GRADING	100%	EXCELLENT	AVERAGE

CAPRICORN - 105W, 3-12" JBL speakers, solid-state (28 transistors, 13 diodes), dual channels, reverb, vibrato, black/aluminum control panel, four inputs, two for each channel, bright switches, ten numbered black knobs with silver skirts (Norm: v, t, b, Vibrato: v, t, m, b, reverb, s, i), ground and power switch on front, optional casters, black alligator covering, silver grille, mfg. 1969-1971.

	N/A	$300 - 350	$260 - 285

SCORPIO - 56W, 2-12" JBL speakers, solid-state (26 transistors, 10 diodes), dual channels, reverb, vibrato, black/aluminum control panel, four inputs, two for each channel, bright switches, ten numbered black knobs with silver skirts (Norm: v, t, b, Vibrato: v, t, m, b, reverb, s, i), ground and power switch on front, optional casters, black alligator covering, silver grille, mfg. 1969-1971.

	N/A	$210 - 250	$170 - 195

TAURUS - 42W, 2-10" JBL speakers, solid-state (26 transistors, 10 diodes), dual channels, reverb, vibrato, black/aluminum control panel, four inputs, two for each channel, bright switches, nine numbered black knobs with silver skirts (Norm: v, t, b, Vibrato: v, t, b, reverb, s, i), ground and power switch on front, optional casters, black alligator covering, silver grille, mfg. 1969-1971.

	N/A	$210 - 240	$170 - 195

Second Series Solid-State

Fender went ten years without a solid-state amp, after they discontinued the first-series and zodiac lines in 1971. In 1981, Fender produced some small solid-state amps and snuck them in with the tube amps. These first two amps were the Harvard and the Harvard Reverb. The Harvard sold for $189 and the Harvard Reverb went for $239. These amps were marketed for the student player and offered the amp with the new Fender Bullet guitar. The tube Champ amp and Harvard were available at the same time. You could get a fully-loaded solid-state Harvard for the same price a wimpy, basic Champ. After this the Champ was switched to the Super Champ, and the bottom line of Fender amplifiers have been solid-states from here on.

At the same time a Bassman Compact amp was released and lasted until 1983. In 1982, Fender released a whole new line of solid-state amplifiers. These amplifiers were mixed right in with the tube amps for the 1983 catalog. These models included the Harvard Reverb II, Yale Reverb, Studio Lead, Stage Lead, the Montreux, London Reverb, Showman, and the Sidekick 10, 20, and 30. All of these amps lasted various lifespans, and had many different styles. Most of these amps were made and sold new between 1981 and 1987. CBS Fender was sold in 1985 and leftover stock of these models were sold into 1987. Remember Fender stopped making these amps in 1985, but they still sold them through 1987.

HARVARD (SOLID-STATE) - 20W, 1-10" speaker, solid-state, new blackface control panel, two inputs, four black knobs (v, b, t, MV with distortion), black tolex covering, silver grille, mfg. 1981-82.

	N/A	$95 - 120	$70 - 85

This model was also available as the Harvard Reverb.

BASSMAN COMPACT - 50W, 1-15" speaker, solid state, new blackface control panel, six silver-top knobs (v, t, m, b, compressor, master volume), black tolex covering, silver grille, mfg. 1981-84.

	N/A	$125 - 150	$95 - 115

SIDEKICK BASS 30 - 30W, 1-12" speaker, solid-state, new blackface control panel, six black-top knobs (V, MV, t, m, b, p), black tolex covering, silver grille, mfg. 1983-85.

	N/A	$100 - 120	$75 - 95

* ***Sidekick Bass 50*** - Similar to the Sidekick Bass 50 except has 50W output and 1-15" speaker.

	N/A	$125 - 150	$100 - 115

HARVARD REVERB II - 20W, 1-10" speaker, solid-state, new blackface control panel, seven black-top knobs (v, gain, master, t, m, b, reverb), black tolex covering, silver grille, mfg. 1983-85.

	N/A	$120 - 145	$95 - 110

* ***Yale Reverb*** - Similar to the Harvard Reverb II except has 50W output and 1-12" speaker.

	N/A	$200 - 250	$160 - 185

STUDIO LEAD - 50W, 1-12" speaker, solid-state, new blackface control panel, dual channels, 11 black-top knobs, (Ch. 1: v, t, m, b, Ch. 2: v, gain, master, t, m, b, r), black tolex covering, silver grille, mfg. 1983-85.

	N/A	$210 - 250	$160 - 195

* ***Stage Lead*** - Similar to the Studio Lead, but a more powerful version, includes 100W output, and 1-12" speaker.

	N/A	$225 - 250	$160 - 200

MONTREUX - 100W, 1-12" speaker, solid-state, new blackface control panel, 12 black-top knobs (Ch. 1: v, t, b, Ch. 2: v, gain, master, t, mid 1, mid 2, b, reverb 1, reverb 2), black tolex covering, silver grille, mfg. 1983-85.

	N/A	$230 - 275	$185 - 215

* ***London Reverb*** - Similar to the Motreux except came as just a head, a 1-12" combo, or a 2-10" combo, included a 5-way equlizer, and were very elaborate amplifiers, especially for the time, mfg. mid 1980's.

	N/A	$230 - 275	$185 - 215

SHOWMAN 112, 212, 115, 210 - 200W, 1-12", 2-12", 1-15" or 2-10" speakers, the model number (112) refers to 1-12" speaker, solid-state, new blackface control panel, 12 black-top knobs (Ch. 1: v, t, b, Ch. 2: v, gain, master, t, mid 1, mid 2, b, reverb 1, reverb 2) plus a 5-way equlizer, black tolex covering, silver grille, mfg. 1983-85.

	N/A	$350 - 425	$275 - 325

SIDEKICK 10, SIDEKICK REVERB 20, 30 (Jap. Mfg.) - 10, 20, & 30W respectively, 1-8", 1-10", 1-12" speakers, respectively, solid-state, 20 and 30 have reverb, new blackface control panel, 10 has five black-top knobs (v, master, t, m, b), 20 has six with an added reverb knob, 30 has seven with reverb and presence knobs, black tolex covering, silver grille, mfg. 1983-85.

10	N/A	$50 - 60	$35 - 45
20-30	N/A	$80 - 100	$50 - 70

The Sidekick 10 was meant to be plugged into a car battery (DC) or optional battery pack. The 30 and 20 reverb models may be worth a little more.

GRADING	100%	EXCELLENT	AVERAGE

B-300 - 300W, head only, solid-state, black control panel, 10 black knobs (v, b, low mid, mid, effects, 3-way equalizer, compressor), rack-mountable, built-in compressor, variable crossover, blanaced line out, no covering just a metal case, mfg. 1980-82.

	N/A	$125 - 150	$100 - 115

This was actually Fender's first solid-state amp in almost 10 years. Even though it wasn't the start of the second line, it was released before the Second Series, and it replaced the 300PS Bass. It was a good effort and sounded decent, but it was terribly expensive. With the deluxe bass enclosure along with 2-15" speakers it cost over $1600! It was simply too much for the public at that time.

Third-Series Solid-State

After CBS sold out in 1985, the Fender Musical Instrument Corporation (FMIC), took over with no amp manufacturing facility. Fender then used up thier old-stock and started to import some solid-state amps including the Squier 15 and Sidekicks. In 1987, FMIC started to pull around and released a few new models, which were American bass BXR amps. In 1988 FMIC released an entire new line of American solid-state amps, which became Fender's third run at solid-state products. This new line of amps used names from earlier amps, like the Deluxe-85, Princeton Chours, and Pro-185, but were nothing like the vintage amps of the same name. In 1989, gray covered amps were introduced with names like the M-80, and Power Chorus. Other amps made their debut in 1990 in gray with the H.O.T., J.A.M.,and the R.A.D.,which were geared toward younger students. By 1992, there were over 25 models in the solid-state line. By this time certain models were phased out, but the whole line was going strong. There are now all kinds of models and variations in this line. Finally after over 20 years of trial and error, Fender has stabilized the solid-state market.

SQUIRE 15 - 15W, 1-8" speaker, solid-state, black control panel, six black knobs (v, gain, master, t, m, b), black tolex covering, silver grille, mfg. 1988-mid 1990's.

	N/A	$45 - 50	$35 - 40

There seems to be some confusion to when this amp was discontinued and what it was changed to. There are the models X-15, the Squier SKX15, and the Sidekick 15 which are all similar to the Squier 15 but may include Reverb, Chorus, etc.

SIDEKICK SERIES - There are many different models and variations made of this amp. There are small guitar amps, bass amps, and key-board amps. They were first introduced in late 1986 and featured in the catalogs in 1987. These amps ranged between 30W up to 100W. Most of these amps had the typical solid-state attire. Volume, treble, bass, distortion, and reverb were on a lot of these amps, but not all of them. There are simply too many variations of these amplifiers to list them separately. The value of these amps isn't high at all, and the price doesn't vary enough between all the models to justify an individual entry for each one. The value is approximately between $75 and $175 for the Sidekick series.

DELUXE 85 - 85W, 1-12" speaker, solid-state, dual channels, 11 red knobs (Ch A: v, t, b, Ch. B: gain, b, m, t, limiter, p, r, v), black tolex covering, black grille, mfg. 1988-1993.

	N/A	$190 - 225	$160 - 180

* 85 - Similar to the Deluxe 85, except only has nine red knobs and only one channel, knobs include (V, t, m, b, r, gain, limiter, p, v),

	N/A	$180 - 210	$150 - 175

M-80 SERIES - This series was introduced in 1989 and was focused on small amps for youth players. These amps feature basic controls plus some have chrous, reverb, and channel select. The most identifying feature about this series was the gray carpet covering on them. Fender hadn't had any covering other than tolex in over 20 years. The models ranged from small to big with the R.A.D. (1-8" 20W), the H.O.T. (1-10" 25W), the J.A.M. (1-12" 25W), and the M-80 (1-12" 90W). The M-80 Chorus (2-12" 2 X 65W), and the BXR 300C (see BXR series), were introduced in 1990. All of the models were remodeled with black tolex covering in 1992. Retail prices for these amps started at $199.99 for the R.A.D. and range up to $719.99 for the M-80 Chorus. Like a lot of Fender solid-state amplifiers these don't hold much value. They were phased out in 1997 and replaced by the Frontline series. You can usually price these amplifiers in the $100 to $200 range.

PERFORMER 1000 (No. 022-6800-000) - 100W, 1-12" speaker, 12AX7 preamp tube, otherwise solid-state, reverb, new blackface control panel, 11 black knobs (Ch. 1: v, t, m, b, Ch. 2: gain, t, m, b, v, Both: reverb and effects mix), black tolex covering, silver grille, three button footswitch, mfg. 1993-95.

	N/A	$225 - 260	$185 - 210

Last MSR was $589.99..

Was also available in head only version (No. 022-6801-000) for $509.99

* Performer 650 (022-6805-000) - similar to Performer 1000 except output is 70W and two button footswitch.

	N/A	$210 - 240	$170 - 200

Last MSR was $459.99.

STANDARD SERIES - These are the higher end solid-state models that were introduced in the late 80's and early 90's. The Champion 110 (1-10" 25W), Princeton 112 (1-12", 35W), Deluxe 112 (1-12", 65W), and Stage 112SE (1-12" 160W) solid-state amps were introduced in 1993. There are many, many models in this series, and many have changed names but kept most of the components. It's very easy to confuse certain models with the right years and options. The Bullet (1-8" 15W) retailed for $164.99 and the Bullet Reverb (see Dyna-Touch section), which is the same amp with reverb retailed for $194.99. These two amps were made between 1993-97.

* Champion 110 - 25W into 8 Ohms, 1-10" speaker, solid-state combo, dual selectable channels (normal and drive), reverb, blackface control panel, one input, seven black knobs (v, gain, v, t, m, b, reverb), black tolex covering, silver grille, mfg. 1993-97.

	N/A	$85 - 100	$70 - 80

Last MSR was $259.99.

* Princeton 112 (Plus) - 35W, 1-12" speaker, solid-state combo, dual selectable channels (normal and drive), reverb, blackface control panel, two inputs, ten black knobs (v, t, m, b, gain, contour, v, t, b, reverb), black tolex covering, silver grille, mfg. 1993-97.

	N/A	$150 - 175	$120 - 135

Last MSR was $364.99.

GRADING	100%	EXCELLENT	AVERAGE

* **Stage 112 SE (No. 022-6700-000)** - 160W into 8 Ohms, 1-12" speaker, dual selectable channels (normal and drive), reverb, blackface control panel, two inputs, mid-switch, ten black knobs (v, t, m, b, gain, contour, v, t, b, reverb), black tolex covering, silver grille, mfg. 1993-97.

| | N/A | $170 - 195 | $150 - 165 |

Last MSR was $579.99.

* **Princeton Chorus (DSP) (No. 022-5700-020)** - 2 X 25W, 2-10" speakers, solid-state combo, reverb, chorus, black control panel, two inputs, eleven black knobs (v, t, m, b, reveb, gain, limiter, presence, volume, rate depth), effects loops footswitch, black tolex covering, silver grille, mfg. 1988-2002.

Fender Princeton Chorus
courtesy Zach Fjestad

Fender Princeton Chorus
courtesy Zach Fjestad

| | $500 | $250 - 300 | $195 - 225 |

Last MSR was $719.99.

This amp underwent a makeover in 1999 and became a stereo amp. There are many different digital effects that are used. DSP stands for Digital Signal Processing. There are a few more knobs in the chrous and reverb, which is where the DSP comes in. This is the same as the old Princeton Chrous in every other way. The old No. was 022-5700-010.

Add $130 for the DSP option. Add $21 for cover.

The ultimate amplifier for the ultimate guitar player.

* **Ultimate Chorus (DSP) (No. 022-6701-020)** - 2 X 65W, 2-12" speakers, solid-state combo, reverb, chorus, black control panel, two inputs,14 black knobs (v, t, m, b, reveb, gain, v, t, m, b, reverb, rate, depth), effects loops footswitch, black tolex covering, silver grille, mfg. 1988-current.

| MSR | $850 | $600 | $425 - 500 | $325 - 375 |

Originally known as the Power Chorus, and was changed to the Ultra Chorus in 1993. The Ultra Chorus was changed to the Ultimate Chorus in 1995, and was changed to a stereo amp (DSP) in 2000. The power and speaker size has remained the same, just some of the effects have changed.

Add $21 for cover.

Automatic Series

This series was introduced in 2000 and lasted a year. and must have been a real cream puff. It was available as the Automatic SE (No. 022-6400-000) retailed for $299.99, or the Automatic GT (No. 022-6300-000) retailed for $339.99. A two button footswitch was available for $54.95. After the raging success of this line, I would say an Automatic with footswitch is worth about as 40 shares of Enron stock.

Bassman Series (Current Production)

The Bassman series have always been popular for Fender. They started to make solid-state models after the original tube Bassman's died out. At the 2002 Summer NAMM show, Fender started to get back into the tube Bassman's. Fender purchased Sunn sometime in the late 1980's or early 1990's and had been producing SUNN amps for a while. Now they are putting Fender's name on SUNN amps. What used to be the SUNN 1200s and 300T are now the Fender Bassman 1200 and 300, respectively.

BASSMAN 1200 - see the Hybrid section of Fender.

BASSMAN 300 - See the Tube section of Fender.

BASSMAN 400 (No. 022-4505-000) - 350W, 2-10" Eminence speakers, 1 8 Ohm compression driver horn, solid-state combo, black control panel, one input, 13 silver-top knobs (gain, room balance, b, t, 6 knob equalizer, compressor, MV), FX loop, mute switch, casters, one-button footswitch, black tolex covering, black metal grille, mfg. 2000-current.

| MSR | $1,350 | $900 | $525 - 600 | $400 - 500 |

* **Bassman 400 Head Only (No. 022-4506-000)** - Same as the Bassman 400, except it is the head unit only, and has two speaker out jacks, mfg 2000-current.

| MSR | $800 | $550 | $350 - 400 | $275 - 325 |

* **Bassman 410H Enclosure (No. 021-1671-010)** - This enclosure matches up exactly to the Bassman 400 Head, as is designed for that application. There are 4-10" Eminence speakers with one compression driver horn with level control, mfg. 2000-current.

| MSR | $600 | $400 | $325 - 275 | $190 - 225 |

GRADING	100%	EXCELLENT	AVERAGE

* Bassman 115 Enclosure (No. 021-1670-010) - This enclosure sits perfectly underneath the Bassman 410, but it can be used for other applications as well. There is 1-15" Eminence speaker with a ported enclosure, mfg. 2000-current.

MSR	$400	$250	$160 - 185	$135 - 150

> Add $21 for cover on the 400. Add $26 for cover on the 410H and 115 enclosure.

BASSMAN 200 (No. 022-4504-000) - 200W, 1-15" Eminence speaker, 1 8 Ohm compression driver horn, solid-state combo, black control panel, one input, eight silver-top knobs (gain, room balance, b, m, mid frequency, t, compressor, master volume), tuner out jack, FX loop, black tolex covering, black metal grille, mfg. 2000-current.

MSR	$900	$500	$375 - 425	$325 - 350

> Add $21 for cover.

BASSMAN 100 (No. 022-4503-000) - 100W, 1-15" Eminence speaker, Piezo horn, solid-state combo, active/passive input pad selector, gain, black control panel, one input, seven silver-top knobs (gain, bass, mid level, mid frequency, treble, compressor, mv), tuner out jack, indicators for tuner mute, power amp, compressor level, and preamp clip, XLR line-out, FX loop, black tolex covering, black metal grille, mfg. 2000-current.

MSR	$730	$475	$300 - 350	$240 - 275

> Add $21 for cover.

BASSMAN 60 (No. 022-4502-000) - 60W, 1-12" Eminence speaker, piezo horn, solid-state combo, active/passive input pad selector, gain, black control panel, one input, five silver-top knobs (gain, bass, mid level, mid frequency, treble), tuner out jack, indicators for tuner mute, power amp, and preamp clip, XLR line-out, FX loop, wedge cabinet design, black tolex covering, black metal grille, mfg. 2000-current.

MSR	$550	$400	$230 - 260	$185 - 215

BASSMAN 25 (No. 022-4501-000) - 25W, 1-10" Eminence speaker, solid-state combo, active and passive inputs, FX loop, headphone jack, aux. input, black control panel, five silver-top knobs (v, t, m, b, aux level), tuner out jack, tuner mute switch with indicator, enhance switch, wedge cabinet design, black tolex covering, black metal grille, mfg. 2000-current.

MSR	$390	$250	$160 - 185	$130 - 150

BXR Series

The BXR series was introduced in 1987 and stood for Bass Extended Range. The first model was the BXR 400 top which came with optional cabinets. This lasted until 1994 and at this point other BXR models started to emerge.Covers were available for most of the larger models and add $20 for the cover.

BXR 400 (No. 022-4000-000) - 400W, Twin 200W amps, speakers were available 1-15", 4-10", or 1-18" and 2-10" in an enclosure, 11 bands of equalization, compressor, only a couple of knobs, black metal casing for the head, black tolex covering for the speaker enclosures, silver grille, mfg. 1987-1994.

	N/A	$375 - 425	$300 - 350

Last MSR was $899.99.

BXR 15 - 15W, 1-8" speaker, solid-state combo, black control panel,one input, headphone jack, external speaker jack, four black knobs (v, l, m, h), black tolex covering, black grille, mfg. 1994-96.

	N/A	$60 - 75	$45 - 55

BXR 25 (No. 022-4403-000) - 25W, 1-10" speaker, solid-state combo, blackface control panel, hi/lo inputs (2), four black-top knobs (v, l, m, h), tape inputs, effects loop, headphone jack, black tolex covering, black grille, mfg. 1992-99.

	$175	$120 - 140	$95 - 110

Last MSR was $299.99.

BXR 60 (No. 022-4404-000) - 60W, 1-10" speaker, solid-state combo, blackface control panel, two inputs, five black knobs (v, l, low mid, high mid, high), tape inputs, effects loop, headphone jack, line out, black tolex covering, black grille, mfg. 1994-99.

	$250	$170 - 195	$140 - 160

Last MSR was $429.99.

BXR 100 (No. 022-4401-000) - 100W, 1-15" speaker, solid-state combo, blackface control panel, two inputs, enhancment buttons, four black knobs (gain, low and high shelving, volume), 7-band equalizer, effects loop, headphone jack, line out, black tolex covering, black grille, mfg. 1993-99.

	$300	$225 - 250	$175 - 200

Last MSR was $529.99.

BXR 200 (No. 022-4405-000) - 200W, various speaker configurations, solid-state combo, chorus, blackface control panel, enhancement buttons, five black knobs (gain, low and high shelving, rate, depth), 9-band equalizer, delta comp switch, footswitch, effects loop, black tolex covering, black grille, mfg. 1995-99.

	$400	$275 - 325	$225 - 260

Last MSR was $729.99.

* BXR 200 HD (No. 022-4406-000) - Similar to the BXR 200 except is the head unit only. The BXR 200 HD was designed for Fender BXR Enclosures. These came in three different styles: the BXR 115B (No. 021-1670-000) 1-15" speaker, last retail $319.99, the BXR 410H (No. 021-1671-000) 4-10" speakers, last retail $549.99, and the BXR 210H (No. 021-1672-000) 2-10" speakers, last retail $399.99. All of these enclosures have matching black tolex covering, and black grille to the BXR 200 HD.

	$275	$185 - 210	$150 - 170

Last MSR was $529.99.

GRADING	100%	EXCELLENT	AVERAGE

BXR 300C (No. 022-4100-010) - 300W, 1-15" speaker, solid-state combo, blackface control panel, two inputs, five black knobs (v, t, m, mid-frequency, b), effects loop, Delta-Comp Limiter, fan cooling, black tolex covering, black grille, mfg. 1987-1999.

	$450	$300 - 350	$250 - 280

Last MSR was $799.99.

***BXR 300R HEAD (No. 022-4107-010)** - Similar to the BXR 300C except is the head unit only, a two-space rack mount. mfg. 1993-95.

	$300	$200 - 225	$170 - 190

Last MSR was $639.99.

Cyber-Twin Series

CYBER-DELUXE (No. 022-9001-000) - 65W, 1-12" Celestion G12T-100 speaker, 64 presets, 16 reverbs, 16 modulation effects, 16 delay types, digital tuner, programmable noise gate and compressor, new blackface control panel, one input, fourteen silver-top knobs (trim, gain, v, t, m, b, master, reverb, mod f/x, delay, amp type, and three others for digital processing, four-button footswitch, black tolex covering, silver grille, New 2002.

Fender Cyber Deluxe
courtesy Fender

MSR	$999.99	$675	$525 - 600	$450 - 500

Dyna-Touch Series

The Dyna-Touch series was introduced in 2000. These are amps that are solid-state and some have three channels. These are meant to deliver the goods in any performance situation. The models include the Stage 100 and 160, the Deluxe 90, Princeton 65, Champion 30, and the Bullet Reverb. The higher end models are equipped with Celestion G12T-100 speakers. All amps include gain, reverb, and various tone knobs. They all come with black tolex covering with a silver grille.

At the 2002 NAMM show Fender introduced the Dyna-Touch amps including DSP on every model. This means every model in this series it now comes with the digital effects that DSP offers.

Add $40 for the one-button footswitch for the Champion 30. (DSP), and $50 for the two-button footswitch for the Princeton 65 (DSP).

Add $20 for cover on any amp for Dyna-Touch series.

STAGE 100 (No. 022-6700-010) - 100W, 2-12" speakers, mfg. 2000-02. A 1-12" enclosure is available (No. 021-1664-000) MSR $299.99.

	$450	$275 - 325	$225 - 250

Last MSR was $649.99.

***Stage 100 Head (No. 022-6900-000)** - Similar to the Stage 100 except is the head unit only. A 4-12" enclosure is available for this model (No. 021-1665-000) MSR $599.99).

	$350	$220 - 250	$185 - 210

Last MSR was $579.99.

STAGE 100 DSP (No. 22-67000-020) - 100W, 2-12" speakers, solid-state chassis, DSP effects, blackface control panel, 14 black knobs, 42 lbs., new 2002. A 1-12" enclosure is available (No. 021-1664-000) MSR $299.99.

MSR	$700	$500	$350 - 400	$275 - 325

***Stage 100 Head DSP (No. 22-69000-010)** - Similar to the Stage 100 except is the head unit only, 24 lbs., new 2002. A 4-12" enclosure is available for this model (No. 021-1665-000) MSR $599.99).

MSR	$650	$475	$325 - 375	$250 - 300

STAGE 160 - 160W, 2-12" speakers, mfg. 2000-02.

	$475	$250 - 300	$200 - 235

Last MSR was $759.99.

STAGE 160 DSP (No. 22-68000-020) - 160W, 2-12" speakers, DSP effects, blackface control panel, 14 black knobs, 53 lbs., new 2002.

MSR	$785.50	$550	$350 - 425	$275 - 325

DELUXE 90 - 90W, 1-12" speaker, three selectable channels, mfg. 2000-02.

	$375	$240 - 275	$200 - 225

Last MSR was $569.99.

GRADING	100%	EXCELLENT	AVERAGE

DELUXE 90 DSP (No. 22-67200-030) - 90W, 1-12" speaker, solid-state chassis, DSP effects, blackface control panel, 12 black knobs, 33 lbs., new 2002.

	MSR	$571	$400	$300 - 350	$225 - 265

PRINCETON 65 - 65W, 1-12" speaker, dual channels, mfg. 2000-02.

	$275	$195 - 225	$160 - 185

Last MSR was $419.99.

PRINCETON 65 DSP (No. 22-67400-030) - 65W, 1-12" speaker, solid-state chassis, DSP effects, blackface control panel, nine black knobs, 28 lbsl, new 2002.

	MSR	$480	$350	$250 - 300	$200 - 225

CHAMPION 30 - 30W, 1-10" speaker, dual channels.

	$200	$125 - 140	$95 - 110

Last MSR was $309.99.

CHAMPION 30 DSP (No. 22-67300-020) - 30W, 1-10" speaker, solid-state chassis, DSP effects, blackface control panel, eight black knobs, 25 lbs., new 2002.

	MSR	$328.50	$235	$175 - 200	$135 - 155

BULLET REVERB - 15W, 1-8" speaker, dual channels, mfg. 2000-02.

	$125	$70 - 85	$50 - 65

Last MSR was $199.99.

BULLET 15 DSP (No. 22-67700-23) - 15W, 1-8" speaker, solid-state chassis, DSP effects, blackface control panel, seven black knobs, 15 lbs., new 2002.

	MSR	$228.50	$165	$120 - 140	$85 - 105

Frontman Amp Series

The Frontman series was introduced in 2000. These are all relatively small amplifiers that are affordable. There are five models of the Frontman, including the 25R, 15R, 15G, and two bass amps the 15B, and 25B. The number and letter indicate what model the amp is. The 25 or 15 indicate the wattage. The G means a basic amp without reverb. The R indicates reverb and the B shows that it's a bass amp. The speakers vary in size according to the wattage. For 15W the speaker is an eight inch. If the amp is a 25W it comes with a 10 inch. Most of the models have volume, gain, and three-way equalizers. Each model comes with a headphone jack as well. The price of these amps are fairly cheap. The Frontman 15G starts at 139.99 and prices range evenly up to 299.99 for the Frontman 25B. Pricing can be found by taking 50% of the retail for an amp in excellent condition.

KXR Series (Keyboard)

The KXR series was designed by Fender for keyboards or self contained P.A. systems. Introduced in the early nineties, around the same time as the BXR series, they have solid-state features. The KXR originally started with the 100 and the 200. Then by 1996, The KXR 60 had made its appearance. The KXR 200 (No. 022-8502-000) offered 200W, 1-15" speaker with a dual piezo high-freq. horn, and a whole lot of controls with four separate channels. This number could keep you busy for hours. The KXR 100, which is still in production (No. 022-8501-000), features 90W, 1-15" speaker with a dual piezo hf horn, and three channels with about half the knobs. It retails for $569.99. The KXR 60 (No. 022-8500-000) has 50W of power, 1-12" speaker, two channels, and retails for $469.99. The 200 was discontinued around 2000.

Misc Solid-State Amplifiers

Fender is always tyring new things and sometimes it's best to stick with what works, but anyway they have introduced the Amp Can. This is a round 15W battery operated amp that can be used for acoustic guitar, voice, electric guitar, keyboard, or whatever. It has a 6" speaker, rechargable battery, distortion and weighs 13 lbs! The Amp Can (No. 022-1200-000) retails for $249.99 and hasn't been on the market long enough to have a solid value on it.

HYBRID AMPLIFIERS (TUBE/SOLID-STATE)

Hybrid Champ Models

CHAMP 25 S/E - 25W, 1-10" speaker, used new "hybrid" circuitry, which combines tubes with transistors, solid-state preamp, 2 X 5881 / 6L6 power output tubes, black control panel, eleven black knobs (norm, v, t, b, m, drive, gain, overdrive, v, t, b, r) black tolex covering, mfg. 1992-94.

	N/A	$235 - 265	$180 - 215

This model came with five custom coverings, including red, white, gray, and snakeskin.

* **Champ 25** -Similar to the Champ 25 S/E, except doesn't have tape inputs, line out, and master volume, and standby switch, mfg. 1992-94.

	N/A	$210 - 245	$160 - 195

Cyber-Twin Series

The Cyber Twin Series is Fender's newest technology. Fender took a wide selection of their vintage amplifiers and by using modern technology were able to put them all into one monster amp. The new technology is called Cybernetic Amp Design. There is a mixture of tubes, capacitors, and resistors, along with analog drive circuits, and the DSP circuits in the stereo amps. There are three preset sections including: your amp collection, Fender Custom Shop, and Player's Lounge. There is a total of 205 different preset possibilites. This amp also makes it possible to create your own amp by mixing the possibiltites. There is a Cyber foot controller (No. 022-9100-000) for the amp that retails for $349.00. For the Cyber Deluxe (no tubes) see solid-state section.

GRADING	100%	EXCELLENT	AVERAGE

CYBER-TWIN (No. 022-9000-000) - 130W, 2-12" Celestian G12 T-100 speakers, 2 X 12AX7 preamp tubes, otherwise solid-state, new blackface control panel with digital display, one input, nine black knobs (trim, gain, v, t, m, b, presence, reverb, master), various buttons and knobs for the digital processor, black tolex covering, silver grille, mfg. 2001-current.

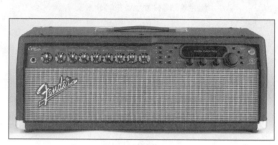

Fender Cyber Twin
courtesy Fender

Fender Cyber Twin
courtesy Fender

MSR	$1,750	$1,250	$850 - 950	$725 - 800

* Cyber-Twin Head Unit Only (No. 022-9002-000) - Similar to the Cyber-Twin Combo but in the head unit only. Designed for use with the Showman 412S Enclosure.

MSR	$1,500	$1,050	$675 - 750	$600 - 650

* Showman 412S Enclosure (No. 021-1675-010) - 4-12" Celestion G12T-75 speakers in a black tolex covering silver grille cabinet. Matches the Cyber Twin Head to create a piggy-back unit.

MSR	$750	$550	$350 - 425	$265 - 300

Bassman Series

BASSMAN 1200 (No. 022-4505-000) - 1200W, 2-space rack mount head-unit only, hybrid design, preamp: 2 X 12AX7, solid-state power amp, dual channels, compression, front black control panel, single input, eleven black knobs, 10-band graphic equalizer, various buttons black covering, black grille, new 2002.

MSR	$1,600	$1,150	$850 - 1,000	$675 - 750

Roc-Pro Series

This series was introduced in 1996 and was meant to be a line of tube driven hybrid amps that were supposed to rock. There were two different amp sizes built with two different speaker cabinets. Inside was a real 12AX7/ECC83 tube to drive it. The design was of a new silver-face control panel with black tolex covering, and a black metal grille. The knobs resembled those of blackface but they were all black. They had one input. The Roc Pro 1000 (No. 022-6808-000) featured 100W, available in head unit or as a combo with 1-12" speaker, two channels, 12 black knobs (Norm: v, t, m, b, Drive: gain 1, gain 2, t, m, b, v, reverb and effects mix) and retailed last for $619.99 for the combo, and $539.99 for the head unit only. The Roc-Pro 700 was the 70W version of the 100, and had two less knobs (gain 2, and effects mix). It retailed for $519.99. There were also speaker enclosures available for the Roc-Pro Head including the GE-112 and the GE-412. The GE-112 (No. 021-1660-000) had 1-12" speaker and retailed for $199.99. The GE-412 (No. 021-1662-000) had 4-12" speakers and retailed for $459.99. There was also a discount when the Roc-Pro 100 and the speaker enclosure were purchased together. This line was discontinued in 2000.

FERNANDES

Amplifiers currently produced in Asia.

Fernandes has made guitars overseas since 1969 and moved to the American market in 1992. Fernandes currently offers some small amplifiers in different colors and has also offered small guitar and bass amps in the past. Nowadays Fernandes has the popular line of HIWATT Amplifiers. Refer to the HIWATT section of the *Blue Book of Guitar Amplifiers* for HIWATT information. The only amplifiers that Fernandes produces now in its own name are hand-held units that are called Skel-Zo and are shaped like the popular Nomad guitar by Fernandes. List price on this unit (available in red, blue-green and a yellow) is $39.98. For more information on these or other Fernandes items, refer to the Fernandes web site (see Trademark Index).

FLITE SOUND

Speaker cabinets currently produced in Danielson, Connecticut.

Flite Sound had been building quality speaker enclosures since 1987. They make a wide variety of bass, guitar, P.A., monitors, and keyboard speakers. For a full line of products and what Flite Sound has to offer, refer to the Flite Sound web site (see Trademark Index).

FRAMUS

Amplifiers currently produced in Markneukirchen, Germany. Distributed by Warwick GmbH & Co. Music Equipment Kg of Markneukirchen, Germany.

When Frederick Wilfer returned to his home town of Walthersgrun at the end of World War II, he realized that the American-controlled Sudetenland area was soon to fall under control of the Russian forces. With the help of the Americans, Wilfer succeeded in resettling a number of violin makers from Schonbach to Franconia (later in the district of Erlangen). Between 1945 to 1947, Wilfer continued to find homes and employment for the Schonbach violin makers.

In 1946, Wilfer founded the Framus production company, the company name an acronym for Franconian Musical instruments. As the company established itself in 1946, Wilfer drew on the knowledge of his violin builder from Schonbach to produce a range of musical instruments including violins and cellos. The new Framus company expanded out of its first couple of production buildings, eventually building a new factory in Bubenreuth in 1955.

The first Framus electric guitars appeared in the 1950's. Due to the presence of American servicemen stationed there, the influence of rock'n' roll surfaced earlier in Germany than other European countries. As a result, German guitar builders had a headstart on answering the demand caused by the proliferation of pop groups during the 1960's. Furthermore, as the German production increased, they began exporting their guitars to other countries (including the U.S.). The Framus company stayed active in producing acoustic and electric guitars, and electric basses until the mid 1970's.

In the 1970's, increased competition and serious price undercutting from firms in the Asian market had a serious effect on established companies. Unfortunately, one aspect was to force a number of firms into bankruptcy - and Framus was one of those companies in 1975. However, Wilfer did have the opportunity to watch his son, Hans-Peter Wilfer, establish his own company in 1982 (see WARWICK). Warwick's success allowed Hans-Peter to re-introduce the Framus trademark to the European musical market in 1996. In honor of his father Frederick, Hans-Peter chose to use the world famous Framus trademark when he began offering guitar models in 1996.

(Source: Hans Peter Wilfer, Warwick GmbH & Co. Music Equipment Kg; and Tony Bacon and Paul Day, The Guru's Guitar Guide)

AMPLIFIERS & SPEAKER CABINETS

Framus produces all-tube handwired amplifiers. They have the Dragon and the Cobra head units, and the Ruby Riot Combo. Prices on the amps start at $2,899. There are speaker cabinets available as well that start at $1,199. For more information on Framus amplication refer to the website (see trademark index).

FULTON WEBB
Amplifiers currently produced in Austin, Texas.

Fulton Webb amplifiers are completely hand-built and are usually delivered 8-10 weeks from the time when ordered. The models that they currently offer are the 17, 31, and 50W models. The DR-45 (Dirty Ryhtyhm) model was just recently released. These amps are all tube, point-to-point wired, and have either a tube or solid-state rectifier switch. For more information or ordering info, refer to the web site (see Trademark Index).

NOTES

F

Section G

GALLIEN-KRUEGER

Amplifiers currently produced in San Jose, California. The Gallien-Krueger trademark was established in 1968.

Robert Gallien is a graduate of Stanford University during the late 1960's, and he took his first hand-built amplifier to a local music store in 1968. Carlos Santana happened to be around when Gallien introduced this amplifier and he bought it the following day. The rest, as we say, is history. Gallien-Krueger has successfully been building quality amplifiers and speaker cabinets for over 30 years now. Some of the artists that play their products include Tom Hamilton of Aerosmith, Toney Kanal of No Doubt, and my favorite, Flea of the Red Hot Chili Peppers. For more information refer to the Gallien-Krueger web site (see Trademark Index).

GRADING	100%	EXCELLENT	AVERAGE

G

ELECTRIC BASS AMPLIFIERS

These are the models from the current Gallien-Krueger catalog. Older models are more hard to come by as far as information. Look for more information on discontinued models of upcoming editions of the *Blue Book of Guitar Amplifiers*.

Bass Head & Combo Units

All head units except for the 400RB-III have dual amplifiers, one to run the woofer, and one to run the horn unit. The 800RB has been in the family for over two decades. This amp differs from the others in the line as it has a gray control panel instead of silver. There are cooling fans in the larger amplifiers. The combo units have a tilt-back cabinet design as well as a regular design.

400RB-III (302-0051-A) - 240W (150W), head-unit only, solid-state chassis, single channel, front silver control panel, single input, nine black knobs (v, c, p, t, h/m, l/m, b, boost, master), direct out line effects loop, voicing filters, black metal covering, 15 lbs., current mfg.

	MSR	$649	$475	$375 - 425	$300 - 330

* **400RB/210 (303-0150-A)** - Similar to the 400RB-III except in combo form with 2-10" speakers, black covering, black metal grille, 65 lbs., current mfg.

	MSR	$999	$699	$500 - 600	$400 - 450

* **400RB/115 (303-0140-A)** - Similar to the 400RB-III except in combo form with 1-15" speaker, black covering, black metal grille, 65 lbs., current mfg.

	MSR	$999	$699	$500 - 600	$400 - 450

* **400RB/112 (303-0130-A)** - Similar to the 400RB-III except in combo form with 1-12" speaker, black covering, black metal grille, 65 lbs., disc 2002.

	$699	$500 - 600	$400 - 450

Last MSR was $999.

700RB (302-0020-A) - 380W + 50W, head-unit only, solid-state chassis, single channel, front silver control panel, single input, eleven black knobs (direct out level, v, c, p, t, h/m, l/m, b, boost, tweeter, woofer), effects loop, voicing filters, black metal covering, 16.5 lbs., current mfg.

	MSR	$799	$575	$475 - 525	$375 - 425

* **700RB/210 (303-0120-A)** - Similar to the 700RB except in combo form with 2-10" speakers, black covering, black metal grille, 82 lbs., current mfg.

	MSR	$1,499	$1,075	$800 - 950	$650 - 725

* **700RB/115 (303-0110-A)** - Similar to the 700RB except in combo form with 1-15" speaker, black covering, black metal grille, 77 lbs., current mfg.

	MSR	$1,499	$1,075	$800 - 950	$650 - 725

* **700RB/112 (303-0100-A)** - Similar to the 700RB except in combo form with 1-12" speaker, black covering, black metal grille, 77 lbs., disc 2002.

	$1,075	$800 - 950	$650 - 725

Last MSR was $1,499.

800RB (302-0060-0) - 300W +100W, head-unit only, solid-state chassis, single channel, front silver and black control panel, single input, nine black and gray knobs (v, t, h/m, l/m, b, boost, f, MV 300, MV100), effects loop, voicing filters, black metal covering, 23 lbs., current mfg.

	MSR	$999	$699	$500 - 600	$425 - 475

1001RB (302-0030-A) - 540W + 50W, head-unit only, solid-state chassis, single channel, front silver control panel, single input, eleven black knobs (direct out level, v, c, p, t, h/m, l/m, b, boost, tweeter, woofer), effects loop, voicing filters, black metal covering, 18 lbs., current mfg.

	MSR	$999	$699	$500 - 600	$425 - 475

* **1001RB/210 (303-0170-A)** - Similar to the 1001RB except in combo form with 2-10" speakers, black covering, black metal grille, 83 lbs., current mfg.

	MSR	$1,699	$1,200	$875 - 1,025	$750 - 825

* **1001RB/115 (303-0160-A)** - Similar to the 1001RB except in combo form with 1-15" speaker, black covering, black metal grille, 77 lbs., current mfg.

	MSR	$1,699	$1,200	$875 - 1,025	$750 - 825

GRADING	100%	EXCELLENT	AVERAGE

2001RB (302-0090-A) - 2 X 500W, 2 X 50W, head-unit only, solid-state chassis, dual channels, front silver control panel, single input, 14 black knobs (Ch. B: g, e, bottom, level B, Ch. A: level A, c, p, t, h/m, l/m, b), boost, tweeter, woofer, effects loop, distortion circuits, voicing filters, 25 lbs., current mfg.

	MSR	$1,699	$1,199	$850 - 1,050	$750 - 800

Gallien-Krueger also makes the 2001RB in a pre-amp or power-amp only version.

MB150S112 (303-0006-0) - 150W, 1-12" speaker, solid-state combo, single channel, front gray control panel, single input, seven black knobs (v, t, h/m, h/l, b, output level, limiter level), effects loop, black covering, black metal grille, 24 lbs., current mfg.

	MSR	$949	$675	$500 - 575	$400 - 450

MB150E112 (303-0011-0) - 150W, 1-12" speaker, solid-state combo, single channel, stereo chorus (with knobs), front gray control panel, single input, nine black knobs (v, t, h/m (freq & level), h/l (freq & level), b, output level, limiter level), effects loop, black covering, black metal grille, 24 lbs., current mfg.

	MSR	$1,099	$775	$600 - 675	$525 - 575

Backline Series

The Backline Series went into full swing at the NAMM show in 2002. The Backline 115 has been around for a while, but the rest of the models were introduced in 2002. There are also speaker cabinets made just for the Backline head. These are available in a 4-10", 1-15", and 2-10" configurations. Retail on the 4-10" is $499.

BACKLINE 250BL - 125W, head-unit only, solid-state combo, dual channels, front silver control panel, single input, ten black knobs (g, level B, level A, c, t, h/m, l/m, b, boost, master, effects loop, footswitch, direct out line, black covering, black metal grille, 55 lbs., new 2002.

	MSR	$399	$285	$220 - 260	$175 - 200

BACKLINE 115 - 125W, 1-15" speaker, solid-state combo, dual channels, front silver control panel, single input, ten black knobs (g, level B, level A, c, t, h/m, l/m, b, boost, master, effects loop, footswitch, direct out line, black covering, black metal grille, 55 lbs., mfg. 2001-current.

	MSR	$599	$425	$325 - 375	$260 - 295

BACKLINE 112 - 70W, 1-12" speaker, solid-state combo, dual channels, front silver control panel, single input, ten black knobs (g, level B, level A, c, t, h/m, l/m, b, boost, master, effects loop, footswitch, direct out line, black covering, black metal grille, 40 lbs., new 2002.

	MSR	$449	$325	$250 - 300	$200 - 225

BACKLINE 110 - 70W, 1-10" speaker, solid-state combo, dual channels, front silver control panel, single input, ten black knobs (g, level B, level A, c, t, h/m, l/m, b, boost, master, effects loop, footswitch, direct out line, black covering, black metal grille, 30 lbs., new 2002.

	MSR	$349	$250	$180 - 220	$150 - 175

Speaker Cabinets

Gallien-Krueger offers high-quality speaker cabinets to match up with their head-units. These cabinets are constructed of birch on the higher wattage models, black carpet, nickel plated casters, heavy-gauge metal black grille, and an interlocking corner system. There are three models in configurations of 4-10", 2-10", or 1-15" for lighter wattage heads (400RB and 800RB). For the higher end models (700RB and up) there are three amps with the same speaker configurations, they can handle twice the power, and have a front loaded port system. For Backline speaker cabinets refer to the Backline section in Gallien-Krueger.

There are also some accessories available for Gallien-Krueger amps and cabinets. Refer to the web site for inoformation (see Trademark Index).

GARNET
Amplifiers previously produced in Canada.

Gar Gillies has been involved in electronics since he started working many years ago. In the mid-1960's, the radio and T.V. repair business Gillies had running turned into the Garnet Amplifier Company. With the help of Gillies' two sons, Russell and Garnet, they formed a partnership and began producing their first amplifiers in the late 1960's. Garnet produced quality tube amplifiers, while the Guess Who started playing as Gar was the roadie for the band in the 1970's. P.A. equipment was also a product offered by Garnet. The late 1970's and 1980's were the heyday for Garnet until 1989. Because of financial hardship after an expansion project, Garnet went out of business as far as an amplifier manufacturing. However, Gar still works on amplifiers, fixing, upgrading, and designing some amplifiers. For a complete history and specs on Garnet amplifiers visit the Garnet web site (see Trademark Index).

(Information for Garnet history from Russell Gillies and www.garnetamps.com).

ELECTRIC TUBE AMPLIFIERS

Garnet did make some neat stuff in its day. The first models to be released were the **Pro, Rebel, and BTO** (stood for Big Time Operator) series. These models had two guitar heads and a P.A. system. The Pro series evolved into the **Pro 200, 400, and 600** models. After this, three Deputy models were released. They also had combo amps such as the **Banshee, Gnome, L'il Rock, Mach 5, Enforcer, Sessionman**, and three **Revolution** models. There were also reverb units made by Gar. For more information on these models, and pictures, go to the Garnet website that has lots of information, especially for a company that has been out of business for over 10 years.

GENESIS
Amplifiers and other electric products currently produced in Sydney, Australia.

Robert Ang is the man who started Genesis Amplifiers. With a degree from the UWA (University of Western Australia-sorry University of Wisconsin). he started work in medicine. Robert then moved into another field after moving to Sydney. Here he makes some amplifiers and preamps (using tubes, of course) in a shop. For a full listing of Genesis' products and what they have to offer visit the web site (see Trademark Index).

GENZ BENZ

Amplifiers currently produced in Scottsdale, Arizona.

Genz Benz is a company out of Arizona that produces amplifers and speaker enclosures. Mainly, Genz Benz makes sound enclosures for bass and electric guitars. They do make amplification systems for acoustic guitars, keyboards, and bass guitars. Their partner company, Tube Works, makes electric guitar amplifers. All of Genz Benz's amplifiers are solid-state units with a variety of head's and combo units. For a full listing and more information on Genz Benz visit their web site (see Trademark Index).

GEORGE DENNIS LTD.

Amplifiers currently produced in the Czech Republic.

George Dennis amplifiers have been produced since 1996, but the story of the company goes back to 1973. The president of the company today, George Burgerstein, was playing in a band with Alex Bajger, who is the designer and developer of the company. Alex showed George an amp he had designed, and George liked it so much he sold his Vox AC-30 and used Alex's exclusively. During the 1980's after the band had broken up, George and another friend, Martin, worked to create "The Blue Amplifier", until Martin was killed in a car accident. In 1996, George met up with Alex again and the two became partners to create the Blue Amplifier, once again. Since these two men have so much experience in the music industry, their prototype amplifier, "The Blue," is a "truly terrific guitar amplifier." Currently, George Dennis Ltd., has a full line of amplifiers and effect pedals. For a complete listing of the George Dennis line, including effect pedals, please visit the web site (see Trademark Index).

ELECTRIC TUBE AMPLIFIERS

George Dennis features many different models for tube amplifiers today. The Blue Series is offered in many versions by itself. The **Blue 60W** is offered as a head and combo, as is the **Blue 100W**. These are the flagship amplifiers for George Dennis and offer these features: four channels, reverb, 5-button footswitch, 12AX7 preamp tubes, EL34 power tubes, and Celestion speakers for all the combos.

Another line of amplifiers are the **Blue Beetle**, and the **Mighty Mouse**. Both of these amplifiers are offered as a head-unit or in combo version. The Blue Beetle is a 15W tube amp powered by 2 X EL84 tubes, and has 1-10" Celestion speaker. The Mighty Mouse has 30W output from 4 X EL84 tubes, and a 12" Celestion speaker. Controls are identical on these amplifiers with dual channels, and reverb.

Recently, bass amplifiers were introduced into the line. The Bassic Tube is offered in two versions, the only difference being wattage and tubes. The **Bassic Tube 120** has 120W output from 4 X EL34 tubes. The **Bassic Tube 200** has 200W from 4 X KT88 tubes.

All amplifiers are covered in a blue vinyl covering. In 2002, for their 10 year anniversary, they are offering all of their tube amps with denim covering and a polished stainless steel control panel. They also have a silver plate on the lower right corner stating the 10 year anniversary.

SPEAKER CABINETS

Just as Marshall did 40 years ago, George Dennis does with their products; offer the stack. There are two different 4-12" cabinets, one that is slanted and one that is straight. These cabinets have Celestion speakers, and can handle up to 200W. A **Blue 412A** and a **Blue 412B** sitting under a Blue 100W head produces a lot of blue. A **Blue 112** cabinet is available with 1-12" speaker and the **Blue 212** cabinet with 2-12" is also in the catalog. For Bass cabinets a enclosure is available in 4-10" and 1-15" configurations. Each of these have a tweeter, and the cabinets can handle 300W for the 15 and 600W for the 4-10.

GERLITZ

Amplifiers currently produced in Salem, Oregon.

The Gerlitz amplifier company was founded to create one specific product. This product is the result of combining two other products into one. The G1 "Revelator" Dual Amp has the sounds of a Marshall Plexi unit and a Fender Blackface. These are two of the most popular amps along with the most recognizable sounds ever produced. The Blackface is based around a Deluxe Super Reverb (mid 1960's) and the Marshall Plexi around a 50 Watt Lead (late 1960's). For a complete description on the Revelator and prices refer to the web site (see Trademark Index).

GERMINO

Amplifiers currently produced in North Carolina.

Greg Germino just moved back to North Carolina to continue producing Germino amplifiers. These amps are handmade in a limited production. All amps go through a complete testing period before they are shipped. If the amp doesn't sound right, it doesn't leave the factory. These amps are somewhat reminiscent of the early Marshall "Plexi's." The electronic components truly make this amp of high quality. For more information regarding Germino amplifiers, please refer to the Germino web site (see Trademark Index).

GIBSON

Amplifiers currently produced in Nashville, Tennessee. Gibson has three facilities to build instruments in Nashville and Memphis, Tennessee, and Bozeman, Montana. Gibson previously produced amplifiers and other instruments in Kalamazoo, Michigan from 1896-1984. All Gibson amplifiers are distributed by the Gibson Guitar Corporation in Nashville. Gibson amplifiers were produced starting circa 1930's.

The roots of Gibson go way back to Orville Gibson when he and other men founded the company in 1902. Gibson guitars were made with the Gibson logo starting in 1896. Gibson amplifiers didn't come into the picture until the late 1930's, however. With the release of the first Gibson electric guitar, the ES-150, a guitar amplifier would be needed to make the new electric pickup useful. The first Gibson amplifiers were the EH series, which debuted in the late 1930's. With World War II going on in the early 1940's, Gibson amplifiers didn't really become a production item until circa 1948. Shipment totals from Gibson were first tracked on amplifiers starting in 1948. Gibson started to produce their popular GA series in the 1950's. Several models exist in this series and they were produced until the early 1970's when all amplifier production was halted. In 1999, Gibson reintroduced their amplifier line with the Goldtone series. Gibson amplifiers are currently produced today. Shipping totals on Gibson amplifiers are known up until 1967.

(Courtesy Walter Carter, Gibson Guitars: 100 Years of an American Icon; and Larry Meiners: Gibson Shipment Totals)

ELECTRIC TUBE AMPLIFIERS

Almost all Gibson Electric Tube amplifiers are in combo form. If they are indeed head-units or piggy back it will be noted in the description, otherwise all models can be assumed to be combos. Gibson uses a system to organize their models. GA stands for Gibson Tube Amplifier, GSS indicates Gibson Solid-State Amplifier, E equals Echo, L means the amp has Lansing speaker(s), R or RV stands for Reverb, and T indicates tremolo. For Example a GA-77RETL is a Gibson

GRADING	100%	EXCELLENT	AVERAGE

Tube Amplifier Model 77 with reverb, echo, tremolo, and has Lansing speakers. This works for almost all Gibson amplifiers. This system essentially started around 1948 when the GA amplifiers were introduced.

Keep in mind that Gibson is sketchy at best in the upper marketing division. Therefore there are a lot of models that are listed in catalogs anywhere and the only information is word-of-mouth. Most of the models up until 1967 are listed, but many after that are still M.I.A. We are constantly updating models when we learn about them and more Gibson amplifiers should be listed in further editions.

Add 10% for original cover on amplifier.

Electric Hawaiian (EH) Series

The first Gibson Electric Steel Guitar was produced around 1935, which was one of the first production amps made. This guitar came with a matching amplifier, the EH-150 (a model EH-100 was also available). These first amplifiers were manufactured by Lyon and Healy. Many times the guitar was sold with the matching amplifier. These amplifiers were produced up until the start of World War II. After the war a new line of amplifiers emerged.

The EH-100, EH-125, and the EH-150 are the three more known amplifiers in the EH series. Gibson offered more models including three AC/DC powered amps. The **EH-110** would run on either AC/DC power and was the same circuit as the EH-100. The **EH-160** was the same AC/DC version of the EH-150. There is also the **EH-195**, which is supposed to be another AC/DC variant, the **EH-185** and the **EH-275**. Research is still underway for these models.

EH-100 - 8W, 1-10" speaker, varying tube chassis, 6N7, 6C8, 6C5, & others for preamp, mainly 6V6 power, single channel, two inputs, no controls, black leatheretter covering, mfg. 1936-1941.

	N/A	$375 - 425	$300 - 325

This model has undergone change almost every year that it was in production. In 1937, a microphone input was added, as an instrument one was taken away, a volume control added, and the covering was changed to a tan color with vertical, dark stripes. In 1938, another input was added, and the covering was changed to a brown covering with horizontal, yellow stripes. In 1940, the covering was changed to a wood natural mahogany finish. The tube chassis has changed numerous times, don't be suprised to find some goofy tubes in the amp.

EH-125 - Wattage unknown, 1-12" speaker, six tube chassis, preamp: 2 X 6SQ7, 1 X 6J5, power: 2 X 6V6, 5Y3 rectifier, three inputs (two instruments, one microphone, microphone volume control, round shouldered cabinet, mfg. 1941-42.

	N/A	$425 - 475	$325 - 375

EH-150 - 15W, 1-10" speaker, various tube chassis: pretty much anything was used (typically six tubes), rear control panel, three inputs (two instruments, one microphone), two volume controls, tone switch, echo speaker jack, square cabinet, aeroplane cloth covering, dark grille, mfg. 1935-1942.

Gibson EH-150
courtesy solidbodyguitar.com, Inc.

Gibson EH-150
courtesy solidbodyguitar.com, Inc.

Gibson EH-150
courtesy solidbodyguitar.com, Inc.

	N/A	$800 - 1,200	$450 - 600

This model was the original amplifier to be released. The tubes have varied over the years, but the power tubes were most consistent with 6L6 tubes. The cabinet style changed in 1937 to become a round shouldered cab that was similar to the EH-125.

Barnes & Reinecke (BR) Series

After World War II was finished, Gibson went to work making guitars and amplifiers again. Barnes Reincke designed these new amps, which had some unusual designs. All of these amps were designed to be used with the Electric Hawaiian guitars. These models were phased out over the next few years when the GA series was released.

BR-1 - 18W, 1-12" speaker, six tube chassis combo, preamp: 1 X 6SJ7, 1 X 6SC7, 1 X 6SN7, power: 2 X 6L6, 5U4 rectifier, dual channels, rear silver control panel, three inputs (two instrument, one microphone), three control knobs (2 volume, 1 tone), dark covering, mfg. 1946-49.

	N/A	$325 - 400	$250 - 275

BR-3 - Wattage unknown, 1-12" speaker, six tube chassis combo, preamp: 2 X 7B4, 1 X 6J5, power: 2 X 6V6, 5Z4 rectifier, dual channels, rear control panel, three inputs (two instrument, one microphone), three control knobs (2 volume, 1 tone), dark covering, mfg. 1946-47.

	N/A	$300 - 400	$250 - 275

BR-4 - 14W, 1-12", six tube chassis, preamp: 1 X 6SJ7, 1 X 6SL7, 1 X 6SN7, power: 2 X 6V6, 5Y3 rectifier, dual channels, rear control panel, three inputs (two instruments, one microphone), three control knobs (2 volume, 1 tone), dark and light covering, mfg. 1946-47.

	N/A	$325 - 400	$265 - 300

GRADING	100%	EXCELLENT	AVERAGE

BR-6 - 10W, 1-10" speaker, five tube chassis, preamp: 1 X 6SL7, 1 X 6SN7, power: 2 X 6V6, 5Y3 rectifier, single channel, rear control panel, two inputs, one volume control, dark covering, three large-slot grille, mfg. 1946-1954.

Gibson BR-6
courtesy solidbodyguitar.com, Inc.

Gibson BR-6
courtesy solidbodyguitar.com, Inc.

N/A	$275 - 400	$230 - 255

In 1948, the model was changed to the BR-6F, an input was added, and a 6SJ7 preamp tube added. Covering was changed to a golden brown and the grille was changed to only two slots on later models.

BR-9 - Wattage unknown, 1-8" speaker, four tube chassis, preamp: 6SN7, power: 2 X 6V6, 5Y3 rectifier, single channel, rear control panel, two inputs, one volume control, dark covering, mfg. 1948-1954.

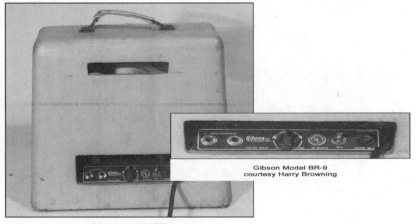

Gibson Model BR-9
courtesy Harry Browning

Gibson Model BR-9
courtesy Harry Browning

Gibson Model BR-9
courtesy Harry Browning

1949-1951	N/A	$250 - 400	$200 - 225
1952-1953	N/A	$200 - 250	$150 - 175

GA Series Models GA-1 - GA-20

GA-CB - 30-40W, 1-15" woofer plus tweeter, 10 tube chassis, preamp: 3 X 6SJ7, 2 X SQ7, 2 X 6J5, power: 2 X 6L6, 5T4 rectifier, dual channels, tremolo, bottom mounted chassis/control panel, four inputs (three instrument, one microphone), six black control knobs (v1, v2, b, t, i, freq), brown covering, six-sloted grille, mfg. 1949-1953.

N/A	$750 - 1,000	$500 - 700

The CB stands for Custom-Built. This is a very rare amp. The *Blue Book of Guitar Amplifiers* suggests getting a second opinion on this amplifier before buying or selling.

GA-1RT (MAESTRO) REVERB-ECHO - 8W, 1-8" speaker, three tube chassis, preamp: 1 X 12AX7, power: 1 X 6BM8, 5Y3 rectifier, single channel, tremolo, reverb, top mounted nickel control panel, two instrument inputs, two black chicken head knobs (v, s), tweed covering, brown grille, mfg. 1961 only.

N/A	$200 - 250	$140 - 185

GA-2RT (MAESTRO) DELUXE REVERB-ECHO - 16W, 1-12" speaker, eight tube chassis, preamp: 4 X 6EU7, 1 X 12AU7, power: 2 X 6V6, 5Y3 rectifier, dual channels, top mounted nickel control panel, four inputs (two per channel), five black and silver knobs (v1, v2, tone, r, one dual purpose s, depth for tremolo), tweed covering, brown grille, mfg. 1961 only.

N/A	$275 - 325	$215 - 240

GRADING	100%	EXCELLENT	AVERAGE

GA-5 LES PAUL JUNIOR - 4W, 5 X 7" special oval type speaker, tubes: 1 X 6SJ7, 1 X 6V6, 1 X 5Y3 rectifier, single channel, rear control panel, two instrument inputs, one volume control, light brown grained covering, gold grille fabric, mfg. 1954-57.

Gibson GA-5 Les Paul Junior
courtesy solidbodyguitar.com, Inc.

Gibson GA-5 Les Paul Junior
courtesy solidbodyguitar.com, Inc.

	N/A	$250 - 400	$100 - 200

GA-5 SKYLARK - 4.5W, 1-8" Jensen speaker, tubes: 1 X 7025, 1 X 6V6, 1 X 5Y3 rectifier, single channel, rear control panel, two instrument inputs, one volume control, light brown grained covering, gold grille fabric, mfg. 1958-1967.

Gibson GA-5
courtesy Savage Audio

Gibson Skylark GA-5
courtesy Dave's Guitar Shop

Gibson Skylark Model GA-5
courtesy Atomic Guitars

1958-1962	N/A	$200 - 250	$150 - 190
1963-1967	N/A	$175 - 215	$130 - 150

The GA-5 Skylark essentially replaced the Les Paul Junior amplifier with a few modifications.

* GA-5T Skylark - Similar to the GA-5 Skylark except has built in tremolo, mfg. 1960-67.

Gibson Skylark Model GA-5T
courtesy TLC Guitars

Gibson Skylark Model GA-5T
courtesy TLC Guitars

1960-1962	N/A	$225 - 275	$165 - 210
1963-1967	N/A	$175 - 200	$125 - 150

GRADING	100%	EXCELLENT	AVERAGE

GA-6 LANCER - 14W, 1-12" speaker, tubes: preamp: 1 X 12AY7, 1 X 6SL7, power: 2 X 6V6, 5Y3 rectifier, dual channels, top control panel, four inputs, three black chicken head knobs (tone, inst v, mic v), two-tone buffalo grained covering, woven Saran grille, mfg. 1948-1961.

Gibson GA-6
courtesy Willie's American Guitars

N/A	$275 - 400	$200 - 225

This amp started life as the GA-6 and was changed to the Lancer in the late 50's or early 60's with no apparent change. This amp was also rated at 10W originally. Newer models have 2 X 7025 tubes for preamps. The cabinet and covering designs have changed over the years as well. There have been dark and light coverings offered on Gibson amps during different years.

GA-7 LES PAUL TV MODEL - 4W, 1-10" speaker, three tubes chassis, preamp: 1 X 6SJ7, power: 1 X 6V6, 5Y3 rectifier, single channel, rear control panel, two instrument inputs, one volume control, light brown covering, gold grille fabric, mfg. 1955-57.

N/A	$300 - 400	$240 - 275

This model is very similar to the GA-5 Les Paul Junior except that fact that the graphics were different on the control panel. This model is rare to come up on the second hand market.

GA-8 GIBSONETTE - 8W, 1-10" speaker, 4 tubes: 6EU7, 6C4, 6BQ5, 6CA4, single channel, top control panel, two instrument inputs, one volume control, light brown grained covering, dark brown flocked grille, mfg. 1952-59.

N/A	$200 - 250	$150 - 180

By 1958 the output had been raised to 9W.

GA-8 DISCOVERER - 10W, 1-12" speaker, 4 tubes: 6EU7, 6C4, 6BQ5, 6CA4, single channel, top nickel plated control panel, two instrument inputs, one volume and one tone control, light vinyl covering, dark cloth grille, mfg. 1960-63.

N/A	$250 - 400	$150 - 200

* **GA-8T Discoverer** - Similar to the GA-8 Discoverer except has built in tremolo, tubes consist of a 7025, 2 X 6BM8, 5Y3, mfg. 1960-66.

Gibson GA-8T
courtesy solidbodyguitar.com, Inc.

Gibson GA-8T
courtesy solidbodyguitar.com, Inc.

1960-1962	N/A	$275 - 400	$200 - 225
1963-1967	N/A	$250 - 300	$175 - 210

GA-9 - 10W, 1-10" Jensen speaker, 4 tubes: 6SJ7, 2 X 6V6, 5Y3 rectifier, single channel, top-mounted chrome control panel, two instrument inputs, one volume and one tone control, light colored covering, dark brown cloth grille, mfg. 1948-1959.

N/A	$250 - 400	$150 - 210

This model was sold with the BR-9 Steel Guitar also.

GA-14 TITAN - 14W, 1-10" speaker, five tube chassis, preamp: 2 X 12AX7, power: 2 X 6V6, 5Y3 rectifier, dual channels, top control panel, four inputs (two per channel), four control knobs (volume and tone per channel), two-tone buffalo grained covering, Saran grille, mfg. 1959-1961.

N/A	$250 - 400	$150 - 200

This model is identical to the GA-6 except that it has a 10" speaker.

GRADING	100%	EXCELLENT	AVERAGE

GA-15 EXPLORER - 14W, speaker configuration unknown, 5 tubes: preamp: 7025, 6SL7, power: 2 X 6L6, 5Y3 rectifier, dual channels, 4 inputs (3 instrument, 1 microphone), two volume controls, one tone control, light tweed covering, dark cloth grille, mfg. 1955-56, 58.

	N/A	$250 - 400	$150 - 225

GA-15RV (MAESTRO) - 14-16W output, 1-12" Jensen speaker, 7 tubes, preamp: 3 X 6EU7, 12AU7, power: 2 X 6V6, 5Y3 rectifier, dual channels, reverb, top chrome control panel, four inputs (two per channel), five black and silver knobs (v1, v2, t, b, r), dark covering, light grille. mfg. mfg. 1961 only.

	N/A	$275 - 400	$150 - 230

GA-15RVT EXPLORER - Output unknown, 1-10" speaker, 5 tubes, preamp: 2 X 6EU7, 12AU7, power: 2 X 6BQ6, single channel, tremolo, reverb, front white control panel, three inputs, 6 control knobs (v, b, t, r, depth, freq.), coarse black tolex covering, gray grille cloth, mfg. 1965-67.

	N/A	$300 - 500	$150 - 250

GA-16T VISCOUNT (MAESTRO) - 14W, 1-10" speaker, 5 tubes, preamp:2 X 12AX7, power: 2 X 6V6, 5Y3 rectifier, single channel, tremolo, top chrome control panel, three inputs, four black chicken head knobs (v, tone, depth, freq.), tweed covering, dark slanted grille cloth, mfg. 1959-1961.

	N/A	$250 - 350	$180 - 215

GA-17RVT SCOUT - output unknown, 1-10" speaker, 6 tubes, preamp: 2 X 6EU7, 12AX7, power: 2 X 6AQ5, 6CA4 rectifier, single channel, tremolo, reverb, top silver control panel, two inputs, four black and silver knobs (v, r, tremolo freq., power switch), brown covering, brown cloth grille, mfg. 1963-67.

	N/A	$300 - 500	$150 - 225

GA-18T EXPLORER - 14W, 1-10" heavy-duty speaker, five tubes, preamp:2 X 6EU7, power: 2 X EL84, 1 X 6CA4, single channel, tremolo, top silver control panel, three inputs, four black chicken head knobs (v, tone, tremolo depth, tremolo freq.), tweed covering, brown cloth grille, mfg. 1959-1963.

	N/A	$325 - 500	$225 - 275

The first year of this amplifier, in 1959, it was only known as the GA-18 without tremolo.

GA-19RVT FALCON - 15W, 1-12" speaker, seven tubes, preamp: 3 X 6EU7, 7199, power: 2 X 6V6, 5Y3 rectifier, dual channels, tremolo, reverb, top silver control panel, two inputs, five black knobs (v, tone, depth, freq, r),footswitch, black tolex covering, light brown grille, mfg. 1961-67.

1961-1963	N/A	$375 - 450	$275 - 325
1964-1967	N/A	$250 - 300	$200 - 225

GA-20 CREST - 12-14W, 1-12" Jensen speaker, six tubes, preamp: 2 X 6SC7, phase splitter: 6SL7, output: 2 X 6V6, 5Y3 rectifier, dual channels, top control panel, four inputs, three controls (v1, v2, tone), light brown covering on bottom, dark brown covering on top, brown cloth grille, mfg. 1950-61.

Gibson GA-20
courtesy solidbodyguitar.com, Inc.

Gibson GA-20
courtesy solidbodyguitar.com, Inc.

1950-1959	N/A	$375 - 450	$275 - 325
1960-1961	N/A	$275 - 350	$200 - 250

In the middle 1950's, the output was raised to 16W. The two tone covering was introduced in 1954. The Crest name on the amp was only used for a couple of years from 1960-61.

GRADING	100%	EXCELLENT	AVERAGE

* GA-20T Ranger - Similar to the GA-20 Ranger except has tremolo circuit with a tube chart of 1 X 12AY7, 7025, 5879, 6SQ7, 2 X 6V6, 5Y3 rectifier, has controls for tremolo (depth and frequency), mfg. 1956-61.

Gibson Ranger Model GA-20T

Gibson Ranger Model GA-20T

| 1956-59 | N/A | $400 - 500 | $300 - 350 |
| 1960-61 | N/A | $325 - 400 | $250 - 300 |

GA-20RVT MINUTEMAN - Wattage unknown, 1-12" speaker, eight tubes, 3 X 6EU7, 2 X 12AU7, 2 X EL84, 5Y3 rectifier, dual channels, reverb, tremolo, white front control panel, four inputs (two per channel), eight knobs (Ch. 1: v, b, t, Ch. 2: v, b, t, s, i, r), footswitch, black tolex covering, gray sparkle grille, mfg. 1965-67.

| | N/A | $250 - 400 | $150 - 200 |

GA Series Models GA-25 - GA-50

GA-25 - 15W, 1-12" & 1-8" speakers, 6 tubes, preamp: 6SJ7, phase: 2 X 6J5, output: 2 X 6V6, rectifier: 5Y3, single channel, four inputs (three instrument, one microphone), one volume and one tone control, brown covering, mfg. 1947-48.

| | N/A | $375 - 425 | $300 - 350 |

Very little is known about this amplifier because it wasn't around very long; it is a little more desireable.

GA-25RVT HAWK - Wattage unknown, 1-15" or 2-10", seven tubes, 4 X 6EU7, 12AU7, 2 X 6V6, 5Y3 rectifier, dual channels, tremolo, reverb, top control panel, four inputs (two per channel), seven control knobs (Ch.1: v, tone, Ch. 2: v, tone, depth, freq., r), footswitch, black tolex covering, light brown grille, mfg. 1965-67.

Gibson Hawk
courtesy Steve Brown

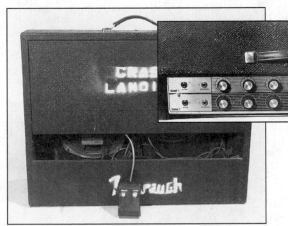

Gibson Hawk
courtesy Steve Brown

| | N/A | $250 - 400 | $150 - 225 |

Late in production, the Hawk had two tone controls for each channel and the tubes were changed to 2 X 6EU7, 3 X 12AU7, 2 X 7591.

GRADING	100%	EXCELLENT	AVERAGE

GA-30 - 14W, 1-12" & 1-8" speakers, six tubes: 1 X 6SC7, 2 X 6SJ7, 2 X 6V6, 5Y3 rectifier, dual channels, rear control panel, four inputs (three instruments, one microphone), two volume controls, one tone control, bass tone expanding switch, brown covering, mfg. 1948-1960.

Gibson GA-30
courtesy solidbodyguitar.com, Inc.

Gibson GA-30
courtesy solidbodyguitar.com, Inc.

1948-1954	N/A	$400 - 500	$300 - 350
1955-1960	N/A	$350 - 425	$275 - 325

Sometime in the 1950's, circa 1958 the GA-30 was designated the GA-30 Invader.

GA-30 INVADER - 14-16W, 1-12" & 1-8" speakers, six tubes: 2 X 12AX7, 1 X 12AU7, 2 X 6V6, 5Y3 rectifier, dual channels, top mounted chrome control panel, four inputs, three control knobs (2 volume, 1 tone), tweed covering, light brown grille cloth, mfg. 1960-61.

	N/A	$350 - 500	$250 - 300

GA-30RV INVADER - 16W, 1-12" & 1-8" speakers, seven tubes: 3 X 6EU7, 1 X 12AU7, 2 X 6V6 power, 5Y3 rectifier, dual channels, reverb (no tremolo), top mounted silver control panel, four inputs (two per channel), four black and silver knobs (v1, v2, tone, r), black tweed covering, brown cloth grille, mfg. 1961 only.

	N/A	$450 - 600	$375 - 425

GA-30RVT INVADER - 25W, 1-12" & 1-8" speakers, nine tubes: 4 X 6EU7, 2 X 12AU7, 2 X 7591, 0A2 rectifier, dual channels, top silver control panel, four inputs (two per channel), seven black and silver knobs (Ch. 1: v, tone, Ch. 2: v, tone, r, Both: trem depth, freq.), black tolex covering, light brown cloth grille, mfg. 1962-67.

	N/A	$400 - 550	$250 - 325

In 1963/64 bass, middle, and treble controls were added to each channel.

GA-35RVT LANCER - Wattage unknown, 1-12" speaker, eight tubes, 2 X 6EU7, 12AX7, 2 X 12AU7, 2 X 7591, 0A2 rectifer, dual channels, tremolo, reverb, front white control panel, four inputs (two per channel), eight knobs (Ch.1: v, b, t, Ch. 2: v, b, t, depth, freq, reverb), black tolex covering, silver sparkle grille, mfg. 1966-67.

	N/A	$400 - 550	$250 - 325

GA-40 LES PAUL - 14W, 1-12" speaker, eight tubes: 3 X 6SJ7, 1 X 6SN7, 3 X 6V6, 5V4 rectifier, dual channels, tremolo, top black control panel, four inputs (three instrument, one microphone), four black chicken head knobs (v1, v2, tone, tremolo), two tone brown covering, basket weave grille with large "LP" letters across the front, mfg. 1952-1960.

Gibson Les Paul Model GA-40
courtesy Savage Audio

Gibson Les Paul Model GA-40
courtesy Savage Audio

	N/A	$850 - 1,200	$500 - 750

In 1956, the model was redesigned with a different two-tone brown covering, but the "LP" design was removed. Another control was added to the control panel as well, the tremolo frequency. Later models have a tube configuration of 2 X 5879, 1 X 7025, 1 X 6SQ7, 2 X 6V6, 5Y3.

GRADING	100%	EXCELLENT	AVERAGE

GA-40T LES PAUL - 25W, 1-12" speaker, seven tubes, 3 X6EU7, 1 X 12AU7, 2 X 7591, 5AR4 rectifier, dual channels, tremolo, top silver control panel, four inputs (two per channel), six black and silver knobs (Ch. 1: v, tone, Ch. 2: v, tone, trem depth & freq), black tolex covering, light brown grille, mfg. 1961-67.

1961	N/A	$850 - 1,200	$500 - 700
1962-67	N/A	$700 - 1,000	$500 - 600

GA-45T SATURN (MAESTRO STANDARD) - 16W, 4-8" speakers, amplifier designed for accordions, seven tubes: 2 X 5879, 6SQ7, 12AX7, 2 X 6V6, 5Y3 rectifier, dual channels, tremolo, top control panel, four inputs (two per channel), six black knobs (v1, v2, b, t, trem depth, freq), tweed covering, brown grille, mfg. 1955-1961.

	N/A	$550 - 800	$400 - 475

This model is quite similar to the GA-40, but it has a treble and bass controls and a different speaker set-up.

* GA-45RV Saturn (Maestro) - Similar to the GA-45T except has reverb instead of tremolo, mfg. 1961 only.

	N/A	$500 - 750	$375 - 450

GA-45RVT SATURN - Wattage unknown, 2-10" speakers, nine tubes: 4 X 6EU7, 1 X 12AU7, 1 X 6CG7, 2 X 6L6, 0A2 rectifier, dual channels, reverb, tremolo, front white control panel, four inputs (two per channel), nine black knobs (Ch. 1: v, t, b, Ch. 2: v, t, b, r, trem depth & freq.), two bright switches, black tolex covering, silver sparkle grille, mfg. 1965-67.

	N/A	$500 - 700	$300 - 400

GA-46 SUPER MAESTRO - 60W, 2-12" speakers, ten tubes: 3 X 7025, 2 X 5879, 1 X 6SN7, 1 X 6V6, 2 X 6550, 5AR4 rectifier, dual channels, tremolo, top control panel, four inputs (two per channel), eight black knobs (Ch. 1: v, b, t, s, depth, Ch. 2: v, b, t), two tone covering, light brown grille, mfg. 1957-1961.

	N/A	$550 - 750	$375 - 450

This is an accordion amplifier.

GA-50 - Wattage unknown, 1-12" & 1-8" speakers, tubes: 2 X 6SJ7, 2 X 6J5, 2 X 6550, 5AR4 rectifier, dual channels, rear control panel, four inputs (three instruments, one microphone), four knobs (v1, v2, b, t), brown covering, mfg. 1948-1955.

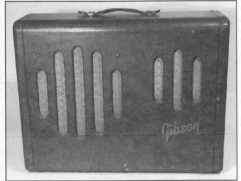
Gibson GA50
courtesy Harry Browning

Gibson GA50
courtesy Harry Browning

Gibson GA50
courtesy Harry Browning

	N/A	$450 - 600	$350 - 400

* GA-50T - Similar to the GA-50 except has tremolo circuit with tubes: 3 X 6SJ7, 1 X 6SN7, 1 X 6SL7, 2 X 6L6, 5V4 rectifier, controls for tremolo (intensity and frequency), mfg. 1948-1955.

	N/A	$500 - 650	$400 - 450

GA Series Models GA- 55 - GA-79

GA-55 RANGER - 18W, 2-12" speakers, six tubes: 2 X 12AY7, 6SC7, 2 X 6L6, 5V4 rectifier, dual channels, top control panel, four inputs (two per channel), four controls (v1, v2, b, t), two-tone brown covering, brown grille cloth, mfg. 1954-58.

Gibson GA55
courtesy C.W. Green

Gibson GA55
courtesy C.W. Green

	N/A	$425 - 550	$350 - 400

GRADING	100%	EXCELLENT	AVERAGE

* GA-55V Ranger - Similar to the GA-55 except has vibrato circuit with vibrato controls, mfg. 1954-58.

| | N/A | $500 - 600 | $400 - 450 |

GA-55RVT RANGER - Wattage unknown, 4-10" speakers, nine tube chassis: 4 X 6EU7, 1 X 12AU7, 1 X 6CG7, 2 X 6L6, 0A2 rectifier, dual channels, reverb, tremolo, front white control panel, four inputs (two per channel), eleven black knobs (Ch. 1: v, b, m, t, Ch. 2: v, b, m, t, trem depth and freq. r), presence swithces, black tolex covering, silver sparkle grille, mfg. 1965-67.

| | N/A | $400 - 475 | $325 - 375 |

The GA-55RVT was available as the GA-55RVTL which had Lansing speakers, mfg. 1967 only.

GA-60 HERCULES - 25W, 1-15" speaker, 5 tube chassis: 2 X 6EU7, 2 X 7591, 5AR4 rectifier, single channel, top silver control panel, two inputs, three knobs (v, b, t), black tolex covering, light brown grille, mfg. 1962-63.

| | N/A | $375 - 500 | $300 - 350 |

GA-70 COUNTRY WESTERN - 25W, 1-15" Jensen, six tube chassis: 1 X 7025, 1 X 12AY7, 1 X 12AU7, 2 X 6L6, 5V4 rectifier, top control panel, four inputs (two per channel), five black chicken head knobs (v1, v2, b, t, fidelity), two tone brown covering, brown grille, Texas longhorn logo on front, 39 lbs, mfg. 1955-58.

| | N/A | $550 - 800 | $350 - 450 |

The new CW model by Gibson was apparantly signaled by the longhorn logo and a new "fidelity" control. Apparently not too hot of an item, as it was discontinued after only a few hundred were made.

GA-75 RECORDING - 25W, 1-15" speaker, seven tube chassis: 6SJ7, 3 X 6SC7, 2 X 6L6, 5V4 rectifier, dual channels, rear control panel, five inputs (four instruments, one microphone), four knobs (v1, v2, b, t), brown covering, mfg. 1950-55.

Gibson GA-75
courtesy Jimmy Gravity

Gibson GA-75
courtesy Jimmy Gravity

| | N/A | $600 - 750 | $475 - 550 |

GA-77 VANGUARD - 25W, 1-15" Jensen speaker, six tube chassis: 12AX7, 12AY7, 12AU7, 2 X 6L6, 5V4 rectifier, dual channels, top control panel, four inputs (two per channel), six black chicken head knobs (v1, v2, b, t, tone, fidelity), two tone brown covering, brown cloth grille, mfg. 1954-1961.

| | N/A | $500 - 700 | $300 - 400 |

GA-77RV VANGUARD - 25W, 1-15" speaker, six tube chassis, dual channels, reverb, top silver control panel, four inputs (two per channel), six black and silver knobs (v1, v2, b, t, tone, r), tweed covering, brown cloth grille, mfg. 1961 only.

| | N/A | $500 - 700 | $300 - 400 |

GA-77RVT VANGUARD - 50W, 1-15" JBL speaker, eight tube chassis: 4 X 6EU7, 12AU7, 7199, 2 X 6L6, dual channels, tremolo, reverb, top silver control panel, four inputs (two per channel), nine black and silver knobs (Ch. 1: v, b, t, Ch. 2: v, b, t, depth, freq. r), black tolex covering, light brown grille, mfg. 1962-67.

| | N/A | $600 - 800 | $450 - 550 |

In 1963/64, a middle switch was added to each channel for a total of eleven total knobs.
This model was available as the GA-77RVTL, which has Lansing speakers.

GA-77RET VANGUARD - Wattage unknown, 2-10" or 1-15" JBL speakers, nine tube chassis: 3 X 6EU7, 2 X 12AU7, 6CG7, 2 X 6L6, 0A2 rectifier, dual channels, tremolo, reverb, top silver control panel, four inputs (two per channel), eleven black and silver knobs (Ch. 1: v, b, m, t, Ch. 2: v, b, m, t, depth, freq, r), black tolex covering, light brown grille, mfg. 1964-67.

| | N/A | $575 - 750 | $350 - 450 |

This model was available as the GA-77RETL, which has Lansing speakers.

GA-78RV MAESTRO 30 - 2 X 15W (Stereo), 2-10" speakers, eight tube chassis: 3 X 6EU7, 7199, 12AU7, 4 X 6BQ5, dual channels, reverb, top silver control panel, five inputs (four mono, one stereo), seven black and silver knobs (Ch. 1: v, b, t, r, Ch. 2: v, b, t), stereo-mono switch, charcoal grey casing, brown grille, cabinet is set up so speakers face away from each other, mfg. 1960-61.

| | N/A | $1,000 - 1,500 | $500 - 750 |

Gibson made four amplifiers as the model GA-78RVT, which had a tremolo unit on it. There were also a few models that were only the model GA-78RV with no reverb.

GRADING	100%	EXCELLENT	AVERAGE

GA-79(RV) STEREO-REVERB - 30W (2 X 15 Stereo), 2-10" speakers, nine tube chassis: 3 X 6EU7, 7199, 12AU7, 4 X 6BQ5, dual channels, reverb, top silver control panel, five inputs (four mono, one stereo), six knobs (Ch. 1: v, tone, depth, freq, Ch. 2: v, tone), mono-stereo switch, footswitch for reverb, six sided cabinet with tweed covering, woven brown Saran grille cloth, mfg. 1961 only.

N/A	$1,350 - 1,650	$1,000 - 1,250

This model was first introuduced in 1960 with out reverb and a few models were produced in 1961 without reverb.

* ***GA-79RVT*** - Similar to the GA-79RV except has tremolo circuit, tubes include one more 6EU7, and 2 X 6L6 power tubes instead of 6BQ5's, depth and frequency controls, treble, bass and middle controls as well (mid was added in 1963/64), mfg. 1961-67.

Gibson GA-79 RVT
courtesy solidbodyguitar.com, Inc.

Gibson GA-79 RVT
courtesy solidbodyguitar.com, Inc.

1961-64	N/A	$1,250 - 1,750	$1,000 - 1,175
1965-67	N/A	$1,100 - 1,300	$875 - 1,000

The GA-79RVT could go for up to $2,000 in mint condition.
This is the most desirable and best sounding Gibson amplifier.

GA Series Models GA-80 - GA-400

GA-80(T) VARI-TONE - 25W, 1-15" speaker, seven tube chassis: 2 X 12AX7, 2 X 5879, 2 X 6L6, GZ34 rectifier, dual channels, top silver control panel, four inputs (two per channel), four black chicken head knobs (Ch.1: v, tone, Ch. 2: v, tone), six button Vari-tone selector switch, tweed covering, brown cloth grille, mfg. 1959-1961.

N/A	$750 - 950	$600 - 700

Later models had a tremolo circuit with volume, depth, and frequency controls.

GA-83 STEREO VIBRATO - 36W (2 X 18W stereo), 4-8" & 1-12" speakers, 13 tube chassis: 4 X 12AX7, 12AU7, 3 X 6CG7, 4 X 6BQ5, GZ34 rectifer, dual channels, tremolo, top silver control panel, four inputs (two per channel), eight black knobs (Ch. 1: v, b, t, trem depth, freq, Ch. 2: v, b, t), six-sided cabinet to project 180 degrees of sound, unknown covering & grille, mfg. 1959-1961.

N/A	$1,400 - 1,700	$1,000 - 1,250

GA-85 - 15W, 1-12" Jensen speaker, detachable control panel, six tube chassis, preamp: 2 X 12AX7, phase: 5V6, power: 2 X 5881, 5V4 rectifier, dual channels, front silver control panel, four inputs (two per channel), five black chicken head knobs (v1, v2, b, t, voicing), two-tone buffalo grain fabric, brown cloth grille with Gibson logo, 39 lbs, mfg. 1957-58.

N/A	$500 - 600	$400 - 450

This model was essentially Gibson's first piggy-back unit where the tube chassis and control panel came off and had an extension cord of 15 feet. Very few of these model were ever made.

GA-86 ENSEMLE, GA-87 MAESTRO STEREO-ACCORDION, & GA-88 STEREO-TWIN - Very little information is known about these models and research is still underway.

GA-90 HIGH FIDELITY - 25W, 6-8" speakers, eight tube chassis: preamp: 2 X 5879, 1 X 12AU7, phase: 2 X 6SN7, power: 2 X 6L6, 5V4 rectifier, dual channels, top silver control panel, four inputs (two per channel), four black knobs (Ch. 1: v, tone, Ch. 2: v, tone), dark brown buffalo-grained fabric covering, woven Saran grille, 38 lbs., mfg. 1953-1960.

N/A	$950 - 1,200	$700 - 850

Later models (after 1958) have treble and bass controls for a total of six knobs, and the grille changed to have a light border around the cloth and logo changed from "Gibson" to " Gibson 90."

GRADING	100%	EXCELLENT	AVERAGE

GA-100 BASS AMPLIFIER - 35W, 1-12" speaker, piggy-back design, nine tube chassis, 6EU7, 2 X 6BD6, 2 X 6FM8, 2 X 6L6, GZ34, 0A2, single channel, front silver control panel, two inputs, three black chicken head knobs (v, t, b), head-unit is mounted in dark covering, cabinet is tweed covering with brown cloth grille, Gibson logo, mfg. 1960-63.

Gibson GA-100 Bass Amp
courtesy Steve Brown

Gibson GA-100 Bass Amp
courtesy Steve Brown

Gibson GA-100 Bass Amp
courtesy Steve Brown

	N/A	$325 - 400	$250 - 300

Add 10% for tripod stand for the tube chassis and control panel (head-unit).

GA-200 RHYTHM KING - 60W, 2-12", 10 tube chassis: 2 X 12AX7, 12 AY7, 2 X 6BJ8, 2 X 6SK7, 6V6, 2 X 6550, GZ34 rectifier, dual channels, top control panel, four inputs (two per channel), six black knobs (Ch. 1: v, b, t, Ch. 2: v, b, t), two-tone buffalo grained covering, brown cloth grille, Gibson 200 logo, Gada-Kart wheel dolly including, 62 lbs., mfg. 1956-1963.

	N/A	$1,000 - 1,250	$750 - 900

Add 15% for the Gada-Kart.

In 1959 covering was changed to tweed and the Gadakart was available as an option.

GA-300RVT SUPER 300 - 60W, 2-12" speakers, tuck away design, eight tube chassis 2 X 6EU7, 3 X 12AU7, 7199, 2 X 6L6, 0A2, 6 diodes, dual channels, tremolo, reverb, compression, top control panel, four inputs (two per channel), nine black and silver knobs (Ch. 1: v, b, t, depth, freq., r, Ch. 2: v, b, t), black tolex covering, light brown grille, mfg. 1962-63.

	N/A	$1,000 - 1,200	$750 - 850

GA-400 SUPER 400 - 60W, 2-12" speakers, twelve tube chassis: 3 X 12AX7, 12AY7, 2 X 6BJ8, 2 X 6SK7, 6V6, 2 X 6550, GZ34 rectifier, three channels, top control panel, six inputs (two per channel), nine black and silver knobs (v, b, t, for each channel), two-tone buffalo grained covering, brown cloth grille, Gibson 400 logo, Gada Kart wheel dolly, 62 lbs., mfg. 1956-1963.

	N/A	$1,100 - 1,300	$850 - 1,000

Add 15% for the Gada-Kart.

In 1959, covering was changed to tweed and the Gadakart was available as an option.

Power Plus Series

These amplifiers were a start to making piggy-back amps for Gibson. Not a whole lot of information is known yet about these amps, but research is still underway. Gibson then released the Medalist series a year later which were the same amps but in combo form.

TITAN I - Wattage unknown, 2-12" speakers, eleven tube chassis, preamp: 3 X 6EU7, 2 X 12AU7, 6FQ7, power: 4 X 6L6, 0A2 rectifier, dual channels, tremolo, four inputs (two per channel), ten control knobs (Ch. 1: v, b, m, t, depth, freq, Ch. 2: v, b, m, t), unknown covering, mfg. 1963-65, 67.

	N/A	$300 - 350	$250 - 275

* **Titan III** - Similar to the Titan I except has 1-15" & 2-10" speakers, mfg. 1963-67.

	N/A	$325 - 375	$250 - 300

* **Titan V** - Similar to the Titan I except has 2-15" JBL speakers, mfg. 1963-67.

	N/A	$350 - 400	$275 - 325

* **Titan Medalist** - Similar to the Titan I except in combo form, mfg. 1964-67.

	N/A	$325 - 400	$275 - 300

MERCURY I - Wattage unknown, 2-12" speakers, eight tube chassis, preamp: 3 X 6EU7, 1 X 6C4, 1 X 6FQ7, power: 2 X 6L6, 0A2 rectifier, dual channels, tremolo, ten control knobs (Ch. 1: v, b, m, t, depth, freq, Ch. 2: v, b, m, t), unknown covering, mfg. 1963-67.

	N/A	$250 - 300	$200 - 225

* **Mercury II** - Similar to the Mercury I except has 1-15" and 1-10" speakers, mfg. 1963-67.

	N/A	$250 - 300	$200 - 225

A few of the Mercury II's were produced as Mercury IIL which had Lansing speakers in 1967.

* **Mercury Medalist** - Similar to the Mercury except in combo form, mfg. 1964-67.

	N/A	$250 - 300	$200 - 225

GRADING	100%	EXCELLENT	AVERAGE

ATLAS IV - Wattage unknown, 1-15" speaker, five tube chassis, preamp: 2 X 6EU7, 6C4, power: 2 X 6L6, single channel, two inputs, three controls, (v, b, t), covering unknown, mfg. 1963-67.

	N/A	$250 - 300	$200 - 225

A few models were produced as Atlas IVL, which had Lansing speakers in 1967.

* Atlas Medalist - Similar to the Atlas IV except in combo form, mfg. 1964-67.

	N/A	$250 - 300	$200 - 225

Gibson Goldtone Series (Current Production)

GA-15 (TGA-BK15) - 15W, 1-10" speaker combo, all tube Class A chassis, single channel, back brown control panel, single input, two gold knobs (v, tone), bright switch, external speaker jack, brown leather covering, dark brown leather grille, current mfg.

MSR	$859	$599	$450 - 525	$350 - 400

* GA-15RV (TGA-BK15RV) - Similar to the Super Goldtone GA-15 except has 1-12" speaker, 3-spring reverb with gold control, triode/pentode switch, and footswitch, current mfg.

MSR	$1,149	$825	$600 - 700	$500 - 550

GA-30RVS (TGA-BK30RVS) - 30W (15 X 2), 2-12" speakers, stereo combo, all tube Class A chassis, dual channel, reverb, back brown control panel, two inputs, three gold knobs (v, tone, r), pull gain on volume, bright switch, effects loop, footswitch, external speaker jack, brown leather covering, dark brown leather grille, current mfg.

MSR	$1,826	$1,299	$800 - 1,000	$675 - 750

GA-30RVH (TGA-BK30RVH) - 30W, head-unit only, all tube Class A chassis, power: 4 X EL84, dual channels, reverb, front brown control panel, single input, twelve gold knobs (Gibson style), (Ch. 1: v, t, m, b, Ch. 2: g, level, t, m, b, r1, r2, MV), effects loop with controls on back panel, speaker out jack, brown leather covering, dark brown leather grille, current mfg.

MSR	$1,995	$1,399	$1,000 - 1,200	$800 - 900

* GA-30RV (TGA-BK30RV) - Similar to the Super Goldtone except in combo form with 1-10" & 1-12" Celestion speakers, current mfg.

MSR	$2,395	$1,699	$1,200 - 1,400	$900 - 1,000

GA-60RV (TGA-BK60RV) - 60W, 2-12" Celestion speakers, all tube Class A/B chassis, power: 2 X EL34, dual channels, reverb, front brown control panel, single input, twelve gold knobs (Gibson style), (Ch. 1: v, t, m, b, Ch. 2: g, level, t, m, b, r1, r2, MV), effects loop with controls on back panel, speaker out jack, brown leather covering, dark brown leather grille, current mfg.

MSR	$2,495	$1,775	$1,250 - 1,500	$1,000 - 1,125

GLOCKENKLANG

Amplifiers currently produced in Germany. Glockenklang amplifiers are distributed in the U.S. by Salwender Int. in Orange, California.

Glockenklang amplifiers are designed and manufactured by Udo Klempt-Giessing in Germany and distributed by Salwender International in the United States. Salwender was looking for a bass-amp system to add to their line up and they ran into Glockenklang before the NAMM show in Winter, 2000. Udo had developed an reference bass amplifier to someone's request, and the rest, as they say, is history. The Bugatti system is the preamp system that was used in the first Glockenklang Bass System. Today Glockenklang offers the Bassware line and the Soul amplifier. For individual listings of amplifiers and speaker cabinets, refer to the web site (see Trademark Index).

GOYA

Amplifiers previously produced in the United States during the late 1960's.

The Goya trademark was originally used by the Hershman Musical Instrument Company in New York City in the 1950's. They imported guitars that were made by the Swedish company, Levin. Levin produced mainly flatop, archtop, and classical guitars. Guitars that were distributed in Sweden were named Levin.

By the late 1950's, Goya jumped on the bandwagon with their own line of electric guitars and basses that were manufactured by Hagstrom, which were also a Swedish company. There are pictures of amplifiers that look like they are from the late 1950's or early 1960's. The first amplifiers I've found in catalogs are in 1967. Avnet (who also owned Guild), bought Goya in 1966. Production shifted from Sweden to Italy where instruments were built by EKO. In 1967, two unusual amplifiers were introduced, the Barracuda and the Bombardier. Very little information is known about these. In the 1960's, there were several other electronics products produced. These included effects, reverb boxes, tremolo units, and other such items. In 1970 Kustom Electronics bought Goya where instruments were probably produced in Japan. In 1976, C.F. Martin bought the rights to Goya and still own them to this day. Currently there are no Goya guitars or amplifiers produced under the Goya name.

(Goya history courtesy of Jack Walsh, www.goyaguitars.com)

ELECTRIC AMPLIFIERS

There is a picture of a Danelectro looking amplifier from circa 1960 on the web site for vintage Goya guitars. Besides this and a briefcase amplifier there is very little known about was produced before Avnet took over in 1966. In 1967, the **Barracuda** guitar amplifier and the **Bombardier** bass amplifier were introduced. These were very peculiar looking amps, which were piggyback amplifiers much like Fender's first run at solid-state models. The controls (knobs and switches on the control panel) were multi-colored, something I've never seen. The Barracuda was a 75W solid-state head running 2-12" speakers in a "Swingaway" cabinet. It had two channels, reverb, tremolo, fuzz tone, and treble boost, and a variety of (rainbow) controls. The Bombardier was a bass amp with 75W going to a 1-18" speaker in a cabinet. This amp had two channels, but not as many features as the Barracuda. These amplifiers were only produced for a year and there are too few on the market to create a price on them.

GRETSCH

Amplifiers previously produced in New York City, New York until 1970, and later produced in Booneville, Arkansas until the late 1970's.

Gretsch dates way back to 1883 when Friedrich Gretsch began manufacturing instruments as the Fred Gretsch Company. Friedrich died in a trip overseas and his son Fred took over the company in 1895 at the age of 15. Business boomed and the company had expanded to percussion, ukuleles, and banjos. In the early 1930's Gretsch introduced their archtop guitars. Fred Gretsch Sr. retired in 1942 and William Walter Gretsch took over until 1948 when Fred Gretsch Jr. became president. The 1950-60's became the heyday for Gretsch as their instruments became endorsed by Chet Atkins and George Harrison. Gretsch Jr., Jimmy Webster, and Charles "Duke" Kramer were all responsible for the success. Kramer was involved with the company until he retired in 1980. In the early 1950's, Gretsch decided to bring in an amplifier line to go with their guitars. Valco, a company that made amplifiers for many companies (Supro, National, Airline, & Oahu), also started to make amplifiers for Gretsch. Naturally, these amps were quite similar to other Valco made amplifiers.

Gretsch went through five distinct changes over the years to the amplifier line. In 1967, Gretsch was bought out by Baldwin, where Gretsch Jr. was made a director. Rumor has it that Baldwin slowed amplifier production after the buyout. Valco continued to make amplifiers for Gretsch until Valco went out of business in 1968-69. Amplifiers were then probably manufactured by Multivox/Premier and the Reverb units were made by OC Electronics. There was a big fire that pretty much wiped out everything in January 1973 (Booneville). This halted guitar production for three months when Bill Hagner of Hagner Musical Instruments formed an agreement with Baldwin to build and sell Gretsch guitars. Baldwin kept the trademark rights, and everything was good until another fire in December of 1973. However, they recovered and squeeked through the 1970's, when Baldwin came in 1978 and took over again. Baldwin bought the Kustom amplifier company in 1978, and it is rumored that some Gretsch amps were actually Kustoms in disguise!

The 1970's took their toll on Gretsch for a number of reasons. Quality control went downhill in a hurry, and it is rumored that disgruntled employees were sabatoging product. Sales were way down and Chet Atkins withdrew his endorsement in 1979. Gretsch stopped producing everything except for drums (produced in Tennesse) in 1981. There were some attempts to get Gretsch going again in the early 1980's, but to no avail. Amplifier production had been long gone by this time. Kramer got Baldwin to sell the rights back to the family and Gretsch III was in charge again. He started producing guitars from Japan that were mainly offered in the U.S. In 1995, Gretsch introduced three reissue models built in the U.S.

(Source for Gretsch History: Michael Wright, Guitar Stories Volume 1; The Gretsch Pages)

DATING GRETSCH AMPLIFIERS

Since Gretsch Amplifiers were produced by Valco, the numbers reflect Valco's date codes. We have the date codes from 1940-1964 for Valco made amplifiers (This works for all amplifiers prodcued by Valco).

G Suffix	**1940-42**
V100-V7500	**1947**
V7500-V15000	**1948**
V15000-V25000	**1949**
V25000-V35000	**1950**
V35000-V38000	**1951**
X100-X7000	**1951**
X7000-X17000	**1952**
X17000-X30000	**1953**
X30000-X43000	**1954**
X43000-X57000	**1955**
X57000-X71000	**1956**
X71000-X85000	**1957**
X85000-X99000	**1958**
T100-T5000	**1958**
T5000-T25000	**1959**
T25000-T50000	**1960**
T50000-T75000	**1961**
T75000-T90000	**1962**
T90000-T99000	**1963**
G5000-G15000	**1963**
G15000-G40000	**1964**

Gretsch amplifiers went through various different style changes. The first was a tweed (similar to Fender). Around 1955 a charcoal gray cloth with silver streaks replaced the tweed. These amplifiers were labled Electromatic and had a wraparound speaker grille. There are two variations of the wraparound; one being a straight grille and the other a slanted grille. Some amplifiers around this time were also available in a "Chet Atkins" covering, which was a white and brown leather. In 1962 a simple cabinet and full grille was introduced. In 1966 piggy-back amps are introduced and controls are moved to the front. By 1967 amps were slowed down in production. The last amps into the 1970's were solid-state and had the sort of "retro" look that solid-state amps of those days had-Serialization information courtesey of the Gretsch Pages (www.gretschpages.com)..

GRADING	100%	EXCELLENT	AVERAGE

ELECTRIC TUBE AMPLIFIERS

6150 - 5W, 1-8" speaker, all tube chassis, preamp: 12AX7, power: 6V6, 5V3 rectifier, single channel, back brown control panel, two inputs, one volume knob, brown tweed covering, brown striped cloth grille, mfg. mid 1950's-late 1960's.

	N/A	$275 - 325	$200 - 225

6150T - Similar to the 6150 except has tremolo unit, tremolo control, tone control, line reversing switch, another tube, and footswitch, mfg. late 1950's-1960's.

	N/A	$300 - 375	$225 - 275

6151 - Similar to the 6150T except produced later.

	N/A	$400 - 500	$300 - 350

This model may have replaced the 6150. The 8" speaker was replaced by a 10" in 1967. Covering's changed according to the dating system.

GRADING	100%	EXCELLENT	AVERAGE

6152 - 5W, 11" X 6" Jensen elliptical speaker, all tube chassis, power: 2 X 6V6, top control panel, reverb, tremolo, three inputs, five knobs (v, tone, r, s, i), black covering, brown grille, mfg. early 1960's-late 1960's.

	N/A	$300 - 375	$225 - 275

In 1967, a 12" Maximum performance speaker was changed from the 11" X 6", and the chassis was upped to 10 tubes.

6154 SUPER BASS - 70W, 2-12" Jensen combo, eight tube chassis, top control panel, two inputs, various knobs including 3-way tone switch, black covering, brown grille, mfg. early 1960's-late 1960's.

	N/A	$350 - 400	$275 - 300

6156 PLAYBOY - 17W, 10" speaker, six tube chassis, 3 X 12AX7, 2 X 6973, 5Y3GT, single channel, tremolo (later models), back brown control panel, three inputs, three knobs (tone, v, i for later models), tweed covering early with brown grille, later charcoal, mfg. late 1940's-1966.

	N/A	$300 - 350	$225 - 275

Around 1961, the speaker was changed from a 10" to a 12" Jensen. This was the flagship amplifier for Gretsch.

6157 SUPER BASS - 35W, 2-15" Maximum performance speakers, piggy-back design, 5 tube chassis, single channel, front control panel, three inputs, three knobs (v, b, t), black covering, brown grille, mfg. late 1960's.

	N/A	$325 - 375	$250 - 285

This amp may have also been available in a combo form.

6159 DUAL BASS - 35W, 2-12" Jensen speakers, seven tube chassis, dual channels, tremolo, top control panel, four inputs, six knobs (Ch. 1: v, tone, s, i, Ch. 2: v, tone), black covering, brown grille, mfg. late 1960's.

	N/A	$350 - 425	$275 - 325

6159 DUAL PLAYBOY TREMOLO - 35W, 2-12" Jensen speakers, tall combo unit, ten tube chassis, dual channels, tremolo, front control panel, three inputs (sometimes four), six knobs (Ch. 1: v, tone, s, i, Ch. 2: v, tone), black covering, brown grille, mfg. late 1960's.

	N/A	$350 - 425	$275 - 300

6160 CHET ATKINS COUNTRY GENTLEMAN - 35W, 2-12" Jensen speakers, nine tube chassis, dual channels, top control panel, five inputs plus one for phonograph, six knobs (Ch. 1: v, b, t, Ch. 2: v, b, t), black covering, brown grille, mfg. 1960-68.

	N/A	$350 - 450	$275 - 325

6161 DUAL TWIN - 14W, 2 11" X 6" Elliptical + 3" tweeter, six tube chassis 2 X 6973 (or 6L6), 3 X 12AX7, 5U4 rectifier, dual channels, tremolo, back control panel, five knobs (v1, v2, tone, s, i), various coverings over the years, mfg. mid 1950's-1960's.

	N/A	$450 - 525	$350 - 400

Wattage was increased to 17W, and speakers were changed to 2-10" Jensen's, and 1-5" tweeter in the early 1960's.

6162 DUAL TWIN REVERB - Similar to the 6161 Dual Twin except has reverb unit, reverb control, and eight tube chassis (2 X 12AX7), mfg. mid 1950's-1960's.

	N/A	$475 - 550	$350 - 425

Wattage was increased to 17W, and speakers were changed to 2-10" Jensen's, and 1-5" tweeter in the early 1960's.

6163 EXECUTIVE - 24W, 1-15" & 1-4" tweeter, eight tube chassis (various tubes), dual channels, tremolo, top control panel, four inputs, various knobs and controls, electromatic style covering, mfg. Mid 1950's-early 1960's.

	N/A	$275 - 325	$200 - 225

6163 CHET ATKINS PIGGYBACK - 70W, 1-15" & 1-12" Maximum performance, 15 tube chassis, dual channels, tremolo, front control panel, four inputs, ten knobs, (Ch. 1: v, t, b, Ch. 2: v, t, b, Both: s, i, tuner v, tone), built in tuner, line reversing switch, black covering, brown grille, mfg. 1966-late 1960's.

	N/A	$500 - 700	$375 - 450

6164 VARIETY - 35W, 2-12" Jensen speakers, nine tube chassis, power: 2 X 6L6, dual channels, tremolo, top control panel, four inputs, eight knobs (Ch. 1: v, b, t, Ch. 2: v, b, t, s, i) hi/lo gain switch, black covering, brown grille, mfg. early 1960's-late 1960's.

	N/A	$350 - 450	$250 - 300

6165 VARIETY PLUS - 35W, 2-12" Jensen speakers, eleven tube chassis, power: 2 X 6L6, dual channels, tremolo, reverb, top control panel, four inputs, nine knobs (Ch. 1: v, b, t, Ch. 2: v, b, t, s, i, r) hi/lo gain switch, black covering, brown grille, mfg. early 1960's-late 1960's.

	N/A	$375 - 450	$250 - 300

6166 FURY - 70W, 2-12" Jensen speakers, 12 tube chassis, 4 X 6V6 outputs, dual channels, tremolo, reverb, top control panel, four inputs, nine knobs (Ch. 1: v, b, t, Ch. 2: v, b, t, tone range selector, i, r), footswitch, black covering, brown grille, mfg. 1960's.

	N/A	$550 - 750	$400 - 475

This amplifier was a unique amp in that it was essentially two amps in one. Each channel was controlled individually into its own preamp and driven to its own speaker. It was also all Class A and it featured a split-chassis.

6169 ELECTROMATIC WESTERN - Similar to the 6161 (in fact identical except for covering) covering was a white leather with brown straps, a steer head on the grille and the metal Gretsch belt-buckle, mfg. late 1950's-early 1960's.

	N/A	$575 - 750	$450 - 525

6169 FURY PIGGYBACK - Similar to the 6166 except now in piggy-back form, 2-12" Maximum Performance speakers, three more tubes, a tone selector, and an external speaker jack, mfg. 1966-early 1970's.

	N/A	$500 - 750	$400 - 450

6170 PRO BASS - 25W (Later models 35W), 1-15" Maximum Performance speaker, 5 tubes and 4 diodes in chassis, single channel, front control panel, three inputs, three knobs (v, b, t), line reverse switch, black covering with brown grille cloth, mfg. 1966-early 1970's.

	N/A	$300 - 425	$250 - 275

GRADING	100%	EXCELLENT	AVERAGE

ELECTRIC SOLID STATE AMPLIFIERS

It is estimated that all the solid-state amplifiers produced by Gretsch were manufactured by Multivox/Premier or GSM. In 1972, Gretsch debuted the Sonax series which included models: 775G, 750G, 730G, 720G, 550B, and 530B. Specifications and other information is sketchy (or print too small to read out of the catalog), but the G stands for guitar amp, the B stands for bass amp, and I'm guessing the second and third numbers indicate wattage. There is also a 330P/480C head unit, but it is not clear what these indicate.

7517 ROGUE - 35 or 40W, 2-12" speakers, solid-state chassis, dual channels, tremolo, reverb, echo, front silver control panel, four inputs plus stereo input, nine silver knobs (Ch. 1: v, b, t, Ch. 2: v, b, t, s, i, r), footswitch, black covering, silver grille, mfg. 1970's.

N/A	$450 - 600	$350 - 425

This amp is very tall.

7763 EXPANDER-G - 300W, head-unit plus two cabinets "single-but-split" either 2-12" or 1-15", solid-state chassis, two or three channels, tremolo, fuzz control, reverb, front silver control panel, various controls and knobs, black covering, black grille, mfg. 1970's.

N/A	$750 - 1,000	$500 - 625

This was a huge unit with two speaker cabinets, which may also have tweeters. On the reverb tank on this model it reads "O.C. Electronics, Folded Line reverb unit. Manufactured by beautiful girls, in Milton, Wisconsin under controlled atmospheric conditions."

GROOVE TUBES
Amplifiers, tubes, and other amplifier equipment currently produced in San Fernando, California.

Aspen Pittman is the genius behind the Groove Tube idea. The trademark was established back in the late 1970's, when Aspen hired some technicians to figure out why tubes acted and performed the way they did. What these people found were new ways to test and perfect tubes. This research is what Groove Tubes used when they first started their business, and what they still use today. Groove Tubes are probably best known for their excellent guitar amp tubes, but they have also ventured in other areas as well. In 1985 GT patented the Fathead, which was a weight that clamped onto the headstock to add weight and sustain. In Fall of 1985, The Speaker Emulator was born along with the company GT Electronics. This is the company that developed the actual guitar pre-amps, tube guitar amps, and guitar speaker systems. The first amps were introduced in 1989. In 1997 the SFX design was debuted (stands for Stereo Field Expansion and is used in the Fender Acoustisonic series). Possibly the best achievement for Aspen and GT is the *Tube Amp Book*. It is currently in it's fourth edition, and there are over 80,000 copies in print.

Keep in mind that besides producing amplifiers and other products you can buy replacement tubes for almost all amplifiers, American or British. Refer to the Groove Tube web site for further information (see Trademark Index).

ELECTRIC TUBE AMPLIFIERS

The first Groove Tube amplifier (not including the Speaker Emulator) was the **D-75 Dual** amp and **Trio Preamp**. The idea behind the Dual 75 was for an amp that could use Fender tubes (6L6) and Marshall tubes (EL34). This amp was designed by Red Rhodes, and it was designed so that flipping between the two channels was in fact switching tubes. The Trio preamp was designed to work in conjunction with the Dual 75. The Trio had three channels (clean, mean, and scream), and when used with the Dual 75, nine possible sounds were available. These amps are still available through the GT custom shop. Also offered are the **D-120 Dual** amp, which has more power.

In 1992 Red Rhodes designed the Soul-o amps. These amps could switch between Class A and Class A/B. The **Solo 75** featured 4 preamp tubes, and a duet of power tubes. The **Solo 150** was essentially the same except with twice the power output. These amps are also available through the custom shop. There are some other amplifiers, including the **STP-B**, and the **STP-G**. Besides these two models, the rest are available to accept many different tube types. The preamp, phase inverter, and power stage are all subject for a number of different tubes.

New for 2002 is the **SINGLE**. This is a guitar amp with a 10" combo, or head unit. Different tubes are acceptable for this amp as well, and it is Class A. There are also speaker cabinets available for these products. For a full line of products, check the Groove Tube web site.

GT ELECTRONICS
See GROOVE TUBES

GUILD
Amplifiers previously produced in New York City from 1952-56; production moved to Hoboken, New Jersey from late 1956-1968, and from Westerly, Rhode Island in 1969-current.

The Guild Guitar company was started in 1952 by Alfred Dronge. They are most known for building fine acoustic and electric guitars. As electric guitars became popular in the late 1950's, Guild started to build guitar amplifiers. The company moved to Hoboken, New Jersey in late 1956 to expand the rapidly growing company. In 1966, Avnet bought the Guild company, and in 1969 they relocated to Westerly, Rhode Island. Alfred Dronge was still president of the company until he was killed in a plane crash in 1973. The vice president, Leon Tell took over the company until 1983. During this period, things started to go. Amplifiers were produced throughout the sixties and the seventies. In 1986, Avnet sold Guild to a management/investment group. This ownership lasted until 1988 when the Faas company of New Berlin, Wisconsin bought them out. At this time electric guitar production was discontinued and amplifier production was long gone. In 1995, the Fender Musical Instrument Corporation bought Guild. Currently they own the trademark and have around 12 models available. Amplifiers are not currently mfg.

ELECTRIC TUBE AMPLIFIERS

It is estimated that Guild has produced many amplifiers, but information is scarce. In the early 1960's, Guild offered the "**Masteramp**" in models 110 and 60. These amps have two tone covering in a TV-style cabinet. Later in the 1960's Guild produced amplifiers similar to Gibson models. We also stumbled upon an interesting contraption (see picture). It is a Guild Acoustic amp that you sit on to get 360 degree sound. With unlimited controls and the soft padding seat it seemed a winner, and editorial man S.P. Fjestad had to have it. Now with a loose connection somewhere, any information on how (or where) to fix would be appreciated (solid-state fix-it shop in the dictionary: the dumpster?!)

Guild G-100 Stereo Acoustic
courtesy S. P. Fjestad

Guild G-100 Stereo Acoustic
courtesy S. P. Fjestad

GUYATONE

Amplifiers previously produced in the 1960's. Currently the company Guyatone produces effects, pedals and other electronic products.

The Guyatone name has been around for the better part of 40 years and have some products behind them. However, information on the product is scarce. Models made in the 1960's are numbered like this; they are GA followed by a 110 numerically up to 810. It is not known what each model features or the specifications. Later models (1970's and possibly early 1980's) are known as the Flip models. Most guyatone amplifiers are solid-state but the Flip's are also hybrid design. The current Guyatone website is strictly for effects and pedals.

NOTES

Section H

HARMONY

Amplifiers currently produced overseas for JC Penney. Previously produced in Chicago, Illinois between the 1940's and 1970's. Some amplifiers may have been produced overseas during the 1980's.

The Harmony Company of Chicago, Illinois was one of the largest American musical instrument manufactures. Harmony has the historical distinction of being the largest "jobber" house in the nation, producing stringed instruments for a number of different wholesalers. Individual dealers or distributors could get stringed instruments with their own brand name on them if they ordered more that 100 pieces. At one time Harmony was producing the largest percentage of stringed instruments in the U.S. market.

The company was founded by Wilhelm J.F. Shultz in 1892. Business expanded exponentially and by 1915 the company already had a 125 person workforce and $250,000 in annual sales. In 1916, Sears, Roebuck & Company purchased Harmony and in 1925 they produced 250,000 units. Most of these guitars were sold through Sears in their catalog (about 35%-40% in 1930). In 1930, they sold 500,000 units, and only sold to wholesalers. Harmony became sort of a steamroller, bought trademarks and kept selling guitars and other equipment faster than they could make.

In the 1940's Harmony began to offer some amplifiers for the increasing popular electric guitar. Through the 1950's and 1960's Harmony kept cruising selling amplifiers and guitars like hotcakes and flapjacks. Information is a lot more frequent on guitars, but amplifiers aren't as well known. They did produce tube and solid-state amps. Products were produced until 1974 when the company dissolved. Sales figures were great right up until the end. Along with Kay and Silvertone, Harmony is classified as a housebrand. A housebrand is defined as a trademark used by distributors, wholesalers, and retailers to represent their respective company instead of the manufacture. In Harmony's case this meant that thousands of guitars were produced at a cheap price and sold at a cheap price. Today prices can be compared to what they were back in the 50's and 60's. A amp that sold for cheap back then is going to be respectively cheap today. Most Harmony amplifiers can be found under the $200 range. Some of the more higher-end models may be worth a little more, but generally a housebrand amp isn't that collectible.

(Source for Harmony History courtesy of Tom Wheeler, American Guitar))

ELECTRIC TUBE AMPLIFIERS

The first Harmony amplifiers were first marketed in the 1940's and the last was produced when the company went under in 1974. Models begin with the letter H and are typically followed by a three digit number. Most amplifiers were labled practice amplifiers, and it wasn't very common to find a professional playing one on stage. Some of the model numbers include an H-191, H-303, and H-500. There are other models as well. Most Harmony amps have basic controls such as a volume and maybe a tone knob. Specs on the amp were pretty basic, such as an 8" or 6" speaker and three tubes. Most of these amps can be valued around $100 and usually under $200.

Harmony Model H303
courtesy S. P. Fjestad

Harmony Model H303
courtesy S. P. Fjestad

ELECTRIC SOLID-STATE AMPLIFIERS

Like most amp companies in the late 1960's, Harmony followed suit with some solid-state amplifiers. In the 1970 catalog, the Rally Stripe Series is listed. There were six different combo units and a couple of speaker cabinets. I'm still waiting for one of these to show up on the market so a secondary-market price hasn't been established on these models. There were probably other models released by Harmony over the years, but information is tough to come by. Research is under way and look for more in upcoming editions of the *Blue Book of Guitar Amplifiers*. For the "new" Harmony amplifiers refer to the web site.

HARTKE

Amplifiers and speaker cabinets currently produced in the U.S.A. Hartke amplifiers are distributed worldwide by the Samson Technology Corp in Syosset, New York.

The Hartke Amplifier company was co-founded by Larry Hartke in 1984. He built a bass cabinet for Jaco Pastorius, which was equipped with eight 10" speakers. What made this cabinet special was that the speakers were aluminum-cone drivers. This cabinet looks quite different from the Hartke cabinets today, but it has a plate on it that states "THE FIRST HARTKE BASS CABINET, CUSTOM BUILT IN 1984 FOR JACO PASTORIUS." Jaco left the company in 1987 but still used the Hartke system in his band Word of Mouth. Hartke has really expanded their line and they offer several models of bass amplifiers, bass cabinets, and bass combo units. A feature that makes Hartke products recognizable, are the polished silver speakers, featured in almost all Hartke products. Hartke recently has released covers for their products. They also have produced some solid-body bass guitars made of wood and aluminum.

GRADING	100%	EXCELLENT	AVERAGE

BASS AMPLIFIERS

Hartke offers several different options to amplify your bass. They have Bass amp heads in a variety of options, combo units and speaker cabinets to make the sound audible. They also offer a **Bass-Gig Pack** (like what Fender does) Where you get a B-15 amp, a Hartke Bass Guitar (red or black finish), guitar strap, gig bag and an instrument cable for a retail price of $429.99.

Bass Amplifier Heads (HA1400, HA2000, HA3500)

All models are of bi-polar design, and are rackmountable (except the 1400).

HA1400 - 140W, head-unit only, solid-state combo, single channel, black front control panel, single input, five black knobs (v, l, l/m, l/h, h), contour switch, compression switch, effects loop, headphone jack, black metal covering, 13 lbs., current mfg.

	MSR	$299.99	$215	$150 - 175	$125 - 140

HA2000 - 200W, head-unit only, solid-state and tube preamp (selectable), front black control panel, two inputs (passive/active), six black and silver knobs (pre-amp A & B, compression, contour low and high pass, MV) 10-band equalizer, black metal covering, 19.5 lbs., current mfg.

	MSR	$519.99	$375	$275 - 325	$225 - 250

HA3500 - 350W, head-unit only, solid-state and tube preamp (selectable), front black control panel, two inputs (passive/active), six black and silver knobs, (pre-amp A & B, compression, contour low and high pass, MV), in/out switch, 10-band equalizer, black metal covering, 25 lbs., current mfg.

	MSR	$639.99	$450	$350 - 400	$275 - 310

BiAmps (HA5000 & HA7000)

HA5000 (BI-AMP) - 500W (250W X 2), head-unit only, solid-state and tube preamp (selectable), front black control panel, two inputs (passive/active), eight black and silver knobs,(pre-amp A & B, compression, contour low and high pass, MV, Crossover freq & balance) in/out switch, 10-band equalizer, black metal covering, 28.5 lbs., current mfg.

	MSR	$749.99	$525	$425 - 475	$350 - 400

HA7000 (BI-AMP) - 700W (350W X 2), head-unit only, solid-state and tube preamp (selectable), front black control panel, two inputs (passive/active), eight black and silver knobs,(pre-amp A & B, compression, contour low and high pass, MV, Crossover freq & balance) in/out switch, 10-band equalizer, black metal covering, 29.5 lbs., current mfg.

	MSR	$999.99	$699	$550 - 625	$450 - 500

Millenium Amps (HA3000 & HA4000)

HA3000 - 300W, head-unit only, solid-state chassis, single channel, shape circuit, front black control panel, two inputs, seven black knobs (v, shape, i, l, m/l, m/h, h), direct XLR out, black covering with description on top of amp, 23 lbs., current mfg.

	MSR	$569.99	$399	$300 - 350	$250 - 275

HA4000 - 400W, head-unit only, solid-state chassis, single channel, shape circuit, front black control panel, two inputs, 12 black knobs (v, shape, i, D-Bass, l, m/l, freq, bandwith, m/h, freq, bandwith, h), direct XLR out, black covering with description on top of amp, 26. 5 lbs., current mfg.

	MSR	$699.99	$499	$400 - 450	$350 - 375

Kickback Combos

KICKBACK 10 - 120W, 1-10" aluminum-cone driver, solid-state combo, single channel, shape control, front black control panel, single input, five black knobs (v, shape, l, m, h), direct XLR line out, headphone jack, stand up or "kickback" stance, black carpet covering, black metal grille, 30 lbs., current mfg.

	MSR	$529.99	$375	$275 - 325	$225 - 250

* **Kickback 12** - Similar to the Kickback 10 except has 1-12" driver, 42 lbs., current mfg.

	MSR	$639.99	$450	$350 - 400	$275 - 325

* **Kickback 15** - Similar to the Kickback 10 except has 1-15" driver, 47 lbs., current mfg.

	MSR	$729.99	$525	$425 - 475	$325 - 375

B-Series Combos

B-15 - 15W, 1-6.5" driver, solid-state combo, single channel, front light brown control panel, two inputs, four black knobs (v, b, m, h), effects loop, line out, headphone jack, black tolex covering, black grille, new 2002.

	MSR	$139.99	$99	$75 - 90	$55 - 65

B-20 - 20W, 1-8" driver, solid-state combo, single channel, front light brown control panel, two inputs, four black knobs (v, b, m, h), effects loop, line out, headphone jack, black tolex covering, black grille, 23.2 lbs., current mfg.

	MSR	$169.99	$125	$90 - 110	$70 - 80

B-30 - 30W, 1-10" driver, solid-state combo, single channel, shape circuit, front light brown control panel, two inputs, five black knobs (v, shape, b, m, h), effects loop, line out, headphone jack, black tolex covering, black grille, 32 lbs., current mfg.

	MSR	$219.99	$160	$125 - 145	$90 - 105

B-60 - 60W, 1-12" driver, solid-state combo, single channel, shape circuit, front light brown control panel, two inputs, five black knobs (v, shape, b, m, h), effects loop, line out, headphone jack, black tolex covering, black grille, 47 lbs., current mfg.

	MSR	$369.99	$275	$200 - 225	$150 - 175

GRADING	100%	EXCELLENT	AVERAGE

B-90 - 90W, 1-15" driver, solid-state combo, single channel, shape circuit, front light brown control panel, two inputs, five black knobs (v, shape, b, m, h), effects loop, line out, headphone jack, black tolex covering, black grille, 62 lbs., current mfg.

MSR	$499.99	$350	$275 - 325	$200 - 225

B-120 - 120W, 2-12" drivers, solid-state combo, single channel, shape circuit, front light brown control panel, two inputs, five black knobs (v, shape, b, m, h), effects loop, line out, headphone jack, casters, black tolex covering, black grille, 74 lbs., current mfg.

MSR	$619.99	$450	$350 - 400	$275 - 325

Combo Amplifiers

HA1410 - 140W, 2-10" aluminum-cone drivers, solid-state chassis, single channel, front black control panel, single input, five black knobs (v, l, l/m, l/h, h), contour button, compression button, effects loop headphone jack, black carpet covering, black metal grille, 59 lbs., current mfg.

MSR	$699.99	$500	$400 - 450	$350 - 375

HA1415 - 140W, 1-15" aluminum-cone driver, solid-state chassis, single channel, front black control panel, single input, five black knobs (v, l, l/m, l/h, h), contour button, compression button, effects loop headphone jack, black carpet covering, black metal grille, 59 lbs., current mfg.

MSR	$649.99	$475	$375 - 425	$325 - 350

HA2115 - 200W, 1-15" aluminum-cone driver, solid-state and tube preamp (selectable), front black control panel, two inputs (passive/active), six black and silver konbs (pre-amp A & B, compression, contour low and high pass, MV) 10-band equalizer, black metal covering, 70 lbs., current mfg.

MSR	$949.99	$675	$550 - 625	$475 - 525

HA2155 - 200W, 1-15" aluminum-cone driver & 1-5" high-frequency speaker, solid-state and tube preamp (selectable), front black control panel, two inputs (passive/active), six black and silver knobs (pre-amp A & B, compression, contour low and high pass, MV) 10-band equalizer, black metal covering, 76 lbs., current mfg.

MSR	$1,249.99	$875	$700 - 800	$550 - 625

VX3500 - 350W, 4-10" aluminum-cone drivers, solid-state and tube preamp (selectable), front black control panel, two inputs (passive/active), six black and silver knobs (pre-amp A & B, compression, contour low and high pass, MV) 10-band equalizer, black metal covering, new 2002.

MSR	$949.99	$675	$550 - 625	$475 - 525

BASS SPEAKER CABINETS

Hartke has a variety of different speaker cabinets in production. The XL series are the flagship amps of Hartke. They come in a variety of different configurations and different wattage capacitys. The Transporter series will get the job done at a more affordable price. The configurations aren't as plentiful, but they are good none the less. New for 2002 are the Professional Series cabinets, and the VX (Very Extreme) cabinets. For prices and a full list of options on these cabinets visit the web site for Hartke (see Trademark Index).

HIWATT

Amplifiers previously produced in England from 1964-current. Currently distributed in North Hollywood, CA in the U.S.

The Hiwatt company was founded in 1964 by Dave Reeves in England. The goal of this new product was to be an "upmarket" compared to Marshall. The first big customer of Hiwatt was Pete Townshend of The Who. Remember, Jim Marshall produced the 8-10" cabinet to Townshend as well. Originally the products were 100W and 50W heads, but combos and other variations were added as the years went on. Reeves died in 1981 and left the company in the hands of some employees. The Hiwatt amp had been virtually untouched up until this point when they decided to do some adjustments. One of these were mounting the preamp and power tubes directly to the circuit board. The vibration and heat caused some problems here and the later Hiwatt amps aren't nearly as dependable as the earlier ones. This makes the early Hiwatt amps much more desirable and more collectible. Hiwatt amps are still produced today with some tube and some solid-state options.

(Courtesy: Ritchie Flieger, Amps!)

ELECTRIC TUBE AMPLIFIERS

Hiwatt is a company that has produced several amps over the years. Unfortunately, no one has written a book about their amps yet. We have listed some of the most popular models that we know about. Anyone who has information on Hiwatt amps can submit it directly to the publisher for upcoming editions of the Blue *Book of Guitar Amplifiers.*

Pricing is also a touchy subject. Some hard-core HIWATT collectors pay top $$ for certain models. We suggest getting a second opinion on these amps before buying or selling, since certain early models can be worth as much as double as what is listed.

LEAD HIWATT 100 - 100W, head-unit only, all-tube chassis, preamp: 4 X 12AX7, power: 4 X EL34, single channel, front black control panel, two inputs (normal and bright), eight black knobs (OD, v, bright, b, m, t, p, MV), black covering, mfg. 1960's-80's.

1964-1981	N/A	$900 - 1,100	$650 - 750
1981-on	N/A	$800 - 1,000	$600 - 700

LEAD HIWATT 100R - 100W, head-unit only, all-tube chassis, preamp: 4 X 12AX7, power: 4 X EL34, dual channels, front black control panel, single input, 12 black konbs (Ch. 1:v, b, t, OD, lead v, Ch. 2: t, m, b, p, MV, r), black covering, mfg. 1960's-80's.

1964-1981	N/A	$950 - 1,125	$675 - 750
1981-disc.	N/A	$800 - 1,000	$600 - 700

GRADING	100%	EXCELLENT	AVERAGE

CUSTOM HIWATT 100 (DR103) - 100W, head-unit only, 8 tube chassis, preamp: 3 X 12AX7, 1 X 12AT7, power: 4 X EL34, single channel, front black control panel, four inputs, seven black knobs (p, MV, normal v, brilliant v, t, m, b), black covering with white piping, mfg. 1960's-80's.

Hiwatt Custom 100 DR 103
courtesy solidbodyguitar.com, Inc.

Hiwatt Custom 100 DR 103
courtesy solidbodyguitar.com, Inc.

Hiwatt Custom 100 Head Unit
w/4-12" Cabinet
courtesy Savage Audio

1964-1981	N/A	$1,000 - 1,200	$750 - 850
1981-disc.	N/A	$800 - 1,000	$600 - 700

The price listed is strictly for the head unit by itself. For a half-stack the price can range anywhere from $1,500 - $2,000. For a full stack that is all original in excellent shape, expect to pay $2,500+.

CUSTOM HIWATT 100 (DR103) - 100W, head-unit only, 8 tube chassis, preamp: 3 X 12AX7, 1 X 12AT7, power: 4 X EL34, single channel, front black control panel, four inputs, seven black knobs (p, MV, normal v, brilliant v, t, m, b), black covering with white piping, current mfg.

LEAD HIWATT 50 - 50W, head-unit only, all-tube chassis, preamp: 4 X 12AX7, power: 4 X EL34, single channel, front black control panel, two inputs (normal and bright), eight black knobs (OD, v, bright, b, m, t, p, MV), black covering, mfg. 1960's-80's.

1964-1981	N/A	$1,100 - 1,350	$875 - 1,000
1981-disc.	N/A	$700 - 1,000	$600 - 700

CUSTOM HIWATT 50 - 50W, head-unit only, all-tube chassis, preamp: 4 X 12AX7, power: 4 X EL34, single channel, front black control panel, two inputs (normal and bright), seven black knobs, black covering, mfg. 1960's-80's.

Hiwatt Custom 50 "2 hole"
courtesy solidbodyguitar.com, Inc.

Hiwatt Custom 50 "2 hole"
courtesy solidbodyguitar.com, Inc.

1964-1981	N/A	$1,100 - 1,350	$875 - 1,000
1981-disc.	N/A	$700 - 1,000	$600 - 700

GRADING	100%	EXCELLENT	AVERAGE

LEAD HIWATT 30 - 30W, 1-12" combo unit, all-tube chassis, preamp: 4 X 7025, power: 2 X EL84, single channel, front black control panel, single input, seven black knobs, black covering, black grille, mfg. 1960's-80's.

Hiwatt Lead 30
courtesy Willie's American Guitars

	N/A	$800 - 1,200	$450 - 650

HOFFMAN
Amplifiers produced currently produced in Pisgah Forest, North Carolina.

Doug Hoffman produces amplifiers along with tube kits and other products to do with amplification. He also sells a whole line of parts that can be mail ordered straight from the Internet. Hoffman no longer puts out a paper catalog, but they do have all the information that anyone could ever want to know posted on the web site. Hoffman currently makes 30W and 50W heads along with a 30W combo. Hoffman has also experimented with 50W and 100W heads. All their units are tube based. Dickie Betts had a 100W head built for him. For a full lineup of the models for Hoffman, or a parts listing visit their web site (see Trademark Index).

HOLLAND
Amplifiers currently produced in Brentwood, Tennessee.

Holland Amplifiers was founded by Mike Holland on April 1, 1992 in Virginia Beach, Virginia while serving in the United States Navy. Mike worked on F14 fighter jets as a structural mechanic. On his kitchen table, using only all American components with specifications that were far above any other amp, Mike created the first Holland Tube Amplifier.

In 1998, Mike contacted Lane Zastrow, President of Lasar Music and former Vice President of Sales and Marketing for the Gibson Guitar Corporation, to handle sales and marketing for Holland Amplifiers. Lane and Mike then decided to become partners and formed L&M Amplifiers in July of 2000. L&M is the corporation that owns Holland Amplifiers. In September of 2000, Holland moved its operations from Virginia Beach to Brentwood, Tennessee. Holland now creates 9 models and is distributed throughout the world. Holland Amplifiers are completely handmade with point-to-point wiring, whether it be a standard model or a custom amp. Holland Amps are compatible with all styles of music including rock, country, jazz and blues.

ELECTRIC TUBE AMPLIFIERS

Holland currently has four different amplifiers in their current series. **The Gibb** is considered the flagship of the Holland line. This amp was created for East coast artist Gibb Droll. It is a 50W chassis available in a head unit, or combo with 10 or 12 inch speakers. It is an all tube amp with blues sounds of the 1950's -1960's. Holland describes it as "reminiscent of ZZ Top. **The Jazz Amp** is also 50W with different power tubes. This amp is also available in a head unit and combo, but no 4 speaker combos (your back says thank you). The Jazz is known for having lots of headroom and great clean power. The **Little Jimi** is a 35W or 50W amp with 2 X 5881 or 6L6 power tubes. This amp is more of a blues amp, which sounds like Hendrix, Clapton, and Stevie Ray Vaughn. The **Mini Jimi** is the Little Jimi with more bite in a 1-12" combo cabinet. Essentially it is the Little Jimi in a smaller package. Holland doesn't have any set retail prices, or at least none that we could find out. The two channel model can be found in 100% condition for about $2,975. The Little Jimi for $1,650 and the Mini Jimi for $1,365. These are not retail prices, but 100% prices.

HONDO
Amplifiers currently produced in Korea. Hondo amplifiers are distributed by MBT International of Charleston, South Carolina.

The Hondo Guitar company was originally formed in 1969 when Jerry Freed and Tommy Moore of the International Music Corporation (IMC) of Forth Worth, Texas combined with the recently formed Samick company. IMC's target was to introduce modern manufacturing techniques and American quality standards to the Korean guitar manufacturing industry.

Hondo was going to offer solid entry level maket instruments at a fair market price. The first Korean instruments were classical and acoustic. In 1972, the first solid-body electrics appeared. Business boomed throughout the 1970's and 1980's as Hondo built a reputation and had distributors in 70 countries world wide. Sales were great until the late 1980's when IMC took an interest in Jackson/Charvel and Hondo went by the wayside in 1987. Jerry Freed started the Jerry Freed International company in 1989 and aquired the rights to the Hondo trademark in 1991. Production of Hondo instruments began at this time, and this time Hondo included amplifiers in the catalogs. The first Hondo amplifiers were included in catalogs around 1985, but there were only three models available. In 1993, the company had moved to Stuart, Florida, and some models were being produced in China and Taiwan. By 1994, a full two pages in the Hondo catalog were dedicated to amplifiers. The Hondo company was purchased by MBT International in 1995 (which also distributes J.B. Player). Currently Hondo offers small guitar and bass amplifiers at an affordable price.

(Source: Michael Wright, Guitar Stories Volume 1)

GRADING	100%	EXCELLENT	AVERAGE

ELECTRIC SOLID-STATE AMPLIFIERS

Currently Hondo offers two guitar amps, two bass amps, and two mini-amps. The **H-10** and **H-20** are guitar amps with small speakers, wattages, and simple controls. The **H-25B** and **H-35B** are bass amps with simple bass controls. There are two mini-amps the **HA-97** and **HA-97S**, which are models that run on a nine-volt battery and turn your headphones into an amplifier. They have a 1/4" jack and three controls. All the current Hondo amplifier units list under $150, with most being much cheaper than this.

Hondo has produced quite a few amplifiers since the mid 1980's. Prices on used amplifiers generally can be found in the $50-150 range.

HONEYTONE

Amplifiers currently produced by Danelectro of Laguna Hills, California. The Honeytone amplifiers are produced in Asia. Refer to the Danelectro section for information.

HUGHES & KETTNER

Amplifiers currently produced in St. Wendel, Germany. Hughes & Kettner is distributed in the U.S. out of Mt. Prospect, Illinois. The Hughes & Kettner trademark was established in the early 1980's.

Hughes and Kettner emerged when amplifier companies all over the country were in the "hurtbag." There was a tube scare looming around the corner where it was estimated that tubes would be no longer available and solid-state was going to be the only way to go. However Hughes & Kettner went to work designing a guitar amp that had the three need channels (clean, cruch, and overdrive), and that would have the effect devices as well. The first product was the AS 64. This amp could store 64 presets, and a number of different amp sounds could come from one machine. This was released in 1985, and they have been developing great tube amplifiers ever since. Hughes & Kettner has had several achievements over the years. Visit the web site for more information and history (see Trademark Index).

ELECTRIC TUBE AMPLIFIERS

Hughes & Kettner make some high-quality amplifiers. Most recently they have introduced the Zen series, which are MIDI equipped and have literally hundreds of digital possibilities. Tube amplifiers are also available in guitar and bass versions.

Guitar Amplifiers

ZENTURA HEAD - 2 X 100W, head-unit only, 2 Sharc 32Bit Floating Point DSP's, 17 amp types, four effects groups, 128 presets, front silver control panel, single input, 15 silver knobs (g, amp type, b, m, t, p, v, preset, mod FX, delay, r, type, para1, para2, MV), digital control panel, black covering, 40 lbs., current mfg.

MSR	$3,299	$2,400	$1,950 - 2,200	$1,500 - 1,700

* **Zentura Combo** - Similar to the Zentura head except in combo form with 2-12" Celestion Vintage 30 speakers, and 2 X 120W output, 60 lbs., current mfg.

MSR	$3,499	$2,500	$2,000 - 2,250	$1,550 - 1,750

ZENAMP HEAD - 2 X 100W, head-unit only, 1 Sharc 32Bit Floating Point DSP, 16 Amp types, 30 presets, MIDI in/out/through, front blue control panel, single input, ten silver knobs (g, b, m, t, p, preset v, FX parameter, r, delay, MV) three black knobs for effects, black covering, 36 lbs., current mfg.

MSR	$1,499	$1,075	$800 - 950	$625 - 725

* **Zenamp Combo** - Similar to the Zenamp head except in combo form with 2-12" Celestion speakers (1 Vintage 30 & 1 Rockdrive Junior), 2 X 60W output, 60 lbs., current mfg.

MSR	$1,499	$1,075	$800 - 950	$625 - 725

PURETONE - 25W, head-unit only, all tube Class A chassis, power: 2 X EL34, single channel, front silver control panel, single input, five silver knobs (growl, b, m, t, v), black covering, mfg. 2001-current.

MSR	$1,999	$1,425	$1,100 - 1,300	$900 - 1,025

* **Puretone Combo** - Similar to the Puretone head except in combo form with 1-12" Celestion Vintage 30 speaker, mfg. 2001-current.

MSR	$2,299	$1,650	$1,300 - 1,500	$1,000 - 1,150

DUOTONE HEAD - 100W, head-unit only, all tube chassis, preamp: 5 X ECC83, power: 4 X EL34, dual channels, front silver control panel, single input, 13 silver knobs (Master: MV1, MV2, p, FX level, OD: b, m, t, MV, g, Clean: b, m, t, v) boost switch, effects loop, footswitch, black covering, clear front panel, current mfg.

MSR	$2,499	$1,750	$1,350 - 1,550	$1,100 - 1,250

* **Duotone Combo** - Similar to the Duotone Head except in combo form with 1-12" Celestion speaker, reverb, 50W output (2 X EL34), current mfg.

MSR	$2,599	$1,800	$1,400 - 1,600	$1,150 - 1,275

TRIAMP MK II HEAD - 100W, head-unit only, all tube chassis, power: 4 X EL34 or 4 X 6L6, three channels, front silver control panel, single input, 21 black knobs (t, b, m, MV, gA, gB, per channel, p, MV, FX mix), effects loop, possible reverb, black covering, clear front panel, current mfg

MSR	$2,999	$2,150	$1,700 - 1,950	$1,450 - 1,575

Bass Amplifiers

There are speaker cabinets available specifically for the Bassbase series. They come in configurations of 2-15", 4-10", or 1-18". They are covered in black covering and have an attractive metal silver grille.

BASSBASE 600 - 650W, rack-mount head-unit, 12AX7 preamp, solid-state power unit, varimetric soundmodes, front silver control panel, 15 black knobs, various lights and buttons, effects looop, dual fan cooling system, current mfg.

MSR	$1,799	$1,275	$975 - 1,100	$750 - 850

GRADING	100%	EXCELLENT	AVERAGE

BASSBASE 400 - 400W, rack-mount head-unit, tube preamp: 12AX7, solid-state power unit, Varimetric soundmodes, front silver control panel, single input, 11 black knobs, various lights and buttons, effects loop, current mfg.

MSR	$1,499	$1,075	$775 - 925	$600 - 700

ELECTRIC SOLID-STATE AMPLIFIERS

There are many solid-state amplifiers that Hughes & Kettner have produced over the years. Not every one is going to be listed here and prices are still unstable on the secondhand market. Look for more information on upcoming editions of the *Blue Book of Guitar Amplifiers*.

Attax Series

The Attax series was recently discontinued. These were solid-state models that were comparable to the high-end tube amps as far as features go. The **Tour Reverb** was available as either a combo or head unit. This model was good for 100W, reverb, and master volume. The **Club Reverb** was a simpler version of the Tour. This had 65W and not as many knobs. The **Metroverb** was a dual channel, 50W amp that could be used for many purposes. Again there were less controls on this model. All the combo units came equipped with Celestion 12" Rock Driver Junior speakers.

Warp 7 Series

WARP 7 HALF STACK - 100W, head-unit only, solid-state chassis, dual channels, front black control panel, single input, ten black knobs (Clean: v, b, m, t, Warp: g, MV, b, m, t, p), effects loop, footswitch, black covering, new 2002.

MSR	$1,149	$825	$650 - 750	$500 - 575

The price listed includes the speaker cabinet that comes with the head. The speaker cabinet is a 4-12" enclosure with 4-12" Celestion RockDriver Junior speakers.

* ***Warp 7 212 Combo*** - Similar to the Warp 7 head unit except has 2-12" Celestion speakers, new 2002.

MSR	$849	$600	$425 - 525	$325 - 375

* ***Warp 7 112 Combo*** - Similar to the Warp 7 212 Combo except with 1-12" speaker, and 80W output, new 2002.

MSR	$649	$475	$350 - 425	$275 - 325

Vortex Series

VORTEX HALF STACK - 80W, head-unit & speaker enclosure, solid-state chassis, dual channels, reverb, front silver V control panel, single input, nine black knobs (clean v, lead g, voicing, lead MV, b, m, t, r, MV), effects loop, speaker cabinet: 4 X 12" Celestion RockDriver Junior speakers, black covering, black grille, current mfg.

MSR	$999	$725	$575 - 650	$450 - 525

Edition Series

Hughes & Kettner also has a budget line of amplifiers for practice of performance. The Edition series are solid-state amps with the bells and whistles of the larger amps. The **Edition Silver 50** has been around for a couple years, and the **Edition Blue 30**, and **Edition Blue 15** are new additions in 2002. The wattage of these amps are indicated in the models. All have two channels and reverb. The 50 comes with a 12" Celestion speaker, the 30 a 10" Jensen and the 15 an 8" Celestion. Retail pricing on these amps start at $199 and go up to $449. These haven't been on the market long enough to come up with a secondary price.

Bassforce Series

The Baseforce Series are combos and heads that are currently not in production. The **XXL Bassforce** is the top model with 300W in a combo or head unit version. It has a 15" driver, and some cool controls including the EQ Matrix. The **XL Bassforce** has 200W, and most of the controls of the XXL. The **Bassforce L** has 100W output, and a basic control panel. All are of good quality and good for practice or performing. The Bassforce XXL is available as a head-unit and matching speaker cabinets are available. All covering is red on these amps with black grille cloth. The Head unit and cabinet are a maroon color with a silver metal grille.

Hughes & Kettner Bass Force
courtesy George McGuire

NOTES

H

Section I

IBANEZ

Amplifiers currently produced in Japan. Ibanez amplifiers are distributed by Ibanez U.S.A. in Bensalem, Pennsylvania.

The Ibanez trademark goes way back to 1932. Hoshino Gakki Ten, Inc. began producing instruments under the Ibanez trademark in 1932. World War II wiped out the Ibanez factory (fire), but the trademark was revived in 1950. By the 1960's, Hoshino was producing instruments under a number of trademarks. Enter Harry Rosenbloom in the mid 1950's. He had opened the Medley Music store outside Philadelphia. With the folk music bloom he started producing acoustic instruments under the Elger name. When Rosenbloom wanted to get solidbody guitars into his lineup, he went to Japan and found Hoshino. They formed a contract and Ibanez guitars were being imported to the U.S. and sold at Rosenbloom's store.

The 1970's gave Ibanez some heat, as they were being sued by Gibson for copying instruments that were almost identical to Gibson, and being sold much cheaper. After this lawsuit was settled, it gave Japanese manufacturers the heads-up to start making their own designs again. Ibanez really popped up during the 1980's and 90's with their many different models and unique designs.

In the late 1990's Ibanez decided that a line of amplifiers would be a good product to sell along with a guitar. The BT and GT bass and guitar amps respectively, were released in 1999. Now Ibanez has a full line of bass and guitar amps.

(Early Ibanez history courtesy: Michael Wright, Guitar Stories Volume One).

GRADING	100%	EXCELLENT	AVERAGE

ELECTRIC GUITAR AMPLIFIERS

TB15R - 15W, 1-8" "Power Jam Jr." speaker combo, solid-state chassis, dual channels, front black control panel, single input, seven black knobs (v, g, v, b, m, t, level), headphone jack, CD input, black covering, gray grille cloth, mfg. 2000-current.

TB25 - 25W, 1-10" "Power Jam" speaker combo, solid-state chassis, single channel, switchable gain, front black control panel, single input, seven black knobs (g, v, v, b, m, t, level), headphone jack, footswitch, black covering, black grille cloth, mfg. 1999 only.

TB25R - 25W, 1-10" "Power Jam" speaker combo, solid-state chassis, reverb, single channel, switchable gain, front black control panel, single input, seven black knobs (g, v, v, b, m, t, r), headphone jack, footswitch, black covering, gray grille cloth, mfg. 1999-current.

TB225C - 50W (2 X 25W stereo), 2-10" "Power Jam" speakers, dual channels, chorus, front black control panel, single input, 13 black knobs (Ch 1: b, m, t, v, Ch. 2: g, b, m, t, v, r, s, depth, MV), effects loop, footswitch, headphone jack, black covering, gray grille cloth, mfg. 2000-current.

TB50R - 50W, 1-12" "Power Jam" speaker, dual channels, front black control panel, single input, eleven black knobs (Ch. 1: g, b, m, t, v, Ch. 2: g, b, m, t, v, MV), effects loop, footswitch, headphone jack, black covering, gray grille cloth, mfg. 2000-current.

GT10DX - 10W, 1-6" speaker combo, solid-state chassis, switchable gain, front black control panel, single input, six black konbs (level, v, clean: v, b, m, t), headphone jack, black covering, black grille, mfg. 1998-99.

	$125	$80 - 100	$55 - 70

* ***GT10DXR*** - Similar to the GT10DX, except has reverb, mfg. 1998-99.

	$130	$85 - 105	$60 - 70

IBZ10 - 10W, 1-6" speaker, solid-state chassis combo, reverb, switchable boost, front black control panel, single input, five black knobs (r, b, m, t, v), black covering, gray grille cloth, mfg. 2000-current.

This amp is part of the Jumpstart package, which comes with a guitar, amp, and distortion box all in one.

ACOUSTIC GUITAR AMPLIFIERS

GT10DXA - 10W, 1-6" speaker, solid-state chassis, single channel, chorus, brown control panel, single input, five black knobs (depth, b, m, t, v), headphone jack, brown covering, brown grille cloth, mfg. 1999 only.

	$125	$80 - 100	$55 - 70

IBZ10A - 10W, 1-6" speaker, solid-state chassis, single channel, chorus, brown control panel, single input, five black knobs (depth, b, m, t, v), headphone jack, brown covering, brown grille cloth, mfg. 2000-current.

TA25H - 25W, 1-10" Ibanez speaker w/ tweeter, solid-state chassis, dual channels, front brown control panel, single input, eight white knobs (mic v, inst v, s, b, m/h, m/l, t, level), brown covering, brown cloth grille, mfg. 2000-current.

TA225 - 50W (2 X 25 stereo), 2-10" "Power Jam" speakers, two tweeters, solid-state chassis, dual channels, chorus, reverb, front brown control panel, mic and instrument inputs, 13 white knobs (Mic: b, t, v, Instrument: b, two parametric, t, v, s, depth, level, v, MV), brown covering, brown cloth grille, mfg. 2000-current.

ELECTRIC BASS AMPLIFIERS

BT10 - 10W, 1-6.5" speaker, solid-state chassis combo, single channel, front black control panel, single input, five black knobs (v, b, m, t, p), headphone jack, black covering, black grille, mfg. 1999-current.

This amp is part of the Jump Start Package with a bass guitar, and bass amp.

IBZ10B - 10W, 1-6." speaker, solid-state chassis combo, single channel, front black control panel, single input, five black knobs (v, b, m, t, p), headphone jack, black covering, black grille, mfg. 2000-01.

SW20 - 20W, 1-8" speaker, solid-state chassis combo, single channel, front black control panel, five black knobs (v, b, m, t, p), headphone jack, CD inputs, black covering, black grille, mfg. 2001-current.

GRADING	100%	EXCELLENT	AVERAGE

SW25 - 25W, 1-10" speaker, solid state chassis combo, single channel, compression, front black control panel, six black knobs (v, threshold, b, m, t, p), headphone jack, shelf port, black covering, black grille, mfg. 1999 only.

SW25DX - Similar to the SW25 except has a tuned front mounted port design, mfg. 2000-01.

SW35 - Similar to the SW25DX except has 35W output & tilt back cabinet design, new 2002.

SW65 - 65W, 1-12" speaker with piezo tweeter, solid-state chassis combo, limiter, black front control panel, single input, six black knobs (g, b, m, t, p, v), CD-inputs, headphone jack, line out, effects loop, black covering, black grille, new 2002.

INTELLI ELECTRONICS INC.

Amplifiers currently produced in China. The Intelli headquarters is located in Korea.

Intelli Amplification is a relatively new company that produces amplifiers and guitar tuners. Currently they have guitar and bass amplifiers in a number of different configurations. Most of the products are entry-level practice units, but there are some high-end models. The amps are solid-state design, and have the basic controls that practice level amplifiers usually have. The A series are guitar amps covered in orange covering that catch the eye. They also make rackmount power amplifiers. For more information, please email the company for questions (see Trademark Index).

Section J

JBL
Speaker Enclosures currently produced in in Northridge California.

JBL doesn't have any amplifiers, but they have everything to do with them. JBL has been around for many years and are probably best known for their speakers. They have produced a number of different items in the electronics field for many years now. Currently they offer the TR series of loudspeakers. These loudspeakers are probably some of the best on the market. The design of the TR series makes so it is almost impossible to blow the speakers. JBL has been around for many years and their speakers (and cabinets) are some of the best out there. Literally they have hundreds of products in the sound industry. For further information refer to the JBL web site (see Trademark Index).

LEE JACKSON AMPLIFIERS
Amplifiers previously produced in Cape Girardeau, Missouri.

Lee Jackson has been involved in many different music companies over the years including B.C. Rich, Fender, Pignose, Metaltronix, Ampeg, and Harmony. Even though he has designed many amplifiers, he didn't get his name put on one until 1993. Harmony Music asked him to design some amplifiers and they would name the company around him. During his time with Harmony he produced XLS-1000 series first and the XLA-1000 followed shortly thereafter. The XLA-1000 amp was a direct copy of the amps that he had built for Zakk Wylde, Steve Vai, and George Lynch. Jackson made amplifiers up until 1996 when Horizon had some problems within the company, and they put the amp project on hold. As they tried to get Lee Jackson amplifiers going again in 2001, the stock market crashed with investors shaking in their boots. This was bad news for Jackson as they were giving a presentation the day the market crashed. The final nail in the coffin was the terrorist attacks on September 11, 2001. All the investors got really scared and pulled out all money and support. Currently Lee Jackson is working on regrouping the company, but no amps are being manufactured. The bumpy ride Lee Jackson has experienced over the years still continues.

JOHNSON (U.S.A.)
Amplifiers previously produced in Sandy, Utah. The Johnson trademark stopped producing amplifiers in July 2002.

The Johnson family of amplifiers has been around just a short time, but the Johnson name in music has been around for 40 years. They are known for producing tube intergrated amp modeling. Johnson actually uses real tubes in the modeling that they do. Johnson also studies the frequency responses, and the EQ curves of vintage amplifiers to store data in modes for instant recall. Johnson stopped producing their current line of amplifiers in July of 2002. They still offer customer support and warranty options. Refer to the Johnson website for further details and more product information (see Trademark Index).

GRADING	100%	EXCELLENT	AVERAGE

ELECTRIC TUBE AMPLIFIERS

JT50 MIRAGE - 50W, Johnson speaker combo, V-Tube technology preamp, 12 amp models, top silver control panel, single input, 14 black knobs, 21 user presets, reverb, effects loop, delay, black covering, gray grille, disc. 2002.
	$600	$475 - 550	$375 - 425

Last MSR was $849.

JM60 MARQUIS - 120W (2 X 60W Stereo), 1-12" Johnson speaker, 1 X 12AX7 preamp tube, 18 amp models, 27 user/27 factory presets, front gold control panel, single input, 12 black knobs, headphone jack, speaker out jack, disc. 2002.
	$800	$600 - 700	$500 - 550

Last MSR was $1,099.95.

An extension speaker cabinet is available to match up with the JM60. It has a 12" Johnson speaker as well.

JM120 MARQUIS STEREO - Similar to the JM60 Marquis execpt in combo form with 2-12" Johnson speakers, disc. 2002.
$950	$750 - 850	$625 - 675

Last MSR was $1,299.

JM150 MILLENIUM - 150W (2 X 75 Stereo), 2-12" Celestion Vintage 30, 2 X 12AX7 preamp tubes, 36 amp models, MIDI, front gold control panel, various knobs and buttons, chromatic tuner, S-DISC II processing, black covering, gray grille, disc. 2002.
$1,500	$1,050 - 1,250	$700 - 850

Last MSR was $2,099.95.

JM250 MILLENIUM - 250W (2 X 125W Stereo), head-unit only, 2 X 12AX7 preamp tubes, 36 amp models, has the featurs of the JM150, disc. 2002.
$1,275	$850 - 1,050	$600 - 750

Last MSR was $1,799.95.

This amp head was sold with two possible speaker cabinets. The cabinets are available as either a slanted or straight front and equipped with 4-12" Celestion Vintage 30 loudspeakers. With two of these and the head you get a full Marshall-like stack.

JOHNSON (FOREIGN)
Amplifiers currently produced overseas.

Currently there are a lot of small practice amps made under the Johnson name showing up everywhere, especially on Ebay. These are all small amps with basic controls, but not a lot is known about them. Typically you can buy one of these amps for under $100.

NOTES

Section K

KMD

Amplifiers previously produced in England.

KMD made amplifiers mainly in the 1980's. However they are out of business now, and little information is known about the company. They did have a slug of amplifiers in various types including tube and solid-state. Typically amps show up on Ebay and in pawn shops for relatively cheap prices. Any information on KMD amps can be submitted directly to the publisher for upcoming editions of the *Blue Book of Guitar Amplifiers*.

KALAMAZOO

Amplifiers previously produced in Kalamazoo, Michigan under Gibson.

Kalamazoo was originally a budget-brand name for Gibson back in the 1930's and 40's. When the economy went sour in the early 1930's, Guy Hart knew that lower priced instruments were going to sell better than the higher priced counterparts. So Gibson introduced some budget lines that released Gibson-made guitars with a different label on the headstock. These guitars were nearly as good as authentic Gibsons except they didn't have the truss rod (or price tag). Kalamazoo disapeared during World War II, but reappeared in the late 1940's. A 1949 catalog offers guitars and amplifiers under the Kalamazoo trademark. Some of the amplifiers were the Model 1, Model 2 with tremolo, Model 3, Model 4 with tremolo, and the Reverb 12 with tremolo. They also had two bass amps, the Bass 30 and Bass 50. Very little is known about these amplifiers. The Kalamazoo name went away again in the 1950's as Gibson went through the roof in sales, and didn't need a budget line to get by. The name came around for one last time in the 1960's for a line of solid-body electric guitars. By 1970, Kalamazoo was R.I.P.

(Source: Walter Carter, Gibson Guitars 100 Years of an American Icon)

KAY

Amplifiers previously in Chicago, Illinois between the 1930's and the 1960's.

The Kay Musical Instrument Company roots go way back to 1890, when the Groeschel Company of Chicago started building bowl-back mandolins. In 1918, the Groeschel name was changed to the Stromberg-Voisenet Company, and incorporated in 1921. C.G. Stromberg was the vice-president, and the company started to produce guitars and banjos under the Mayflower trademark. Henry Kay Kuhrmeyer offered to use his middle name on the instruments, and Kay Kraft was born. Kuhrmeyer bought the company in 1928, and changed the name of the company to Kay Musical Instruments in 1931. At this time they started to mass-produce stringed instruments. At this point the company became a "house brand" company.

Early guitar amplification for the Stromberg company (before Kay) is thought to go way back to 1928! Amplification was just being explored and the quest for portable amplification was underdevlopment in the mid 1920's. The first Stromberg amplifier is guessed to have a 12" Jensen speaker driven by old tubes (71A power tubes), and put out 3 Watts. These amps were very basic and little is known about them.

When the economy rebounded in the mid 1930's, Kay (previously Stromberg), went back to developing a guitar amplifier. The depression had halted this research, but many advances had come to surface by 1939. When the electric guitar became popular and technology came along, amplifiers were starting to be produced again. The company was sold to Sydney Katz in 1955. Kay's heyday was between 1955-65. In 1965, the guitar market was super-saturated and Kay was feeling the pinch of the economy. Katz sold the company to Seeburg, a large jukebox manufacture in Chicago. They owned the company for two years and sold to Valco guitars. Kay wanted to buy Valco but Bob Keyworth suggested the opposite; that they sell to Valco. Kay then produced amplifiers up until 1969 when the bills weren't being paid anymore, and an investment group showed up to the plant and changed the locks on the doors. Kay (and Valco) were out of business by 1970.

(Kay history and model information courtesy: Michael Wright, Guitar Stories Volume 2)

ELECTRIC TUBE AMPLIFIERS

Most of Kay's amps ran in series. Before 1952 most amplifiers were here and there with odd or no model number destinations. In 1952 the K prefix appeared on amplifiers. In 1957 four new models were introduced, two more in 1960, two more in 1961, and nine new models in 1962. In 1966 there were 13 new models introduced, but only in production until 1968 when the company folded shortly thereafter. Kay amplifiers are generally tube amps in the early years, and by 1962 a good portion of these amps were solid-state. The K prefix lasted from 1952 until they went under in 1968. Generally speaking Kay amplifiers are very basic with few controls and are supposed to be practice amps. There were some amplifiers that were higher end with features such as reverb and tremolo.

Since Kay amps were budget amps at the time in the 50's and 60's, they hold about the same price today. Most Kay amps can be found between the price range of $100-$200. Some smaller models can even be found for $50. For rare models and units loaded with features, the price may be rise over the $200 line.

The first Kay amplifier, technically, can be dated back to 1928-29 as the Stromberg amp. As talked about in the heading, this amp was basic, used ancient tubes, and doesn't exactly show up on the second-hand market to often. The price tag on this amp would be considerably higher, but an average retail market price can't be established since not many of them are known to exist. Kay didn't start putting their name on amplifiers until the late 1930's. In between this time there were some Ward, Oahu, and Gretsch amps made by Kay (these were all made by Valco). In 1945 Kay debuted its post-war amp. In 1947, the Model F475 High Fidelity Amp was released. In 1952, Kay's amplifier line expanded rapidly as they debuted the K series. Each model was designated with a K then followed by a three digit number. Most early models are K500's and a couple K600's & K300's. In 1962 the model designations were all K700's. As of now there are probably around 35 models known in the Kay line.

KITCHEN-MARSHALL

Amplifiers previously produced in England by Marshall.

Kitchen-Marshall is just another Marshall amp in disguise. Like CMI and Park, Kitchen came to Marshall to build some amps for them. The Kitchen chain of music shops was located in North England in the late 1960's. Marshall agreed to and built the amps (Marshall), under the name Kitchen-Marshall. Guitar and P.A. amp heads were made along with some 4-12" speaker cabinets bearing the name Kitchen-Marshall. These amps looked exactly like Marshall amps except with a Kitchen spelled before Marshall in the block logo. These amps are very rare today, and, like Narb amplifiers, are more valuable to the collector than the player.

(History courtesy: Michael Doyle, The History of Marshall)

KOCH

Amplifiers currently produced in Amersfoort, The Netherlands. Koch amplifiers are distributed in the United States by Eden Electronics in Montrose, Minnesota.

GRADING	100%	EXCELLENT	AVERAGE

Dolf Koch has developed an amplifier company that is dedicated to creating an amplifier that is perfectly tonally balanced. This company is rather new but they have some strongly built materials. They also have a custom shop that can make modifications on a special request. Everything that goes into the amplifier is carefully constructed. Visit the Koch web site for more information (see Trademark Index).

ELECTRIC TUBE AMPLIFIERS

Koch produces one preamp unit, the **Pedaltone** and the **Loadbox**. The Pedaltone is equipped with 4 X 12AX7 tubes and has four channels. The Load Box is a unit that reduces the sound output coming out of the amp (Similar to the Marshall powerbreak). Since some amplifiers need to be run wide-open to get that sound, this will keep that sound but reduce the volume at different percentage levels.

Koch LB120
courtesy Koch

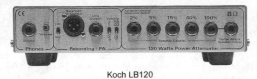

Koch LB120
courtesy Koch

Koch Pedaltone
courtesy Koch

TWINTONE - 50W, head-unit only, all tube chassis, preamp: 1 X 12AX7WA, 2 X 12AX7, power: 1 X 12AX7, 2 X EL34, dual channels, front black and silver control panel, dual inputs, ten black knobs (Clean: v, b, m, t, OD: g, v, p, b, m, t), footswitch, effects loop, headphone jack, black tolex covering, gray grille, current mfg.

Koch Twintone
courtesy Koch

Koch Twintone Combo
courtesy Koch

Koch Twintone Combo
courtesy Koch

MSR	$1,480	$1,050	$850 - 950	$700 - 800

* **Twintone Combo** - Similar to the Twintone except in combo form with 1-12" Koch/Jensen VG12-90, current mfg.

MSR	$1,684	$1,199	$900 - 1,050	$750 - 850

MULTITONE 50 - 50W, head-unit only, all tube chassis, preamp: 1 X 12AX7WA, 2 X 12AX7, power: 1 X 12AX7, 2 X EL34 or 4 X 6V6, dual channels, front black and silver control panel, two inputs, 14 black knobs (Pre: b, m, t, v, drive, v, Post: g, v, p, b, m, t, Master: MV, r), effects loop, footswitch, black tolex covering, gray grille cloth, current mfg.

Koch Multitone 50w
courtesy Koch

MSR	$1,990	$1,450	$1,100 - 1,300	$925 - 1,025

* **Multitone 50 Combo** - Similar to the Multitone 50 head except in combo form with 2-12" Koch/Jensen VG12-90 speakers, current mfg.

MSR	$2,415	$1,750	$1,300 - 1,500	$1,100 - 1,200

MULTITONE 100 - Similar to the Multitone 50 except has 100W output from either 4 X EL34/6L6 or 2 X EL34 + 2 X 6L6, current mfg.

MSR	$2,030	$1,475	$1,150 - 1,350	$950 - 1,050

GRADING	100%	EXCELLENT	AVERAGE

Multitone 100 Combo - Similar to the Multitone 100 head except in combo form with 2-12" Koch/Jensen VG12-90 speakers, current mfg.

Koch Multitone 100w Combo
courtesy Koch

Koch Multitone 100w Combo
courtesy Koch

MSR	$2,452	$1,799	$1,350 - 1,550	$1,150 - 1,250

POWERTONE - 120W, head-unit only, all tube chassis, preamp: 1 X 12AX7WA, 2 X 12AX7, power: 1 X 12AX7, 4 X EL34, dual channels, reverb, front black and silver control panel, two inputs, 14 black knobs (Clean: b, m, t, v, Gain: g, m, ultra g, v, p, b, m, t, Master: MV, r), effects loop, footswitch, black tolex covering, silver metal grille, current mfg.

Koch Powertone
courtesy Koch

MSR	$2,074	$1,499	$1,150 - 1,350	$950 - 1,050

This model is also available with 6550 power tubes (4).

Add $150 for the 6550 tube option.

SPEAKER CABINETS

Koch produces a fine line of speaker cabinets to match up with their amplifier heads. All cabinets have 12" Koch/Jensen VG12-90 speakers. These cabinets are available in configurations of 1-12", 2-12", & 4-12" speakers. Each speaker in a cabinet can handle 90W and they multiply by how many speakers. For more information and specifications on the cabinets, visit the web site.

KONA
Amplifiers currently produced overseas.

The Kona line of guitars are distributed by M & M Merchandisers in the United States. M & M has been around since 1976 as a factory with roots in the pawn shop business dating back to 1917. The Kona line of guitars was introduced in 2001 and the amps followed suit in January of 2002.

ELECTRIC SOLID-STATE AMPLIFIERS

Currently Kona offers five different amplifiers; three are guitar and two are bass amps. The Guitar amps start at a 10W, 1-5" speaker amp, which is model # **KA-10**. This retails for $79.99. The **KA-20** has 20W, an 8" speaker and two channels. This retails for $149.99. The **KA-35R** has 35W, a 10" speaker, two channels, reverb, and retails for $249.99. The smaller bass amp is the **KB-30**, which features 30W and a ten inch speaker for $239.99. The larger bass amplifier is the model **KB-50** with 50W of power, a 12" speaker, and reverb. This model goes for $269.99. All amplifiers have the following features: volume, treble, and bass knobs, black tolex covering, a black grille, silver control panel, top handle, and metal corners.

KUSTOM
Amplifiers previously produced in Chanute, Kansas during the 1970's. Currently produced by Kustom Incorporated.

Kustom amps were introduced in the 1970's when transistor amplification was the latest fad. While most people think of transistor amp companies of the 1970's as "one hit wonders," Kustom had a unique touch. The Kustom amps were covered in their "tuck and roll" padded vinyl. A person cannot mistake a Kustom amp as Ritchie Flieger describes it as a cross between a 1957 Chevy and its radio. These amps were very retro looking, and the cosmetics had to have something with the company surviving as long as it did. Beyond the cosmetics, there are electronics inside that were built very well. The best thing about these neat looking, usually working, amps is that they can be found for fairly cheap. Even if an old Kustom amp doesn't work (and don't try to fix it $$$), hey, at least it looks cool.

Kustom amps are now being produced once again and the headquarters are in Cinncinnati, Ohio. They are now producing a wide aray of amplifiers, however they still are solid-state in most cases. They do offer some tubes in products, but nothing too serious. They have also re-released the tuck and roll series in their different colors. The Kustom web site has more information on everything they have to offer (see Trademark Index).

ELECTRIC TUBE AMPLIFIERS

The only tube amps that Kustom has are the Tuck and Roll amps of vintage style, but they have tubes in them now. These new tuck and roll amplifiers are available in red, blue, black, or charocal covering.

Tuck and Roll Series (Current Production)

TRT50H - 50W, head-unit only, all tube chassis, preamp: 4 X 12AX7, power: 2 X 6L6, dual channels, reverb, front black control panel, two inputs, 12 black and silver knobs (b, m, t, g, r, v, per channel), footswitch, tuck & roll covering (various colors), 38 lbs., current mfg.

TRT100H - 100W, head-unit only, all tube chassis, preamp: 4 X 12AX7, power: 4 X 6L6, dual channels, reverb, front black control panel, two inputs, 12 black and silver knobs (b, m, t, g, r, v, per channel), footswitch, tuck & roll covering (various colors), 42 lbs., current mfg.

TRB400H - 400W, bass head-unit only, tube/solid-state chassis, preamp: 1 X 12AX7, solid-state power supply, dual channels, chorous, compressor, front black control panel, two inputs, 16 black and silver knobs (voice, voice, ratio, depth, g, g, threshold, rate, 7-band equalizer, v), footswitch, tuck & roll covering (various colors), 42 lbs., current mfg.

SPEAKER CABINETS - Kustom has four different speaker cabinet configurations to match the tuck and roll heads. All speakers are Jensen's, and can handle at least 100W. The cabinets are the TR212 (2-12"), TR215 (2-15"), TR410 (4-10"), and TR412 (4-12").

ELECTRIC SOLID-STATE AMPLIFIERS

Kustom has tuck and roll amps only in solid-state during the late 1960's and early 1970's. The solid-state amps of today are the K series, which are affordable but have some cool effects and options.

Tuck and Roll Series

Kustom has made several head and speaker cabinets in the past. This means that there were many combinations of head units and speaker cabinets. Generally speaking Kustom made 50, 100, 150, and 200W head units. Within these head units there were several different configurations of inputs, knobs, and other effects. When you throw in a speaker cabinet with a number of different possibilities (i.e. 1-15" or 2-10"), the head/cabinet combinations are nearly endless. However most Kustom setups that are seen on the market today are sold as head/cabinet combinations. It is nearly impossible to list all the combinations of everything, and there are some models that we don't know about (any early Kustom catalogs or information would be appreciated). Usually a common head/cab combo (i.e. K100 head with a 1-15" speaker cab) can be found in between the $400-500 range. Prices listed in the Tuck and Roll series are for either only the combo or the head listed. Generally speaking, if the cabinet is sold with the head you can approximately double the price (i.e. a K-100 worth $200 with the matching 2-12" cabinet could be valued around $400). For models not listed prices can be generally between $200-400 for combos. Any information on Kustom amplifiers is welcome and will be published in upcoming editions of the *Blue Book of Guitar Amplifiers*.

The Tuck and Roll series were available in several colors. Most common, are black, gray sparkle, gold sparkle, blue sparkle, red sparkle, and teal sparkle. Other colors are entirely possible as well.

K-50-2 - 50W, 1-12" speaker combo, solid-state chassis, front black control panel, two inputs, six black and silver knobs, tuck and roll covering (various colors), black grille, mfg. 1970's.

Kustom K50-2
courtesy Dave Rogers

N/A $150 - 200

Kustom K50-2
courtesy Dave Rogers

$100 - 125

GRADING	100%	EXCELLENT	AVERAGE

K-100-C7 - 100W, 2-12" speaker combo, solid-state chassis, front black control panel, two inputs, 10 knobs, tuck and roll covering (various colors), black grille, casters, mfg. 1970's.

Kustom K100 Ct
courtesy Dave Rogers

Kustom K100 C7
courtesy Dave Rogers

N/A	$275 - 350	$175 - 225

K-100-C8 - 100W, 4-10" speakers, solid-state chassis combo, front black control panel, two inputs, 10 black and silver knobs, tuck and roll covering (various colors), black grille, mfg. 1970's.

Kustom K-100 C-8
courtesy Dave Rogers

Kustom K-100 C-8
courtesy Dave Rogers

N/A	$300 - 375	$200 - 250

K-100 - 100W, head-unit only, solid-state chassis, front black control panel, two inputs, six black and silver knobs, tuck and roll covering (various colors), mfg. 1970's.

Kustom K100
courtesy Dave Rogers

Kustom K100
courtesy Dave Rogers

N/A	$200 - 250	$125 - 175

GRADING	100%	EXCELLENT	AVERAGE

2-150-1 - 150W, head-unit only, solid-state chassis, front black control panel, dual channels, four inputs, eight black and silver knobs (Ch. 1: v, b, t, bright, Ch. 2: v, b, t, bright), tuck and roll covering (various colors), mfg. 1970's.

Kustom 2-150-1
courtesy Dave Rogers

N/A	$200 - 250	$125 - 175

K-200-B3 - 200W, head-unit only, solid-state chassis, dual channels, front black control panel, four inputs, 10 black and silver knobs (Ch. 1: v, b, t, boost, Ch. 2: v, b, t, bright, boost v, selective boost), harmonic clipper, tuck and roll covering (various colors), mfg. 1970's.

Kustom K200 B-3
courtesy Dave Rogers

N/A	$225 - 275	$150 - 200

The K Series

There are several amps in the K series. The ones listed below are all guitar amps, there are also acoustic/electric amps, bass amps, and keyboard amps. The amps are generally on the same line with a few modifications to work for the certain application.

KGA10 - 10W, 1-6.5", solid-state chassis, voice control, single channel, top silver control panel, single input, three black and silver knobs (g, voice, v), headphone jack, overdrive switch, black covering, gray grille, current mfg.

MSR	$77.95	$55	$40 - 50	$25 - 35

KGA16 - 16W, 1-8" Celestion speaker combo, solid-state chassis, single channel, top silver control panel, two inputs, six black and silver knobs (g, v, rhythm v, l, m, h), headphone jack, overdrive switch, black covering, gray grille, current mfg.

MSR	$113.95	$80	$60 - 70	$45 - 55

* KGA16R - Similar to the KGA16 except has reverb circuit with control, current mfg.

MSR	$154.95	$110	$85 - 95	$65 - 75

KGA30 - 30W, 1-10" Celestion speaker combo, solid-state chassis, reverb, chorus, single channel, top silver control panel, two inputs, eight black and silver knobs (g, v, rhythm v, l, m, h, r, chorus), headphone jack, overdrive switch, footswitch, black covering, gray grille, current mfg.

MSR	$257.95	$199	$150 - 175	$115 - 135

KGA65 - 65W, 1-12" Celestion speaker combo, solid-state chassis, digital effects, dual channels, top silver control panel, two inputs, 11 black and silver knobs (Lead: g, l, m, h, v, Rhythm b, m, t, v, digital effects level, program), eight preset effects, headphone jack, overdrive switch, footswitch, black covering, gray grille, footswitch, current mfg.

MSR	$359.95	$270	$190 - 225	$150 - 170

Section L

LANEY

Amplifiers previously produced in Birmingham, England during the 1960's and 1970's. Currently they are produced as an "affordable" tube amp, from Cradley Heath West Midlands, England.

Laney was founded in the late 1960's by Lyndon Laney and Bob Thomas. Laney produced quality tube amplifiers througout the 1970's, but didn't keep up with what guitarists wanted. Their popularity waned, and they stopped producing Laney amplifiers in 1980. Recently, Laney began manufacturing their amplifiers again. They emerged with the A.O.R., which is the Advanced Overdrive Response. They are currently producing several different types of amplifiers from tube guitar amps to acoustic amplifiers.

(Early Laney information courtesy: Aspen Pittman, The Tube Amp Book)

ELECTRIC TUBE AMPLIFIERS

Laney amplifiers are split up under early (vintage) tube amps and current production models.

Early Valve Amplifiers

Laney has been around for over 30 years and produced quite a few amplifiers during the early years. However, there is very little information about these old Laney amps. They are quite similar to Marshall and Hiwatt head units of the same era. Most head units are either 50W or 100W and equipped with EL34 power tubes. Model identification is tricky on these models. We have come across a model that they call the Supergroup 4 X 1550 MK I. There are quite a few more models out there, but we haven't seen a whole lot of them.

Laney Supergroup 4X1550 100W MK I
courtesy solidbodyguitar.com, Inc.

Laney Supergroup 4X1550 100W MK I
courtesy solidbodyguitar.com, Inc.

Pricing on early Laney amplifiers is tricky. Most amps are fairly rare, but not always collectible. Common amplifiers prices can be seen between the $400 - 700 range. For other amps that are rare, the price could rise up to $1,000. The *Blue Book of Guitar Amplifiers* suggests having a second opinion on old Laney amplifiers before buying or selling.

GRADING	100%	EXCELLENT	AVERAGE

AOR100 SERIES II - 100W, head-unit only, all tube chassis, preamp: 4 X 12AX7, power: 4 X EL34, dual channels, front black control panel, two inputs, eight black knobs (p, b, m, t, v, clean channel preamp, OD v, OD channel preamp), effects loop, footswitch, black rough covering, mfg. 1980's.

	N/A	$275 - 350	$175 - 225

Valve Amplifiers (Current Production)

VH100R - 100W, head-unit only, tube chassis, power: 4 X 5881, or EL34, dual channels, reverb, front silver control panel, two inputs, 17 black chicken head knobs, effects loop, footswitch, black covering, gray grille, current mfg.

MSR	$1,399.99	$999	$725 - 825	$600 - 650

VC100 - Similar to the VH100R except is in combo form with 2-12" HH Premier Vintage 60W speakers, control panel reversed, current mfg.

VC50 - Similar to the VC100 except has 50W output, current mfg.

MSR	$1,399.99	$999	$750 - 850	$625 - 675

VC30-112 - 30W, 1-12" HH Invader speaker combo, all tube chassis, 12AX7 preamp tubes, 4 X EL84 power tubes, dual channels, reverb, front silver control panel, two inputs, eight black knobs (clean v, drive, drive v, b, m, t, r, effects level), effects loop, footswitch, dark blue covering, blue/gray grille, current mfg.

MSR	$899.99	$640	$475 - 550	$375 - 425

* VC30-212 - Similar to the VC30-112 except has 2-12" speakers, current mfg.

MSR	$1,099.99	$775	$600 - 700	$510 - 560

* VC30-210 - Similar to the VC30-210 except has 2-10" speakers, current mfg.

MSR	$999.99	$690	$500 - 600	$400 - 450

CHROME-O-ZONE - 30W, 2-10" HH Special Edition, all tube chassis, 4 X EL84 outputs, dual channels, reverb, front chrome control panel, two inputs, 17 silver knobs, effects loop, footswitch, gray covering, black grille cloth, current mfg.

GH100L - 100W, head-unit only, all tube chassis, preamp: 12AX7's, power: 4 X 5881, dual channels, front silver control panel, two inputs, seven black chicken head knobs (p, b, m, t, MV, g, drive), vaious switches, effects loop, black covering, gray grille, current mfg.

MSR	$999.99	$699	$500 - 600	$400 - 450

GRADING	100%	EXCELLENT	AVERAGE

GH50L - Similar to the GH100L except has 50W output (2 X 5881 power tubes), current mfg.

	MSR	$899.99	$650	$475 - 550	$400 - 430

GH100TI - 100W, head-unit only, all tube chassis, 4 X EL34 output tubes, permanent gain channel, front silver control panel, two inputs, six black knobs (p, b, t, m, MV, g), effects loop, black covering, black metal grille, current mfg.

	MSR	$1,099.99	$775	$600 - 700	$510 - 560

This amp was designed specially for Tony Iommi. It is in permanent gain, sorry country folks, no twang. There are also special speaker cabinets for this that will be listed in the speaker cabinet section.

LC15 - 15W, 1-10" HH Invader, all tube chassis, output: 2 X EL84, single channel, front silver control panel, two inputs, five black knobs (g, b, m, t, v), black covering, gray grille, current mfg.

	MSR	$399.99	$295	$175 - 225	$125 - 150

* LC15R - Similar to the LC15 except has reverb circuit, effects loop, footswitch, current mfg.

	MSR	$499.99	$375	$275 - 325	$215 - 240

LC30-II - 30W, 1-12" HH Invader, all tube Class A chassis, 4 X EL84 output, dual channels, reverb, front silver control panel, two inputs, eleven black knobs (v, b, m, t, drive, MV, b, m, t, r, effects), effects loop, footswitch, black covering, gray grille, current mfg.

	MSR	$879.99	$625	$475 - 550	$375 - 425

LC50-II - Similar to the LC30-II except has 50W output (2 X 5881), and 1-12" HH Premier speaker, current mfg.

* LH50R-II - Similar to the LC50-II except in head-unit only, current mfg.

Tube Fusion

TF50 - 30W, 1-10" HH Vintage, dual channels, reverb, front slanted silver control panel, two inputs, seven silver knobs (v, drive, v, b, m, t, r), effects loop, footswitch, black covering, gray grille, current mfg.

	MSR	$329.99	$245	$190 - 215	$150 - 175

TF100 - 50W, 1-10" HH Vintage, dual channels, reverb, front slanted silver control panel, single input, eleven silver knobs (v, b, m, t, drive, v, b, m, enhance, t, r), effects loop, footswitch, black covering, gray grille, current mfg.

	MSR	$479.99	$350	$250 - 300	$195 - 225

TF200 - 65W, 1-12" HH Vintage, three channels, reverb, front slanted silver control panel, single input, fourteen silver knobs (v, b, m, t, drive, v, g, m, enhance, b, m, enhance, t, r), effects loop, footswitch, black covering, gray grille, current mfg.

	MSR	$629.99	$450	$325 - 375	$275 - 300

TF300 - 120W, 1-12" HH Vintage, ECC83 preamp tube, three channels, reverb, front slanted silver control panel, single input, fifteen silver knobs (v, b, m, t, drive, v, enhance, g, m, enhance, b, m, enhance, t, r), effects loop, footswitch, black covering, gray grille, current mfg.

	MSR	$749.99	$525	$400 - 475	$325 - 375

TF320 - 120W, 2-12" HH Vintage, ECC83 preamp tube, three channels, reverb, front slanted silver control panel, single input, fifteen silver knobs (v, b, m, t, drive, v, enhance, g, m, enhance, b, m, enhance, t, r), effects loop, footswitch, black covering, gray grille, current mfg.

	MSR	$839.99	$599	$450 - 525	$350 - 400

TF400 - 120W, 2-12" HH Premier, ECC83 preamp tube, four channels, reverb, front slanted silver control panel, single input, 22 silver knobs (and why not?), effects loop, footswitch, black covering, gray grille, current mfg.

	MSR	$859.99	$625	$450 - 525	$350 - 400

TF500M - Similar to the TF400 except has MIDI send & recieve, current mfg.

			$699	$500 - 600	$400 - 450

TF700 - Similar to the TF300 & TF320 except in head-unit only, current mfg.

	MSR	$549.99	$399	$275 - 335	$200 - 235

TF800 - Similar to the TF400 except in head-unit only, current mfg.

	MSR		$525	$400- 450	$325 - 375

Tube Fusion X

TFX200 - 65W, 1-12" HH Vintage speaker combo, 1 X ECC83 preamp tube, three channels, digital processor, front silver control panel, single input, 15 silver knobs (v, b, m, t, effects, drive, drive v, g, master, enhance, b, m, t, effects, effects level), various buttons, black covering, gray grille, current mfg.

	MSR	$769.99	$550	$399 - 450	$310 - 360

TFX300 - Similar to the TFX200 except has 120 W output, current mfg.

	MSR	$879.99	$625	$475 - 550	$400 - 435

TFX320 - Similar to the TFX300 except has 2-12" speakers, current mfg.

			$700	$525 - 600	$425 - 475

TFX700 - Similar to the TFX300 & TFX320 except in head unit version, current mfg.

	MSR	$699.99	$499	$375 - 425	$325 - 350

ELECTRIC SOLID-STATE AMPLIFIERS

Laney also produces solid-state amplifiers. These are much cheaper and less desirable than the tube couterparts.

Hard Core Series

The Hard Core Series by Laney are the more affordable solid-state models for the more hard rock/heavy metal scene. These amps come in a variety of configurations for bass and guitar players. The small amp is the 30W with or without reverb and it climbs all the way up to a 120W head unit.

Richter Bass Series

These are amps that are designed specifically for bass instruments. These are also available in a number of different configurations, starting at a 65W up to a 300W earth mover. Some of the smaller units are tilt-back designs, and there are also head-units available.

ACOUSTIC AMPLIFIERS

For some reason, it seems all companies make their acoustic amplifiers in a brown color. Laney follows suit here and they offer the EA and LA series of Acoustic Guitar amplifiers. The LA series are smaller with either 30W or 60W output. The EA series has either 65W or 120W for output along with an electro channel.

LESLIE
Speaker cabinets and amplifiers currently produced out of Addison, Illinois.

Leslie has made one of the most interesting products in the musical genre. Most often a Leslie is associated with a Hammond organ. A Hammond organ would be plugged in, and the sound that came out of the powered Leslie amplifier was unmatched by any other product. Leslie had a rotary horn unit that would spin in the top part of the cabinet to give sort of a reverbish sound. They produced these amps/cabinets first around the 1960's, and they are still producing them today. Even though the Hammond and Leslie are legendary together, a guitar can be plugged into the Leslie for a truly unique sound.

ELECTRIC AMPLIFIERS

The two amplifiers that Leslie are most known for are the Model 122 and Model 147. Both of these amps are driven by a 12AU7 & OC3 preamp tubes, and 2 X 6550 for output. You can now buy completely new Leslie tube amps that are replacements for the old ones. Prices on these new amps are around $500-$600. On older speaker cabinets and other amplifiers pricing is sketchy. There are several speaker cabinets, and amplifiers that show up all over. Look for more information on upcoming editions of the *Blue Book of Guitar Amplifiers*.

Leslie
courtesy S. P. Fjestad

Leslie
courtesy S. P. Fjestad

LINE 6
Amplifiers and other modeling devices currently produced in Agoura Hills, California. The Line 6 trademark was established in 1996.

Line 6 is a relatively new company, yet in their seven years of existence have been very successful. Line 6 products can be described as taking musical products, such as amplifiers, and combining with up-to-date technology. Line 6's first patent was a digital modeling amp, which almost all amplifier companies have given a try at now. This was a result of realizing the need to get a number of amplifier tones out of one amplifier. Not only was this Line 6's idea, but this is the theory behind all modeling amps. The AxSys 212 was the first product to hit the shelfs in 1996, and many amplifiers were to follow. Shortly thereafter, another idea was tackled by the staff at Line 6; to make an amplifier that would sound great in the recording studio. The POD was the answer to this, as it could plug into a tape recorder, or even a computer. This is a kidney shaped device that has all the effects with a line out jack for recording purposes. Line 6 is currently still producing state-of-the-art amps and leading the industry as far as technology.

ELECTRIC AMPLIFIERS

Since Line 6 uses digital technology in a lot of their amplifiers, they can't really by classified into either tube or solid-state driven. Besides the combo amplifiers and head-units that Line 6 has, they also have the P.O.D. units, which are very popular and useful. There are also other foot pedals and studio modulers that Line 6 produces. For more information on these products, visit the Line 6 web site (see Trademark Index).

L

GRADING	100%	EXCELLENT	AVERAGE

Duoverb Series

DUOVERB COMBO - 100W, 2-12" Custom Celestion speakers, modeling amp design, 16 amp models, dual amp capability, spring reverb, front black control panel, single input, seventeen white knobs, various switches, black covering, brown grille cloth, 63 lbs., new Fall, 2002.

Line 6 Duoverb
courtesy Line 6

Prices were not available when this edition went to press.
A FBV Shortboard footcontroller can be added, which features 36 possible presets, a chromatic tuner, and more.

DUOVERB HEAD - Similar to the Duoverb combo except in head-unit version, 29 lbs., new Fall 2002.
Prices were not available when this edition went to press.

Vetta Series

VETTA HEAD - 200W, head-unit only, modeling amp, amp, effect, and cabinet models, front silver control panel, single input, 12 black knobs, various other buttons, black covering, 40 lbs., current mfg.

Line 6 Vetta Head
courtesy Line 6

MSR	$2,400	$1,625	$1,200 - 1,400	$950 - 1,100

VETTA COMBO - 100W, 2-12" Custom Celestion speakers, modeling amp, amp, effect, and cabinet models, front silver control panel, single input, 12 black knobs, various other buttons, brown/red, reddish grille cloth, covering, 65 lbs., current mfg.

Line 6 Vetta Combo
courtesy Line 6

MSR	$2,400	$1,625	$1,200 - 1,400	$975 - 1,100

VETTA SPEAKER CABINETS - There are a couple speaker cabinets that match up with the Vetta series, including a couple 4-12" cabinets and a couple 2-12" cabs. One of the 12" cabinets matches exactly to the Vetta 2-12" combo.

Flextone Series

The Flextone series is an amp that is targeted not as budget, but to a guitarist who wants a variety of great tones. Each flextone amp has 32 amp models and 16 digital effects, along with four programmable channels. The **Flextone II** is a 60W mono amp with 1-12" speaker. The **Flextone II** Plus has a 60W mono along with a 100W stereo amp. The **Flextone II XL** is strictly a 100W stereo amp.

Line 6 Flextone II Combo
courtesy Line 6

Spider Series

The Spider series are amps that are for anyone from beginners (S. P. Fjestad) to the more experienced (Z.R. Fjestad). The Spider doesn't come with a 101 amp models like some amps do, but it has 6 amp models and 7 digital effects. These are more than plenty of models to get started with this technology. The Spider comes in three configurations currently. The Spider 212 has 2-12" speakers, the Spider 112 has 1-12" speaker and the Spider 210 has 2-10" speakers, so there are many possiblities to your heart's content. The Spider is capable of putting out 100W (2 X 50W) stereo.Prices on these amps start at $600 retail for a 1-12" combo.

NOTES

Section M

MAESTRO
See GIBSON

MAGNATONE
Amplifiers previously built in California betweed the 1940's and 1960's.

Magnatone was originally founded as the Dickerson Brothers in Los Angeles, California circa 1937. The company began building phonographs, lap steels, and amplifiers. In 1947, the company changed its name to Magna Electronics. They produced many amplifiers, but wanted a guitar to accompany it. In the early 1950's, they jumped on the bandwagon and began producing electric Spanish hollow-body guitars, which were designed by Paul Bigsby. In 1959, Magna merged forces with Estey Electronics. In 1966, Magnatone moved to Pennsylvania from Torrance. Magnatone continued to produce amplifiers in California during the 1950's and 1960's until Magnatone was bought out by a toy company in 1971.

ELECTRIC TUBE AMPLIFIERS

Magnatone produced many amplifiers during their existence. Information on every model is skecthy in parts. The model listings, typically, are three digit numbers. Amplifiers began being produced around 1937 when the Dickerson amplifiers were introduced with the **Student**, **Standard**, and **Semi De Luxe** models. These are probably the rarest of the Magnatone amplifiers and are hard to put a price on since there is little secondary market on them.

Models weren't typically numbered until circa 1951. Models up until this point were also named Oahu, Silver Grey, and the Gourley along with Magnatone. Around 1952, the models became all Magnatone brand with model numbers. It is estimated that Magnatone produced at least 35 different amplifiers during the 1950's, and probably more. At this point there are too many models to list individually.

As far as pricing on Magnatone amplifiers, most fall into the $100-300 price range. However, there are many exceptions with these amps. There are some Model M amps that were produced in the mid 1960's that can go up to $500 in excellent shape. Early models such as Dickerson amplifiers could also be worth up to $500.

There is a web site that is helpful in model identification. www.vibroworld.com has a link to the unofficial Magnatone web site. On the site there are several models listed with pictures and other useful information. Look for more model listings and information in upcoming editions of the *Blue Book of Guitar Amplifiers*.

Here are some examples of Magnatone amplifiers.

Magnatone Custom 280
courtesy Willie's American Guitars

Magnatone Custom

Magnatone M7
courtesy The Music Shoppe

M

MARSHALL
Amplifiers currently produced in Milton Keynes, England. Marshall Amplification is distributed in England and through the U.S.A. in New York City by Marshall USA. The Marshall trademark was established circa 1962 in Hanwell, England.

Jim Marshall was born on July 29, 1923 in Kensington, England. Jim suffered tuberculosis of the bones, and spent most of his school years in a plaster cast up to his arms. He was only in school for three months and left at the age of 13 1/2. From here he started a variety of jobs. He worked for his dad at a fish and chip shop, a scrap metal yard, builder's merchant, a bakery, was a salesman, and held a number of other jobs. He worked wherever they needed him. He wasn't able to go into the forces for World War II, because of his illness, so he went to work at Cramic Engineering. He was able to explore his interest in engineering and electronics and used this engineering experience by working at Heston Aircraft in Middlesex as a tool maker in the late 40's. Jim's interest in music started when he was 14, when he learned how to tap dance. Originally Jim was a drummer and played in a band around 1942. In 1946, he started to take lessons to sharpen up his skills, which it did. Two years later, he had learned all there was to. So in 1949 he started teaching drums to people who would one day become famous (i.e. Mitch Mitchell of Jimi Hendrix). He made enough money to start his own business. Marshall's Music opened around 1960. At first the shop was just for drums and drummers, but shortly thereafter Jim started to stock guitars and amps due to popularity in American instruments. Fender and Gibson were quite popular according to Jim.

In 1960, Jim started to build bass and PA cabinets in his garage, because of popular demand for a good bass amp. These 25W amps with a 12", 15" or 18" speaker were included on a sale sheet. Since Jim's company had been just buying other amplifiers and selling them, Ken Bran, the new service engineer, suggested that they start building their own amplifiers. Jim and Ken looked at Fenders since they were their favorites, and were going to try to make them better. The first Marshall amp was a 2 X 12" 50W lead. That wasn't what they were looking for, and the speakers kept blowing. This lead to the 4 X 12" cabinet, which was accidentally the most convenient size. Marshall Amplifiers began to take shape after this. Originally the cabinets were straight up front, but later Jim had them sloped to match up to the head unit.

Orders began to pour in, and by 1964 Marshall Amplifiers had expanded three times! The Marshall Amplifier factory in Hayes was 6,000 square feet with 16 people making 20 amplifiers a week. Jim began to distribute his amps throughout England. In 1965, he signed a world-wide distribution agreement with Rose-Morris for around 15 years. Jim had been distributing to his friend Johnny Jones, but this was lost after the signing of the 15 year deal. Jim then introduced Park, a new line of amplifiers, for Johnny to distribute. What a nice guy, huh? In 1966 the factory was moved to Milton Keynes, England.

The British Invasion was in full swing now, and bigger amps were in demand, especially by Pete Townshend. Jim sent Ken to built a 100W amp. Pete also wanted an 8 X 12" cabinet to play through. Jim produced and Pete's roadies complained of achy backs. Pete suggested to "cut it in half", but what Jim did was create two 4 X 12" cabinets and stack them onto each other. The Marshall stack was born as a combined idea of Pete Townshend and Jim Marshall. Pete did end his stint with Marshall and began using Hiwatt amplifiers later on.

As Jimi Hendrix, The Who, Cream, Roy Orbison, and many others started to use Marshall Amplifiers, sales went through the roof. In just a few short years, Marshall had established themeselves as king of the rock guitar amplfier. The 70's lead to, like many other companys tried, new and unusual products. Bass amps, PA cabinets, and mixer designs. There are many different models and colors introduced at this time. In 1981, Jim ended the 15 year deal with Rose-Morris and started to distribute on his own. The early 80's presented a tough time for Marshall, as many models were discontinued, and Britain was in a recession, but all guitar and amp manufactures were seeing this at the time. Marshall pulled around in 1982 as they released their 20th anniversary amplifiers. In 1984, Marshall was presented with the Queen's award for export, which meant they could use the Queen's Award logo on letterheads and any advertising, which gave a sense of pride. In 1985, Jim was invited to put his handprints in the sidewalk of Hollywood. Along with him was Les Paul, Leo Fender, and Eddie Van Halen. In 1987, Marshall celebrated 25 years in amplification and 50 years in music. In 1990, Marshall announced the long-awaited JCM 900 series. Jim was giving a lot of time to many charities and organizations. In 1992, Marshall celebrated 30 years with a couple of new amps. In 1993, Marshall got the contract to build the reissue of the Vox AC30, whom Marshall was in direct competition with back in the 60's! How the times have changed. In the early 1990's Marshall introduced Valvestate, which are solid-state amplifiers with the Marshall sound.

As Jim and Marshall Amps look to the 21st century, they still produce some of the finest amps on the market. They are also expanding every year and haven't looked back since. In 1998, they released the JCM2000 and in 2000 the VS2000 was introduced. Nearly every famous rock musician has had an experience with Marshall amps. For many people this is the best. Every year Jim signs posters and calenders at NAMM. Where else do you sen 175 4-12" cabinets stacked on top of each other? I can't think of another company!

(Source for Marshall History: Michael Doyle, The History of Marshall: The Sound of Rock)

DATING MARSHALL AMPLIFIERS

Dating Marshall amplifiers isn't a difficult task to do, since they don't have overlapping models and numbers like a lot of other companys have. The cosmetics of the amp and serial numbers are the best way to determine date of manufacture. Note that these numbers are very accurate, but not set in stone. There will always be exceptions and overlaps in numbers. The only date on a Marshall is on the Celestion speaker. There aren't any other dated-parts on the amp, inlcuding the potentiometer. The serial number on the amps are a dating tool as well. The chassis had a signed sticker that was also dated, but most of these are difficult to read.

Marshall Dating

October 1962-December 1964 -The easiest way to determine the make between these dates, is the cosmetics of the amps. The serial numbers, which were started when production amplifiers were, started at 1001. You can find these numbers stamped in the back panel of the chassis, with an occasional model number. The numbers ran numerically, when 1964 rolled around, and the number was started at 2001. The 2 is for the second year of production.

January 1965-June 1969 - The best way to determine this era is by the cosmetics and electronics, as many of the plexiglas panels were subcontracted out. To find the date, check the Celestion speaker chart later in this section and then find the model number in the serial number by the chart below:

July 1969-September 1992 - The Marshall date coding system was introduced in 1969. Aluminum back panels were also introduced. The serial number Is broken down into three different parts. These are the model code, serial number, and date code. The charts are listed for the model and date codes, and the serial number is simply the production ranking. These serial numbers are on the back most of the time, except for the years 1979-1981 when they were on the front panel. The model code is pretty close to that of the old one, but different enough. These codes have been used both up to the late seventies. Watch for these codes when dating as either one of them could come up on your amp. On the date codes, they started at A in July 1969 and that ran until December 1970. They then skipped the letter B and went to C to avoid confusion (or create it?). O, I, and Q weren't used since they looked too much like numbers. Up until 1983, the order is model code, serial number, then date code. In 1984, It switched to model code, date code, and serial number.

MODEL CODE (65-69)	MODEL CODE (69-92)	MODEL TYPE
/A	A/	200-WATT
SL/	SL/A	100-WATT SUPER LEAD
SB/	SB/A	100-WATT SUPER BASS
SP/	SP/	SUPER PA
ST/	ST/A	100-WATT TREMOLO
S/	S/A	50-WATT
T/	T/A	50-WATT TREMOLO
-	RI	REISSUE

DATE CODES IN THE SERIAL NUMBERS

A 1969 & 1970	C-1971	D-1972
E-1973	F-1974	G-1975
H-1976	J-1977	K-1978
L-1979	M-1980	N-1981
P-1982	R-1983	S-1984
T-1985	U-1986	V-1987
W-1988	X-1989	Y-1991
Z-1991 & 1992		

October 1992-Current - A new bar code introduced along with the serial number being applied by a sticker instead of being stamped on. This new system consists of nine numbers and resembles Gibson guitars serilaization. The first two numbers are the year, the next five are the five-digit serial number, and the last two indicates the month. i.e. 991018905 is amp number 10189 made in May of 1999 .

GRADING	100%	EXCELLENT	AVERAGE

Date Codes on Celestion Speakers

Early date codes were stamped on the gasket of the speaker, and on later models the number was stamped onto the frame itself. There are three types of date codes that have been stamped onto the speakers dating back to the 50's. Type 1 ran from 1956-1967, type 2 ran from 1968-1991, and type 3 after 1991. The charts for the earlier two are here. Remember, the chances of having original speakers in an original Marshall chassis, is very rare. A lot of the time the cone has been replaced in a speaker or a couple of speakers may have been replaced. If this has happened ,then the speakers aren't going to give the right year that the amp was made. A keen eye is the best factor here, and using your best judgement. For type 1 there are two numbers first followed by two letters. The first two numbers indicate the day of the month the speaker was made (i.e. 1-31 are the numbers). Then the first letter is month and the second letter is the year, which can be found by the corresponding chart. Type 2 date codes are reversed. The letters come first followed by the number's which are the day of the month again. The letters are also the same. Notice in 1961 or 62, they discontinued using the letter I because of confusion with the number 1. Examples of this system are 20 CG would be a speaker made March 20, 1962. A date code of FQ 26 would be a speaker made on June 26, 1982.

MONTH 1956-1961/1962

A-JANUARY	B-FEBRUARY	C-MARCH	D-APRIL	E-MAY	F-JUNE
G-JULY	H-AUGUST	I-SEPTEMBER	J-OCTOBER	K-NOVEMBER	L-DECEMBER

MONTH 1962/1963-CURRENT

A-JANUARY	B-FEBRUARY	C-MARCH	D-APRIL	E-MAY	F-JUNE
G-JULY	H-AUGUST	J-SEPTEMBER	K-OCTOBER	L-NOVEMBER	M-DECEMBER

YEAR TYPE 1 1956-1967

A-1956	B-1957	C-1958	D-1959	E-1960	F-1961
G-1962	H-1963	J-1964	K-1965	L-1966	M-1967

YEAR TYPE 2 1968-1991

A-1968	B-1969	C-1970	D-1971	E-1972	F-1973
G-1974	H-1975	J-1976	K1977	L-1978	M-1979
N-1980	P-1981	Q-1982	R-1983	S-1984	T-1985
U-1986	V-1987	W-1988	X-1989	Y-1990	Z-1991

Marshall Covering and Grille Cloth

Mashall has used numerous vinyls and grille cloths over the years. For Marshall vinyl coverings, black has been the most poputlar. This has been offered on almost all the models since the beginning. There was a black on green that was used here and there in the late '60's. In 1967 and 1968, orange, purple, red and blue Levant coverings were all offered in Marshall catalogs. A yellow and a silver were also available but not as popular. In 1975, the Levant coverings were changed to the new Elephant covering. Black was still standard on all models. Light brown, dark brown, red, and white Elephant coverings have been used on some models since then. Blue Levant covering was used on the 30th Anniversary Series, and Silver Levan was used on the Silver Jubilee Series. Black is now standard on all Marshall models

Marshall cloths have changed over the years as well. In 1962, at the birth of Marshall, white cloth was used. In 1965, this was changed to a new cloth called Grey Bluesbreaker which was used until 1968. There was a brown Bluesbreaker cloth that was used around the same time but is very rare. In 1968, the Bluesbreaker cloth was changed to a two-tone brown weave and that was changed to a grey basket weave in 1968. The Chequerboard weave was introduced around 1972 and lasted until 1975 (1981 in the United States). In 1976, a light black, almost grey, cloth was introduced as standard. This cloth faded easily and was replaced in the eighties with the now standard black weave. There have been other cloths used as well including: brown basket weave used mainly on purple cabinets, light straw used mainly on Club and Country models, Black and Silver weave, and the black and white stiped for reissues.

(Marshall Dating all courtesy Michael Doyle: The History of Marshall.)

ELECTRIC VALVE AMPLIFIERS

Many Marshall amps are sold as the head-unit only. They sell cabinets that are separate, yet universal for almost all applications. We list the heads throughout, but the speaker cabinets are in one part at the end of the section.

JTM 45 Series

This was Marshall's first line of amplifiers in 1962. Since this was Marshall's first stab at mass producing amplifiers, the cosmetics changed quite frequently. When parts would run out, they would just go out and buy whatever was handy. For a series of amps there are many different looking models that bear the same name. The electronics didn't change much except for a tube here and there. JTM stands for Jim and Terry Marshall, Terry is Jim's son.

JTM-45 (NO MODEL NUMBER) - 45W, Head Unit only, tubes: 12AX7, 2 X 5881, GZ34 Rectifier, Lead guitar application, 2 channels, 4 inputs, various front looks, black leather covering, typically six knobs (presence, b, m, t, high t, normal) occasionally volume knobs, mfg. 1962-64.

1962 Marshall JTM-45 (Off-set chassis) courtesy solidbodyguitar.com, Inc.	1962/63 Marshall JTM-45 courtesy solidbodyguitar.com, Inc.	1963/64 Marshall JTM-45 MK II (sandwich front) courtesy solidbodyguitar.com, Inc.
N/A	**$2,300 - 2,800**	**$1,600 - 2,000**

The first Marshall amplifier, very desirable and hard to find. The offset chassis is very rare.

GRADING	100%	EXCELLENT	AVERAGE

* JTM-45 (No. 1963) - Similar to the JTM-45 lead except Super PA version, 50W output, four channels, eight normal inputs, bears the name MK III on front panel, mfg. 1965-66.

| | N/A | $1,800 - 2,300 | $1,400 - 1,600 |

* JTM-45 (No. 1985) - Smiliar to the JTM-45 lead except PA version, 45W, output, bears the name MK II, mfg. 1965-66.

1965 Marshall JTM-45 MK II P.A. (gold block logo)
courtesy solidbodyguitar.com, Inc.

1965 Marshall JTM-45 MK II P.A. (gold block logo)
courtesy solidbodyguitar.com, Inc.

| | N/A | $1,750 - 2,200 | $1,300 - 1,600 |

* JTM-45 (No. 1986) - Similar to the JTM MK II except in bass version, high treble and normal channels, mfg. 1965-66.

| | N/A | $2,000 - 2,400 | $1,500 - 1,800 |

* JTM-45 (No. 1987) - Similar to the JTM-45 MK II except in lead version, high treble and normal channels, mfg. 1965-66.

| | N/A | $2,300 - 2,700 | $1,600 - 2,000 |

Also available with Tremolo as an option, model number T1987.

* JTM-45 (No. 1989) - Similar to the JTM MK II except designed for electric organs, mfg. 1965-66.

| | N/A | $2,100 - 2,500 | $1,500 - 1,900 |

Also available with Tremolo as an option, model number T1989.

JTM-45 REISSUE (No. 1987) - Original reissue of the JTM-45 (No. 1987) re-released in 1989, mfg. 1989-current.

| 1989-1995 | N/A | $650 - 750 | $550 - 600 |
| MSR | $1,650 | $1,175 | $925 - 1,025 | $750 - 850 |

JTM-45 LIMITED EDITION HALF STACK 2255HS - Reissue of the original offset-chassis JTM-45 (only three made) with matching speaker cabinet, current mfg.

MSR $5,000

Back in 1962, three JTM-45 heads were built with an off-set chassis (you WON'T find a real one). Recently they went to work recreating this model piece by piece all hand-wired and made to look original. Only 300 of these will be made and when they are gone, they are gone. Pricing is highly inaccurate right now. When they sell out, it will be a different story.

Bluesbreaker Series

This series was the first combo design from Marshall. Eric Clapton is known for playing through these amps on John Mayall's Bluesbreakers album, which is where the nickname comes from. There are two different series with these amps. The difference here was a new cabinet which was introduced in 1966. It should be noted that models between the years 1969 and 1972 are not plexi units.

BLUESBREAKER (No. 1961) - 45W, 4-10" speakers, tube combo, tubes: KT66's, GZ 34 rectifier, lead amplifier, tremolo, top control panel, known as the first series Bluesbreaker, the grill is split about 4 inches down from the top, black levant covering, white covering on grille in 1965, gray "bluesbreaker" covering from then on, mfg. 1965-1972.

Marshall Bluesbreaker
courtesy Savage Audio

Marshall Bluesbreaker
courtesy Savage Audio

1965-66	N/A	$3,800 - 4,600	$2,900 - 3,500
1967-69	N/A	$3,500 - 4,200	$2,600 - 3,200
1969-1972	N/A	$2,400 - 3,000	$1,500 - 2,100

GRADING	100%	EXCELLENT	AVERAGE

In 1966, the second series was introduced and featured a revised cabinet, JTM 50 MKII appeared on front panel, and power increased to 50W. In 1968, the amp was changed on the front to a plain grille.

This model was made popular by Eric Clapton and is quite popular today, especially if you don't dig the Marshall stack.

* Bluesbreaker (No. 1962) - 45W, 2-12" tube combo, tubes: KT66's, GZ34 rectifier, same as the Bluesbreaker No. 1961 except for speaker configuration. mfg. 1965-1972.

Marshall Bluesbreaker
courtesy solidbodyguitar.com, Inc.

Marshall Bluesbreaker
courtesy solidbodyguitar.com, Inc.

Marshall Bluesbreaker Series 2 Model 1962
courtesy solidbodyguitar.com, Inc.

1965-66	N/A	$4,000 - 4,800	$3,000 - 3,800
1967-69	N/A	$3,750 - 4,500	$2,850 - 3,500
1969-1972	N/A	$2,500 - 3,100	$1,600 - 2,200

In 1966 the second series was introduced and featured a revised cabinet, JTM 50 MKIV appeared on front panel, and power increased to 50W. In 1968 the amp was changed on the front to a plain grille and was the last of the original Bluesbreakers.

BLUESBREAKER (No. 1962 REISSUE) - 50W, 2-12" tube combo, tremolo, a reissue of the late 60's Bluesbreaker model 1962, mfg. 1989-current.

1989-1995	N/A	$900 - 1,100	$750 - 825
MSR	$2,150	$1,500	$1,150 - 1,300	$950 - 1,050

50 Watt Series

This series was introduced in 1966 when Marshall was undergoing big changes. There were some tube changes amongst other electronics inside the amp, while the cosmetics on the outside were changing as well. In 1967, the "JTM 50" and "MK II" labels had been replaced by JTM. In 1968, the steel chassis was introduced and the initials JMP (Jim Marshall Products) were added. In 1969, the Plexiglas panel were changed to gold aluminum. These are the amps that really started to make the "Marshall Stack" known to the world.

MODEL 1963 - 50W, Head unit only, tubes: EL34 valves, solid-state rectifier, PA application, black levant covering, various grill coverings, front control panel, four channels, eight inputs, various knobs, mfg. 1966-68.

	N/A	$1,600 - 2,000	$1,300 - 1,500

MODEL 1987 - 50W, Head unit only, tubes: EL 34 valves, solid-state rectifier, lead application, two channels, four normal inputs, black levant covering, various grille coverings, mfg. 1966-68.

Marshall 50w Lead Model 1987
courtesy Savage Audio

Marshall 50w Lead Model 1987
courtesy Savage Audio

	N/A	$2,200 - 2,500	$1,500 - 1,900

This model came from the original JTM 45 series. Tremolo was available as an option until 1975.

* Model 1985 - Similar to the Model 1987 lead, except for PA application, mfg. 1966-68.

	N/A	$1,600 - 2,000	$1,300 - 1,500

* Model 1986 - Similar to the Model 1987 lead, except is for bass application, high treble and a normal channel, mfg. 1966-1981.

1966-69 PLEXI	N/A	$1,600 - 2,000	$1,300 - 1,500
1969-1976	N/A	$875 - 1,700	$650 - 850
1977-1981	N/A	$600 - 750	$525 - 575

GRADING	100%	EXCELLENT	AVERAGE

Model 1987S - Reissue of the Model 1987 lead, mfg. 1988 only.

	N/A	$550 - 650	$475 - 525

This reissue was available with a matching 4-12" cabinet with Celestion G12 75" speakers, and 70's Chequerboard cloth.

Model 1987X - Second Reissue of the Model 1987, with the Plexiglas panels, mfg. 1992-mid 1990's.

	N/A	$500 - 625	$450 - 500

1987XL - Third reissue of the 50W Super Lead Plexi circa 1966-1969, has true bypass Series FX loop, new 2002.

MSR	$1,650	$1,175	$950 - 1,050	$750 - 850

Model 1989 - Similar design to the 1987, except was designed for organ applications, mfg. 1966-1975.

1966-69	N/A	$1,700 - 2,100	$1,300 - 1,600
1969-1973	N/A	$1,200 - 1,500	$800 - 950
1974-75	N/A	$700 - 800	$575 - 675

This model also came with tremolo as an option and sold as the model T1989.

Model 2187 - Similar to the model 1987 except is the combo version with 2-12" speakers, mfg. 1974-1981.

	N/A	$650 - 800	$500 - 625

ARTIST MODEL 2040 - 50W, 2-12" combo, tubes, lead application, reverb, two channels, four inputs, eight knobs (Ch. 1: r, v, b, t, Ch. 2: v, t, b, Both: master presence control), black levant covering, Chequerboard cloth, mfg. 1971-78.

	N/A	$750 - 900	$600 - 700

This model was a newer version of the standard series, and was named the Artist.

Artist Model 2041 - Similar to the model 2040 except was in half-stack version, mfg. 1971-78.

	N/A	$950 -1,200	$750 - 900

Artist Model 2048 - Similar to the Artist model 2040 except was head-only version, mfg. 1971-78.

	N/A	$700 - 800	$575 - 650

MODEL 2100 - 50W, 2-12" speaker combo, lead and bass application, tubes, two channels, four inputs, top control panel, various knobs, black levant covering, black grille, mfg. 1973-76.

	N/A	$800 - 1,000	$600 - 750

Model 1964 - Similar to the Model 2100 except is head unit only, two channels, four inputs, mfg. 1973-76.

	N/A	$700 - 875	$525 - 675

MODEL 2204 - 50W, Head unit only, lead application, one channel, master volume, various knobs, black levant covering, various grille coverings, mfg. 1975-1981.

	N/A	$600 - 750	$500 - 575

Model 2104 - Similar to the model 2204 except in combo form with 2-12" speakers, mfg. 1975-1981.

	N/A	$650 - 800	$525 - 600

Model 2144 - Similar to the Model 2204 except in combo form with 2-12" speakers, has reverb, and boost, mfg. 1978 only.

	N/A	$675 - 800	$550 - 625

100 Watt Series

The 100 series project was launched in 1965. With the 50 Watt series being released shortly after the 100 Watts, these amps had a lot more punch than the 50's and there wasn't anything out there at the time that could match it. The 100 Watt amplifiers were designed because of the demands for more power, but more importantly, Pete Townshend wanted them. These amps made their way onto the market in 1966.

MODEL 1959 - 100W, Head unit only, tubes: 4 X 6V6 valves, GZ 34 rectifier, two channels, four inputs, super lead application, front gold control panel, six knobs, black levant covering, mfg. 1966-1981.

Marshall 100w Lead MK III
courtesy Savage Audio

Marshall 100w Lead MK III
courtesy Savage Audio

Marshall 100W Super Lead
courtesy solidbodyguitar.com, Inc.

1966-69	N/A	$1,800 - 2,500	$1,400 - 1,700
1969-1973	N/A	$1,100 - 1,500	$750 - 1,100
1974-1981	N/A	$675 - 1,000	$550 - 650

This model was known as the Super Lead. It was also available with tremolo in the model T1959. This was discontinued in 1973. This model was changed to the JCM 800 1959 in 1981.

Model 2159 - Similar to the Model 1959 except is in a combo version with 2-12" speakers, mfg. 1977-1981.

	N/A	$600 - 750	$525 - 575

Model 1959S - Reissue of the 70's Model 1959, mfg. 1988 only.

	N/A	$600 - 750	$525 - 575

GRADING	100%	EXCELLENT	AVERAGE

* Model 1959X - Second reissue of the model 1959, based on the 60's Plexiglas models, mfg. 1991-93.

	N/A	$600 - 750	$525 - 575

* Model 1959SLP - Third reissue of the model 1959, mfg. 1993-1995

	N/A	$600 - 750	$525 - 575

* Model 1959SLPX - Fourth reissue of the 100W Super Lead Plexi circa 1967-1969, has true bypass Series FX loop, new 2002.

MSR	$1,950	$1,399	$1,100 - 1,250	$900 - 1,000

MODEL 1968 - 100W, Head unit only, tubes, PA application, four channels, eight inputs, similar feaures to those of the Model 1959, mfg. 1966-1975.

1966-69		N/A	$1,600 - 2,000	$1,200 - 1,500
1969-1973		N/A	$900 - 1,500	$650 - 875
1974-75		N/A	$750 - 950	$600 - 700

Known as the "Super PA" amp.

MODEL 1992 - 100W, Head unit only, tubes, bass spplication, two channels, four inputs, smiliar controls to those of the model 1959, mfg. 1966-1981.

1966-69		N/A	$1,600 - 2,000	$1,200 - 1,500
1969-1973		N/A	$900 - 1,500	$650 - 875
1974-1981		N/A	$750 - 950	$600 - 700

Known as the Super Bass amp. It was available with tremolo as the model T1992. This option was discontinued in 1972.

MODEL 2068 - 100W, Head unit only, tubes, lead application, two channels, four inputs, reverb, known as the artist, mfg. 1971-78.

	N/A	$750 - 850	$625 - 700

* Model 2059 - Similar to the Model 2068, except was a combination of the 2068 with a matching 4-12" cabinet, was sold as a complete set, mfg. 1971-78.

	N/A	$1,000 - 1,250	$875 - 950

MODEL 2203 - 100W, Head unit only, tubes: 4 X EL34, one channel, two inputs, six control knobs, master volume, mfg. 1975-81.

Marshall JMP Model 2203
courtesy Savage Audio

Marshall JMP Model 2203
courtesy Savage Audio

	N/A	$700 - 800	$600 - 675

This was Marshall's first stab at designing a master volume amp.

* Model 2103 - Similar to the Model 2203 except is a 2-12" combo, mfg. 1975-81.

	N/A	$725 - 850	$625 - 700

MODEL 2959 - 100W, Head unit only, tubes, reverb, boost, no master volume, foot switch for reverb, mfg. 1978-1980.

	N/A	$750 - 900	$650 - 725

This model was the last introduced in the first 100 Watt series, and was discontinued shortly after its introduction. Only about 150 of these were made. This model was a combination of new features without master volume.

18 And 20 Watt Series

This series of amps was debuted in the Summer of 1965, right around the same time as the 100 Watt heads. The 18 Watt amps were released first and then in 1967 were replaced by the 20 Watt amps. These two amps were identical as far as cosmetics, but the electronics inside were completely different. The 18 Watts are more desirable than the 20 Watts.

MODEL 1958 (18W) - 18W, 2-10" combo, tubes: 3 X ECC83 preamps, 2 X EL84 outputs, EZ81 rectifier, (ECC86 for reverb), lead application, dual channels, four inputs, tremolo on first channel, black covering, gray and white striped cloth, mfg. 1966-68.

	N/A	$2,300 - 2,900	$1,700 - 2,200

Add $200-$400 for reverb.

* Model 1958 (20W) - Similar to the 18W except has 20W output, tubes: 2 X ECC83 preamps, rectifier was solid-state, reverb no longer an option, mfg. 1968-1973.

1968-69		N/A	$1,800 - 2,300	$1,500 - 1,700
1969-1973		N/A	$1,200 - 1,600	$950 - 1,100

GRADING	100%	EXCELLENT	AVERAGE

MODEL 1973 (18W) - 18W, 2-12" combo, tubes: 3 X ECC83 preamps, 2 X EL84 outputs, EZ81 rectifier, (ECC86 for reverb), lead and bass application, dual channels, four inputs, tremolo on first channel, black covering, gray and white striped cloth, mfg. 1966-68.

Marshall 18W Combo Model 1973
courtesy solidbodyguitar.com, Inc.

Marshall 18W Combo Model 1973
courtesy solidbodyguitar.com, Inc.

| | N/A | $2,500 - 3,200 | $1,700 - 2,400 |

Reverb was available as an option.

* Model 1973 (20W) - Similar to the 18W Model 1973 except has 20W ouput, tubes: 2 X ECC83 preamps, rectifier was solid-state, reverb no longer an option, mfg. 1968-1973.

Marshall 20w Lead Model 1973
courtesy Savage Audio

Marshall 20w Lead Model 1973
courtesy Savage Audio

| 1968-69 | N/A | $1,800 - 2,300 | $1,500 - 1,700 |
| 1969-1973 | N/A | $1,200 - 1,600 | $950 - 1,100 |

* Model 1973 (Lead & Bass 20) - Similar to the Model 1973 except came as a head and a cab, 1-12" speaker, ported cabinet, mfg. 1973 only.

| | N/A | $1,100 - 1,500 | $875 - 1,000 |

This model was never listed in the Marshall catalogs and there is some confusion about what model number this really was. It has been seen as Model 2061, as well as the 1973.

MODEL 1974 (18W) - 18W, 1-12" combo, tubes: 3 X ECC83 preamps, 2 X EL84 outputs, EZ81 rectifier, (ECC86 for reverb), lead and bass application, dual channels, four inputs, tremolo on first channel, black covering, gray and white striped cloth, mfg. 1966-68.

| | N/A | $1,700 - 2,200 | $1,200 - 1,600 |

Reverb was available as an option.

* Model 1974 (20W) - Similar to the model 1974 18W, except has 20W output, tubes: 2 X ECC83 preamps, solid-state rectifier, reverb no longer an option, mfg. 1968-1973.

| 1968-69 | N/A | $1,700 - 2,300 | $1,300 - 1,600 |
| 1969-1973 | N/A | $1,300 - 1,700 | $950 - 1,200 |

MODEL 2019 - 20W, 4-10" speakers, bass head and cabinet unit, tubes: 3 X ECC83 preamps, 2 X EL84 outputs, EZ81 rectifier, (ECC86 for reverb), bass application, dual channels, four inputs, black covering, gray and white striped cloth, mfg. 1968-1973.

| 1968-69 | N/A | $2,000 - 2,600 | $1,500 - 1,900 |
| 1969-1973 | N/A | $1,400 - 1,900 | $1,000 - 1,300 |

* Model 2022 - Similar to the Model 2019 except is for a lead application, and tremolo was an option, mfg. 1968-1973.

| 1968-69 | N/A | $2,000 - 2,600 | $1,500 - 1,900 |
| 1969-1973 | N/A | $1,400 - 1,900 | $1,000 - 1,300 |

* Model 2061 - See Model 1973 in this section.

GRADING	100%	EXCELLENT	AVERAGE

MODEL 1917 - 20W, 2-10" or 2 13" X 8" ellipticals, Head unit and cabinets, tubes, dual channels, four inputs, mfg. 1967-1973.

Marshall 20w Head Pa
courtesy solidbodyguitars.com, Inc.

| 1968-69 | N/A | $1,900 - 2,500 | $1,400 - 1,800 |
| 1969-1973 | N/A | $1,400 - 1,750 | $1,000 - 1,350 |

This model was sold as a setup of 1 head and two cabinets.

200 Watt Series

This series was introduced after the success of the 100 Watt heads and the increasing "power race." By the late 60's and early 70's people were looking for more and more power and liked what many other companies were doing, and Marshall followed suit. These amps were first known as the Marshall 200, but in 1968 the name was changed to the Marshall Major. These models came in a lead, bass, and PA version. The series was discontinued in 1974.

MODEL 1967 - 200W, Head unit only, tubes: 3 X ECC83 preamp valves, 4 X KT88 output valves, lead application, small gold control panel three knobs (t, b, v), two inputs, one channel, active tone controls, black covering, mfg. 1967-74.

1967	N/A	$1,600 - 2,000	$1,300 - 1,500
1968-1969	N/A	$1,400 - 1,700	$1,100 - 1,300
1969-1974	N/A	$900 - 1,200	$700 - 850

In 1968, the cosmetics were overhauled from the small chassis to the more conventional look, two channels were standard, four inputs, and passive tone controls were added.

* Model 1966 - Similar to the Model 1967 except was meant for a PA application, four channels, eight inputs, mfg. 1968-1971.

| 1968-1969 | N/A | $1,200 - 1,600 | $950 - 1,100 |
| 1969-1971 | N/A | $1,000 - 1,200 | $850 - 975 |

* Model 1968 - Similar to the Model 1967 except was meant for Bass application, mfg. 1967-1974.

| 1967-1969 | N/A | $1,300 - 1,700 | $1,000 - 1,200 |
| 1969-1974 | N/A | $900 - 1,200 | $700 - 875 |

2000 Series

In April 1981 Marshall released some new workhorse amps that had wattage of over 200. These were known as the most powerful Marshalls built. The design from these came from many rock personalities, including AC/DC. These amps produced lots of power, and had features that many traditional Marshalls never fooled with. These amps would lead into the JCM-800 series to be released later in 1981. These amps never caught on for a number of reasons, including their weight, cost, and technology that no one really knew how to use them. Only a few hundered are known to exist.

2000 LEAD - 200W, Lead head-unit only, tubes: 6 X ECC83 premamp valves, 6 X 6550 output valves, dual channels (A & B), two inputs, front control panel, eleven knobs (Ch. A: p, b, m, t, v, Ch. B: preamp gain, t, m, m sweep, b, MV), effects loops on back that could be patched between channels, preamp jack for other systems, XLR jacks, standby and power were on the back, black covering, black grille, mfg. 1981 only.

| | N/A | $650 - 750 | $525 - 625 |

2001 BASS - 300W, Bass head-unit only, tubes: 2 X ECC83 and 3 X ECC81 preamp valves, 8 X 6550 output valves, dual channels, front control panel, eight knobs (Ch. A: gain, t, m, mid-frequecy select, b, Ch. B: gain, t, b), similar controls on the back to the 2000 Lead, footswitch, compression circuit, black covering, black grille, mfg. 1981 only.

| | N/A | $650 - 750 | $525 - 625 |

JCM-800 Series

This series was released in 1981 at the end of Rose-Morris' contract for distribution. The early 80's were tough times for the music industry and Marshall felt the same hurt that everyone else did. Therefore a new amp to bring them into the new decade was needed. The JCM-800 series which was named after Jim Marshall's license plate (JCM is James Charles Marshall), was virtually identical to the Master Volumes and the Super Leads of the 70's. The big change was the cosmetics of the amp. A new black cloth with white piping (spelling Marshall) and the control panel spanning the entire width of the amp. Jim's signature was also on the front with JCM 800 in bold, black letters. They took the old, familiar models and made them the JCM-800 series. However, the new combos

GRADING	100%	EXCELLENT	AVERAGE

were different designs and new models. In 1983 they brought on the channel switching in the amps. The JCM-800 series lasted about 10 years and was replaced by the JCM-900 series. The good news around this time was no more Rose-Morris, which opened Marhsall's opportunities up a lot.

JCM-800 MODEL 1959 - 100W, Head-unit only, tubes, lead application, two channels, four inputs, six knobs (presence, b, m, t, volume 1, volume 2), black covering, new black cloth grille, the JCM-800 version of the Super Lead, mfg. 1981-1991.

| | N/A | $600 - 675 | $500 - 575 |

JCM-800 MODEL 1986 - 50W, Head-unit only, tubes, bass application, two inputs, six knobs (slope, b, m, mid-sweep, t, v), black covering, new black grille cloth, mid-sweep from 400 Hz to 1 kHz, active tone circuit, JCM-800 version of the Model 1986 Bass, mfg. 1981-87.

| | N/A | $575 - 650 | $475 - 550 |

JCM-800 MODEL 1987 - 50W, Head-unit only, tubes, lead application, two channels, four inputs, six knobs (presence, b, m, t, volume 1, volume 2), black covering, new Marshall grille, JCM-800 version of the Model 1987 lead, mfg. 1981-1991.

| | N/A | $600 - 675 | $500 - 575 |

JCM-800 MODEL 1992 - 100W, Head-unit only, tubes, bass application, two channels, four inputs, six knobs (slope, b, m, mid-sweep, t, v), mid-sweep from 400 Hz to 1 kHz, active tone controls, black covering, new Marshall cloth grille, JCM-800 version of the Model 1992, mfg. 1981-86.

| | N/A | $600 - 700 | $500 - 575 |

JCM-800 MODEL 2203 - 100W, Head-unit only, tubes, lead application, two inputs (high and low), one channel, six knobs (presence, b, m, t, MV, preamp v), black covering, new Marshall grille, JCM-800 version of the Model 2203, mfg. 1981-1990.

| | N/A | $575 - 650 | $500 - 550 |

* JCM-800 Model 4010 - Similar to the JCM-800 Model 2203 except is in a combo form with a 1-12" speaker, mfg. 1981-1990.

Marshall JCM-800 Model 4010
courtesy Savage Audio

Marshall JCM-800 Model 4010
courtesy Savage Audio

| | N/A | $425 - 475 | $350 - 400 |

* JCM-800 Model 4104 - Similar to the JCM-800 Model 2203 except is in a combo form with 2-12" speakers, mfg. 1981-1990.

Marshall JCM-800
courtesy Savage Audio

Marshall JCM-800
courtesy Savage Audio

| | N/A | $475 - 525 | $400 - 450 |

JCM-800 MODEL 2204 - 50W, Head-unit only, tubes, lead application, two inputs (high and low), one channel, six knobs (presence, b, m, t, MV, preamp v), black covering, new Marshall grille, JCM-800 version of the Model 2203, mfg. 1981-1990.

| | N/A | $575 - 650 | $500 - 550 |

* JCM-800 Model 2204S - Similar to the JCM-800 Model 2204, except is the mini-stack version, mfg. 1986-87.

| | N/A | $600 - 725 | $525 - 575 |

* JCM-800 Model 4103 - Similar to the JCM-800 Model 2204, except is in a combo form with 2-12" speakers, mfg. 1981-1990.

| | N/A | $500 - 600 | $425 - 475 |

GRADING	100%	EXCELLENT	AVERAGE

JCM-800 MODEL 2210 - 100W, Head-unit only, tubes, split channel, one input, reverb, six 11 knobs (presence, v, reverb, Drive Channel: b, mid, t, v, g, Clean Channel: b, t, v), black covering, new Marshall cloth grille, mfg. 1983-1990.

	N/A	$600 - 700	$500 - 575

This model was only available as a JCM-800, and it became one of the best selling Marshall distortion amps.

* JCM-800 Model 4211 - Similar to the JCM-800 Model 2210, except is in combo form with 2-12" speakers, mfg. 1983-1990.

	N/A	$600 - 700	$500 - 575

JCM-800 MODEL 2205 - 50W, Head-unit only, tubes, split channel, one input, reverb, six 11 knobs (presence, v, reverb, Drive Channel: b, mid, t, v, g, Clean Channel: b, t, v), black covering, new Marshall cloth grille, mfg. 1983-1990.

	N/A	$600 - 675	$500 - 575

* JCM-800 Model 4210 - Similar to the JCM-800 Model 2205, except is in combo form with 1-12" speakers, mfg. 1982-1990.

	N/A	$425 - 500	$350 - 400

* JCM-800 Model 4212 - Similar to the JCM-800 Model 2205, except is in combo form with 2-12" speakers, mfg. 1983-1990.

	N/A	$475 - 575	$400 - 450

2203X - Reissue of the JCM-800 circa 1981-1990, has true bypass Series FX loop, new 2002.

MSR	$1,950	$1,399	$1,100 - 1,250	$900 - 1,000

LIMITED EDITION ORIGINAL CLASSIC - This series of amps was designed to look like the 1969 Marshalls, but they got it all wrong. The grille was from that of a 70's. They had an ugly green-black vinyl that didn't match the early 60's style, bad speakers, and the electronics inside were that of the new JCM-800 series of the time! These amps were very short-lived Marshall released the real 1969 amps later on and they became a much greater success.

Silver Jubilee Series

The Silver Jubilee series was introduced in 1987 to commemorate Jim Marshall's 25 years in amplification and 50 years in music. These amps were based on the 2203 and 2204 Master Volume models, but they did have other changes in the electronics as well. The wattage could be dropped (cut in half) by a switch when less sound was needed. There were three different gain modes as well. These amps were covered in silver-vinyl (for 25 years), and featured chrome-plated control panels. The Jubilee series was only produced for that year, 1987, and after that the name was changed to the Custom Series for the next year or so. These were discontinued in 1990, around the same time ast the JCM-800 series.

SILVER JUBILEE MODEL 2550 - 50W (switchable to 25W), head-unit only, tubes: (need to get), lead application, gain switching, pentode/triode output section, one input, seven silver knobs, effects loop on back, silver covering, black grille, mfg. 1987-89.

	N/A	$800 - 950	$700 - 775

In 1988, the silver covering, and chrome control panel was replaced with traditional black covering and gold control panel.

* Model 2551A, 2551AV, 2551B, 2551BV Speaker Cabinets - These cabinets were made to match the Silver Jubilee series heads. The 2551A and 2551B came with 4-12" G12 70 & 75 speakers, while the 2551AV and 2551BV came with 4-12" Vintage 30 speakers, essentially a 1960 cabinet with the silver vinyl, mfg. 1987-88.

MODEL 2551 A & B	N/A	$500 - 600	$400 - 475
MODEL 2551 AV & BV	N/A	$500 - 600	$400 - 475

* Model 2553 - Similar to the Model 2550, except is a smaller head-unit built for a mini-stack, discontinued when the Custom Series was launched, mfg. 1987 only.

	N/A	$750 - 850	$600 - 700

* Model 2554 - Similar to the Model 2550 except in combo version with 1-12" speaker, mfg. 1987-89.

	N/A	$750 - 875	$625 - 700

* Model 2555 - Similar to the Model 2550 except has 100W (switchable to 50W) output, mfg. 1987-89.

	N/A	$975 - 1,200	$875 - 950

* Model 2556A, 2556AV, 2556B, 2556BV Speaker Cabinets - These cabinets were made to match the Silver Jubilee Model 2553, which is the smaller version. These cabinets came with 2-12" speakers. The 2556 A & B have G12 70 & 75 speakers, and the 2556 AV & BV have Vintage 30 speakers, mfg. 1987-88.

MODEL 2556 A & B	N/A	$375 - 425	$300 - 350
MODEL 2556 AV & BV	N/A	$375 - 425	$300 - 350

* Model 2558 - Similar to the Model 2550 except is in combo form with 2-12" speakers, mfg. 1987-89.

	N/A	$850 - 1,000	$725 - 800

The 9000 Series

These are Marshall "Rack amps." By the late '80's, different people wanted different products, even though the Marshall stack was still the standard. The Rack system were used by musicians that wanted to put all of their effects along with an amp into a rack box. This way there could be several effects within a hand's reach. There were some models that were strictly preamps, and there were models that were the power amps. The prototype was announced at the 1989 NAMM show, but the product was dramatically altered before it was released. All of the models were in black cases, 19" wide for rack-mounts, and labeled 9000. The first of this series ran through 1993 when a couple new models were released. The models 9010 and 9030 were prototypes that were advertised but never put into production.

JCM-900 Series

The JCM-900 amps came out after the JCM-800 was discontinued. The amps came with two basic models the Hi-Gain Master Volume MK III and the Hi Gain Dual Reverb. These amps started to focus on more distortion and effects loops. The most signifigant change is what Nigel Tufnel of Spinal Tap help think of. The gain had two different knobs and the second one had numbers that went from 10 to 20! There was an effects loop on the back as well as fail LED lights to inform when valves weren't working.

GRADING	100%	EXCELLENT	AVERAGE

One of the best changes was the way Marshall numbered the models. A system was actually developed and the numbers actually stood for something (It only took them 25 years to figure this one out, thanks mostly to Rose-Morris). Most models previously had four numbers as well as the new system did. The first number was a 2 or a 4, with the 2 indicating Hi Gain Master Volume and 4 meaning a Hi Gain Dual Reverb. The second and the third number were a 50 or a 10 indicating how much power the amp put out. 50 was for 50 watts and 10 was for 100 watts. The final number was a 0, 1, or 2 indicating the configuration. A 0 is a head, a 1 is a 1-12" combo, and 2 is a 2-12". By looking at the model number now it was easy to tell what the specs were on the amp. Note that this only works for the JCM-900 series and nothing before that.

The JCM-900 series brought Marshall into the 90's with vigor and kept them going. Marshall, for the first time was able to take the skill they had in amplifiers and apply it to marketing in combination to create a great product. The JCM-900 series ran through the late '90's when it was replaced by the JCM-2000. These amps are generally great sounding and can be found rather cheaply.

JCM-900 MODEL 2100 (SL-X) - 100W (Switchable to 50W), head-unit only, tubes: 3 X ECC83 preamp valves, 4 X 5881 output valves, one input, eight knobs (presence, b, m, t, volume A, volume B, gain (10-20), preamp volume), effects loop, output valve protection, pentode/triode output stage, footswitch for volume switching, black covering, gold control panel, black grille, mfg. 1990-1998.

Marshall JCM-900 MKIII
courtesy Dave's Guitar Shop

Marshall JCM-900 MKIII
courtesy Dave's Guitar Shop

| 1990-93 | N/A | $600 - 650 | $525 - 575 |
| 1993-98 | N/A | $625 - 700 | $550 - 600 |

In 1993, the 2100 was changed to the 2100 SL-X and an extra ECC83 preamp tube was added for more gain! This was another derivative of the 2203/2204 series. Known as the Hi Gain Master Volume MK III. It had two master volume controls. A clean sound is available, but this amp is designed for the uncompromising player who demands a no-compromise sound.

* JCM-900 Model 2101 - Similar to the JCM-900 Model 2100 except in combo form with 1-12" speaker, controls on the panel are reversed, mfg. 1990-93.

| | N/A | $525 -600 | $450 - 500 |

JCM-900 MODEL 2500 (SL-X) - 50W (Switchable to 25W), head-unit only, tubes: 3 X ECC83 preamp valves, 2 X 5881 output tubes, dual channels, one input, eight knobs (presence, b, m, t, volume A, volume B, gain (10-20), preamp volume, effects loop, output valve protection, pentode/triode output stage, black covering, gold control panel, black grille, mfg. 1990-1998.

| 1990-93 | N/A | $600 - 650 | $525 - 575 |
| 1993-98 | N/A | $600 - 750 | $525 - 575 |

In 1993, the 2500 was changed to the 2500 SL-X with the addition of another ECC83 preamp tube for added gain.

* JCM-900 Model 2501 - Similar to the JCM-900 Model 2500 except is in combo form with 1-12" speaker, controls on the panel are reversed, mfg. 1990-93.

| | N/A | $500 -550 | $425 - 475 |

* JCM-900 Model 2502 - Similar to the JCM-900 Model 2500 except in combo form with 2-12" speakers, controls on the panel are reversed, mfg. 1990-93.

| | N/A | $525 -575 | $450 - 500 |

JCM-900 MODEL 4100 - 100W (Switchable to 50W), tubes: 3 X ECC84 preamp valves, 4 X 5881 output valves, dual channels, one input, ten knobs (Ch B: v, reverb, Ch. A: v, reverb, Both: presence, b, m, t, lead gain, gain), effects loop, output valve protection, pentode/triode output stage, footswitch for channel switching, black covering, gold control panel, black grille, mfg. 1990-98.

| | N/A | $575 -675 | $475 - 550 |

This model was known as the Hi-Gain Dual Reverb.

* JCM-900 Model 4101 - Similar to the JCM-900 Model 4100 except is in combo form with 1-12" speaker, controls are reversed, mfg. 1990-98.

| | N/A | $500 -575 | $400 - 475 |

* JCM-900 Model 4102 - Similar to the JCM-900 Model 4101 except has 2-12" speakers, mfg. 1990-98.

| | N/A | $525 -600 | $425 - 500 |

JCM-900 MODEL 4500 - 50W (Switchable to 25W), tubes: 3 X ECC84 preamp valves, 2 X 5881 output valves, dual channels, one input, ten knobs (Ch B: v, reverb, Ch. A: v, reverb, Both: presence, b, m, t, lead gain, gain), effects loop, output valve protection, pentode/triode output stage, footswitch for channel switching, black covering, gold control panel, black grille, mfg. 1990-98.

| | N/A | $500 -575 | $400 - 475 |

* JCM-900 Model 4501 - Similar to the JCM-900 Model 4500 except in combo form with 1-12" speaker, reversed controls, mfg. 1990-98.

| | N/A | $475 -525 | $400 - 450 |

* JCM-900 Model 4502 - Similar to the JCM-900 Model 4501 except has 2-12" speakers, mfg. 1990-98.

| | N/A | $500 -575 | $425 - 475 |

GRADING	100%	EXCELLENT	AVERAGE

30th Anniversary Series

As Marshall had done with the 25/50 Anniversary, they released a series of amps for the 30th Anniversary in 1992. This amp was the result of a triple-channel JCM-900 that wasn't ready for release when the Hi-Gain and Hi-Gain Dual Reverb were. They saved it for the 30 year anniversary, covered it in blue vinyl, and it was the most advanced amplifier they had ever released. The three different channels are what made this amp something. The first channel was for clean tone and by using a switch the sound could be switched from Marshall sound in the out to Fender sound pushed in. Channel 2 presented three different modes (A, B, & C), that could be used all together. The Lead/JTM 45, a 2203, and a JCM-900 could all be heard through this amp in channel 2. Channel 3 was a whole different animal with distortion like no other. All of these could be used through a footswitch. The power selection was also new. Not only was there a triode/peontode selection switch, but a new power selection switch was added. This allowed the selection between two or four tubes.

The series lasted for the better half of the 90's. For the year 1992, the amp was covered in blue Levant vinyl, but after that it was changed to standard black like the JCM-900's. This series was discontinued in 1998, around the same time as the JCM-900 series. All of these models are meant for lead applications.

30TH ANNIVERSARY MODEL 6100 - 100W (Switchable to 50W or 25W), head-unit only, tubes (11): 7 X ECC83 preamp valves, 4 X EL34 output valves, triple channels, MIDI, speaker emulator, one input, seventeen gold knobs (Master: v, presence, effects, Ch. 3: b, m, t, v, gain, Ch. 2: b, m, t, v, g, Ch.3: v, m, t, v), contour and gain boost controls, effects loop, multiple outputs on back, footswitch for channel switching, blue Levant covering, black grille, mfg. 1992-98.

1992	N/A	$900 - 1,100	$750 - 875
1993-98	N/A	$875 - 1,050	$700 - 850

The Blue covering only ran for the year 1992, after that it was changed to standard black.

* 30th Anniversary Model 6101 - Similar to the Model 6100 except is in combo form with 1-12" speaker, controls are reversed and stacked in two rows instead of one, back panel is reversed as well, mfg. 1992-98.

N/A	$800 -900	$650 - 750

* 30th Anniversary Model 6100LE - Similar to the Model 6100 except is the limited edition model. This includes a brass plated chassis, with the valve caps, spring retainers, and transformer covers all covered in brass. A signature plate was mounted on the chassis with the serial number, mfg. 1992 only.

N/A	$875 -1,000	$750 - 850

There were only 800 units made of this model.

* 30th Anniversary Model 6101LE - Similar to the Model 6101 except is the limited edition model. This includes a brass plated chassis, with the valve caps, spring retainers, and transformer covers all covered in brass. A signature plate was mounted on the chassis with the serial number, mfg. 1992 only.

N/A	$875 -1,000	$725 - 850

There were only 500 units in the combo form made.

6912 & 6960 SPEAKER CABINETS - There were special speaker cabinets made for this series with the blue Levant covering. See the Marshall cabinet section in the *Blue Book of Guitar Amplifiers*.

JCM-2000 Series

Following up the JCM-900 series was a tough thing to do, but Marshall released the powerful JCM-2000 series in 1998. The first models were the Dual Super Leads (DSL) in the traditonal 100W and 50W heads. With the extreme success of these amps Marshall released the Triple Super Lead shortly thereafter. The feature that DSL amps boast are the dual channels with two modes in each of them. What this means is that these four modes are individually voiced as an amp in its own right. The TSL amps have three independent channels, all with their own controls. These amps are the most current valve amps that Marshall has to offer.

It appears that Marshall has also made the model numbers useful in this series. The three letters are either DSL or TSL which is Dual or Triple Super Lead. The numbers that follow indicate wattage and speakers if there are any. The numbers are 100, 60, 50, 40, and 20. These are all how much wattage that amp puts out. The last number indicates if it is a combo amp or not. An ending in 0 is a head unit, 1 is a 1-12" combo and a 2 is a 2-12" combo. The TSL-122 makes no sense, so just assume that they thought it would be cool and throw out a curve ball; (must have talked to Gibson about it!)

DUAL SUPER LEAD (DSL) 100 - 100W, head-unit only, tubes: 4 X 12AX7 preamp valves, 4 X EL34 output valves, dual channels, reverb, one input, ten gold knobs (presence, t, m, b, Ch.A reverb, Ch.B reverb, Ch.B volume and gain, Ch. A volume and gain), tone switch, deep switch, effects loop, footswitch, black Levant covering, gold control panel, black grille, mfg. 1998-current.

MSR	$1,650	$1,175	$850 - 975	$700 - 775

* DSL-50 - Similar to the DSL-100 except has 50W output and only 2 X EL34 output tubes, mfg. 1998-current.

MSR	$1,500	$1,050	$800 - 900	$675 - 750

DSL 401 - 40W, combo unit with 1-12" speaker, tubes: 4 X 12AX7 preamp valves, 4 X EL84 output tubes, three channels, one input, twelve gold knobs (Clean: gain, t, m, b, Overdrive: gain, v, t, m, b, Master: FX mix, reverb, v), parallel effects loop, footswitch, second overdrive channel, black Levant covering, gold control panel, black grille, reversed control panel, mfg. 1998-current.

MSR	$1,025	$699	$500 - 575	$400 - 450

* DSL-201 - Similar to the DSL 401 except has 20W output, only 2 X EL84 output tubes, two channels, mfg. 1998-current.

$499	$350 - 425	$275 - 325

TRIPLE SUPER LEAD (TSL) 100 - 100W, head-unit only, tubes: 4 X ECC83 preamp, 4 X EL34 output, triple channels, reverb, one input, 21 gold knobs (why not?), (one for each channel clean and lead crunch: presence, FX mix, reverb, one of these for each channel, lead, crunch, and clean: b, m, t, v, gain), two effects loops, black Levant covering, gold control panel, black grille, mfg. 2000-current.

MSR	$2,050	$1,475	$1,100 - 1,300	$900 - 1,000

* TSL 122 - Similar to the TSL 100 except in combo form with 1-12" speaker, reversed control panel, mfg. 2000-current.

MSR	$2,450	$1,750	$1,300 - 1,500	1,075 - 1,175

GRADING	100%	EXCELLENT	AVERAGE

TSL 60 - 60W, head-unit only, tubes: 4 X ECC83, 2 X EL34, triple channels, reverb, one input, 16 gold knobs (Clean: gain t, m, b, Lead: gain, v, t, m, b, Crunch: gain, v, Master: presence, FX mix, clean reverb, volume, OD reverb), effects loop, five-way footswitch, black Levant covering, gold control panel, black grille, mfg. 2000-current.

	MSR	$1,575	$1,150	$850 - 975	$700 - 775

* **TSL 601** - Similar to the TSL 60 Head unit except is in combo form with 1-12" speaker, reversed controls, mfg. 2000-current.

	MSR	$1,675	$1,199	$850 - 1,000	$725 - 800

* **TSL 602** - Similar to the TSL 601 except has 2-12" speakers, mfg. 2000-current.

	MSR	$1,775	$1,275	$950 - 1,100	$750 - 850

Misc. Valve Amps

1930 POPULAR - 10W, combo with 1-12" speaker, tubes: 1 X ECC83 preamp, 2 X ECL86 output, dual channels, tremolo, four inputs (two for each channel), six knobs (v, t, v, t, s, i), footswitch, mfg. 1972-73.

N/A	$1,300 -1,800	$900 - 1,200

2046 SPECIALIST - 25W, combo with 1-15" speaker, tubes: 1 X ECL86 & 2 X ECC83 preamp valves, 2 X EL34 output valves, reverb, tremolo, two inputs, five knobs, black covering, chequerboard grille, mfg. 1971-73.

N/A	$1,250 -1,600	$875 - 1,150

This model was the first Marshall amp to have a printed circuit board in the electronics. This was a model designed for a jazz application.

2060 MERCURY - 5W, combo with 1-12" speaker, hybrid design with a solid-state preamp, 1 X EL84 output valve, one channel, two inputs, four knobs (s, i, tone, v), red or orange covering, chequerboard grille, Marshall logo on a piece of metal running across front of amp, mfg. 1972-73.

N/A	$275 -325	$225 - 250

This model was available through mail order catalogs only.

MODEL 2150 - 100W, combo with 1-12" speaker, tubes: (need the valves), dual channels, four inputs (two for each channel), 7 knobs, Master volume design, mfg. 1978-1980.

N/A	$400 -475	$325 - 375

This model was the only Marshall amp to have four inputs with a Master Volume control. Rose-Morris called it the "Rock n' Roll Baby."

MODEL 4001 (STUDIO 15) - 15W, combo with 1-10" speaker, tubes: 6V6 output tubes, ECC83 preamp, one channel, one input, five gold knobs (gain, t, m, b, v), black covering, gold control panel, black grille, mfg. 1986-1992.

Marshall Studio 15 Model 4001
courtesy Willie's American Guitars

N/A	$375 -425	$300 - 350

This Marshall amp was the first for the company in many ways. It was the first to have the 6V6 tubes, Clestian Vintage 30 speakers, and to have a headphone jack.

CLUB AND COUNTRY SERIES - 100W, combos, tubes: KT77 valves. These amps were targeted at the country market. Marshall hadn't made anything close to something for the country music industry so far. These amps were covered in brown vinyl (Brown Oak), and straw-colored grilles, mfg. 1978-1982.

* **Model 4140** - Club and Country Series with 2-12" speakers, dual channels, (guitar and mic), two inputs, 10 knobs.

N/A	$575 -650	$450 - 525

* **Model 4145** - Club and Country Series with 4-10" speakers, similar to the Model 4140.

N/A	$600 -700	$475 - 550

* **Model 4150** - Club and Country Series bass amplifier, 4-10" speakers, nine knobs.

N/A	$575 -650	$450 - 525

These models were initially going to be called Reverb Twins. Funny the resemlance to the Fender Twin and Super Reverbs?!

4203 ARTIST - 30W, combo with 1-12" speaker, tubes: 1 X ECC83 preamp, 2 X EL34 outputs, solid-state tone network, one input, nine knobs, black covering, gold control panel, black grille, mfg. 1986-1991.

3203 (HEAD ONLY)	N/A	$350 -400	$300 - 325
4203	N/A	$375 -425	$325 - 350

This model was designed around the model 3203 mini-stack.

GRADING	100%	EXCELLENT	AVERAGE

CAPRI - 5W, combo with 1-8" speaker, tubes: 1 X ECC83 preamp, 1 X EL84 output, two inputs, volume and tone controls, red custom vinyl, white grille, mfg. 1966-67.

| | N/A | $225 -250 | $175 - 200 |

There were only around 100 of these made.

Reissue & Limited Edition Amps

For the JTM-45 series reissues, please refer to the JTM-45 series.

ZAKK WYLDE SIGNATURE HEAD (2203ZW) - 100W, head-unit only, all tube chassis, 4 X 6550 power tubes, single channel, front custom control panel, two inputs, six gold knobs (presence, b, m, t, MV, v), black covering, TV fret cloth, mfg. 2002 only.

| | $2,000 | $1,750 - 1,900 | $1,350 - 1,550 |

Last MSR was $2,250.

This amp is one of only two that have been signature amps at Marshall. This amp is a reissue of the JCM-800 2203 made signature for Zakk. When shipped it came equipped with Zakk Wylde guitar picks, a custom cover, and certificate of authenticity. There were only 600 made and they sold out within half a year. There are speaker cabinets to match up with this head that are listed in the Speaker Cabinet section.

VALVESTATE AMPLIFIERS (HYBRID)

With Marshall having their postion at the top for tube (valve) amplifiers, they realized that they could excel in other areas of the amplifier industry. This is where Valvestate came in. Valvestate isn't a just a valve amp or a solid-state amp, but a combination of the two. This is also known as a hybrid design. This new series featured tubes in the preamp section to get the real Marshall tone and drive. The output section was then solid-state. This made Marshall amplifiers now available for those who didn't need, want, or could afford the tube-design models. In a sense this was more of a budget line, but surprisingly these amps really sounded good and got the job done.

Valvestate Series I

The first Valvestate series came in four models with matching cabinets. In 1991, they introduced a 100W head with matching 4 X 12 cabinet, two power amps, and a mircro-stack. Models then followed in 1992 with the popular 8200 head-unit, and combo 8240. A new feature on this series, with the exception of the 10W model, was a contour knob. This knob worked with the mid-frequencies to go from metal to blues.

MODEL 8100 - 100W, head-unit only, hybrid design, dual channels, reverb, two modes in each channel, one input, 13 gold knobs (Norm: gain, b, m, t, Boost: gain, b, m, t, contour, v, Master: effects, reverb, v) effects loop on front, footswitch, black covering, gold control panel, black grille, mfg. 1991-98.

| | N/A | $275 -325 | $200 - 250 |

There is a cabinet made especially to fit the model 8100. It is a 4-12" cabinet model 8412 listed in the cabinet section.

* Model 8080 - Similar to the model 8100 except is in combo form with 1-12" speaker, mfg. 1991-98.

| | N/A | $250 -300 | $180 - 225 |

MODEL 8040 - 40W, combo with 1-12" speaker, hybrid design (ECC83 preamp), dual channels, reverb, one input,10 gold knobs (Norm: gain, b, m, t, Boost: gain, contour, b, t, volume, master reverb), preamp out, power amp in jacks, line out, footswitch, black covering, gold control panel, black grille, mfg. 1991-98.

| | N/A | $160 -200 | $100 - 135 |

MODEL 8020 - 20W, combo with 1-10" speaker, hybrid design, dual channels, reverb, one input, eight gold knobs (Norm: gain, b, t, Boost: gain, contour, presence, v, master reverb), headphone jack line out, footswitch, black covering, gold control panel, black grille, mfg. 1991-98.

| | N/A | $75 -90 | $50 - 65 |

MODEL 8010 - 10W, combo with 1-8" speaker, hybrid design, one input, five gold knobs (gain, master volume, b, m, t) headphone jack, line output, black covering, gold control panel, black grille, mfg. 1991-98.

| | N/A | $50 -60 | $35 - 45 |

* Model 8001 - Similar to the 8010, except in micro-stack version, mfg. 1991-98.

| | N/A | $225 -275 | $175 - 200 |

MODEL 8200 - 100W x 2, head-unit only, hybrid design, dual channels, Overdrive 1/2 switch in boost, chorus, reverb, one input, 17 gold knobs (Norm: gain, b, m, t, Boost: gain, b, m, t, contour, v, Master: effects, reverb, v, Chorus: rate and depth controls for Normal and Boost channels), various switches, effects loop, black covering, gold control panel, black grille, mfg. 1993-98.

| | N/A | $275 -325 | $200 - 250 |

There is a cabinet, model 8222, to match the 8200 head listed in the cabinet section.

* Model 8280 - Similar to the Model 8200, except is in combo form with 80W output, mfg. 1993-98.

| | N/A | $325 -375 | $275 - 300 |

* Model 8240 - Similar to the Model 8280, except has 40W output, two less knobs, effects loop on control panel, mfg. 1993-98.

| | N/A | $265 -300 | $215 - 250 |

MODEL 8004 & 8008 - 40 X 2, 80 X 2 respective output, power amp, rack mount, hybrid design, 8008 has dual volume controls, originally finished in black, but changed to gold in 1993, mfg. 1991-98.

| 8004 | N/A | $100 - 120 | $70 - 90 |
| 8008 | N/A | $110 - 135 | $75 - 95 |

GRADING	100%	EXCELLENT	AVERAGE

Valvestate Series II

This series is based on the success of the first line of Valvestate amps. Marshall took what they had and added some features and more power. The second series of Valvestate lasted until 2001 when the Advanced Valvestate Technology series was debuted.

VS 15(R) - 15W, 1-8" combo, Valvestate power stage hybrid (ECC83 preamp), one channel, reverb on the VS15R model, one input, seven gold knobs (gain 1, gain 2, t, contour, b, master volume, reverb on VS 15R only), head phone jack and line out, mfg. 1998-2001.

	N/A	$50 - 65	$35 - 45

VS 30 R - 30W, 1-10" combo, Valvestate power stage hybrid (ECC83 preamp), dual channels, reverb, one input, nine gold knobs (Ch 1: v, b, t, Ch 2: gain, b, contour, t, v, reverb), line out, headphone jack, footswitch, mfg. 1998-2001.

	N/A	$135 -160	$100 - 125

VS 65 R - 65W, 1-12" combo, Valvestate power stage hybrid (ECC83 preamp), dual channels, reverb, one input 11 gold knobs (Ch 1: v, b, m, t, Ch 2: gain, b, contour, t, v, FX mix, reverb), effects loop, line out, headphone jack, footswitch, mfg. 1998-2001.

	N/A	$265 -295	$225 - 250

VS 100 RH - 100W, head-unit only, Valvestate power stage hybrid (ECC83 preamp on all 3 channels), 3 channels (clean, OD1,OD2), spring reverb, one input, 15 gold knobs (Clean: v, b, m, t, Overdrive 1: gain, v, Overdrive 2: gain, contour, v, Overdrive EQ: b, m,t, All: FX mix, clean reverb, OD reverb), channel switches, effects loop, footswitch, black covering, gold control panel, black grille, mfg. 1998-2001.

	N/A	$240 -275	$180 - 220

* VS 100 R - Similar to the VS 100 R except is in combo form with 1-12" speaker, mfg. 1998-2001.

	N/A	$250 -300	$200 - 235

* VS102R - Similar to the VS 102 R except is in combo form with 2-12" speakers, mfg. 1998-2001.

	N/A	$325 -375	$260 - 300

VS 230 - 2 X 30W, combo with 2-10" speakers, Valvestate power stage hybrid, two independent channels (clean and overdrive), chorus, reverb, one input, 11 gold knobs (Clean: v, b, t, Overdrive: gain, b, contour, t, v, reverb, speed, depth), headphone jack, stereo line out, black covering, gold control panel, black grille, mfg. 1998-2001.

	N/A	$225 - 250	$175 - 200

* VS 232 - Similar to the VS 230 except has 2-12" speakers, mfg.1998-2001.

	N/A	$260 - 295	$200 - 235

VS 265 - 2 X 65W, combo with 2-12" speakers, Valvestate power stage hybrid, three channels (Clean, Overdrive 1 and 2), chorus, reverb, one input, 17 gold knobs (Clean: v, b, m, t, Overdrive 1: gain, volume, Overdrive 2: gain, contour, volume, EQ: b, m, t, All: FX mix, clean reverb, overdrive reverb, s, depth), effects loop, headphone jack, black covering, gold control panel, black grille, mfg. 1998-2001.

	N/A	$375 -450	$300 - 350

Advanced Valvestate Technologyl (AVT) Series

The Advanced Valvestate Technology series is in the line of VS2000 amps. This is known as the VS 2000 series with AVT and the number indicating what model it is. These amps are even more advanced then the earlier Valvestates. The most noted addition is the digital effects touting. This lets the user use different digital effects in the amp. This is the most current Valvestate series.

M

AVT 20 - 20W, 1-10" combo, Valvestate power with a ECC83 preamp, one channel, overdrive, reverb, one input, six gold knobs (gain, v, b, m, t, depth), CD input, DI emulation input, headphone jack, External Speaker jack, black covering, gold control panle, black grille, mfg. 2002-current.

MSR	$449	$325	$235 - 275	$195 - 210

This model is also available as a limited edition with white covering and checkered grille cloth.

AVT 50 - 50W, 1-12" combo, Valvestate power with a ECC83 preamp, dual channels, reverb, one input, ten gold knobs (Clean: gain, v, b, t, Overdrive: gain, v, b, m, t, reverb depth), CD and headphone jacks, effects loop, emulated DI output, footswitch, black covering, gold control panel, black grille, mfg. 2002-current.

MSR	$699	$499	$360 - 425	$275 - 325

* AVT 50H - Similar to the AVT 50 except is the head-unit only, mfg. 2002-current.

MSR	$649	$450	$350 - 400	$265 - 300

There are extension cabinets made especially for the AVT series, the AVT412A, AVT412B, and the AVT 112. See the cabinet section.

AVT 100 - 100W, 1-12" combo, Valvestate power with a ECC83 preamp, three channels, reverb, 16 built in DFX (digital effects), one input, 18 gold knobs (gain and volume for clean, OD1, and OD2 channels, b, m, t, for clean and overdrive, Master Volume, presence, mix, DFX mix, Adjust, and program selection knob), parallel effects loop, footswitch, black covering, gold control panel, black grille, mfg. 2002-current.

MSR	$999	$699	$500 - 600	$400 - 450

AVT 150 - 150W, 1-12" combo, Valvestate power with a ECC83 preamp, four channels (Acoustic simulator, Clean, OD1, and OD2), The Clean and Overdrive channels are the same as the AVT 100, reverb, one input, 24 gold knobs (gain and voulme for Clean, OD1, and OD2, Ac. Sim and voulme for Acoustic, b, m, t, for clean and overdrive, master volume, presence, FX loop mix (2), DFX mix, adjust and program selection for clean and overdrive channels), effects loop, footswitch, black covering, gold control panel, black grille, mfg. 2002-current.

MSR	$1,149	$825	$575 - 675	$475 - 525

* AVT 150H - Smilar to the AVT 150 except is in head-unit version, mfg. 2002-current.

MSR	$999	$699	$500 - 575	$400 - 450

GRADING	100%	EXCELLENT	AVERAGE

AVT 275 (STEREO) - 2 X 75W, 2-12" combo, Valvestate power with a ECC83 preamp, four channels, (Acoustic simulator, Clean, OD1, and OD2), The Clean and Overdrive channels are the same as the AVT 150, reverb, one input, 24 gold knobs (gain and volume for Clean, OD1, and OD2, Ac. Sim and volume for Acoustic, b, m, t, for clean and overdrive, master volume, presence, FX loop mix (2), DFX mix, adjust and program selection for clean and overdrive channels), effects loop, footswitch, black covering, gold control panel, black grille, mfg. 2002-current.

MSR	$1,299	$925	$750 - 850	$625 - 675

SOLID-STATE AMPLIFIERS

Marshall has also released a solid-state line of amplifiers. These are more budget-lined models but have a lot of features that the Valvestate and all-tube amps have. In 2000 the G solid-state series was released, but it was replaced by the MG series in 2002. They current line is MG III series.

MG Series

These models include the **MG10CD**, which includes 10W output, 1-6.5" speaker, two channels, and a CD-input, MSR is $99. The **MG15CD** has 15W output, 1-8" speaker, two channels, and CD-input, MSR is $139. The **MG15CDR** is the same as the MG15CD except has reverb and retail is $179. The **MG15DFX** is the same as the MG15CD except has DFX capabillities and retails for $219. The **MG30DFX** has 30W output, 1-10" speaker, DFX effects and retails for $349. There are models **MG50DFX, MG100DFX** and the model **MC250DFX**. These models have wattage aooording to their model number and 12" speakers in combo versions. There is no retail pricing on these at this time.

The MG series differs from the MG III series and these are the two that are listed in the catalog and price list respectively, go figure!

Bass-State Combos

Marshall made Bass-State combos that were solid-state. These models were made only in 2001 and there isn't a lot known about them. Look for more information in upcoming editions of the *Blue Book of Guitar Amplifiers*..

MARSHALL SPEAKER CABINETS

Marshall is known for making amplifiers that put out ea-crunching sounds. They are also known for the cabinets that the amps went through. As noted earlier in the section, Jim Marshall developed the "stack", which is a cabinet or two stacked on top of each other with a head-unit amp on the top. When first released they surely looked like monsters towering over most people. Nowadays, these are standerd equipment for most hard-rockers. Marshall didn't release heads and cabinets together usually. This gives musicians the availabiltiy to play a different amp through different cabinets for a number of possibilities. No other company had done this and Marshall was considered the pioneer of this. The most popular style of the stack is a head-unit sitting on top of two 4 X 12" speaker cabinets (one angled). It's almost impossible to go to a rock concert today and not see a Marshall stack.

As listed in the dating of Marshall Amplifiers earlier in the section, it can be done by the speakers if they are original. There are also cosmetic features that indicate the year as well. This will be helpful in idenitifying the year of the speaker cabinet.

1962-1966 - Marshall cabinets introduced and included a yellow materlal made of foam for an acoustic insulator. This was discontinued around 1966.

1970 & 1971 - The black baffle board in the back was changed from plywood to chipboard. Chequerboard cloth replaced the basket-weave grille cloth also.

1972 & 1973 - The metal grab handles on 4 X 12" models were changed over to plastic ones.

1975 - Black grille cloth replace the Chequerboard cloth in the U.K. It changed over in the U.S.A. in 1981.

There are literally hundreds of Marshall cabinets. We will try to list as many as possible, but not everything can be listed. That's an impossibility. Make sure to read the fine print, because some models may be known as others. There are three different categories of cabinets Lead, bass, and PAs. Almost all Marshalls have Celestion speakers. If other speaker name appears, then it is different, otherwise assume Celestion. All models are listed numerically. The color is assumed black unless otherwise noted. When there is the same model number with an A and a B that refers to a straight cabinet from an angeled. Usually they are the same in price. If no, then they will be listed differently in the pricing.

Add 25% for custom cabinet colors.

Lead Cabinets

These are cabinets that are meant for guitars to plug in through. Some may be for more than one application (i.e. Lead & Bass). We'll try to list them as accurately as possible.

1912 - 150W, 1-12", extension cab for JCM900 1-12" combo's, mfg. 1989-1998.

	N/A	$150 -175	$115 - 140

1922 - 150W, 2-12", extension cabinet for JCM900 2-12" combos, stereo/mono switching, G12T75 speakers, similar to the model 1936, mfg. 1989-1998.

	N/A	$250 -300	$185 - 225

1931A & 1931B - 75W, 1-12", angle cabinet for model 3310, G12T75 speakers, mfg. 1989-1991.

	N/A	$140 -175	$100 - 125

1933 - 65W, 1-12", extension cabinet, for the model 4010 and 4210 head's, G12 65 speakers, mfg. 1984-89.

	N/A	$140 -175	$100 - 125

In 1986 the output was increased to 70W and the speakers were changed to G12M70's.

1936 - 140W, 2-12", extension cabinets for full-sized heads, mfg. 1981-current.

	N/A	$275 -325	$225 - 260

In 1986 the speakers were changed to G12T75's. Switches from 16 Ohms Stereo to 8 Ohms Mono.

1551 - 2-15" Bass cabinet.

	N/A	$260 - 300	$200 - 250

GRADING	100%	EXCELLENT	AVERAGE

1960 - 60W, 4-12, lead & bass application, angled front cabinet for full-sized heads, mfg. 1964-1979.

Marshall 1960A speaker cabinet
courtesy solidbodyguitar.com, Inc.

1964-65	N/A	**$1,600 - 2,100**	**$1,000 - 1,500**
1966-1970	N/A	**$1,250 - 1,650**	**$900 - 1,150**
1971-79	N/A	**$675 - 950**	**$500 - 650**

In 1965, the output was increased to 75W. In 1970, the output was increased to 100W and was changed to a lead only application. The 1960 was the first production cabinet with 4-12" speakers and it only came as an angled front. The 1960 series was revamped in 1979 when it was split up into two categories, the 1960A and 1960B. A stands for the angle front and B indicates the straight front.

1960A & 1960B - 260W, 4-12", angled front cabinet or straight front cabinet for full-sized heads, G12 65 speakers, mfg. 1979-current.

1979-1983	N/A	**$450 - 525**	**$350 - 425**
1984-1986	N/A	**$425 - 500**	**$350 - 425**
1987-1990	N/A	**$425 - 500**	**$350 - 425**
MSR	$950	**$650**	**$400 - 475**	**$325 - 400**

In 1983, the output was raised to 280W and speakers were changed to G12M70's. In 1986, the output was raised to 300W and speakers were changed to G12T75's. In 1990 the cabinet was changed to mono/stereo switching speakers. The cabinets are currently 4/16 Ohms for mono and 8 Ohms for stereo.

* 1960AC & 1960BC - Similar to the 1960A & 1960B except has 100W output and speakers are mono Classic 25's 16 Ohms, mfg. 1990-current.

MSR	$1,100	**$650**	**$425 - 475**	**$350 - 400**

* 1960AS & 1960BS - Similar to the 1960 A & B, except is a reissue to fit the 1987S and 1959S reissue heads, 4-12" speakers, G12T75 speakers, mfg. 1988 only.

	N/A	**$475 - 525**	**$375 - 450**

* 1960AV & 1960BV - Similar to the 1960A & B except has 280W output, stereo/mono switching, 4-12" Vintage 30 speakers, 4/16 Ohms mono, 8 Ohms stereo, mfg. 1990-current.

MSR	$1,200	**$675**	**$500 - 600**	**$400 - 475**

* 1960AX & 1960BX - Similar to the 1960A & B except has 100W output, reissue cabinet for the 1987X & 1959X reissue heads, 4-12" mono Classic 25 speakers, mfg. 1990-93.

	N/A	**$450 - 525**	**$350 - 425**

* 1960ST - Similar to the 1960B except is stereo/mono switching, 4-12" G12T75 speakers, mfg. 1989 only.

	N/A	**$450 - 525**	**$350 - 425**

This cabinet was only available in straight front version (B). This was Marshall's first stab at a stereo 4-12" cabinet. Meant for the JCM 900 series.

* 1960TV - Similar to the 1960B except has 100W output, extra-tall cabinet, mono, 4-12" Classic 25 speakers, mfg. 1990-mid 1990's.

	N/A	**$450 - 525**	**$350 - 425**

1961A & 1961B - 150W, 2-12" G12T75 speakers, extension cabinet for the 3315 head, mfg. 1988-1990.

	N/A	**$260 - 300**	**$200 - 250**

1965A & 1965B - 140W output, 4-10" speakers, extension cabinet for "mini-stack" 3210/3203 heads, mfg. 1984-1991.

	N/A	**$300 - 375**	**$240 - 275**

1966A & 1966B - 150W, 2-12" G12 75 speakers, extension cabinet for "mini-stack" 3210/3203 heads, mfg. 1985-1991.

	N/A	**$250 - 300**	**$180 - 225**

1972 - 50W, 2-12" speakers, Lead, Bass, & Organ applications, extension cabinet for 1962 combo, mfg. 1966-68.

	N/A	**$875 - 1,100**	**$650 - 850**

Initially in 1966, this cabinet was designed with 2 horizontal mounted speakers. In 1967, the speakers were changed to the more common vertical design. The horizontal cabinet is very rare.

1966	N/A	**$1,000 - 1,250**	**$800 - 950**
1967-1968	N/A	**$900 - 1,100**	**$700 - 850**

GRADING	100%	EXCELLENT	AVERAGE

1982 & 1982B - 100W, 4-12" speakers, extension cabinet for full-sized heads, mfg. 1967-1980.

1967 - 1969	N/A	$950 - 1,300	$800 - 900
1970 - 1980	N/A	$625 - 850	$500 - 600

These cabinets are high-powered 1960's. They can be used for lead or bass applications. In 1970, the output was raised to 120W.

1982A & 1982B - 320W, 4-12" speakers, high-powered extension cabinets for full-sized heads, mfg. 1981-1987.

	N/A	$500 - 600	$375 - 475

In 1982, the output was raised to 400W for a truly high-powered speaker cabinet.

1990 - 80W, 8-10" speakers, extension cabinet for full-sized heads, mfg. 1967-1978.

1967 - 69	N/A	$750 - 900	$575 - 700
1970 - 78	N/A	$550 - 750	$475 - 525

In 1973, the output was increased to 100W. This cabinet is a slightly smaller version of the 2034 speaker cabinet.

2032 - 80W, 4-12" speakers, extension cabinet for full-sized heads, mfg. 1970-74.

	N/A	$600 - 700	$500 - 575

In 1973 the output was increased to 100W. This cabinet is in similar size to the model 2034 cabinet.

2034 - 120W, 8-10" speakers, extension cabinet for full-sized heads, mfg. 1970-73.

	N/A	$650 - 800	$525 - 600

This model along with the 1990 and 2032 are all in the same family. This model is a heavy-duty version of the model 1990 and is slightly larger in size.

2035B - 75W, 4-12" speakers & horn, Lead & Organ application, mfg. 1970-74.

	N/A	$650 - 750	$525 - 625

In 1973, the power was increased to 100W.

* 2036B - Similar to the 2035B except has 120W output, mfg. 1970-74.

	N/A	$700 - 850	$575 - 675

2038 - 60W, 4-10" speakers, extension cabinet for smaller amps, about the size of a 4-12" cabinet, mfg. 1972 only.

	N/A	$550 - 650	$400 - 525

2045 - 60W, 2-12" speakers, Lead, Bass, & Organ applications, extension cabinet for smaller amps, mfg. 1972-76.

	N/A	$425 - 500	$325 - 400

2049 - 60W, 2-12" speakers, 4 foot tall extension cabinet for 50W Artist series, mfg. 1973-77.

	N/A	$425 - 475	$350 - 400

2052 - 125W, 1-15" speaker, Lead & Organ application, horn loaded in rear with Powercel, extension cabinet for full-sized heads, mfg. 1973-79.

	N/A	$300 - 350	$225 - 275

2053 & 2053B - 100W, 1-12" speaker, lead & organ application, extension cabinet sized for a 4 X 12" with flared "picture frame" cosmetics, 2053B has castor cups, mfg. 1972-73.

	N/A	$350 - 400	$300 - 325

2054 & 2054B - 125W, 1-15" speaker, lead & organ application, extension cabinet with flared picture fram front, same size as a 4 X 12 cabinet, 2054 has castero cups, mfg. 1972-73.

	N/A	$350 - 400	$300 - 325

2064 & 2064B - 100W, 1-12" Powercel speaker, lead & organ application, extension cabinet for full-sized heads, both straight front cabinets, 2064B has castor cups, mfg. 1973-75.

	N/A	$325 - 375	$275 - 300

2065 & 2065B - 125W, 1-15" Powercel speaker, lead & organ application, extension cabinet for full-sized heads, both straight front cabinets, 2065B has castor cups, mfg. 1973-75.

	N/A	$350 - 400	$275 - 325

2069 - 120W, 4-12" speakers, tall extension cabinet for 100W Artist series, mfg. 1973-77.

	N/A	$475 - 550	$400 - 450

2196 - 100W, 2-12" 80W speakers with 4 Ohms impedance, lead & bass application, extension cabinet for 2195 head, mfg. 1976-1980.

	N/A	$425 - 475	$350 - 400

MARTIN

Amplifiers previously built in Nazareth, Pennsylvania in the early 1960's and again in the late 1980's.

World renowned guitar company, Martin, tried their go at building their own amplifiers, which turned out to be a flop, twice. Martin has been building mainly acoustic guitars since 1833 when the company was founded in New York. They moved to Nazareth, Pennsylvania in 1939, where they have been ever since. Fast forward to the 1960's, when Martin began producing solid-body electric guitars and amplifiers. The amps lasted until the mid 1960's when the idea was put into mothballs, but emerged again in 1988 as the FX Acoustic series. The second run of amps lasted two years and they haven't produced an amplifier since. Electric guitars have been retired for almost 20 years now. For a full history on Martin guitars, see the *Blue Book of Acoustic Guitars*.

ELECTRIC & ACOUSTIC AMPLIFIERS

There were a few models released in the 1960's, such as the 110T, 112T and the SS140. Needless to say, Martin isn't known for their electric insturments and the amps weren't very popular. Then in the late 1980's, Martin gave it a run again under the Stinger name. These were amps that were named the FX series. They were available in a small ten watt combo up to a 60 watt combo. This time the series of amps lasted about two years from 1988-1990. These amps rarely

GRADING	100%	EXCELLENT	AVERAGE

show up on the second hand market, since they aren't very desireable. But when they do appear, an amp in excellent condition should be able to be scored for about $125 (maybe a little more for the 60W). Prices on the older Martins are probably as much as someone wants to pay for having a Martin amplifier.

MASCO

Amplifiers previously produced in Long Island, New York.

Masco made small amplifiers in the 1950's. The name MASCO stands for Mark Alan Sampson Company. They were generally small amps used for guitars, P.A.s and even harps. Masco has been long out of business now, and little is known about the company and what they made. Any information on Masco or Masco amplifiers is welcome for upcoming editions of the *Blue Book of Guitar Amplifiers*.

MATCHLESS

Trademark currently produced in Los Angeles, California from 1999-present. Matchless amplifiers were also previously produced in North Hollywood, California from 1989-1994, Santa Fe Springs, California from 1994-97, and Pico Rivera, California from 1997-98.

The Matchless Amplifier Company was founded by Mark Sampson and Rick Perrotta, in 1989. Mark was born and raised in Iowa where he built streetrods and racecars while playing in a band as a hobby. In the late 1980's, Mark and his family moved to the west coast. Mark then worked in various enterprises relating to music and instrument manufacture. Rick had an incredible collection of vintage radio and tube instruments. The two came together to form a partnership in 1989 to put together an amplifier. They spent two years forming the first prototype amplifier after extensive research and trial and error. Finally in 1991, they had an amp that wasn't too complicated to make or operate; therefore creating a product that would be reliable. This was the 30W series. The first amp had features that the ones produced today still have including: shock-mounted tubes, 1-watt resistors, and Teflon wiring. Mark stayed with the company until 1998. In 2000, Mark began doing freelance work and became involved with BadCat amplifiers. All currently manufactured and most older models are made using point-to-point hand wiring, made in the U.S. Matchless uses this philosophy in their business: To build the best most versatile amplifier possible. Today Matchless still produces quality amplification under new management. There was a period of time in 1999 when no amplifiers were produced. Essentially the Matchless trademark was reintroduced in 2000 with original names for models.

Mark Sampson and Rick Perrotta

ELECTRIC TUBE AMPLIFIERS

Matchless amplifiers not only have excellent circuitry, but the cabinets are available in eight custom colors! Black is the standard color. Optional colors are Crimson Red, Dark Burgundy, Elk Beige, Green, Grey, White, Shower Curtain Turquoise, and Shower Curtain Black. For optional colors add $100.

Matchless amplifiers have several factors that give away the fact that it's a Matchless. They have the chicken head knobs (usually available in ivory or black). They also have a light on the inside of the cabinet the illuminates the insides as well as the label and controls on the outside (sort of a car dashboard design).

15W MODELS

All 15W amps made prior to January 1997 were in small cabinet size and had a full cloth grille cloth front. In January, 1997, the cabinets were enlarged and started using the grille cloth they looked like the DC-30 amps. Head units first came available in 1997 and 2-12" combos were introduced in 1998.

SPITFIRE - 15W, 1-12" speaker combo, all tube chassis, preamp: 2 X 12AX7, power: 2 X EL84, 5AR4 rectifier, single channel, front black control panel, three control knobs (v, tone, MV), various color covering, gray grille cloth, mfg. 1994-97.

N/A	$1,100 - 1,250	$850 - 975

Last MSR was $1,499.

This amp was available as a head-unit for a short while in 1997. It was also available as a 2-10" combo for a while. The combos offer a slight premium over the head unit in value.

TORONADO - 15W, 1-12" speaker combo, all tube chassis, preamp: 2 X 12AX7, power: 2 X EL84, 5AR4 rectifier, single channel, tremolo, front black control panel, four control knobs (v, tone, s, depth), various color covering, gray grille cloth, mfg. 1994 only.

N/A	$1,250 - 1,500	$1,000 - 1,100

Last MSR was $1,290.

This amp was available identical to the Spitfire except with tremolo. This model was replaced by the Hurricane.

HURRICANE - 15W, 1-12" speaker combo, all tube chassis, preamp: 2 X 12AX7, power: 2 X EL84, 5AR4 rectifier, single channel, tremolo, front black control panel, five control knobs (v, tone, s, depth, MV), various color covering, gray grille cloth, mfg. 1994-97.

N/A	$1,150 - 1,300	$950 - 1,050

Last MSR was $1,599.

This amp was available as a head-unit for a short while in 1997. It was also available as a 2-10" combo for a while. The combos offer a slight premium over the head unit in value.

GRADING	100%	EXCELLENT	AVERAGE

LIGHTNING - 15W, 1-12" speaker combo, all tube chassis, preamp: 3 X 12AX7, power: 2 X EL84, 5AR4 rectifier, single channel, front black control panel, four control knobs (v, B, T, MV), various color covering, gray grille cloth, mfg. 1994-98.

Matchless Lightning 112
courtesy Willie's American Guitars

1994-98	**N/A**	**$1,250 - 1,500**	**$1,000 - 1,100**
MSR $1,999	**$1,400**	**$1,000 - 1,200**	**$700 - 850**

This amp was available as a head-unit for a short while in 1997. It was also available as a 2-10", and 2-12" combo for a while. The combos offer a slight premium over the head unit in value.

* Lightning 212 (LG-212) - Similar to the Lightning 112 except has 2-12" speakers, mfg. 1994-current.

1994-98	**N/A**	**$1,300 - 1,500**	**$1,050 - 1,200**
MSR $2,199	**$1,500**	**$1,050 - 1,250**	**$725 - 875**

* Lightning 210 - Similar to the Lightning 112 except has 2-10" speakers, mfg. mid 1994-98.

$1,450	**$1,000 - 1,250**	**$725 - 875**

Last MSR was $1,899.

LIGHTNING REVERB - 15W, 1-12" speaker combo, all tube chassis, preamp: 5 X 12AX7, power: 2 X EL84, 5AR4 rectifier, single channel, reverb, front black control panel, five control knobs (v, B, T, r, MV), various color covering, gray grille cloth, mfg. 1997-98.

N/A	**$1,250 - 1,500**	**$1,050 - 1,150**

Last MSR was $2,349.

This amp was available as a head-unit for a short while in 1997. It was also available as a 2-10", and 2-12" combo for a while. The combos offer a slight premium over the head unit in value. The Last MSR on the 2-12" combo was $2,549.

30W MODELS

SC-30 - 30W, 1-12" speaker combo, all-tube chassis, preamp: 3 X 12AX7, 1 X EF86, power: 4 X EL84, 5AR4 or 2 X 5V4 rectifiers, two channels, front black control panel, four inputs, seven black knobs (Ch. 1: v, b, t, Ch. 2: v, tone, Both: Cut, MV), hi/lo power switch, impedance selector switch, light gray vinyl covering (later other colors), gray grille cloth, mfg. 1990-98, 2000-current.

1990-98	**N/A**	**$2,500 - 2,750**	**$2,000 - 2,200**
MSR $3,099	**$2,500**	**$2,000 - 2,300**	**$1,500 - 1,750**

Last MSR was $3,249.

This was the first production Matchless amp introduced in mid 1990. Early models used the 5AR4 rectifier. In 1992, burgundy became a color option and in 1993, a multitude of colors were available. Before 1993 effects loop was optional however few were produced with them.

* DC-30 - Similar to the SC-30 except has 2-12" speakers, mfg. 1991-98, 2000-current.

1991-98	**N/A**	**$2,600 - 2,800**	**$2,100 - 2,300**
MSR $3,395	**$2,800**	**$2,250 - 2,500**	**$1,900 - 2,100**

Last MSR was $3,449.

This was the second production Matchless model.

* HC-30 - Similar to the SC-30 in head-unit only, mfg. 1991-98, 2000-current.

	N/A	**$1,750 - 1,950**	**$1,450 - 1,600**
MSR $2,699	**$2,250**	**$1,500 - 1,800**	**$1,200 - 1,350**

Last MSR was $2,899.

* TC-30 - Similar to the SC-30 except has 2-10" speakers, mfg. 1998 only.

N/A	**$2,250 - 2,500**	**$1,950 - 2,100**

Last MSR was $3,449.

* 410-C30 - Similar to the SC-30 except has 4-10" speakers, mfg. 1991-93.

N/A	**$2,750 - 3,250**	**$2,400 - 2,600**

Last MSR was $2,450.

This amp was available on special order after 1993. It was replaced by a head unit with a 4-10" speaker cabinet

RMC-30 - 30W, rack-mount head, all-tube chassis, preamp: 3 X 12AX7, 1 X EF86, power: 4 X EL84, 5AR4 or 2 X 5V4 rectifiers, two channels, front black control panel, four inputs, seven black knobs (Ch. 1: v, b, t, Ch. 2: v, tone, Both: Cut, MV), hi/lo power switch, impedance selector switch, light gray casing with black lettering, mfg. 1991-94.

N/A	**$1,500 - 1,750**	**$1,000 - 1,200**

Last MSR was $1,890.

GRADING	100%	EXCELLENT	AVERAGE

RA-30 - 30W, power amp only, rack mount head, all-tube chassis, front chrome control panel, three ivory chicken head knobs (input level, brilliance, MV), mfg. 1998 only.

	N/A	$1,200 - 1,400	$950 - 1,100

JOHN JORGENSEN SIGNATURE - 30W, 1-12" speaker combo, all tube Class A chassis, preamp: 1 X EF86, 4 X 12AX7, power: 4 X EL84, rectifier: 5AR4 or 2 X 5V4, single channel, front control panel, two inputs, seven white knobs (v, master tone, s, depth, r, cut, MV), hi/lo power switch, speaker phase switch, sparkle red, white, blue or silver covering, black grille cloth, mfg. 1997-98.

	N/A	$2,800 - 3,200	$2,500 - 2,650

This amp was designed with John Jorgensen who was playing with Elton John at the time. It is the only Matchless amp to be made in the 30W configuration with reverb.

CHIEFTAIN SERIES (40W)

CHIEFTAIN CH-40 - 40W, head-unit only, all tube Class A chassis, preamp: 5 X 12AX7, power: 2 X EL34, 5AR4 rectifier, single channel, reverb, front black control panel, single input, seven white knobs (v, b, m, t, brillance, MV, r), effects loop, switchable output impedance, various color covering, gray cloth grille, mfg. 1994-98, 2001-current.

1994-98		N/A	$1,800 - 2,100	$1,500 - 1,650
MSR	$2,449	$2,250	$1,750 - 2,100	$1,400 - 1,600

* **Chieftain CH-112** - Similar to the Chieftain CH-40 execpt in combo form with 1-12" speaker, mfg. 1994-98, 2001-current.

1994-98		N/A	$2,150 - 2,350	$1,650 - 1,800
MSR	$2,749	$2,450	$2,000 - 2,250	$1,500 - 1,750

* **Chieftain CH-212** - Similar to the Chieftain CH-40 except in combo form with 2-12" speakers, mfg. 1994-98, 2001-current.

1994-98		N/A	$2,200 - 2,500	$1,950 - 2,100
MSR	$3,099	$2,650	$2,150 - 2,400	$1,900 - 2,050

* **Chieftain CH-210** - Similar to the Chieftain CH-40 except in combo form with 2-10" speakers, mfg. 1994-98.

	N/A	$2,000 - 2,200	$1,700 - 1,825

Last MSR was $2,749.

* **Chieftain CH-410** - Similar to the Chieftain CH-40 except in combo form with 4-10" speakers, mfg. 1994-98.

	N/A	$2,250 - 2,500	$2,000 - 2,150

Last MSR was $3,099.

MID WATTAGE AMPS (CLUBMAN 35, BRAVE, BOLT 45)

CLUBMAN 35 - 35W, head-unit only, all tube Class A chassis, three variations, current (3rd variation; see below for others) preamp: 2 X 12AX7, 1 X EF86, power: 2 X EL34, 5AR4 rectifier, single channel, front black control panel, two inputs, five white knobs (v, b, t, brilliance, MV), effects loop, various color covering, gray cloth grille, mfg. 1993-98, 2001-current.

1993-98		N/A	$1,050 - 1,250	$850 - 950
MSR	$1,899	$1,250	$950 - 1,100	$700 - 825

There were three variations of this amp produced (as far as electronics). The first variation had a tube chassis of 1 X 6AT6, 1 X 6SH7, 1 X 12AX7, 2 X EL34, and 1 X 5AR4 rectifier. The second variation featured 2 X 12AX7, 1 X 6SH7, 2 X EL34, and 1 X 5AR4 rectifier. The third variation is listed in the model description. By mid 1994, the Clubman 35 was using the third variation.

BRAVE 112 - 40W, 1-12" speaker combo, all tube Class A chassis, preamp: 2 X 12AX7, power: 2 X EL34, 5AR4 rectifier, single channel, front black control panel, two inputs (high/lo), four knobs (v, b, t, MV), various color covering, gray cloth grille, mfg. 1997-98.

	N/A	$1,500 - 1,750	$1,200 - 1,350

Last MSR was $2,249.

This amp was a stipped down version of the Chieftain.

* **Brave 212** - Similar to the Brave 112 except has 2-12" speakers, mfg. 1997-98.

	N/A	$1,550 - 1,800	$1,250 - 1,400

Last MSR was $2,499.

BOLT 45 112 - 45W, 1-12" speaker combo with flip-top head design, all tube chassis with solid-state rectifier, preamp: 2 X 12AX7, power: 2 X EL34, 5U4 rectifier, single channel, front black control panel, five knobs (v, b, t, brilliance, MV), tube/s.s. rectifier switch, various color covering, gray cloth grille, mfg. 1997-98.

	N/A	$2,000 - 2,200	$1,650 - 1,800

Last MSR was $2,799.

This amp was the guitar version of the Thunderman bass amp (see Bass amp section)

* **Bolt 45 115** - Similar to the Bolt 45 112 except has 1-15" speaker, mfg. 1997-98.

	N/A	$2,000 - 2,200	$1,650 - 1,800

Last MSR was $2,799.

HIGH WATTAGE AMPS (HC-85, HC-90, SUPERCHIEF 120)

HC-85 - 85W, head-unit only, all tube chassis, preamp: 3 X 12AX7, 1 X EF86, power: 4 X EL34, rectifier: 2 X 5R4, or 2 X 5U4, two channels, front black control panel, four inputs, seven black knobs (Ch. 1: v, b, t, Ch. 2: v, tone, Both: Cut, MV), hi/lo power switch, impedeance selector switch, light gray vinyl covering (later other colors), gray grille cloth, mfg. 1991-93.

	N/A	$2,200 - 2,400	$1,600 - 1,800

Last MSR was $2,355.

All of these models had a fan installed. In 1992 burgundy became a color option and in 1993, a multitude of colors were available. Before 1993 effects loop was optional. However, few were produced with them. This amp used the same cabinet as the HC-30.

GRADING	100%	EXCELLENT	AVERAGE

HC-90 - Similar to the HC-85 except has 90W output, mfg. 1993 only.

	N/A	$2,500 - 3,000	$2,000 - 2,250

This model replaced the HC-85 before the Superchief 120 replaced this model. Only a handful of the HC-90s were built.

SUPERCHIEF 120 - 120W, head-unit only, all tube chassis, preamp: 3 X 12AX7, power: 4 X EL34, rectifier: 2 X 5U4, single channel, front black control panel, single input, six black knobs (v, b, m, t, brilliance, MV), hi/lo power switch, impedeance selector switch, various color covering, gray grille cloth, mfg. 1994-98.

	N/A	$1,850 - 2,150	$1,400 - 1,600

Last MSR was $2,699.

CHIEF 100 - 100W, head-unit only, all tube chassis, preamp: 5 X 12AX7, power: 4 X EL34, single channel, reverb, front black control panel, single input, seven white knobs (v, b, m, t, brilliance, MV r), various color covering, brown grille (combo only), mfg. 1997-98.

	N/A	$2,000 - 2,300	$1,700 - 1,900

Last MSR was $2,799.

This amp is the version of the Chieftan.

* Chief 100 212 - Similar to the Chief 100 except in combo form with 2-12" speakers, mfg. 1997-98.

	N/A	$2,500 - 2,750	$2,100 - 2,300

Last MSR was $3,349.

* Chief 100 410 - Similar to the Chief 100 except in combo form with 4-10" speakers, mfg. 1997-98.

	N/A	$2,500 - 2,750	$2,100 - 2,250

Last MSR was $3,349.

BASS AMPS "THUNDER AMPS"

THUNDERCHIEF - 200W, head-unit only, all-tube chassis, preamp: 2 X 12AX7, 1 X 12AU7, 1 X 12BH7, power: 4 X KT88, rectifier: 2 X 5U4, single channel, front black control panel, single input, six white knobs (input level, v, b, m, t, MV), deep switch, hi/lo switch, various color covering, gray grille cloth, mfg. 1994-98.

	N/A	$1,500 - 1,750	$1,200 - 1,350

This amp was meant to be mated with 1-15" ported cab or a 4-10" closed back cabinet.

THUNDERMAN 45 - 45W, 1-15" or 2-1" speaker combo in a flip-top design, all tube chassis, preamp: 2 X 12AX7, power: 2 X 6L6, rectifier: 5U4, single channel, front black control panel, four knobs (v, b, t, sensitivity), compression switch, chrome cage over chassis, various color covering, black grille cloth, mfg. 1997-98.

	N/A	$1,700 - 1,900	$1,450 - 1,550

Last MSR was $2,349.

This is a recording bass amp.

THUNDERMAN 100 - 100W, 1-15" or 2-10" speaker combo in a flip-top design, all tube chassis, preamp: 2 X 12AX7, power: 4 X 6L6, rectifier: 5U4, single channel, front black control panel, five knobs (v, b, t, sensitivity, definition), chrome cage over chassis, various color covering, black grille cloth, mfg. 1998 only.

	N/A	$2,200 - 2,500	$1,950 - 2,100

Last MSR was $3,249.

This is the big brother of the Thunderman 45.

SUPERLINER SERIES

The Superliner series is a stripped down Matchless amp. All amps in this series are made on a circuit board and not point-to-point wired. There are no internal lights or lights behind the logo like there are on other Matchless amps. There were two chassis one a 15W that came in a 1-12" cabinet and a 40W in a 2-12" cabinet. In the 15W range was the **Clipper**, a basic amp, the **Skyliner** with two channels, and the **Skyliner Reverb**. The 40W series had the **Slipstream Reverb** with a single channel and reverb, The **Starliner** with two channels, and the **Starliner** Reverb. These models were produced for a short while during 1998.

EXTENSION SPEAKER CABINETS

ESS - 30W capability, 1-12" Celestion speaker, 8 Ohm, open back design, various color covering, gray grille, mfg. 1991-current.

MSR	$679	$400	$300 - 350	$225 - 275

ESD - 40W capability, 2-12" Celestion speakers, 4 Ohm, open back design, various color covering, gray grille, mfg. 1991-current.

MSR	$899	$550	$425 - 500	$350 - 400

ES-210 - 70W capability, 2-10" Celestion speakers, 8 Ohm, open back design, various color covering, gray grille, mfg. 1993-98.

	N/A	$450 - 550	$350 - 400

Last MSR was $799.

ES-410 - 140W capability, 4-10" Celestion speakers, 8 Ohm, open back design, various color covering, gray grille, mfg. 1993-98.

	N/A	$600 - 700	$475 - 550

Last MSR was $999.

ES-412 - 120W capability, 4-12" Celestion speakers, 8 Ohm, open back design, various color covering, gray grille, mfg. 1993-98.

	N/A	$800 - 900	$650 - 725

Last MSR was $1,139.

* ES-412D - Similar to the ES-412 except has a closed back, mfg. 1993-98.

	N/A	$800 - 900	$650 - 725

Last MSR was $1,249.

M

GRADING	100%	EXCELLENT	AVERAGE

ES-1012 - 120W capability, 2-12", & 2-10" Celestion speakers, 8 Ohm, open back design, various color covering, gray grille, mfg. 1993-98.

N/A   **$800 - 900**   **$650 - 725**

Last MSR was $1,139.

EB-115 - 200W capability, 1-15" Celestion speaker, 8 Ohm, closed back, ported design, various color covering, gray grille, mfg. 1997-98.

N/A   **$550 - 650**   **$450 - 500**

Last MSR was $799.

Very few of these models were produced.

EB-410 - 200W capability, 1-15" Celestion speaker, 8 Ohm, closed back, ported design, various color covering, gray grille, mfg. 1997-98.

N/A   **$600 - 700**   **$450 - 525**

Last MSR was $999.

Very few of these models were produced.

MCINTOSH
Amplifiers previously produced in Binghamton, New York.

The McIntosh amplifier company was started in the early 1950's as a company that produce tube amplifier units. They also made loudspeakers, and numerous other audio components. McIntosh is known for having a tube amp that would produce Hi-Fi sound. They made mono and stereo amplifiers from wattages between 30W up to 75W. One of the first McIntosh amplifiers was produced with 6L6 tubes in 1949. Any information on McIntosh amplifiers and products is welcome for upcoming editions of the *Blue Book of Guitar Amplifiers*.

(McIntosh information courtesy: Aspen Pittman: The Tube Amp Book)

MEGA AMPLIFIERS
Amplifiers currently produced in Korea. Mega is part of WooSung Chorus Industries.

Mega is a company from Korea that stands for Megatone. They are a relatively young company and produce mainly small practice, solid-state amplifiers. Recently they have released an acoustic line and a couple tube amplifiers. For the complete lineup and specifications refer to the web site (see Trademark Index).

ELECTRIC AMPLIFIERS

Mega has quite a few series going on. For guitars they have the DL, SL, ML, WL, SL, and VL series. Within each of these series are about four amps that are for guitar and sometimes bass. They also have a line of acoustic amplifiers, the AC series, a line of tube amplifiers, the T series, and the mini-series. They also offer footswitches and effects for their products.

MESA/BOOGIE
Amplifiers currently produced in Petaluma, California.

Mesa Boogie was started by Randall Smith in the early 1970's. Randall had a life-altering experience as a young boy. He was working on a Boy Scout project and for a merit badge he had to go to his scout leader with some wood carvings. The leader took him into this shop, an electronics lab. Cut up his wood carvings in a band saw, and told him, this is what I think of your projects and you! The leader explained to Smith that he wouldn't want that showing up one day when he was making decent stuff and would ask himself, embarassly, "I did that?" Randall took an instant liking from the electronics lab, and began learning from his oddly-made friend. He also took a liking to cars (Mercedes in particular). He would repair cars for friends. In 1966, the hippie movement came through San Francisco, and music was the thing. Randall got a drumset to get into the scene and joined a band. One day an amp blew in the band and shortage of funds made fixing it at a shop not feasible. So Randall took a look at it and fixed it in 15 minutes. The band instantly thought they should open up a shop. Prune Music was then set up in N. Berkeley, California. Randall fixed amps in the back of the store and a lot of great artists would come in such as the Greatful Dead and Jefferson Airplane. Randall also would modify amps for people, and as Smith states, "What started out as a joke became the foundation of the company." Barry Melton's roadies came in and wanted something to be done to make his Princeton amp "melt." Randall stripped the chassis, put a chassis from a 4-10" Bassman, and carefuly installed a 12" JBL D-120 speaker. However the amp still looked stock. He got some regular customer to plug into it and was blown away by the new 60W Bassman/Princeton. Things really changed when Carlos Santana came in and played the concoction. Carlos quoted that, "This little amp really boogies." Viola, the name was established. It is estimated that 200 of these Princetons were converted before Fender stopped supplying Randall with product.

By 1970 Randall left Prune Music, thinking Prune would buy him out. He actually got zero money and was out of a job. So he started fixing cars to get cash and would build amps at night. At this point he formed MESA Engineering as a company that suppliers would take seriously. He built amps for a while until Lee Michaels, an "equipment junkie," got his hands on these new Crown DC300 solid-state power amplifiers. Many companies had tried to make a preamp for this but they all had no tone. Randall was summoned where he worked his magic in the circuitry and came up with the winning combination. Randall had found something and thought it was for Carlos Santana himself. Carlos got an amp and people were coming after Randall wondering if the guy making amps in the shack was for real. The idea behind this amp was cascading preamp, which is having the preamp stages lined up into each other that would produce ehanced distortion and gain.

So Boogie had an amp that they described as an instrument. These Boogies were wood cabinets with a wicker grille. They sort of look like some old chairs or lamps. The first amps were MKI's but they didn't get labled this until the second series (MKII) was released. Boogies had some innovations that a lot of other amp companies failed to see (executives can't build an amplifier, only shuffle paper). Mesa/Boogie amps took off after that and released the MKII-B in the 1980's, and the MKII-C with an improved effects loop and footswitch. In 1989, they developed the dual and triple rectifier heads, which have been a staple throughout the 1990's.

Mesa/Boogie is now producing the Mark IV series (MK IV), along with solo, dual, and triple rectifier heads. They also have a full line of products for all types of guitarists and bass players.

(Mesa/Boogie history courtesy: Ritchie Flieger, Amps!)

ELECTRIC TUBE AMPLIFIERS

Add $150 for Custom color vinyl or grille.

Add $250 for whole hide or Suede leather covering.

Add $350 for embossed custom leather.

GRADING	100%	EXCELLENT	AVERAGE

Add $425 for AAA grade flame or quilted maple built cabinets.

All amps and cabinets that come standard with vinyl are open for the above options. Most of these are custom ordered.

Mesa Boogie is responsible for some fine tube amplifiers in combos, heads, preamps, and power amps. The MK series is listed with the models from MK I up until MK IV. All the current amp combos and heads are listed. There are other preamps and power amps that Mesa builds that aren't listed yet. Look for more information on this and other discontinued models in upcoming editions of the *Blue Book of Guitar Amplifiers*.

MK Models

MK-1 - 100W, 1-12" speaker, all tube chassis, dual channels, cascading gain, front black control panel, two inputs, six black knobs (v1, v2, MV, t, b, m), wood covering, wicker cane grille, mfg. 1970's.

Boogie Mesa
courtesy Dave Rogers

Boogie Mesa
courtesy Dave Rogers

N/A	$1,000 - 1,400	$700 - 850

This amp was also available in some custom coverings including snake skin. This amp was also available in a head-unit only version.

MK-1 REISSUE - 100W, 1-12" Celestion Custom 90 speaker combo, all tube Class A/B chassis, 4 X 12AX7, 1 X 12AT7, power: 4 X 6L6, two modes, reverb, front black control panel, two inputs, six black knobs (v1, v2, MV, t, b, m), half power switch, effects loop, Imbuya hardwood or cream vinyl coverings wicker cane or brown cloth grille, current mfg.

MSR	$1,099	$799	$575 - 650	$475 - 525

* **MK-1 Reissue Head** - Similar to the MK-1 Reissue except in head-unit version, current mfg.

MSR	$999	$725	$550 - 625	$450 - 500

MK-II - Similar to the MK-I original except has added switches for preamp, five band equalizer, some early model's have a solid-state device to replace the preamp tubes, and had internal switch between channels, mfg. late 1970's-early 1980's.

N/A	$825 - 1,050	$600 - 750

* **MK-IIA** - Similar to the MK-II, except featured footswitching channels, mfg. early 1980's.

N/A	$850 - 1,050	$625 - 750

* **MK-IIB** - Similar to the MK-II except, has the patented Simul-Class power tube, mfg. 1980's.

Mesa/Boogie MK IIB
courtesy Savage Audio

Mesa/Boogie MK IIB
courtesy Savage Audio

N/A	$900 - 1,100	$675 - 775

* **MK-IIC** - Similar to the MK-II, except has an improved effects loop and quieter footswitching, mfg. 1980's.

N/A	$900 - 1,100	$675 - 775

MK-III - Similar to the MKIIC, except featured a three channel design, mfg. 1980's.

N/A	$700 - 900	$500 - 550

GRADING	100%	EXCELLENT	AVERAGE

MARK IV (MK IV) - 85W, head-unit only, all tube chassis, preamp: 5 X 12AX7, power: 4 X 6L6, Simul-Class power, three channels, reverb, front black control panel, single input, eighteen black knobs, five band equalizer, half power switch, fan cooled, six-button footswsitch, black vinyl covering, black grille, mfg 1990-current.

MSR	$1,599	$1,150	$850 - 975	$650 - 750

This head unit is available as a short head, medium width, or as a rackmount. The unit is also available in the wood covering, with the wicker grille.

* Mark IV Widebody Combo - Similar to the Mark IV head, except in combo form with 1-12" Celestion Custom 90 speaker, current mfg.

MSR	$1,699	$1,200	$900 - 1,025	$700 - 800

* Mark IV Combo - Similar to the widebody combo, except has an Original EVM 12L speaker, current mfg.

MSR	$1,799	$1,275	$950 - 1,100	$750 - 850

Single, Dual, & Triple Rectifier Series

SINGLE RECTIFIER SOLO 50 HEAD - 50W, head-unit only, all tube Class A/B chassis, preamp: 5 X 12AX7, power: 2 X 6L6, two channels, five modes, front black control panel, two inputs, twelve chrome knobs (g, b, m, t, p, MV per channel), two black knobs (output level, solo level), effects loop, two button footswitch, black covering, polished diamond front, current mfg.

MSR	$1,099	$775	$600 - 700	$475 - 525

RECT-O-VERB - Similar to the Single Rectifier Solo 50 except has reverb circuit with knobs for reverb, current mfg.

MSR	$1,199	$850	$650 - 750	$550 - 600

* Rect-o-verb Combo - Similar to the Rect-O-Verb, except has 1-12" Celestion 90 speaker, current mfg.

MSR	$1,299	$925	$750 - 850	$625 - 675

DUAL RECTIFIER SOLO HEAD - 100W, head-unit only, all tube Class A/B chassis, preamp: 5 X 12AX7, power: 4 X 6L6, rectifiers: 2 X 5U4, three channels, eight modes, front black control panel, two inputs, 14 chrome knobs (g, b, m, t, p, MV per channel), one black knob (output level), rectifier selector, effects loop, five button footswitch, black covering, polished diamond front, current mfg.

MSR	$1,499	$1,050	$725 - 825	$600 - 650

TRIPLE RECTIFIER SOLO HEAD - 150W, head-unit only, all tube Class A/B chassis, preamp: 5 X 12AX7, power: 6 X 6L6, rectifiers: 3 X 5U4, three channels, eight modes, front black control panel, two inputs, 14 chrome knobs (g, b, m, t, p, MV per channel), one black knob (output level), rectifier selector, effects loop, five button footswitch, black covering, polished diamond front, current mfg.

MSR	$1,599	$1,100	$825 - 950	$700 - 750

ROAD KING - 150W (switchable to 100 or 50W), head-unit only, all tube chassis, preamp: 5 X 12AX7, power: 4 X 6L6 & 2 X EL34, rectifiers: 2 X 5U4, four independent channels, reverb, front black control panel, two inputs, 24 silver knobs (g, b, m, t, p, r per channel), five position tube selector, output and solo level controls, effects loop, nine-button footswitch, black covering, current mfg.

MSR	$2,499	$1,750	$1,250 - 1,500	$1,025 - 1,150

Add $149 for the diamond plate front panel.

* Road King Combo - Similar to the Road King head except has 2-12" Celestion Custom 90 speakers, current mfg.

MSR	$2,699	$1,900	$1,400 - 1,600	$1,150 - 1,250

MAVERICK - 35W, head-unit only, all tube Class A chassis, preamp: 6 X 12AX7, power: 4 X EL84, 5AR4 rectifier, two channels, reverb, front black control panel, single input, 13 black knobs (v, t, m, b, r, MV per channel, output level), bright/fat switch, effects loop, fan cooled, one button footswitch, vanilla vinyl covering, tan grille cloth, current mfg.

MSR	$1,099	$775	$600 - 675	$500 - 550

* Maverick 2X12 Combo - Similar to the Maverick head, except in combo version with 2-12" Celestion Vintage 30 speakers, current mfg.

MSR	$1,299	$925	$700 - 800	$600 - 650

* Maverick 4X10 Combo - Similar to the Maverick head, except in combo version with 4-10" Jensen Vintage Alnico speakers, current mfg.

MSR	$1,349	$950	$725 - 825	$600 - 650

BLUE ANGEL - 38W (switchable to 33W & 15W), head-unit only, all tube Class A chassis, preamp: 5 X 12AX7, power: 2 X 6V6, 4 X EL84, 5AR4 rectifier, single channel, reverb, front blue control panel, two inputs, six black knobs (v, t, m, b, r, progressive linkage), effects loop, fan cooled, black covering, black grille cloth, current mfg.

MSR	$999	$725	$575 - 650	$475 - 525

This model has a tube switching feature where either 6V6 or EL84 tubes can be used or they can be combined.

* Blue Angel 1X12 Combo - Similar to the Blue Angel head unit, except in combo version with 1-12" Celestion Custom 90 speaker, current mfg.

MSR	$1,099	$775	$600 - 675	$500 - 550

* Blue Angel 4X10 Combo - Similar to the Blue Angel head unit, except in combo version with 4-10" Jensen Vintage Alnico speakers, current mfg.

MSR	$1,249	$900	$700 - 800	$600 - 650

A 2X10 Combo has been offered as well in the catalog but doesn't appear in any price lists.

Nomad Series

NOMAD 45 - 45W, head-unit only, Dyna-Watt power, all tube chassis, preamp: 5 X 12AX7, power: 4 X EL84, three channels, six modes, reverb, front black control panel, single input, eighteen black knobs, effects loop, five button footswitch, black covering, black grille, current mfg.

MSR	$999	$725	$575 - 650	$475 - 525

GRADING	100%	EXCELLENT	AVERAGE

* Nomad 45 Combo - Similar to the Nomad 45, except in combo form with 1-12" Celestion Vintage 30 speakers, current mfg.

MSR	$1,199	$850	$650 - 750	$550 - 600

NOMAD 55 - 55W, head-unit only, all tube Class A/B chassis, preamp: 5 X 12AX7, power: 2 X 6L6, three channels, six modes, reverb, front black control panel, single input, eighteen black knobs, effects loop, five button footswitch, black covering, black grille, current mfg.

MSR	$1,199	$850	$650 - 750	$550 - 600

This head is available in a medium or long width head.

* Nomad 112 Combo - Similar to the Nomad 55, except in combo form with 1-12" Celestion Custom 90 speaker, current mfg.

MSR	$1,299	$925	$700 - 800	$600 - 650

* Nomad 212 Combo - Similar to the Nomad 55, except in combo form with 2-12" Celestion Custom 90 speakers, current mfg.

MSR	$1,399	$1,000	$775 - 875	$675 - 725

* Nomad 410 Combo - Similar to the Nomad 55, except in combo form with 4-10" Jensen Vintage Alnico speakers, current mfg.

MSR	$1,499	$1,050	$825 - 925	$725 - 775

NOMAD 100 - 100W, head-unit only, all tube Class A/B chassis, preamp: 5 X 12AX7, power: 4 X 6L6, three channels, six modes, reverb, front black control panel, single input, eighteen black knobs, half power switch, effects loop, six button footswitch, black covering, black grille, current mfg.

MSR	$1,499	$1,075	$850 - 950	$725 - 775

* Nomad 212 Combo - Similar to the Nomad 55, except in combo form with 2-12" Celestion Custom 90 speakers, current mfg.

MSR	$1,699	$1,200	$900 - 1,050	$750 - 825

F-Series

All F-Series models here are shown as the combo units. All the units are available as head units as well. Subtract $50 for the F-30 and F-50 models. Subtract $150 for the F-100 head unit.

F-30 - 30W, 1-12" Celestion Vintage 30 speaker combo, all tube Dyna-Watt chassis, preamp: 4 X 12AX7, power: 2 X EL84, two channels, reverb, front black control panel, single input, fourteen black knobs (g, b, m, t, r, MV per channel, pull bright, contour switch), effects loop headphone output, three button footswitch, black covering, black grille cloth, new 2002.

MSR	$799	$575	$450 - 525	$350 - 400

F-50 - 50W, 1-12" Celestion Vintage 30 speaker combo, all tube Class A/B chassis, preamp: 4 X 12AX7, power: 2 X 6L6, two channels, reverb, front black control panel, single input, fourteen black knobs (g, b, m, t, r, MV per channel, pull bright, contour switch), effects loop headphone output, three button footswitch, black covering, black grille cloth, new 2002.

MSR	$999	$725	$550 - 650	$450 - 500

F-100 - 100W, 2-12" Celestion Vintage 30 speakers combo, all tube Class A/B chassis, preamp: 4 X 12AX7, power: 4 X 6L6, two channels, reverb, front black control panel, single input, fourteen black knobs (g, b, m, t, r, MV per channel, pull bright, contour switch), effects loop headphone output, three button footswitch, black covering, black grille cloth, casters, new 2002.

MSR	$1,299	$925	$750 - 850	$650 - 700

Misc. Models

HEARTBREAKER - 100W, head-unit only, all tube Class A/B chassis, preamp: 7 X 12AX7, power: 4 X 6L6, 5AR4 rectifier, two channels, black front control panel, two inputs, eleven black knobs (v, t, m, b, r per channel, overall level), half-power switch, various other switches and buttons, one button footswitch, crocodile skin covering, brown cloth grille, mfg. current mfg.

MSR	$1,499	$1,050	$800 - 925	$650 - 725

* Heartbreaker 2X12 Combo - Similar to the Nomad 55, except in combo form with 4-10" Jensen Vintage Alnico speakers, current mfg.

MSR	$1,699	$1,200	$925 - 1,050	$775 - 850

Bass Models

Mesa/Boogie has had a couple of different designs of bass amps and cabinets over the years. Currently they offer the Walkabout bass amp, a 2-rack space amp, the M-Pulse 360 and M-Pulse 600, also 2 rack spaces, and the Bass 400+, which takes four rack spaces. All of these have preamp tube chassis and a good part of them have tube power output as well. Mesa also offers the Basis M2000, which is a 600W unit. For more model listing information and options refer to the Mesa/Boogie web site.

In the bass series there are two different series of bass speaker cabinets. The Powerhouse is the bottom line amps and the Roadready are the more elaborate designs with more options. These cabinets are available in quite a few configurations and wattage.

GUITAR SPEAKER CABINETS

Mesa/Boogie makes several different speaker cabinets to match up to the guitar heads (For bass heads refer to the Bass series under Electric Tube Amplifiers.) Boogie has the Thiele design, which are cabinets with closed backs and ported fronts. These come standard with a Celestion 90 speaker at $299 retail, and with an upgradeable cabinet with a 200W EVM 12L speaker at $419. The same cabinets come with an open back (non-Thiele design) for $20 less per piece, respectively. They are also available in a widebody version for the same price as the Thiele designs.

The three-quarter back designs come with a turned 3/4 closed back and include 12" Celestion Custom 90 speakers in configurations of 1-12" (90W), 2-12" (180W), and 4-12" (360W). Prices are $299, $499, and $799 respectively.

The Rectifier Cabinets have the most configurations currently offered by Mesa/Boogie. These cabinets start with a 12" Celestion Vintage 30 at $299 and work all they way up to a 4-12" cabinet with Celestions and retail for $799. For a complete listing of these cabinets visit the Mesa/Boogie web site.

MILL HILL

Amplifiers and other audio equipment currently produced in Camarillo, California.

Mill Hill creations was founded by Johnathon E. Glynn in California. Mill Hill claims to build the "World's Finest Amplifier." They currently have four different models, the Juma, Love, Summer, and Phoenix Rising. These are all tube amplifiers that are built to the finest quality. Mill Hill Creations also do resorations and modifications to other amplifiers and do some hot-rodding. For more information on John, or Mill Hill Creations, please refer to the web site (see Trademark Index).

MOTION SOUND

Amplifiers currently produced in Salt Lake City, Utah.

Motion Sound was established in 1994 by three people, one an electronics engineer and musician, one a mechanical engineer and the other a financial guy. John H. Fischer is the current president. At the 1995 NAMM show, they introduced the Pro-3 a rotating hybrid amplifier. This unit could produce the large sound of big rotating systems (such as a Leslie) in a much smaller model. Later on they started making products for guitars. In 2001, John Johnson joined the team to help market. Currently Motion Sound has these rotating horn units for all types of applications.

HYBRID AMPLIFIERS

Motion Sound built their foundation off of rotating horn cabinets, built mainly as speaker cabinets. Later on they started making Keyboard amplifiers, and now they have entered the acoustic and electric guitar market. The Pro-3, which was their first amp, is still offered but as the Pro-3T model. Motion Sound compares it to the Leslie 147. All amps have the 12AX7 tube in the preamp circuit with a solid-state power amp.

The guitar amps offered by Motion Sound are the **AR-112**, which is a 100W electric rotary guitar amp with a 12" speaker and has reverb. The **SR-112** is a speaker cabinet that can be hooked up to the AR-112 or can be powered by any other amplifier as well. It features a 12" speaker that can handle 150W, and full rotary speed control of the unit. The **AG-110H** is a electric acoustic amplifier with a unique rotary speaker that can produce sound in several directions.

MULTIVOX

Amplifiers previously produced in New York City and Hauppauge, New York.

The Multivox company was started in the late 1940's by Peter Sorkin Music to manufacture amplifiers as a subsidary to the company. The company produced amplifiers for many years until around 1984. They also produced some guitars and other products under the same name. A lot of products were produced in the same factory Multivox was in, just under different names (Strad-O-Lin & Premier). The Multivox company produced many patents as far as amplifiers, which included the "Organ-Tone Tremolo" circuit. In the 1960's Multivox broke away from the Sorkin company and in 1970 when Sorkin closed down, Multivox kept going. They produced amplifiers throughout the 1970's and stopped producing amplifiers in 1984. Any information on the Multivox trademark and models is welcome for upcoming editions of the *Blue Book of Guitar Amplifiers*.

ELECTRIC AMPLIFIERS

Multivox start out with tube amplifiers in the late 1940's and by the time the company closed its doors in 1984, they were producing mostly solid-state amplifiers. Needless to say there are a lot of models and information during those 35 years or so. Most of the models that show up on today's market are the models that were built in the 1970's and 1980's. These amps can usually be landed in the range of $25-100 in excellent shape (in my book, that's a buy!). These amps will typically show up in pawn shops and such for dirt cheap prices.

Early models were the Model 50 and Model 110. These two amps were introduced around 1948 and had an 8" and 10" speaker respectively. The Premier series was first introduced in the late 1940's with the models Premier 66 (17W, 1-12" speaker, tremolo), Premier 88, and the Premier 120 (20W, 1-12" speaker). From then on pretty much all Multivox amps were of the Premier series. These amps rarely show up on the second-hand market, so a price is hard to come up with. For the more elaborate models (such as high-wattage, dual speakers, and tremolo), will add a premium over other models.

MUSICLORD

Amplifiers and speaker cabinets currently produced in Kent (Seattle), Washington.

Musiclord was started in 1984 by the same man who is president today, Glen Huttenlocker. They produce amplifiers and speaker cabinets in a variety of color coverings. Queensryche and Tim Bachman are a couple of artists that use Musiclord products. Musiclord has expanded steadily since their birth in 1984 and their products are now distributed across the world. They currently have guitar and bass amplifiers along with speaker cabinets. Most cabinets and amplifiers can be ordered to the customers specs, including the covering color. For more information and how to order refer to the Musiclord website (see Trademark Index).

MUSICMAN

Amplifiers previously produced in Fullerton, California during the 1970's and early 1980's.

The Music Man company was formed in March of 1972 by two ex-Fender executives, Tom Walker and Forrest White. They started to produce amplifiers keeping Fender ideas in mind. The amps were very succesful early and they decided to release a solid body guitar. In 1976, they released their first guitar, designed and built by Leo Fender. After abiding by a ten year "no compete" clause in the sale of the Fender Electric Instrument Company in 1965, Music Man produced guitars up until 1979. Music Man made amplifiers throughout the 1970's and kept producing up until 1984. Ernie Ball bought out Music Man in 1984 and they stopped producing amplifiers at this time.

Music Man produced some of the first hybrid amplifiers. This meaning the preamp was often tube and the power section was driven by a solid-state component. Early models did have power tube drivers. Typically the Music Man amplifiers weren't a good solution for overdrive and hard rock applications. They generally sounded best for country and jazz applications.

ELECTRIC TUBE AMPLIFIERS

Music Man did something that just about every other company out there could learn a thing or two from. There models were named after the configuration of the amp. The speaker configuration was listed first followed by the wattage. If there are any letters following speaker configs, it indicated either an RP, which stood for Reverb Phase, or an RD, which indicated Reverb Distortion. Therefore not can you only identify the model of the amp on the grille cloth, but it stated the configurations of the amplifier as well. Example: 112 RD Fifty is a 50W amp with a 12" speaker and reverb distortion.

Generally the early models (with tube power sections), would have the wattage written out in lettering (i.e. Sixty Five instead of 65). These are typically the better sounding ones, which means more collectible as well.

GRADING	100%	EXCELLENT	AVERAGE

Fifty Watt Models

110 RD FIFTY - 50W, 1-10" speaker, tube chassis, preamp: 7025, power: 2 X 6L6, dual channels, tremolo, reverb, front black control panel, single input, separate bass, treble, and volume controls, reverb, black covering, gray grille, mfg. 1980-83.

	N/A	$350 - 400	$250 - 300

112 RD FIFTY - 50W, 1-12" speaker, tube chassis, preamp: 7025, power: 2 X 6L6, dual channels, tremolo, reverb, front black control panel, single input, separate bass, treble, and volume controls, reverb, black or custom color covering, gray grille, mfg. 1980-83.

Ernie Ball Music Man Model 112 RD   Ernie Ball Music Man Model 112 RD

	N/A	$375 - 425	$275 - 325

RD FIFTY HEAD - Similar to the 112 RD fifty combo units except in head version only, mfg. 1973-1983.

	N/A	$275 - 325	$200 - 225

Sixty-Five Watt Models

112 SIXTY FIVE - 65W, 1-12" speaker, tube chassis, preamp: solid-state, power: 2 X 6L6, dual channels, tremolo, front black control panel, four inputs, separate bass, treble, and volume controls, black covering, gray grille, mfg. 1978-1983.

	N/A	$350 - 425	$250 - 300

* 112 RD Sixty Five - Similar to the 112 Sixty Five, except has reverb distortion, mfg. 1978-1983.

	N/A	$375 - 425	$275 - 325

* 112 RP Sixty Five - Similar to the 112 RD Sixty Five, except has built in phaser, mfg. 1978-1983.

	N/A	$375 - 425	$275 - 325

* Sixty Five Head - Similar to the 112RD Sixty Five, except in head-unit only, mfg. 1973-1983.

	N/A	$275 - 325	$275 - 325

115 SIXTY FIVE - 65W, 1-15" speaker, tube chassis, preamp: solid-state, power: 2 X 6L6, dual channels, tremolo, reverb, front black control panel, four inputs, separate bass, treble, and volume controls, reverb control, black covering, gray grille, mfg. 1978-1983.

	N/A	$325 - 400	$225 - 275

410 SIXTY FIVE - 65W, 4-10" speaker, tube chassis, preamp: solid-state, power: 2 X 6L6, dual channels, tremolo, reverb, front black control panel, four inputs, separate bass, treble, and volume controls, reverb control, black covering, gray grille, mfg. 1973-1983.

	N/A	$450 - 550	$350 - 400

Seveny-Five Watt Models

410 SEVENTY FIVE - 75W, 4-10" speakers, preamp: solid-state, power: 2 X 6L6, dual channels, tremolo, reverb, front black control panel, four inputs, separate bass, treble, and volume controls, reverb control, black covering, gray grille, mfg. 1981-1983.

	N/A	$450 - 550	$350 - 400

One-Hundred Watt Models

112 RD ONE HUNDRED - 100W, 1-12" speaker, tube chassis, preamp: solid-state, power: 2 X 6L6, dual channels, tremolo, reverb, front black control panel, four inputs, separate bass, treble, and volume controls, reverb control, black covering, gray grille, mfg. 1978-1983.

	N/A	$375 - 450	$275 - 325

GRADING	100%	EXCELLENT	AVERAGE

* 112 RP One Hundred - Similar to the 112 RD One Hundred except has built in phaser, mfg. 1973-1983.

Ernie Ball Music Man Model 112 RP
courtesy Willie's American Guitars

	N/A	$400 - 475	$300 - 350

One-Hundred Thirty Watt Models

210 HD 130 - 130W, 2-10" speakers, preamp: 7025, power: 4 X 6CA7, dual channels, reverb, tremolo, front black control panel, four inputs (two per channel), 12 black and silver knobs (Ch. 1: v, b, m, t, Ch. 2: v, b, m, t, r, s, i, MV), effects loop, black covering. gray grille, mfg. 1973-1983.

	N/A	$450 - 525	$350 - 400

212 HD 130 - 130W, 2-12" speakers, preamp: 7025, power: 4 X 6CA7, dual channels, reverb, tremolo, front black control panel, four inputs (two per channel), 12 black and silver knobs (Ch. 1: v, b, m, t, Ch. 2: v, b, m, t, r, s, i, MV), effects loop, black covering. gray grille, mfg. 1973-1983.

	N/A	$475 - 575	$375 - 425

HD 130 - 130W, head-unit only, preamp: 7025, power: 4 X 6CA7, dual channels, reverb, tremolo, front black control panel, four inputs (two per channel), 12 black and silver knobs (Ch. 1: v, b, m, t, Ch. 2: v, b, m, t, r, s, i, MV), effects loop, black covering. gray grille, mfg. 1973-1983.

	N/A	$275 - 325	$200 - 235

One-Hundred Fifty Watt Models

210 HD 150 - 150W, 2-10" speakers, preamp: 7025, power: 4 X 6CA7, dual channels, reverb, tremolo, front black control panel, four inputs (two per channel), 12 black and silver knobs (Ch. 1: v, b, m, t, Ch. 2: v, b, m, t, r, s, i, MV), effects loop, black covering. gray grille, mfg. 1973-1983.

	N/A	$500 - 600	$400 - 450

Section N

NARB

Amplifiers previously produced in England during the mid 1970's.

Narb is another amplifier that Marshall produced for a dealer with a different name on the amp. Sound City was a dealer in Charing Cross Road, London, wanted a Marshall amp, but didn't want to call it a Marshall. Ken Bran was Jim Marshall's second hand man for many years. They decided to call it a Bran (they used Jim's last name, might as well use Ken's), however Bran is a type of cereal and they didn't want to be associated with that. So an inventive mind and some quick thinking went into action, and they turned Bran around to come up with Narb. So the Narb amplifier name came from Ken Bran's last name spelled backwards. Another reason for building these Narb amplifiers were to use up some old components around. However, there were only a few of these made (less than 50), and are extremely rare. The Narb name stuck around for a only a short while before it was retired.

(History courtesy Michael Doyle, The History of Marshall)

ELECTRIC TUBE AMPLIFIERS

Once again (like CMI and Park) these are Marshall amplifiers with different identification. They made a handful of amp heads, and a speaker cabinet with 4-12" speakers. I've only seen to Narb amplifier heads. Serial number 0008 is owned by the good fellows up at solidbodyguitars.com Inc. in Mounds View, Minnesota, and 0011 is owned by Aspen Pittman. Both of these models are 100W heads with tremolo. This would be a rare Marshall find, let alone the Narb brand. Needless to say pricing on the second hand market is very hard to determine. The *Blue Book of Guitar Amplifiers* stongly suggests keeping options open when either selling or buying a Narb. These amps are much more valuable to a collector than to someone who would want to play it.

100W TREMOLO - 100W, head-unit only, all tube chassis, 4 X EL34 power tubes, dual channels, front silver control panel, four inputs, eight black knobs (p, b, m, t, v1, v2, s, i), black covering, white piping, mfg. circa 1974.

Narb Tremolo 100w
courtesy solidbodyguitar.com, Inc.

Narb Tremolo 100w
courtesy solidbodyguitar.com, Inc.

Pricing on this amp is difficult to establish on the secondary market.

NATIONAL

Amplifiers previously produced in Chicago, Illinois under the company Valco.

The National name goes way back to the early 1920's, when John and Rudy Dopyera started producing banjos in Southern California. Guitarist George Beauchamp approached the company with an idea on how to solve the lack of volume in the instruments of the vaudevill orchestra. His idea was taking an aluminum resonator in a guitar body to amplify the sound. With this idea, John Dopyera and four brothers formed National in 1925. This was the birth of possibly the greatest resonator guitar company.

National ran into financial hardship because of the Depression in the early 1930's. Louis Dopyera owned more than 50% of Dobro and bought out National in the early 1930's. He merged the two companies together and called in National-Dobro. In 1936, the company was moved to Chicago, Illinois, where many companies were mass producing instruments (i.e. Kay, Harmony). Victor Smith, Al Frost, and Louis concerned in 1943 to change the name of the company to VALCO (The initials of their three first names). Valco worked on war materials during WWII, and returned to start producing instruments afterwards.

Amplifiers first appeared in the 1930's and had a strikingly similar appearance to the acousic resonator instruments that they also produced. Some of these amps are known as "chicken feet." In the early 1940's, National began to produce amps with their National badge as the front grille. They also had some models with elaborate designs on the grille, such as the moon and stars.

After the war, Valco began producing amplifiers under the name National. Valco also produced amplifiers for other companys including Super, Oahu, Gretsch and Airline. Most of these amps were built between the late 1940's and the 1960's, and are typically mates to other companies amplifiers only with a different name. National had some models called the Dynamic, Glenwood, and the Newport 50.

In 1969 or 1970, Valco went out of business. The assests were auctioned off, and the rights to the National trademark were bought by the Chicago, Illinois-based importers Strum'n Drum. Since Valco went out of business, there was no one to make amplifiers anymore, and production was halted. Only the National brand survived for guitars. This company had been importing Japanese guitars under the Norma trademark. National instruments are still being produced today, but amplifiers were never to be seen again.

(Early company history courtesy Bob Brozeman, the History and Artistry of National Resonator Instruments.)

ELECTRIC TUBE AMPLIFIERS

Since the early National amplifiers are tough to come up with information on, we have them grouped into the early and later models. The early models run from around 1930 up until the late 1950's. The later models have amps from the early 60's until the company's end in the late 1960's.

Early Models

National has amps going back to the 1930's with their original acoustic resonator cover over the speaker. It is a lot tougher to find these amplifiers the older they are. The Chicken Foot amps are a rare find, but it's tough. Prices on these amps can have a range from anywhere to $150-500. Later models include the Stagester and the Tremo-tone. Information is welcome on National amps for further editions of the *Blue Book of Guitar Amplifiers*.

GRADING	100%	EXCELLENT	AVERAGE

NATIONAL DOBRO 100 - 40W, 1-12" speaker, all tube chassis, single channel, three inputs, three knobs, brown wood covering, National badge style grille, mfg. 1940's.

National Dobro

National Dobro

N/A	$300 - 400	$225 - 275

The amp picture isn't stock from factory. The vibrato shown on the back panel was added sometime in the 1950's.

Later Models

Later models are the amps that were made from about 1960 until National's (Valco's) end. National also tried their smarts with a solid-state amp line around 1965. They made an FET head and a Budget combo model. They probably made some other models of this era, but no information is to be had about them. There are two models the Val Trem and the Val Verb that we don't have info on. Look for more information on these models in upcoming editions.

SMALL MODEL (NO MODEL NAME) - Wattage unknown, 1-8" Jensen speaker, three tube chassis, 12AX7, 6V6GT, 5Y3GT rectifier, single channel, front chrome control panel, three inputs, one volume knob, black with random colored stiching covering, brown grille, mfg. 1960's.

National Small
courtesy George McGuire

National Small
courtesy George McGuire

N/A	$225 - 275	$165 - 195

DYNAMIC - 20W, 2-8" Jensen speakers, all tube chassis, preamp: 2 X 6EU7, power: 2 X 6973, 5Y3GT rectifier, single channel, front chrome control panel, three inputs (1 treble, 2 regular), two knobs (v, tone), black with random colored stiching covering, brown grille, mfg. 1960's.

National Dynamic
courtesy George McGuire

National Dynamic
courtesy George McGuire

N/A	$300 - 375	$200 - 250

GRADING	100%	EXCELLENT	AVERAGE

VALPRO - Wattage unknown, 2-8" Jensen speakers, all tube chassis, preamp: tubes unknown, dual channels, front chrome control panel, four inputs (2 per channel), five knobs, black with random colored stiching covering, brown grille, mfg. 1960's.

| | N/A | $325 - 400 | $225 - 275 |

NEWPORT 50 - 50W, 2-10" Jensen speakers, all tube chassis, preamp: 4 X 12AX7, power: 3 X 6973, 5Y3GT rectifier, dual channels, reverb, tremolo, front chrome control panel, four inputs (2 per channel), eight knobs (Ch. 1: v, tone, Ch. 2: r, i, v, tone), chrome rear control panel with tremolo speed, tone switches, black with random colored stiching covering, brown grille, mfg. 1960's.

National Newport
courtesy George McGuire

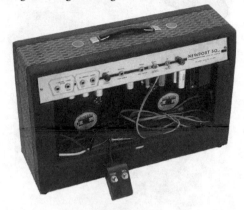

National Newport
courtesy George McGuire

| | N/A | $350 - 425 | $250 - 300 |

GLENWOOD - Wattage unknown, 2-12" or 2-10" Jensen speakers, all tube chassis, preamp: 3 X 6EU7, 2 X 12AX7, 1 X 6973 power: 2 X 6L6, 5U4 rectifier, dual channels, front chrome control panel, four inputs (in rear, 2 per channel), eight knobs (Ch. 1: v, t, b, Ch. 2: r, i, v, b, t), chrome rear control panel with tremolo speed, tone switches, black with random colored stiching covering, brown grille, mfg. 1960's.

National Glenwood
courtesy George McGuire

National Glenwood
courtesy George McGuire

| | N/A | $400 - 500 | $300 - 350 |

N

NAYLOR

Amplifiers previously produced in Detroit Michigan.

Joe Naylor was co-founder of J.F. Naylor Engineering. The company produced amplifiers for a while in the late 1990's before Joe left the company to start Reverend in 1997. Naylor made fine quality amplifiers that were all-tube of course. Reverend now produces both guitars and amplifiers.

ELECTRIC TUBE AMPLIFIERS

SUPER CLUB 38 - Wattage unknown, 1-12" speaker combo, all tube chassis, top control panel, various knobs, wood covering, brown grille, mfg. 1990's.

Naylor Super Club 38
courtesy S. P. Fjestad

Naylor Super Club 38
courtesy S. P. Fjestad

This model is tough to put a price on since there is little second market on them. This model is signed by Joe Naylor and appears to be the fifth model produced.

NEMESIS

Amplifiers and speaker cabinets currently produced in Montrose, Minnesota. Nemesis are produced and distributed by Eden Electronics.

Nemesis makes bass amp heads, combos, and speaker enclosures. All of their amps are FET powered, and their speaker cabinets are of the finest quality. The cabinets are made of composite materials instead of plywood. All of their equipment is lighter, stronger, and sounds better, than the typical cabinets that are out on the market. They have quite a few models of speaker cabinets in different configurations. The flagship amp head is a 600W RMS unit with some good features. All combo models feature a 225W amp head in a varation of different speakers. For more information visist the Eden Electronics web site or contact them directly (see Trademark Index).

Section O

OAHU

Amplifiers previously distributed by the Oahu Publishing Company of Cleveland, Ohio. The Oahu trademark was established circa 1930.

The Oahu Publishing Company first offered Hawaiian and Spanish style guitars, lap steels, sheet music, and other accessories during the 1930's. As electric guitars began to take off during the late 1930's, Oahu began to distribute amplifiers as well. With the World War coming on in the 1940's, the amps really didn't take off until the late 1940's and the 1950's. Most of the amplifiers were produced during this time. Catalogs stress the fact that the company was a "Major Music Distributor," which still poses the question who actually produced these amplifiers (and guitars). There have been some reissues made by other companies in recent years that include the names Jester and Valco.

GRADING	100%	EXCELLENT	AVERAGE

ELECTRIC TUBE AMPLIFIERS

OAHU LAPSTEEL

Oahu Lapsteel
courtesy Harry Browning

Oahu Lapsteel
courtesy Harry Browning

OAHU AMPLIFIER (NO MODEL NAME)

TONEMASTER 112 - 20W, 1-12" Rola speaker, all tube chassis: preamp: 1 X 6SL7, 1 X 1273, power: 2 X 6V6, 5Y3 rectifier, single channel, three input jacks, one volume and tone knob, light-bulb for a Oahu sign on amp, covering unknown, mfg. late 1940's-early 1950's.

	N/A	$200 - 300	$125 - 175

* Tonemaster 230K - Similar to the Tonemaster, mfg. late 1940's-early 1960's.

	N/A	$200 - 250	$100 - 150

OLIVER

Amplifiers previously produced in Westbury, New York during the late 1960's.

The Oliver Sound Company was started after Jess Oliver was left Ampeg and went to start his own business. The company was started with Oliver and a technician from Ampeg, Gene Andre. Most of these amps were based off of Ampeg's designs. The Oliver Powerflex was one of the best designs that they had, which would elevate the head out of the speaker cabinet on a platform. They also had some combo amps, and a rotating speaker cabinet. The elevating platform amp (P500) could draw up to $1,000 in excellent shape.

(History courtesy: Gregg Hopkins & Bill Moore, Ampeg: The Story Behind the Sound)

ORANGE

Amplifiers previously currently produced in London England. The Orange trademark was established in 1968 and lasted until the mid 1980's. The Orange trademark was revived in 1993 and is currently producing amplifiers to this day under the Orange Musical Electronic Company Limited in London. Orange amps are distributed in the U.S. by the Orange Musical Electronic Company Limited in Atlanta, Georgia. Solid-state amplifiers are produced in Korea.

The Orange amplifier trademark was established by Mr. Clifford Cooper in September of 1968. Cooper started a shop in London, England selling musical insturments. Being a young man and not widely known, he was unable to develop many dealerships in his shop. So Cooper decided to build amplifiers if he couldn't get any to sell. Cooper hired some of the best engineers, including Matthew Mathias, around to build amplifiers, and with acquiring some vinyl in the color orange (maybe the price was right?), they started covering the amps with this fabric. Instead of naming the company Cooper, he named it after the color the amps sported, and Orange amplifiers were born. There were amps sold as "Matamp" in the north part of England. This was similar to the Marshall and Park situation.

The success of these amplifiers had to do with the fact that they were covered in this oddly colored vinyl, but the fact they were really decent sounding amps. It really didn't take long for Orange amps to take off in the 1970's when solid-state products were being introduced. Solid-state being innovative (but we all know where they stand next to good old valves!), people needed POWER! So, Orange began making PA units that were full of power, along with bass combos, large guitar amps, mixing boards, disco units, & other products. Orange really had their heyday in the 1970's.

The 1980's didn't do Orange amplification any favors, that's for sure. With a troubled economy, solid-state became a useful option, finally, and with synthesizers taking over, Orange went into a tailspin. Besides Marshall, it seems that every tube-making amplifier company either had to resort to solid-state, or check to see if McDonald's was hiring. For a good part of the 1980's Orange condensed considerably and didn't do much business at all. As the 1980's drew to a close (thank God) and people began to appreciate the warmth of a valve amp, there was opportunity for the company. New amplifiers began to show up in 1993 and in 1994 Orange, in a sense, was revived. In 1997, with the introduction of the "OTR" system, which was a completely new innovation for Orange, put the company back where they wanted to be. Orange continues to produce orange colored tube amps to this day, with the founder, Clifford Cooper, now CEO of the company.

Orange amplifiers have several identification features. Unless you are color-blind, the orange coloring of these amps are one-of-a-kind (besides some Marshall's) and can be identified from a football field distance away. If you're a little hungover and have a tough time with this, here are some other features about these amps. They typically tend to have brown cloth grilles with the Orange logo with the "Voice of the World" symbol above it. The controls on early models are kind of cool. Instead of just the typical descriptions of what the controls do they were also accompanied by a picture. The tone controls had treble and bass clef symbols for each one. The H.F. Drive control had a fist punching, the gain has a speaker blaring, the echo has two mountains with a sound bouncing off of it, and power a lightning bolt.

(Source for Orange history: www.orange-amps.com by Mo Morgan the Media Manager at Orange)

ELECTRIC TUBE AMPLIFIERS

Orange has produced many amplifiers in the heyday of rock & roll in the 1970's, but we can't forget what they are producing these days. They have recently produced the OTR amp, and have an entire line of new amplifiers. This section is broken up into the early model's, such as the OR120, and the AD series.

Early Orange Models

OR120 - 120W, head-unit only, all tube chassis, preamp: 3 X ECC83, power: 4 X EL34, front silver control panel, two inputs (hi and lo), five black knobs (F.A.C., b, t, H.F. Drive, g), echo return and send jacks, orange vinyl covering, brown grille, mfg. 1968-1981.

Orange OR120
courtesy Willie's American Guitars

Orange OR120
courtesy Willie's American Guitars

N/A	$900 - 1,200	$600 - 700

* OR120 Combo - Similar to the OR120 except in combo form with 2-12" speakers, mfg. 1968-1981.

N/A	$950 - 1,250	$650 - 750

OR80 - 80W, head-unit only, all tube chassis, preamp: 3 X ECC83 (7025), power: 2 X EL34, front silver control panel, two inputs (hi and lo), five black knobs (F.A.C., b, t, H.F. Drive, g), echo return and send jacks, orange vinyl covering, brown grille, mfg. 1968-1981.

N/A	$850 - 1,025	$600 - 750

"AD" Series & Custom Shop Models

AD15 (#AD1512) - 15W, 1-12" Celestion Vintage 30 speaker, all tube Class A chassis combo, preamp: 2 X ECC83, power: 2 X EL84, GZ34 rectifier, single channel, top silver control panel, single input, five black knobs (g, b, m, t, MV), standby, 8 & 16 Ohm external speaker jacks, orange vinyl covering, light brown grille, mfg. 2000-current.

MSR	$1,089	$775	$550 - 650	$425 - 475

GRADING	100%	EXCELLENT	AVERAGE

* AD15 (#AD1510) - Similar to the AD1512 except has 1-10" Jensen Alnico speaker, mfg. 2000-current.

| MSR | $1,059 | $750 | $525 - 625 | $425 - 475 |

AD30H - 30W, all tube chassis Class A head-unit, preamp: 2 X ECC83, power: 4 X EL84, GZ34 rectifier, single channel, front silver control panel, two inputs, five black knobs (MV, t, m, b, g), standby, orange vinyl covering, mfg. 2000-current.

| MSR | $1,099 | $800 | $600 - 700 | $475 - 525 |

* AD30R - Similar to the AD30H except is in combo form with 2-12" Celestion Vintage 30 speakers and 3-spring reverb circuit with an additional black knob, mfg. 2000-current.

| MSR | $1,539 | $1,100 | $850 - 975 | $700 - 775 |

AD30HTC - 30W, all tube chassis Class A head-unit, preamp: 4 X ECC83, power: 4 X EL84, GZ34 rectifier, dual channels, single input, ten black knobs (for each channel: MV, t, m, b, g), channel switch, orange vinyl covering, mfg. 2001-current.

| MSR | $1,299 | $900 | $725 - 850 | $575 - 650 |

* AD30TC - Similar to the AD30HTC except is in combo form with 2-12" Celestion Vintage 30 speakers, mfg. 2001-current.

| MSR | $1,819 | $1,325 | $1,000 - 1,175 | $850 - 950 |

AD140TC - 140W, all tube chassis Class AB head-unit, preamp: 4 X ECC83, power: 4 X EL34, dual channels, single input, ten black knobs (for each channel: MV, t, m, b, g), channel switch, orange vinyl covering, mfg. 2001-current.

| MSR | $1,869 | $1,350 | $1,000 - 1,200 | $850 - 950 |

AD200B (#AD200B) - 200W, all tube chassis bass head-unit, hand wired point-to-point, preamp: 1 X ECC81, 1 X ECC83, power: 4 X 6550, single channel, front silver control panel, two inputs (high and low), five black knobs (MV, t, m, b, g), standby, orange vinyl covering, mfg. 2000-current.

| MSR | $2,329 | $1,650 | $1,250 - 1,450 | $1,000 - 1,100 |

This amp is now part of the Custom Shop.

RETRO 50 - 50W, all tube chassis head-unit, hand wired point-to-point, single channel, front silver control panel, two inputs (high and low), five black knobs (MV, t, m, b, g), standby, 8 & 16 Ohm speaker outputs, orange vinyl covering, mfg. 2000-current.

| MSR | $2,499 | $1,799 | $1,400 - 1,600 | $1,150 - 1,250 |

This model is part of the Custom Shop.

Orange Speaker Cabinets

Currently Orange offers four speaker cabinets, two guitar and two bass. When Orange was making cabinets back in the 1970's they also had a variety of models. It isn't known to us how many they exactly had, but the 4 X 12" was by far most popular. Typically you can find these cabinets with original speakers in the $500-700 price range, for excellent condition. More information will be included about these cabinets in upcoming editions of the *Blue Book of Guitar Amplifiers*. An orange half stack can be found around $2,000 and even up to $3,000 for a full stack.

Orange OR120 Half Stack
courtesy Willie's American Guitars

Orange 4-12" Speaker Cabinets
courtesy Willie's American Guitars

The current Orange guitar amplifiers are the **4 X 12 (Model # PPC412)** and the **2 X 12 (Model # PPC212)**. Both cabinets are equipped with Vintage Celestion 30 speakers and have a plywood shell faced with 18 ply birch. The 4 X 12 retails for $1,069 and the 2 X 12 retails for $789. The bass cabinets are available in a 4 X 10 (Model OBC 410) or a 1X 15" (Model OBC 115) version. The 4 X 10" cabinet has 4-10" speakers and a HF horn which can handle 600W. This retails for $1,169. The 1 X 15 cabinet has 1-15" speaker, which can handle 400W. This prices at $899. The bass cabinets are constructed in the custom shop and also have dark brown grille cloth. For cabinets in 100% condition, value can be approximately 50% of retail price.

ELECTRIC SOLID-STATE AMPLIFIERS

Orange makes practice amplifiers in solid-state form. These are constructed in Korea and are labeled the "Crush" series. These are small amps with all the features of the big boys at affordable prices.

Crush Series (Solid-State)

CRUSH 10 (CR10) - 10W, 1-6" heavy-duty speaker, solid-state combo, single channel, top silver control panel, single input, six black knobs (g, v, MV, l, m, h), headphone jack, orange vinyl covering, light brown grille, mfg. 2000-current.

| MSR | $99 | $75 | $50 - 65 | $35 - 45 |

GRADING	100%	EXCELLENT	AVERAGE

CRUSH 15 (CR15) - 15W, 1-8" heavy-duty speaker, solid-state combo, single channel, top silver control panel, single input, six black knobs (g, v, MV, l, m, h), gain in/out switch, headphone jack,, orange vinyl covering, light brown grille, mfg. 2000-current.

MSR	$139	$90	$65 - 80	$50 - 60

*** Crush 15 (CR15R)** - Similar to the Crush 15 except has reverb circuit and knob for reverb, mfg. 2000-current.

MSR	$179	$115	$90 - 105	$70 - 80

OVATION

Amplifiers previously produced in New Hartford, Connecticut. The Ovation trademark was established in 1967.

Ovation are probably most known for their fine acoustic guitars. Shortly after the company was incorporated, they tried their luck at the Electric market with solid-body guitars in the early 1970's. It is known that they also produced at least one electric guitar amplifier during the 1970's. The specifications of this amp are unknown, but the few that have been seen for sale are generally priced in the $200-300 range in excellent condition. More information is underway and should appear in upcoming editions of the *Blue Book of Guitar Amplifiers*.

O

Section P

PARK

Amplifiers previously produced by Marshall from 1965 until 1982, and again from 1993 until 2000. The Park trademark was established by Marshall for a distributor in England.

Park amplifiers are essentially Marshall amps with a different name on the front. Why would Marshall like to take their fine amps and put a different name on them? Answer: Because Jim Marshall is a nice guy and wanted to help out a friend. When Marshall was first established in 1962 a guy named Jonny Jones was the man to sell most of the Marshall amps through his shop, Jones and Crossland. He was to be the main distributor in North England. As Marshall began to expand business in 1964, Jim began looking for a big-time distributor, and in early 1965, Rose-Morris owned world-wide rights of distribution of Marshall. This left buddy, Jonny Jones out in the dark on Marshall amps. Jim felt a bit guilty, I'm guessing, and started to produce another line of amplifiers solely for Jonny. He was able to do this through an option in his contract if he built them under another name. The name chosen; Johnny's wife's maiden name, Park.

These amps were distributed under Cleartone Musical Instruments (CMI), where another line of amps would come in the late 1970's. Park amplifiers were Marshall amps in disguise with different cosmetic features but virtually identical electronics. The first Park amps were JTM 45's. Information is also more sketchy on Park amps as compared to Marshall. Park amps did have their own models and ideas later in 1970's. Steve Grindrod was in charge of making a lot of these models, including the Rock Head. Park amps also always had the edge on prices as compared to Marshall.

When Rose-Morris' contract was up with Marshall in 1981, Jim took over as the sole distributor of his product. Since Park wasn't making Marshall any money, CMI was gradually consolidated. In 1982, Park amplifiers were discontinued. Park amplifiers were reintroduced in 1992 as the solid-state line of amps for Marshall. Once again they were the Epiphone of Gibson. Park produced these small solid-state amps until 2000, when Marshall started to make solid-state amps in their name.

(Source for Park History: The History of Marshall by Michael Doyle).

ELECTRIC TUBE AMPLIFIERS

Identifying the different years of Park amplifiers is a tougher thing to do rather than Marshall. The serial numbers aren't as documented as they are on the Marshall side, this makes it difficult to date by serial number. Cosmetic features are the best identifying feature as far as Park goes. The earliest Park amps have a top mounted control panel, but were later moved to the front. These also had a black and white grille as well. Black was introduced shortly after that. The label has also changed over the years. Early on the P in Park was separate from the ark (you need to be familiar with the logo). In the early seventies the P was joined with the ark in the logo and in the late seventies the Park logo moved to the middle of the amplifier

Add 25% for custom colors.

GRADING	100%	EXCELLENT	AVERAGE

Early Models

JTM45 (PARK) - 45W, head-unit only, all tube chassis, preamp: 12AX7, power: 2 X 5881, GZ34 rectifier, lead guitar application, dual channels, front or top black plexi control panel, four inputs, typically six knobs (p, b, m, t, high t, v), black covering, mfg. 1965-66.

Park 45 Top Mount
courtesy solidbodyguitar.com, Inc.

Park 45 Top Mount
courtesy solidbodyguitar.com, Inc.

| N/A | $2,250 - 3,000 | $1,250 - 1,500 |

This amp is essentially a Marshall JTM45 with a Park nametag. This amp was available as a top mount control panel or a front mount. The top-mount is rarer.

100W P.A. AMPLIFIER - 100W, head-unit only, all tube chassis, four channels, front black control panel, eight inputs (high and low for each channel), eight white knobs (v1, v2, v3, v4, b, m, t, brightness), 8 & 16 Ohm speaker output, black covering, mfg. 1966-1972.

| N/A | $1,750 - 2,500 | $1,250 - 1,500 |

* 50W P.A. Amplifier - Similar to the 100W version except has 50W output and two less channels, mfg. 1966-1972.

| N/A | $1,750 - 2,500 | $1,250 - 1,500 |

100W BASS/LEAD/ORGAN - 100W, head-unit only, all tube chassis, two channels, front black control panel, four inputs (high and low for each channel, six white knobs (v1, v2, b, m, t, brightness), black covering, mfg. 1966-1972.

| N/A | $1,750 - 2,500 | $1,250 - 1,500 |

* 50W Bass/Lead/Organ - Similar to the 100W version except has 50W output, mfg. 1966-1972.

| N/A | $1,750 - 2,500 | $1,250 - 1,500 |

GRADING	100%	EXCELLENT	AVERAGE

Models With Model Number Designations

1001L - 75W, head-unit only, lead-application, all tube chassis, front silver control panel, four inputs (two per channel), 6 silver knobs (v1, v2, b, m, t, brightness), 4, 8, & 16 Ohm Speaker output, black covering, mfg. 1972-75.

Park Model 75
courtesy solidbodyguitar.com, Inc.

Park Model 75
courtesy solidbodyguitar.com, Inc.

	N/A	$750 - 1,050	$500 - 700

   * **1001B** - Similar to the 1001L, except designed for bass applications, the first channel bass boosted, mfg. 1972-75.

	N/A	$750 - 1,050	$500 - 700

1002L - 150W, head-unit only, lead-application with first channel treble boosted, all tube chassis, front silver control panel (slightly offset), four inptus (two per channel), six silver knobs (v1, v2, b, m, t, brightness), 4, 8, & 16 Ohm speaker output, black covering, mfg. 1972-75.

	N/A	$800 - 1,100	$500 - 700

   * **1002B** - Similar to the 1002L, except designed for bass applications, the first channel bass boosted, mfg. 1972-75.

	N/A	$800 - 1,100	$500 - 700

1005L - 100W, head-unit only, lead-application with first channel treble boosted, all tube chassis, front silver control panel, four inptus (two per channel), six silver knobs (v1, v2, b, m, t, brightness), 4, 8, & 16 Ohm speaker output, black covering, mfg. 1972-75.

	N/A	$800 - 1,000	$500 - 700

   * **1005B** - Similar to the 1005L, except designed for bass applications, the first channel bass boosted, mfg. 1972-75.

	N/A	$800 - 1,000	$500 - 700

1206 - 50W, head-unit only, lead-application, all tube chassis, high-input gain, single channel, master volume, front silver control panel, two inputs, six silver knobs (v, MV, b, m, t, brightness), black covering, mfg. 1976-1982.

	N/A	$500 - 650	$375 - 450

   * **1207** - Similar to the 1206, except has 100W output, mfg. 1976-1982.

	N/A	$500 - 700	$400 - 450

1210 (ROCK HEAD) - 100W, head-unit only, lead-application, all tube chassis, dual channels, front silver control panel, four inputs (two per channel), unknown controls, MV, black covering, mfg. mid 1970's.

	N/A	$1,200 - 1,500	$800 - 1,000

This amp was derived from the Marshall 2150 100W combo, but very little is known about it and not that many were produced.

   * **1240** - Similar to the 1210 Rock Head, except in combo version with 1-12" speaker, mfg. mid 1970's.

	N/A	$1,500 - 2,000	$1,000 - 1,250

1212 - 50W, 2-12" speakers, all tube chassis combo, lead application, dual channels, reverb, top black control panel, two inputs, seven black and silver knobs (v1, v2, r, b, m, t, brightness), black covering, black and white grille cloth, mfg. 1975-78.

	N/A	$600 - 900	$400 - 525

   * **1213** - Similar to the 1212, except has 100W output, mfg. 1975-78.

	N/A	$650 - 900	$400 - 525

1214 - 50W, 2-12" speakers, all tube chassis combo, lead application, single channel, master volume, top black control panel, two inputs, six black and silver knobs (v1, MV, b, m, t, brightness), black covering, black and white grille cloth, mfg. 1975-78.

	N/A	$600 - 850	$400 - 500

   * **1215** - Similar to the 1214, except has 100W output, mfg. 1976-1982, .

	N/A	$650 - 850	$400 - 500

1216 - 50W, head-unit only, bass application, all tube chassis, dual channels, front silver control panel, four inputs, six silver knobs (v1, v2, b, m, t, brightness), black covering, mfg. 1975-1982.

	N/A	$500 - 700	$400 - 450

   * **1217** - Similar to the 1216, except has 100W output, mfg. 1975-1982.

	N/A	$500 - 750	$400 - 450

1228 - 50W, head-unit only, lead application, all-tube chassis, dual channels, front silver control panel, four inputs (two per channel), six silver knobs (brightness, b, m, t, v1, v2), black covering, mfg. 1975-76.

	N/A	$600 - 800	$450 - 550

   * **1229** - Similar to the 1228 lead model, except has 100W output, mfg. 1975-76.

	N/A	$600 - 800	$450 - 550

GRADING	100%	EXCELLENT	AVERAGE

1231 VINTAGE 20LE - 20W, 1-12" Celestion speaker, all tube chassis, preamp: 2 X ECC83, power: 2 X EL84, various knobs, brown vinyl covering, black and white grille cloth, mfg. mid 1970's.

	N/A	$750 - 1,000	$500 - 600

* 1273 - Reissue of the Vintage 20, mfg. 1980-82.

	N/A	$500 - 700	$375 - 450

1238 - 50W, 1-12" speaker, all-tube chassis, bass application, single channel, front silver control panel, two inputs, seven black and silver knobs (v, b, t, m1, m2, m3, e), black covering, black and white grille cloth, mfg. 1976-1982.

	N/A	$600 - 800	$450 - 550

1239 - 1-12" speaker, all-tube chassis, lead application, single channel, reverb, master volume, front silver control panel, two inputs, seven black and silver knobs (g, MV, t, m, b, brightness, r), black covering, black and white grille cloth, mfg. 1976-1982.

	N/A	$600 - 800	$450 - 550

ELECTRIC SOLID-STATE AMPLIFIERS

It should be noted that there is a noticeable gap in Park amplifiers when it comes to what is collectible and what is not. The solid-state models that were released pre-1982 are part of the more collectible Park amps. The recent models (1990's) were strictly budget amps that Marshall produced rather than putting their name on them.

Early Park Solid-State (1965-1982)

1211 - 50W, 2-12" speakers, solid-state combo, single channel, tremolo, front black control panel, two inputs (normal and bright), eight black and silver knobs (g1, g2, b, m, t, d, f, MV), black covering, black and white grille, mfg. mid 1970's.

	N/A	$700 - 1,000	$400 - 600

1218 - 100W, narrow head unit-only, solid-state chassis, single channel, front black control panel, two inputs, six black and silver knobs (g, t, m, b, brightness, MV), black covering, mfg. 1976-1982.

	N/A	$500 - 750	$350 - 450

1230 - 8W, 1-8" speaker, practice solid-state combo, single channel, various controls, mfg. 1977-1982.

	N/A	$150 - 200	$75 - 125

Recent Mfg. Park (1992-2000)

In 1992, Marshall brought back the Park trademark to market their solid-state amps. They made many small models from 10W up to 100W. These amps were produced through 2000 when Marshall started to put their own name on the solid-state models. Since we haven't been able to find a catalog on any of these amps, we're not sure of what models were made, what options they had, and when they were produced. There were the G series, the PG series, the MG series and B indicated Bass models. The number following the letters indicates the wattage. With these letters and numbers in the models it's fairly easy to determine what model you have.

Most models of these amps can be found between the $50 and $200 depending on condition and features. If it is a G-10 (10W practice amp), you're probably looking around $75 max.

PARK SPEAKER CABINETS

Park, like Marshall offered speaker cabinets to be matched up with their different amplifier heads. Unlike most companys, these two pieces of equipment aren't considered "one." There are many cabinets out there and we will try to list the major ones. Usually the 4-12" cabinets have an "A" model which means the cabinet is angled. Early Park speaker cabinets are original in that the angle started at the bottom of the cabinet (Marshall's angle starts in the middle). The later Park models (from about 1975 on) have Marshall style speaker cabinets. All prices are the same as the flat front cabinet unless noted. There are other models intended for P.A. application (i.e. Models, 1014, and 1015) but information and pricing is scarce. Early models don't carry a model number on the speaker cabinet. Look for more information on upcoming editions of the *Blue Book of Guitar Amplifiers*.

1008 - 4-12" Speaker Cabinet, lead-application, 4-12" Celestion 25W speakers (100W capability), mfg. 1970's.

	N/A	$750 - 1,000	$400 - 600

1009 - 4-12" Speaker Cabinet, bass-application, 4-12" heavy duty Celestion 25W speakers (100W capability), mfg. 1970's.

	N/A	$750 - 1,000	$400 - 600

1010 - 2-15" Speaker Cabinet, bass/lead application, 2-15" 50W Celestion speakers, no angled front, mfg. 1970's.

	N/A	$400 - 600	$250 - 350

1011 - 1-18" Speaker Cabinet, bass application, 1-18" 100W Celestion speaker, no angled front, mfg. 1970's.

	N/A	$450 - 700	$300 - 400

1209 - 2-12" Speaker Cabinet, bass/lead application, 2-12" 50W speakers (100W capability), mfg. 1976-1982.

	N/A	$400 - 600	$250 - 350

1222 - 4-12" Speaker Cabinet, lead application, 4-12" speakers (100W capability), mfg. 1976-1982.

	N/A	$450 - 700	$300 - 400

1223 - 4-12" Speaker Cabinet, lead application, 4-12" heavy-duty speakers (120W capability), mfg. 1976-1982.

	N/A	$450 - 700	$300 - 400

P

GRADING	100%	EXCELLENT	AVERAGE

PAUL REED SMITH

Amplifiers previously produced by PRS in Annapolis, Maryland. PRS made amplifiers between 1988 and 1989. The PRS trademark was established in 1985 and the company is now located in Stevensville, Maryland.

Luthier Paul Reed Smith devised an electric guitar that became very influential in the 1980's. With the success of the electric guitars, Smith decided to move into other markets, including the amplifier business. As American companies were looking like they were going to dump the tube amp idea with the lack of surplus in tubes, Smith thought solid-state was the way to go. The circuitry for these amps was developed by Eric Pritchard. However, the amps weren't well received, especially by *Guitar World* magazine. Only 350 units were shipped and high cost of the amp caused the project to fold in 1989. The circuitary which was used in the amps was a Harmonic Generator. This is where the HG comes from in the model names.

Source for Paul Reed Smith Amplifier history: (The Paul Reed Smith book by Dave Burrluck)

PAUL REED SMITH AMPLIFIERS (SOLID-STATE)

In the short life of PRS amplifiers, there were three different models produced. The two amps produced both contained the "Harmonic Generator," which added harmonics to the tone. The HG-70 was a head unit and the HG-212 was the combo unit with 2-12" speakers. There was also a cabinet with 4-12" speakers.

HG-70 - 70W, head-unit only, solid-state, two separate preamps (to create a "Vintage American" and a "Vintage English" sound), dual channels, reverb, front black control panel, single input, 14 black knobs (Rhythm Ch. r, MV, bright, b, m, t, g, Solo Ch. MV, p, b, m, t, gate, g), effects loop, speaker switching (16, 8, & 4 Ohm), XLR out, luminescent rear panel, black covering, black/gray grill, mfg. 1988-89.

N/A	$300 - 375	$225 - 275

* HG-212 - Similar to the HG-70 except has 2-12" speakers, mfg. 1988-89.

N/A	$350 - 450	$250 - 300

412 SPEAKER CABINET - Speaker cabinet with 4-12" speakers, meant to match up with the HG-70 head-unit, mfg. 1988-89.

N/A	$275 - 350	$200 - 250

PEAVEY

Amplifiers currently produced in Meridian and Leaksville, Mississippi. Peavey Electronics are distributed by the Peavey Electronics Corporation of Meridian, Mississippi. The Peavey trademark was established in 1965.

Peavey Electronics is one of the very few major American instrument manufactures still run by the original founder and owner. Hartley Peavy grew up in Meridian, Mississippi and spent time working in his father's music store repairing record players. While he was in high school, he gained recognition, locally, for guitar amplifiers he built by hand. Before college graduation, he decided that he was to go into business for himself. Peavey Electronics was established in 1965 out of the basement of his parent's house. The first amps Hartley began producing were P.A. amps and their components. The young Peavey's company took off in a hurry and the first shop was built in 1968 along with hiring another staff member. By 1970, there were 150 people working for Peavey. At this time they were still making P.A. amps primarily, but guitar and bass amps were popular as well.

After a decade of making amplifiers, Peavey emerged as a guitar builder as well. Throughout the 1980's and 1990's, Peavey nailed the market at the perfect time. The tube scare of the 1980's couldn't have come at a better time as they were producing all solid-state amps. In the 1990's, Peavey released the EVH5150, which was an amplifier developed in conjunction with Edward Van Halen. This amp has been one of Peavey's most successful amplifiers and later on they released a series of guitars with Van Halen.

Peavey still makes many different models of guitars and amplifiers to this day in Hartley's hometown. Recent models include the 5150 II, and the digital Session 2000. Along with guitar amplifiers, Peavey is responsible for bass amplifiers, rack mount equipment, preamps, power amps, speaker enclosures, subwoofers, and guitar effects.

ELECTRIC TUBE AMPLIFIERS

Yes, Peavey does make Tube amps. Their tweed amps have a variety of options and Eddie Van Halen has his own line in the 5150 series. There are also other series of tube amps.

Classic Series

BLUES CLASSIS - 50W, 1-15" speaker combo, all tube chassis, two channels, reverb, top chrome control panel, two inputs, nine black knobs, tweed covering, brown grille cloth, mfg. mid 1990's.

Peavey Blues Classic
courtesy S. P. Fjestad

N/A	$400 - 450

Peavey Blues Classic
courtesy S. P. Fjestad

$300 - 350

GRADING	100%	EXCELLENT	AVERAGE

CLASSIC 30 - 30W, 1-12" Blue Marvel speaker, all tube chassis, preamp: 3 X 12AX7, power: 4 X EL84, two channels, reverb, top chrome control panel, single input, seven black knobs (normal v, pre gain, post gain, r, b, m, t), effects loop, optional footswitch, tweed or black vinyl covering, brown or black grille, mfg. 1994-current.

	MSR	$579.99	$425	$325 - 375	$250 - 285

This model in black vinyl covering and a black grille is known as the Classic 30 BT.

* ***Classic 30 Limited Edition Signature Series*** - Similar to the Classic 30 except has quilted maple cabinet, with a hand-painted, hand-sanded finish, new 2002.

	MSR	$1,099.99	$775	$600 - 700	$475 - 550

DELTA BLUES - 30W, 1-15" Blue Marvel speaker, all tube chassis, preamp: 3 X 12AX7, power: 4 X EL84, two channels, reverb, tremolo, top chrome control panel, single input, nine black knobs (normal v, pre gain, post gain, r, b, m, t. i. s), effects loop, optional footswitch, tweed covering, brown grille, current mfg.

	MSR	$649.99	$475	$350 - 425	$275 - 325

* ***Delta Blues 210 BT*** - Similar to the Delta Blues in circuitary, except has 2-10" Blue Marvel speakers, black tweed coveirng, and black grille cloth, current mfg.

	MSR	$649.99	$475	$350 - 425	$275 - 325

CLASSIC 50 HEAD - 50W, head-unit only, all tube chassis, preamp: 3 X 12AX7, power: 4 X EL84, dual channels, reverb, front chrome contol panel, two inputs (normal and bright), nine black knobs (normal v, pre g, post g, r, b, m, t, MV, p), effects loop, footswitch, black tweed covering, current mfg.

	MSR	$749.99	$525	$400 - 475	$300 - 350

* ***Classic 50/212*** - Similar to the Classic 50 head in circuitry, in combo form with 2-12" Blue Marvel speakers, tweed covering, brown grille, mfg. 1990-current.

	MSR	$899.99	$650	$475 - 575	$350 - 400

* ***Classic 50/212 BT*** - Similar to the Classic 50/212 except in black tweed covering, and black cloth grille, current mfg.

	MSR	$899.99	$625	$450 - 550	$350 - 400

* ***Classic 50/410*** - Similar to the Classic 50 head in circuitry, in combo form with 4-10" Blue Marvel speakers, tweed covering, brown cloth grille, mfg. 1990-current.

	MSR	$929.99	$650	$475 - 575	$350 - 400

5150 Series

The 5150 series were developed with Eddie Van Halen. For you youngsters, Eddie Van Halen is lead guitar player for Van Halen, and 5150 is a hit album from the mid 1980's. All 5150 products have Eddie's signature on them, and are built with his specifications.

5150 HEAD - 120W (16, 8, or 4 Ohms), head-unit only, all tube chassis, preamp: 5 X 12AX7, power: 4 X 6L6GC, dual channels, front silver control panel, two inputs, nine black knobs (rhythm pre g, lead g, l, m, h, rhythm post g, lead post g, resonance, p), bright and crunch switches, effects loop, preamp out, footswitch, black covering, black metal grille, 48 lbs., mfg. 1995-present.

	MSR	$1,199.99	$850	$625 - 725	$500 - 550

5150 II HEAD - 120W (16, 8, or 4 Ohms), head-unit only, all tube chassis, preamp: 6 X 12AX7, power: 4 X 6L6GC, dual channels, front silver control panel, two inputs, 14 black knobs (Rhythm: pre, l, m, h, post, Lead: pre, l, m, h, post, resonance & p per channel), bright and crunch switches, effects loop, preamp out, black covering, footswitch, black metal grille, 48. 3 lbs., mfg. 1995-present.

	MSR	$1,299.99	$900	$675 - 775	$550 - 600

5150 COMBO - 60W, 2-12" Sheffield 1200 speakers, all tube chassis combo, preamp: 5 X 12AX7, power: 4 X 6L6GC, dual channels, top silver control panel, two inputs, nine black knobs (rhythm pre g, lead g, l, m, h, rhythm post g, lead post g, resonance, p), bright and crunch switches, effects loop, preamp out, footswitch, black covering, black metal grille, 84.5 lbs., mfg. 1995-present.

	MSR	$1,249.99	$875	$650 - 750	$525 - 575

Triple XXX Series

TRIPLE XXX HEAD - 120W (16, 8, or 4 Ohms), head-unit only, all tube chassis, preamp: 4 X 12AX7, power: 4 X 6L6GC (or EL34), three channels, reverb, front black control panel, single input, 15 silver knobs (Clean: v, b, m, t, Crunch & Lead: b, v, bottom, body, hair, MV, r), power amp switch, effects loop, line out, footswitch, black covering, brushed aluminum face, current mfg.

	MSR	$1,249.99	$875	$650 - 750	$550 - 600

TRIPLE XXX 212 COMBO - Same as the Triple XXX head in circuitary, in combo form with 2-12" Triple XXX chrome-plated speakers, black and silver grille cloth, current mfg.

	MSR	$1,399.99	$999	$750 - 850	$600 - 675

ELECTRIC SOLID-STATE AMPLIFIERS

Solid-State amps have done the best in Peavey. Since these amps weren't hard to build, they were affordable yet with great quality. Now Peavey produces several different models with endless features. Most recently the developed the Transtube design, which gives tube sound without the tubes.

Early Solid-State Models

Peavey has been producing solid-state guitar amps for many years now. Most of these amps were affordable in the 1980's and early 1990's, they are still affordable today. Small combos such as 1-10" and 1-12" amps can usually be found for under $200 in excellent shape. Bigger models with 2 speakers go for a slightly higher premium. We are looking to list more models for upcoming editions.

P

GRADING	100%	EXCELLENT	AVERAGE

BANDIT STUDIO PRO - 65W, 1-12" speaker, solid-state design, two channels, reverb, front black control panel, two inputs, 10 black knobs, effects loop, footswitch, black covering, black grille, mfg. 1980's-1995.

Peavey Bandit Studio Pro 110
courtesy Dave's Guitar Shop

N/A	$140 - 180	$100 - 120

Transtube Series

SPECIAL 212 - 200W, 2-12" Sheffield speakers, solid-state Transtube design, three channels, reverb, front blue control panel, two inputs, 16 black knobs, T-Dynamics control, effects loop, footswitch, black covering, black grille, mfg. 1995-current.

Peavey Special 212
courtesy Dave's Guitar Shop

Peavey Special 212
courtesy Dave's Guitar Shop

MSR	$699.99	$499	$375 - 425	$275 - 325

REVOLUTION 112 - 100W, 1-12" Sheffield speaker, solid-state Transtube design, three channels, reverb, front blue control panel, two inputs, 14 black knobs, T-Dynamics control, effects loop, footswitch, black covering, black grille, mfg. 1995-current.

MSR	$599.99	$425	$325 - 375	$225 - 275

BANDIT 112 - 80W, 1-12" Sheffield 1230 speaker, solid-state Transtube design, two channels, reverb, front blue control panel, two inputs, 12 black knobs, T-Dynamics control, effects loop, footswitch, black covering, black grille, mfg. 1995-current.

MSR	$499.99	$350	$250 - 300	$175 - 225

STUDIO PRO 112 - 65W, 1-12" Blue Marvel speaker, solid-state Transtube design, two channels, reverb, front blue control panel, two inputs, 11 black knobs, T-Dynamics control, effects loop, footswitch, black covering, black grille, mfg. 1995-current.

MSR	$399.99	$285	$200 - 250	$150 - 175

ENVOY 110 - 40W, 1-10" Blue Marvel speaker, solid-state Transtube design, two channels, reverb, front blue control panel, two inputs, 10 black knobs, T-Dynamics control, headphone jack, footswitch, black covering, black grille, mfg. 1995-current.

MSR	$299.99	$225	$150 - 175	$115 - 130

RAGE 158 - 15W, 1-8" Blue Marvel speaker, solid-state Transtube design, two channels, front blue control panel, two inputs, six black knobs, T-Dynamics control, headphone jack, footswitch, black covering, black grille, mfg. 1995-current.

MSR	$109.99	$79	$60 - 70	$45 - 55

BLAZER 158 - Similar to the Rage 158 except has reverb with level control, mfg. 1995-current.

MSR	$159.99	$115	$85 - 100	$60 - 75

GRADING	100%	EXCELLENT	AVERAGE

Transtube HeadAmps (Supreme, XXL, Wiggy)

SUPREME - 100W (16, 8, or 4 Ohm), head-unit only, solid-state Transtube design, two channels, reverb, front black control panel, two inputs, 12 black knobs, T-Dynamics control, effects loop, footswitch, black covering, black grille, current mfg.

MSR	$569.99	$399	$285 - 335	$225 - 250

XXL - 100W (16, 8, or 4 Ohm), head-unit only, solid-state Transtube design, three channels, reverb, front black control panel, single input, 16 silver knobs, T-Dynamics control, effects loop, footswitch, black covering, silver striped grille, current mfg.

MSR	$699.99	$499	$375 - 425	$275 - 325

WIGGY - 100W (16, 8, or 4 Ohm), semi-circle shaped head-unit only, solid-state Transtube design, two channels, reverb, front silver control panel meant to emulate a car dashboard, two inputs, controls are gain (RPM), master volume (MPH), Batt, oil, and temp for 3-band equalizer, presence and T-Dynamics control, various lights and knobs, effects loop, footswitch, lighted control panel, purple covering, current mfg.

MSR	$1,099.99	$775	$600 - 675	$475 - 550

For the matching speaker cabinet refer to the Speaker Cabinet section.

Transtube EFX Series

TRANSTUBE 258 - 25W, 1-8" speaker, solid-state chassis with digital processing, front black and red control panel, single input, six black knobs, three black and silver knobs (EFX), three programmable presets, black covering, black grille, new 2002.

MSR	$239.99	$175	$125 - 150	$90 - 105

This model used to be the Transtube 208 with 20W of power.

TRANSTUBE 112 - 65W, 1-12" Blue Marvel speaker, solid-state chassis with digital processing, front black and red control panel, single input, nine black knobs, three black and silver knobs (EFX), three programmable presets, black covering, black grille, new 2002.

MSR	$539.99	$399	$300 - 350	$250 - 275

TRANSTUBE 212 - 80W, 2-12" Blue Marvel speaker, solid-state chassis with digital processing, front black and red control panel, two inputs, 11 black knobs, three black and silver knobs (EFX), three programmable presets, black covering, black grille, new 2002.

MSR	$699.99	$499	$350 - 425	$275 - 325

Transformer Series

TRANSFORMER 112 - 50W, 1-12" speakers, solid-state chassis, TransTube preamp & power amp, 24-bit processing, 12 amp models, 32 presets, front blue control panel, two inputs, 14 black knobs, built in tuner, footswitch, black covering, black grille, current mfg.

MSR	$849.99	$599	$450 - 525	$350 - 400

TRANSFORMER 212 - 100W (50W per side stereo), 2-12" speakers, solid-state chassis, TransTube preamp & power amp, 24-bit processing, 12 amp models, 32 presets, front blue control panel, two inputs, 14 black knobs, built in tuner, footswitch, black covering, black grille, current mfg.

MSR	$1,099.99	$775	$600 - 700	$500 - 550

ACOUSTIC & STEEL AMPLIFIERS

Currently, Peavey has one steel amplifier and one acoustic amplifier. Imagine that, the acoustic amplifier is brown. Peavey is a rarity in that they produce an amplifier that is strictly for steel guitars. Twang-twangers rejoice!

Steel Amplifiers

NASHVILLE 1000 - 300W, 1-15" Black Widow 1501-4SB speaker, digtial power amp, front black control panel, eight black knobs, pre-EQ patch loop send and return, presence control, footswitch, black covering, black grille, current mfg.

MSR	$999.99	$699	$550 - 625	$450 - 500

For the Matching speaker cabinet refer to the Speaker Cabinet section.

Acoustic Amplifiers

ECOUSTIC 112 - 100W, 1-12" Blue Marvel coax speaker, solid state chassis, two channels, reverb, front brown control panel, instrument input, and mic input, seven brown knobs 2 five-band equalizers, various buttons, brown covering, brown grille cloth, current mfg.

MSR	$649.99	$475	$375 - 425	$275 - 325

BASS AMPLIFIERS

Bass amplifiers are a good line for Peavey as well as the guitar amps. They have kept up with the features that the guitars amps have and they sound pretty decent.

Bass Amp Combos (Current Production)

MICROBASS - 20W, 1-8" Blue Marvel speaker, solid-state chassis, DDT compression, single channel, front black control panel, single input, four black knobs (g, l, m, h), headphone jack, external speaker jack, black covering, black metal grille, mfg. 1988-current.

MSR	$169.99	$125	$85 - 105	$65 - 75

MINX 110 - 35W, 1-10" Blue Marvel speaker, solid-state chassis, DDT speaker protection, single channel, front black control panel, single input, four black knobs (g, l, m, h), headphone jack, external speaker jack, effects loop, black covering, black metal grille, mfg. 1988-current.

MSR	$299.99	$225	$160 - 190	$130 - 150

P

GRADING	100%	EXCELLENT	AVERAGE

BASIC 112 - 50W, 1-12" Blue Marvel speaker, solid-state chassis, DDT speaker protection, single channel, front black control panel, single input, six black knobs (pre-g, l, l/m, m/h, h, v), bright/normal switch, active/passive switch, headphone jack, external speaker jack, effects loop, black covering, black metal grille, mfg. 1996-current.

MSR	$359.99	$265	$200 - 230	$150 - 175

TKO 115 - 75W, 1-15" Blue Marvel speaker, solid-state chassis, DDT speaker protection, ported enclosure, single channel, front black control panel, single input, four black knobs (pre-g, l, h, v), seven-band equalizer, bright/normal switch, normal/contour switch, active/passive switch, headphone jack, external speaker jack, effects loop, black covering, black metal grille, mfg. 1988-current.

Peavey TKO 115 Bass
courtesy Ryan Muetzel

Peavey TKO 115 Bass
courtesy Ryan Muetzel

MSR	$489.99	$350	$250 - 300	$185 - 225

TNT 115 - 150W, 1-15" Blue Marvel speaker, solid-state chassis, DDT speaker protection, ported enclosure, single channel, chorus, front black control panel, single input, four black knobs (pre-g, l, h, v), seven-band equalizer, bright/normal switch, normal/contour switch, active/passive switch, headphone jack, external speaker jack, effects loop, black covering, black metal grille, mfg. 1996-current.

MSR	$599.99	$425	$325 - 375	$260 - 290

COMBO 115 - 210W, 1-15" Blue Marvel speaker, solid-state chassis, DDT speaker protection, ported enclosure, active crossover, single channel, chorus, front black control panel, two inputs, five black knobs (v, l, h, crossover frequency, v), seven-band equalizer, bright/normal switch, normal/contour switch, active/passive switch, headphone jack, external speaker jack, effects loop, black covering, black metal grille, mfg. 1996-current.

MSR	$729.99	$525	$375 - 450	$285 - 335

BAM 210 - 500W, 2-10" cast frame woofers, horn-loaded tweeter, solid-state modeling amp, effects, front black control panel, single input, 14 black knobs (input trim, input preset, compressor squeeze, level, model selector, pre g, l, m, shift, h, post g, effects adj, depth, MV), various buttons and switches, on two wheel casters with dolly handle (adjustable like a suitcase), current mfg.

MSR	$1,499.99	$1,075	$800 - 925	$625 - 700

This amp is also available in a head-unit only. Refer to the Bass Amp head section under current mfg.

Bass Amp Heads (Current Production)

DELTABASS - 160W, head-unit only, solid-state chassis, DDT speaker protection with switch, single channel, front black and red control panel, seven black knobs (pre-g, c, l, m, m-shift, h, v), tuner output, XLR output, effects loop, current mfg.

MSR	$399.99	$285	$200 - 250	$150 - 175

NITROBASS - 450W, head-unit only, solid-state chassis, DDT speaker protection with switch, single channel, front black and red control panel, eight black knobs (pre-g, c, l, m, m-shift, h, v, line out level), tuner output XLR output, effects loop, current mfg.

MSR	$589.99	$425	$325 - 375	$275 - 300

FIREBASS 700 - 700W, head-unit only, solid-state chassis, DDT speaker protection with switch, single channel, front black and red control panel, ten black knobs (pre-g, c, l, m, m-shift, h, v, line out level, freq, balance), tuner output XLR output, X over outs, effects loop, current mfg.

MSR	$759.99	$550	$400 - 475	$325 - 375

PRO 500 - 500W, rackmount head unit, tube preamp, solid-state power amp, black control panel, single input, 14 white knobs, tuner send, footswitch, new 2002.

MSR	$999.99	$700	$500 - 600	$400 - 450

SPEAKER CABINETS

Currently Peavey produces many variations of guitar and bass speaker enclosures. They also have powered speaker units that are listed here.

Guitar Speaker Cabinets

CLASSIC 412E - 4-12" Sheffield 1230 speakers, stereo or mono operation, stackable configuration, straight front, black or regular tweed covering, black or brown grille, current mfg.

MSR	$679.99	$489	$350 - 425	$275 - 325

This model is also available in a slanted version as the model 412ES.

GRADING	100%	EXCELLENT	AVERAGE

TRIPLE XXX 412 - 4-12" Triple XXX speakers, stackable configuration, black covering, black and silver grille, current mfg.

MSR	$699.99	$499	$350 - 425	$275 - 325

This model is also available in a slanted version as the model 412ES.

5150 ENCLOSURE - 300W, 4-12" Sheffield 1200 speakers, straight or slanted front, stackable configuration, straight front, black covering, black grille, current mfg.

MSR	$799.99	$575	$445 - 500	$350 - 400

This model is also available in a slanted version as the model 412ES.

WIGGY 212 ENCLOSURE - 150W, 2-12" Sheffield speakers, stereo or mono operation, straight front, purple covering, silver grille, current mfg.

MSR	$549.99	$399	$275 - 325	$215 - 250

This model is also available in a slanted version as the model 412ES.

PX300 - 300W digital powered amplifier, 1-15" 1501-4 Black Widow speaker, can be used to add stereo capability to amps or as an extension speaker, current mfg.

MSR	$849.99	$599	$450 - 525	$375 - 425

112SX GUITAR - 75W, 1-12" Sheffield speaker, closed back, black covering, black grille, 36.4 lbs., current mfg.

MSR	$299.99	$215	$150 - 180	$110 - 130

412M GUITAR - 300W, 4-12" Sheffield speaker, closed back, stereo or mono operation, casters, straight front, black covering, black grille, 89.7 lbs., current mfg.

MSR	$599.99	$425	$325 - 375	$250 - 300

This model is also available in a slanted version as the model 412MS.

Bass Speaker Cabinets

210TVX BASS - 175W, 2-10" Sheffield, 1-dome tweeter, closed back cabinet, black covering, black grille, 60.8 lbs., current mfg.

MSR	$449.99	$325	$250 - 300	$190 - 220

115BVX BASS - 350W, 1-15" Black Widow, closed back cabinet, black covering, black grille, 75.7 lbs., current mfg.

MSR	$449.99	$325	$250 - 300	$190 - 220

410TVX BASS - 350W, 4-10" Sheffield, one-horn loaded tweeter, closed back cabinet, black covering, black grille, 95.2 lbs., current mfg.

MSR	$649.99	$475	$350 - 400	$285 - 325

412TVX BASS - 350W, 4-12" Sheffield, one-horn loaded tweeter, closed back cabinet, black covering, black grille, 129.1 lbs., current mfg.

MSR	$799.99	$575	$450 - 500	$375 - 425

810TVX BASS - 400W, 8-10" Sheffield, one-horn loaded tweeter, closed back cabinet, black covering, black grille, 161.7 lbs., current mfg.

MSR	$979.99	$699	$525 - 600	$425 - 475

PRO 210 - 700W, 2-10" high performance cast frame bass guitar speakers, 1-1" horn tweeter, black carpet covering, silver metal grille, new 2002.

MSR	$799.99	$575	$450 - 525	$350 - 400

PRO 115 - 700W, 1-15" high performance cast frame bass guitar speakers, 1-1" horn tweeter, black carpet covering, silver metal grille, new 2002.

MSR	$799.99	$575	$450 - 525	$350 - 400

PRO 410 - 700W, 4-10" high performance cast frame bass guitar speakers, 1-1" horn tweeter, horn tweeter protection, tweeter level control, black carpet covering, silver metal grille, new 2002.

MSR	$999.99	$699	$525 - 600	$425 - 475

PIGNOSE

Amplifiers currently produced in Las Vegas, Nevada.

Pignose amplifiers have been around since 1972. A kid went to a distributor in Oakland with this prototype amp that was built in a wooden box. The idea of a portable, battery operated amp wasn't taken by storm from the distributor in Oakland. He later gave a prototype to Terry Kath of Chicago who took interest in the idea. The volume knob kept coming loose and he brought it his tech. The rubber knob was melted and when it was fixed, Terry said that it looked like a pig's nose. Some of the first models were produced with these "pignose" knobs, and there only two of them known in existence. It's funny how names sometimes come about.

This amp was one of the first that was completely portable amplifier. Now Pignose offers amps that are run strictly on DC battery power along with a rechargeable model. Not only are these amps novel ideas, they are also fairly cheap. They currently offer a wide range of products, including some tube models.

ELECTRIC AMPLIFIERS

The bread and butter to Pignose is the model **7-100**. This was the first practice amp that they had in production, and has been produced since 1972. With a brown vinyl type covering and a small speaker, these amps can be found used in the range of $50-75 in excellent shape. Mint models could go for $100. A brand new model retails for only $109. The models **7-200** and **7-300** are portable amps with more features. The 7-200 has a overdrive feature and the 7-300 is meant for a bass, keyboard, or acoustic guitar.

Pignose now has a line of tube amp heads and combos. They have a **G-40V** combo amp that has 40W of power going through a 10" speaker. It features a 3 band equalizer and presence, volume, and master volume controls for a retail price of $399.95. The **G-60VR** combo has 60W through a 12" speaker and all the features of the G-40V plus reverb. This model goes for $649.95 and comes in a head-unit, **G-60VRH** for $539. The "big dawg" is a 100W bass amp in a combo unit, **B-100V**, and a head unit **B-100VH**. The combo has a 15" driver, but is still portable and affordable at $749 retail. The head unit is $539.

Pignose also offers some P.A. amplification in a to-go package. For further information on Pignose, please refer to the Pignose web site.

P

GRADING	100%	EXCELLENT	AVERAGE

POLYTONE

Amplifiers currently produced in North Hollywood, California.

The Polytone company was started in 1968 by Tommy Gumina. The motto for the company is "Made by Musicians for Musicians." Tommy started to build small, portable amps with the Polytone sound. The Mini-Brute line of amps debuted in 1976. Since then they have been working with musicians to build products to the highest industry standards. Currently they have a full line of amplifiers and accessories. The Mini-Brute series is still the most popular to the company and have produced many different versions of the amp.

ELECTRIC AMPLIFIERS

Most of the Mini-Brute amplifiers are going to be the ones showing up on the market. Currently in production they offer the Mini-Brute, Mini-Brute II, Mini-Brute IV, and the Mini-Brute V. Each model increases in power, features and price as the suffix goes higher. They also offer the Mega-Brain, which is an amp that weighs only 8 lbs., and can fit under an airplane seat. Retail prices on Polytone range from about $700 and top out at the $1,000 mark. Two bass models are also offered in combo forms (not so portable). The Sonic Circuit is the newest innovation on the block for Polytone, which is like having four amps in one.

In the past they produced many different versions of the Mini-Brute. Including that was a not-so-popular Baby-Brute. Editor S.P. Fjestad cut a deal at a guitar show and picked one of these derilics up. The coolest feature about it is the black felt/plushy grille fabric.

Polytone Baby-Brute
courtesy S. P. Festad

Polytone Baby-Brute
courtesy S. P. Festad

PREMIER

Amplifiers previously produced in New York City, New York.

Premier was the brand name of the Louis Sorkin Music Company. They started producing amplifiers in the late 1930's, World War II halted production of any products, and they came with vigor to the 1947 NAMM show. They advertised the new "Premier Multivox Amplifier with Push-Button tuning." These new amplifiers were manufactured by Multivox with the Premier name on them. It's obvious to tell that these two companies as later Multivox models are exact copies, even the model name to Premier's models. Premier focused more on the guitars that they built during their existence. They made amplifiers with random designs and applications. Such early models were the 76, 88, and the 120, which would become Multivox later. Premier manufactured amplifiers until the late 1960's. Premier officially stopped guitar production in 1973 or 74. No more amplifiers were made after this time.

ELECTRIC AMPLIFIERS

Multivox conveniently numbered most of their amplifiers, which makes them easier to identify. Amplifier production began around 1946 (not counting pre-war) and models at this time had lyre grilles. In the early 1960's a dark brown/light brown two-tone covering was introduced (similar to Gibson amps of the same era). In the late 1960's the amps were covered in a dark woodgrain.

The most common models are the Model 50, Model 76, Model 88, and the Model 120. Most common Premier amplifiers can be found in between the price range of $200-400 depending on condition. Excellent condition Premiers can bring a premium of as much as $600 or more. The 1940 and 1950 model Premiers are quite more desirable than the 1960 models.

PRIME

Amplifiers currently distributed by Music Industries Corporation in Garden City, New York.

Prime amplifiers are mainly practice amps for many instruments offered at a competitive price. Among the applications are guitar amps, acoustic amps, P.A. amps, keyboard amps, and bass amps.

ELECTRIC AMPLIFIERS

Prime amps have lots of features and are affordable. The most any Prime amplifier is, is the big Acoustic amp at a retail price of $399.95. The electric and acoustic guitar amps are grouped together under guitar amplifiers.

Guitar Amplifiers

CG-25RC - 25W, 1-8" speaker guitar combo, solid-state chassis, single channel, reverb, chorus, front silver control panel, two inputs, nine black knobs, three band equalizer, seperate mic volume, black covering, black grille, current mfg.

MSR	$209.95	$150	$100 - 125	$70 - 85

P

GRADING	100%	EXCELLENT	AVERAGE

CG-40RC - 40W, 1-12" speaker guitar combo, solid-state chassis, single channel, reverb, chorus, front silver control panel, two inputs, nine black knobs, three band equalizer, separate mic volume, black covering, black grille, current mfg.

MSR	$299.95	$215	$150 - 175	$100 - 125

CA-30RC - 30W, 1-8" speaker, 2-3" tweeters, solid state chassis acoustic combo, reverb, chorus, single channel, front black control panel, single input, eight black and yellow knobs, mic input, oak cabinet, black grille, current mfg.

MSR	$319.95	$225	$155 - 180	$100 - 125

CA-60RC - 60W, 2-6.5" speakers, 2-3" tweeters, solid state chassis acoustic combo, reverb, chorus, single channel, front black control panel, single input, eight black and yellow knobs, five-band equalizer, mic input, oak cabinet, black grille, current mfg.

MSR	$399.95	$285	$200 - 250	$150 - 175

Other Amplifiers

Prime has four practice amplifiers that range in retail price from $40 to $120. They also have two bass amplifiers the PBA-20 for $129.95, and the CB-50 $299.95. There is a P.A. and a keyboard amp also available at reasonable prices.

P

NOTES

Section Q

QSC AUDIO PRODUCTS

Amplifiers currently produced in Costa Mesa, California.

QSC was developed in 1968 from two people running into each other and becoming friends. Barry Andrews broke down on his motorcycle in California and while waiting for it to get fixed, he struck up a conversation with Pat Quilter working in a garage. Barry was a cabinet maker while Pat was designing and building amplifiers. Shortly thereafter Pat needed help with his business and he called Barry. This was the roots for the small company that was named Quilter's Sound Company. Later it would be renamed QSC Audio Products, Inc.

The early years of QSC were that of a small company building guitar amplifiers and other items of the same caliber. In the late 1970's, they took a look at the market and decided to focus on building power amplifiers. This is when the business really took off. In 1978, Pat developed the AC Coupled Amplifier Circuit. In 1982 the Series three and Series One models were released. A lot of their units could be used for guitars, but they were starting to branch out to pro audio, such as theaters.

Currently they offer several amplifiers in high wattages, and in several different industries. Visit the QSC web site and see what the new 81,000 square foot facility is producing today. They also have a full company history in detail on the website (see Trademark Index).

ELECTRIC TUBE AMPLIFIERS

Most guitar players use QSC as a power amp, and another brand for a preamp. Most guitar players use these amps because they are lightweight and pack a lot of power for not a lot of space. No guitar player will often complain of a lack of power on these models. Since the QSC company has so many different applications it's tough to pinpoint any second-hand prices. These amps are typically used for playing (often hard), and the playing function is the selling factor.

Q

NOTES

Section R

RMS AUDIO

Amplifiers currently produced overseas and in the United States. RMS is a division of MBT International.

RMS makes a handful of guitar and bass amplifiers along with a slug of other products. They build their speaker cabinets in U.S.A, but their other products are built overseas. Among their other products are P.A. mixers, microphones, and audio snakes. For guitar and bass amplifiers, they offer the Standard and Pro Drive Series. The Standard series are smaller wattage amps that are used more for the beginner and practice. The Pro-Drive series are sounded more for the performing musician. These amps are available in wattage up to 100 and chorus amps are available. Bass amps are also available in both series. Prices are very reasonable on all products. For more information, refer to the MBT web site (see Trademark Index).

RAEZER'S EDGE

Speaker cabinets currently built in Swarthmore, Pennsylvania.

Rich Raezer currently builds quality speaker cabinets for many applications. He started buliding these cabinets, because there was a void in the industry: a small cabinet that would produce big sounds. Performers were getting sick of carrying around heavy speaker cabinets, and there was a demand for a lightweight design. With a lot of research, Rich found the perfect ratio, where the cabinet is small enough, but won't sacrifice the sound. Raezer's Edge's motto is "A Big Focused Sound in a Small Portable Cabinet." Raezer's Edge makes a small line of guitar and bass cabinets in different configurations. Most cabinets have a brown strip on the bottom and the rest of the cabinet is black. Prices start around $400 for a new cabinet. For more information on products and pricing vist the website (see Trademark Index).

RANDALL

Amplifiers currently produced in St. Mundelein, Illinois. Randall is a division of Washburn International.

Don Randall worked with Leo Fender way back in the 1940's when Fender was just starting out. Don was responsible for designing many amps for Fender. Eventually, Don broke away and started his own company. He wanted to design some more radical designs that never happened at Fender. The Randall Amplifier Company was then started. Amplifiers built today are mostly solid-state, but they are built with the great tube tone in mind and are very reliable. Randall uses the finest materials available to produce some fine amplifiers.

ELECTRIC AMPLIFIERS

Randall produces mostly solid-state guitar amplifiers. All guitar amplifiers are in this section. More research is underway on earlier Randall amplifiers since not much is known about them. All the new models are listed and there is a brief description on discontinued models.

Early Models

Randall amplifiers have been manufactured for quite some years. Some of the popular models include the Commander II, and the early RG-series. Most Ranadall amplifiers can be found in the $200-400 range ,depending on model and condition.

MTS Series

The MTS series is a new modeling amp. This modeling amp is a different design than others. Start with the preamp, which is a 4-module tube chassis. Then there are 10 different amp models that can be plugged into four slots onto the preamp. These 10 amps are of classic design s (Marshall Plexi, Fender Black-face), up to current Randall sounds. Each different model can be purchased for $249.90. The preamp unit retails for $699.90 alone. Then a power amp is needed to drive the sound outward. This is a novel design, but can prove costly to get all the effects that a guitarist may want.

A 50W combo with 1-12" speaker and 2-modules is available for a retail price of $999.90. It includes a 12" Celestion Century G12 and 6L6 power tubes.

GRADING	100%	EXCELLENT	AVERAGE

Warhead Series

These amps were designed with Dimebag Darrell of Pantera. This is his signature series. For Warhead speaker cabinets, see the Speaker Cabinet section.

WARHEAD HEAD - 300W, head-unit only, solid-state chassis, two channels, front black control panel, single input, 14 black and silver knobs, 9-band equalizer, 16 D.D. EFX, 6 equalizer knobs, independent gain and master, effects loop, footswitch, black covering, black metal grille, current mfg.

MSR $1,299.90	$925	$700 - 800	$575 - 650

WARHEAD COMBO - 150W, 2-12" Celestion Vintage 30 speakers, same chassis as the head, black covering, side handles, black metal grille, current mfg.

MSR $1,399.90	$999	$750 - 850	$625 - 675

Colossus Series

The Colossus Series was designed with Paul Stanley of Kiss. The Colossus series is now discontinued.

COLOSSUS HEAD - 300W, head-unit only, solid-state chassis, two channels, front black control panel, single input, eight black and silver knobs (v, b, m, t per channel), effects loop, footswitch, black covering with white piping, disc. 2002.

	$800	$650 - 725	$550 - 600

XL Series

VMAX - 300W, head-unit only, hybrid design, dual preamps (one solid-state, one tube), solid-state power amp, front silver control panel, single input, 17 black knobs, six-band graphic equalizer, effects loop, five-button footswitch, black covering, black grille, current mfg.

MSR $1,599.90	$1,125	$900 - 1,000	$750 - 825

R

GRADING	100%	EXCELLENT	AVERAGE

CYCLONE - 300W, head-unit only, solid-state chassis, two channels, reverb, front black control panel, single input, 13 black knobs, nine-band graphic equalizer, effects loop, black covering, black grille, two-button footswitch, current mfg.

MSR	$1,199.90	$850	$650 - 725	$550 - 600

TITAN - 300W, head-unit only, solid-state chassis, two channels, reverb, front black control panel, single input, nine black knobs, effects loop, two-button footswitch, black covering, black grille, current mfg.

MSR	$899.90	$650	$475 - 550	$375 - 425

Misc Head Amps

RH100 - 100W, head-unit only, solid-state chassis, two channels, reverb, front black control panel, single input, 13 black knobs, headphone jack, two-button footswitch, black covering, black grille, current mfg.

MSR	$449.90	$325	$240 - 285	$185 - 225

Combo Guitar Amplifiers

RG230SC - 40W (2 X 20W stereo), 2-10" Randall Jaguar speakers, solid-state chassis, two channels, chorus, reverb, front black control panel, single input, eleven black knobs, line out, headphone jack, black covering, black grille, current mfg.

MSR	$379.90	$275	$195 - 225	$150 - 175

RG75 - 75W, 1-12" Custom 80W Celestion speaker, solid-state chassis, two channels, reverb, front black control panel, single input, 13 black knobs, line out, headphone jack, two-button footswitch, black covering, black grille, current mfg.

MSR	$449.90	$325	$250 - 295	$175 - 205

RG100SC - 100W, 2-12" Custom 80W Celestion speakers, solid-state chassis, two channels, stereo chorus, reverb, front black control panel, single input, 15 black knobs, line out, headphone jack, two-button footswitch, black covering, black grille, current mfg.

MSR	$579.90	$425	$300 - 350	$250 - 275

X Series

The X series are small practice amplifiers that have a lot of features. All guitar amp combos in this series are solid-state and offer two channels. The **RG15XM** is a 15W amp with 1-6.5" speaker and retails for $99.90. The **RG15RXM** is the same as the RG15XM, except has reverb circuit and goes for $139.90. The **RG25RXM** is a 25W guitar amp with 1-8" speaker, reverb, and an effects loop. This one lists for $179.99. For the RB30XM refer to the Bass Amplifier Section.

BASS AMPLIFIERS

All the current bass amps produced are listed along with a brief description of the older RB series.

Current Production Models

RB200/115 - 200W, 1-15" Eminence Legend speaker, solid-state combo, single channel, front silver control panel, single input, eight black knobs, nine-band graphic equalizer, effects loop, balanced XLR out, headphones, black carpet covering, black metal grille, current mfg.

MSR	$999.90	$699	$500 - 600	$375 - 450

RB200/410 - Same as the RB200/15 in circuitary has 4-10" Eminence Coaxial speakers, current mfg.

MSR	$1,099.90	$775	$575 - 675	$475 - 525

RB100 - 100W, 1-15" Eminence Legend speaker, solid-state combo, single channel, front silver control panel, single input, eight black knobs, nine-band graphic equalizer, effects loop, balanced XLR out, headphones, black carpet covering, black metal grille, current mfg.

MSR	$849.90	$599	$450 - 525	$350 - 400

RB30XM - 30W, 1-10" speaker, solid-state combo, front black control panel, two inputs (active/passive), five black knobs, effects loop, headphone jack, black covering, black metal grille, current mfg.

MSR	$159.90	$120	$80 - 100	$60 - 70

RB Series (Discontinued Models)

Randall's earlier bass amps typically carried the RB model prefix. These amps were found in combo units as well as heads. Such examples of models are the RB-60, RB-35, and RBA-500ES head unit. These units can be usually found in the price range of $100-300.

SPEAKER CABINETS

Along with the speaker cabinets listed here, there are two isolation cabinets available. These are speaker cabinets that are meant for live recording with a microphone, essentially a recording studio in a box. This cabinet blocks out outside sounds to make recording possible. They are available for guitar for $399.90 and for bass for $499.90.

XL Series

R412XLT - 280W, 4-12" Celestion V30 speakers, 4/16 mono/8 stereo, straight front, angled baffle, black covering, black metal grille, current mfg.

MSR	$999.90	$699	$500 - 600	$400 - 450

RA412XLT - 280W, 4-12" Celestion V30 or G12T-75 speakers, 4/16 mono/8 stereo, angled front, black covering, black metal grille, current mfg.

MSR	$999.90	$699	$500 - 600	$400 - 450

* RS412XLT - Simlar to the RA412XLT, except in straight front cabinet, current mfg.

MSR	$999.90	$699	$500 - 600	$400 - 450

GRADING	100%	EXCELLENT	AVERAGE

RA412XL - 280W, 4-12" Celestion V30 or G12T-75 speakers, 4/16 mono/8 stereo, angled front, black covering, black grille cloth, current mfg.

	MSR	$899.90	$650	$450 - 550	$375 - 425

   * RS412XL - Simlar to the RA412XL, except in straight front cabinet, current mfg.

	MSR	$899.90	$650	$450 - 550	$375 - 425

MTS Series

RA412CS - 280W, 4-12" Celestion V30 speakers, 4/16 mono/8 stereo, straight front, black covering, Vintage Silver grille cloth, current mfg.

	MSR	$1,049.90	$750	$550 - 650	$450 - 500

R212CS - 120W, 2-12" Celestion V30 speakers, 8 Ohm mono, angled front, black covering, Vintage Silver grille cloth, current mfg.

	MSR	$649.90	$475	$350 - 400	$250 - 300

Signatures Series

RS412W - 280W, 4-12" Celestion V30 speakers, 4 stereo/8 mono, straight front, black covering, stainless steel and metal grille cosmetics, current mfg.

	MSR	$1,099.90	$775	$575 - 675	$450 - 525

RS215W - 400W, 2-15" Jaguar speakers, 8 Ohm mono, straight front, black covering, stainless steel and metal grille cosmetics, current mfg.

	MSR	$999.90	$699	$500 - 600	$400 - 450

Misc. Cabinets

R412CXM - 320W, 4-12" Custom 80W Celestion speakers, 4 stereo/8 mono, straight front,angled baffle, black covering, metal grille, current mfg.

	MSR	$649.90	$475	$350 - 400	$250 - 290

R212CX - 160W, 2-12" Custom 80W Celestion speakers, 4/16 mono/8 stereo, straight front, black covering, metal grille, current mfg.

	MSR	$449.90	$325	$225 - 275	$175 - 200

RAT FINK

Amplifiers currently produced in Huntington Beach, California.

Rat Fink is a series of amplifiers and guitars that are based on characters that were created by "Big Daddy" Ed Roth. These products were released at the Winter NAMM show in 2002. There was an animated video of these characters playing in the Lace booth featuring the new amps and guitars. Rat Fink has appeared more on show cars and other related memorabilia. Ken Mitchroney has painted designs on Rat Fink guitars as well.

ELECTRIC AMPLIFIERS

Currently Rat Fink has two amplifiers in production, which were both new in 2002. The smaller model is the **RF-15** and the larger model is the **RF-40**. Each model is covered in Red Tolex and features the Rat Fink character in the lower right hand corner. The RF-40 has considerably more controls and features than the RF-15. The RF-15 retails for $169, and the RF-40 is listed at $399.

Rat Fink 40
courtesy Rat Fink

REVEREND

Amplifiers currently produced in Warren, Michigan.

Reverend amplifiers started in 1997 when Joe Naylor and Dennis Kager started designing amps together. Joe Naylor founded Naylor Amps years ago, and Dennis Kager has roots with Ampeg. Together they came up with a high end amplifier and a workingman's price. Currently their Hellhound series is the flagship product. They are now a factory direct order company, which eliminates the middle man.

GRADING	100%	EXCELLENT	AVERAGE

ELECTRIC TUBE AMPLIFIERS

Add $25 for amp cover.

HELLHOUND 40/60 - 60W (switchable to 40W), head-unit only, all-tube chassis, preamp: 4 X 12AX7, power: 2 X 6L6, single channel, front black control panel, single input, schizo switch (US to UK), seven black knobs (g, v, t, m, b, p, r), effects loop, black custom tooled vinyl, gray/white peppered grille cloth, 24.5 lbs., mfg. 1997-current.

MSR	$799	$600	$450 - 525	$350 - 390

HELLHOUND 40/60 COMBO - Similar to the Hellhound in circuitry, has 1-12" Alltone 1250 speaker, 36 lbs., mfg. 1997-current.

Reverend Hellhound 40-60

MSR	$899	$650	$500 - 575	$400 - 450

GOBLIN 5/15 - Same features as the Hellhound 40/60, 15/5 switchable watts, available in a head-unit or 1-10" combo, new Summer 2002.

SPEAKER CABINETS

112 GUITAR CABINET - 1-12" Alltone 1250 speaker, 8 Ohm, compact open back, black custom tooled vinyl, gray/white peppered grille, 24 lbs., current mfg.

MSR	$399	$299	$200 - 250	$150 - 175

This amp matches up with the Hellhound 1-12" combo or head.

410 GUITAR CABINET - 4-10" Alltone 1030 speakers, 8 Ohm, compact open back, black custom tooled vinyl, gray/white peppered grille, 45 lbs., current mfg.

MSR	$399	$299	$200 - 250	$150 - 175

This amp matches the Hellhound head.

RHINO

Amplifiers currently produced in El Paso, Texas.

Rhino is a very young company that was formed in November of 2000. Robert Turner is the president of the company. In just two years, they have released a lot of tube amplifiers that have some unique designs. As of Fall 2002, Rhino was now going to have several more dealers in the United States and they are going to be sold in Japan as well. Yngwie Malmsteen has a new signature amp with Rhino, the Blackstar YJM-50. This amp was released recently at the NAMM Summer Show, 2002. They have a full listing of amplifiers and features on their web site (see Trademark Index).

ELECTRIC TUBE AMPLIFIERS

The new Yngwie Malmsteen amplifier was released at NAMM Summer session in 2002. The amp is going to be a 50W amp with specifications to Yngwie. The head unit retails for $1049, and the 2-12" combo is $1,424. All the other models are listed.

The Beast Series

The Beast series has it's own speaker cabinets that come in a 4-12" or 2-12" configurations. The 4-12" comes in a slanted version for retail of $744, or a straight front for $722. The 2-12" comes only in a straight front for $468. Rhino advertises the Beast in a full stack for retail price of $2,434, or a half stack for $1,712.

THE BEAST - 100W (switchable to 50W), head-unit only, all tube chassis, preamp: 5 X 12AX7, 1 X 12AT7, power: 4 X 6L6/EL34, two channels, reverb, front black control panel, single input, 13 black knobs, effects loop, line out, speaker impedance control, black covering, black metal grille, current mfg.

MSR	$968	$699	$500 - 600	$400 - 450

THE BEAST COMBO - Same as The Beast in circuitary, in combo form with 2-12" speakers, current mfg.

MSR	$1,343	$950	$725 - 825	$575 - 650

GRADING	100%	EXCELLENT	AVERAGE

The Bad Boy Series

The Bad Boy series has its own speaker cabinets that come in a 4-12" or 2-12" configurations and match the head unit. The 4-12" comes in a slanted version for retail of $744, or a straight front for $722. The 2-12" comes only in a straight front for $468. Rhino advertises the Beast in a full stack for retail price of $2,361, or a half stack for $1,639.

THE BAD BOY - 100W (switchable to 50W), head-unit only, all tube chassis, preamp: 5 X 12AX7, 1 X 12AT7, power: 4 X 6L6/EL34, two channels, reverb, definition, front black control panel, single input, nine black knobs, effects loop, line out, speaker impedance control, black covering, silver metal grille, current mfg.

MSR	$895	$650	$475 - 550	$375 - 425

THE BAD BOY COMBO - Same as The Bad Boy in circuitry, in combo form with 2-12" speakers, current mfg.

MSR	$1,270	$899	$675 - 750	$575 - 625

The Texas Tone-Ranger Series

THE TEXAS TONE RANGER - 100W (switchable to 50W), 2-12" speaker combo, all tube chassis, preamp: 5 X 12AX7, 1 X 12AT7, power: 4 X 6L6/EL34, two channels, reverb, definition, front black control panel, single input, 12 black knobs, effects loop, line out, speaker impedance control, brown covering, black metal grille, current mfg.

MSR	$1,321	$925	$700 - 800	$550 - 625

The Texas Tone Ranger can be teamed up with a 2-12" speaker cabinet. The 2-12" comes only in a straight front for $468.

The Baby Rhino Series

THE BABY RHINO - 100W (switchable to 50W), head-unit only, all tube chassis, preamp: 4 X 12AX7, power: 4 X 6V6, two channels, reverb, definition, front black control panel, single input, eight black knobs, effects loop, line out, speaker impedance control, black covering, black metal grille, current mfg.

MSR	$872	$625	$475 - 525	$375 - 425

RICKENBACKER
Amplifiers previously produced in Santa Ana, California.

The Rickenbacker company has been producing instruments that date back to 1931. In 1925, John Dopyera (and brothers) joined up with George Beauchamp and Adolph Rickenbacker. They formed National and started to build resonator guitars. Dopyera left the company and Rickenbacker, Beauchamp, and Dopyera's nephew, Paul Barth, started to build electric lap steel guitars. Beauchamp left in the late 1920's and the company was in the hands of Rickenbacker and Barth. In 1931, they started building aluminum versions of the electric Frying Pan prototype. Rickenbacker was added to the headstock around 1933, and the company was born. Instruments were produced as the Electro String Instrument company until 1953 when F.C. Hall bought the company.

In 1965, the Rickenbacker company was formed as an organizational change. Electro was building the instruments, and Rickenbacker was putting the name on the units. Amplifiers started to appear at this time (however there were some models made in the late 1950's). One of the first (and really the only Rickenbacker amp I see), was the Transonic. This is a trapezoid in shape and controls galore. You really have to see one to appreciate it. Amplifier production information is really scarce, and production of amps occurred off and on during the 1970's and 1980's. There are no current amplifiers produced by Rickenbacker.

ELECTRIC TUBE AMPLIFIERS

There are only a handful of tube amplifiers that Rickenbacker is known for building. Some of the early ones were produced in the 1950's. The Richenbacher (note spelling) M-8 is one of the first specimen. This amp was released before they had everything say Rickenbacker. This amp can generally be found between $100-$200 depending on condition. There are also other tube amps made over the years, but little is known about them. The Rickenbacker web site provides a schematic of the tube amplifiers, that may help in identification.

We have found a B-14A tube amp that is early 1960's. This particular model has tremolo. Pricing is difficult since this is the only one we've seen!

Rickenbacker B-14A
courtesy Savage Audio

Rickenbacker B-14A
courtesy Savage Audio

GRADING	100%	EXCELLENT	AVERAGE

ELECTRIC SOLID-STATE AMPLIFIERS

I can't explain why the one amp that is collectible from Rickenbacker is solid-state, but I do think that it has a lot to do with the looks. The Transonic series is the one amp that comes to mind when anyone mentions Rickenbacker amps. There are quite a few other Rickenbacker amplifiers out there in solid-state form and they usually are found between $125-$300 depending on features and condition.

TRANSONIC SERIES - This amp comes in a couple of versions, a 200, and 100 probably wattage, that are known. The TS-100 has 2-12" speakers and a control panel for rocket scientists. The amp is shaped like a trapezoid and has blue/green grille cloth. Knobs, buttons, and gauges are just some of the feature(there are plenty). These amps were produced in the late 1960's. Speaker configurations are different in every model as well. Pricing is tricky on these amps because that they are so odd, off-the-wall, and rare, that they are becoming ever so collectible. I have seen amps in excellent condition take as much as $2,000. Anywhere between $1,400-$1,800 is probably accurate for excellent and around $1,000 for average pieces. The *Blue Book of Guitar Amplifiers* would suggest getting a second opinion when either selling or buying a Transonic.

Rickenbacker Transonic 75-100
courtesy Dave Rogers

Rickenbacker Transonic 75-100
courtesy Dave Rogers

Rickenbacker Transonic 75-100
courtesy Dave Rogers

RIVERA

Amplfiers currently produced in Sylmar, California.

Paul Rivera has been involved in music all his life. Paul started in a repair shop in New York City repairing amplifiers. He also modified amplifiers for many famous musicians. He then moved to the west coast in 1972, where he continued to modify and started to help design new amplifiers. In 1976, Rivera Research Development & Co. was formed, and the first client of the company was Yamaha. Paul then worked with Fender in the early 1980's, trying to bail them out. He is responsible for the only great amps of the 80's from Fender, the Super Champ, Concert, and Twin Reverb II.
In 1985, Paul began producing his own amplifiers, and the first design was the rack-mount TBR-1. Ever since then, amplifier production has expanded rapidly. They offer many products now, including combo amps, amp heads, and speaker cabinets. Not only does Rivera build quality components but they are built to withstand road wear. A couple of places you may have seen Rivera amps was Clinton's Inaugural bash and the Grammy Awards.

ELECTRIC TUBE AMPLIFIERS

Rivera has produced quite a few models over the years. Some of the models that have been recently discontinued include the Bonehead series. This was a 100W head that was aimed to be built for a half or a full-stack. The Jake and Rake amps were also recently discontinued. Look for more information on these models and pricing in upcoming editions of the *Blue Book of Guitar Amplifiers*.

The Tube Rack Series

Rivera used to make a tube Rack series that was known as the TBR series. TBR-1M, TBR-2SL, and the TBR-3 were some of the models that used to be available. The TBR-3 and TBR-5 were strictly power amps. There is more information on these out of production amps on the Rivera web site (see Trademark Incex).

The KnuckleHead Series

KNUCKLEHEAD REVERB 55 - 55W, head-unit only, all tube chassis, preamp: 5 X 12AX7, power: 2 X 6L6GC or EL34, three channels, reverb, front black control panel, single input, 17 black knobs, various boosts and knobs, black covering, black metal grille, 36 lbs., disc. 2001.

$1,050	$800 - 900	$625 - 700

Last MSR was $1,495.

KNUCKLEHEAD 100 - Similar to the Knucklehead Reverb 55 except has 100W output with 4 power tubes, disc. 2002.

$1,275	$950 - 1,100	$800 - 875

Last MSR was $1,795.

R

GRADING	100%	EXCELLENT	AVERAGE

KNUCKLEHEAD REVERB COMBO 55 - 55W, 1-12" Celestion V-30 or G12T-75 speaker, all tube chassis, preamp: 5 X 12AX7, power: 2 X 6L6GC or EL34, three channels, reverb, front black control panel, single input, 17 black knobs, various boosts and knobs, black covering, black metal grille, current mfg.

MSR	$2,295	$1,650	$1,300 - 1,500	$1,050 - 1,200

KNUCKLEHEAD REVERB COMBO 100 - 100W, 2-12" Celestion V-30 or G12T-75 speaker, all tube chassis, preamp: 5 X 12AX7, power: 4 X 6L6GC or EL34, three channels, reverb, front black control panel, single input, 17 black knobs, various boosts and knobs, black covering, black metal grille, current mfg.

MSR	$2,495	$1,775	$1,400 - 1,600	$1,075 - 1,225

The R Series

R30-112 - 30W, 1-12" Celestion G12L-55 speaker, all tube chassis, preamp: 5 X 12AX7, power: 2 X EL34, two channels, reverb, front black control panel, two inputs, eleven black knobs (v, b, m, t, MV per channel, r), effects loop with level controls, black covering, black grille cloth, current mfg.

MSR	$1,095	$775	$650 - 725	$525 - 575

R55-112 - 55W, 1-12" Celestion G12L-85 speaker, all tube chassis, preamp: 5 X 12AX7, power: 2 X EL34, two channels, reverb, front black control panel, two inputs, twelve black knobs (v, b, m, t, MV per channel, r, p), effects loop with level controls, black covering, black grille cloth, current mfg.

MSR	$1,295	$925	$775 - 850	$675 - 725

R100-112A - 100W, 2-12" Celestion G12L-85 speakers, all tube chassis, preamp: 5 X 12AX7, power: 4 X EL34, two channels, reverb, front black control panel, two inputs, twelve black knobs (v, b, m, t, MV per channel, r, p), effects loop with level controls, black covering, black grille cloth, current mfg.

MSR	$1,795	$1,275	$950 - 1,100	$800 - 875

The Fandango Series

FANDANGO 112 - 55W, 1-12" Celestion G12T-75 speaker, all tube chassis, preamp: 5 X 12AX7, power: 2 X EL34, two channels, reverb, front black control panel, two inputs, 13 black knobs (v, b, m, t, MV per channel, r, p, focus), effects loop with level controls, cream Tolex covering, brown grille cloth, 65 lbs., current mfg.

MSR	$1,695	$1,199	$900 - 1,025	$750 - 850

* Fandango Top - Similar to the Fandango 112 except in head-unit version, current mfg.

MSR	$1,495	$1,050	$800 - 900	$650 - 750

FANDANGO 212 (55W) - 55W, 2-12" Celestion G12T-75 speakers, all tube chassis, preamp: 5 X 12AX7, power: 2 X EL34, two channels, reverb, front black control panel, two inputs, 13 black knobs (v, b, m, t, MV per channel, r, p, focus), effects loop with level controls, cream Tolex covering, brown grille cloth, 73 lbs., current mfg.

MSR	$1,895	$1,350	$1,000 - 1,200	$750 - 850

* Fandango Top (100W) - Similar to the Fandango, except in combo form, 100W output, with 4 X EL34 tubes, current mfg.

MSR	$1,695	$1,199	$900 - 1,000	$750 - 825

* Fandango 212 (100W) - Similar to the Fandango, except has 100W output, with 4 X EL34 tubes, 80 lbs., current mfg.

MSR	$2,095	$1,475	$1,150 - 1,350	$900 - 1,000

The Quiana Series

QUIANA 212 (55W) - 55W, 2-12" Celestion Vintage 30 speakers, all tube chassis, preamp: 5 X 12AX7, power: 2 X 6L6GC, two channels, reverb, top black control panel, two inputs, 13 black knobs (v, b, m, t, MV per channel, r, p, focus), effects loop with level controls, red Tolex covering, Vintage blonde grille cloth, 65 lbs., current mfg.

MSR	$1,895	$1,350	$1,000 - 1,200	$750 - 850

QUIANA 410 (55W) - Similar to the Quiana 212, except has 4-10" Eminence speakers, current mfg.

MSR	$1,995	$1,399	$1,025 - 1,200	$750 - 850

QUIANA STUDIO TOP - 100W, head-unit only, all tube chassis, preamp: 5 X 12AX7, power: 4 X 6L6GC, two channels, reverb, top black control panel, two inputs, 13 black knobs (v, b, m, t, MV per channel, r, p, focus), effects loop with level controls, red Tolex covering, Vintage blonde grille cloth, current mfg.

MSR	$1,495	$1,050	$800 - 900	$650 - 750

QUIANA STUDIO 112 - 100W, 1-12" Celestion Vintage 30 speaker, all tube chassis, preamp: 5 X 12AX7, power: 4 X 6L6GC, two channels, reverb, top black control panel, two inputs, 13 black knobs (v, b, m, t, MV per channel, r, p, focus), effects loop with level controls, red Tolex covering, Vintage blonde grille cloth, current mfg.

MSR	$1,695	$1,199	$950 - 1,075	$800- 875

QUIANA STUDIO 212 - Similar to the Quiana Studio 112, except has 2-12" speakers, current mfg.

MSR	$2,095	$1,475	$1,150 - 1,325	$900 - 1,000

The Chubster & Suprema Series

CHUBSTER 40W - 40W, 1-12" Celestion G12L-55 speaker, all tube chassis, preamp: 5 X 12AX7, power: 2 X EL34, two channels, reverb, front black control panel, two inputs, twelve black knobs (v, b, m, t, MV per channel, r, p), footswitch, red covering, Vintage Blonde grille cloth, 45 lbs., current mfg.

MSR	$1,195	$850	$650 - 725	$550 - 600

R

GRADING	100%	EXCELLENT	AVERAGE

CHUBSTER 55W - 55W, 1-12" Celestion G12T-75 speaker, all tube chassis, preamp: 5 X 12AX7, power: 2 X EL34, two channels, reverb, front black control panel, two inputs, twelve black knobs (v, b, m, t, MV per channel, r, p), footswitch, red covering, Vintage Blonde grille cloth, 56 lbs., current mfg.

	MSR $1,395	$999	$750 - 850	$650 - 700

CHUBSTER 55W - 55W, 1-12" Celestion Vintage 30 speaker, all tube chassis, preamp: 5 X 12AX7, power: 2 X EL34, two channels, reverb, front black control panel, two inputs, twelve black knobs (v, b, m, t, MV per channel, r, p), effects loop with level controls, footswitch, black Tolex covering, Tri-Tone Silver/Black grille cloth, 70 lbs., current mfg.

	MSR $1,595	$1,125	$900 - 1,000	$750 - 825

ACOUSTIC-ELECTRIC TUBE AMPLIFIERS; THE DOYLE DOKES & SEDONA SERIES

SEDONA 55 - 55W, head-unit only, all tube chassis, preamp: 5 X 12AX7, power: 2 X EL34, two channels, reverb, front black control panel, two inputs, 14 black knobs (v, b, m, t, MV per channel, r, p, 2 anti-feedback knobs), effects loop with level controls, footswitch, brown Tolex covering, Di-Tone Brown/Cream grille cloth, current mfg.

	MSR $1,595	$1,125	$900 - 1,000	$750 - 825

* **Sedona 55 Combo** - Similar to the Sedona 55 head-unit, except in combo form with 1-12" JBL speaker, current mfg.

	MSR $1,995	$1,399	$1,100 - 1,250	$875 - 975

SEDONA 100 - 100W, head-unit only, all tube chassis, preamp: 5 X 12AX7, power: 4 X EL34, two channels, reverb, front black control panel, two inputs, 14 black knobs (v, b, m, t, MV per channel, r, p, 2 anti-feedback knobs), effects loop with level controls, footswitch, brown Tolex covering, Di-Tone Brown/Cream grille cloth, current mfg.

	MSR $1,795	$1,275	$1,000 - 1,125	$800 - 900

* **Sedona 100 Combo** - Similar to the Sedona 100 head-unit except in combo form with 1-15" JBL speaker, current mfg.

	MSR $1,995	$1,399	$1,100 - 1,250	$875 - 975

SPEAKER CABINETS & POWERED SUBS

Rivera has speaker cabinets along with power sub-woofers to enhance the quality of sound coming from either a head-unit of a combo amp.

Extension Speaker Cabinets

QUIANA 212 - 2-12" Vintage 30 Celestion speakers, closed back, matches the Quiana head unit and combos, current mfg.

	MSR $795	$575	$425 - 485	$325 - 375

* **Quiana 412** - Similar to the Quiana 212, except has 4-12" speakers, current mfg.

	MSR $995	$699	$525 - 600	$425 - 475

FANDANGO 212 - 2-12" Celestion G12T-75speakers, closed back, matches the Fandango head unit and combos, current mfg.

	MSR $795	$575	$425 - 485	$325 - 375

* **Fandango 412** - Similar to the Fandango 212, except has 4-12" speakers, current mfg.

	MSR $995	$699	$525 - 600	$425 - 475

SEDONA (DOYLE DYKES) 112 - 1-12" JBL speaker, 2-way cabinet, matches the Sedona head unit and combos, current mfg.

	MSR $695	$499	$375 - 425	$275 - 325

* **Sedona 115** - Similar to the Sedona 112, except has 1-15" speaker, current mfg.

	MSR $995	$699	$525 - 575	$425 - 475

K212 - 2-12" Celestion Vintage 30 speakers, stackable enclosure, matches the Knucklehead head unit and combos, current mfg.

	MSR $795	$575	$425 - 485	$325 - 375

K412B - 4-12" Celestion Vintage 30 speakers, bottom enclosure, matches the Knucklehead head unit and combos, current mfg.

	MSR $995	$699	$525 - 600	$425 - 475

* **K412T** - Similar to the K412B, except is the top, angled version, current mfg.

	MSR $995	$699	$525 - 575	$425 - 475

Powered Sub-Woofers

LOS LOBOTTOM SUB 1 - 300W, 1-12" JBL powered subwoofer, black or blonde Tolex covering, silver/black or blonde grille cloth, current mfg.

	MSR $895	$650	$475 - 550	$390 - 425

Add $100 for wide version.

LOS LOBOTTOM SUB 2 - 500W, 1-12" JBL powered subwoofer, black or blonde Tolex covering, silver/black or blonde grille cloth, current mfg.

	MSR $1,395	$999	$725 - 825	$600 - 650

K312 SUB 1 - 300W (Sub 1), 1-12" JBL powered subwoofer, 2-12" Vintage Celestion 30 Speakers, black or blonde Tolex covering, silver/black or blonde grille cloth, current mfg.

	MSR $1,495	$1,075	$800 - 900	$700 - 750

R

GRADING	100%	EXCELLENT	AVERAGE

ROCCAFORTE

Amplifiers currently produced in Brea, California.

Doug Roccaforte has been producing tube amplifiers for a few years now. Doug started building amps when he was the type of guy who would take an amplifier, and modify it into something way better. His first victims were usually Fenders that he would soup up into a Marshall chassis. The first amp was a 1978 or 1979 Marshall 50W Master Lead that he rebuilt with a completely different circuit. His buddy, Mark Dickerson, really like the tone of the amp and told Doug that he thought he could sell a lot of them. He built some amps, mainly custom orders, before his business really started to get going. Now he produces amplifiers on a regular basis and some of his endorsers include Cesar Rosas, Marc Ford, and Scott Weiland of Stone Temple Pilots. Amplifiers and information are available on the web site and orders can be taken by phone (see Trademark Index). Doug also repairs amps (tube amps only). Currently Doug describes himself as a "Marshall guy."

(Roccaforte information courtesy of Tonequest, August, 2002)

ELECTRIC TUBE AMPLIFIERS

Doug Roccaforte builds four basic models of amplifiers.They come in a Custom 18, 40, or 80, and a Hi-Gain 100. These amps resemble Marshall in controls, and by the EL34 tubes. The look of the amplifiers are that of an early Marshall (1960's) head when the chassis didn't run all the way across the amplifier.

Roccaforte offers most of their models in either head or combo versions. The Levant series are amps that are covered in levant covering (there are several choices of color), and the Flame Series that are wood cabinets in an attractive solid flame maple wood, and custom inlay.

Most Roccaforte designs are truly great sounding amps, and they look great as well. Check the website for all the options and what a Roccaforte amp has to offer. Orders can be place directly.

ROCKTRON

Amplifiers currently produced in Battle Creek, Michigan. Rocktron is a division of the GHS corporation.

Rocktron has been around for about 20 years. Earlier their products were pedals and effects, but they are venturing into amplifiers more now. Rocktron first started producing solid-state amps, and recently have moved onto tube amplification. Rocktron now offers their DSP effects in their latest product, the Digital Tube Replication. The new amps are the RepliTone series. Essentially this is a modeling amp with all the classic amp sounds along with effects. For more information log on to their website (see Trademark Index).

ELECTRIC TUBE AMPLIFIERS

The Vedetta is the current tube series offered by Rocktron. This amp was designed by Bruce Egnator. It features a 100W output and EL34 output tubes. There are numerous controls on the amp, as it has four channels. It is available as a combo unit or a head unit that can be played through the matching 4-12" speaker cabinet (Vintage Celestion 30 speakers). Unfortunately, we don't have any retail prices on Rocktron products as they were not available when this book went to press. Used head units can be found between $800-1,200 depending on condition.

The Repli-Tone technically isn't a tube amplifier, but it is a digital tone replicator. Since it features a lot more effects and costs more than solid-sate we put it in the tube amplifier section. These amps have the digital effects of a slug of different amplifiers and a big list of effects. It also has the standard knobs that an amp of this caliber would have.

ELECTRIC SOLID-STATE AMPLIFIERS

The current line of solid-state amplifiers are known as the Rampage series. There are quite a few models offered within the series. Chorus amps are among the most flashy as they have 2 speakers to make stereo chorus. Then they have the typical 10, 20, 30, and 50W amplifiers with features increasing as the wattage goes up. Used amplifiers are generally pretty cheap in the Rampage series.

ROLAND

Amplifiers and other audio equipment currently produced in Japan. Roland Amplifiers are distributed in the U.S. by Roland Corporation U.S. in Los Angeles, California.

The Roland company was founded in Japan in 1974. They are known as one of the premier synthesizer builders in the world today. They started out with keyboards and other synthesizers and later moved on to building amplifiers and guitars. They have produced a number of amplifiers over the years in a different variety of applications. One of Roland's designs was to build a guitar with a synthesizer sort of built into it. This worked with a guitar with 10 buttons on it that plugged into a Roland unit where the sounds could be processed. The problem with this is that you would have to buy both the guitar and synthesizer together as a package for either one to work.

Today Roland produces several items in the audio industry. They make amplifiers, mixers, digital drum sets, effects, pedals, you name it. They have produced both tube and solid-state amps during the 1980's and 1990's. At the 2002 Summer NAMM show, Roland released their Cube 15 and their Cube 30, which are little solid-state guitar amps, but the effects on them are unbelievable. Having a booth across from Roland at NAMM, I heard first-hand what the Cube 30 can do (3 full days to be precise).

ELECTRIC TUBE AMPLIFIERS

There are three tube amplifiers in one series that I know of made by Roland Boss. The Bolt Series was in production during the 1980's and included three models, the Bolt-30, the Bolt-60, and the Bolt-100. The numbers indicate the wattage of the amp. These were small combo amps with 12" speakers, 12AT7 preamp tubes, and 2 X 6L6 output tubes. The Bolt-30 had a 7391 power tube. Prices are relatively cheap, falling in the $200-400 range. Lower for the 30 model and higher for the 100W model.

ELECTRIC SOLID-STATE AMPLIFIERS

We have split up the sections into the different series. Some of these series have both current and non-current amplifiers listed.

GRADING	100%	EXCELLENT	AVERAGE

Jazz-Chorus Series

JC-55 JAZZ CHORUS - 50W (2 X 25W Stereo), 2-8" speakers, solid-state combo, distortion, reverb, chorus, front black control panel, two inputs, eight black and silver knobs (v, b, m, t, distortion, r, chorus rate, depth), black covering, black and silver grille, mfg. 1980's.

	N/A	$250 - 300	$175 - 225

JC-77 JAZZ CHORUS - 70W (2 X 35W Stereo), 2-10" speakers, solid-state combo, distortion, reverb, chorus, front black control panel, two inputs, nine black and silver knobs (v, b, m, high t, t, distortion, r, chorus rate, depth), black covering, black and silver grille, mfg. 1980's.

	N/A	$300 - 350	$225 - 275

JC-90 JAZZ CHORUS - 80W (2 X 40W Stereo), 2-10" speakers, solid-state combo, distortion, reverb, chorus, front black control panel, two inputs, ten black and silver knobs (v, b, m, high t, t, distortion, r, chorus rate, depth), black covering, black and silver grille, current mfg.

MSR	$799	$525	$375 - 450	$275 - 325

JC-120 JAZZ CHORUS - 120W (2 X 60W Stereo), 2-12" speakers, solid-state combo, distortion, reverb, chorus, vibrato, front black control panel, two inputs, 13 black and silver knobs (v, b, m, high t, t, distortion, r, chorus rate, depth,s, i), black covering, black and silver grille, mfg 1975-current.

Roland Jazz Chorus-129
courtesy Savage Audio

Roland Jazz Chorus-129
courtesy Savage Audio

1975-1985	N/A	$500 - 575	$400 - 450
MSR	$1,099	$775	$550 - 650	$450 - 500

The Cube Series

CUBE 15 - 15W, 1-8" speaker, solid-state combo, two channels, overdrive, distortion, metal and metal stack sounds, 3-band equalizer, black covering, top control panel, black grille, new 2002.
> Roland's Price list these at $999, but at the NAMM show I heard that they were going to be around $299. We didn't recieve closure when this book went to press.

CUBE 20 - 20W, 1-8" speaker, solid-state combo, two channels, various knobs and buttons, black covering, black grille, mfg. late 1970's-1980's.

	N/A	$150 - 200	$100 - 125

CUBE 30 - 30W, 1-10" speaker, solid-state combo, two channels, DSP circuit, 8 COSM guitar amp models, EFX section, various knobs and buttons, black covering, top control panel, black grille, new 2002.
> Roland's Price list these at $999, but at the NAMM show I heard that they were going to be around $299. We didn't recieve closure when this book went to press.

CUBE 40 - 40W, 1-10" speaker, solid-state combo, two channels, various knobs and buttons, effects loop, black coveirng, black grille, mfg. late 1970's-1980's.

	N/A	$175 - 225	$125 - 150

CUBE 60 - 60W, 1-12" speaker, solid-state combo, two channels, various knobs and buttons, effects loop, black coveirng, black grille, mfg. late 1970's-1980's.

	N/A	$200 - 250	$150 - 175

The BluesCube Series

BC-30 - 30W, 1-12" speaker, solid-state combo, two channels, top control panel, six knobs, cream covering, brown grille cloth, made in the U.S.A., current mfg.

MSR	$379	$275	$210 - 250	$160 - 185

    * **BC-30/210** - Similar to the BC-30, except has 2-10" speakers, current mfg.

MSR	$479	$340	$250 - 300	$200 - 230

GRADING	100%	EXCELLENT	AVERAGE

BC-60 - 60W, 1-12" speaker, solid-state combo, two channels, reverb, top control panel, various knobs, cream covering, brown grille cloth, made in the U.S.A., current mfg.

MSR	$599	$425	$325 - 375	$250 - 275

* BC-60/310 - Similar to the BC-30, except has 3-10" speakers, current mfg.

MSR	$779	$550	$425 - 475	$350 - 400

The V-Guitar Series

VGA-3 - 50W, 1-12" speaker, digital solid-state chassis, 11 COSM digital amp models, 10 digital memories presets, front black control panel, single input, 11 black and silver knobs, various buttons and switches, black covering, black grille cloth, current mfg.

MSR	$649	$475	$375 - 425	$300 - 350

VGA-5 - 65W, 1-12" speaker, digital solid-state chassis, 11 COSM digital amp models, 10 digital memories presets, front silver control panel, two input, 16 black and silver knobs, various buttons and switches, effects-loop, casters, black covering, black grille cloth, current mfg.

MSR	$999	$699	$500 - 600	$400 - 450

VGA-7 - 130W (2 X 65 Stereo), 2-12" speaker, digital solid-state chassis, 20 COSM digital amp models, 26 guitar models, 80 digital memory presets, front silver control panel, two input, a whole bunch of black and silver knobs, various buttons and switches, effects-loop, casters, black covering, black grille cloth, current mfg.

MSR	$1,699	$1,200	$950 - 1,100	$750 - 850

ACOUSTIC SOLID-STATE AMPLIFIERS

AC-100 - 100W (50W, 2 X 25W), 1-12" + 2-5" speakers, solid-state chassis, two channels, chorus, reverb, front gold control panel, four inputs (two per channel), 14 black and gold knobs, anti-feedback system, brown covering, brown grille cloth, mfg. 1995-current.

MSR	$1,195	$850	$625 - 725	$525 - 575

Gee, another brown acoustic amp, whoever made the first brown acoustic amplifier must be a millionaire.

BASS SOLID-STATE AMPLIFIERS

DB-500 - 160W, 1-12" speaker + horn tweeter, solid-state chassis, digital COSM modeling, D-Chorus effect, shape controls, 2 programmable memories, top control panel, various knobs and buttons, black covering, gray grille, current mfg.

MSR	$999	$699	$525 - 600	$400 - 450

DB-700 - 250W, 1-15" speaker + horn tweeter, solid-state chassis, digital COSM modeling, D-Chorus effect, shape controls, 2 programmable memories, top control panel, various knobs and buttons, black covering, gray grille, current mfg.

MSR	$1,299	$925	$750 - 850	$650 - 700

DB-900 - 320W, 7-speaker cabinet including 4-10", 2-12" and a horn tweeter, solid-state chassis, digital COSM modeling, D-Chorus effect, shape controls, 2 programmable memories, front control panel, various knobs and buttons, black covering, gray grille, current mfg.

MSR	$1,999	$1,425	$1,100 - 1,250	$900 - 1,000

NOTES

Section S

SMF

Amplifiers currently produced in Newport Beach, California.

SMF stands for Sonic Machine Factory, LLC, which was founded in 2002 by Rick Hamel. Rick was working in San Diego with his line of SIB effects pedals. Mark Sampson (Matchless, Badcat) was brought in to do the engineering. Mark has several years of experience in the Class A tube design. These new SMF amps were just released with two models. All amplifiers are hand-assembled right here in the U.S.A.

ELECTRIC TUBE AMPLIFIERS

SMF has two models in their current line. The arsenal consists of the 15 Watter and the 30 Watter. The 15 is in a combo with 1-12" Celestion speaker, 2 X EL84 power output tubes, a footswitch, and retails for $2,199. The 30 is also a combo with 2-12" Celestion speakers, 4 X EL84 tubes, reverb, and retails for $2,999. Both models have two channels (Clean and Hi-Gain), and a Sonic Hatch tunable cabinet. The front of these amps have their own look to them as well, with a sort of an off-set oval grille cloth.

SWR

Amplifiers currently produced in Sun Valley, California.

SWR was founded in 1984 by Steve W. Rabe (SWR are his initials). The company was formed with the idea that their products would serve the creative needs of musicians beyond their expectations. Daryl Jamison is currently the president/CEO at the company. They have grown from a company that started with a power amp in 1984 to having a half-dozen lines of amps. They specialize in bass amplication and acoustic amps. In 2002, they won two awards from the MIPA (Musikmesse International Press Award) for making the best bass cabinets in the world and for the Mo' Bass soundstation. There is more information on the SWR web site (see Trademark Index).

GRADING	100%	EXCELLENT	AVERAGE

ACOUSTIC AMPLIFIERS

For the Blonde on Blonde model, refer to the speaker cabinet section in SWR.

STRAWBERRY BLONDE - 80W, 1-10" + a tweeter acoustic combo, solid-state chassis, single channel, reverb, front strawberry-colored control panel, single input, eight cream knobs, effects loop, headphone jack, XLR direct out, cream covering, cream metal grill, mfg. 1996-current.

	MSR	$699	$499	$375 - 425	$275 - 325

CALIFORNIA BLONDE - 120W, 1-12" + a tweeter acoustic combo, solid-state chassis, two channels, reverb, front brown control panel, instrument and mic input, 13 cream knobs, effects loop, headphone jack, XLR direct out, tuner out, cream covering, brown metal grill, mfg. 1996-current.

	MSR	$1,099	$775	$575 - 675	$450 - 500

ELECTRIC BASS AMPLIFIERS

SWR produced only Bass amplifiers until 1996. Therefore they have some great designs and some power that will relocate house if used right (or wrong).

Professional Series (Head-Units)

MO' BASS - 900W (400W per side stereo), rack-mount head unit only, tube preamp, solid-state power amp, single channel, chorus, overdrive, front silver control panel, two inputs (passive and active), 23 silver knobs, headphone jack, lots of speaker and line outs, blue casing, 3-space rack mount, 29 lbs., mfg. 2000-current.

	MSR	$1,999	$1,450	$1,100 - 1,300	$950 - 1,000

Add $250 for master footswitch (Mo' Control).

SM-500 - 500W (250W per side stereo), rack-mount head unit only, tube preamp, solid-state power amp, single channel, front black control panel, two inputs (passive and active), 11 black knobs, four-band equalizer, lots of speaker and line outs, black casing, 2-space rack mount, 20 lbs., current mfg.

	MSR	$1,649	$1,175	$900 - 1,050	$725 - 800

SM-900 - 900W (400W per side stereo), rack-mount head unit only, tube preamp, solid-state power amp, single channel, limiter, crossover, front black control panel, two inputs (passive and active), 17 black knobs, switchable equalizers, lots of speaker and line outs, footswitch, black casing, 2-space rack mount, 26 lbs., current mfg.

	MSR	$2,299	$1,625	$1,250 - 1,450	$1,025 - 1,125

BASS 350 - 350W, rack-mount head unit only, tube preamp, solid-state power amp, single channel, limiter, front black and silver control panel, two inputs (passive and active), eight black knobs, lots of speaker and line outs, effects loop, black casing, 2-space rack mount, 16.5 lbs., current mfg.

	MSR	$999	$699	$500 - 600	$400 - 450

BASS 350X - Similar to the Bass 350 except has SubWave circuitry and one more control knob, silver casing, new 2002.

	MSR	$1,099	$775	$550 - 650	$400 - 450

GRADING	100%	EXCELLENT	AVERAGE

BASS 750 - 750W, rack-mount head unit only, tube preamp, solid-state power amp, single channel, limiter, front black and silver control panel, two inputs (passive and active), nine black knobs, lots of speaker and line outs, effects loop, black casing, 2-space rack mount, 16.5 lbs., current mfg.

	MSR	$1,499	$1,075	$800 - 900	$700 - 750

BASS 750X - Similar to the Bass 750 except has SubWave circuitry (with overdrive), and one more control knob, silver casing, new 2002.

	MSR	$1,599	$1,150	$850 - 950	$725 - 775

POWER 750 - 750W power amp only, rack mount head-unit, silver and black control panel, single volume knob, four LED lights, silver casing, 32 lbs., current mfg.

	MSR	$1,199	$850	$625 - 725	$550 - 600

This model received a facelift in 2002, older models are going to have polished look, the new one has ribs.

INTERSTELLAR OVERDRIVE PREAMP - preamp only, rack mount head-unit, silver and black control panel, two inputs, eight black knobs, four LED lights, single rack-mount space, 10 lbs., current mfg.

	MSR	$899	$625	$475 - 550	$375 - 425

Baby Blue, Black Beauty, & Super Redhead Series

BABY BLUE HEAD - 160W (120W @ 4 Ohms), head-unit only, tube preamp, solid-state power amp, single channel, front blue control panel, single input, seven black knobs, effects loop, headphone jack, tuner out, black carpet covering, 12 lbs., current mfg.

	MSR	$899	$650	$475 - 550	$375 - 425

Baby Blue II - Same chassis as the Baby Blue Head, in combo form with 2-8" speakers + a tweeter, silver metal grille, current mfg.

	MSR	$1,399	$999	$750 - 850	$625 - 675

Baby Baby Blue - Same chassis as the Baby Blue Head, in combo form with 1-10" speakers + a tweeter, silver metal grille, current mfg.

	MSR	$1,099	$775	$600 - 675	$500 - 550

BLACK BEAUTY - 350W, 1-15" speaker + a tweeter, tube preamp, solid-state power amp, single channel, front black control panel, single input, nine black knobs, black vinyl covering, black metal grille, 95 lbs., new 2002.

	MSR	$1,499	$1,100	$825 - 925	$700 - 750

Add $75 for chrome grille.

SUPER REDHEAD - 350W, 2-10" speaker + a tweeter, tube preamp, solid-state power amp, single channel, front red control panel, single input, nine black knobs, black vinyl covering, black metal grille, front black cover also serves as a tilt-back floor stand, 80 lbs., mfg. 1988-current.

	MSR	$1,999	$1,450	$1,050 - 1,250	$850 - 950

Workingman's Series

WORKINGMAN'S 2004 - 200W, head-unit only, solid-state chassis, single channel, limiter, compression, front black control panel, two inputs, nine silver knobs, headphone jack, tuner out jack, black rough covering, 27lbs., current mfg.

	MSR	$599	$425	$300 - 350	$225 - 250

WORKINGMAN'S 4004 - 400W, head-unit only, solid-state chassis, single channel, limiter, compression, front black control panel, two inputs, five silver knobs, five-band equalizer, headphone jack, tuner out jack, black rough covering, 33 lbs., current mfg.

	MSR	$799	$575	$425 - 475	$325 - 375

WORKINGMAN'S 8004 T/O/P - 800W, head-unit only, solid-state chassis, single channel, limiter, compression, front black control panel, two inputs, nine silver knobs, headphone jack, tuner out jack, black rough covering, 49 lbs., new 2002.

	MSR	$799	$575	$425 - 475	$325 - 375

WORKINGMAN'S 10 - 80W, 1-10" + a tweeter combo, solid-state chassis, single channel, limiter, compression, top black control panel, two inputs, six black knobs, headphone jack, tuner out jack, effects loop, black rough covering, black metal grille, 32 lbs., current mfg.

	MSR	$599	$425	$300 - 350	$225 - 250

WORKINGMAN'S 12 - 100W, 1-12" and a tweeter combo, solid-state chassis, single channel, limiter, compression, top black control panel, two inputs, seven black knobs, headphone jack, tuner out jack, effects loop, black rough covering, black metal grille, 50 lbs., current mfg.

	MSR	$799	$575	$425 - 475	$325 - 375

Models produced before 2002 had a different situated control panel as it was set back on top of the cabinet.

WORKINGMAN'S 15 - 160W, 1-15" and a tweeter combo, solid-state chassis, single channel, limiter, compression, top black control panel, two inputs, nine black knobs, headphone jack, tuner out jack, effects loop, black rough covering, black metal grille, 70 lbs., current mfg.

	MSR	$999	$699	$525 - 625	$425 - 475

Models produced before 2002 had a different situated control panel as it was set back on top of the cabinets.

LA Series

The LA series are little amplifiers, hence the abbreviation. These little devils are aimed at anyone who wants to plug into an amplifier, that anyone can afford. They start at a 30W 1-8", in the model LA 8. This retails for $299. The LA 12 has 60W output with 1-12" speaker, and lists at $399. The LA 15 is a 100W model with a 15" speaker and tweeter that goes for $499. All amps have black covering, a black top control panel, various knobs, and a black grille.

GRADING	100%	EXCELLENT	AVERAGE

SPEAKER CABINETS

The speaker cabinets are broken up into their respective series. The professional series cabinets are the highest quality end cabinets, the Custom Pro series typically have smaller configurations. The Workingman's cabinets are meant to go with the heads. The Acoustic amp matches the California Blonde model.

Professional Series Speaker Cabinets

SON OF BERTHA - 350W, 1-15" speaker + a tweeter, black covering, chrome metal grille, 60 lbs., current mfg.

MSR	$799	$575	$425 - 500	$350 - 390

GOLIATH JUNIOR III - 350W, 2-10" speaker + a tweeter, 4 or 8 Ohm, black covering, chrome metal grille, 55 lbs., current mfg.

MSR	$799	$575	$425 - 500	$350 - 390

GOLIATH III - 700W, 4-10" speaker + a tweeter, 4 or 8 Ohm, black covering, chrome metal grille, 89 lbs., current mfg.

MSR	$1,099	$775	$600 - 675	$500 - 550

GOLIATH SENIOR - 1,000W, 6-10" speaker + a tweeter, 4 Ohm, black covering, chrome metal grille, 115 lbs., current mfg.

MSR	$1,499	$1,075	$800 - 950	$650 - 725

MEGOLIATH - 1,200W, 8-10" speaker + a tweeter, 8 or 4 Ohm, black covering, chrome metal grille, 154 lbs., current mfg.

MSR	$1,999	$1,475	$1,125 - 1,325	$900 - 1,000

A.K.A. "The Chiropracters special," luckily there are wheels and handles to wheel it along. The *Blue Book of Guitar Amplifiers* doesn't suggest carrying it up the stairs by yourself.

Custom Pro Specialist Series Speaker Cabinets

BIG BEN - 400W, 1-18" subwoofer, 8 Ohm, black covering, chrome metal grille, 73 lbs., current mfg.

MSR	$799	$575	$425 - 500	$350 - 400

TRIAD 1 - 400W, 1-15" driver, 1-10" driver, high-frequency tweeter, 4 Ohm, black covering, chrome metal grille, 80 lbs., current mfg.

MSR	$1,049	$750	$550 - 625	$450 - 500

HENRY THE 8X8 - 480W, 8-8" drivers, high-frequency tweeter, 4 Ohm, black covering, chrome metal grille, 100 lbs., current mfg.

MSR	$1,299	$925	$725 - 825	$600 - 650

BIG BERTHA - 700W, 2-12" drivers, high-frequency tweeter, 4 Ohm, caster wheels, black covering, chrome metal grille, 98 lbs., current mfg.

MSR	$1,349	$950	$750 - 825	$625 - 675

12-STACK ROCK BOX - 800W+, 4-12" drivers, ported cabinet, removable caster wheels, brown leatherish covering, black metal grille, 107 lbs., new 2002.

MSR	$999	$699	$500 - 600	$400 - 450

12-PACK ROCK BOX - 400W+, 2-12" drivers, ported cabinet, removable caster wheels, brown leatherish covering, black metal grille, 63 lbs., new 2002.

MSR	$699	$499	$350 - 425	$250 - 300

BASS MONITOR 12 - 250W+, 1-12" driver, high-frequency tweeter, tilt-back cabinet design, black covering, black metal grille, 33 lbs., reintroduced 2002.

MSR	$399	$299	$200 - 250	$150 - 175

Workingman's Series Speaker Cabinets

WORKINGMAN'S 1X10T - 100W, 1-10" driver, high-frequency tweeter, ported front slot, black covering, black metal grille, 26 lbs., current mfg.

MSR	$269	$199	$125 - 175	$90 - 105

This cabinet matches perfectly up with the Workingman's 10 combo amp.

WORKINGMAN'S 1X15T - 200W, 1-15" driver, high-frequency tweeter, ported front slot, black covering, black metal grille, 45 lbs., current mfg.

MSR	$499	$350	$250 - 300	$175 - 225

WORKINGMAN'S 2X10T - 200W, 1-10" driver, high-frequency tweeter, ported front slot, black covering, black metal grille, 60 lbs., current mfg.

MSR	$499	$350	$250 - 300	$175 - 225

WORKINGMAN'S 4X10T - 400W, 4-10" driver, high-frequency tweeter, ported front slot, black covering, black metal grille, 97 lbs., current mfg.

MSR	$799	$565	$425 - 500	$350 - 390

WORKINGMAN'S TOWER - 800W, 8-10" driver, high-frequency tweeter, ported front slot, black covering, black metal grille, 110 lbs., current mfg.

MSR	$1,299	$925	$675 - 775	$550 - 600

GRADING	100%	EXCELLENT	AVERAGE

Acoustic Speaker Cabinets

BLONDE ON BLONDE - 80W, 1-12" speaker with a high-frequency tweeter, volume control, horn on/off switch, speaker jack, cream covering, brown metal grille, current mfg.

MSR	$699	$499	$350 - 425	$250 - 300

This unit is capable of giving the acoustic series stereo output as well as a monitoring system.

SAMSON AUDIO

Amplifiers and other audio equipment currently distributed out of Syosset, New York.

Samson has been building power amplifiers and other audio equipment for over 10 years now. Most of the staff are musicians, which is a strong point to have in the music industry. Samson produces rack-mount power amplifiers in a number of different wattages. They also build signal processors, and equalizers, which musicians can use. They focus more on the DJ seen more with mixers, speaker cabinets, and microphones. For more information and what Samson has to offer refer to the web site (see trademark index).

SAVAGE AUDIO

Amplifiers currently produced in Burnsville, Minnesota.

Savage Audio is run by Jeff Krumm. Along with him, there are other great employees down in Burnsville, fixing, building, and jamming on amplifiers all day long. Savage Audio is mainly a fix-it shop where they specialize in tube amps, but will also fix solid-state models as well. The repair shop here can do almost anything from repair, to rebuilding, to restoration. With all the know-how around there, they started to produced their own amplifiers, The store used to be located in Savage (a stone's throw away from Burnsville), and the name fit for the store and the new line of amplifiers. Kudos out to the guys who know so much about these boxes that make noise, thanks again. See Trademark Index for company information.

ELECTRIC TUBE AMPLIFIERS

Currently Savage produces three main amplifiers. the Blitz 50, the Glas 30, and the Rohr 15 (See the PPGS for chassis pictures). All amplifiers are hand built, tube design to provide optium performance. All the information is on the web site, but talking to the knowledgable men at Savage will give you a good idea what they have to offer, and what would be the right fit for you.

Savage Audio Blitz 50
courtesy Savage Audio

Savage Audio Blitz 50
courtesy Savage Audio

SELMER-LONDON

Amplifiers previously produced in London, England.

Selmer goes way back to before the Franco-Prussian war in the 1800's! Henry Selmer developed a clarinet that was much better than anything else that was out there. This became the first Selmer instrument. Ben Davis was a gentleman that formed the Selmer instrument company after meeting with Selmer. This was in the early 1930's. By the time World War II came around, Selmer was the largest producer of instruments in the U.K. The company really took off in the 1950's and 1960's when amplifiers came around.

Selmer amps go back to when they took over a small company named RMS. They produced amps under this name for a while in the late 1940's and early 1950's. Selmer then began putting their own names on amps. The company went through some changes and by the 1970's things started to dissipate. By the mid 1970's, amp production had been discontinued all together. Selmer still produces musical instruments, but focuses more in the woodwind and brass industry. For more information refer to the Selmer Truvoice web site (unofficial).

(The author would like to thank Tim Fletcher and Steve Russell for contributing information to this section.)

ELECTRIC TUBE AMPLIFIERS

The only information that I have been able to find has come from the unoffical Selmer Truvoice web site that Tim Fletcher and Steve Russell have developed. Not only is this about the only info I have been able to find, but they have spent a lot of time developing it and including as much information as possible. Since the web address is really long, I would suggest going to a search engine and looking up Selmer Truvoice amps to access this site. More information is to come in future edtions of the *Blue Book of Guitar Amplifiers*.

Here are two examples of Selmer amps circa 1960's.

Selmer Truvoice Constellation 20
courtesy solidbodyguitar.com, Inc.

Selmer Truvoice Zodiac Twin Thirty
courtesy solidbodyguitar.com, Inc.

SEYMOUR DUNCAN

Amplifiers previously produced in Santa Barbara, California.

Seymour Duncan is both a guitar player and guitar repairman. He is probably most noted for the pickups he has made over the past two decades. Early in life he learned how to play guitar and became a noted musician. His first experience winding a pickup came when his Tele's lead pickup broke and he rewound it on a 33 1/3 RPM record player. He spent time with musicians including Les Paul and Roy Buchanan, and he realized it was his pickups that were keeping him from getting that tone. He moved to England as a suggestion by Les Paul and learned all about pickups. He fixed and rewound pickups for many notables including Jimmy Page and Pete Townshend, among others. Seymour moved back to the states in the mid 1970's, and along with more experience, started his own company. Seymour Duncan pickups was established in 1978 with Cathy Carter Duncan.

Shortly after they started producing pickups, they began producing amplifiers. Seymour Duncan produced both tube and solid-state designs. One of the innovations that they had at Seymour was the Convertible series, where the amps were capable of holding interchangeable modules, for all kinds of different amp sounds. For one reason or another, they only produced amplifiers for about a decade. By the early 1990's, amp production had been phased out and production was focused on pickups. Today Seymour Duncan has over 60 employees and produce some of the finest pickups out on the market.

ELECTRIC TUBE AMPLIFIERS

CONVERTIBLE 60W - 60W, 1-12" Celestion speaker, tube chassis, preamp: 2 X 12AX7, power: 2 X EL34, two channels, reverb, space for 5 amp modules, front black control panel, two inputs, eight black knobs, black covering, black grille, mfg. 1980's.

N/A	$275 - 325	$200 - 235

CONVERTIBLE 100W - 100W, 1-12" Celestion speaker, tube chassis, preamp: 3 X 12AX7, power: 4 X EL34, 5 amp module with preamp tube for each, two channels, reverb, front black control panel, two inputs, 13 black knobs (OD, MV, t, m, b, r per channel, wattage selector), black covering, black grille, mfg. 1980's.

N/A	$350 - 425	$260 - 300

84-40 COMBO - 40W, 1-12" speaker, tube chassis, preamp:12AX7, power: 4 X EL84, two channels, front black control panel, single input, eight black knobs, black covering, black grille, mfg. 1980's.

N/A	$350 - 425	$275 - 300

84-50 COMBO - 50W, 1-12" speaker, tube chassis, preamp:12AX7, power: 4 X EL84, two channels, three boost stages, front black control panel, single input, eight black knobs, black covering, black grille, mfg. 1980's.

N/A	$375 - 425	$275 - 325

SIEGMUND

Amplifiers currently produced in Tujunga, California.

The Siegmund guitar and amplifier company currently produces amplifiers along with other custom guitars (acoustic, electric, and resophonic). The current line of amplifiers is the Midnight series. These are all tube amplifiers that are open for custom options as far as tone and other features. Contact Siegmund to get a list of options and features that they have to offer (see Trademark Index).

SILVERTONE

Amplifiers previously produced during the 1950's-1960's.

Silvertone is a company that never actually produced or had a factory to build amplifiers (or guitars). Amplifiers were made by the Danelectro company, which also produced solid-body guitars for Silvertone. Silvertone was the brandname for Sears and Roebuck that was used between 1941 and 1970. The acoustic instruments and other guitars were usually made by Harmony, Valco, and Kay. Silvertone amps for the most part were made by Danelectro from the get-go. Since Silvertone amps were typically sold out of the Sears and Roebuck mail order catalog, they were entry-level models. Silvertone guitars were known as house-brand instruments, and amplifiers can be thought of in the same way. Danelectro closed its doors around 1969, and naturally all amplifier production was finished. Silvertone was terminated after Sears and Roebuck stopped selling their instruments and amps in the catalog.

ELECTRIC TUBE AMPLIFIERS

Since Silvertone amplifiers were budget, entry level, practice instruments when they were first produced, they still are today. This doesn't mean that they are bad amplifiers, it just isn't collectable. Silvertone amps are basically Danelectro amplifiers with a different name on them. This means that Danelectro descriptions will match most Silvertone descriptions (funny how that works). In some ways you can cross reference Danelectro with Silvertone (just a helpful hint).

Silvertone amplifiers were typically numbered with a four-digit identification. Unfortunately in the catalogs that I have seen, the numbers are linked with the different models. Therefore we can't get every model with the correct identification. Most Silvertone amplifiers can be found relatively cheap. Almost all models can be found priced under $250. There are a couple exceptions to this. One is the Twin 12 (Model 1484) model that was introduced in the mid 60's. This was a piggy-back unit that is typically found on the market in the $300-450 range, depending on condition.

MODEL 1457 - 5W, 1-8" speaker, all tube chassis, guitar case with built in amp, single channel, tremolo, four knobs (v, tone, s, strength), black case with gray grille, red lining inside, mfg. 1960's.

Silvertone Model 1457
"Amp in the Case"
courtesy S. P. Fjestad

Silvertone Model 1457
"Amp in the Case"
courtesy S. P. Fjestad

Silvertone Model 1457
"Amp in the Case"
courtesy S. P. Fjestad

| N/A | $300 - 375 | $200 - 250 |

Price includes the guitar in the case. The Guitar is a model 1457 as well as the amplifier. For information on the guitar refer to the *Blue Book of Electric Guitars*.

SIMMS-WATTS
Amplifiers previously produced in England.

Simms-Watts is a company that produced amps that were of Marshall and Hiwatt kin. They basically made a 100W head unit that was recognizable with the orange control panel. Controls are comparable to that of Marshall-era. People compare the sound to a more country sounding unit that the hard-rock that Marshall was known for. These amps were made for a short while in the 1970's and built to a very high quality standard. They are pretty rare today.

SOLDANO
Amplifiers currently produced in Seattle, Washington.

Soldano amplifiers have been in the works for more than two decades, but serious production didn't start until 1988. Michael Soldano has been working and building things from the ground up ever since he was a kid. At age 21 he began playing guitar, and because of a shortage of cash while going to college he built his own amplifier. His first amp was a Bassman copy that would pretty much blow up every night. He started fixing it and found that they were fun to actually work on. Mike's knowledge of amplifiers really took off when he picked up some tube books from the library where his mom worked. They were throwing them away as they thought tube technology was obsolete. Doug Roberts helped Mike build his first amp in 1980. The first amp wasn't much but it was a learning experience. He was building an amp on a chassis that he named Mr. Science. After he had saved enough money he bought a Mesa Boogie MK II. He decided that it needed some modifications and started a five year building process to make the "ultimate guitar amp." Mike moved to L.A. from Seattle and back with very little success. He had a couple SOL-100, which were the Super Overdrive Lead 100W amp, and had sold a few to friends and players. Tony Antidormi started working for Mike and tried to get the amp out on the music scene. Mike took a job as a roadie for a gig. When he got done with that gig, word had been spread like wildfire about the Soldano amp. The rest, like they say, is history. In 1987 and 1988 some big names bought Soldano amps, like Eric Clapton, and Mark Knopfler of Dire Straits. Later on came the Soldano/Caswell motorized preamp. Business has boomed ever since.

Currently Soldano produces a full line of amplifiers that have proved to be some of the best amplifiers on the market. Solidbodyguitars.com is a dealer of Soldano and sell them only because they are "the best amps out there." They now make a full range of head-units, combo amps, and speaker cabinets.

(Soldano history courtesy of Ritchie Flieger: Amps!)

ELECTRIC TUBE AMPLIFIERS

There are various series for all types of electric guitar amplification in the Soldano line. The color of an amp is also an option. They do come standard in black, red, snakeskin, and purple. For a fee (usually $200) custom colors can be used on both the head units and speaker cabinets.

Add $150 for custom colors.

GRADING	100%	EXCELLENT	AVERAGE

SLO (Super Lead Overdrive) Series

SLO 100 - 100W, head-unit only, all tube chassis, two channels, front silver control panel, single input, eight black and silver knobs, footswitch, various color covering, black metal grille, current mfg.

Soldano SLO-100
courtesy Soldano

MSR	$3,499	$2,500	$1,950 - 2,200	$1,500 - 1,700

* SLO 100 212 Combo - Similar to the SLO 100, except in combo form with 2-12" speakers, current mfg.

MSR	$3,849	$2,750	$2,100 - 2,350	$1,750 - 1,950

Hot Rod Series

HOT ROD 50 - 50W, head-unit only, all tube chassis, single channel, front silver control panel, two inputs, six black knobs, footswitch, various color covering, black metal grille, current mfg.

Soldano Hot Rod 50
courtesy Soldano

MSR	$1,439	$1,050	$850 - 975	$700 - 800

* Hot Rod 212 Combo - Similar to the Hot Rod 50, except in combo form with 2-12" speakers, current mfg.

MSR	$1,739	$1,250	$950 - 1,100	$750 - 850

GRADING	100%	EXCELLENT	AVERAGE

HOT ROD 50+ - 50W, head-unit only, all tube chassis, dual channels, front silver control panel, two inputs, eight black knobs, various color covering, black metal grille, current mfg.

Soldano Hot Rod 50
courtesy Soldano

	MSR	$2,159	$1,525	$1,100 - 1,300	$900 - 1,000

* Hot Rod 212 Combo - Similar to the Hot Rod 50, except in combo form with 2-12" speakers, current mfg.

	MSR	$2,459	$1,750	$1,250 - 1,500	$1,000 - 1,100

Reverb-O-Sonic & Decatone Series

REVERB-O-SONIC - 50W, 2-12" speakers, all tube chassis, two channels, reverb, front silver control panel, single input, nine black knobs, effects loop various color covering, silver cloth grille, current mfg.

	MSR	$2,459	$1,750	$1,300 - 1,500	$1,050 - 1,200

DECATONE - 100W, head-unit only, all tube chassis, three channels, front black control panel, single input, 13 black knobs, footswitch, effects loop, various color covering, black metal grille, current mfg.

	MSR	$2,879	$2,050	$1,600 - 1,900	$1,200 - 1,400

* Decatone 212 Combo - Similar to the Decatone, except in combo form with 2-12" speakers, current mfg.

	MSR	$3,179	$2,250	$1,750 - 2,000	$1,400 - 1,600

Lucky 13 Series

LUCKY 13 HEAD 100 - 100W, head-unit only, all tube chassis, two channels, separate reverb, front black control panel, single input, 12 black knobs, various color covering, black grille cloth, current mfg.

Soldano Lucky 13 Head
courtesy Soldano

	MSR	$2,499	$1,750	$1,300 - 1,500	$1,050 - 1,200

* Lucky 13 Combo 100 - Similar to the Lucky 13 head 100, except in combo version with 2-12" speakers, current mfg.

	MSR	$2,899	$2,050	$1,600 - 1,800	$1,250 - 1,400

LUCKY 13 HEAD 50 - 50W, head-unit only, all tube chassis, two channels, separate reverb, front black control panel, single input, 12 black knobs, various color covering, black grille cloth, current mfg.

	MSR	$2,299	$1,625	$1,250 - 1,450	$1,000 - 1,100

* Lucky 13 Combo 50 - Similar to the Lucky 13 head 50 except in combo version with 2-12" speakers, current mfg.

	MSR	$2,699	$1,899	$1,500 - 1,700	$1,200 - 1,350

GRADING	100%	EXCELLENT	AVERAGE

Astroverb Series

ASTROVERB 16 - 20W, head-unit only, all tube chassis, single channel, reverb, front silver control panel, single input, seven black knobs, various color covering, black or silver grille cloth, current mfg.

Soldano Astro Head
courtesy Soldano

MSR	$899	$650	$475 - 550	$400 - 435

* **Astroverb 16 112 Combo** - Similar to the Astroverb head 50, except in combo version with 1-12" speaker, current mfg.

MSR	$999	$699	$525 - 625	$425 - 475

* **Astroverb 16 212 Combo** - Similar to the Astroverb head 50, except in combo version with 2-12" speaker, current mfg.

MSR	$1,299	$925	$700 - 800	$575 - 625

SPEAKER CABINETS

Soldano features several speaker cabinet options to be teamed up with the head unit amplifiers. All cabinets, including their combo units, are equipped with Eminence Legend speakers. The configurations consist of 4-12" and 2-12" cabinets in either straight or angled fronts. For prices and other options on speaker cabinets visit the Soldano web site (see Trademark Index).

SOUNDBOARD

Amplifiers currently produced in Kaukauna, Wisconsin by the High Cliff Company.

Soundboard is a company that makes acoustic amplifiers. They are all built of the highest quality and hand assembled by luthier Bruce Petros in the United States. These amps are carefully built and tested to ensure great sound and reliability. Instead of having a standard grille cloth covering the speaker, these amps have a real spruce soundboard where the sound is aimed to. This replicates what a real acoustic guitar does instead of using the harsh overtones that a speaker produces. The soundboard actually has a soundhole that is about the size of one on a guitar. Essentially these amps replicate the sound of an acoustic guitar the most accurately with a wood soundboard (no cheese).

ACOUSTIC AMPLIFIERS

The Acoustic Soundboard amp has the series 2 model HC 125/M currently on the market. This is an 85W amplifier with two channels, separate gain controls, a 7 band Timbre control equalizer, and effects loop. It is available in a brown vinyl covering, or in Dovetailed oak. The controls and general color is brown since it is an acoustic amp (imagine that!). Speaker cabinets are also available to match up with the respective amp. Prices start at just under $1,000 for an amp that is bought factory direct (list is somewhat higher). Refer to the web site for more information and pricing (see Trademark Index).

SOUND CITY

Amplifiers previously produced in England.

Sound City was a company out of England that produced amps that were of similar resemblence to Marshall and Hiwatt heads. They also made combos and speaker cabinets. They produced amplifiers during the 1960's and 1970's. They made a few different models, but not much information is known about them. They are fairly rare today and are slightly collectible on the vintage market today.

SOUNDKING

Amplifiers and other audio equipment currently produced in Ningbo, China.

SoundKing produces a full line of electronic equipment. They make power amps, preamps and guitar amplifier combos. Along with these guitar products they have mixers, speakers, speaker cabinets, stands, cables, and other accessories. Among their amplifiers are the Professional series. The power units are of different wattages and mostly rack-mounts. The guitar combos are small practice units along with some larger (50W) models.

SOVTEK

Amplifiers currently produced in Russia.

Sovtek is a company in Russia that produces amplifier tubes along with their own line of guitar amplifiers. Their current amplifiers are bass units that are known as the Bassov Blues Midget. These are tube amplifiers at reasonable prices. They also distribute Electro-Harmonix amps. For more information refer to the web site (see Trademark Index).

SPEEDSTER

Amplifiers previously produced in Gig Harbor, Washington.

Speedster amps were built for a while in the late 1990's. These amps were only made for a few years, but featured some interesting designs. These amps look a little like an old radio from the 1930's or 1940's. They also had great circuitry with tubes and other effects. The cabinets were available in many different colors and and wood grains. They made some anniversary models for such occasions as the 100th Anniversary of NAMM. Luckily, the web site is still up and running so you can get information on the amps even though they are no longer produced. More information is to come on Speedster amplifiers in upcoming editions of the *Blue Book of Guitar Amplifiers*.

Speedster
courtesy solidbodyguitar.com, Inc.

Speedster
courtesy solidbodyguitar.com, Inc.

SQUIER

Amplifiers currently produced in Mexico, Korea, and China. Distributed by the Fender Musical Instrument Company in Scottsdale, Arizona.

Squier instruments began in 1983 in Matsumoto, Japan at the Fugi Fen Gakki. Fender had established Fender Japan in 1982 in conjunction with Kanda Shokai and Yamano music. This trademark came from the V.C. Squier company that produced strings for in the 1950's. Fender aquired the trademark in 1965 and it remaned unused until 1982. The Squier name was originally going to be for the European market, but Fender quickly realized that they could use it in the U.S. for an entry level brand of instruments. They first started producing guitars that were all Fender designs, built overseas that could be sold cheaply. Shortly after this they started producing small solid-state amplifiers. Among the most popular Squier amps are the Champ series, based off the popular line by Fender. Squier amplifiers only appear now in the Strat-Pak and Bass-Pak. These are all-in-one packages where you get the guitar, amp, strings, cord, strap, picks, and a video. Refer to Fender in the Trademark Index for more information.

ELECTRIC SOLID-STATE AMPLIFIERS

The Squier amplifiers really never were produced with the intention of being performance units. All were on the entry-level and practice type. Most amplifiers are either 10 or 15 Watts. These amps are based on the Fender Blackface series and some have black grilles. These models can usually be found for under $100 used.

STANDEL

Amplifiers previouslly produced in Newark, New Jersey. Distributed by Standel of Temple City, California. Previous Standel Amplifiers were produced during the 1950's-circa 1971. Currently produced in Los Angeles by the Requisite Audio Engineering Company.

The Standel company was founded by Bob Crooks, an electronic engineer, in the early 1950's. Crooks learned electronics from correspondance courses and began working for Lockheed. After a while he was promoted to engineer in charge of their electronics to build amplifiers. Crooks had a radio repair business that was called Standard Electronics where they derived the name of the company from. Standel's first amplifiers were of tube design and were some of the first designs in the amp industry. Such musicians like Joe Maphis, Merle Travis, and Chet Atkins played Standel amplifiers. The first brochure for Standel amplifiers was published in 1954.

Crooks began experimenting with semi-conductors in 1961 and within two years had developed a solid-state amplifier. The company was successful in the 1960's as they beat Fender to the punch by releasing a solid-state amp by 1964. The 1970's proved to be very unlucky to Standel as they had faulty parts and components that faulted often. This led to erosion of the Standel quality reputation. Crooks sold the company to CMI in Chicago and worked for them for two years. Later Crooks worked at Barcus Berry learning more about tube and solid-state amps. He developed the Sonic Maximizer, which was a unit that compensated for speaker errors by modifying the signal going into the amplifier. The product is still being produced by the BBE Sound Corporation in the Long Beach, California. Bob Crooks passed away in 1999.

Stanel amplifiers are back in business producing amplifiers that made them famous in the first place. Danny McKinney is now the current president of the company. They are now producing amplifiers after about a 25 year absence from the music industry.

(Source: Willie Moseley, Vintage Guitar magazine, and Deke Dickerson)

ELECTRIC TUBE AMPLIFIERS

Bob Crooks first started building amplifier out of his garage in 1953. The first model (and most popular) was the 25L15. These amplifiers were typically completely custom made from the speaker size to the color of covering. This is the model that Standel re-released when they came back in the late 1990's. The unique thing about Standel amplifiers is that they beat the big companies to the punch with several designs, including the piggyback and the front mounted control panel. There is a complete history, including a list of the first 25L15 models built on the Requisite Audio web site done by Deke Dickerson. Pricing on these early tube Standel amps is difficult since most of them don't come up on the second hand market. If you have a Standel amplifier, chances are you have a real unique amplifier with some great innovative designs of the 1950's.

GRADING	100%	EXCELLENT	AVERAGE

ELECTRIC SOLID-STATE AMPLIFIERS

Standel started producing solid-state dinosaurs in the early 1960's. They beat Fender, Vox, and Ampeg to the punch with this one once again. They produced amplifiers throughout the 1960's until faulty parts and the amps started failing. Around 1971 Standel sold the company and stopped producing amplifier shortly thereafter. Standel remained in mothballs until the late 1990's, when they revived the name just in time for the original founder, Bob, to see it. They are currently producing a couple of solid-state amplifiers, the Studio 12, and the Custom 15. For more information refer to the web site (see Trademark Index).

Stantel Studio X
courtesy George McGuire

Stantel Studio X
courtesy George McGuire

SUNN

Amplifiers previously produced in Portland, Oregon and in Kentucky. Sunn is now part of the Fender Musical Instrument Corporation of Scottsdale, Arizona.

The Sunn Amplifier company was founded by Norm Sundholm and his brother Conrad. Norm played bass in the band the Kingsmen. He played through a Fender Bandmaster, but needed more power out of it. He changed speakers with improvement, but later changed the actual amp to a Hi-Fi amplifier, leaving only the cabinet the original part of the Bandmaster. So he figured he could build the box and get the components for much chepaer than what a Fender cost. Norm bought the parts to build the box and would buy the power amp from Dynakits. His first amplifiers were named BAMCO, which stood for Burke Aarons Music Company. Enter Norm's brother Conrad, who knew a little about woodworking. Conrad (Con for short) built some amps after school for Norm, as he was on the road with the Kingsmen. They started putting Sunn on the amplifiers for the first time and Sunn Musical Equipment Company was born. They chose Sunn rather than Sun because of Sun Tachometers in all the cars that could be a problem. This idea came from Barry Curtis.

In 1965, Con hired the first full time employee, and in late 1965 they decided they needed a factory to build amps. They moved to Tualtain, Oregon, which was right outside Portland. Their building was actually an old public swimming pool that had gone out of business. They filled in the hole with dirt, cemented it over and it became the factory. Employees included Jim Peterson and Gene Matheny, and later Bob Teneyck as an engineer.

In 1969, the brothers of the company started to disagree and Con bought out Norm's part of the company. However, in three years Con sold Sunn to the Hartzell. When Hartzell took over they moved the factory to Williamstown, Kentucky so they would be closer to Cinncinati and the east coast. Amps were heavy and speaker cabinets were only coming from Kentucky (the amplifiers were still produced in Oregon). They ended up moving back to Oregon in the late 1970's where they manufactured amps until the company was sold to a rebuilding Fender organization in 1987. Fender took Sunn and put them in mothballs until Fender became reorganized in their own name. Either Fender took a long time to reorganize or they forgot about Sunn amps never producing them until 1998. Sunn amplifiers were mainly for the bass players like they had been in the seventies. By 2002, the Sunn name did not appear on amplifiers as Fender put their own name on Sunn amps. Fender bass amps are now Sunn in disguise.

(Courtesy Ritchie Fliegler: Amps!)

ELECTRIC TUBE AMPLIFIERS

The Sunn amplifiers are split up into two sections, vintage and non-vintage. No tube amplifiers were manufactured during the 1980's and early 1990's making a big gap between the series. This makes it easy to date them and tell the difference.

Vintage Amps (Pre-1980)

100S - 60W head-unit, came with speaker cabinet loaded with 1-15" JBLspeaker + high frequency horn, all-tube chassis, preamp: 1 X 7025, 1 X 12AU7 1 X 6AN8, power: 2 X 6550 (or KT-88), 1 X GZ34 rectifier, single channel, front silver control panel, two inputs (hi and lo), three black knobs (v, b, t), black covering, silver grille, 150 lbs., (amp and cabinet), mfg. late 1960's-mid 1970's.

N/A	$575 - 650	$450 - 500

This price includes both the amp and the head unit, if one or the other is missing the price can be reduced by 60% on each.

200S - 60W head-unit, came with speaker cabinet loaded with 2-15" JBLspeakers, all-tube chassis, preamp: 1 X 7025, 1 X 6AN8 (or 7199), power: 2 X 6550 (or KT-88), 1 X GZ34 rectifier, single channel, front silver control panel, two inputs (hi and lo), three black knobs (v, b, t), black covering, silver grille, 150 lbs., (amp and cabinet), mfg. late 1960's-mid 1970's.

N/A	$650 - 750	$500 - 575

This price includes both the amp and the head unit, if one or the other is missing the price can be reduced by 60% on each.

GRADING	100%	EXCELLENT	AVERAGE

2000S - 120W head-unit, came with two speaker cabinet loaded with 2-15" JBLspeakers, all-tube chassis, preamp: 1 X 7025, 1 X 6AN8 (or 7199), power: 4 X 6550 (or KT-88), 2 X GZ34 rectifiers, single channel, front silver control panel, four inputs (hi and lo), four black knobs (v, b, t, contour), black covering, silver grille, 200 lbs., (amp and cabinets), mfg. late 1960's-mid 1970's.

	N/A	$950 - 1,100	$700 - 825

This price includes both the amp and the head unit, if one or both of the speaker cabinets are missing the price can be reduced by 75% on the value.

MODEL T - 120W head-unit only, all-tube chassis, preamp: 3 X 12AX7, power: 4 X 6550, dual channels (normal and bright), front silver control panel, five inputs (normal and bright), seven black knobs (norm v, bright v, b, m, t, p, MV), black covering, silver grille, mfg. late 1960's-mid 1970's.

	N/A	$350 - 450	$275 - 325

Recent Manufacture (1998-2001)

Sunn (Fender) re-released the Model T series in the late 1990's. It was available as a head unit with 100W output, two channels, and a power switch. This can be teamed up with a Model T 412 speaker enclosure that matches the head and can handle 300W. The amp is available as a combo unit, model T50C, that has 50W output, 1-12" speaker and all the features of the head-unit. There is a 1-12" speaker cabinet that can match up with this as well. These models pop up quite a few places on the second hand market and can be found for $600-$700 for the head unit and about $750 - 900 for the combo.

Sunn also released a couple bass amps that are completey tube driven. The 1200s is available with 1200W of power (but it is solid-state).

ELECTRIC SOLID-STATE AMPLIFIERS

Sunn had pretty much gone completely solid-state by the mid 1970's. About the only amp that survived the transistor stage was the Model T (with no gold chains). Most Sunn amplifiers have fallen off the face of the Earth for one reason or another. Before CBS bought out Sunn there isn't very much information on these amplifiers that we know of. Any information on Sunn amps (tube or solid-state) would be appreciated for future editions of the *Blue Book of Guitar Amplifiers*.

SUPERTONE

Amplifiers previously sold by Sears & Roebuck. Amplifiers were made by various companies.

Supertone is another brandname trademark that was used by Sears & Roebuck between 1914 and 1941. These amplifiers were manufactured by a number of different companies including Harmony, which was a subsidiary of Sears. Sears used the Supertone trademark on a full range of amplifiers, guitars, lap steels, banjos, mandolins and ukuleles. In 1940, then-company president Jay Krause bought Harmony from Sears by acquiring the controlling stock, and continued to expand the company's production. In 1941 Sears retired the Supertone name in favor of the Silvertone trademark, which was brand new. Harmony produced amps and guitars to Sears with other names. Supertone made a handful of amplifiers during the 1920's and 1930's.

SUPRO

Amplifiers previously produced by the National Dobro company.

The Supro trademark was the budget brand of the National Dobro company (See NATIONAL or VALCO), who also supplied Montgomery Wards with Supro models under the **Airline** trademark. National offered budget versions of their designs under the Supro brand name beginning in 1935.

When National moved to Chicago in 1936, the Supro name was on wood-bodied lap steels, amplifiers, and electric Spanish arch top guitars. The first solid body Supro electrics were introduced in 1952, and the fiberglass models began in 1962 (there's almost thirty years of conventionally built guitars in the Supro history).

In 1962, Valco Manufacturing Company name was changed to Valco Guitars, Inc. (the same year that fiberglass models debuted). Kay purchased Valco in 1967, so there are some Kay-built guitars under the Supro brand name. Kay went bankrupt in 1968, and both the Supro and National trademarks were acquired by Chicago's own Strum 'N Drum company. The National name was used on a number of Japanese-built imports, but not the Supro name.

Archer's Music of Fresno, California bought the rights to the Supro name in the early 1980s. They marketed a number of Supro guitars constructed from new old stock (N.O.S.) parts for a limited period of time.

(Source: Michael Wright, Vintage Guitar Magazine)

Section T

THD

Amplifiers currently produced in Seattle, Washington.

THD Electronics has been producing amplifiers since 1987. They are a company that specializes in tube amplification and other products that have to deal with tube amps. Most recently, THD released the BiValve 30 at the 2002 Summer NAMM show. They also make other amps, speaker cabinets, and tube converters. For more information please refer to the THD Electronics web site (see Trademark Index).

TECAMP

Amplifiers currently produced in China.

Tecamp are amplifiers that are produced by the Sino-Amp Company. The China factory is located in Tianjin where all amps are built. The amps are distributed in the U.S. by Sino-Amp that is located in Los Angeles. They produce a full line of guitar and bass amplifiers. They also are involved in building mixers and speaker cabinets (as well as monitors). For more information on specific material, check the Tecamp web site (see Trademark Index).

TECH 21

Amplifiers currently produced in New York City.

Tech 21 is a company that produces many products including guitar amplifiers. Their most popular line of amplifiers are probably the Trademark series. These are amps that come in a variety of configurations. They can produce many different wattages and have a great channel switching feature. They also offer the Bronzewood and Landmark series. For more information on Tech 21 amplifiers and other products, visit the Tech 21NYC web site (see Trademark Index).

TEISCO

Amplifiers previously produced in Japan between 1956 and 1973. Teisco amplifiers were distributed in the U.S. by Westheimer Musical Instruments of Evanston, Illinois.

In 1946, Mr. Atswo Kaneko and Mr. Doryu Matsuda founded the Aoi Onpa Kenkyujo company, makers of the guitars bearing the Teisco and other trademarks (the company name roughly translates to the **Hollyhock Soundwave or Electricity Laboratories**). The Teisco name was chosen by Mr. Kaneko, and was used primarily in domestic markets. Early models include lap steel and electric-Spanish guitars. By the 1950s, the company was producing slab-bodied designs with bolt-on necks along with guitar amplifiers. In 1956, the company name was changed to the Nippon Onpa Kogyo Co., Ltd. - but the guitars still stayed Teisco!

As the demand for guitars in the U.S. market began to expand, Mr. Jack Westheimer of WMI Corporation of Evanston, Illinois started to import Japanese guitars and amplifiers in the late 1950s, perhaps circa 1958. WMI began importing the Teisco-built Kingston guitars in 1961, and also used the Teisco Del Rey trademark extensively beginning in 1964. Other Teisco-built guitars had different trademarks (a *rebranding* technique), and the different brand names will generally indicate the U.S. importer/distributor. The Japanese company again changed names, this time to the Teisco Co. Ltd. The Teisco line included all manners of solid body and semi-hollowbody guitars, and their niche in the American guitar market (as entry level or beginner's guitars) assured steady sales.

In 1967, the Kawai Corporation purchased the Teisco company. Not one to ruin a good thing, Kawai continued exporting the Teisco line to the U.S. (although they did change some designs through the years) until 1973. Due to the recent popularity in the Teisco name, Kawai actually produced some limited edition Teisco Spectrum Five models lately in Japan, although they were not made available to the U.S. market.

(Source: Michael Wright, Vintage Guitar Magazine.)

TELE-STAR

Amplifiers previously produced in Japan circa late 1960's to 1983.

The Tele-Star trademark was distributed in the U.S. by the Tele-Star Musical Instrument Corporation of New York, New York. Tele-Star offered a full range of acoustic, thinline acoustic/electric hollow body, and solid body electric guitars and basses. They also offered select guitar amplifiers. Many were built by Kawai of Japan.

(Source: Michael Wright, Vintage Guitar Magazine.)

TOKAI

Amplifiers currently produced in Japan since the early 1960's.

Tokai instruments were very good Fender and Gibson-based replicas produced during the mid to late 1970s. After 1978. the company built instruments based on these classic American designs, then further branched out into some original designs and "superstrat" models. Along with guitars based on the popular brands they have also produced some amplifiers. Information on these models is scarce, however.

TONY BRUNO CUSTOM AMPLIFIERS

Custom Amplifiers currently produced in Woodside, New York.

Tony Bruno is the man behind Tony Bruno Custom Amplifiers. He builds amplifiers so that they sound absolutely perfect to him before they leave the factory. Each amplifier is tested by him with the point-to-point wiring and components being checked each individually. He also takes each amp before it leaves and plays it in a band to make sure that it has the right tone. If an amp isn't cutting it, he takes it appart and makes adjustments to his liking. Each Bruno amp leaves the shop with that "Bruno tone." Tony has over 1000 designs to his name and has won awards for his amplifiers. For information and to see what Tony can make for you please refer to the Tony Bruno Amp web site (see Trademark Index).

TOP HAT

Amplifiers currently produced in Anaheim, California.

The Top Hat Amplifier company is owned by Brian Gerhard. Top Hat makes guitar amps that are all hand built with point-to-point wiring and an all-tube circuit. They are also built with great strength in the United States, and they are advertised as some of the best sounding amplifiers on the market. Check out the web site for more player and product information (see Trademark Index).

GRADING	100%	EXCELLENT	AVERAGE

ELECTRIC TUBE AMPLIFIERS

Currently Top Hat breaks up their amplifiers into two series. The Flagship and the Club Series have different series within them. Then there are models within each of those series. Top Hat just recently released the Studio Series line of amps. These are small 5 watt amps that are tube driven. More information is coming on these models. Most Top Hat amps are available in different color coverings and grille clothes. Check the website for availability.

Flagship Series

KING ROYALE TH-K35 - 35W, head-unit only, all tube Class A chassis, power tubes: 4 X EL84, GZ34, 5AR4 rectifier, two channels, front black control panel, four inputs (two per channel), eight white chicken head knobs, various color covering, current mfg.

MSR	$2,449	$1,799	$1,400 - 1,600	$1,150 - 1,275

* **King Royale TC-K35** - Similar to the King Royale TH-K35, except in combo version with 2-12" speakers, current mfg.

MSR	$2,799	$1,999	$1,500 - 1,750	$1,250 - 1,400

AMBASSADOR 35 TH-A35 - 35W, head-unit only, all tube Class A chassis, power tubes: 4 X 6V6, one channel, reverb, front black control panel, two inputs, eight white chicken head knobs, various color covering, current mfg.

MSR	$2,499	$1,799	$1,400 - 1,600	$1,150 - 1,275

* **Ambassador 35 TC-A35** - Similar to the Ambassador TH-A35, except in combo version with 2-12" speakers, current mfg.

MSR	$2,849	$2,050	$1,550 - 1,800	$1,250 - 1,400

AMBASSADOR 50 TH-A50 - 50W, head-unit only, all tube Class AB chassis, power tubes: 2 X 6L6, one channel, reverb, front black control panel, two inputs, eight white chicken head knobs, various color covering, current mfg.

MSR	$2,549	$1,850	$1,425 - 1,625	$1,150 - 1,300

* **Ambassador 50 TC-A50** - Similar to the Ambassador 50 TH-A50, except in combo version with 2-12" speakers, current mfg.

MSR	$2,899	$2,075	$1,575 - 1,825	$1,250 - 1,450

AMBASSADOR 100 TH-A100 - 100W, head-unit only, all tube Class AB chassis, power tubes: 4 X 6L6, one channel, reverb, front black control panel, two inputs, eight white chicken head knobs, various color covering, current mfg.

MSR	$2,699	$1,925	$1,450 - 1,700	$1,150 - 1,300

* **Ambassador 100 TC-A100** - Similar to the Ambassador 100 TH-A100 except in combo version with 2-12" speakers, current mfg.

MSR	$2,999	$2,150	$1,650 - 1,900	$1,300 - 1,500

EMPLEXADOR 50 TH-E50 - 50W, head-unit only, all tube Class AB chassis, two channel, reverb, front black control panel, two inputs, eight white chicken head knobs, various color covering, current mfg.

MSR	$2,349	$1,650	$1,250 - 1,400	$950 - 1,100

* **Emplexador 100 TC-E100** - Similar to the Emplexador 50 TH-E50, except has 100W output, current mfg.

MSR	$2,499	$1,750	$1,300 - 1,500	$1,050 - 1,150

Club Series

CLUB BAJO TC-B115 - 40W, 1-15" speaker combo bass amp, all tube Class A chassis, preamp: 1 X 12AY7, 1 X 12AX7, 1 X 12AU7, power tubes: 2 X 6L6, one channel, top black control panel, two inputs, six white chicken head knobs, various color covering, current mfg.

MSR	$1,649	$1,175	$850 - 975	$650 - 750

* **Club Bajo TC-B212** - Similar to the Club Bajo TC-B115 except has 2-12" speakers, current mfg.

MSR	$1,899	$1,350	$950 - 1,100	$725 - 850

The Club Bajo is also available as a custom order with 2-10" or 4-10" speakers.

CLUB ROYALE TC-R1 - 20W, 1-12" speaker combo, all tube Class A chassis, power tubes: 2 X EL34, one channel, top black control panel, two inputs, six white chicken head knobs, various color covering, current mfg.

MSR	$1,549	$1,099	$775 - 900	$600 - 700

* **Club Royale TC-R2** - Similar to the Club Royale TC-R1 except has 2-12" speakers, current mfg.

MSR	$1,849	$1,325	$950 - 1,075	$725 - 850

CLUB DELUXE TC-D1 - 20W, 1-12" speaker combo, all tube Class A chassis, power tubes: 2 X 6V6, one channel, top black control panel, two inputs, six white chicken head knobs, various color covering, current mfg.

MSR	$1,549	$1,099	$775 - 900	$600 - 700

* **Club Deluxe TC-D2** - Similar to the Club Deluxe TC-D1 except has 2-12" speakers, current mfg.

MSR	$1,799	$1,299	$950 - 1,075	$725 - 850

SPEAKER CABINETS

Naturally, Top Hat offers speaker cabinets to match up with their head-units. These are sold separately from the heads and come in a vareity of configurations. They are available in a 1-12", 2-12", 4-12", and 4-10" configurations. Most speakers in these cabinets are Celestion G12H, but Celestion Greenback, Vintage 30 and Jensen C12N speakers are available as options. For more information on these speaker cabinets refer to the Top Hat website (see Trademark Index).

TORRES ENGINEERING
Amplifiers currently produced San Mateo, California.

Torres Engineering is a company that sells not only guitar amplifiers, but tubes, and other electronic equipment. They sell a couple of guitar amps that are custom kits, one being a Fender tweed amp. They also sell kits to make your own amplifiers along with pickups and other electronics. Books are also available on the web site on tube amplifiers and other products. Referto the web site for more information (see Trademark Index).

TRACE ELLIOT

Amplifiers currently produced in Essex, England. Trace Elliot amplifiers are distributed in the U.S. by Trace Elliot America in Elgin, Illinois as a part of Gibson.

Trace Elliot is probably most noted for their bass amplifiers that they have produced over the years. The company was formed in the late 1970's in a small music shop located in Essex, England. The bass amplifier that first emerged was a result of what bass players were looking for in an amp that wasn't available on the market. This new amp was one that had flexibility and power along with quality components that were reliable. Trace Elliot nailed the bass amp market, then looked to expand to other industries. The next product that came along was the acoustic line of amplifiers.

Recently Trace Elliot teamed up with the Gibson Guitar company and are offering more products, which include a line of guitar amplifiers. Trace Elliot still produces fine amplifiers for all kinds of industries now.

BASS AMPLIFIERS

Trace Elliot has several bass amplifiers, we are still doing research on other models not listed below.

V-Type Bass Amplifiers

Trace Elliot makes tube powered bass amplifiers. These hogs put out 400W of power (The V-8 model) from 8, yes 8 KT88 fan cooled power tubes, and have 7 X ECC83 or 12AX7 preamp tubes with1 X EM84 display tube. The controls are fairly basic with gain controls, a three knob EQ section, and compressor knobs. Along with this model there is a V-Type 300H, which is a hybrid model with a tube preamp section powered by MOSFET.

12-Band Bass Amplifiers

The 12-band series indicates the 12 band equalizer and is based on the GP12X preamp. All head units are available as a rack mount and indicated by an "R" in the model.

AH1000-12 - 1000W, head-unit only, solid-state chassis, single channel, front black control panel, two inputs (passive and active), seven black knobs, 12-band equalizer, various buttons, compression, black covering, green accents, current mfg.

AH500-12 - 500W, head-unit only, solid-state chassis, single channel, front black control panel, two inputs (passive and active), seven black knobs, 12-band equalizer, various buttons, compression, black covering, green accents, current mfg.

AH300-12 - 300W, head-unit only, solid-state chassis, single channel, front black control panel, two inputs (passive and active), seven black knobs, 12-band equalizer, various buttons, compression, black covering, green accents, current mfg.

1210H COMBO - 300W, 4-10" speaker combo, HF horn, solid-state chassis, single channel, front black control panel, two inputs (passive and active), seven black knobs, 12-band equalizer, various buttons, compression, black covering, green accents, black metal grille, current mfg.

122H COMBO - 300W, 2-10" speaker combo, HF horn, solid-state chassis, single channel, front black control panel, two inputs (passive and active), seven black knobs, 12-band equalizer, various buttons, compression, black covering, green accents, black metal grille, current mfg.

1215 COMBO - 300W, 1-15" speaker combo, solid-state chassis, single channel, front black control panel, two inputs (passive and active), seven black knobs, 12-band equalizer, various buttons, compression, black covering, green accents, black metal grille, current mfg.

7-Band Bass Amplifiers

The 7-band series indicates the 7 band equalizer and is based on the GP7 preamp.

AH300-7 - 300W, head-unit only, solid-state chassis, single channel, front black control panel, two inputs (passive and active), three black knobs, 7-band equalizer, various buttons, compression, black covering, green accents, current mfg.

AH150-7 - 150W, head-unit only, solid-state chassis, single channel, front black control panel, two inputs (passive and active), three black knobs, 7-band equalizer, various buttons, compression, black covering, green accents, current mfg.

7210H COMBO - 300W, 2-10" speaker combo, HF horn, solid-state chassis, single channel, front black control panel, two inputs (passive and active), three black knobs, 7-band equalizer, various buttons, compression, black covering, green accents, black metal grille, current mfg.

7215 COMBO - 300W, 1-15" speaker combo, solid-state chassis, single channel, front black control panel, two inputs (passive and active), three black knobs, 7-band equalizer, various buttons, compression, black covering, green accents, black metal grille, current mfg.

712 - 130W, 1-12" speaker combo, solid-state chassis, single channel, front black control panel, two inputs (passive and active), three black knobs, 7-band equalizer, various buttons, compression, black covering, green accents, black metal grille, current mfg.

715 - 150W, 1-15" speaker combo, solid-state chassis, single channel, front black control panel, two inputs (passive and active), three black knobs, 7-band equalizer, various buttons, compression, black covering, green accents, black metal grille, current mfg.

TRAINWRECK

Amplifiers previously produced during the 1980's.

Trainwreck was an amplifier companys formed by Ken Fischer in 1980. Ken Fischer worked for Ampeg back when they were really swinging. He learned a lot from that company, but left it to start restoring Vox amplifiers. In 1980, he started building his own amps. Trainwrecks aren't the usual amps that you find used at a music shop. These are amps that are built entirely out of wood, with Trainwreck engraved on the front along with a design (very elaborate). Trainwreck amps were also only available as a head-unit as Ken thought a separate head/cabinet provided many sound possiblities rather than a combo. There are three designs that Ken made, the Rocket, the Liverpool, and the Express. Ken kept the designs simple and the Express is along a Fender Bassman in design. He handbuilt each one individually and instead of using a serial number on the amp he came up with a woman's name for each amp. Not only can he recall names of the amps, but when they were built. Now that's hard-core.

These amps were produced for a very short time, very few were made, and very few show up on the market. Needless to say that when they come along they are not cheap. If you own a Trainwreck, chances are it's going to mature in value over the years. If you can buy one for cheap, tell the guy (or gal) you'll pay cash. We have an example of a Trainwreck Express amp, enjoy!

(Courtesy Aspen Pittman, The Tube Amp Book.)

Trainwreck Express
courtesy solidbodyguitar.com, Inc.

Trainwreck Express
courtesy solidbodyguitar.com, Inc.

TRAYNOR
Amplifiers currently produced by Yorkville Sound.

Pete Traynor has been making amplifiers since 1963. He had been a musician for many years and had fixed his own amplifier during his stint. He started off in Toronto, Canada making amplifiers until he moved to Nova Scotia in the late 1970's. Many different bands have played through Traynor amplifiers. Today Traynor amps are still built by Yorkville Sound, but are smaller solid-state amps. All old Traynor amps are tube designed with various features and functions.

TUBE WORKS
Amplifiers currently produced in Scottsdale, Arizona. Tube Works is a division of Genz Benz (See Genz Benz for other information).

Tube Works is a company out of Arizona that produces amplifers and the famous Tube Works "Tube Driver" guitar pedal. In the late 1970',s this guitar pedal was designed to give the warm feeling of a tube amplifier run through a footswitch. They now have an actual footpedal with a preamp (12AX7) tube in it. Tube Works now makes guitar amplifiers, bass amplifiers, and Mosvalve amps. Tube Works has also come up with the Integrated Valve Augmented Circuitry design. This design has the preamp tube as the center where all tone is shaped at. They also make some head unit amplifiers along with speaker cabinets.

Section U

ULTRASOUND

Amplifiers currently produced in Adel, Iowa. Ultrasound is a division of UJC Electronics.

Ultrasound amplifiers are acoustic amps with digital technology. They are a relatively young company but offer one of the finest acoustic guitar amplifiers on the market. They have digital effects on most of the amps with many acoustic applications such as reverb, chorus, and delay. They also have the least amount of backround noise when the unit is on. They offer many different configurations along with extension speaker cabinets to provide a stereo effect. For more information on everything Ultrasound amps can do, please visit the website (see Trademark Index).

GRADING	100%	EXCELLENT	AVERAGE

ACOUSTIC AMPLIFIERS

AG-30 - 30W, 1-8" + 1-2" tweeter, solid-state chassis, sweepable notch filter, top black control panel, single input, four black knobs (v, b, t, notch), effects loop, line out, brown leatherette covering, black grille, current mfg

Ultrasound AG-30
courtesy Jason Scheuner

MSR	$279.95	$185	$140 - 160	$100 - 115

AG-50 - 50W, 2-8" + 1-2" tweeter, solid-state chassis, sweepable notch filter, top black control panel, single input, four black knobs (v, b, t, notch), effects loop, line out, brown leatherette covering, black grille, disc 2001.

	$300	$225 - 275	$175 - 200

* AG-50R - Similar to the AG-50, except has reverb circuit with knob, disc 2001.

	$350	$275 - 325	$200 - 225

AG-100 - 100W, 4-8" + 1-2" tweeter, solid-state chassis, sweepable notch filter, top black control panel, single input, four black knobs (v, b, t, notch), effects loop, line out, brown leatherette covering, black grille, disc 2001.

	$425	$300 - 350	$175 - 200

* AG-100R - Similar to the AG-100, except has reverb circuit with knob, disc 2001.

	$475	$375 - 425	$250 - 300

GRADING	100%	EXCELLENT	AVERAGE

AG-50DS - 50W, 2-8" + 1-2" tweeter, solid-state chassis, single channel, sweepable notch filter, digital effects, top black control panel, two inputs (mic & instrument), six black knobs (digital effect level & mode, level, b, t, notch), effects loop, line out, brown leatherette covering, black grille, disc 2001.

Ultrasound AG-50
courtesy Jason Scheuner

	$500	$400 - 450	$300 - 350

AG-100DS - 100W, 4-8" + 1-2" tweeter, solid-state chassis, single channel, sweepable notch filter, digital effects, top black control panel, two inputs (mic & instrument), six black knobs (digital effect level & mode, level, b, t, notch), effects loop, line out, brown leatherette covering, black grille, disc 2001.

	$625	$500 - 550	$400 - 450

AG-50DS2 - 50W, 2-8" + 1-2" tweeter, solid-state chassis, dual channels, sweepable notch filter, digital effects, top black control panel, two inputs (mic & instrument), ten black knobs(Mic: b, t, level, Inst: digital effect level & mode, level, b, t, notch, MV), effects loop, line out, brown leatherette covering, black grille, current mfg.

Ultrasound AG-50DS2
courtesy S. P. Fjestad

Ultrasound AG-50DS2
courtesy S. P. Fjestad

	MSR	$749.95	$525	$425 - 475	$350 - 400

AG-100DS2 - 100W, 4-8" + 1-2" tweeter, solid-state chassis, dual channels, sweepable notch filter, digital effects, top black control panel, two inputs (mic & instrument), ten black knobs(Mic: b, t, level, Inst: digital effect level & mode, level, b, t, notch, MV), effects loop, line out, brown leatherette covering, black grille, current mfg.

	MSR	$939.95	$650	$525 - 600	$400 - 450

PAMM (PREAMP MINI MIXER) - Preamp only, solid-state chassis, four inputs, 13 black knobs, tape/cd in, main out, cased in a black box, current mfg.

	MSR	$229.95	$150	$100 - 125	$75 - 90

EXTENSION SPEAKER CABINETS

AG-50E - 50W powered extension speaker cabinet, 2-8" speakers, top control panel, single volume control, brown leatherette covering, black grille, current mfg.

	MSR	$419.95	$275	$200 - 250	$140 - 175

AG-1050E - 100W powered extension speaker cabinet, 2-8" speakers, top control panel, single volume control, brown leatherette covering, black grille, current mfg.

	MSR	$599.95	$400	$300 - 350	$225 - 250

UNIVOX

Amplifiers previously produced in the United States and Japan. They were distributed by the Merson Musical Supply Company of Westbury, New York. Currently they are produced overseas.

Univox amplifiers were originally produced between the 1960's and 1970's. At first Univox amplifiers were completely made in the U.S. as tube amplifiers with Jensen speakers. By the late 1960's, Univox started using Japanese parts to assemble their amplifiers in American made cabinets. By 1971, Univox was offering several different designs and solid-state models were part of the regular line. Univox produced amplifiers throughout the 1970's and by 1980, all amplifiers were produced by Westbury, the company that had supplied the cabinets for Univox. Westbury amps were made up until 1982. Univox was purchased by Korg in 1985. Univox amplifiers are now appearing again as small practice solid-state models.

(Early History courtesy: Michael Wright, Guitar Stories Volume One)

ELECTRIC AMPLIFIERS

Univox has produced several amplifiers over the years. Unfortunately, very little information is known about these models. Models that do show up aren't exactly wallet-busters. Usually Univox amps can be found for a relatively cheap price. Tube amps are the more desirable models than the solid-state later counterparts. Any infromation on Univox amplifiers can be submitted directly to the publisher.

NOTES

Section V

VHT AMPLIFICATION
Amplifiers currently produced in Sun Valley, California.

VHT amplifiers are hand built in California by president Stevie Fryette, and crew of the company. Stevie feels that a guitarist is born with their own tone and it takes a certain product (amplifier) to develop the sound so the world can hear. This is what VHT amplifiers are about. They are all-tube amplifiers that come in head and combo units. Not only are these units hand checked before they leave the factory, but they are checked by the pres himself! For more information refer to the web site (see Trademark Index).

PITTBULL ELECTRIC TUBE AMPLIFIERS

VHT guitar amplifiers are called Pittbulls. They have various combos and head units within this series that all have different names. There are also power amps and speaker cabinets that are listed in different sections. No prices were available when this edition went to press.

Ultra Lead & Hundred/CLX series

ULTRA-LEAD HEAD G-100-UL - 120W, head-unit only, all tube chassis, KT-88 power tubes, three channels, front black control panel, two inputs, 14 black knobs, various buttons, half power mode, variable line out, effects loop, footswitch, cover, black or spruce vinyl covering, black grille, current mfg.
This model is also avaiable as the model G-100-UL/EQ, which features a six band graphic equalizer.

HUNDRED/CL HEAD G-100-CL - 100W, head-unit only, all tube chassis, 6L6/EL34 power tubes, 5U4 tube rectifiers, two channels, front black control panel, two inputs, 13 black knobs, various buttons, half power mode, variable line out, effects loop, footswitch, cover, black or spruce vinyl covering, black grille, current mfg.
This model is also available with an optional 6-band graphic equalizer and 3-spring Acccutronics reverb.

* **Fifty/CL Head G-50-CL** - Similar to the Hundred/CL head, except has 50W output and has a Class A operation switch, current mfg.

Pittbull Fifty Series

FIFTY/ST HEAD G-5034-L - 50W, head-unit only, all tube chassis, EL34 power tubes, two channels, reverb, front black control panel, two inputs, 11 black knobs, effects loop, variable line out, class A switch, footswitch, black or spruce vinyl, black grille with white piping, current mfg.

FIFTY/TWELVE 2 X 12 COMBO C-5034-L - Similar to the Fifty/ST head, except has 2-12" speakers, current mfg.

Pittbull Forty-Five & Super 30 Series

FORTY-FIVE HEAD G-5084-T - 45W, head-unit only, all-tube chassis, EL84 power tubes, two channels, reverb, front ivory control panel, two inputs, 11 black chicken-head knobs, effects loop, line out, footswitch, black, spruce, or ivory vinyl covering, black grille, current mfg.

* **Forty-Five 2-10" Combo C-5084-TW10** - Similar to the Forty Five head in chassis, has 2-10" speakers, current mfg.
* **Forty-Five 2-12" Combo C-5084-TW12** - Similar to the Forty Five head in chassis, has 2-12" speakers, current mfg.
* **Forty-Five 1-12" Combo C-5084-T** - Similar to the Forty Five head in chassis, has 1-12" speaker, and no master controls, current mfg.

SUPER THIRTY C-3084-S - 30W, 1-12" speaker combo, all tube Class A chassis, EL84 power tubes, two channels, front black control panel, nine black chicken head knobs, various buttons, effects loop, line out, footswitch, black covering, black grille with white piping, current mfg.

VALCO
See NATIONAL

Louis Dopyera bought out the National company, and as he owned more than 50% of the stock in Dobro, "merged" the two companies back together (as National Dobro). In 1936, the decision was made to move the company to Chicago, Illinois. Chicago was a veritable hotbed of mass produced musical instruments during the early to pre-World War II 1900s. Manufacturers like Washburn and Regal had facilities, and major wholesalers and retailers like the Tonk Bros. and Lyon & Healy were based there. Victor Smith, Al Frost, and Louis Dopyera moved their operation to Chicago, and in 1943 formally announced the change to VALCO (the initials of their three first names: V-A-L company). Valco worked on war materials during World War II, and returned to instrument production afterwards. Valco produced the National/Supro/Airline/Oahu Amplifiers in the 1950s and 1960s, as well as other instruments. In the late 1960s, Valco was absorbed by the Kay company (See KAY). In 1968, Kay/Valco Guitars, Inc. went out of business. Both the National and the Supro trademarks were purchased at the 1969 liquidation auction by Chicago's Strum 'N Drum Music Company.
(Source: Tom Wheeler, American Guitars)

VERO AMPS
Amplifiers currently produced in Joliet, Illinois.

The Vero Amplifier company was formed in 1998 in Joliet, Illinois. The company has taken guitar amps and brought them to an artistic level. Their amps typically feature an elaborate wooden cabinet with old-school tube technology going on inside. Vero also lets the customer design the amp to his/her specs therefore making each amplifier entirely custom. Fender Custom Shop eat you heart out! As Vero's website describes it, the options are essentially endless as far as color and design of the cabinet. Now someone could actually match an amp to be as custom as a 5-necked guitar.

ORDERING VERO AMPS

Vero can make a guitar amplifier for pretty much anyone. To order an amp call up Vero and expect to put a $1,000 deposit and then let the brainstorming begin. They have the possibility to choose the power section, preamp section, tubes, as well as the cosmetics. If I want to create the Zach Fjestad model, they can create the Zach Fjestad model (guaranteed hot seller!). The general turn around time on these amps are about six weeks. For more infromation refer to the web site (see Trademark Index).

VICTORIA
Amplifiers currently produced in Naperville, Illinois.

Mark Baier is the president of Victoria amplifiers. Victoria have made tweed amplifiers that are close to the original Fender tweed's. They aren't Fenders inside out, they have had several modern updates to make them some of the finest amps out there. How can you not like the look of good tweed either? Victoria has a full website where you can look at all their models and get more information on the company (see Trademark Index).

VOX
Amplifiers currently produced in Erith, Kent. Vox Amplification is distributed in England and through the U.S.A. in Melville, New York by Vox Amplification. The Vox trademark was established circa 1957 in Dartford, Kent.

The Vox Amplifier company was started mainly by two people, Tom Jennings and Dick Denney. Tom Jennings was the man who started his own retail business and the Univox portable accordion/organ. Dick Denney came up with the first amp that went on to be the first Vox Amplifier.

Tom Jennings was born on February 28, 1917 in Hackney England. After school he took up the hobby of the piano/accordion. As World War II raged on, he was called up to duty in 1940, but discharged medically in 1941. He then went to work in a munitions plant where he and fellow colleagues learned to entertain themselves musically. This is where he was inspired to go into music and did so after the war was over. In 1944, he formed his own business trading accordians and other musical instruments. In 1946, his co-worker back at the ammunition plant, Dick Denney, came to work with Tom. Denney was into amplifying instruments and set out to make an amplifier for a Hawaiian guitar. Denney and Jennings went their different ways as the war ended and many war-industry workers were laid-off.

Tom kept on with the small business and hired a new electric technician. Shortly thereafter the Univox, a portable piano/accordion, was released. With the slow growing of the Univox and Jennings being a successful business man, The Jennings Organ Company was started in 1951. Jennings made organs and the Univox throughout the 1950's when he decided that a new line of product was necessary. Dick Denney had employed himself in radio and electronics as a repairer and an engineer. He also developed an amplifier during his sickness, which restricted him from working on a normal basis. One of Denney's buddies took this new 15W amp down to Jennings shop and Tom was very interested. Tom ended up hiring Dick as the chief design engineer for Jenning's new company to be called Vox. After ten years of hardly taking to each other, Tom and Dick were now in the process of releasing the first Vox amplifier. Denney's 15W amp would become the AC15.

As Rock & Roll exploded into Britain in 1958, Vox picked up a couple of endorseres like Cliff Richard and The Shadows. Later in 1958, Vox released two new amps without the vibrato that the AC-15 had. Then the "big dawg," the AC-30, made its debut in late 1959. This amp was to compete with the Fender Twin of the same type. The AC-30 became an unqualified success and then the Beatles happened. As we all know, the Beatles played Vox amplifiers from day one when Brian Epstein traded in their old AC-15's, for new AC-30's. The rest is what they say history. Vox landed the best endorsement deal they could have ever dreamed of, and sales just roared.

Amid the heyday, Vox was experiencing in the mid 1960's, financial woes were on the horizon. This caused Tom Jennings to sell the company to the Royston Group in 1964. The Thomas Organ Company arranged a deal where Vox could now be imported into the United States. Under new ownership now, the company was run in a different way and felt that solid-state was the way to go. These amps just couldn't keep up with what Marshall and other companies were producing and times became tough. After a fire in 1966 at the factory, and declining numbers, Tom Jennings resigned in 1967. Shortly thereafter Royston was liquidated and Corinthian Securities took over. This proved to be a bad ownership, as Corinthian had no connection with the previous staff and they discontinued almost all of the guitars in the catalog. The few that remained were manufactured in Japan from then on. This ownership didn't last long and Stolec bought them out in 1970. CBS-Arbiter bought out Vox again in 1972 for the third change of ownership in as many years.

When CBS-Arbiter took over it looked like things may change around for Vox. The return of the Vox organs came along with many new amplifiers and effects. But the 1970's had it's tole on Vox, as it did with other manufactures as well. CBS took a loss during the 1970's and were forced to sell again, this time to the long-time distributor of Marshall, Rose-Morris. RM had just lost the rights of Marshall and were looking for something to get them back with amplifiers. The company name was now Vox Ltd. Rose Morris released quite a bit of new products, and in a sense kept Vox going through the tough 1980's. Dick Denney endorsed the new AC-30 Limited Edition in 1990. But in 1992, with an economic recession hurting the company, Rose Morris looked to sell the company for the fifth time. Korg now becomes the distributor of Vox instruments. In 1993, Vox went back to their bread and butter with the AC-30 bringing it back to its almost original design from the 1960's. The original amplifier now kept the company going over 30 years later.

Vox is now producing instruments with great quality and new and innovative designs every year. In 2001, they released the Valvetronix series along with a bunch of new models. They continue into the 21st century as one of the big amp companies.

(Source for Vox History: David Petersen & Dick Denney, Vox: The Vox Story.)

DATING VOX AMPLIFIERS

The only way to date Vox amplifiers is to know when and what models were made during certain times. Since ownership has changed so many the times over this manufacture's lifespan, the serialization records haven't survived through today. Cosmetics and a niche for looking at Vox amps is the best way to date amps so far. It should be noted that Vox has made U.S. and British amps. Some were special only to the U.S. or Britain and others were equivalents of each other. Make sure to take note as not to mix things up.

Here is a list of changes that happened during the years as far as cosmetics, and other features that can be detected by looking at it.

COVERING - Vox started making amps with Blonde covering in 1958. Some of the early coverings were a two-tone gray/cream. Blond covering was used until around 1962 when dark covering was introduced. There have been some models found in 1961 and 1962 that had black, red or blue samples. Cabinets remained covered in dark covering up until current.

GRILLES - In 1958 the original grille cloth was brown latticed however a plain cloth is known to exist. The brown latticed covering was in use until 1964 when it was changed to black latticed. The black grille covering is in use today.

CONTROL PANELS - The original Vox control panel was black with gold legend. This was used for two years between 1958 and 1959. In 1960, the panel was changed to a copper and this lasted until 1964. In 1965, a dark gray panel was introduced with a metallic legend. In 1978, the control panel was changed to a spray paint/screen print legend with the same color.

FEATURES ON THE AMP - There are other certain features on the amp that were changed throughout the years that help identify the approximate year.

* *1958* - At the beginning of 1958, amps had small letters for the Vox emblem, a small Jennings embossing on the frame, round control knobs, a small 10 or 15 badge on the lower left, Audiom speakers, brass ventilators, and a handle.

GRADING	100%	EXCELLENT	AVERAGE

* **1959** - Knobs were now pointer (chicken head knobs), all models have 4 inputs, an "A J.M.I. Product" legend appears between the input jacks, otherwise same as 1958.
* **1960** - 6-input models with three channels, otherwise same as 1958.
* **1961** - Blue "Vox" speakers in amplifiers, a J.M.I Product logo on lower right part of control panel.
* **1962** - Top Boost models made their first appearance. These models would have treble and bass controls on the back.
* **1963** - Injection-molded vents introduced, dark covering varies in texture from smooth to rough, quite random.
* **1964** - Top Boost controls now part of the control panel, corner protectors added to cabinet, and hardware injection molding.
* **1965** - Black speaker cloth introduced, speakers in lead models are changed to a silver color, and the mains switch is changed to a 5-way rotary.
* **1966** - Black ventilators introduced.
* **1967** - Solid-state amplifiers begin to take off.
* **1968** - "A Vox Product" logo introduced on control panel, the GZ34 rectifier is replaced with a solid-state system.
* **1969-1991** - Information is tough to come by with all of the changes in ownership over the years. Research still underway.

(Source for Vox History: David Petersen & Dick Denney, Vox: The Vox Story).

ELECTRIC TUBE AMPLIFIERS

AC Series

This is Vox's claim to fame here. The AC-15 is the first model to be released by Vox with the AC-30 following shortly thereafter. The AC-30 is by far the most successful and powerful of Vox amps. As seen in 1993, the AC-30 was redesigned almost to its original and kept the company running.

AC-4 - 3.5W, 1-8" Elac speaker, tubes: preamp: 7025, 6267, power: EL84, 6V4, single channel, top control panel, two inputs, three black pointer knobs (v, tone, s), blond covering, brown grille, mfg. 1958-early 1960's.

	N/A	$1,050 - 1,300	$850 - 975

This model was originally the AC-2 with a 6 inch speaker but changed quickly to the AC-4 when the earlier one didn't sell very well.

AC-10 - 12W, 1-10" Vox speaker, tubes: preamp: EF86, ECF82, ECC83, power: 2 X EL84, EZ81, dual channels, top control panel, four input jacks, five knobs (2vol, tone, tremolo speed, tremolo depth), blond covering, brown grille, mfg. 1958-early 1960's.

	N/A	$1,200 - 1,500	$900 - 1,050

* **AC-10 Twin** - Similar to the AC-10 except has 2-10" speakers, mfg. 1958-early 1960's.

Vox AC-10
courtesy solidbodyguitar.com, Inc.

Vox AC-10
courtesy solidbodyguitar.com, Inc.

	N/A	$1,250 - 1,600	$950 - 1,100

* **AC-10 Reverb Twin** - Simiar to the AC-10 except a piggyback version with reverb and reverb control, mfg. early 1960's.

	N/A	$1,250 - 1,600	$1,000 - 1,125

AC-15 - 18W, 1-12" Vox Celestion speakers, combo, tubes: EL84 output tubes, dual channels, top control panel, four inputs, six knobs (2v, tone, brilliance, vib/tremolo speed, VT select), blond covering, brown grille, mfg. 1958-1960's.

	N/A	$1,100 - 1,500	$850 - 950

* **AC-15 Twin** - Similar to the AC-15 except has 2-12" speakers, mfg. 1958-1960's.

	N/A	$1,200 - 1,500	$950 - 1,050

GRADING	100%	EXCELLENT	AVERAGE

AC-30 TWIN - 36W combo, 2-12" Vox Celestion Alnico speakers, tubes: preamp: 4 X 7025, 12AU7 power: 4 X EL84, 5AR4 rectifier, three channels, vibrato/tremolo, top control panel, six inputs (two per channel, vib/trem, normal, brilliant), six black pointer knobs (vib/trem speed, vib/trem depth, three volumes, one per channel, tone), blond covering, brown grille, mfg. 1959-1970's.

Vox AC-30
courtesy solidbodyguitar.com, Inc.

Vox AC-30
courtesy solidbodyguitar.com, Inc.

Vox AC-30 w/stand
courtesy Savage Audio

	100%	EXCELLENT	AVERAGE
1959-1960	N/A	$5,000 - 6,000	$2,750 - 3,500
1960-1970	N/A	$3,500 - 4,250	$1,950 - 2,850

This model was originally known as the AC-30/4 but meant it only had four input jacks. It was changed in 1960 to the AC-30/6 with six jacks. Early models of the AC-30 have Audiom 60 speakers. Later models have Clestion Model G12 speakers made especially for Vox. This model was also available later with 2-15" Vox Celestion speakers. In 1963, dark covering was introduced. The Original Top-Boost AC-30 came from a separate bass and treble control mounted on the back of the amp separately from the control panel.

* AC-30 Super Twin - Similar to the AC-30 except in a piggyback version with 2-12" Vox Clesetion speakers, mfg. 1962-mid 1960's.

	N/A	$2,500 - 3,500	$1,750 - 2,250

* AC-30 Super Twin Reverb - Similar to the AC-30 Super Twin (Piggyback) except has reverb, tubes: 2 X 7025 added for reverb, total of 6 X 7025, mfg. 1960's.

	N/A	$2,750 - 3,500	$2,000 - 2,500

AC-30 TWIN TOP BOOST - 36W combo, 2-12" Vox Celestion Alnico speakers, tubes: preamp: 7 X 7025, 12AU7 power: 4 X EL84, three channels, vibrato/tremolo, top control panel, six inputs (two per channel, vib/trem, normal, brilliant), eight black pointer knobs (vib/trem speed, vib/trem depth, three volumes, one per channel, b, t, cut), blond covering, brown grille, mfg. 1961-mid 1960's.

1961-63	N/A	$4,000 - 5,000	$3,000 - 3,500
1964 on	N/A	$3,000 - 3,500	$2,000 - 2,500

In 1963, the covering was changed to a dark or black.

* AC-30 Super Twin Top Boost - Similar to the AC-30 Twin Top Boost except in piggyback version with a sloping cabinet, mfg. 1961-mid 1960's.

	N/A	$3,500 - 4,250	$2,500 - 3,000

* AC-30 Super Twin Top Boost Reverb - Similar to the AC-30 Super Twin Top Boost except has reverb, mfg. 1961-mid 1960's.

	N/A	$3,500 - 4,250	$2,500 - 3,000

AC-50 SUPER TWIN - 50W, Piggyback with a 2-12" cabinet with a mid-range horn, tubes: preamp: 3 X 7025, 12AU7, power: 2 X EL34, 5AR4 rectifier, dual channels, top control panel, four input jacks, six black knobs (2v, 2b, 2t one for each channel), black covering, dark grille, mfg. mid 1960's.

Vox AC-50
courtesy solidbodyguitar.com, Inc.

Vox AC-50
courtesy solidbodyguitar.com, Inc.

	N/A	$900 - 1,200	$500 - 700

This model was originally aimed for the bassist.

GRADING	100%	EXCELLENT	AVERAGE

AC-100 SUPER DELUXE - 100W, Piggyback, cabinet contains 4-12" Vox Celestion Alnico speakers and 2 midrange horns, tubes: preamp: 7025, 2 X 12AU7, power: 4 X EL34, one channel, top control panel, two inputs, three black knobs (v, b, t), black covering, dark grille, mfg. 1964-late 1960's.

	N/A	$2,000 - 2,500	$1,500 - 1,750

This model was meant to be used with the new Beatle speaker cabinet.

AC-120 - 120W, 2-12" heavy-duty speakers, tube combo with 4 X EL34 power tubes, dual channels, reverb, distortion, top control panel, four inputs (two normal, two bright), 14 black knobs (v1, v2, b, m, t, presence, five band harmonic balance knobs, distortion, r, MV), brown covering, brown diagonal grille, mfg. 1975-late 1970's.

	N/A	$1,000 - 1,300	$750 - 900

AC-30 LIMITED EDITION - 36W combo, 2-12" Vox Celestion Alnico speakers, tubes: preamp: 7 X 7025, 12AU7 power: 4 X EL84, three channels, vibrato/tremolo, top control panel, six inputs (two per channel, vib/trem, normal, brilliant), eight black pointer knobs (vib/trem speed, vib/trem depth, three volumes, one per channel, b, t, cut), blond or brown covering, brown grille, mfg. 1990-91.

	N/A	$1,000 - 1,250	$500 - 750

These models were available in a blonde or dark finish covering. There is a label inside indicating the 30th anniversary of the AC-30 inside. These amplifiers were built to commemorate the original AC-30 of the early 1960's.

* **AC-30 Top Boost Vintage Head and Speaker Cabinet** - Similar in chassis to the AC-30 Limited Edition, Is a head-unit that sits atop a 4-12" speaker cabinet, available in blonde or black covering, mfg. 1990-91.

	N/A	$1,250 - 1,750	$750 - 1,000

* **AC-30 TB Collector** - Similar to the AC-30 Limited Edition, except finished in a mahogany cabinet, mfg. 1990-91.

	N/A	$1,750 - 2,000	$1,000 - 1,250

* **AC-30TBR (Reverb)** - Similar to the AC-30, except has reverb with reverb controls, mfg. 1990-91.

	N/A	$1,250 - 1,750	$750 - 1,000

AC-30/6 TOP BOOST (CURRENT PRODUCTION) - 33W, 2-12" G12M-25W "Greenback" speakers, tube combo, preamp:5 X ECC83, ECC82, power, 4 X EL84 (class A), GZ34 rectifier, three channels, vibrato/tremolo, top control panel, six inputs (three per channel), eight black pointer knobs (v for each channel, vib/trem speed, vib/trem, b, t, cut), black covering, diagonal brown grille, three handles, mfg. 1993-current.

MSR	$2,150	$1,599	$1,100 - 1,300	$850 - 975

* **AC-30/6 TBX** - Similar to the AC-30/6 Top Boost except has 2-12" Celestion G12 "blue" speakers, mfg. 1993-current.

MSR	$2,675	$1,849	$1,200 - 1,450	$950 - 1,100

    Add $200 for the Chrome stand.

    Add $45 for cover.

AC-15 TOP BOOST (CURRENT PRODUCTION) - 15W. 1-12" Bulldog speaker, tube combo, preamp: 5 X ECC83, ECC82, power: 2 X EL84, 5Y3 rectifier, single channel, top control panel, two inputs, seven black pointer knobs (v, t, b, reverb, s, depth, MV), black covering, diagonal brown grille, mfg. 1996-current.

MSR	$1,375	$800	$575 - 725	$450 - 525

* **AC-15TBX** - Similar to the AC-15 Top Boost, except has 1-12" Celestion G12 Alnico Vox "blue" speaker, mfg. 1996-current.

MSR	$1,675	$950	$700 - 825	$550 - 650

    Add $200 for chrome stand.

    Add $50 for cover.

U.S.A. Models Released from 1964-69

PATHFINDER (V-101) - 4W, 1-8" speaker, tubes unknown, single channel, tremolo, top mounted control panel, two input jacks, five knobs (v, t, b, s, depth for tremolo), black covering, brown diagonal grille, mfg. 1967-69.

	N/A	$300 - 400	$150 - 225

PACEMAKER (V102) - 17W, combo, 1-10" Bulldog speaker, tubes: preamp: 3 X 7025, 12AU7, power: 2 X EL84, EZ81, single channel, tremolo, top mounted control panel, three input jacks, five black knobs (v, t, b, s, depth for tremolo), mid-range switch, built in E-tuner, black covering, brown diagonal grille, mfg. 1964-67.

	N/A	$500 - 700	$300 - 425

* **Cambridge Reverb (V103)** - Similar to the Pacemaker except has reverb circuit, reverb depth control in place of mid range switch (M.R.B.), footswitch for mid-range control, mfg. 1964-67.

	N/A	$500 - 700	$300 - 425

* **Berkeley II (V104)** - Similar to the Cambridge reverb except in piggy-back form, pressure cabinet with 2-10" speakers, mfg. 1964-67.

	N/A	$550 - 750	$350 - 450

"V" Series V-125 Stack and V-15 Combo

These amplifiers were the first efforts of Rose-Morris. The Escort Series (solid-state) debuted at the same time. Since these models were released in England and didn't get over to the U.S. much, very little are showing up in the American market. We haven't been able to establish a price on these since there are so few of the around.

V-15 - 15W, 2-10" speakers, five tube chassis combo, preamp: 2 X ECC83, 1 X ECC81, power: 2 X EL84, single channel, top mounted control panel, two input jacks, five black knobs (v, t, m, b, MV), black covering, brown diagonal grille, mfg. 1980-mid 80's.

GRADING	100%	EXCELLENT	AVERAGE

V-125 LEAD - 125W, piggy-back, head unit only, eight tube chassis, preamp: 2 X ECC83, 1 X ECC82, 1 X ECC81, power: 4 X EL34, single channel, top mounted control panel, two input jacks (one normal, one brilliant), six control knobs (v, sensitivity, three equalizer knobs, MV), black covering, brown diagonal grille, mfg. 1980-mid 1980's.

  * *VR212* - Speaker cabinet to match up with the V-125 Lead head-unit, has 2-12" speakers, mfg. 1980-mid 1980's.
  * *Climax* - Similar to the V-125 except is the combo version, with 2-12" speakers, and has distortion circuit, distortion knob in place of sensitivity, mfg. 1979-mid 1980's.
  * *V-125 Bass* - Similar to the V-125 except has cabinets with 1-15" speakers, and the equalizer consists of the frequencies of 50, 100, 250, 500, and 1500 Hz, mfg. 1980-????

Concert Series

This series was introduced after the Venue series. The first model in the Concert series, The Concert 501, was basically a 50W version of the Dual 100 in the Venue series.

CONCERT 501 - 50W, 1-12", nine tubes chassis, preamp: 5 X 7025, power: 4 X EL84, dual channels, reverb, gain, front black control panel, two inputs (hi and lo), eleven black and white control knobs (Ch. 1: v, b, m, t, Ch. 2: gain, b, m, t, v, Both: r, MV), effects loop, extension speaker jack, headphone jack, black covering, black grille, mfg. 1984-87.

	N/A	$300 - 400	$150 - 250

  * *Concert 501/2* - Similar to the Concert 501, except has 2-10" speakers, mfg. 1984-87.

	N/A	$350 - 450	$200 - 300

CONCERT 100 - 100W, head-unit with 2 cabinets consisting of 4-12" speakers in each, eight tube chassis, preamp: 4 X 7025, power: 4 X EL34, single channel, front black control panel, two input jacks, six control knobs, (gain, t, m, b, MV, presence), output jacks for speakers, black covering, diagonal black grille cloth, mfg. 1986-87.

HEAD UNIT	N/A	$300 - 400	$175 - 250
SPEAKER CAB	N/A	$350 - 450	$200 - 300

ELECTRIC SOLID-STATE AMPLIFIERS

AC Series Solid-State

Vox tried its first transistor amp with the T-60, which was a bass amp. They took the AC-30 and made it a solid-state, and issued a couple new AC amps that were solid-state as well.

AC-30 SOLID-STATE - 40W, 2-12" speakers, solid-state combo, tremolo, top control panel, six inputs (three per channel), seven black control knobs (v1, v2, v3, t, b, tone, s), tremolo on/off, footswitch for tremolo, black covering, diagonal brown grille, mfg. 1975-1980's.

T-60 BASS - 60W, Piggyback, cabinet with 1-15" Vox Celestion Alnico HD and 1-12" Vox Celestion Alnico, solid-state, single channel, rear control panel, four input jacks, three knobs (v, t, b), black covering, black diagonal grille, mfg 1964-67.

Vox T-60 Bass
courtesy Dave's Guitar Shop

This model was also available for a short time with blond covering in 1964.

U.S.A. Models Released from 1964-69.

The first few models listed here were originally tube amplifiers. By 1967, all Vox amps had become transistor (solid-state). Since they were originally tube amps check the tube section of Vox if the models match up with those listed.

PATHFINDER (V1011) - 25W, unknown speaker, solid-state combo, single channel, tremolo, top mounted control panel, two input jacks, five knobs (v, t, b, s, depth for tremolo), black covering, brown diagonal grille, mfg. 1964-69.

	N/A	$225 - 325	$100 - 200

Last MSR was $109.90.

GRADING	100%	EXCELLENT	AVERAGE

PACEMAKER (V1020, V1021, V1022) - 17W, 1-10" speaker, solid-state combo, single channel, tremolo, top mounted control panel, three input jacks, six control knobs (v, b, t, m, s, depth tremolo), built in E-tuner, black covering, brown diagonal grille, mfg. 1964-69.

Vox Pacemaker (Solid-State)
courtesy S. P. Fjestad

Vox Pacemaker (Solid-State)
courtesy S. P. Fjestad

N/A	$250 - 350	$150 - 225
		Last MSR was $149.90.

This model had a couple model number changes. In 1969, it was switched to V1022.

CAMBRIDGE REVERB (V1031) - Similar to the Pacemaker except has reverb and mid-range switch on footswitch, reverb depth control replaced mid range switch, mfg. 1967-69.

N/A	$400 - 500	$200 - 300
		Last MSR was $229.

In 1969, the model number was switched to V1032.

BERKELEY II (V1081) - Similar to the Cambridge Reverb, except is in piggy-back form with a pressure cabinet containing 2-10" speakers, mfg. 1967-69.

N/A	$500 - 600	$350 - 450

* _Berkeley III_ - Similar to the Berkeley, except is has 32W, three button footswitch, updated version of the Berkeley II, mfg. 1967-68.

N/A	$600 - 700	$300 - 500

BUCKINGHAM (V1121, V1122) - 35W, piggyback design with 2-12" Vox Heavy Duty Bulldog speakers, solid-state chassis, two channels, reverb, MRB, two inputs, five knobs, chrome roller stand, footswitch, mfg. 1964-68.

Vox Buckingham V1121
courtesy Gurney Brown

N/A	$600 - 700	$400 - 550
		Last MSR was $695 for V1122 and $725 for the V1121.

The difference between the V1122 and the V1121 is the V1121 had a remote controlled footswitch distortion booster.

KENSINGTON BASS (1241) - 22W, 1-15", solid-state combo, top mounted control panel, single channel, two input jacks, two controls (v, tone-X), built in G-tuner, chrome roller stand, black covering, brown diagonal grille, mfg. 1967-69.

N/A	$400 - 600	$250 - 350

ESSEX BASS (V1043) - 35W, 2-12" Vox Bulldog bass speakers, solid-state combo, top mounted control panel, single channel, two input jacks, two controls (v, tone-X), Watchdog limiter, footswitch for Tone-X, chrome roller stand, black covering, brown diagonal grille, mfg. 1965-68.

N/A	$400 - 500	$250 - 350

GRADING	100%	EXCELLENT	AVERAGE

WESTMINSTER BASS (V1181) - 120W, 1-18", solid-state combo, dual channels, top mounted control panel, six controls (v1, v2, t1, t2, b, Tone-X), built-in G-tuner, footswitch for Tone-X, black covering, brown diagonal grille, mfg. 1964-67.

	N/A	$350 - 550	$200 - 300

Last MSR was $850.

* Westminster Bass (V1182) - Similar to the Westminster Bass V1181, except has the Watchdog limiter, mfg. 1968 only.

	N/A	$400 - 600	$250 - 350

SUPER BEATLE (V1141) - 120W, piggy-back, cabinet with 4-12" speakers and 2 Midax, three channels, tremolo, reverb, distortion, top mounted control panel, six input jacks (two per channel), 14 knobs total, nine on top (Ch. 1: v, b, t, Ch. 2: v, b, t, Ch. 3: v, t, Tone X) five on back (trem speed, trem depth, MBR selector, reverb selection switch, reverb depth), built in E-tuner, five button footswitch, black covering, brown diagonal grille, mfg. 1964-66.

	N/A	$1,800 - 2,100	$1,300 - 1,700

Last MSR was $1,225.

* Super Beatle (V1142) - Similar to the Beatle model 1141, except has a four button footswitch, mfg. 1965-67.

	N/A	$2,000 - 2,500	$1,500 - 1,900

Last MSR was $1,195.

* Super Beatle (V1143) - Similar to the Beatle model 1141, except has a five button footswitch, mfg. 1964-68.

	N/A	$2,000 - 2,500	$1,500 - 1,900

This model was designated the V1143J or the V1143A. Each designated what speakers the amp contained. The J indicated JBL and the A stood for Altec Lansing speakers.

BEATLE POWER STACK (V1262) - 120W, piggyback cabinet design with 8-12" speakers, three channels, reverb, tremolo, top control panel, six inputs, "Watchdog load limiter," various control knobs, five button footswitch, E-tuner, line reverse, black vinyl covering, Vox diamond grille cloth, mfg. 1969 only.

Pricing on this model is highly inaccurate because of the rarity of this amplifier. We suggest getting a second opinion on this model.

ROYAL GUARDSMAN (V1131, V1132, V1133) - 60W, piggyback design with 2-12" Vox Heavy Duty Bulldog speakers, solid-state chassis, two channels, two inputs, various knobs, chrome roller stand, black covering, brown Vox diagonal grille cloth, mfg. 1964-68.

	N/A	$650 - 850	$400 - 550

Last MRS was $895 for the V1132 and $925 for the V1131.

The difference between the V1132 and the V1131 is the V1131 had a remote control distortion booster.
This model was also available as the Super Beatle (V1142), which only had a three button footswitch. This eliminated the distortion switch.

4 & 7 Series Solid-State

These were the first real series developed for solid-state. This happened when Jennings sold to Royston and they were looking to get this into the market. The 7 series were guitar amps and the 4 series were bass amps. These amps got some play with endorsers but overall the market rejected them and were removed shortly thereafter. There are corresponding bass models to the guitar models supposedly. This means there is a 415, 430, and 460 with the same basic specs as the 7 series.

Pricing on this amp is highly inaccurate because of the lack of distribution in the U.S. Most of these amplifiers were sold in England and never made it over to North America.

4120 - 120W, Piggyback, 2 cabinets with 4-12" G12H25 W speakers & 2-10" Celestion speakers, solid-state, dual channels, bottom front control panel, two inputs, eight knobs (v, b, t, m, v, b, t, m), bright switch, boost switch, black covering, diagonal black covering, mfg. 1966-mid 1970's.

* 460 - Similar to the 4120 except has 60W output, and a speaker configuration of 4-12", 2-12" or 2-10" speakers, mfg. 1966-mid 1970's.

* 430 - Similar to the 460 except has 30W output, mfg. 1966-mid 1970's

* 415 - Similar to the 460 except has 15W output, mfg. 1966-mid 1970's.

7120 - 120W, Piggyback, 4-12" Vox Celestion Aninco speakers & 2 Midax HF horns in a cabinet, solid-state, dual channels, front control panel, four input jacks, eight knobs (Ch.1: v, t, m, b Ch. 2: v, t, m, b), black covering, diagonal black covering, mfg. 1966-mid 1970's.
This model was also available in a 2-cabinet system.

* 760 - Similar to the 7120 except has 60W output, cabinet with 2-12" Celestion G12H 25W speakers & 2-10" Celestion 10W speakers, mfg. 1966-68.

730 - 30W, 2-12" or 2-10" speakers, Piggyback, solid-state, dual channels, front control panel, four input jacks, six knobs (Ch. 1: v, t, b, Ch. 2: v, t, b), bright and boost switches, black covering, diagnoal black grille, mfg, 1966-68

* 715 - Similar to the 730 except with 15W output, mfg. 1966-68.

British Models Introduced After 1966

These models are hard to put a price on since they were all made in England. At this point in time, Vox produced only models in England or the U.S. Many of these amps never made it to the U.S., therefore there aren't enough to create a second market on them.

VIRTUOSO - 30W, 2-10" speakers, solid-state combo, dual channels, tremolo, reverb, distortion, top control panel, four input jacks, 14 control knobs (Ch. 1: v, b, t, Ch. 2: v, b, t, bright switch, mid-range (MRB) switch, mid-range select, s, trem depth, reverb switch, reverb depth, distortion knob), three button footswitch, black covering, brown diagonal grille, mfg. 1966-1970's.

* Conqueror - Similar to the Virtuoso, except is in piggy-back form, with a 2-12" cabinet, mfg. 1966-1970's.

* Defiant - Similar to the Conqueror, except has 50W output and the cabinet contains a Midax with the speakers, mfg. 1966-1970's.

* Supreme - Similar to the Defiant, except has 100W, a cabinet with 4-12" speakers and 2 Midax, and has a Watchdog limiter, mfg. 1966-1970's.

GRADING	100%	EXCELLENT	AVERAGE

DYNAMIC BASS - 30W, piggy-back, cabinet with 1-15" speaker, solid-state, dual channels, distortion switch, top control panel, four input jacks, eight control knobs (v1, v2, t, b, Tone-X, distortion, mid-range switch, mid-range select), black covering, brown diagonal grille, mfg. 1966-1970's.

* *Foundation Bass* - Similar to the Dynamic Bass, except has 50W output and a cabinet with 1-18" speaker, mfg. 1966-1970's.
* *Super Foundation Bass* - Similar to the Foundation Bass, except has 100W output, mfg. 1966-1970's.

Escort Series

ESCORT 30 - 30W, 1-12" speaker, solid-state combo, three channels, distortion, top-mounted control panel, three input jacks, seven black chicken head knobs (v1, v2, v3, fuzz intensity, t, m, b) footswitch for fuzz (distortion), brown covering, brown diagonal grille, mfg. 1970's.

| | N/A | $100 - 150 | $50 - 100 |

ESCORT BATTERY - 3W, 1-5.5" speaker, solid-state combo, single channel, top control panel, two input jacks (one normal, one brilliant), two control knobs (v, tone), black covering, brown diagonal grille, mfg. 1970's

| Vox Escort | Vox Escort | Vox Escort |
| courtesy Dave's Guitar Shop | courtesy Dave's Guitar Shop | courtesy Rick Wilkiewicz |

| | N/A | $100 - 200 | $75 - 90 |

This amp was modeled after the ever so popular AC-30 but in mini-form.

* *Escort Battery/Mains* - Similar to the Escort Battery, except has an output socket that feeds a signal into the main amplifier (i.e. AC-30), has third control knobs which is a supply selector, mfg. 1970-mid 70's.

| | N/A | $125 - 175 | $75 - 100 |

ESCORT 50 - 50W, 1-12" speaker, solid-state combo, single channel, top control panel, two input jacks, five control knobs (v, t, m, b, harmonics), black covering, brown diagonal grille, mfg. 1970-mid 70's.

| | N/A | $125 - 175 | $75 - 100 |

Venue Series

LEAD 100 - 100W, 1-12" speaker, solid-state combo, single channel, reverb, overdrive, front black control panel, two input jacks, seven black and white knobs (v, t, m, b, r, overdrive, MV), footswitch for overdrive and reverb, black covering, black grille, mfg. mid 1980's.

| | N/A | $175 - 250 | $100 - 150 |

* *Lead 50* - Similar to the Lead 100, except has 50W output and no overdrive circuit, mfg. mid 1980's.

| | N/A | $150 - 200 | $75 - 125 |

BASS 100 - 100W, 1-15" speaker, solid-state combo, single channel, front black control panel, two input jacks, four black and white knobs (v, t, m, b), effects loop, extension speaker jack, headphone jack, black covering, black grille, mfg. mid 1980's.

| | N/A | $175 - 200 | $100 - 150 |

* *Bass 50* - Similar to the Bass 100, except has 50W output and 1-12" speaker, no extension speaker jack, mfg. mid 1980's.

| | N/A | $150 - 200 | $75 - 125 |

KEYBOARD 100 - 100W, 1-15" speaker and a H.F. horn, solid-state combo, three channels, reverb, six input jacks (three per channel), 12 black and white knobs (v, b, & t for each channel, presence, r, MV), effects loop, footswitch, extension speaker jack, headphone jack, black covering, black grille, mfg. mid 1980's.

| | N/A | $175 - 250 | $100 - 150 |

PA-120 - 120W, piggy-back unit, two cabinets with 1-12" speaker and a H.F. horn in each, solid-state, four channels, reverb, front control panel, eight input jacks (two per channel), 15 control knobs (v, t, & b for each channel, presence, r, MV), effects loop, footswitch, headphone jack, black covering, black grille, mfg. mid 1980's.

| | N/A | $150 - 200 | $100 - 125 |

GT-100 - 100W, 1-12" and H.F. horn, solid-state combo, dual channels, reverb, front control panel, three input jacks (two for Ch. 2), 12 control knobs (Ch. 1: v, mid sweep, m, t, b, Ch. 2: v, mid sweep, m, t, b, r, MV), footswitch for lots of controls, extension speaker jack, headphone jack, black covering, black grille, mfg. mid 1980's.

| | N/A | $175 - 250 | $100 - 150 |

GRADING	100%	EXCELLENT	AVERAGE

BUSKER - 4W, 1-8" speaker, solid-state combo, single channel, front black control panel, two input jacks, four black knobs (v, m, t, MV), headphone jack, operable on AC or DC, black covering, black grille, mfg. mid 1980's.

	N/A	$100 - 150	$50 - 75

This model is essentially the Escort now in the Venue series.

DUAL 100 - 100W, 1-12", solid-state combo, dual switchable channels, reverb, gain, front black control panel, two inputs (hi and lo), eleven black and white control knobs (Ch. 1: v, b, m, t, Ch. 2: gain, b, m, t, v, Both: r, MV), extension speaker jack, headphone jack, black covering, black grille, mfg. mid 1980's.

	N/A	$200 - 300	$100 - 175

LEAD 30 - 30W, 1-10" speaker, solid-state combo, single channel, reverb, front mounted control panel, two input jacks, six black control knobs (v, t, m, b, r, MV), slave jack, headphone jack, black covering, black grille, mfg. mid 1980's.

	N/A	$175 - 225	$125 - 150

"Q" Series

BASS 100 MOSFET - 100W, 1-15" speaker, solid-state combo, single channel, front black control panel, two inputs, eight black knobs (three compressors, b, mid-freq, mid, t, MV), five-band equalizer, effects loop, extension speaker jack, headphone jack, black covering, black grille, mfg. 1988-1990.

	N/A	$175 - 225	$110 - 145

LEAD 100 MOSFET - 100W, 1-12" speaker, solid-state combo, dual channels, reverb, front black control panel, three input jacks, eight black knobs (v1, v2, t, mid-freq, mid, b, MV, r), five-band equalizer, effects loop, extension speaker jack, headphone jack, black covering, black grille, mfg. 1988-1990.

	N/A	$200 - 250	$150 - 175

GT 100 MOSFET - 100W, 1-12" and H.F. horn, solid-state combo, dual channels, reverb, front control panel, three input jacks (two for Ch. 2), 12 control knobs (Ch. 1: v, mid sweep, m, t, b, Ch. 2: v, mid sweep, m, t, b, r, MV), footswitch for lots of controls, extension speaker jack, headphone jack, black covering, black grille, mfg. 1988-1990.

	N/A	$175 - 250	$100 - 150

KB 50 MOSFET - 50W, 1-12" speaker, solid-state combo, reverb, three channels, front black control panel, six input jacks (two per channel), 14 black knobs (v, mid-freq, mid & b for each channel, r, MV), effects loop, extension speaker jack, headphone jack, black covering, black grille, mfg. 1988-1990.

	N/A	$125 - 165	$95 - 110

Pathfinder Series (Current Production)

These are small practice amplifiers that were introduced in 1999. These are solid-state amps that are affordable to have in your bedroom to practice with. The Pathfinders have all of the features that the larger amps have but in a smaller package.

PATHFINDER 10 (V9106) - 10W, 6.5" speaker combo, solid-state, clean/overdrive switch, top control panel, one input, four black pointer knobs (gain, v, b, t), headphone jack, black covering, brown diagonal grille, mfg. 2001-current.

MSR	$99	$70	$50 - 60	$40 - 45

PATHFINDER 15 (V9168) - 15W, 1-8" speaker combo, solid-state, clean/overdrive switch, tremolo, top control panel, one input, six black pointer knobs (gain, v, b, t, s, d), headphone jack, footswitch, black covering, brown diagonal grille, mfg. 1999-current.

MSR	$150	$90	$65 - 75	$50 - 65

* Pathfinder 15R (V9168R) - Similar to the Pathfinder 15, except has reverb and an extra control on panel for reverb, mfg. 1999-current.

MSR	$175	$105	$75 - 90	$60 - 70

Add $27.50 for cover on 15 and 15R.

Add $35 for footswitch.

New Bass Solid-State Amplfiers

As of 2002, Vox has two amps specifically made for bass guitars. The T-60 is derived from the amp back in the 1960's and the T-25 is a new model name coming up. These are also affordable models with some decent abilities.

T-15 - 15W, 1-8" Vox speaker combo, solid-state, single channel, top control panel, one instrument input, tape/CD input, four black pointer knobs (v, t, m, b), headphone jack, black covering, diagonal brown grille, new 2002.

MSR	N/A	$115	$75 - 90	$60 - 70

T-25 - 25W, 1-10" Vox speaker and horn combo, solid-state, single channel, top control panel, two inputs (high and low), five black knobs (v, t, high-mid, mid-low, b), "bassilator switch," black covering, diagonal brown grille, mfg. 2000-current.

MSR	$270	$145	$105 - 120	$85 - 95

Add $35 for cover.

T-60 - 60W - 1-12" with horn combo, solid-state, single channel, top control panel, two inputs (active and passive), five black knobs (v, t, high-mid, low-mid, b) "bassilator switch," headphone jack, FX loop, external speaker jack, black covering, brown diagonal grille, mfg. 2001-current.

MSR	$450	$250	$195 - 225	$150 - 175

Add $40 for cover.

GRADING	100%	EXCELLENT	AVERAGE

ELECTRIC HYBRID AMPLIFIERS

Vox was a little behind on this one, but they still gave it a go around. While most companies were toying with a tube amp mixing with a solid-state amp in the early 90's, Vox didn't come out with one until 1999 with the Cambridge series. This series lasted a couple of years and the new Vavletronix series was introduced in 2001. The Cambridge 30 Reverb is still in production.

Cambridge Series

CAMBRIDGE 15 (9310) - 15W, 1-8" Vox/Celestion Bulldog speaker, hybrid design, 1 X 12AX7 preamp, solid-state power section, single channel, tremolo, top control panel, one input, six black pointer knobs (gain ,v, t, b, s, d), footswitch, headphone jack, black covering, black diagonal grill, mfg. 1999-2000.

	$250	$150 - 175	$100 - 125

CAMBRIDGE 30 REVERB - 30W, 1-10" Vox/Celestion Bulldog speaker, hybrid design, 1 X 12AX7 preamp, solid-state power section, dual channels, gain, tremolo, reverb, top control panel, one input, 10 black pointer knobs (Ch 1: v, t, b, Ch 2: gain, t, b, v, Both: s, d, reverb), footswitch, headphone jack, line output, extra speaker jack, black covering, black diagonal grille cloth, mfg. 2000-current.

MSR	$399	$225	$200 - 250	$150 - 175

* Cambridge 30 Reverb Twin - Similar to the Cambridge 30 Reverb, except has 2-12" speakers, mfg. 2000 only.

	$300	$225 - 275	$150 - 200

Valvetronix Series

This is the newest product to be released by Vox. This is the new digital modeling amplifier. It was being demonstrated at Winter NAMM 2002, and it really had some neat features. With the digital features and the power of Vox amps a person is able to create an unlimited number of possibilities in sound. This amp truly has to be played around with to get all the effects It can do. With the digital preamp and the odd tube in the power section, this is truly an effective hybrid amplifier.

AD60VT - 60W, 1-12" Custom voiced Celestion combo, digital preamp, 12AX7 power section, 16 amp models, 21 effects, top blue control panel, two inputs (high and low), nine black pointer knobs (pedal, amp type, gain, v, t, m, b, presence, master), modulation, delay and reverb effects, programming, black covering, diagonal black grille cloth, mfg. 2001-current.

MSR	$899	$699	$400 - 475	$325 - 375

Add $45 for cover.

* AD120VT - Similar to the AD60VT, except has 120W output, and 2-12" Custom voiced Celestion speakers, mfg. 2001- current.

MSR	$1,199	$899	$475 - 600	$400 - 450

Add $50 for cover.

Add $200 for footswitch controller (VC-4).

Add $99 for Additional Volume Pedal for footswitch controller.

NOTES

Section W

WEM
See WATKINS
WEM was another name change for the Watkins company.

WALLER AMPLIFICATION
Amplifiers currently produced in Clarkston, Michigan. Waller amps are a division of ISP (Intelligent Signal Processing).
Waller Amps are a part of ISP, which has developed many sound and audio innovations. ISP came around after the founder of Rocktron sold out of that company to form a new one. After ISP had established itself with some products, they put these ideas out into guitar amplifiers. As a result they have several products out now from combos to head units. Most amplifiers have one or a combination of the effects and other products that ISP has produced. For more information visit the ISP web site (see Trademark Index).

WATKINS
Amplifiers previously produced in England.
Watkins was an amplifier company out of England that produced amps during the 1960's. Not much is known about this amp company except they produced an amplifier that featured speakers that faced away from each other. It was also covered in a greenish/white material. Any information on the Watkins trademark can be submitted directly to the publisher.

Watkins Dominator
courtesy solidbodyguitar.com, Inc.

Watkins Dominator
courtesy solidbodyguitar.com, Inc.

WARWICK
Amplifiers currently produced in Markneukirchen, Germany by Warwick Gmbh & Co., Music Equipment KG. Warwick amplifiers are distributed exclusively in the U.S. by Dana B. Goods of Santa Barbara, California.
Hans Peter Wilfer, son of Framus' Frederick Wilfer, established the Warwick trademark in 1982 in Erlangen (Bavaria). Wilfer literally grew up in the Framus factories of his father, and learned all aspects of construction and production 'right at the source'. The high quality of Warwick basses quickly gained notice with bass players worldwide.

In 1995, Warwick moved to Markneukirchen (in the Saxon Vogtland) to take advantage of the centuries of instrument-making traditions. Construction of the new plant provided the opportunity to install new state-of-the-art machinery to go with the skilled craftsmen. The Warwick company continues to focus on producing high quality bass guitars.

Recently Warwick established an amplifier line to team up with their basses. They have taken tube and solid-state technology and combined them to create the best sound that they could. Like they have from the beginning, Warwick works with musicians to develop the best amplifiers they can. Warwick focused on keeping the controls simple, which can be seen on the control panel. They now have a full line of bass amps that are available in head units, combos, and speaker enclosures are available.

ELECTRIC BASS AMPLIFIERS

The amplifiers listed are ones that are currently on Warwick's price list. Warwick does make other amplifier models, but not all of them are available in the U.S. For more information on models not available in the U.S. visit the website (see Trademark Index).

GRADING	100%	EXCELLENT	AVERAGE

Preamps
QUADRUPLET - preamp only, one space rack-mount head, tube preamp circuit, single channel, front black control panel, single input, seven silver knobs, effects loopheadphone jack, various buttons, black casing, current mfg.

	MSR	$999	$699	$450 - 550	$375 - 425

GRADING	100%	EXCELLENT	AVERAGE

Rack-Mount Amplifiers

PRO FET II - 250W, two-space rack-mount head-unit only, MOSFET solid-state chassis, single channel, front black control panel, single input, eight silver knobs, various buttons, effects loop, black casing, current mfg.

MSR	$599	$425	$300 - 375	$225 - 275

PRO FET IV - 400W, two-space rack-mount head-unit only, MOSFET solid-state chassis, single channel, front black control panel, single input, three silver knobs, eight-band equalizer, various buttons, effects loop, black casing, current mfg.

MSR	$699	$499	$350 - 425	$275 - 325

QUAD VI - 600W, two-space rack-mount head-unit only, all-tube preamp, MOSFET solid-state power amp, single channel, front black control panel with silver grilles, singel input, seven silver knobs, various buttons, effects loop, black casing, silver handles, current mfg.

MSR	$1,999	$1,425	$1,000 - 1,200	$800 - 900

Combo Amplifiers

CL COMBO - 150W, 1-12" peaker with horn, solid-state chassis, single channel, front black control panel, single input, six silver knobs, various buttons, effects loop, black covering, black metal grille with large "W," wheels with retractable luggage handle, current mfg.

MSR	$1,198	$850	$625 - 725	$500 - 550

CCL COMBO - 250W, 1-15" peaker with horn, solid-state chassis, single channel, front black control panel, single input, eight silver knobs, various buttons, effects loop, black covering, black metal grille with large "W," wheels with retractable luggage handle, current mfg.

MSR	$1,398	$999	$700 - 800	$600 - 650

SPEAKER CABINETS

410 PRO - 300W handling, ported cabinet, 4-10" speakers, black covering, black metal grille with large "W," current mfg.

MSR	$779	$550	$400 - 475	$325 - 375

411 PRO - 600W handling, ported cabinet, 4-10" speakers with horn, black covering, black metal grille with large "W," current mfg.

MSR	$1,049	$750	$600 - 675	$500 - 550

115 PRO - 400W handling, ported cabinet, 1-15" speaker, black covering, black metal grille with large "W," current mfg.

MSR	$749	$525	$400 - 450	$325 - 375

TERMINATOR - 450W handling, ported cabinet, 2-15" & 2-10"speakers and horn, bandpass design, black covering, black metal grille with large "W," current mfg.

MSR	$1,499	$1,050	$775 - 875	$650 - 700

WA XV - 300W slave cabinet for cabinets, 1-15""speaker, black covering, black metal grille with large "W," current mfg.

MSR	$1,088	$775	$575 - 650	$475 - 525

Section Y

YAMAHA

Amplifiers currently produced in U.S., Taiwan, and Indonesia. Distributed in the U.S. by the Yamaha Corporation of America, located in Buena Park, California. Amplifiers previously produced in Japan. Yamaha company headquarters is located in Hamamatsu, Japan.

Yamaha has a tradition of building musical instruments for over 100 years. The first Yamaha solid body electric guitars were introduced to the American market in 1966. While the first series relied on designs based on classic American favorites, the second series developed more original designs. In the mid 1970s, Yamaha was recognized as the first Oriental brand to emerge as a prominent force equal to the big-name US builders.

Production shifted to Taiwan in the early 1980s as Yamaha built its own facility to maintain quality. In 1990, the Yamaha Corporation of America (located in Buena Park, California) opened the Yamaha Guitar Development (YGD) center in North Hollywood, California. The Yamaha Guitar Development center focuses on design, prototyping, and customizing both current and new models. The YGD also custom builds and maintains many of the Yamaha artist's instruments. The center's address on Weddington Street probably was the namesake of the Weddington series instruments of the early 1990s. Recently Yamaha released the DG-1000 & DG100-212 digital guitar amplifiers

The Yamaha company is active in producing a full range of musical instruments, including band instruments, stringed instruments, amplifiers, and P.A. equipment. .

GRADING	100%	EXCELLENT	AVERAGE

ELECTRIC GUITAR AMPLIFIERS

Yamaha has produced several amplifiers over the years. They have numerous other models besides the ones we have listed. There just isn't a lot of information on Yamaha amplifiers. Since they are such a large music manufacturing company, nobody has focused just on that part of the operation. If someone were to do a book on all the Yamaha products produced over the years, it could be 10,000+ pages easily. Look for more information in upcoming editions of the *Blue Book of Guitar Amplifiers.*

YAMAHA G50-112 - 50W, 1-12" speakers, solid-state chassis, single channel, front black control panel, two inputs (high and low), seven black and silver knobs, black covering, black grille, mfg. 1980's-1990's.

Yamaha G50-112
courtesy S. P. Fjestad

N/A   **$150 - 200**

Yamaha G50-112
courtesy S. P. Fjestad

$100-125

GRADING	100%	EXCELLENT	AVERAGE

YAMAHA JX-20 - 20W, 1-10" speaker, solid-state chassis, single channel, reverb, front brown control panel, two inputs (high and low), five knobs (v, MV, t, b, r), brown covering, brown grille, mfg. 1980's-1990's.

Yamaha JX-20
courtesy S. P. Fjestad

Yamaha JX-20
courtesy S. P. Fjestad

N/A $150 - 200 $100-125

YORKVILLE

Amplifiers and other audio equipment currently produced in Pickering, Ontario. Yorkville products are distributed in the U.S. by Yorkville Sound Inc. in Niagra Falls, New York.

Yorkville was founded in Toronto in 1963. Pete Traynor developed a bass amplifier (see Traynor amps) when he was a repairman at the shop, Long & McQuade. Jack Long started Yorkville with Traynor's bass amp along with other amps. In the 1960's, Yorkville started to produce P.A. amps along with guitar amps and by 1965 had started to sell to the U.S. The 1970's were time of expansion to Europe and North America. In the 1980's, they developed some speaker cabinets, and other audio products.

Currently Yorkville employs over 185 people in their manufacturing facility that is just outside of Toronto. They work on several products now including all kinds of amplifiers to speaker cabinets. Their engineers and builders develop some of the best designs out there.

Section Z

ZAPP

Amplifiers previously produced in the 1970's.

Not much is known about the amplifier company, Zapp. They produced amplifiers during the 1970's, when small practice amplifiers were beginning to take off. A couple small solid-state models exist, but information is scarce on them. Any information on Zapp amplifiers would be appreciated for upcoming editions of the *Blue Book of Guitar Amplifiers.*

Z

TRADEMARK INDEX

A.R.T. (Applied Research and Technology)
215 Tremont Street
Rochester, NY 14608
Phone: 585-436-2720
Fax: 585-436-3942
cserve@artproaudio.com
www.artroch.com

Acoustic
A division of Samick Corp.
18521 Railroad Street
City of Industry, CA 91748
Phone: 626-964-4700
Fax: 626-964-8898
www.acoustic.mu

Acoustic Image
7517 Precision Dr Suite 102
Raleigh, NC 27617
Phone: 919-598-3113
Fax: 919-957-3294
info@acousticimg.com
www.acousticimg.com

Aguilar
599 Broadway 7th Floor
New York, NY 10012
800-304-1875
Phone: 415-831-8200
Fax: 415-831-0243
info@aguilaramp.com
www.aguilaramp.com

Alembic
3005 Wiljan Court
Santa Rose, CA 95407
Phone: 707-523-2611
Fax: 707-523-2935
alembic@alembic.com
www.alembic.com

Alessandro
Phone: 215-355-6424
hounddogcorp@msn.com
www.alessandro-products.com

Allen
1325 Richwood Road
Walton, KY 41094
Phone: 859-485-6423
Fax: 859-485-6424
tonesavor@fuse.net
www.allenamps.com

Ampeg
Division of St. Louis Music
1400 Ferguson Ave.
St. Louis, MO 63133
1-800-738-7563
Phone: 314-569-0141
twilson@stlouismusic.com
www.ampeg.com

Ashdown Engineering
Distributed by HHB
Communications
1410 Centinela Ave.
Los Angeles, CA 90025-2501
Phone: 310-319-1111
Fax: 310-319-1311
sales@hhbusa.com
www.ashdownmusic.co.uk

Badcat
2621 Green River Road Suite # 105
Pmb # 406
Corona, CA 92882
Phone: 909-808-8651
Fax: 909-279-6383
badcatamps@earthlink.net
www.badcatamps.com

BGW
13130 Yukon Ave.
Hawthorne, CA 90250
800-468-2677
Fax: 310-676-6713
info@bgw.com
www.bgw.com

Blockhead
Phone: 845-528-2229
Fax: 212-888-1374
blockheadamp@aol.com
www.blockheadamps.com

Blue Tone
Springhill House 94 - 98
Kidderminster Road
Bewdley , Worcs DY12 1DQ United
Kingdom
Phone: +44 (0) 1299 402552
sales@bluetoneamps.com
www.bluetoneamps.com

Blues Pearl
92 Litchfield Ave.
Babylon, NY 11702
Phone: 516-422-8661
Fax: 516-422-7030

Bogner
11411 Vanowen St.
North Hollywood, CA 91605
Phone: 818-765-8929
Fax: 818-765-5299
www.bogneramplification.com

Bruce Bennett Music Labs
64 Allie Ln
Rossville, GA 30741
Phone: 423-355-1750
bbml@bellsouth.net
www.bennettguitars.com

Brunetti
Distributed by Salwender
International
1140 N. Lemon "M"
Orange, CA 92867
Phone: 714-538-1285
info@brunetti.it
www.brunetti.it

Budda
37 Joseph Court
San Rafael, CA 94903
Phone: 415-492-1935
Fax: 415-492-1663
buddatone@budda.com
www.budda.com

TRADEMARK INDEX

Callaham Vintage Amplifiers
114 Tudor Drive
Winchester, VA 22603
Phone: 540- 955-0294
callaham@callahamguitars.com
www.callahamguitars.com

Carr Amplifiers
433 W. Salisbury St.
Pittsboro, NC 27312
Phone: 919-545-0747
info@carramps.com
www.carramps.com

Carvin
12340 World Trade Drive
San Diego, CA 92128
800-854-2235
Phone: 858-487-1600
www.carvin.com

Cornford Amplification
48 Joseph Wilson Industrial Estate
Millstrood Road
Whitstable, Kent CT5 3PS England
Phone: 44 (0) 1227 280000
Fax: 44 (0) 1227 771158
info@cornfordamps.com
www.cornfordamps.com

Crate
A Division of St. Louis Music
1400 Ferguson Avenue
St. Louis , MO 63133
1-800-738-7563
Phone: 314-569-0141
pstevenson@stlouismusic.com
www.crateamps.com

Danelectro
P.O. Box 73010
San Clemente, CA 92673
Phone: 949-498-9854
Fax: 949-369-8500
info@danelectro.com
www.danelectro.com

Dean Markley
P.O. Box 507
Bloomfield, CT 06002-0507
800-647-2244
Phone: 860-243-7941
Fax: 860-243-7287
info@deanmarkley.com
www.deanmarkley.com

Demeter
15730 Stagg Street
Van Nuys, CA 91406
Phone: 818-994-7658
Fax: 818-994-0647
info@demeteramps.com
www.demeteramps.com

Diaz
www.cesardiaz.com

Diezel
Distributed by Salwender
International
1140 North Lemon Street "M"
Orange, CA 92867
800-464-3525
Phone: 714-538-1285
www.salwender.com

Dinosaur
Distributed by Eleca International Inc.
21088 Commerce Points Drive
Walnut, CA 91789
1-888-GO-ELECA
Phone: 909-468-1382
Fax: 909-468-1652
info@eleca.com
www.dinosauramps.com

Dr. Z
17011 Broadway Ave.
Maple Heights, OH 44137
Phone: 216-475-1444
Fax: 216-475-4333
drz@drzamps.com
www.drzamps.com

EBS
Distributed by Matthews & Ryan
68 - 34th Street
Brooklyn, New York 11232-2004
Phone: 718-832-6333
ebs.sweeden@bass.se
www.ebs.bass.se

Eden, David
Distributed by Eden Electronics
P.O. Box 338 310 1st Street
Montrose, MN 55363
Phone: 763-675-3650
Fax: 763-675-3651
eden@eden-electronics.com
www.eden-electronics.com

Edward Amplification
41 Corman Place
Stoney Creek, Ontario L8G 4W6
Canada
Phone: 905-664-1274
Fax: 905-664-5319
www.edwardamp.com

Egnator
196 Oakland Suite D-209
Pontiac, MI 48342
Phone: 248-253-7300
Fax: 248-253-7301
frank@musicproductsgroup.com
www.egnator.com

Electro-Harmonix
info@ehx.com
www.turnstyle.com/ehx/

Emery Sound
Phone: 510-236-1176
Fax: 510-236-1176
amps@emerysound.com
www.emerysound.com

TRADEMARK INDEX

Engl
Distributed by ji concept us inc
6440 Antgua Place
West Hills, CA 91307
Phone: 818-610-2892
Fax: 818-610-2894
info@jiconcept.com
www.engl-amps.com

Enhancer
3501 Interstate 35-E S.
Waxahachie, TX 75165
Phone: 972-937-8424

Epiphone
645 Massman Drive
Nashville, TN 37210
1-800-4GIBSON
Phone: 615-871-4500
Fax: 615-872-7768
relations@gibson.com
www.epiphone.com

Euphonic Audio
P.O. Box 10
Toms River, NJ 08753
Phone: 866-878-0009
Fax: 866-878-1642
info@euphonicaudio.com
www.euphonicaudio.com

Evans Custom Amplifiers
2734 Woodbury Drive
Burlington, NC 27217
Phone: 336-437-0703
Fax: 336-437-0703
evans@evansamps.com
www.EvansAmps.com

Fender
Fender Musical Instrument
Corporation
8860 E. Chaparral Road Suite 100
Scottsdale, AZ 85250
Phone: 480-596-9690
Fax: 480-596-1384
www.fender.com

Fernandes
8163 Lankershim Blvd.
North Hollywood, CA 91605
800-318-8599
Phone: 818-252-6799
Fax: 818-252-6790
info@fernandesguitars.com
www.fernandesguitars.com/

Flite Sound
80 Mashentuck Road
Danielson, CT 06239
Phone: 860-774-9374
Fax: 860-7799-6066
flite@flitesound.com
www.flitesound.com

Framus
Distributed by Dana B. Goods in
the U.S.
P.O. Box 10100
Gewerbegebiet Wohlhausen,
Markneukirchen Germany
1-888-123-4556
Phone: 49-37422-555-0
Fax: 49-37422-55599
info@danabgoods.com
www.framus.com

Fulton-Webb
1110 South Lamar
Austin, TX 78704
Phone: 512-801-4332
www.fultonwebb.com

Gallien-Krueger
2240 Paragon Drive
San Jose, CA 95131
1-800-555-5855
Phone: 408-441-7970
Fax: 408-441-8085
info@gallien-krueger.com
www.gallien-kruger.com

Garnet
No current production
info@garnetamps.com
www.garnetamps.com

Genesis
info@audio-genesis.com
www.audio-genesis.com

Genz Benz
7811 East Pierce Street
Scottsdale, AZ 85257
1-888-978-4529
Phone: 480-941-0705
Fax: 480-946-2412
info@GENZBENZ.com
www.GENZBENZ.com

George Dennis Ltd.
Nostrasnicka 39
Prague 10, CZ-100 00 Czech
Republic
Phone: 420-2-7822758/9
Fax: 420-2-7822584
georgede@vol.cz
www.george-dennis.cz

Gerlitz
1380 Hines St. SE
Salem, OR 97302
Phone: 503-364-3774
Fax: 503-364-1860
harvey@gerlitzamps.com
www.gerlitzamps.com

Germino
921 East Gilbreath Street
Graham, NC 27253
Phone: 336-437-0317
greg@germinoamps.com
www.germinoamps.com

Gibson
1818 Elm Hill Pike
Nashville, TN 37210
1-800-4GIBSON
Phone: 615-871-4500
Fax: 615-871-4060
relations@gibson.com
www.gibson.com

TRADEMARK INDEX

Glockenklang
Distributed by Salwender
International in the U.S.
1140 North Lemon Street "M"
Orange, CA 92867
800-464-3525
Phone: 714-538-1285
www.salwender.com

Groove Tubes
1543 Truman Street
San Fernando, CA 91340
Phone: 818-361-4500
Fax: 818-365-9884
sales@groovetubes.com
www.groovetubes.com

Hartke
Distributed by Samson Technologies
Corp.
P.O. Box 9031
Syosset, NY 11791
Phone: 516-364-2244
sales@samsontech.com
www.hartke.com

HIWATT
8163 Lankershim Blvd.
North Hollywood, CA 91605
800-318-8599
Phone: 800-318-8599
Fax: 818-252-6790
info@hiwatt.com
www.hiwatt.com

Hoffman
190 Lakeland Dr.
Pisgah Forest, NC 28768
hoffmanamps@hoffmanamps.com
www.hoffmanamps.com

Holland
500 Wilson Pike Circle Suite 204
Brentwood, TN 37027
Phone: 615-377-4913
Fax: 615-373-4986
mike@hollandamps.com
www.hollandamps.com

Hondo
Distributed by Musicorp/MBT
P.O. Box 30819
Charleston, SC 29417
800.845.1922
Phone: 803.763.9083
Fax: 803.763.9096
www.mbtinternational.com/hondo/amplifie.htm

Hughes & Kettner
1848 S. Elmhurst Road
Mt. Prospect, IL 60056
800-452-6771
Phone: 847-439-6771
Fax: 847-439-6781
info@hughes-and-kettner.com
www.hughes-and-kettner.com/

Ibanez
Hoshino Inc.
1726 Winchester Road
Bensalem, PA 19020
Phone: 215-638-8670
www.ibanez.com

Intelli Electronics Inc.
4F, Seoil B/D Suknam-dong
Seo-gu
Incheon, Korea
Phone: 82-32-584-6217
Fax: 82-32-584-6219
intellituner@netsgo.com

JBL
Pro Audio
8400 Balboa Blvd.
Northridge, CA 91329
Phone: 818-894-8850
www.jblpro.com

Johnson (U.S.A.)
www.johnson-amp.com

Koch
Distributed by Eden Electronics
Arnhemseweg 152
Amersfoort, 3817 CL
The Netherlands
Phone: 31-33-4634533
Fax: 31-33-4655274
info@koch-amps.com
www.koch-amps.com

Kustom
A division of HHI (Hanser Holdings
Inc.)
4940 Delhi Pike
Cinncinati, OH 45328
Phone: 513-451-5000
Fax: 513-347-2298
www.kustom.com

Laney
P.O. Box 2632
Mount Pleasant, SC 29465-2632
888-860-1668
Fax: 888-863-0763
sales@laneyusa.com
www.laneyusa.com

Leslie
Hammond Suzuki, Inc.
733 Annoreno Drive
Addison, IL 60101
Phone: 630-543-0277
Fax: 630-543-0279
hammondsuzuki@worldnet.att.net

Line 6
29901 Agoura Rd.
Agoura Hills, CA 91301-2513
Phone: 818-575-3600
Fax: 818-575-3601
Info@line6.com
www.line6.com

Marshall
Distributed by Korg
Denbigh Road Bletchley
Milton Keyes, MK1 1DQ England
www.marshallamps.com

TRADEMARK INDEX

Marshall USA
Distributed by Korg
316 South Service Road
New York, NY 11747-3201
800-872-5674
Fax: 800-289-5674

Matchless
2105 Pontius Ave
Los Angeles, CA 90025
Phone: 310-444-1922
sales@matchlessamplifiers.com
www.matchlessamplifiers.com

Mega
Part of WooSung Chorus Industries
857-37 Jakjun-dong
Kaeyang-ku
Inchon, 407-823 Korea
Phone: 82-32-543-7940
Fax: 82-32-543-7941
sales@wscmusic.com
www.wscmusic.com

Mesa/Boogie
1317 Ross Street
Petaluma, CA 94954
Phone: 707-778-6565
Fax: 707-765-1503
info@mesaboogie.com
www.mesaboogie.com

Mill Hill
Camarillo, CA
1-877-Mill-Hill
Fax: 805-987-7335
jonathan@millhillaudio.com
www.millhillaudio.com

Motion Sound
Salt Lake City, UT
Phone: 801-265-0917
Fax: 801-265-0978
sales@motion-sound.com
www.motion-sound.com

Musiclord
1761 Central Ave. South
Kent, WA 98032-1832
Phone: 206-878-8038
glen@musiclord.com
www.musiclord.com

Nemesis
Distributed by Eden Electronics
P.O. Box 338 1st Street
Montrose, MN 55363
Phone: 763-675-3650
Fax: 763-675-3651
eden@eden-electronics.com
www.eden-electronics.com/nemesis.html

Orange
World Headquarters (Orange
Musical Electronic Company
Limited)
28 Denmark Street
London, WC2H8NJ England
44-20-7240-8292
Fax: 44-20-7240-8112
info@orangeamps.com
USA Office (Orange Musical
Electronic Company, Inc.)
P.O. Box 421849
Atlanta, GA 30342
404-303-8196
Fax: 404-303-7176
info@orangeusa.com
www.orange-amps.com

Peavey
711 A Street
Meridian, MS 39301
Phone: 601-483-5365
Fax: 601-486-1278
humanresources@peavey.com
www.peavey.com

Pignose
3430 Precision Drive
North Las Vegas, NV 89030
1-888-369-0824
Phone: 702-648-2444
Fax: 702-648-2440
pss@pignose.com
www.pignose.com

Prime
A division of Music Industries
Corporation
625 Locust Street Suite 300
Garden City, NY 11530
800-431-6699
Phone: 516-794-1888
Fax: 516-794-4099
prime@musicindustries.com
www.primeamps.com

QSC Audio Products
1675 MacArthur Blvd.
Costa Mesa, CA 92626
1-800-854-4079
Fax: 714-754-6174
ryan_white@qscaudio.com
www.qscaudio.com

Raezer's Edge
726 Girard Ave.
Swarthmore, PA 19081
Phone: 610-328-5466
Fax: 610-328-3857
rraezer@rcn.com
www.raezers-edge.com

Randall
A division of Washburn International
444 East Courtland Street
Mundelein, IL 60060
1-800-877-6863
Phone: 847-949-0444
Fax: 847-949-8444
randall@randallamplifiers.com
www.randallamplifiers.com

Rat Fink
5561 Engineer Drive
Huntington Beach, CA 93649
Phone: 714-898-2776
Fax: 714-893-1045
info@agi-lace.com
www.agi-lace.com/ratfink/amps.html

Reverend
27300 Gloede Unit D
Warren, MI 48088
Phone: 586-775-1025
www.reverenddirect.com

TRADEMARK INDEX

Rhino
11900 Montana Ave.
El Paso, TX 79936
Phone: 915-855-4922
Fax: 915-855-3080
info@rhinoamps.com
www.rhinoamps.com

Rivera
13310 Ralston Ave.
Sylmar, CA 91342
Phone: 818-833-7066
Fax: 818-833-9656
rivera@rivera.com
www.rivera.com

RMS Audio
101 Colony Park Drive Suite 400
Cumming, GA 30040
Phone: 678-947-3982
Fax: 678-947-3984
rms@rms-audio.com
www.rmsaudio.com

Roccaforte
307 West Avenida Gaviota
San Clemente, CA 92672
Phone: 949-369-7862
Fax: 949-369-7864
RoccaforteAmps@aol.com
www.roccaforteamps.com

Rocktron
A division of GHS Corporation
2813 Wilber Ave.
Battle Creek, MI 49015
Phone: 616-968-3351
Fax: 616-968-6913
info@rocktron.com
www.rocktron.com

Roland
5100 S. Eastern Ave. P.O. Box
910921
Los Angeles, CA 90091-0921
Phone: 323-890-3700
Fax: 323-890-3701
www.rolandus.com

Samson Audio
575 Underhill Blvd. P.O. Box 9031
Syosset, NY 11791-9031
Phone: 516-364-2244
Fax: 516-364-3888
audio@samsontech.com
www.samsontech.com

Savage Audio
12500 Chowen Ave S. Suite 112
Burnsville, MN 55337
Phone: 952-894-1022
Fax: 952-894-1536
savrok@prodigy.net
www.savageaudio.com

Siegmund
Tujunga, CA
Phone: 818-353-5558
Fax: 818-353-0218
chris@siegmundguitars.com
www.siegmundguitars.com

Soldano Custom Amplification
1537 NW Ballard Way
Seattle, WA 98107
Phone: 206-781-4636
Fax: 206-781-5173
www.soldano.com

Soundboard
A division of the High Cliff
Company
345 Co. Rd CE
Kaukauna, WI 54130
Phone: 920-766-5941
Fax: 920-766-5941
info@soundboard.net
www.soundboard.net

Soundking
Panhuo Industry Development Areaa
Ningbo, 315105 China
Phone: 86-574-88237437-82235195
Fax: 86-574-88235763-88238178
sales@soundking.com
www.soundking.com

Sovtek
info@newsensor.com
www.sovtek.com

Speedster
No current production
www.speedster-amplifiers.com

Standel
Phone: 818-247-2047
Fax: 818-247-4498
danmckinney@earthlink.net
www.requisiteaudio.com

SWR
9130 Glenoaks Blvd.
Sun Valley, CA 91532-2611
Phone: 818-253-4797
Fax: 818-253-4799
support@swrsound.com
www.swrsound.com

Tecamp
A division of Sino-Amp Inc.
1624 N. Indiana St.
Los Angeles, CA 90063
Phone: 323-262-8308
Fax: 323-262-8038
jtecamp@aol.com
www.tecamp.com

Tech 21
Phone: 973-777-6996
Fax: 973-777-9899
info@tech21.com
www.tech21nyc.com

THD
4816 15th Ave. NW
Seattle, WA 98107-4717
Phone: 206-781-5500
Fax: 206-781-5508
info@thdelectronics.com
www.thdelectronics.com

TRADEMARK INDEX

Tony Bruno Custom Amplifiers
251 West 30th St. 6th. Fl
New York, NY 10001
Phone: 212-967-5626
brunoamps@mindspring.com
www.brunoamps.com

Top Hat
www.tophatamps.com

Torres Engineering
1630 Palm Ave.
San Mateo, CA 94402
Phone: 650-571-6887
Fax: 650-571-1507
www.torresengineering.com

Trace Elliot
Part of Gibson
1150 Bowes Road
Elgin, IL 60123
1-800-4-GIBSON
www.trace-elliot.com

Traynor
A division of Yorkville Sound
4625 Witmer Industrial Estate
Niagra Falls, NY 14305
Phone: 716-297-2920
Fax: 716-297-3689
sales@yorkville.com
www.traynor.com

Tube Works
A division of Genz Benz
7811 E. Pierce Street
Scottsdale, AZ 85257
Phone: 480-941-0705
Fax: 480-946-2412
info@genzbenz.com
www.genzbenz.com

UltraSound
A division of UJC Electronics
5110 Park Ave.
Des Moines, IA 50321-1247
1-888-308-1557
Fax: 888-993-4550
info@ultrasoundamps.com
www.ultrasoundamps.com

Vero Amps
22436 S. River Road
Joliet, IL 60431
Phone: 815-467-7093
info@veroamps.com
www.veroamps.com/home.html-ssi

VHT Amplification
9130 Glenoaks Blvd.
Sun Valley, CA 91352-2611
Phone: 818-253-4848
Fax: 818-253-4780
info@vhtamp.com
www.vhtamp.com

Victoria
1504 Newman Court
Naperville, IL 60564
Phone: 630-369-3527
Fax: 630-527-2221
bisbee@mc.net
www.victoriaamp.com

Vox
Korg USA
316 S. Service Road
Melville, NY 11747
Phone: 516-333-9100
Fax: 516-333-9108
www.voxamps.co.uk

Waller Amplification
A division of ISP Technologies Inc.
7508 M.E. Cad Blvd Unit C
Clarkston, MI 48348
Phone: 248-620-6795
Fax: 248-620-6796
shellwaller@hotmail.com
www.isptechnologies.com

Warwick
Distributed in the U.S.A. by Dana
B. Goods
4054 Transport St. Unit A
Ventura, CA 93003
800-741-0109
Phone: 805-644-6621
Fax: 805-644-6332
sales@danabgoods.com
www.danabgoods.com

Yamaha
6600 Orangethorpe Ave.
Buena Park, CA 90620
Phone: 714-522-9011
www.yamaha.com

Yorkville
4625 Witmer Industrial Estate
Niagra Falls, NY 14305
Phone: 716-297-2920
Fax: 716-297-3689
info@yorkville.com
www.yorkville.com

REFERENCE SOURCES

Maybe the best advice any amp hound will ever get is "For every amp you purchase, buy 5 books." It's still a good rule of thumb. In terms of the major trademarks, it's pretty much over – most of the good books are already out there. All you have to do is buy 'em and read 'em. Some are even out of print, and have already become very collectible (expensive).

If you're a player, collector, or just kind of an all-around average amp hound, you gotta do your homework. And there have never been more ways to bone up on your chosen homework assignments. Even though the web does a good job of performing many basic guitar amplifier information services, it's still not a book. It's also necessary that you subscribe to a few good magazines within your area (please refer to Periodicals listing).

The following titles represent a good cross sectional cut of those reference that are outstanding in their field(s). Spending $300 annually to have these valuable books at your fingertips is the cheapest insurance policy you'll every buy. If you're serious about your amps, this information could also save you thousands of dollars and a lot of bad attitude. So bone up or bail out! No whining either – it's a pretty cool homework assignment.

Most of the books listed below can be obtained through:

JK Lutherie
11115 Sand Run
Harrison, OH 45030
Phone: 800.344.8880
www.jklutherie.com
Guitar@jklutherie.com

JK Lutherie also attends many major guitar shows annually, and you may want to stop by the booth to either purchase or inquire about any new releases. Many video releases are also available, and can be found on his web site.

Bechtoldt, Paul & Doug Tulloch, *Guitars from Neptune*, Backporch Publications, 1995.

Brosnac, Donald, *The Amp Book - An Guitarist's Introductory Guide to Tube Amplifiers*, Westport, CT, The Bold Strummer, Ltd., 1987.

Burrluck, Dave, *The PRS Guitar Book - A Complete History of Paul Reed Smith Guitars*, updated edition, San Francisco, CA, Backbeat Books, 2002.

Carter, Walter, *Epiphone - The Complete History*, Milwaukee, WI, Hal Leonard Publishing Corporation, 1995.

Day, Paul, *The Burns Book*, Westport, CT, The Bold Strummer, Ltd., 1990.

Doyle, Michael, *The History of Marshall, The Illustrated Story of "The Sound of Rock"*, Milwaukee, WI, Hal Leonard Publishing Corporation, 1993.

Fliegler, Ritchie, *AMPS! The Other Half of Rock 'n' Roll*, Milwaukee, WI, Hal Leonard Publishing Corporation, 1993.

Gruhn, George & Walter Carter, *Gruhn's Guide to Vintage Guitars - An Identification Guide for American Fretted Instruments*, 2nd Edition, San Francisco, CA, Miller Freeman Books, 1999.

Hopkins, Gregg & Bill Moore, *Ampeg - The Story Behind the Sound*, Milwaukee, WI, Hal Leonard Publishing Corporation, 1999.

Meiners, Larry, *Gibson Shipment Totals 1937-1979*, Chicago, IL, Flying Vintage Publications, 2001.

Morrish, John, *The Fender Amp Book*, San Francisco, CA, Miller Freeman Books, 1995.

Petersen David & Dick Denney, *The Vox Story - A Complete History of the Legend*, Westport, CT, The Bold Strummer, Ltd., 1993.

Pittman, Aspen, *The Tube Amp Book 4.1th Edition*, Sylmar, CA, Groove Tubes, 1995.

Teagle, John & John Sprung, *Fender Amps - The First Fifty Years*, Milwaukee, WI, Hal Leonard Publishing Corporation (in cooperation with Fender), 1995.

Wright, Michael, *Guitar Stories Volume One*, Bismarck, ND, Vintage Guitar Inc., 1995.

Wright, Michael, *Guitar Stories Volume Two*, Bismarck, ND, Vintage Guitar Inc., 2000.

PERIODICALS

You've bought this book so you're obviously interested in guitar amplifiers. Being knowledgeable about any subject is a good idea and having the up-to-the-minute news is the best form of knowledge. We recommend the following publications for information, collecting news, updates and show announcements, artist insights and loads of other information that might interest you.

20th Century Guitar
Seventh String Press, Inc., 135 Oser Avenue, Hauppauge, New York 11788
Phone number: 631-273-1674,
Fax: 631-434-9057
www.tcguitar.com
Published monthly. 12 month subscription is $15.00 in the USA.

Acoustic Guitar
String Letter Publishing, Inc., 255 W. End Ave.,
San Rafael, California 94901
Phone number: 415-485-6946,
Fax: 415-485-0831
www.acousticguitar.com
Email: slp@stringletter.com
Published monthly. 12 month subscription is $29.95 in the USA.

Bass Player
2800 Campus Dr.
San Mateo, CA 94403
Phone number: 650.513.4300
Fax: 650.513.4642
www.bassplayer.com
bassplayer@musicplayer.com
Published monthly. 12 month subscription is $29.95.

Downbeat
102 N. Haven Road, Elmhurst, Illinois 60126-3379.
630-941-2030 Fax: 630-941-3210
Published monthly.

Gitarre & Bass (Germany)
MM-Musik-Media-Verlag GmbH,
An Der Wachsfabrik 8, Koln, 50996 Germany
Phone number: 011-39-2236-96217
Fax: 011-39-2236-96217-5
Published monthly.

Guitar Digest
P.O. Box 66, The Plains, Ohio 45780
Phone number: 740-797-3351
or 740-592-4614
www.guitardigest.com
www.ohioguitarshow.com
Email: alexmack@frognet.net
Published 6 times a year. A six issue subscription is $10.00 in the USA.

Guitar for the Practicing Musician
Cherry Lane Magazines, LLC,
Six East 32nd St., 11th Flr., New York, NY 10016
Phone number: 212-561-3000
Fax: 212-251-0840
Published monthly. 12 month subscription is $22.95 in the USA, and a two year subscription is $37.95 in the USA.

Guitar One ·
Cherry Lane Magazines, LLC, Six East 32nd St., 11th Flr., New York, NY 10016
Phone number: 212-561-3000
Fax: 212-251-0840 Published monthly.
Available on the newstands for $4.95 per issue in the USA.

The Guitar Magazine (UK)
IPC Focus House Dingwall Avenue, Croyden CR9 2TA, England.
Phone number: 011.44.208.774.0600
Fax: 011.44.208.774.0934
Published every 4 weeks - 16 per year.

Guitar Player
2800 Campus Dr.
San Mateo, CA 94403
Phone number: 650.513.4300
Fax: 650.513.4642
www.guitarplayer.com
Published monthly. 12 month subscription is $24.00 in the USA.

Guitar World
Harris Publications, Inc.,
1115 Broadway, 8th Flr.
New York, New York 10010
Phone number: 800-866-2886
Email: sounding.board@guitarworld.com
http://www.guitarworld.com
Published monthly. 12 month subscription is $23.94 in the USA.

Guitar World Acoustic
Harris Publications, Inc.,
1115 Broadway, 8th Flr.
New York, New York 10010
Phone number: 212-807-7100,
Fax: 212-627-4678
Email: sounding.board@guitarworld.com
http://www.guitarworld.com
Published monthly. $16.97 for 6 issues, publisher every other month.

Guitarist (UK)
Alexander House, Forehill, Ely,
Cambs CB7 4AF, England
Phone number: 011-44-1353-665577
Fax: 011-44-1353-662489
Email: guitarist@musicians-net.co.uk
Published monthly.

Guitarist (France)
10, Rue De la Paix, Boulogne, France 92100

JazzTimes
8737 Colesville Rd., 9th Floor,
Silver Spring, MD 20910
Phone: 301.588.4114 Fax: 301.588.5531
wwwjazztimes.com
Published 10 times/year. A one year subscription is $23.95 in the USA.

Just Jazz Guitar
P.O. Box 76053, Atlanta,
Georgia 30358-1053
Phone number: 404-250-9298
Fax: 404-250-9951
www.justjazzguitar.com
Published 4 times a year. A one year subscription is $40 in the USA.

Musico Pro
Music Maker Publications, Inc., 5412 Idylwild Trail, Suite 100, Boulder, Colorado 80301
Phone number: 303-516-9118
Fax: 303-516-9119
www.recordingmag.com
Email: info@recordingmag.com
A music/gear magazine is published in Spanish (available in U.S., Argentine, Chile, Mexico, and Spain).
Published 12 times a year. Subscription is $19.95 in the USA.

Staccato
Manfred Hecker and Carsten Durer, Editors.
Akazienweg 57, Cologne, 50827 Germany
Phone number: 011-39-221-5301560
Fax: 011-39-221-5302286
Email: staccato@vva.com

The ToneQuest Report
Mountainview Publishing
235 Mountainview st. Ste # 23
Decatur, GA 30030-2027
1-877-MAX-TONE
Email: tonequest@aol.com
Published Monthly. 12 month subscription is $98.

Vintage Guitar Magazine
Alan J. Greenwood, P.O. Box 7301,
Bismarck, North Dakota 58507
Phone number: 701-255-1197
Fax: 701-255-0250
www.vintageguitar.com
Published monthly. 12 month subscription is $24.95 in the USA.

In addition to the regular publications put out by these publishers, most offer Special Edition (i.e., yearly buyers' guides, new product reviews, market overviews, etc.) magazines that are released annually, or bi-annually. Please contact them directly for more information.

SHOW TIME
2002 - 2003
On the road with Blue Book Publications, Inc.

BLUE BOOK
PUBLICATIONS, INC.

Here are the shows that we will be at! This is perhaps your best chance to see/talk to us on a one-to-one basis while we're on the road. If you're lucky, we'll even throw in a free insult! If we're exhibiting, please consult each event's show directory for our location. If BBP is attending only, then it would be a good idea for you to contact us to arrange an appointment.

For more information on these shows, please use the contact information provided below. For a complete recap of each show, including new and interesting products, please click on the Show Time portion of our web site. If you can't be there, this is the next best thing.

Oct. 19-20, 2002
Arlington Guitar Show (sponsored by the 4 Amigos)
(show open to public, BBP will be exhibiting)
Arlington Convention Center
Arlington, TX

Jan. 16-19, 2003
Winter NAMM (National Association of Musical Merchandisers)
(semi-annual industry trade show, BBP will be attending)
Anaheim Convention Center
Anaheim, CA
www.namm.com

Mar. 22-23, 2003
26th Annual Dallas Guitar Show
(annual show open to public, BBP is a sponsor and will be exhibiting)
Dallas Fair Park
Dallas, TX
www.guitarshow.com

July 18-20, 2003
Summer NAMM
Nashville Convention Center
Nashville, TN
(industry trade show only – not open to the public)
www.namm.com

FYI – An industry trade show is typically not open to the general public, and is usually restricted to industry professionals, including manufacturers, distributors, dealers, and in some cases, the press. All shows open to the public typically have an admission charge. Again, please use the show contact information to find out more about pricing, show hours, the exact location, and in some cases, hotel/motel accommodations.

INDEX

P.S.

So you think having the ability to turn your amp up to 20 (Marshall's JCM-900 inspired by Nigel Tufnel) is going to make things loud? Try fitting this tube into your High Gain Master Volume. The tube displayed in the middle is a transmitter tube from a radio station, circa 1930. The output of this tube is unknown, but chances are if you can get it rigged into your favorite Marshall or Fender, it's going to rattle eardrums. To put things into proportion, a typical 6L6 output tube is shown directly below. Along with these tubes there are some very rare KT66 power tubes that are very tough to find. Anyone looking for those G&C tubes from England? Good luck, we displayed the two we know of. All of these tubes are to be housed in the General Electric Tube Caddy (except the monster radio transmitter). On the right is a tube tester from the late 1930's and a Weston amp meter that dates back to the 1900's. Also displayed is an early RCA mike model DX-77 from the early 1950's, Fender schematics from a Fender Vibroverb, and authentic hanging tags from Savage Audio. Talk about Vintage tubes!

Props by Savage Audio.
Photography and layout by Zach Fjestad and Clint Schmidt.